MW00572386

Perspectives on
Canadian Federalism

Edited by

R. D. Olling
Mount Allison University

M. W. Westmacott
University of Western Ontario

Prentice-Hall Canada Inc., Scarborough, Ontario

To F. C. Engelmann

Professor Emeritus, University of Alberta

Canadian Cataloguing in Publication Data

Main entry under title:

Perspectives on Canadian federalism

Bibliography: p.
ISBN 0-13-660424-2

1. Federal government — Canada. 2. Federal-provincial relations — Canada.* I. Olling, R. D. 1949- . II. Westmacott, Martin.

JL27.P47 1988   321.02'0971   C87-094791-5

Prentice-Hall, Inc., Englewood Cliffs, New Jersey
Prentice-Hall International, Inc., London
Prentice-Hall of Australia, Pty., Ltd., Sydney
Prentice-Hall of India Pvt., Ltd., New Delhi
Prentice-Hall of Japan, Inc., Tokyo
Prentice-Hall of Southeast Asia (Pte.) Ltd., Singapore
Editora Prentice-Hall do Brasil Ltda., Rio de Janeiro
Prentice-Hall Hispanoamericana, S.A., Mexico

ISBN 0-13-660424-2

1 2 3 4 5 AP 92 91 90 89 88

Production Editor: Maurice Esses
Copyeditor: Stan Draenos
Cover Designer: Elaine Cohen
Production Coordinator: Matt Lumsdon
Typesetting: Jaytype Inc.

Printed and bound in Canada by The Alger Press Limited

Every reasonable effort has been made to find copyright holders. The publishers would be pleased to have any errors or omissions brought to their attention.

Contents

Section Seven: Perspectives on Political and Constitutional Reform   365

Preface

In 1982, decades of constitutional discussion and intergovernmental conflict ended with the patriation of the Canadian Constitution. This event marked an important moment in the evolution of the Canadian federal state.

In response to the intense and protracted nature of the intergovernmental conflict, many studies of Canadian politics have offered a decidedly pessimistic assessment of the future of the Canadian federal state. Consider the titles of some of the major texts published in the last decade: *Unfulfilled Union, Canada in Question, Divided Loyalties, Must Canada Fail?, and No One Cheered.* The fact remains that, despite predictions to the contrary, the Canadian federation continues to endure and to provide an effective form of political organization for Canadians.

What are some of the uniquely Canadian ways of dealing with the problems that are faced by federations? It is our contention that the Canadian approach to federalism reflects some of the basic values of the country itself—pragmatism, respect for, and tolerance of, linguistic and cultural diversity, and deference to political authority and to political elites.

In Canada, federalism is central to virtually every major policy debate. The jurisdictional boundaries of authority of each level of government and the appropriate degree of federal-provincial consultation are the subject of continued discussion. The Canadian way often emphasizes questions of procedure at the expense of substantive policy issues. Canadians endorse a commitment to sharing both the costs and benefits of Confederation and agonize over the problem of regional inequalities. Yet we often fail to recognize that it may well be beyond the capacity of government to reduce these regional inequalities significantly.

This volume contains essays that focus on the evolution of the Canadian federal system since 1945. It is designed to acquaint students with the basic institutions, processes and issues that have dominated intergovernmental relations over the past forty years—a period of dramatic and significant change for the Canadian federal state. The collection is organized by topic and is divided into seven sections. Section One examines the concept of federalism as a form of political organization and places the Canadian federal state in a comparative context. Section Two reviews some of the central institutions and processes of Canadian federalism: the constitution and the distribution of powers between the two levels of government, the Supreme Court, and judicial review. Section Three focuses on the impact of regionalism on the federal system. Section Four identifies the enduring issues surrounding fiscal federalism. Section Five examines the institutions and processes associated with intergovernmental negotiation and decision-making. Section Six chronicles Ottawa's postwar relations with each of the main regions of the country. Section Seven offers a perspective on future constitutional and political reforms. An appendix presents the full text of the *1987 Constitutional Accord.*

The authors for the essays were chosen individually for their acknowledged expertise in a field and collectively for the diversity of their approaches to the subject matter. Abridgement has been limited to ensure that the reader is exposed to the flow of each author's argument. (A row of three asterisks indicates that material has been omitted.) Some of the articles selected for this volume represent seminal studies in Canadian political science. They are works of enduring value because of the unique contributions to the field. Other articles were selected because they provide a summation and synthesis of a body of literature previously scattered in a variety of sources. Finally, a number of essays were specially commissioned for publication in this volume. These essays bring to the reader important new insights and effectively supplement the existing literature.

This collection by no means exhausts the literature on Canadian federalism. Because of limitations of space, a number of excellent essays had to be excluded. However, at the conclusion of each essay there is a list of basic bibliographic references which serve as a starting point for further research.

Students may use this volume in several ways. As a comprehensive collection of readings, this book may serve as a core text for the study of Canadian federalism or as a supplemental text for the general study of Canadian government and politics. With its wide range of perspectives and approaches, this book may also serve as a text for seminar discussion and as a research tool.

The editors wish to thank the authors and publishers who granted permission for the reprinting of their material. We also wish to express our appreciation to our colleagues at several universities who offered their advice in the preparation of this volume. We are particularly grateful to Professors N. J. Ruff, Ian Stewart, and R. B. Woodrow for their helpful remarks as reviewers of the manuscript. Editorial assistance at Prentice-Hall Canada Inc. was provided by project editor David Jolliffe, production editor Maurice Esses, and copyeditor Stan Draenos. Finally, we wish to acknowledge the contribution of our past students, as well as the editorial assistance of Mrs. Janet Horowitz, Mrs. Penny Westmacott, and Ms. Anna Vandendries.

R. D. Olling
Sackville, New Brunswick

M. W. Westmacott
London, Ontario

May 1988

Notes on Contributors

Paul Barker is assistant professor of political science at The University of Western Ontario. He has held positions in evaluation and policy analysis in government departments at the provincial level. He is currently conducting research on the formulation and implementation of Canadian health policy.

André Blais is associate professor of political science at l'Université de Montréal. His interests include electoral behaviour, public-choice theory, and tax systems. As a research coordinator for the Macdonald Royal Commission on the Economic Union and Development Prospects for Canada, he edited the volume *Industrial Policy* and wrote *A Political Sociology of Public Aid to Industry*.

Albert Breton currently teaches at the University of Toronto. He is the author of many books and articles on economic theory and policy. Professor Breton was vice-chairman of the Applebaum-Hébert Federal Cultural Policy Review Committee and commissioner with the Macdonald Royal Commission on the Economic Union and Development Prospects for Canada. He has an LL.D. *(honoris causa)* from the University of Manitoba, is a Fellow of the Royal Society of Canada, and is an Officer of the Order of Canada.

Alan C. Cairns has written extensively on Canadian federalism and is recognized as one of Canada's foremost authorities on Canadian government and politics. He is a member of the department of political science at the University of British Columbia. He is a former president of the Canadian Political Science Association and has served as a research director for the Macdonald Royal Commission on the Economic Union and Development Prospects for Canada.

Thomas J. Courchene is a professor in the department of economics at The University of Western Ontario. Professor Courchene has written on a wide variety of topics in the field of fiscal federalism and in particular on the subject of equalization payments. He is a former chairman of the Ontario Economic Council and is a Fellow of the Royal Society of Canada.

J. Stefan Dupré is a professor of political science at the University of Toronto. His principal published works deal with intergovernmental relations, research policy, and regulatory administration. He has served as member or chairman of a number of federal and provincial councils, commissions, and task forces. Professor Dupré is a past president of the Institute of Public Administration, a recipient of the Institute's Vanier Medal, and an Officer of the Order of Canada.

Rand Dyck is chairman of the political science department at Laurentian University. His research interests centre on Canadian welfare policy, Canadian federalism, and the federal and provincial electoral systems. He is the author of *Provincial Politics in Canada*.

David Elton is a professor of political science at the University of Lethbridge. He is also president of the Canada West Foundation. Dr. Elton has consulted with both industry and government on a wide range of national resource and intergovernmental policy issues. He is the author of numerous monographs and articles on constitutional issues and on the Canadian West.

Frederick C. Engelmann is a member of the department of political science at the University of Alberta, where he served as chairman from 1982 to 1985. From 1985 to 1986 he was president of the Canadian Political Science Association. He is the co-author (with Mildred Schwartz) of *Canadian Political Parties: Origin, Character, Impact.*

Philippe Faucher is associate professor of political science at l'Université de Montréal. He has published major works on Brazilian politics *(Le Brésil des militaires)* and Crown corporations *(Hydro-Québec: la société de l'heure de pointe)*. He continues to work on industrial policy, especially on technology markets.

Elliot J. Feldman was director of the University Consortium for Research on North America at Harvard University from 1978 to 1987. He is the author or co-author of seven books, including three on Canada and Canadian-United States relations. He has served on Canadian working-groups or study-groups for the Atlantic Council of the United States, the Council on Foreign Relations, the American Assembly, the Atlantic Provinces Economic Council, the World Peace Foundation, and the Institut Québecois des Relations Internationales. Dr. Feldman, a graduate of Harvard Law School and at one time Special Project Officer to the Assistant Secretary of Defense, is an attorney.

Lily Gardner Feldman is associate professor of political science at Tufts University where she teaches international relations. She is the author of *The Special Relationship between West Germany and Israel* and numerous articles on the Middle East, Germany, Canada, and Canadian-United States relations. Professor Gardner Feldman is co-director of the Canadian-United States Relations Project at Harvard University. There she is also co-chair of the German Study Group, co-chair of the Seminar on the European Community, and co-editor of *German Politics and Society.*

Alain-G. Gagnon is assistant chairman of the department of political science at Carleton University. A specialist in Canadian and Quebec political economy, he has published such works as *Quebec: State and Society, Le Développement régional, L'État et les groupes populaires, Intellectuals in Liberal Democracies* (forthcoming) and *Politics and Political Parties in Canada* (with A. Brian Tanguay, forthcoming).

Joseph Garcea is assistant professor in the department of political studies at the University of Saskatchewan. He previously lectured at Carleton University and the University of Ottawa. He also served as a Parliamentary Intern.

Thomas O. Hueglin is an associate professor of political science at Wilfrid Laurier University. He has been affiliated with the European University Institute (Florence, Italy), Konstanz University (West Germany) and Queen's University. In his research he has focused on federalism, regionalism, and the comparative analysis of advanced industrial societies. His recent publications include *Federalism and Fragmentation, Regionalism in Western Europe,* and *The Politics of Fragmentation in an Age of Scarcity.*

Samuel LaSelva is a member of the department of political science at the University of British Columbia. He has recently published articles on liberalism and on various aspects of the Canadian Charter of Rights and Freedoms, such as "Federalism and Unanimity: The Supreme Court and Constitutional Amendment," "Justifying Tolerance" (with R. A. Vernon), and "Mandatory Retirement: Intergenerational Justice and the Canadian Charter of Rights and Freedoms."

Rory Leishman is an editorial writer with *The London Free Press*. He joined the editorial board of the paper in 1975. Earlier Mr. Leishman had been a lecturer on Canadian federalism and Quebec politics in the department of political science at The University of Western Ontario.

J. Peter Meekison is academic vice-president and professor of political science at the University of Alberta. He was formerly Deputy Minister of Federal and Intergovernmental Affairs for the Province of Alberta. He is the editor of *Canadian Federalism: Myth or Reality?* and has written a wide variety of articles on the constitutional reform process.

Gordon Robertson was Secretary to the Federal Cabinet from 1963 to 1977 and Secretary to the Cabinet for Federal-Provincial Relations from 1975 to 1979. In both capacities he was very active in federal-provincial relations and interministerial conferences.

Peter H. Russell has been teaching political science at the University of Toronto since 1958. In his scholarly work he has focused on constitutional and judicial politics. He has served on royal commissions and task forces dealing with bilingualism and biculturalism, with reform of the R.C.M.P., and with aboriginal land claims.

Donald J. Savoie is executive director of the Canadian Institute for Research on Regional Development and professor of public administration at l'Université de Moncton. He has published widely on federalism, regional development, and government organization. He is the author of *Federal-Provincial Collaboration: Canada/New Brunswick General Development Agreement* and *Regional Economic Development: Canada's Search for Solutions*.

Richard Simeon is director of the School of Public Administration and professor of political studies at Queen's University. He has written extensively on federalism, regionalism, and public policy in Canada. He is author of *Federal-Provincial Diplomacy* and co-author (with David Elkins) of *Small Worlds: Provinces and Parties in Canadian Political Life*. Richard Simeon was research coordinator (Institutions) for the Macdonald Royal Commission on the Economic Union and Development Prospects for Canada, and was previously director of the Institute of Intergovernmental Relations at Queen's University.

D. V. Smiley is a distinguished research professor of political science at York University. He is a Fellow of the Royal Society of Canada, past editor of *Canadian Public Administration*, and past president of the Canadian Political Science Association. He has written numerous studies in the field of Canadian federalism. His most recent publication is *The Federal Condition in Canada*.

Garth Stevenson is professor of politics at Brock University. He previously taught at Carleton University and at the University of Alberta. He is the author of *Unfulfilled Union: Canadian Federalism and National Unity* and of *The Politics of Canada's Airlines: From Diefenbaker to Mulroney*.

Richard Vernon is professor and chairman of the department of political science at The University of Western Ontario. His publications include *Citizenship and Order*, and *Commitment and Change: Georges Sorel and the Idea of Revolution*. He has also edited *The Principle of Federation* by P. J. Proudhon.

Robert A. Young is associate professor of political science at The University of Western Ontario. He has written on Canadian federalism, politics in the Maritime provinces, free trade between Canada and the United States, and industrial policy. His current interests include development policy in New Brunswick and Ontario.

SECTION ONE

FEDERALISM AND THE ORGANIZATION OF POLITICAL LIFE

Approximately half of the world's population lives in a federal regime of one kind or another. What exactly is federalism and why has this form of political organization proven to be so popular? What factors influence the choice of a federal form of political organization and what are the benefits and advantages inherent in such a political union? How does Canada differ from other federal states, such as the United States, Australia, Switzerland, or West Germany? This section explores the *concept* of federalism and the variations in the *structure* of federal states. The objective is to place the Canadian federal state in a cross-national context.

On the most basic level, federalism involves a particular division of sovereignty within a nation-state. To understand this, it is perhaps best to contrast federalism with three other forms of political organization. In a *unitary state*, legislative authority (i.e., sovereignty) resides in a single legislative body. Great Britain provides the classic example of a unitary system of government. A *confederal system* involves the joining together of sovereign states and their delegation of limited legislative authority to newly created central institutions composed of representatives appointed by these component states. The first American constitution of 1781 (the Articles of Confederation) created a "confederation."

An *economic association* constitutes a limited form of confederal arrangement in which politically independent states enter into an agreement (i.e., an international treaty) on such matters as common tariffs, common currency and rates of exchange, and the free flow of capital and labour. An economic association between Canada and a politically independent Quebec was the objective of the "sovereignty-association" option advocated by the Parti Québécois during the 1980 Quebec referendum.

Federalism is most often defined in terms of the *division* of sovereignty within a state, the existence of independent and autonomous governments *within a single political system*, and a union of *territorial communities* that are differentiated by language, religion, ethnicity, culture, or economic condition. In practice, the internal organization of federal states can vary significantly in such matters as the number, size, and wealth of component units (asymmetrical federalism), the distribution of

1

legislative authority (interstate federalism), regional representation in central institutions (intrastate federalism), and the methods of resolving intergovernmental disputes (conflict management).

Authors differ in their views of the objective of the federal form of political association. Economists often see the union of previously independent states as motivated by a desire to create a larger economic market, to increase international bargaining power, and to achieve greater economies of scale through the sharing of common governmental functions (such as the construction of transportation facilities). Sociologists frequently identify federalism with the institutional recognition and protection of group or community interests, whereas political scientists emphasize its protection of the individual citizen. For some authors, federalism is viewed as a means of achieving territorial expansion or military security in the face of an external threat. Other authors emphasize the enhancement of personal freedom and the limitation of the power of the state through the division of legislative authority among competing governmental units.

The initial essay, written by Richard Vernon, explores the objectives of federalism from the perspective of the citizen. Vernon argues that citizenship does not lend itself easily to dual political allegiance and that a federal system fosters both conflicting and mutually reinforcing loyalties to both the nation and the local community (state or province). Federal states reflect internal societal tensions and divisions, and if conflict is to be managed, institutional arrangements must permit the effective expression of these competing civic loyalties.

The essay by Thomas Hueglin examines how three mature, industrialized Western federal states—Canada, the United States and West Germany—confront the problems of a postindustrial society. His study compares the form of political institutions that express "the federal fact" in each society, the degree of fiscal self-sufficiency of the territorial units and the particular mechanisms employed to redistribute wealth within each federal state. Despite the persistence of strong regional attachments and some institutional failure, when viewed comparatively, Canadian federalism emerges as a relatively effective and stable form of political organization for its citizenry.

1. THE FEDERAL CITIZEN

Richard Vernon

Federalism has traditionally been defined in terms of constitutional law as a system in which powers are divided between central and regional authorities, each governing directly and independently within its own defined sphere, and neither being able to modify the division of powers unilaterally.[1] From time to time, indeed, social scientists appear to have felt uneasy about relying upon constitutional law for their categories, and thus have been led to criticize the traditional definition. Should we not, as some have argued, adjust our categories to the realities of social and political process, not constitutional forms?[2] But to interest oneself in federalism is necessarily to interest oneself in a constitutional category, for it is in constitutional terms that the otherwise disparate polities termed "federal" are related. It may or may not be the case that all the polities termed "federal" are acted upon by some common social or political factor that makes them all federal. But even if they are all acted on this way, what *defines* them as federal has to be distinguished from what *explains* their federal character. Finally, even if we are looking for explanations of why some polities are federal, it would be quite wrong to suppose that constitutional features are mere effects and not causes, for it is plainly the case that constitutions can exercise important influences over politics and, in the longer run, over society too.

For these reasons, then, anxiety about relying upon a constitutional definition is largely misplaced. Such a definition is adequate to the task. A federation, as opposed to a unitary state, is a regime of coordinate authority, in which

some division of jurisdiction between centre and region is constitutionally protected.

All that is proposed here is a change of, so to speak, a tactical nature. Instead of looking at federalism from the top down, in terms of the imposition of authority, we may look at it from the other angle, that is, from the perspective of its members, and define it in terms of coordinate *citizenship*. A federation is a system in which each participant enjoys a constitutionally protected membership in two polities, one regional and one central. This does nothing to the substance of the above definition. It merely changes perspectives on it from that of *obeying* to that of *belonging*. But this switch of perspective may be of some use in bringing to light an intriguing question. Can the concept of citizenship lend itself to dual political allegiance?

The theme of citizenship has been an important one in Western political thought. It has always had strongly hierarchical implications, in the sense that "citizens" have been viewed as people with a single overriding object of loyalty. Machiavelli (in the *Discourses*) and Rousseau (in *Emile*) propose somewhat caricatured examples. Machiavelli recommends Brutus as a model citizen, because he sacrificed his sons to save Rome, while Rousseau admires the story of the Spartan mother who cared nothing for her children's lives, as long as Sparta won the battle. The citizen, as described in such classical texts, is not attractive as a friend, still less as a parent. But even in less overdrawn pictures, citizens are required to be alive to the general interests of a political community and to set particular interests aside when necessary. They are supposed to attach importance to their membership in a political community, at the expense sometimes of their membership in families or professional or

An original essay written especially for this volume.

regional communities; and they are supposed to define their own interests, at least in certain contexts, in terms of the interests of the political community to which they belong. It is this, traditionally, that has distinguished the "citizen" from the mere "subject". While subjects are "subjected" to law in a manner no different from that of a foreign visitor, citizens see membership in a community as something that in part defines who and what they are and arrange their priorities accordingly.

Now it is this aspect of citizenship that places federalism in an interesting light and may also render it problematic. The citizen, as viewed by political theorists, sets the general above the particular and ranks his or her attachments. To be a citizen is to put one's priorities in strict order. But to be a *federal* citizen, as we at once see, must be different. A federal citizen has *two* official loyalties. This is simply not the same as having one official loyalty and all sorts of other unofficial loyalties—loyalties to be set aside, when necessary, in order to be a good citizen, as theorists such as Machiavelli and Rousseau so vividly recommend. Federal constitutions explicitly provide that neither provincial nor national authorities are supreme over the other, that obligations are owed to each within their defined spheres. Because authority is divided in this way, the citizen too is divided.

What is the point of drawing attention to this notion of divided loyalty?[3] It may provide a basis for explaining why federalism matters, what difference it makes, and why it might be worth having. It helps to explain what federalism might have to do with widely accepted values such as democracy and freedom—a question which is often raised, but which is remarkably hard to answer. It also helps to explain why some recent Canadian debates about the *mode* of federalism are important. They are debates about how to make sense of the difficult notion of competing civic loyalties in a specific political context.

But this is to run ahead of the argument. First, I must explain why federalism needs de-fending at all; second, I must explain why a "competing civic loyalties" argument is better than other proposed defences; and finally, I must attempt to show how this rather abstract idea connects with political debate.

I

Why, first of all, does federalism require a defence? The answer is simple: federalism has been declared to be quite pointless. Here fashions in criticizing federalism have changed. For an earlier generation of critics, federalism was malign because it impeded central planning, hindered firm political action, prevented national majorities from enjoying their due, and defended local prejudices and tyrannies. An eloquent statement of such a view is Harold Laski's "The Obsolescence of Federalism" (1939),[4] prompted by economic depression and the (federal) state's inability to respond effectively.

Similar sorts of objections were provoked by the protection apparently afforded by federalism to racist policies in American states and to Nazism in pre-war Germany. Federalism gets in the way of urgently needed change. But more recent criticisms attribute no efficacy to federalism at all, not even the efficacy in doing the evil which earlier critics saw in it. Their spirit is well conveyed by the subtitle of an essay by W. H. Riker: "Does Federalism Exist and Does it Matter?"[5] In particular, recent critics have attempted to discredit the idea that federalism has any connection with freedom, which they take to be the value which is supposed to give federalism its point. They have certainly succeeded in casting doubt upon the case that they believe has been made for federalism. What are their arguments?[6]

Federalism is a system in which governing powers are constitutionally dispersed between different governmental levels. If federalism has a point, it must be shown that such a dispersal of power promotes some significant and widely shared value. The first and most obvious possibility is that a federal arrangement, in dispersing power between national and provincial governments, thereby limits the power of national majorities to do as they wish, and thus protects minorities. Interest- or opinion-groups which have no hope of becoming a national majority may become a provincial majority or at least a minority strong enough that provincial majorities must reckon with them. Thus, a structure of government assigning powers to provincial majorities or their representatives certainly enhances the position of such groups. But unfortunately for the argument, if it is wrong to give national majorities power over provincial minorities, it must also be wrong to give provincial majorities power over provincial minorities, which is what federalism does. It subjects black minorities to white majorities in white majority states, even though the cause of black minorities may be supported by a national majority. In such cases it is hard indeed to suppose that the federal dispersal of power is an instrument of freedom. But we cannot disapprove of the federal dispersal of power when we dislike the consequences and approve of it when we like the consequences, just as we cannot (consistently) deny national majorities the right to impose upon minorities while constitutionally confirming the right of provincial majorities to do exactly the same thing.

Alternatively, we could seek to defend federalism, not in terms of protecting minority freedom, but in terms of protecting a whole society's freedom against the undue concentration of power, the abuse of power, or both. A famous maxim of political science is that power can be checked only with power. What better way of checking power than by multiplying governments, so that they restrain and limit one another? They will do so, however, only if they have opposed interests or values. If they act in concert they will not check one another. If they do check one another, that may be because they reflect a diversity of interests or values in society—a diversity which, if there were no federal system, would probably find political reflection

by other means (such as the party system). So if "the real cause for the existence of liberty is the pluralist structure of society"[7] and not a federal constitution, then the significance of the federal constitution is clearly limited. And when a national mood of fear or anger overrides social pluralism—anti-communist paranoia, for example—governments act concertedly and liberties receive no protection from the federal system.

But surely there are some arguments for decentralization? Of course there are. There are arguments based upon the efficiency of service provision, which is likely to be improved if there is a mixture of governmental levels rather than a single distant central distributor. There are values based upon the merits of democratic participation, which is often thought to be enhanced by the provision of relatively small and relatively homogeneous units. There are arguments based upon the preservation of local cultures, to which political decentralization may offer one route. There are, doubtless, many other arguments too. All of them, however, run into a serious difficulty: the objection that unitary states, too, can be decentralized. Here the example of Britain, a (politically) decentralized but (constitutionally) unitary state, is frequently cited and clearly is instructive. In the British political tradition local self-government and the limitation of central power are themes often stressed. The British process of state formation is often contrasted with the French case, in which the state grew by systematically demolishing local powers instead of coming into counterpoise with them. But it is plainly not federalism that explains this difference; it is explained by a complex of political factors. Observers impressed by this fact have made the claim that decentralization does not require federalism at all. "All that is needful," J. S. Mill wrote, "is to give a sufficiently large sphere of action to the local authorities."[8]

A possible reply, however, is that only a federation can give adequate constitutional protection to the subnational governments. The Greater London Council can be abolished at will by the British Parliament, but the Province of Ontario cannot be abolished by the Canadian Parliament. At any given point, in other words, there may be as much decentralization in some unitary states as in some federations. But over time, the chances of preserving the powers provinces have in a federation are better than the chances of preserving the powers subordinate governments have in a unitary state. Such a view has been attributed to the American founders,[9] and also to Proudhon. It is not obviously unreasonable. If it is true that federations arise when smaller territories desire some unity but fear complete absorption into a unitary state, then some such view must presumably be held by the inhabitants or leaders of the smaller territories, or else they would have no reason to choose federation. But the view is not in any unqualified sense true. A federal constitution has not protected subnational governments in the U.S.S.R.; and in cases where subnational governments *have* retained their powers, they have done so, not only because of the federal constitution, but because of many other contributing factors (including, of course, those factors which incline political actors to accept constitutional provisions!). The claim, then, needs to be weakened: federation may be one of the ways in which subnational autonomies are protected, though it is neither (always) a necessary nor (ever) a sufficient condition.

II

One approach to defending federalism, currently popular and apparently promising, must be mentioned here, if only to be rejected. This is an approach based on the logic of social choice. Let us suppose that a political society (like an economy) is made up of individuals who make choices and want to get as many as possible of the things they choose. What scale of organization will best enable them to get what they choose? Here we seem to face a dilemma. Relatively

small organizations will, of course, be relatively more responsive to any individual's choices—in a group of ten, each counts for one-tenth; in a group of one million, each counts for only one-millionth. To this we may add the further consideration that the smaller the groups which make decisions, the better the chance of homogeneity, so that the choices of one group of like-minded citizens are less likely to be constantly thwarted by the choices of other groups with different interests. So for these reasons, organizations should be small.

But that is only half the picture. The smaller the organization, the smaller its jurisdiction. If we draw the boundaries narrowly, we shall be less able to exercise control over events which impinge upon the community from outside its boundaries. The smaller the organizations, the more of them there will be, and thus there will be more "externalities," that is, effects generated by one community's choices which spill over into another community's life. And the more fragmented decision-making is, the more likely we are to encounter unwanted policy results which only concerted common action could avert. Each community may derive benefits from its own polluting industries which far outweigh the costs specifically attributable to its own pollution, but the benefits may be outweighed by the costs imposed by *everyone's* pollution cumulatively. So organizations should be large, permitting allowance to be made for such cumulative costs.

The outcome of this logic, as was argued by the authors of a study of *Size and Democracy* in 1973, is a "complex federated polity" in which small and large political organizations coexist.[10] When responsiveness is essential and diversity precludes consensus, we assign powers to small organizations. Where "externalities" abound or where joint action is essential, we assign powers to large organizations. Such a view has more recently been elaborated by Vincent Ostrom and offered specifically as a reply to Riker's critique.[11] Ostrom's argument is more refined and detailed than the mere sketch offered above and should be consulted by anyone who is interested in the spirited construction of ingenious defences. But the trouble is, it is not really a defence of *federalism*. It is a defence of a system in which "citizens confront several purveyors of public goods and services" so that they can "search out an appropriate mix of public goods and services." That says nothing, however, about the constitutional form of such a system. It thus misses the point of the objection: whatever is claimed for decentralization can also be claimed for a unitary state. The point is made by Ostrom's appeal to examples such as the "fragmented" but (he claims) exemplary management of water use in Southern California. While the United States is a federal system, the State of California is a unitary system, and the West and Central Basin Replenishment District is not a partner in a federal arrangement but (legally speaking) the creature of a superior government. And if such agencies *are* to be regarded as components of "federalism," then logically it could make no difference if the states themselves were merely creatures of the federal government, so that we no longer had federalism in the relevant (constitutional) sense.

Worse than that, the "federalism" defended in the above way ideally demands fluid boundaries, defined by intersecting preferences, and redefined constantly as salient issues shift. While it would be satisfying to suppose that the division of jurisdiction in any actual federation might more or less correspond to this model, it would in fact be entirely irrational to do so. The provinces of Canada may or may not correspond to relatively homogeneous communities of interest. They may be too small: a unified Atlantic region might fit the social choice model better than four provinces. They may be too big: Northern Ontario and Metro Toronto should be separate actors, not subsumed under one province. It may also be that more than two levels of organization are needed to give optimal expression to the distribution of choices, as Ostrom indeed says.[12] But there is no evidence that federal regimes are more hospitable to multiple levels of organization than unitary regimes are. Indeed, confronted with a predatory federal centre, provinces may seek to concentrate power jealously and to minimize the autonomy of sub-provincial (municipal) organizations.[13] So if the "federalism" defended by social choice theorists demands multiple, functionally defined jurisdictions, then it provides us with a critique rather than a defence of what federalism is generally taken to be.

It may be revealing, though, to ask what is wrong with the social choice approach, and whether there is some general reason why it leads us away from understanding federalism. The answer, surely, is that it treats the citizen only as a *consumer* of quantifiable goods. Anything quantifiable can vary indefinitely in quantity, and any desire to consume can vary indefinitely in relation to other desires. Here we scarcely have a promising basis for any constitutional arrangement, least of all for federalism. If federalism is to be defended as constitutionally-protected decentralization, we remove any possibility of using an economic model to defend it. For if economic models derive their persuasive power from their flexibility in relation to shifting preferences, federalism derives whatever persuasive power it has from its resistance to shifting preferences, and from its protection of a distribution of power against whatever majorities happen to want.

III

Now it is perfectly true that the consumption of desired things is an integral part of politics. Politics *is* about who gets what, when, and how. Any view of politics which neglects this fact is doomed to hopeless irrelevance. Politics *is* consumption. But that is not all it is. It is also a matter of self-identification, that is, of declaring not merely what one wants but who one is. To vote (or work) for a nationalist party, or for a provincialist party such as the Parti Québécois, or for a class party such as the British Labour Party is to declare something about how one sees oneself and which of the various identifications one might adopt is most salient. And this is prior to the act of wanting: what one takes oneself to *be* is logically prior to determining the salience of various possible wants and desires. A sort of spurious realism attaches to the idea that wants are somehow primary or given, that reflection on self-identification is a luxury of dubious political importance. What seems to be realism is actually nothing more than excessive neatness. Wants affect what one decides to be; what one decides to be governs what one wants. There is a two-way process, and any desire to reduce it to a one-way process displays impatience with the complexity of human motivation.[14]

Where, then, should one look? Let us examine very briefly three texts which establish a connection between federalism and the process of self-definition, where membership involves determining where one belongs, and which of one's attachments have priority. That, it was suggested above, is the point of introducing the notion of federal *citizenship*. A citizen, ideally viewed, is concerned, not simply with identifying the rules which he or she is subject to, but wants to view himself or herself as a participant in a political community, and thus attaches value to belonging to one community rather than another. The three texts to be briefly discussed may help to illustrate the importance of this point in justifying federalism's significance.

1. For a defence of federalism it is natural to turn first to *The Federalist*, written during the constitutional debates in the United States in the 1780s and an unrivalled statement of American political philosophy.[15] However, to turn to *The Federalist* is to be disappointed, for there is rather little about federalism in it. The object of the authors, Madison, Hamilton, and Jay, is to make a case for a more unified constitution than

the original Articles of Confederation had provided, and their best known and most powerful arguments would serve to justify a unitary state as well as a federation.

Take, for example, the famous argument of Letter 10. A democracy, by which Madison means a direct democracy, can exist only in a small society, but in a small society minorities are constantly imperilled by "factions" or self-interested majorities. A larger society places more obstacles in the path of factious majorities: "Extend the sphere, and you take in a greater variety of parties and interests; you make it less probable that a majority of the whole will have a common motive to invade the rights of other citizens."

Madison's argument concerns the extent of political organization, not its form. Something a little more promising follows at once: "The influence of factious leaders may kindle a flame within their particular States, but will be unable to kindle a general conflagration through all the States." This part of the argument entails local political autonomy as well as sheer diversity. But we have seen that local autonomy arguments are not necessarily federalism arguments, and it is interesting to note that when the same argument is used later by Tocqueville, it is intended to support, not federalism, but simply administrative decentralization.

What, then, are the specifically federalist arguments of *The Federalist*? In Letter 17, Hamilton speaks of the state governments as a "counterpoise . . . to the power of the Union," and this might seem a natural argument for theorists of checks and balances to use. The division of powers between State and Union, on such an argument, could be defended in the same way as the separation of powers between branches of government, or between upper and lower branches of the legislature.

Such a connection is hinted at in Madison's Letter 51, perhaps the fullest statement of his pluralistic point of view: "In the compound republic of America, the power surrendered by the people is first divided between two distinct governments, and then the portion alloted to each, subdivided among distinct and separate departments. Hence a double security arises to the rights of the people. The different governments will controul each other; at the same time that each will be controuled by itself." But very little is made of this, and one cannot fail to gather the impression that if federalism is important for this reason, it is not very high on Madison's list of priorities. Even in Letter 17, where Hamilton speaks of "counterpoise," the context is the extremely limited one of persuading states that there is no risk of federal encroachment on their powers—a task quite different from that of explaining why (if at all) it is a good thing that states should *have* any powers. At best, it explains why "local" (that is, state) government is necessary: "It is a known fact of human nature that its affections are commonly weak in proportion to the distance or diffuseness of the object," and there is thus a necessary place in political schemes for objects of local attachment.

But this notion of "affection" points towards a different line of argument, premised not upon balance but upon *competition*. People will have affections for various objects, and the affections that they have for nearer objects will normally be stronger than their affections for more distant objects. "The operations of the national government . . . will be less apt to come home to the feelings of the people; and, in proportion, less likely to inspire a habitual sense of obligation and an active sentiment of attachment." But something may intervene to change this normal pattern: maladministration, tyranny, or corruption.

Hamilton offers two examples. The first is that of feudal Europe, where power was divided between a sovereign and his feudatories (or barons). Being "immediate lords" of their subjects rather than a distant sovereign whose power was mediated through subordinates, barons generally enjoyed a more secure authority. For short periods, a "vigorous" sovereign "of superior

abilities" could redress the balance, and in the long run, the barons' oppression of their subjects was so intolerable that the latter formed an alliance with the king against the barons. "Had the nobles, by a conduct of clemency and justice, preserved the fidelity and devotion of their retainers and followers, the contests between them and the prince must almost always have ended in their favour." The second example, that of the decline of the clans of Scotland after the Act of Union, adopts a similar tack. Hamilton then goes on to compare with these examples the federal situation, the same in displaying "the rivalship of power." Here we have at least a plausible defence of federalism: by systematically dividing loyalties, it sets authorities in competition for the affection of followers. If it does so, then presumably it will enhance at least one democratic value, that of the responsiveness of government to opinion. Civic efficacy is greater, *The Federalist* in effect claims, when the objects of civic affection are multiple and thus potentially in contestation.

2. It is *not* natural to turn for illumination to *The Principle of Federation*, a book written in 1863 by P.-J. Proudhon, better known as an anarchist than as a federalist thinker.[16] What he proposes is in detail too radical, too eccentric, and still too imbued with anarchist feeling to serve as a guide to the modern federal state. Whereas Madison and Hamilton were arguing for the *aggregation* of thirteen semi-independent states into a closer union, Proudhon was arguing for nothing less than the *dis*aggregation of France into (about) eighteen provinces and for the replacement of nation-states by "federations." But although this conclusion takes him far afield, his *principle* does tell us something about federalism.

Nothing could be more misleading than the assumption that Proudhon, because he believed in the disaggregation of large units into small ones, is therefore the victim of a cult of smallness. What he is against is the cult of monism or the exaggerated belief in unity. Like so many French thinkers of both the left and the right, he believed that the centralization of the French state had been carried to absurd lengths, thanks in part to the French Revolution. "In the social contract as imagined by Rousseau and the Jacobins the citizen divests himself of sovereignty, and the town and the Department and province, absorbed by central authority, are no longer anything but agencies under direct ministerial control."[17] But it is not Proudhon's intention to set against this vision of the indivisible sovereign state a counter-vision of an indivisible town or province. His is a thesis of the systematic divisibility of power. No level of government is to assume a dominant position on the horizons of individuals' lives.

Higher levels of government, Proudhon believed, must keep their hands off local administration, which is not only something better accomplished locally, but also a realm of action in which civic virtues are best displayed; the centralized state reduces the citizen to a passive and pathetic role, leaving him nothing to do but "perform his little task . . . relying for the rest upon the providence of government,"[18] while the federal state cultivates local initiative. In that sense it is the local or provincial government that is the agent of freedom, if freedom is taken to mean activity rather than passivity, self-assertiveness rather than dependence. But in at least two other senses the federal state itself is the agent of freedom. For one thing, if it is to keep its hands off administration, it has a correspondingly dignified role as "prime mover and general director" and as "the highest expression of progress." It is thus the state that expresses and gives direction to freedom in the sense of a society's capacity to initiate, to change its own circumstances, and to achieve common objectives. For another thing, the locality or province, no less than the state, can become oppressive to the individual, and it is necessary to set a federal state above it in order to act as a guarantor of

individual rights. In Proudhon's account the idea of "freedom" takes on rich and complex forms, and it would be instructive to compare his account with the rather mechanical and impoverished view of freedom which critics of federalism tend to adopt.

The extraordinary interest of Proudhon's argument does not lie, as I have noted above, in the details of what he has to offer—details which are open to innumerable criticisms. His argument is interesting because he believes in "citizenship" but not in "cities"; that is, he values above all else the sort of virtues that citizens are supposed to display—self-sacrifice, responsibility, concern for shared goals—but he does not want these virtues to be directed towards any single focus. Indeed, he believed that if civic loyalty is directed towards any single object it will be destroyed, that citizenship is compatible only with multiple loci of attachment. Perhaps more than any other theorist, he exemplifies the value of what has recently and aptly been called "agnosticism about community";[19] that is, Proudhon does not believe that any level of organization inherently expresses one's sense of who one is and what one belongs to, and that this sense can best be realized when feelings of belonging are in competition. To the extent that one is obliged to choose one obligation over another, one is less free to choose between potentially rival attachments, and, consequently, to choose one identity rather than another. To the extent that "the federal principle" leaves open the question of priority, permitting individuals to balance one attachment against another, it permits more scope, Proudhon believes, for self-determination.

3. The third example is a remarkable essay entitled "Nationality" by Lord Acton,[20] a British liberal of the Victorian period, published one year before Proudhon's *Principle of Federation*. Acton's concern is scarcely with federalism as we know it. Although he mentions Switzerland and the United States he also offers a passionate defence of "the British and Austrian multiracial empires." That, of course, at once distances him rather sharply from Proudhon, for whom "federalism" and "empire" were antitheses. Yet the interesting thing is that, despite enormous distance of what we might call an ideological kind, Acton's liberal imperialism is remarkably in tune with Proudhon's socialist anarchism.

Like Proudhon, Acton dreads above all the creation of single, supreme, and unqualified loyalties, and values federalism precisely because it sets loyalties in permanent competition. Like Proudhon, too, he sees the pernicious source of undivided loyalty in the democratic principle of the French Revolution, which sought to represent political society as the expression of an undivided common will. On the French democratic view, Acton complains, "nationality is founded on the perpetual supremacy of the collective will, of which the unity of the nation is the necessary condition, to which every other influence must defer, and against which no obligation enjoys authority, and all resistance is tyrannical . . . . Whenever a single definite object is made the supreme end of the state, be it the advantage of a class, the safety or the power of the country, the greatest happiness of the greatest number, or the support of any speculative idea, the State becomes for the time inevitably absolute."

Acton contrasts this absolutist view with a liberal one. Instead of requiring submission to a "single definite object," liberals seek to establish conditions under which multiple and various desired objects can coexist, liberty being a precondition for the pursuit of diverse ends. Liberty is possible only when one end is not supposed to be all-inclusive or all-important. That is why it is so necessary to separate ends, to divide loyalties, and to ensure that political structures do not wholly coincide with other objects of loyalty. "The presence of different nations under the same sovereignty is similar in its effect to the independence of the Church in the State. It provides against the servility which flourished under the shadow of a single authority, by balancing interests, multiplying associations, and giving to

the subject the restraint and support of a combined opinion. In the same way it promotes independence by forming definite groups of public opinion, and by affording a great source and centre of political sentiments, and of notions of duty not derived from the sovereign will."

Here Acton's argument plainly shares something with Madison as well as with Proudhon. Acton is Proudhon-like in demanding recognition of a diversity of wills which resists subsumption under a general will. He is Madison-like in demanding an association which is "the vastest that can be included in a state." But Acton's introduction of the church-state analogy introduces a wholly new dimension. Madison and Proudhon speak of the division of interests and of the advantage of separating interest-representing mechanisms. Acton speaks, also, of the advantage of separating *kinds* of interests, so that states do not become overbearing in the sort of attachment that they invite or demand. To fuse the state and the nation, in other words, is to do much the same as to fuse the state and the church. It is to overload politics with aspirations and passions which appropriately belong elsewhere. Federalism, then, is the means of confining politics to its proper scope, by setting other loyalties in a position of rivalry with loyalty to the state.

Here, then, we have three different approaches, written in quite different political contexts and with quite different ideological assumptions, that nevertheless have something important in common: they promote federalism because it divides civic loyalty. The arguments are not the same, of course. *The Federalist*—to the extend that it *is* federalist—wants to enhance the responsiveness of government to shades and diversities of opinion that could simply vanish in a majoritarian unitary state. Proudhon wants to cultivate a certain kind of moral responsibility, which he believes can be cultivated only where responsibilities are both specific and tangible, and not swamped by the demands of a (fictitious) "people." Acton wants to protect a certain style of politics by excluding from politics those obsessive and redemptive passions which churches, but not states, can sustain. These arguments are so interesting, and so richly diverse, that one suspects that a very much better case could be made for federalism than the case which critics of federalism delight in overturning.

IV

There could then be reasons why citizenship should be divided. But *how* can citizenship be divided? How can something traditionally thought to be exclusive by its very nature, come to be directed to two objects at once? Such a thing may go against the grain of one's expectations. It did so in the Canadian case. It was the belief of Sir John A. Macdonald, among many others, that provincial identities would wither away as the Canadian state gained increasing saliency as a focus of political attention and an outlet for political ambition.[21] But as one careful examination of political loyalties in Canada concludes, "citizens generally see no need to 'choose sides'—to renounce either their federal or their provincial loyalties or identities."[22] The authors continue: "The perceptions of citizens and the policies of governments . . . reflect a balance of unity and diversity, of convergence and divergence, of loyalties to larger and smaller units . . . . The tension and conflict so obvious to any observer indicate that no one view, no one loyalty, no one identity has any predominance, nor is it likely to in the near future."

One way of explaining this situation is as follows. Provincial and federal loyalties share something in that they are political loyalties. They entail legal obligations, the legitimate use of coercion, the official expression of conflict, and the symbolism of sovereignty. But although they are similar in type, they can differ in content. Some official powers can belong to one level, others to another level. So just as in private life people can readily adjust to the existence of authorities in different spheres—children, for example, expect-

ing instructions of one kind from parents, another kind from teachers—so federal citizens adapt to dual political allegiances. There are, as it were, two states, occupying themselves with distinct areas of each individual's life. If the division of powers has been appropriately settled, the provincial state will concern itself with matters of primary concern to a region, while the federal state will concern itself with matters of general interest. This is what has been termed "interstate" federalism—a federalism which divides powers between two states or political systems, each of which has its own political life, neither impinging in any primary way upon the other.[23]

What is called "intrastate" federalism, however, contains a different and more complex relationship between the two levels of identification, which are pictured as parts of a single political system. The stress does not fall on the independence of provinces as (partially) self-governing entities, and thus upon the division of responsibilities which gives them this status: rather, the stress falls upon the fact that provinces retain *an identity as political actors in federal politics*. If Canada were a unitary state, Ontario could simply vanish as a distinct interest or a distinct voice in national policy-making. In a Canadian federation of an "intrastate" kind, on the other hand, Ontario's interests and views must be taken into account in formulating what the Canadian general interest *is*.

One could say that intrastate federalism is a form of democratic theory in which the constituencies are regional ones, as opposed to professional or social or economic ones. In pluralist democracy as once understood in the United States, policies reflected the interplay of "groups" with varied demands and varying degrees of leverage, whereas in intrastate federalist democracy the crucial interplay occurs among provincial demands, perhaps with the difference that provincial demands are already more likely than "group" demands to represent aggregation, compromise, and democratic legitimation. They are already the demands of citizens, citizenship finding its locus not merely at one level, as in pluralist democracy, nor in two separate realms, as in interstate federalism, but in two realms, one of which is embraced by the other.

Here, though, we evidently face a choice. Are provinces or provincial governments to be represented at the federal centre? The difference is enormous. Provincial governments, as political elites, have some political objectives which non-elites do not share. Even if provincial governments perfectly reflect provincial majorities, it makes a difference whether or not a federal government can mobilize "dispersed majorities," or majorities lacking decisive strength in any one province. Even with respect to reflecting the views of provincial majorities, a federal government can change those views by manipulating alternatives or offering inducements, if it is able to bypass provincial governments and seek the support of provincial opinion directly. A version of intrastate federalism permitting federal government to do that is evidently more "centralist" in its potential. It gives federal government itself the possibility of becoming the outlet for important provincial demands, thus undercutting the claim of provincial governments to be the sole voice of provincial interests. Conversely, of course, a version of intrastate federalism in which provincial governments were the sole voice of provinces would tend to be highly decentralist. The federal government would be constrained in its role of national government not only by the federal division of powers but also by the fact that, even in exercising its *own* powers, it would be impeded by the opposition of provincial governments with interests different from its own and from each other's. In the latter case, *federal* citizenship would seem to be quite attenuated. Federal politics would be intergovernmental politics, and federal citizenship would be expressed only in a periodic national vote which of necessity could exercise only remote influence with respect to any given issue.

It is in the "centralist" version of "intra-state" federalism, then, that the idea of divided citizenship is pushed to the most interesting lengths. Here we have a situation in which, ideally viewed, two distinct kinds of judgment are made systematically available to every citizen, perhaps, even, with respect to one and the same issue. First, one is required to judge which of two or more outcomes is preferable in relation to one's own interests, when set in the context of other (*provincial*) interests with which one's own interests may be highly interdependent. Second, one is required to judge which of two or more outcomes is preferable when set in the context of other (*national*) interests, where even more complex sets of interdependencies exist. This would seem to require great sophistication—certainly more than Machiavelli required Brutus to exercise, or Rousseau required the Spartan mothers to exercise in condemning their children in the name of a single unambiguous standard. Yet it appears not altogether unrealistic to expect such sophistication.

These three conceptions of federal citizenship naturally affect conceptions of federalism itself and are notably prominent in discussions of constitutional change. *How* they affect constitutional proposals is a question which, although intriguing, goes beyond the scope of this paper.[24] All that can be said here is that assessments of any given federation, and proposals for amending its constitution, may helpfully be examined in the light of the broad themes mentioned above: democratic responsiveness, the openness of choice of identification, and the preservation of politics from (unqualified) nationalism. If none of these themes find any reflection in political fact, then we may have to agree that federalism makes no difference. If one or more of them *do* find concrete expression, then the federal character of a polity will have to be taken as seriously as its democratic, its liberal, or its pluralist character, for its federal character bears upon the most fundamental issue that can be raised about it—namely, what it means to be a citizen within it.

Notes

1. A clear and careful definition is provided by Peter W. Hogg: "In a federal state governmental power is distributed between a central (or national or federal) authority and several regional (or provincial or state) authorities, in such a way that every individual in the state is subject to the laws of two authorities, the central authority and a regional authority . . . . The central authority and the regional authorities are 'coordinate,' that is to say, neither is subordinate to the other." *Constitutional Law of Canada*, revised edition (Toronto: Carswell, 1985), 80.

2. See especially W. S. Livingston, *Federalism and Constitutional Change* (Oxford: Clarendon, 1956).

3. For an exploration of this theme in the Canadian context, see Edwin R. Black, *Divided Loyalties: Canadian Concepts of Federalism* (Montreal: McGill-Queen's, 1975).

4. *The New Republic*, vol. 98, May 3, 1939, 367-9.

5. *Comparative Politics* 2 (1969), 135-46.

6. The following arguments are assembled from three sharply critical texts: Franz Neumann, "On the Theory of the Federal State," in *The Democratic and the Authoritarian State* (New York: Free Press, 1957), 216-32; William H. Riker, *Federalism: Origins, Operation, Significance* (Boston: Little, Brown, 1964); Preston King, "Against Federalism," in R. Benewick et al., eds., *Knowledge and Belief in Politics* (London: Unwin, 1973), 151-76.

7. Neumann op. cit., 220.

8. J. S. Mill, *Utilitarianism, On Liberty and Considerations of Representative Government* (London: Dent, 1910), 375.

9. See Martin Diamond, "The Ends of Federalism," in *Daniel J. Elazar*, ed., *The Federal Polity* (New Brunswick, N.J.: Transaction, 1974), 129-52.

10. Robert A. Dahl and Edward R. Tufte, *Size and Democracy* (Stanford: Stanford University Press, 1973), 137.

11. "Can Federalism Make a Difference?" in Elazar, *Federal Polity*, 197-237.

12. Ibid., 204-5.

13. See for example Neumann, "Theory of the Federal State," and for a Canadian case, Robert A. Young, "Remembering Equal Opportunity: Clearing the Undergrowth in New Brunswick," *Canadian Public Administration* (forthcoming).

14. For a fluent and wide-ranging discussion, see Charles Taylor, "Alternative Futures: Legitimacy, Identity and Alienation in Late Twentieth-Century Canada," in Alan Cairns and Cynthia Williams, eds., *Constitutionalism, Citizenship and Society in Canada* (Toronto: University of Toronto Press, 1985), 183-229.

15. The edition I have used is *The Federalist Papers* by Alexander Hamilton, James Madison and John Jay (New York: Bantam, 1982).

16. See Richard Vernon, ed. and trans., *The Principle of Federation* by P.-J. Proudhon (Toronto: University of Toronto Press, 1979).

17. Ibid., 59.

18. Ibid., 60.

19. See Reginald Whitaker, "Federalism and Democratic Theory," Institute of Intergovernmental Relations, Queen's University (Discussion Paper #17), 1983, 45.

20. In Acton's *Essays in the Liberal Interpretation of History* (Chicago: University of Chicago Press, 1967), 131-59. A more recent discussion sharing something with Acton's is P. E. Trudeau, *Federalism and the French Canadians* (Toronto: Macmillan, 1968).

21. See for example Gordon Stewart, "The Origins of Canadian Politics and John A. Macdonald," in R. Kenneth Carty and W. Peter Ward, eds., *National Politics and Community in Canada* (Vancouver: University of British Columbia Press, 1986), 15-47.

22. David J. Elkins and Richard Simeon et al., *Small Worlds: Provinces and Parties in Canadian Political Life* (Toronto: Methuen, 1980), 308.

23. See Alan C. Cairns, "From Interstate to Intrastate Federalism in Canada," Institute of Intergovernmental Relations, Queen's University (Discussion Paper #5), 1979.

24. Discussions include Alan C. Cairns, Recent Federalist Constitutional Proposals: A Review Essay," *Canadian Public Policy* 5 (1979): 348-65.

Selected Readings

Simeon, R. "Criteria for Choice in Federal Systems." *Queen's Law Journal*, 8:1 and 2 (Fall 1982, Spring 1983), 131-58.

Smiley, D.V. *The Federal Condition in Canada.* Toronto: McGraw-Hill Ryerson Ltd., 1987.

Trudeau, P. E. *Federalism and the French Canadians.* Toronto: Macmillan of Canada, 1968.

Vernon, R., ed. and trans. *The Principle of Federation by P.-J. Proudhon.* Toronto: University of Toronto Press, 1979.

Whitaker, Reginald. *Federalism and Democratic Theory.* Kingston: Institute of Intergovernmental Relations, Queen's University, Discussion Paper #17, 1983.

2. FEDERALISM IN COMPARATIVE PERSPECTIVE

Thomas O. Hueglin

The Canadian federal polity has recently experienced three fundamental crises which may well be regarded unique in the context of politics in the Western industrialized world. The Quebec crisis brought the country to the brink of political disintegration. The negative outcome of the 1980 referendum on sovereignty-association and the defeat of the Parti Québécois in 1986 must be seen today as a consequence of the fundamentally changed role of Quebec in Confederation. The separatist thrust declined with the success of province-building and the ascent of francophone influence in Ottawa.

Secondly, the energy crisis, which culminated in the oil war between Ottawa and Alberta in 1980-81, exposed the brittleness of Canadian economic union in an unprecedented way. While western separatism remained a short-lived emotional outburst of alienation and the collapse of the world oil price after 1982 brought to a halt the boom of prairie province-building, a considerable shift in the focus of national economic policy-making nevertheless marked the end of the Trudeau years. The conservative electoral victory of 1984 was clearly based on the promise "to bring the west back in." Ironically, this has meanwhile resulted in some degree of alienation of Ottawa's traditionally most faithful ally, Ontario, over, for instance, the free trade issue.

Finally, and closely linked to the Quebec and western crises, the long-standing controversy over the question of constitutional patriation reached a dramatic climax in 1981. Based on an ambiguous Supreme Court judgement, the Constitutional Accord was agreed upon by nine provinces and the federal government, but left Quebec "out in the cold." While the adoption of a Charter of Rights must be interpreted as a centralist victory with hardly forseeable legal consequences, the further entrenchment of provincial resource ownership rights as well as the amending formula and opting-out clause basically confirm the decentralist dynamic of the previous two decades. In essence, this outcome is more of a symbolic than practical political consequence, as the amending process is now patriated, but remains largely immobilized.

Canadians have tended to attribute the roots of this interrelated set of political, social, and economic crises to the peculiar fabric and decentralizing dynamic of Canadian federalism,[1] although not all have gone so far as to denounce this dynamic as a lack of political sanity.[2] In comparative perspective, however, the record of Canadian federalism can only be established in a meaningful way when the uniquely Canadian crisis symptoms are clearly distinguished from those which are affecting all advanced industrial

An original essay written especially for this volume.

states—although both may be mutually reinforcing in the Canadian setting. This exercise requires us to redefine federalism in the context of advanced or postindustrial society.

FEDERALISM REVISITED: STRUCTURES AND PROCESSES

With nearly 40 percent of the world's population now living under some form of federal government[3] and trends of federalization affecting the fabric of some of the most stubbornly Jacobin unitary states,[4] one ought to assume that the study of federalism (as a concept of political organization) and the analysis of existing or emergent federations would be among the most fascinating topics in social science. Far from it. The excitement over past federal-provincial conflict in Canada cannot obscure the fact that both conceptual discussion and comparative analysis of federalism have remained somewhat stale, strangely insulated from mainstream political discourse.

A number of reasons for this can be given. During the postwar reconstruction period and after the experience with fascist totalitarianism in Europe, the discussion of federalism focused on the constitutional aspects of a vertical separation of power which was to protect liberal societies against the central usurpation of power. The American model obviously served as the classical yardstick. By the late 1960s, the focus had shifted from constitutional design to the analysis of federal practice. Still based on the American model, a gap began to open between the narrow focus of the principles of federalism and the "infinite variety" of federation in practice.[5]

By now the conceptualization of federalism appears both too narrow *and* too wide. It is too narrow where federalism remains defined as structural variety—two or three constitutionally guaranteed levels of government, and the cooperation between them,[6] commonly confined to the framework of pluralistic society. This latter narrowness does not so much stem from the obvious exclusion of non-pluralist or socialist types of federalism, but from the limits of pluralism itself. If the most advanced pluralists concede themselves that their concept suffers from a contradiction between *form* (unrestrained group diversity) and *content* (the domination of business over all other groups),[7] then structural variations or the constitutional procurement of such a contradiction do not appear to become any more meaningful.

The concept of federalism appears too wide, on the other hand, when it tries to provide a "broad church" of approaches encompassing everything and anything that can be roughly squared with the federalist spirit of sharing, mutualism, or covenant.[8] A recourse to the philosophical tradition of covenanted mutualism is a badly needed counterpoint to the competitive "cash-nexus" of modern capitalist life,[9] but it can hardly serve as a point of conceptual clarification or comparative analysis in a world whose institutions are for the most part designed and governed by a cash-nexus.

The combination of a narrow set of institutional principles with the generous supposition of a broad federal philosphy tends to lead the analysis to the wrong issues and perspectives. Taking intergovernmental cooperation and/or conflict as an indication of a "living" system of federalism may blind the analysis to the existence of dominant socio-economic forces which either operate outside this system or instrumentalize it for purposes which hardly qualify as "mutual sharing." Focusing primarily on nation-state politics and structures, federal analysis neglects the fact that the political stage of the nation-state is losing relevance. Global interdependence makes intergovernmental squabbles appear as not much more than buck-passing. And while policy-making is rapidly passing from the *logic* of active public policy formation to the *logistics* of reactive damage control to economic crisis and governmental overload, fiscal policy is still treated as an independent analytical variable.

What is missing, then, is an appropriate conceptual as well as analytical framework within which the politics and policy of federalism can be re-examined. Much federal theorizing has focused on the question of whether the politics of federalism is a result of the cultures and ideologies of federal societies, or whether it is the governments of federalism which have made society "responsive to its demands."[10] As recent theories of the modern capitalist state have suggested, the ideological, political, and economic substructures of modern societal systems must be seen as interdependent and at the same time operating in *relative autonomy* of one another, albeit with the economic substructure ultimately determining the other two.[11] This is the framework in which the analysis of federalism and federation must be placed.

First, in the realm of political ideology dramatic changes have been noted over the past two decades. While Robert Lane still could forsee a universal trend of "politics of consensus in an age of affluence" in the mid-1960s[12], the situation is now characterized by rapid value change and ideological fragmentation. Samuel Huntington correctly predicted that the structural adjustments to such postindustrial fragmentation would bring along with them an enormous expansion of mobilized participatory demands which would make postindustrial societies difficult to govern.[13] In this context federal analysis needs to examine to what extent intergovernmental conflict may be influenced and reinforced by an increase of regionalized cultural identity.

Second, the main institutional challenge to liberal capitalist societies throughout the postwar period has been the dramatic increase in public political interventionism. Administering the transition from the postwar period of growth to the current period of (relative) economic stagnation, the Keynesian interventionist state became caught

in the contradictory webs of a market-oriented restructuring of the capitalist economy and the welfare state as its most important support system. In the context of the duplication of government in federal systems, this has typically meant the "growth of government at both levels," and an often immobilizing and counterproductive degree of federal-provincial competition.[14]

Finally, the political economy of the postindustrial state is characterized by rapid structural change and an increasing degree of socioeconomic polarization resulting from it. Leaving behind the epoch of postwar economic reconstruction, capitalism is now confronted with the constraints of a volatile international market place experiencing unprecedented competition and saturation in many sectors. Domestically contrained by fiscal crisis and sectoral decline, the capitalist state has to administer painfully selective choices of economic restructuring and investment priority. Postindustrial societies are presently witnessing an alarming degree of socio-economic polarization between corporate mergers and business bankruptcies, sunbelt and rustbelt industries, winners and losers. According to the spatial division of labour and productivity, this polarization adds particular strains to federal systems which appear doubly divided: between winner and loser provinces on the one hand, and between regional and national economic priorities on the other.

In this context a re-evaluation of the federal principle is warranted. Power-sharing among institutionally autonomous levels of government is meaningless when it is not accompanied by a sufficient socio-economic power base. The insistence on sufficient economic means is likewise irrelevant without the socio-cultural persistence of regional identity, otherwise people would simply move closer to where such means are available. Federalism as a meaningful yardstick for the analysis of federations—and their distinction from unitary states—is therefore defined as a system of political organization characterized by the constitution of at least two levels of institutional political autonomy, the retention of a substantial degree of regional cultural identity, and by the provision of a minimal degree of economic self-sufficiency for all jurisdictions.

By definition, the ultimate goal of federal systems is to maintain a balance between the two levels of government. The maintenance of "unity in diversity" is a matter of centralization and decentralization, which in turn depends on the style and dynamic of intergovernmental conflict regulation. Other than in the contractualist market-place, federalism typically is a political arrangement in which the weaker get more than they can pay for: equal rights and opportunities regardless of size and power. This is often a matter of style. Given the ambiguity of overlapping jurisdictions, governments at either level may try to resort to unilateral action when they believe that they can get away with it; both levels of government may perceive intergovernmental relations as an arena for competitive struggle with changing rounds of winners and losers; or they may rely on consensual bargaining as the intrinsically federal mode of conflict regulation.

The institutional set-up of divided jurisdictions and the high degree of policy interdependence in complex industrial societies make federal cooperation on the basis of mutual bargaining inevitable. This does not mean, however, that unilateralism and competitiveness do not loom behind the facade of consensual federal brotherhood. Participants at the federal negotiating table will try to improve their bargaining position by unilaterally changing the balance of power in their favour, and/or they will try to win support from their respective electorates by competitively promoting alternative policy packages. The relative dominance of each of these modes of conflict regulation will ultimately depend upon the quality, dynamic, and stability of federal systems.

The quality of the Canadian federal polity can now be discussed in this framework. The comparative focus will be on those two other major federations in the Western industrialized world which are at the same time similar enough to allow meaningful comparisons and yet sufficiently different from one another to point out the specific character of the Canadian federation in the context of a general federal typology: West Germany and the United States.

AUTONOMY, SELF-SUFFICIENCY, IDENTITY: THE COMPARATIVE RECORD

The Political Structures of Federalism

According to classical theory the duplication of governments in federal systems means a vertical separation of powers. Neatly separated spheres of jursidiction are to prevent the abuse of political power and to ensure the autonomy of the component member-states. In modern societies such a system of dual federalism cannot work, though, and it is doubtful if it ever has.[15] Given the complexity of modern industrial life, jurisdictional competencies can hardly ever be separated cleanly, and the relationship between the two levels of government must rather be described as one of competition and/or cooperation. Cooperative federalism typically encompasses both the legislative and executive branches of government. Its most important political structures are known as the system of bicameralism and the wide field of intergovernmental relations.

Bicameralism means that the federal legislature is composed of two chambers: a lower house where members are elected on a nation-wide basis and an upper house composed of regional (state/provincial) representatives. Thus the states/provinces participate in federal legislation. While the American Senate is composed of two popularly elected senators from each state, the German *Bundesrat* (Federal Council) consists of appointed representatives of the ten West German *Laender*. These are typically the Prime Ministers of the Laender and/or their cabinet ministers. Moreover, as opposed to the U.S. Senate, voting in the Bundesrat is weighted, giving more votes to the larger and more populus Laender than to the smaller ones.

This distinction of the senate and council principle is very important for the character of the two legislative systems. U.S. senators are directly responsible to the population in their home states, but they can vote independently from government policy in these states. The members of the German *Bundesrat* are instructed delegates of their *Laender* governments, and their votes are given unanimously according to this instruction from the *Laender* governments. Thus the *Laender* governments can influence federal legislation much more directly than in the American case.

Canada is the only federation in the world which does not possess a meaningful second chamber in the federal legislature. It does have a Senate, but its members are appointed by the federal government. It is not inappropriate to describe the Canadian Senate as a refuge of patronage posts occupied by lobbyists for (sometimes regionally) organized interests.[16] The ongoing debate about senate reform in Canada[17] is obviously not only spawned and guided by the lack of provincial representation at the national level of government, but also by the apparent embarrassment about the present situation. Because of the political insignificance of the Canadian upper house, which stems from the British tradition of Westminster parliamentarism, federal-provincial cooperation in Canada has to rely exclusively on intergovernmental relations. While all other federations allow for a significant degree of provincial/state participation in the national legislative process (intrastate federalism), Canadian federalism is best described as a system of "federal-provincial diplomacy" (interstate federalism).[18]

Of course, other federations also have developed various channels of intergovernmental relations which reflect the complexity of policy-making in advanced industrial societies. In West Germany this cooperation between the two levels of government is highly formalized through the constitutional establishment of various intergovernmental councils and committees involved in all important policy areas.[19] In the United States, on the other hand, the process of intergovernmental cooperation is informal and incrementalist, growing parallel to the hundreds of Congress-enacted individual grant programs rather than trying to create generally integrated patterns of policy-making.[20]

Canada is different again in this context. Because federal-provincial cooperation has to rely on interstate federalism alone, the arena of intergovernmental relations has grown to appalling proportions. Seven hundred and eighty-two federal-provincial conferences and meetings at all levels of the government bureaucracy have been counted for one typical year.[21] Critics have consequently held that Canadian politics has degenerated into a bureaucratic jungle of *executive federalism* which is too far removed from popular (i.e., legislative) control.[22] With the media attention on the highly visible First Ministers' Conferences, the process of intergovernmental coordination has moreover often become overly politicized, pouring oil on the flames of general federal-provincial conflict, rather than focusing on the functional coordination of individual policy issues.

Another and often neglected aspect of federalism pertains to the structural incorporation of the local or municipal level of government. Canada and West Germany have unicameral state/ *Laender* legislatures. (An exception is the Bavarian Senate, which has little political power and can be compared to the Canadian Senate.) The vertical separation of power is therefore incomplete in these countries. While federal governments have to live with the constraint of bicameral control, provincial or *Laender* governments exercise almost "feudal" power over their territories. In the United States the principle of bicameralism is reproduced at the state level as well (with the exception of Nebraska). Representation by county or district, rather than population, led to rural over-representation and legislative neglect of the growing problems of urbanization. This in turn spawned federal grant programs, which increasingly influenced urban renewal policy. Recent Supreme Court decisions therefore ordained that representation in both state chambers be more or less apportioned on a population basis.[23]

Typically, however, this democratic principle of representation on the basis of population is exactly what appears modified in federal systems: two senators from each state sit in the American Senate, regardless of the states' size and population, and although the votes in the German *Bundesrat* are weighted according to the population basis of the Laender, the smaller ones among them are still over-represented. Thus their share of the vote exceeds their share of the population. Second chambers in federal systems modify the democratic principle of majority rule. Votes are not taken on the representative basis of a nation-wide majority, as in the lower houses, but on the basis of a majority among the component units, states or *Laender*. Federalism thus appears as a balance between the interests of national majorities (represented through the lower house) and regional minority interests (represented through the upper house). The legislative process in bicameral federal systems can therefore be defined as a system of *compound majoritarianism*.[24] In Canada, on the other hand, it is probably appropriate to speak of a system of "dual majoritarianism," as the two levels of government operate independently of each other, and the collective will of the provinces can only be voiced through the channels of intergovernmental relations.

The extent to which the component units in federal systems can exercise their influence upon national legislations varies according to the for-

mal distribution of powers between the two chambers.[25] The American Senate possesses powers equal or "symmetrical" to those of the House, i.e., all legislation must be passed by both chambers. The West German constitution (Basic Law), on the other hand, distinguishes between legislation which must secure majorities in both chambers (constitutional amendments and laws which affect the competencies of the *Laender*) and other legislation, where the negative vote of the *Bundesrat* can be overridden by the lower House (*Bundestag*).[26]

While these "asymmetrical" provisions seem to establish that the *Bundestag* has the edge over the *Bundesrat*, the powers of the two chambers are in reality nearly equal because the division of competencies between the two levels of government in the West German federal system is different from most other federations. Instead of enumerating distinct spheres of legislative competencies, the Basic Law concentrates almost all important legislative powers at the federal level and leaves most of the powers and regulations of implementation to the *Laender*. Hence, *Laender* interests are almost always affected by federal legislation, and the *Bundesrat's* veto power in fact extends to all major bills. Its composition (representatives of the *Laender* governments) and voting behaviour (government-instructed block voting) make it one of the most powerful upper houses in the world. The crucial task of legislative coordination lies with a Mediating Committee, composed of members from both Houses.

Obviously, Canadian bicameralism is extremely asymmetrical. Although the Canadian Senate formally possesses co-equal powers, its composition through appointment by the federal executive (on a rather arbitrary basis of regional representation) deprives it of any political legitimacy. House bills are passed routinely—albeit after minor amendments. At best, the Senate's input to legislation can be described as "legislative craftsmanship" with regard to the final formulation of a bill. Occasional opposition is only voiced when "major business and financial concerns" are at stake.[27]

This is why the balance between national and regional interests has to be accomplished through intergovernmental relations alone. For a number of reasons these relations are often strained and confrontational. The lack of adequate regional representation at the federal level of government is reinforced by a highly decentralized party system. Some provinces are governed by regional parties which are not represented at the federal level at all (e.g., Social Credit in British Columbia and, recently, the Parti Québécois in Quebec). And the three nationally dominant parties not only have asymmetrical regional power bases (e.g., the lack of any representation west of Winnipeg in the governing Liberal caucus during the last Trudeau years), but are also divided internally along regional lines (e.g., the looming conflict between the Alberta and federal Conservatives).

Representative asymmetry is compounded by the majoritarian, winner-take-all electoral system, which typically does not translate regional percentage shares of the vote into House seats. While the same is true for the United States, the effects are mitigated by the larger number of states and greater dispersion of partisanship. In contrast, the West German electoral system is *proportional*, i.e., all parties gain seats equivalent to their shares of the vote.

A second and most important source of conflict is the peculiar division of powers in the Constitution Act of 1867, which assigned the ownership of natural resources to the provinces (Section 92) while giving Ottawa the general competence over economic management (Section 91). Given the importance of natural resources such as oil and gas for the Canadian economy, these constitutional provisions proved critical for Canada's style of conflict regulation. Competitively trying to secure the lion's share of revenues, a major oil conflict erupted in 1980-81 when Ottawa unilaterally announced new price

and revenue sharing regimes (National Energy Program), and Alberta retaliated by consecutive five percent cuts in eastward-bound oil production.[28] In the end a compromise was reached which left both parties better off than either one of their unilateral proposals would have.[29]

Federal-provincial conflict has finally been reinforced by the growth of government at both levels in general and the establishment of an intergovernmental bureacracy in particular. While government growth is a consequence of public policy expansion in all advanced industrial societies, its duplication in federal systems opens new areas for conflict. The particular growth of a new intergovernmental bureaucracy occurred over the conflicts about language rights and resource revenues. Special departments for intergovernmental affairs have been established at both levels of government since the early 1960s. This institutionalization may well have reinforced conflict, as intergovernmental executives (including First Ministers) tend to politicize the jurisdictional and symbolic dimension of policy issues formerly handled by line departments.[30]

The style of intergovernmental relations in Canada is clearly competitive, but the overlapping nature of jurisdictional competencies ultimately requires compromise. Originally designed as a strongly centralizing document, the Canadian Constitution Act has nevertheless contributed to the retention and even expansion of substantial provincial political autonomy. In contrast to this decentralizing dynamic of the Canadian federal polity, the United States and West Germany have gone the opposite way.

As in the Canadian case, centralization and decentralization of political power in the United States are determined by two potentially conflictive constitutional provisions. The supremacy clause (Article VI.2) gives general legislative superiority to the federal level of government, whereas the 10th Amendment assigns to the states all legislation which is not explicitly enumerated as a federal competence (i.e., residual competence lies with the states). Contrary to the evolution of Canadian federalism, however, and supported by a long history of Supreme Court decisions, the 10th Amendment must today be considered as of not much more than declaratory value.[31] Especially in conjunction with the clauses referring to welfare, commerce, and taxation, the federal government can enact whatever legislation it deems opportune "in the national interest." In particular the abysmal federal grant system has subordinated the states' share of power to the "permission and permissiveness of the national government." A new label has therefore been suggested for the American system of federalism: permissive federalism.[32] Because of the magnitude of programs, and the large number of participants, American intergovernmental relations seem uncoordinated and pragmatic.

In sharp contrast, intergovernmental relations in West Germany are highly institutionalized and structured, as might be expected in a country with a long and unbroken legal tradition. The peculiar division of powers (federal legislation and *Laender* administration) left little room for subnational autonomy, and soon after the West German state had been established through the Basic Law in 1949, unitary federalism became its commonly accepted label. Very few competencies remained exclusively under *Laender* jurisdiction (mainly police and education). On the other hand, and contrary to the system of dual administration in Canada and the United States, the German federal government does not possess an extensive administrative bureaucracy of its own. This gives the *Laender* administrations a great deal of discretion in the implementation of federal provisions.

Until the late 1960s the main characteristic of intergovernmental relations was the horizontal self-coordination of the *Laender* in numerous commissions and committees. This changed radically after the constitutional reforms of 1967-69. A system of interlocking federalism emerged

which was characterized by "vertically cartelized bureaucracies."[33] After the experience of the first postwar economic recession in the mid-1960s there was general belief that the German state needed a centrally coordinated Keynesian management ("global economic steering"), and the constitutional reform was in fact implemented by a grand coalition between the two major political parties (Conservatives and Social Democrats). Financial and economic planning commissions were established and even the *Laender* self-coordination in the cultural and educational policy field was overlaid by a Joint Commission for Educational Planning. Most importantly, the *Laender* discretion in the administration of three crucial policy fields was curtailed by the constitutional entrenchment of "joint tasks" (regional development, higher education, and science). Moreover, the decentralization of law and order, designed as a democratic safeguard for the new German polity, became more and more integrated between the *Laender* police, the Federal Office for Crime Detection, and the paramilitary border police, potentially allowing a degree of surveillance (against growing civil protest and terrorism) which has provoked another label for the West German state: the security state. Finally, and in the same spirit of centralized efficiency and planning phobia, the historical structure of local government was eventually reduced from 24 000 to 8 500 units.[34]

The interlocking nature of West German federalism extends to both the legislative and executive sphere of government. Hailed as a model of stability and management efficiency by its constitutional designers, German-style federalism has also been criticized for major deficiencies. The roots of these deficiencies lie in the overly centralized party system composed of three major parties representing dominant interest orientations: business and agriculture in the case of the Christian Democrats (CDU/CSU), the professional middle classes in the case of the Liberals (FDP), and organized labour in the case of the Social Democrats (SPD). As coalition governments are the general rule at both levels of government and all the important policy programs require federal action including the cooperation of both Houses, "all major policies toward the private sector have required the formal agreement of all three parties." The adoption of policies "against the opposition of a major private interest group" has become extremely difficult,[35] especially when the two levels of government (and therefore *Bundestag* and *Bundesrat*) are dominated by concurrent party majorities. With the establishment of a new fourth party (the Greens), the problems have become even more complicated. The result of this system of multiple consensus requirements is a political culture and style of conflict avoidance and policy immobilism. The success and stability of the West German federation stem from an efficiently homogenized political economy rather than its interlocking political structures. They would hardly befit a country such as Canada, which neither avoids conflict nor is homogeneous.

The Political Economy of Federalism

Given the rapid structural changes forced upon advanced industrial societies by the volatility of national and international markets, the content of formally decentralized political power becomes very much a measure of subnational economic self-sufficiency. The capacity of provinces, states, or *Laender* to adapt to these structural changes depends on various factors: the degree of industrial diversification, including the procurement of resources; infrastructure and know-how; the capacity to raise revenues; and finally a system of fiscal transfers routinely compensating for structural disparities.

Being the richest country in the world, the United States still has almost unlimited resources.

Its industries are also highly diversified and spread well across the country. Nevertheless, the states' capacities to secure economic stability are unevenly distributed. Innate in the capitalist system of production is a secular trend towards centralization complemented by a spatial division of labour. Capitalism, in this sense, is incompatible with the principle of federalism. The political economy of federalism has to rectify these trends in order to maintain its political legitimacy.

The American system, however, reinforces this incompatibility for a number or reasons. Its bias towards government non-intervention and its lack of horizontal equalization belies the federal principle of mutual sharing. Federal Darwinism prevails instead. On the one hand, American market liberalism allows the structural shifts between rustbelts and sunbelts, growing and decaying industries, and winners and losers, to go unfettered. On the other hand, regional response to structural change is kept in the lead-strings of Congressional legislative permissiveness, particularly with the conditional grant system: he who pays makes the rules and vice versa. In addition, the uncoordinated and concurrent tax system has led to a grave imbalance between revenue and expenditure (to some extent typical of all federal systems). The federal government collects most of the taxes, and the lower levels of government spend most of the money.[36] The dependency of state and local governments on federal grant transfers becomes inevitable. President Reagan's "new federalism" has turned out to be a largely rhetorical attempt to rectify this situation. While he has successfully resisted new commitments to intergovernmental assistance, no formal devolution of authority has occurred. Reagan's ultimate goal has not been to reform federalism, but to extricate the federal government from the responsibility for nationally uniform standards in the public services.[37]

There can be no doubt that some fundamental reform of fiscal federalism in the United States would be appropriate. On the one hand, given the mismatch between federal revenues and state and local expenditures, the plethora of federal transfers under the categorical grant (492 programs in 1978) and general revenue sharing system (general purpose federal assistance to approximately 38,000 local governments)[38] has reduced the federal government to a "transfer agency, shifting funds to other units of government which had become the main providers of direct services to the public." On the other hand, and especially given the predominance of categorical grants (75 percent of all federal grant outlays by 1980) which inevitably involve "strings" (e.g., matching requirements and/or program specifications), the proliferation of the transfer system has meant a major "infringement upon state and local administrative freedom."[39]

Moreover, by focusing on recipient groups and projects instead of regions, the transfer system has reinforced rather than alleviated problems of fiscal inequality. While the grant system has given freely to everyone, regardless of regional need in time of abundance, the cuts now administered likewise affect everyone, regardless of the fact that some states run fiscal surpluses and others deficits.

The current "new federalism" debate does not address these issues. Instead intergovernmental relations have become a battleground between the (old) liberal and (new) conservative visions of nationhood. The conservative agenda in relation to federal transfer cuts is to strengthen their primary national goals—in the words of U.S. Vice-President George Bush, "to assure the national defense and, domestically, to make freedom work." While this agenda works under the pretext of giving authority back to the states, its aggressive assertion of federal jurisdictional supremacy at the same time (including a "deathwatch on liberal members of the U.S. Supreme Court") aims at exactly the opposite: a national determination of how exactly freedom ought to work.

On the liberal side, goals and the critique of government action are similarly confused. De-ploring the return to a system of dual federalism as a return to the "dark ages of states' rights," liberals are in reality opposing the kind of policies promoted by it. Committed to a New Deal universalism, the liberal agenda of "making freedom work" would substitute military for domestic spending, but it would also entail a further federal encroachment of states' rights.[40] Thus American federalism seems to be in both a conceptual and operational crisis. A serious re-sorting of federal/state functions and competencies is nowhere in sight. Given the dependency of national policy-making upon the concerns of the industrial-military complex, the resurgence of institutional and jurisdictional muscle-flexing appears to be little more than rearguard action in a battle already lost.

Contrary to the American situation, the "equality of living conditions" for all citizens, regardless of their place of residence, is enshrined in West Germany's Basic Law (Article 72.2). Consequently, fiscal equalization has become the most prominent feature of German intergovernmental relations. All major taxes are shared and distributed among the three levels of government according to a constitutionally prescribed formula. Distribution adjustments are likewise prescribed when the revenue/expenditure relation begins to differ substantially between the federal and *Laender* level of government.[41] In addition, there are two major mechanisms of equalization which ensure that West Germans live in one of the regionally most homogeneous federations in the world. Negotiated federal payments (out of the federal share of the turnover tax) to the poorer *Laender* constitute a "fatherly" system of vertical equalization. It is complemented by a "brotherly" scheme of horizontal equalization which redistributes funds directly from the richer to the poorer *Laender* on the basis of their tax capacities. These interstate transfers nearly bring the overall tax income of the poorer *Laender* up to the national average.[42]

Compared to the dependency of American

states upon the whims of the permissive grant system and the volatility of unfettered market capitalism, West German federalism seems to be blessed with the happy coincidence of industrial homogeneity aided by a political commitment to regional infrastructural development and a scheme of "brotherly" fiscal equalization providing equal public services and living conditions. The picture is deceiving. If it can be said that American economic federalism "has all but disappeared"[43] under a national regime of economic concentration, the same can be said in the case of Germany—albeit for different reasons.

A close look at the West German political economy reveals a unique pattern of centralized interaction between the industrial, financial, and government sectors in all important economic policy matters. Given Germany's limited national market capacity and lack of indigenous resources, the industrial sector appears strongly unified in its persistent export orientation. A close interrelationship between industrial and financial capital bridges the polycentric structure of the German economy. Dominated by three giants, German banks effectively control "seventy percent of the shares of the 425 largest firms . . . accounting for three-quarters of the value of all the shares on the stock exchange."[44] Through ideological ties with two of the three major political parties (CDU and FDP) as well as through the regime of corporatist intermediation (direct bargaining between government and the highly centralized peak organizations of capital and labour), major economic policies cannot be implemented without the consent of the dominant financial/export/government bloc. Tied into this scheme of interlocking politics through the *Bundesrat*, the *Laender* governments will either support or obstruct economic policy-making along partisan lines (depending on the majority situation in the upper house), but they will rarely if ever promote regional economic interests. West German federalism is therefore overshadowed, not only by an overly centralized

party system, but also and more importantly by the asymmetry of organized interests. Federal legitimacy remains subordinated to national economic efficiency.

This is precisely what some Canadian economists and policy makers would want. They deplore the fact that Canadian provinces "balkanize" the national economy by making use of jurisdictional ambiguities in order to strengthen and protect their uneven economic bases (province-building). The main grievances are the diversification of regional staple economies through forced industrialization; discriminatory purchasing policies; and provincialist barriers to trade, transportation, and labour mobility—the latter especially achieved through such "artificial incentives to stay" as equalization payments and regional development programs. It is almost funny how the same line of argument which blames concurring factions of business for interprovincial conflict and competition at the same time cries out for national market forces to redress Canada's economic ills.[45]

Given the highly uneven economic bases of Canada's regions, neither tax sharing (with some provinces opting out)—the most elaborate scheme of fiscal equalization (considering 29 provincial revenue sources)—nor shared-cost programs (Established Programs Financing, Canada Assistance Plan, and a wide array of conditional grant programs) have been able to eradicate basic disparities in the provinces' economic and fiscal status.[46] Ontario's heavy manufacturing sector, for example, outweighs the Canadian average by 50 percent.[47] Due to this industrial concentration, Ontario's share of federal transfers lies at 25 percent, while that of Prince Edward Island amounts to 56 percent.[48] Because of the revenues accruing from natural resources in the three westernmost provinces and because of the lack of direct horizontal ("brotherly") transfers from the richer to the poorer provinces, the equalization system puts considerable strain on the federal budget, despite a recent imposition of limits and ceilings. On the other hand, the resource revenue field is volatile, as the recent decline in world oil prices and other events demonstrate. In the case of the British Columbian lumber industry, the postwar boom ended when the forest resource became less valuable to U.S. investors due to a drop in demand, costly technological change, organized labour power, and the depletion of the most valuable timber holdings.[49]

More recently, the very commitment of the Canadian federal state to equalization has been called into question. What has so far been regarded as an indispensable if costly precondition for democratic legitimation, i.e., the provision of equal public services and acceptable living conditions for all Canadians regardless of their regional place of residence, is now being denounced as a harmful system of transfer dependency which not only weakens the national economy as a whole, but hurts the regional transfer recipients themselves. The main argument is that transfer payments make poor regions even poorer, because "easy handout[s]" prevent them from seeking "to alter the conditions which create their underdevelopment," and because they allow an artificially high standard of living, preventing the "natural" adjustment of the regional price and wage system. A drastic reduction of transfers would instead lead to "natural" conditions of cheap labour (attractive for external investment) and out-migration (balancing labour markets).

Critics belonging to the dependency theory school have argued instead that the desired consequences of such transfer reductions are far from certain because the principal cause of peripheral underdevelopment is not a lack of initiative or indigenous deficiency, but the central exploitation of the peripheries' resources and "reserve army" of labour. Most importantly in the context of federalism, however, they argue that the transfer dependency approach is based on an instrumentalist economic view which "tends to divorce considerations of economic

well-being from broader social and cultural value orientations," in particular the values of those "who wish to remain in Canada's dependent regions."[50]

As long as the commitment to equalization remains intact, the Canadian polity can be regarded as living up to the federal yardstick of sharing and of balancing regional group liberty with national individual liberty. This retention of regional values and group identities is what the critics of the decentralizing forces of Canadian federalism have for a long time denounced as "hallowed nonsense."[51]

The Political Culture of Federalism

One of the most famous and yet least seriously considered statements about the nature of politics is Schattschneider's observation that all political systems have a specific "bias in favor of the exploitation of some kinds of conflict and the suppression of others."[52] Federal systems will therefore accentuate intergovernmental conflict, but that does not necessarily mean that the major social conflicts of a society do not get addressed. Rather, they are channelled through the institutions of federalism in a particular way. Given the regional division of labour, conflicts between capitalist factions, which occupy the central political stage in unitary systems, may typically take on intergovernmental characteristics in federal states. Likewise, class conflict may take the form of centre-periphery conflict. It is therefore unclear whether federal societies set the agenda of intergovernmental conflict, or whether the governments of federalism make federal societies "responsive to their demands."[53] It is safe to say that while the formation of federal systems is usually based on the pre-existence of strong regional identities, the retention of such identities is reinforced by the federal organization of politics.

Whether political institutions address the kinds of conflicts prevalent in society is a question of legitimacy. On the basis of American mass culture, William Riker argues that federal institutions are "specious and unreasonable" because they do not promote what American society seeks most: individual freedom.[54] A good argument can be made, however, that it is exactly the other way around. The institutions of American federalism promote mass culture in order to suppress that kind of conflict which would make the notion of individual freedom meaningful: class conflict.

The lack of socialism in the United states has been an object of academic puzzlement and curiosity for many years. Theodore Lowi contends the "balkanization" of state and local government structures did not allow a "socialist critique of American capitalism as a whole to develop."[55] Given the centralist bias of socialism this argument seems plausible, but it puts the blame on the inflexibility of the socialist counter-ideology rather than on the structure of federalism itself. The point is not whether federal, state or local governments are responsible for America's "victory over socialism," but how the same political elites occupying all political structures can successfully insulate themselves from social responsibility by passing the buck from one level of government to another. American federalism thus stabilizes society by suppressing social conflict. A legitimation crisis may erupt as regional identities are being sharpened through the experience of uneven economic development, the spatial effects of sectoral economic decline, or the impact of interregional ethnic diversification.[56]

Political stability in West Germany, on the other hand, is maintained through the interlocking of the two major ideological blocs or "pillars" in the structures of intrastate federalism (business/CDU/FDP, and labour/SDP). Not only are class conflicts dampened and "internalized" by this cartel of dominant socio-economic interests, but also the already poorly developed regional identities are further weakened as federal policy-making is organized towards one exclusive goal: the achievement of economic efficiency.

A potentially delegitimizing consequence of cartelizing the two major special interest organizations into a dominant power bloc is a decline of mass integration resulting from "diffuse protest postures, apathy, and 'being fed up with the state' (*Staatsverdrossenheit*)."[57] While these attitudes have affected the entire nation, it nevertheless strengthens regional identities as the growing power of various protest movements and the Green Party is essentially based on the exploitation of regional and local issues and conflicts. Because of its overly centralized and cartelized structures, West German federalism tends to polarize a society which is increasingly bifurcated into a dominant bloc occupying the political centre and various marginalized segments allying themselves with regional and local concerns. The institutionalized process of politics becomes obsolete when the dominant bloc primarily relies on direct negotiations with government, bypassing parliamentary control, while protest and opposition increasingly take to the streets. It is not without reason that the Greens insist their future efforts lie both inside and outside the parliamentary process.

What is a relatively new phenomenon in the United States as well as in West Germany is that innovative socio-political protest comes from the periphery. In Canada, this is the norm. Both the drive towards a modern welfare system and the efforts to reduce the vulnerability of the staples economy have originated in the west. Quebec has certainly succeeded in changing the fabric of Canadian federalism once and for all. Atlantic Canada has shown a remarkable resistance to the national forces of uniformity and migration. While the slow process of "Canadianization" has assimilated both regional "expectations and preferences with respect to most areas of public policy" and provincial "patterns of public expenditure," Canadians have remained "highly sensitized to regional differences."[58]

There are various explanations for this persistence of "dual loyalties." The relative autonomy of both levels of government prevents the strategy of passing the buck to avoid salient social issues. It likewise leaves more space for ideological diversity. And most importantly, the French factor remains a catalyst for the persistence of provincial aspirations. The recent flirtations of Canada's Conservative Government with the political style south of the border notwithstanding, there is no "American way" to a Canadian future.

THE CANADIAN WAY

Among the three federations considered, Canada is the weakest and most incomplete in a formal and institutional sense. But the lack of intrastate federalism might well correspond to the strongly regionalized character of the Canadian socioeconomic system. Institutionalizing federal-provincial conflict in a bicameral system lacking the central permissiveness of American federalism or the conflict-avoiding political culture prevailing in West Germany would probably be a cure worse than the disease. The legitimation deficits of Canadian executive federalism might be better addressed through more political transparence and the institutionalization of policy-oriented interprovincial cooperation.

As everywhere, the political institutions of democracy are in danger of becoming obsolete to the modes of policy formation dictated by the national and international political economy. There is little if any convincing evidence that the strongly decentralized forces of Canadian federalism contribute to this process of democratic erosion and delegitimization. Rather, the provincial jurisdiction over natural resources has provided a rationale for alternative responses to the challenges of economic globalization. As a consequence, the political economy of federalism is more strongly developed in Canada than in either the United States or Germany. Ironically, the source of this strength is at the same time Canada's greatest weakness: the continued dependence on the extraction of natural resources and their volatile world markets. If it is true that the dominating influence of American capital upon the Canadian economy exacerbates federal-provincial conflict (via the rivalries of factions of American capital interests and their Canadian "bridgeheads"), then this appears to be a problem of Canada's dependent capital structure and not of Canadian federalism as such.

Finally, while the political and economic structures of Canadian federalism certainly shape societal behaviour, it would appear to be a reductionist simplification to neglect the decentralizing elements in Canadian political culture itself. The political, economic, and cultural substructures of the Canadian federal polity must be seen as both interdependent and relatively autonomous. That the conflict in all three arenas tends to be reinforcing rather than cross-cutting makes Canada a difficult country to govern and a difficult fatherland to identify with. On the other hand, when compared to the potentially delegitimizing conflicts between economic centralism and societal bifurcation in West Germany or between federal supremacy and regional decline in the United States, the relative congruence of politics, economy, and culture in Canada ought to be considered a strength and not a liability.

Notes

1. Compare Donald V. Smiley. *Canada in Question* (Toronto: McGraw-Hill Ryerson, 1980), 252-83.

2. See Garth Stevenson, *Unfulfilled Union* (Toronto: Gage, 1982), preface.

3. See Max Frenkel, *Foederalismus und Bundesstaat* vol. 1 (Berne: Lang, 1984), 19.

4. See Yves Meny and Vincent Wright, eds., *Centre-Periphery Relations in Western Europe* (London: Allen and Unwin, 1985).

5. See Valerie Earle, ed., *Federalism* (Itasca: Peacock, 1968); S. Rufus Davis, *The Federal Principle* (Berkeley: University of California Press, 1978); William H. Riker, *Federalism* (Boston: Little, Brown and Co., 1964); the most useful definition within the liberal-pluralist paradigm is still Daniel J. Elazar, "Federalism" in *International Encyclopedia of the Social Sciences* (USA: Macmillan, 1968) vol. 5, 353-65.

6. See typically Stevenson, *Unfulfilled Union*, 8, although he then proceeds to talk about Canadian federalism mainly in economic terms.

7. See John F. Manley, "Neo-Pluralism: A Class Analysis of Pluralism I and Pluralism II," *American Political Science Review* 77 (1983): 368-83.

8. See John Kincaid and Daniel J. Elazar, eds., *The Covenant Connection* (Chapel Hill: Carolina Academic Press, 1987).

9. See Robert Skidelsky, "The Decline of Keynesian Politics," in Colin Crouch, ed., *State and Economy in Contemporary Capitalism* (New York: St. Martin's, 1979), 64.

10. Alan C. Cairns, "The Governments and Societies of Federalism," *Canadian Journal of Political Science* 10:4 (1977): 695.

11. See Martin Carnoy, *The State and Political Theory* (Princeton: Princeton University Press, 1984), 89-97.

12. Robert Lane, "The Politics of Consensus in an Age of Affluence," *American Political Science Review* 59 (1965): 874-95.

13. Samuel P. Huntington, "Postindustrial Politics: How Benign Will It Be?" *Comparative Politics* 6 (1974): 163-91.

14. Alan C. Cairns, "The Other Crisis of Canadian Federalism," *Canadian Public Administration* (Summer 1979): 177.

15. See Carl J. Friedrich, *Trends of Federalism in Theory and Practice* (London: Pall Mall, 1969), 19-20.

16. See John McMenemy, "Business Influence and Party Organizers in the Senate Imperil the Independence of Parliament," in Paul W. Fox, ed., *Politics: Canada* (Toronto: McGraw-Hill Ryerson, 1982), 541-8.

17. The literature is abundant; see recently Donald V. Smiley and Ronald L. Watts, *Intrastate Federalism in Canada* (Toronto: University of Toronto Press, 1985), chapter 7.

18. Richard Simeon, *Federal-Provincial Diplomacy* (Toronto: University of Toronto Press, 1972), as well as Smiley and Watts, *Intrastate Federalism in Canada*.

19. See Nevil Johnson, *State and Government in the Federal Republic of Germany* (Oxford: Pergamon, 1983), 136-41.

20. See *Studies in Comparative Federalism: Australia, Canada, the United States and West Germany* (Washington, D.C.: Advisory Commission on Intergovernmental Relations, 1981), 27-9.

21. Ibid., 33-4.

22. See Smiley, *Canada in Question*, chapter 4 and Leo Panitch, "The Role and Nature of the Canadian State," in L. Panitch, ed., *The Canadian State* (Toronto: University of Toronto Press, 1977), 11.

23. See M. Glenn Abernathy, *Civil Liberties under the Constitution* (New York: Harper & Row, 1977), 600-19.

24. See Daniel J. Elazar, "Confederation and Federal Liberty," *Publius: The Journal of Federalism* 12:4 (Fall 1982): 4.

25. See Arend Lijphart, *Democracies* (New Haven: Yale University Press, 1984), 95-9.

26. See Johnson, *State and Government in the Federal Republic of West Germany*, 126.

27. Roger Gibbins, *Conflict and Unity* (Toronto: Methuen, 1985), 318-9; see also pp. 119-20.

28. See John F. Conway, *The West* (Toronto: Lorimer, 1983), 209-17.

29. See John F. Helliwell and Robert N. McRae, "Resolving the Energy Conflict: From the National Energy Program to the Energy Agreements," *Canadian Public Policy* 8:1 (1982): 14-23.

30. Compare Gibbins, *Conflict and Unity*, 246-9.

31. See Robert F. Cushman, *Leading Constitutional Decisions* (New York: Appleton-Century-Crofts, 1971), 93-8.

32. Michael D. Reagan and John G. Sanzone, *The New Federalism* (New York: Oxford University Press, 1981), 175.

33. Gerhard Lehmbruch, "Party and Federation in Germany: A Developmental Dilemma," *Government and Opposition* 13:2 (1978): 170-1.

34. Johnson, *State and Government in the Federal Republic of West Germany*, 151.

35. Fritz W. Scharpf, Bernd Reissert and Fritz Schnabel, "Policy Effectiveness and Conflict Avoidance in Intergovernmental Policy Formation," in Kenneth Hanf and F. W. Scharpf, eds., *Interorganizational Policy Making* (London: Sage, 1978), 95-6.

36. See Daniel J. Elazar, "Fiscal Questions and Political Answers in Intergovernmental Finance," in Deil S. Wright and Harvey L. White, eds., *Federalism and Intergovernmental Relations* (Washington, D.C.: American Society for Public Administration, 1984), 159.

37. See George E. Peterson, "Federalism and the States," in John L. Palmer and Isabel V. Sawhill, eds., *The Reagan Record* (Cambridge: Ballinger, 1984), 256-9.

38. *Studies in Comparative Federalism*, 96.

39. Ibid., 63-4.

40. See John Kincaid and Stephen L. Schechter, "The State of American Federalism — 1985," *Publius: The Journal of Federalism* 16:3 (Summer 1986): 1-5.

41. See *Studies in Comparative Federalism*, 41-2.

42. See ibid., 69-70.

43. Theodore J. Lowi, "Why Is There No Socialism in the United States? A Federal Analysis," *International Political Science Review* 5:4 (1984): 379.

44. Peter A. Hall, "Patterns of Economic Policy: An Organizational Approach," in Stephen Bornstein, David Held, and Joel Krieger, eds., *The State in Capitalist Europe* (London: Allen and Unwin, 1984), 25.

45. See Stevenson, *Unfulfilled Union*, 104-24.

46. For details, see *Studies in Contemporary Federalism*, 54-62.

47. Paul Phillips, *Regional Disparities* (Toronto: Lorimer, 1982), 39.

48. Donald J. Savoie, "Defining Regional Disparities", in D. J. Savoie, ed., *The Canadian Economy: A Regional Perspective* (Toronto: Methuen, 1986), 176.

49. See Patricia Marchak, "The Rise and Fall of the Peripheral State: The Case of British Columbia," in Robert J. Brym, ed., *Regionalism in Canada* (Toronto: Irwin, 1986), 123-54.

50. On the question of transfer dependency vs. dependency theory, see Ralph Matthews, "Two Alternative Explanations of the Problem of Regional Dependency in Canada," in Savoie, *The Canadian Economy*, 64-81.

51. See Stevenson, *Unfulfilled Union*, 123.

52. E. E. Schattschneider, *The Semi-Sovereign People* (New York: Holt, Rinehart and Winston, 1960), 71.

53. See above, note 10.

54. Riker, *Federalism*, 139-45 and 151.

55. Lowi, "Why Is There No Socialism in the United States?", 375-8.

56. See Amitai Etzioni, *An Immodest Agenda* (New York: McGraw-Hill, 1983), chapter 7.

57. Joachim Hirsch, "Developments in the Political System of West Germany," in Richard Scase, ed., *The State in Western Europe* (London: Croom Helm, 1980), 128.

58. Richard Simeon and David J. Elkins, "Conclusion: Province, Nation, Country and Confederation," in D. J. Elkins and R. Simeon, eds., *Small Worlds* (Toronto: Methuen, 1980), 287-90.

Selected Readings

Bakvis, Herman. *Federalism and the Organization of Political Life: Canada in Comparative Perspective*. Kingston: Institute of Intergovernmental Relations, Queen's University, 1981.

Riker, W. H. *Federalism: Origin, Operation, Significance*. Boston: Little, Brown, 1964.

Sawer, G. F. *Modern Federalism*. London: C.A. Watts and Co. Ltd., 1969.

Watts, R. L. *Multicultural Societies and Federalism*. Studies of the Royal Commission on Bilingualism and Biculturalism, No. 8, Ottawa: Information Canada, 1970.

Wheare, K. C. *Federal Government*. 4th ed., London: Oxford University Press, 1963.

THE CONSTITUTION, THE COURTS, AND JUDICIAL REVIEW

A constitution may be defined as "a set of fundamental laws, customs, and conventions which provide the framework within which government is exercised in a state."[1] More specifically, a constitution fulfills several functions. It sets out the rule of law, outlines the major elements of the political regime, defines the legitimate role of government within society, and acts as a unifying symbol expressing the fundamental goals and values of a nation.

The written constitution is central to the very existence of a federal state. In the words of the British constitutional scholar K. C. Wheare: "Federal government exists . . . when the powers of government . . . are divided substantially according to the principle that there is a single independent authority for the whole area in respect to some matters, and that there are independent regional authorities for other matters, each set of authorities being coordinate with, and not subordinate to, the others within its own prescribed sphere."[2] A written constitution divides sovereignty and sets out the legislative authority of each level of government within a federal political system. Constitutional change may be initiated either by a formal amendment procedure enshrined in the constitution or by judicial interpretation that will give flexibility and clarity to the written document.

Until 1982, the British North America Act served as Canada's "core" constitutional document. However, as a result of a series of intergovernmental discussions initiated in 1968, the Canadian constitution was patriated with the enactment of the Constitution Act of 1982. A Charter of Fundamental Rights and Freedoms and a comprehensive amending formula were constitutionally entrenched and provincial ownership of natural resources was clarified and strengthened.

Garth Stevenson's article was originally prepared as a background study for the Royal Commission on the Economic Union and Development Prospects for Canada

---

1. Task Force on Canadian Unity, *Coming to Terms: The Words of the Debate* (Ottawa: Minister of Supply and Services, 1979), 29.
2. K. C. Wheare, *Federal Government*, 4th ed. (New York: Oxford University Press, 1963), 35.

(the MacDonald Commission). The article defines the allocation of federal and provincial responsibilities under the Constitution Act of 1867 and explains the criteria utilized by the Fathers of Confederation. Furthermore, Stevenson traces the evolution of the division of powers since 1867, thereby illustrating the changing federal-provincial balance from the highly centralized "quasi-federalism" of the MacDonald era to the more decentralized federal state of the 1980s. The article concludes with an explanation and assessment of the ever-increasing jurisdictional interdependence between governments. This functional interdependence has forced Ottawa and the provinces into an intricate system of joint decision-making and intergovernmental diplomacy.

Peter Meekison served as Deputy Minister of Federal and Intergovernmental Affairs for the Government of Alberta during the 1980-81 constitutional discussions. His essay chronicles the historical background of the amending formula, assesses the strategies and tactics employed by federal and provincial governments during the constitutional negotiations, and describes in detail the provisions of the amending formula.

An analysis of the provisions of the amending formula is essential in order to assess the possibility of major constitutional changes that could alter the distribution of powers between governments and facilitate reform of central political institutions such as the Senate, the House of Commons, and the Supreme Court. It is clear that these new constitutional "rules of the game" will influence the "politics" of constitutional reform as well as the approach of both federal and provincial government to future constitutional negotiations.

Since the passage of the Constitution Act of 1982 there has been considerable debate within both the academic and legal communities with regard to the limitations placed on the legislative authority by the entrenchment of the Charter of Fundamental Rights and Freedoms. Unique to the Canadian Charter is the so-called "notwithstanding clause" which allows for a legislative override in matters pertaining to fundamental freedoms, legal rights, and equality rights. Samuel LaSelva's essay asserts that questions related to the protection of individual rights and freedoms are not easily disassociated from federalism.

The balance of power within the Canadian federal system has been significantly influenced by the process of judicial review. The decentralizing thrust of the decisions of the Judicial Committee of the Privy Council have been extensively documented and debated in the academic literature. Since the Supreme Court of Canada became the final court of appeal in 1949, it has been argued that the Supreme Court possessed a centralist bias. Peter Russell reviews the major decisions of the Supreme Court since 1949 and concludes that, on balance, the Court has not exhibited a noticeable bias in favour of either Ottawa or the provinces. His article concludes with an assessment of the impact of the Supreme Court's decisions on the political strategies employed by federal and provincial governments within the intergovernmental decision-making process.

3. THE DIVISION OF POWERS

Garth Stevenson

INTRODUCTION

Among modern writers on federalism, the division of powers between the central and regional governments is usually regarded as a fundamental attribute of a federal constitution. "The distribution of powers," according to A.V. Dicey, "is an essential feature of federalism."[1] K. C. Wheare views the existence of a constitutionally entrenched division of powers as the primary feature that distinguishes federal from unitary states, and defines the federal principle as "the method of dividing powers so that the general and regional governments are each, within a sphere, coordinate and independent."[2] For W. H. Riker, "The essential institutions of federalism are, of course, a government of the federation and a set of governments of the member units, in which both kinds of governments rule over the same territory and people and each kind has the authority to make some decisions independently of the other."[3] Depending on how many kinds of decisions the central government can make alone, Riker classifies particular federalisms as centralized or peripheralized.

Canadian federalism in recent years, and indeed throughout most of its history, has been characterized by conflict and controversy regarding the division of powers. Federal and provincial governments have sought to expand their de facto, and at times de jure, sphere of legislative power at one another's expense, and have frequently accused governments at the other level of trespassing on the powers guaranteed them by the Constitution. Private interests have often challenged the actions of governments by arguing that such actions violated the constitutional division of powers, while at other times private interests have encouraged the expansion of governmental activity without much regard for whether the jurisdiction of the other level of government was being invaded. Repeatedly, the judiciary has been called upon to define the scope of legislative powers confided to one or the other level of government, with results that have rarely failed to cause disappointment or resentment among some of those interested in the outcome. Formal changes in the division of powers have been rare, difficult and controversial, although in recent years at least there has been no lack of suggestions concerning changes that might be made. Clearly for Canadians the division of powers is an important subject.

*   *   *

Garth Stevenson, "The Division of Powers," in *Division of Powers and Public Policy,* ed. Richard Simeon, vol. 61 of Research Studies for the Royal Commission on the Economic Union and Development Prospects for Canada (Toronto: University of Toronto Press, 1985), 71-123. Reprinted by permission of University of Toronto Press. © Minister of Supply and Services Canada, 1985. The essay has been abridged and edited to suit the needs of this volume.

Powers to Tax

Taxation is mainly an instrumental power, providing the state with the revenue needed to perform its various functions. It can also serve other purposes; for example, it can provide financial incentives or disincentives to various kinds of behaviour. A high tariff discourages the consumption of imported goods, and a high tax on tobacco might discourage smoking. It is, however, mainly as a source of revenue that taxation is vitally important to the state, and indeed a precondition for all its other activities. Former premier Maurice Duplessis of Quebec was fond of asserting that "the power to tax is the power to govern," and few would dispute the truth of the observation.

Canada's federal Constitution gives Parliament the power to raise money "by any Mode or System of Taxation": section 91(3). The provincial legislatures are given the power of "Direct Taxation within the Province in order to the raising of a Revenue for Provincial Purposes": section 92(2) and the power to issue licences "in order to the raising of a Revenue for Provincial, Local or Municipal Purposes": section 92(9). The new section 92A, added to the Constitution in 1982, allows the provinces to impose indirect as well as direct taxation in respect of mineral resources, forest resources and hydro-electric power, provided that such taxation does not discriminate between consumption within the province and consumption in other parts of Canada. Although a royalty is not, strictly speaking, a tax, it should also be noted that the provinces can impose royalties in return for the right to extract minerals, section 109, and charges for the sale of timber from Crown lands, section 92(5). Finally, section 125 provides that neither level of government can tax the other level. With the growth of state enterprises and Crown corporations at both levels, this provision is of far more practical importance than it appeared to be in 1867.

Powers to Regulate

"Powers to regulate" comprise a more complex category, and are dealt with at much greater length in Canada's federal Constitution. Subjects that can be regulated by Parliament or its agencies include Trade and Commerce: section 91(2); Navigation and Shipping, 91(10); Quarantine, 91(11); Fisheries, 91(12); Ferries, 91(13); Banking, 91(15); Savings Banks, 91(16); Weights and Measures, 91(17); Bills of Exchange and Promissory Notes, 91(18); Interest, 91(19); Legal Tender, 91(20); Bankruptcy and Insolvency, 91(21); Indians, 91(24); Interprovincial or international works and undertakings and other works declared to be for the general advantages of Canada, 92(10); Agriculture, 95; and Immigration, 95. Jurisdiction over the criminal law, 91(27), confers, in addition to the specific powers, a very broad general power to regulate.

Provincial powers to regulate, although much less numerous, are substantial. They include powers over Hospitals, Asylums, Charities and Eleemosynary Institutions, 92(7); Local Works and Undertakings, 92(10); The Solemnization of Marriage, 92(12); Property and Civil Rights, 92(13); and local or private matters generally, 92(16). The provinces share with the federal government the power to regulate agriculture and immigration, although federal legislation is paramount. Provincial regulatory powers are reinforced by the power to impose fines, penalties or imprisonment for enforcing any law relating to the enumerated areas of provincial jurisdiction, 92(15).

Powers to regulate can be divided into a number of subcategories. There are broadly defined and general regulatory powers such as the federal powers over Trade and Commerce and the Criminal Law, or the provincial powers over Property and Civil Rights and "Matters of a merely local or private Nature." Somewhat more specific powers are those directed toward particular sectors of the economy, such as Fisheries, 91(12); Banking, 91(15) and 91(16); Transportation, 91(10), 91(13), and 92(10); and Agriculture, 95. There are two regulatory powers related to particular categories of persons: Indians, 91(24), and Aliens, 91(25).

Finally, there are powers to regulate specific activities or situations such as Weights and Measures, 91(17); Bills of Exchange and Promissory Notes, 91(18); Interest, 91(19); or Bankruptcy and Insolvency, 91(21).

Powers to confer recognition or status are an aspect of regulatory powers and are shared between the two levels of government. Parliament can provide for the incorporation of banks, section 91(15); Patents, 91(22); Copyrights, 91(23); Naturalization, 91(25); and Marriage and Divorce, 91(26). The provincial legislatures can provide for "The Incorporation of Companies with Provincial Objects," 91(11). The courts have ruled that Parliament can also incorporate by virtue of its general power to make laws for the peace, order and good government of Canada.

Powers to Spend

"Powers to spend" do not seem to be explicitly limited by the federal Constitution, and there has been controversy over what limitations, if any, should exist, particularly in relation to the powers of Parliament. At the very minimum, each level of government can obviously spend in relation to the matters over which it has specific jurisdiction; for example, both levels can spend in relation to agriculture. Usually, Parliament's power over "The Public Debt and Property" is considered to confer a very broad, and perhaps unlimited, spending power. In practice, both levels of government have made a variety of subsidies and payments to individuals and organizations, as well as to other governments, and they have acted as though the power to spend were virtually unlimited.

Powers to Provide Services

A final category consists of "powers to provide services." Although the service-providing func-

tions of the state were far less developed in 1867 than they became subsequently, a considerable number of service-providing powers are specifically assigned by Canada's federal Constitution. Services to be provided by the federal level of government include Postal Service, section 91(5); The Census and Statistics, 91(6); Militia, Military and Naval Service and Defence, 91(7); Beacons, Buoys, Lighthouses, 91(9); Quarantine and Marine Hospitals, 91(11); Currency and Coinage, 91(14); and Penitentiaries, 91(28). Subsequent amendments added unemployment insurance, pensions and survivors' benefits, although, in relation to the last two items, provincial legislation has paramountcy over federal. Services to be provided by the provincial governments include Public and Reformatory Prisons, section 92(6); Hospitals, Asylums, Charities and Eleemosynary Institutions, 92(7); Municipal Institutions, 92(8); The Administration of Justice, 92(14); and Education, section 93.

It may be noted that some of the enumerated heads of jurisdiction in Canada's federal Constitution include both a regulatory power and a power to provide services, with the choice apparently left to the discretion of Parliament or the legislature. For example, jurisdiction over education includes both the power to regulate the curriculum of private schools and the power to provide education through a system of public schools. The same may be said of the provincial power over "Hospitals, Asylums, Charities and Eleemosynary Institutions." Although it is phrased so as to suggest that the provinces themselves would provide such services, in practice, until long after Confederation, they did little more than regulate them. Generally, governments seem to have moved from regulating activities in their traditional areas to providing services directly, while their regulatory involvement has extended into new fields of activity. This tendency will be discussed later as one aspect of the changing role of the state in modern society. . . .

CRITERIA FOR DISTRIBUTING LEGISLATIVE POWERS

*   *   *

Avoidance of Externalities

Avoidance of externalities means that provinces or other component units within a federation should not be assigned powers that would enable them to affect the interests of people residing outside their own boundaries. That this was a major concern of the Fathers of Confederation is evident from a reading of the Constitution Act, 1867. Eight of the sixteen subsections of section 92 include the qualifying phrase "in the Province" or "within the Province," and, in fact, the word "province" or "provincial" occurs in every subsection, leaving no doubt that provincial governments and legislatures would be rigidly confined to the jurisdiction affecting only their own territories and populations. The prohibition of indirect taxation was also intended to serve the same purpose; an "indirect" tax was then understood to mean a tax that could be passed on by the person taxed to someone else—and thus to someone residing outside the province.

Parliament, on the other hand, was given powers over matters affecting interests or activities in two or more provinces, such as interprovincial transportation; the banking system, which must move capital freely between the provinces; trade and commerce, which implies the movement of commodities; and fisheries (fish are notorious for their disregard of provincial or even national boundaries). Parliament could also assume jurisdiction over "works" within a province if it believed them to be for "the general Advantage of Canada." (John A. Macdonald illustrated the need for this provision by referring to the Welland Canal, which was located within Ontario but was of obvious interest to Quebec as part of the St. Lawrence water-

way.) Additional safeguards against externalities were provided by the lieutenant governor's power to reserve provincial legislation, the federal government's power to disallow it, and Parliament's power to ignore provincial powers if their exercise would obstruct the implementation of imperial treaties.

From the standpoint of avoiding externalities, the Constitution is no longer as effective today as it once was. The powers of reservation and disallowance are now too controversial to be used, and Canada's independence has deprived section 132, dealing with imperial treaties, of any practical consequence. Of greater significance, however, is the fact that a more advanced, interdependent economy, a more mobile population, and modern means of transport and communication have created many more types of externalities. Provinces now create externalities when they regulate the trading in securities that are purchased by residents of other provinces; when they speed up or slow down the extraction of their energy resources; when they reduce or increase the operating grants of universities whose graduates do not necessarily remain within the province; or when they seek to regulate the relations between corporations and unions whose operations transcend the provincial boundary. Given the vested interests and the emotions that have grown up around the provinces since Confederation, resolving these problems will be no easy task.

Capacity to Act Effectively

There are a number of different aspects to the capacity to act effectively. Provincial governments might be unable to exercise a power effectively because they lack the necessary financial resources or because there are economies of scale that make it more efficient for one government to do so than for ten governments. It would obviously be foolish, for example, if each of the ten provinces had its own military forces. For the same reason, some provinces do not even have their own police forces, preferring to hire the services of the federal police force on a contract basis. Provinces might be unable to act effectively for less obvious reasons as well. For example, provincial regulation of environmental standards or labour conditions might prove futile if the regulated industry could simply move to a province whose regulations were less onerous. To avoid being penalized for their high standards by a flight of jobs and investment, provinces might prefer to have uniform regulations imposed by the federal government.

The criterion of capacity to act effectively does not necessarily suggest placing all powers in the hands of the federal government, however. For one thing, the federal government and administration, and particularly Parliament, could not act effectively if they were overloaded with too many tasks and responsibilities. The transfer of responsibility for decisions that create no significant externalities to the provincial governments and legislatures leaves Parliament and the federal government with more time and administrative resources to perform the functions they perform best. Also, for many types of decisions, the more effective government may be one that is smaller, less cumbersome, closer to the grass roots and able to adapt its policies to local needs and conditions. It would make no sense if decisions about the installation of sewers or street lights in Edmonton were made in Ottawa. Few Canadians would wish to emulate the minister of education under Napoleon III, who boasted that he could look at his watch and know what page of what book every school child in France was reading at that moment.

Simplicity and Accountability

Simplicity and accountability are perhaps easy to understand but the most difficult to realize. To apply them, a federal constitution should minimize the overlap between the powers and responsibilities of different levels of government. Ideally, each government should be able to make policies and exercise powers in its own spheres of activity, without having to pay any attention to the activities of other governments. Thus, if one power is assigned to the provincial level of government, then closely related powers should also be assigned to that level. Responsibilities for particular functions should not be shared, either in theory or fact. Governments should not have to coordinate their activities, or to consult one another about related activities, or to make their policies jointly through a process of intergovernmental negotiation. Each government would be accountable only to its own electorate, and each voter would know precisely which government deserves the credit or blame for a particular output of public policy. There are many practical reasons why this ideal cannot readily be achieved, or why simplicity and accountability must be sacrificed for the sake of other criteria, but simplicity and accountability are nonetheless worth pursuing and should not be neglected.

The Fathers of Confederation probably believed that they had achieved a high degree of simplicity and accountability by placing federal and provincial powers in exclusive, watertight compartments, but they consciously violated the principle by including under section 93 such anomalous provisions as disallowance, reservation, and the possibility of remedial legislation. They allowed some unnecessary overlapping between categories such as "Prisons" and "Penitentiaries" or "Marriage and Divorce" and "The Solemnization of Marriage." They provided for shared powers over agriculture and immigration, perhaps because they could not agree among themselves as to which level of government should have those powers. Over time, many more areas of overlapping have developed through the vagueness of broad powers like "Property and Civil Rights," through the exercise of undefined spending powers, and through the competitive occupation, by both levels, of new fields of jurisdiction.

Spatial Distribution of Policy Preferences

The spatial distribution of policy preferences can be illustrated by a simple example. Imagine a hypothetical country with two regions. In one, 90 percent of the population believe that motorists should be required to wear seat belts; in the other, 90 percent believe that freedom of choice is more important than safety. Assuming that the two regions are equal in population, any decision on this issue by the national government would automatically displease half the voters. If regional governments were allowed to make the decision, each would presumably respond to the wishes of the majority in its region, and only 10 percent of the voters would be dissatisfied.

The Fathers of Confederation were well aware of this criterion, and they governed themselves accordingly. In predominantly Catholic Quebec, prevailing opinions about education, about the operation of charities and hospitals, and about who should have the right to perform a marriage ceremony were known to differ from opinions in other parts of the country. Therefore, these subjects were placed under provincial jurisdiction so that the majority in Quebec, as well as majorities elsewhere, could receive the kinds of policies that they preferred.

In Canada today there are many more fields of public policy, and thus many more potential differences of opinion, than there were in 1867. (Public opinion polls also make it much easier to measure the differences today.) However, opinion on most kinds of issues seems to be surprisingly uniform across the country. Where there are pronounced interprovincial differences of opinion, they tend to be on issues such as the price of oil,

the preferential recruitment of bilingual people for the public service, equalization payments, or the tariff protection of secondary industry. These issues, however, have a special character that explains the pattern of opinions in relation to them. While issues such as seat belt legislation are properly described as conflicts of taste, issues such as those listed above are really conflicts of claim between regions.[4] That is to say, giving the people of one region what they want will automatically deprive people in another region of benefits, regardless of the level of government that makes the decision. It is therefore not necessarily appropriate to place such decisions under provincial jurisdiction. Indeed, provided that decision-making procedures in the federal government are equitable and fair, it may be more appropriate to place them under federal jurisdiction.

Concern for Subnational Communitarian Identities

This leads us, finally, to the most difficult and dangerous issue: concern for subnational communitarian identities. If a group of people have a strong sense of collective identity and mutual attachment and if one of the provincial governments is identified with that group in the minds of its members, then such a body may simply demand that the provincial government be given or retain a wide range of powers, regardless of any of the other issues discussed above. Such sentiments are difficult to measure, and there is disagreement about their importance in present-day Canada, but they obviously cannot be dismissed.

RECENT EVOLUTION OF THE DIVISION OF POWERS

In any federal constitution, the formal division of powers provides no more than a starting point for a continuous process of distributing powers between the two levels of government. New problems arise to which governments must react, and new objects of public policy are invented or discovered. Groups who attempt to persuade governments to take initiatives on their behalf rarely allow the formal division of powers to dictate their choice as to which level of government will be the principal target of their representations. Governments themselves seek to expand their authority and to increase their popularity with little concern for the formal boundaries of their jurisdiction. In any event, the roles of the formal heads of power listed in the constitution are soon found to be imprecise, incomplete and overlapping. In a sense, the formal division of powers begins to become obsolete almost as soon as it is enacted.

In discussing the recent evolution of the division of powers, therefore, one must be concerned not only with formal amendments and with judicial interpretations of the written constitution, but with the largely unplanned and uncoordinated expansion of activity by both levels of government in the era of the interventionist state. It is appropriate to begin with the Depression of 1929-39 because, prior to that time, the functions of the state and their distribution between the federal and provincial levels of government had remained substantially congruent with the arrangements made in 1867. Over the last half-century, however, changes have been far more extensive. The somewhat chaotic division of powers that has emerged de facto almost defies concise description, and it certainly bears little resemblance to the terms of the federal Constitution.

There is probably little point in attempting to compare the actual division of powers today (or at any other time) with the formal division of powers enacted in 1867, for the two are not strictly comparable. A "power" that exists on paper arguably has no reality until it is used and until the courts have had the opportunity to rule on whether it was used legitimately. Its meaning may be unclear until confirmed by actual experi-

ence, particularly if it is couched in such broad and general terms as "Property and Civil Rights" or "The Regulation of Trade and Commerce." A power formally conferred may in practice be unused or unusable, a notable example being Parliament's alleged power to protect the educational rights of religious minorities through remedial legislation. Alternatively, a significant constitutional power to deal with some new subject of concern may be discovered by reference to a section that was drafted with quite different purposes in mind.

Formal changes in the division of powers have been few, although it is interesting to note that there have been four since 1940, in contrast to the total absence of such changes in the first seventy-three years of Canadian federalism. In 1940, by a constitutional amendment, Parliament gained the powers to provide unemployment insurance. It gained power to legislate concerning old age pensions in 1951 and concerning supplementary benefits in 1964, although provincial legislation in relation to these fields has paramountcy over federal legislation, a peculiarity that was apparently the price paid for Quebec's consent to both amendments. The amendments of 1940, 1951 and 1964, which facilitated federal assumption of responsibility for income support programs, were all necessitated by the 1937 decision of the Judicial Committee of the Privy Council in the Employment and Social Insurance Act reference, a decision that struck down an early federal initiative in this area. It cannot be said, however, that the gains of federal power through the amendments represented a loss of provincial power in any real sense, since the provinces had never effectively occupied the fields in question and were perhaps never in a position to do so. This is a reminder of the significant fact that the division of powers is not, in practice, always a zero-sum game. Both levels of government have expanded their power more at the expense of the private sector than at the expense of each other.

The fourth and most recent formal amendment to the division of powers is the lengthy and complex provision concerning natural resources, which now appears as section 92A of the Constitution Act, 1867. Included as part of the package of constitutional changes that took effect in 1982, it increases provincial powers to legislate concerning mineral, forest and hydro-electric resources traded interprovincially, and for the first time gives the provincial legislatures a limited right to impose indirect taxation. Because federal paramountcy in relation to the regulation of trade and commerce is explicitly retained by the terms of section 92A, it does not appear that Parliament's powers have been reduced by this amendment, so this amendment also illustrates the non-zero-sum character of the division of powers.

Informal changes in the division of powers are of course much less easy to identify and measure than are formal changes, although they have been considerably more important and extensive. Although no claims are made for the precision of the method, some indication of the scope and direction of changes in the concerns of the federal and provincial levels of government can be seen by comparing the lists of ministerial portfolios in the cabinets of Canada and a medium-sized province (Alberta) for the years 1934, 1959 and 1984.[5] The overall impression gained from this exercise is one of expanding government activity at both levels, particularly in the years since 1959. Moreover, the size of cabinets has increased at almost exactly the same rate in both jurisdictions. The federal cabinet increased from 16 members in 1934 to 21 in 1959 and to 37 in 1984. The Alberta cabinet increased from 11 members in 1934 to 15 in 1959, and to 27 in 1984. The extensive overlapping of de facto powers and responsibilities between the two levels is also suggested by the fact that many federal and provincial ministers hold similar titles, a tendency that becomes more pronounced as the cabinets expand.

Looking first at the federal level, the changes between 1934 and 1959 seem related mainly to the expansion of Canada's international role and status, rather than to a redistribution of power internally. Portfolios added to the cabinet in this period include External Affairs (an office occupied by the prime minister until 1946), Veterans Affairs, Citizenship and Immigration, Defence Production, and the position of associate minister of National Defence. In addition, the Department of Mines and Resources was divided into two new departments: Mines and Technical Surveys, and Northern Affairs and Natural Resources. Two other departments gained new names, reflecting the expansion of federal activities into new fields. Railways and Canals became Transport, thus incorporating the new field of civil aviation, and Pensions and National Health became National Health and Welfare.

In the Alberta government, changes during the 1934-59 period were even less extensive. The Department of Lands and Mines was divided into two successor departments: Mines and Minerals, and Lands and Forests. The three new departments created were Highways, Labour, and Public Welfare, none of which suggested an expansion of provincial jurisdiction at the expense of the federal government.

Betweeen 1959 and 1984, changes at both levels were far more extensive, with both cabinets nearly doubling in size. At the federal level, the positions of postmaster general and associate minister of National Defence disappeared, but these changes implied no erosion of federal powers and responsibilities. Defence Production was replaced by a Ministry of Industry with a broader mandate. Citizenship and Immigration became Employment and Immigration. Entirely new portfolios included Energy, Communications, Supply and Services, Science and Technology, Fitness and Amateur Sport, Consumer Affairs and Environment. Ministries of State for Economic and Social Development were also added, the list reflecting the new dimensions and priorities of government activity. Junior ministries were added, too, with responsibility for specific client groups such as women, youth, multiculturalism and small business.

Changes in the Alberta cabinet were remarkably similar, suggesting a competitive expansion of the two levels of government into the same fields of activity. Mines and Minerals was replaced by Energy and Natural Resources; and Highways became Transportation, the result of provincial involvement in the field of civil aviation. While the office of provincial secretary disappeared, new portfolios were added, parallelling some of the new portfolios in Ottawa; for example, Consumer and Corporate Affairs, Manpower, Environment, Tourism and Small Business, and Recreation. Advanced Education was separated from Education; Personnel Administration, Housing, and Workers' Health, Safety and Compensation appeared for the first time. Unabashed incursions into federal areas of jurisdiction were indicated by the emergence of portfolios for International Trade, Native Affairs, and Federal and Intergovernmental Affairs, the last of which conducts extensive dealings with foreign governments as well as other Canadian governments.

Both levels of government have frequently accused each other of intruding on areas of jurisdiction that are supposedly beyond the scope of their powers. The report of Quebec's Tremblay Commission in 1956 and the lists of alleged federal "intrusions" collected by the Western Premiers' Task Force on Constitutional Trends in the 1970s are examples of provincial perceptions in this regard, while former Prime Minister Pierre Elliot Trudeau responded to provincial claims by accusing the provincial governments of trespassing on federal areas of jurisdiction and "balkanizing" the country without regard for the national interest. Given the emotion and the vested interests that surround both sets of claims, it is not easy to evaluate them with any semblance of impartiality; and it is also not always clear

what standards of evaluation should be used. If the intentions of Sir John A. Macdonald are the relevant criterion, it is clear that the provinces have become too powerful, but Sir John might also have been astonished could he have known of some of the activities in which the federal government is now engaged. If the written text of the Constitution Act, 1867, is the appropriate criterion, one is faced with the problem of deciding the meaning of the words in the document, a task that can be performed with varying results, as the history of judicial interpretation bears witness. Moreover, the different perceptions of the two sides of this controversy rely on different evidence; the situation suggests the blind men in the poem, who reach varying conclusions about the elephant by touching different parts of its anatomy. If a federal "intrusion" in one area is matched against a provincial "intrusion" in another, who is to decide which outweighs the other in importance? Finally, and perhaps most significantly, there is the problem of those government activities that were simply not envisaged at all in 1867. Federal enthusiasts tend to assign all such matters to the residual category of "Laws for the Peace, Order and Good Government of Canada," and thus they believe that only the federal government should be involved in them. Provincialists—although in recent years they have tended not to base their arguments on the written Constitution—seem implicitly to believe that these new activities are "Matters of a merely local or private Nature," or perhaps that they pertain to "Property and Civil Rights."

It would seem that there have been some intrusions by both levels of government into areas of policy that belong to the other level. The federal government has a long history of limited involvement in the forest, mining and petroleum industries, all based on resources that are owned by the provinces. Since the early 1970s, intervention in the petroleum industry has become increasingly pronounced, to the point where that industry has become one of the major preoccupations of the federal government. The governments of the petroleum-producing provinces have viewed this trend with considerable resentment and suspicion, as have many of the people who reside in them. In fairness, however, it must be noted that the uncertain global situation with regard to petroleum over the last decade has arguably made it a subject directly related to the "Peace, Order and Good Government of Canada."

The federal government has also been involved in various aspects of education. From 1952 until 1967, direct federal grants were made to universities, although since 1967 the federal government has made its contributions through the intermediary of the provincial governments, and since 1977 it has virtually abandoned any control over how its contributions are spent. At the same time, the federal government continues to subsidize research in the universities and second-language education in the schools. Federal involvement in manpower training programs, which the provinces tend to view as a part of education, has been extensive since 1960.

Public health has been another area of federal concern for several decades. Conditional grants for various health programs began in 1948 and those for hospital insurance began a decade later. The replacement of conditional grants for medical insurance, with the Established Programs Financing arrangements in 1977, lessened federal influence over the health and hospital sector; but the Canada Health Act, introduced in Parliament in 1983, indicated the federal government's renewed desire to become involved.

These instances of federal involvement in provincial fields must be balanced, however, against the evidence of federal self-denial in other areas. The declaratory power of Parliament under section 92(10)(c) has not been used since 1961, and the regulation of highway transportation has been left to the provincial governments, even though the Judicial Committee of the Privy Council determined in 1954 that international

and interprovincial "undertakings" by truck or bus fell under federal jurisdiction. Family allowances, a purely federal program when they were first introduced—and one upheld by the Supreme Court of Canada—have been administered since 1974 in collaboration with the provincial governments, which are now permitted to vary the schedule of payments depending upon the age of children or the number of children in a family.

In addition, the provincial governments, through their own initiative, have become involved in many areas of federal jurisdiction. Most of the larger provinces are active in the area of international trade and commerce, with government departments and agencies dedicated to this purpose, visits made abroad by premiers and ministers, and networks of permanent missions established in foreign capitals and commercial centres. The larger provinces also assert the right to deal directly with foreign governments on a variety of issues, with Quebec and Alberta having embryonic foreign ministries and quasi-diplomatic activities, much as Canada itself did before the Statute of Westminster. Fisheries is another area of federal jurisdiction in which some provinces, particularly Newfoundland, are very active. The western provinces and Quebec are also intruding on the federal jurisdiction over "Indians, and Lands reserved for the Indians," a development that is viewed with disfavour by the Indians themselves. Eight of the ten provinces have full-time officials dedicated to the field of civil aviation, which the Judicial Committee of the Privy Council assigned to exclusive federal jurisdiction in 1932. Alberta operates a network of savings banks in the guise of "Treasury Branches," and appears to ignore the federal jurisdiction over this field of activity. Ontario and Quebec are both active in the field of television broadcasting, for which they claim authority because of the allegedly educational nature of the programs, although all broadcasting was placed under exclusive federal jurisdiction by the

Judicial Committee of the Privy Council in 1932.

In areas of government activity that are entirely new, so that the federal Constitution does not specifically assign them to either level of government, the general rule is for both levels of government to be involved, either cooperatively or competitively. There are a few exceptions, such as atomic energy, over which Parliament assumed jurisdiction by using its declaratory power, and civil aviation and broadcasting, both of which the Judicial Committee of the Privy Council placed under the rubric of "Peace, Order and Good Government" during its brief and untypical display of enthusiasm for the federal power. In general, however, the law and the courts have provided little guidance for the assignment of new fields of public policy, and the

result has been to leave such fields open to initiatives by either level of government. . . .

To summarize the present de facto division of powers, it is useful to refer to the categorization mentioned earlier: taxing, regulating, spending, and providing services. Table 3-1 shows the share of various types of revenue that went to the central government in 1979-80. It can be seen that the only sources monopolized by the central government are those related to international movements of goods or capital. Local governments and school boards monopolize the field of real estate taxes, while provincial governments have a monopoly on health insurance premiums and a virtual monopoly on natural resource revenues and licence and permit fees. The remaining sources of revenue are shared;

Table 3-1   Share Going to Federal Government by Source of Revenue, 1979-80

Source	Percent
Customs Duties	100.0
Oil Export Charge and Petroleum Levy	100.0
Income Tax on Interest and Dividends Sent Abroad	100.0
Universal Pension Plan Levies	74.0
Corporation Tax	69.6
Other Social Insurance Levies	63.1
Personal Income Tax	61.0
Sale of Goods and Services	48.2
Sales Taxes (Except Motor Fuel)	47.1
Other Revenue from Own Sources	37.8
Return on Investment	37.7
Miscellaneous Taxes	34.4
Motor Fuel Taxes	19.1
Privileges, Licences, Permits	3.7
Natural Resource Revenue	0.5
Health Insurance Premiums and Taxes	0.0
Other Business Taxes	0.0
Property Taxes	0.0

Source: Canadian Tax Foundation, *The National Finances*, 1982-83, p. 29.

provincial governments take the larger share of sales taxes (particularly those on motor fuel), and the federal government takes the larger share of social insurance premiums, corporation tax and personal income tax. However, the federal share of corporation tax and personal income tax has declined sharply; in 1969-70 it was 76.7 percent and 72.6 percent, respectively, versus 69.6 percent and 61.0 percent in 1979-80. Succession duties and estate taxes, once an important source of revenue, have disappeared, while the 19th century distinction between direct and indirect taxation has become almost meaningless.

Regulatory powers and activities have multiplied at both levels of government. In accordance with the terms of the Constitution Act, 1867, the federal government regulates most imports (through the Tariff Board and the Anti-Dumping Tribunal), exports of certain commodities (through the National Energy Board), as well as railways, water carriers, banks and savings banks. Through judicial decision, it has acquired and now exercises regulatory powers over airlines and broadcasting. The federal government regulates the major telephone system in Central Canada as an interprovincial work or undertaking, while other telephone systems and utilities are regulated by the provinces. The provinces regulate highway transport, as Parliament has delegated its authority over interprovincial and international undertakings of this nature. The provinces regulate the industries exploiting their natural resources and also regulate such traditional provincial areas of concern as horse racing, the professions and the sale of alcoholic beverages in restaurants or bars. Censorship of films and other media is also a provincial power. Industrial relations, except in a few federally regulated industries, and stock exchanges are regulated by the provinces. Among the newer areas of concern, as noted earlier, foreign direct investment is mainly regulated by the federal government, human rights mainly by the provinces, and responsibility for the environment and the protection of consumers appears to be shared by both levels. Rent regulation, which might be seen as an aspect of consumer protection, is an undertaking of some provinces. Quebec, through its language charter, regulates the language of work in business and industry, which may in some sense be an aspect of industrial relations.

Spending powers have developed in a way that is even less obviously related to the formal Constitution, a fact that is understandable because the federal government has traditionally claimed the right to spend in areas outside its formal jurisdiction. Table 3-2 shows the federal government's share of spending in various categories, as accounted for in 1979-80. (It excludes the general purpose federal grants such as equalization payments.) Defence and foreign affairs are the only categories apparently monopolized by the federal government, and even the latter is questionable in view of the quasi-diplomatic activities undertaken by certain provinces. No category is totally monopolized by the provincial governments, but the provinces are clearly dominant in their traditional fields of education and health (albeit subsidized through EPF) and, to a somewhat lesser extent, in the protection of persons and property. The federal government accounts for most spending on the economy, apart from transportation where, as Harold Innis noted, its dominant position did not survive the transition from railways to highways.[6]

The distribution of spending on some of the less traditional fields of government activity is less predictable. The federal government appears heavily dominant in scientific research, while the provinces are almost equally dominant in recreation and culture. Housing is mainly federal, but regional planning is mainly provincial. Social services are mainly federal, but the provincial governments account for most spending on the environment.

Powers to provide services are clearly much more important today than they were in 1867, although they were apparently not negligible then

Table 3–2   Share Spent by Federal Government by Category of
Spending, 1979–80

Category	Percent
Defence	100.0
Foreign Affairs	100.0
Research Establishments	95.2
Labour, Employment, Immigration	84.2
Social Services	66.5
Housing	61.6
Resource Conservation and Industrial Development	59.0
Transfers to Own Enterprises	54.9
Debt Charges	49.5
General Services	37.6
Transport and Communications	34.7
Protection of Persons and Property	22.4
Recreation and Culture	17.5
Regional Planning and Development	12.9
Environment	9.8
Health	2.4
Education	1.9
Other Spending	1.8

Source: Canadian Tax Foundation, *The National Finances*, 1982–83, p. 29.

either. Both the federal and provincial levels of government continue to provide the kinds of services outlined in relevant provisions of sections 91, 92 and 93 of the Constitution Act, 1867. They also provide various other kinds of services, through government departments and through various other agencies such as Crown corporations, state enterprises, independent commissions and marketing boards. Both levels of government are heavily involved in the transportation of persons and of goods by road, rail, air and water. Most of the provinces exercise a virtual monopoly over the generation and sale of electricity, and all do so over the sale of alcoholic beverages. Three provinces operate their own telephone systems. All eleven governments are involved in the marketing of agricultural produce. Most provide services of various kinds to business enterprises, such as assistance in exporting their products. Specific in-

dustries such as mining and fishing benefit from services designed to fit their needs. People involved in cultural activities, such as painters and musicians, benefit from other types of services, which are also provided by both federal and provincial governments.

The municipal level of government, frequently ignored in constitutional discussions, is exceedingly important in the provision of public services. Municipalities provide water purification, sewage and garbage disposal, public transportation, snow removal, parks, libraries, health clinics, police and fire protection, and a variety of other services. Some operate utilities such as electric power or telephone service. The constitutional subservience of municipalities to the provinces, and the municipalities' lack of financial independence, hardly do justice to their real importance.

EXPLANATIONS FOR THE RECENT EVOLUTION

Judicial Interpretation

In seeking explanations for the way in which the division of powers has evolved, attention often focusses on the judiciary and its interpretations of the formal Constitution. Judicial review, like the division of powers itself, is often viewed as a necessary condition of federalism. A.V. Dicey, while acknowledging that judicial review of national legislation did not exist in federal Switzerland, identified federalism in general with conservatism and legalism, characteristics which he attributed to the power exercised by the judiciary.[7] A once highly influential school of thought about Canadian federalism attributed the growth in provincial power—and the frustration of Sir John A. Macdonald's hopes for a quasi-unitary state—to the interpretations of the division of powers by the Judicial Committee of the Privy Council.[8] The belief that the Judicial Committee had both disregarded the intentions of the founders and ignored the real needs of the country for effective government contributed to the abolition in 1949 of appeals from Canadian courts to that tribunal. Abolition of appeals, however, did not end the controversy over judicial review. Since 1949, and especially in the last decade, supporters of provincial autonomy have argued that the Supreme Court of Canada has excessively curtailed provincial legislative powers and enlarged those of Parliament.

Judicial review has undoubtedly contributed to the defining of the powers of both Parliament and the provincial legislatures, particularly so with regard to taxing and regulating powers. Powers to spend, to provide services and to confer status or recognition have not been subjected to much restriction by the courts. This is partly because these powers are more vaguely defined by the Constitution than are the taxing or regulating powers, and partly because individuals and

corporations are less likely to litigate against governments that do them favours than against those that tax them or prohibit them from doing what they wish.

Parliament's taxing powers appear to be virtually unlimited, except that its power to earmark special funds for purposes of social insurance or income support was definitely established only after the constitutional amendments of 1940, 1951 and 1964. The legislatures have been constrained by the familiar, although somewhat questionable, distinction between direct and indirect taxation. The judiciary decided as early as 1887 that corporation taxes could be imposed by the provinces, and retail sales taxes were declared to be "direct" in 1943. Business taxes that directly increase the price of commodities, however, or that have a prohibitive impact on activities falling under federal jurisdiction, are likely to be struck down by the courts. In general, the evolution of Canadian public finance has been far more influenced by economic trends than by judicial decisions.

The regulatory powers of Parliament have been a popular subject for consideration by the judiciary, frequently with controversial results. At times the courts have interpreted the general power to make laws "for the Peace, Order and Good Government of Canada" broadly as a residual power, while at other times they have viewed it narrowly as being, in the absence of an "emergency" situation, subordinate to the enumerated powers of the provincial legislatures. Two of Parliament's enumerated regulatory powers have also been considered frequently by the courts, namely "The Regulation of Trade and Commerce," 91(2) and "The Criminal Law," 91(27). The former has, on the whole, been viewed more restrictively than has the comparable power of Congress under the constitution of the United States. On the other hand, the criminal law power has sometimes been interpreted broadly enough to legitimize its use for the regulation of economic activity.

In strict theory, the judiciary, in making decisions, cannot either enlarge or restrict the regulatory powers of Parliament; it merely discovers the powers already inherent in the Constitution and applies them to specific situations. In practice, however, this may not be the case. Some decisions have the effect of enlarging or restricting a regulatory power because Parliament's role is perceived differently after the decision, in a way that affects the subsequent behaviour of both government and the private sector. Thus, the Judicial Committee of the Privy Council ruled in 1916 that Parliament lacked a general power to regulate the insurance industry; in 1922 that it could not regulate hoarding or control prices in peacetime; in 1925 that it could not regulate labour-management relations except in the industries explicitly placed under federal jurisdiction; in 1937 that it could not regulate the marketing of agricultural products consumed within the province of origin; and in the same year that it could not implement a treaty that purported to regulate the conditions of labour.[9] On the other hand, the Judicial Committee declared in 1915 that Parliament could incorporate companies by virtue of the preamble to section 91.[10] In 1931 it decided that Parliament could use its criminal law power to regulate combines and mergers in industry, and in 1932 that it could regulate the new fields of aeronautics and broadcasting.[11]

The Supreme Court of Canada after 1949 appeared more permissive than the Judicial Committee in defining Parliament's regulatory powers, but there were no really dramatic departures from the previous trends of interpretation. Since about 1975, the Supreme Court has become somewhat more restrictive in its approach, and portions of some acts of Parliament have been declared *ultra vires*. The overall impact of the Court on the evolution of federal government activity, however, would seem to be relatively insignificant.

The regulatory powers of the provincial legislatures have also received extensive consideration from the courts and, before that, from the Judicial Committee of the Privy Council. Although often criticized for its narrow interpretations of Parliament's powers, the Judicial Committee frequently did protect those powers against trespassing by the provinces, particularly with respect to the regulation of interprovincial works or undertakings, or of corporations chartered by Parliament. The Supreme Court since 1949 has had similar concerns and has also been wary of provincial enactments that regulate trade and commerce.

Judicial review of provincial legislation has at times been controversial, particularly since the abolition of appeals to the Judicial Committee of the Privy Council, an event that caused misgivings on the part of some provincial governments. In the 1950s, several Quebec enactments relating to civil liberties were struck down by the Supreme Court on the grounds that they related to criminal law.[12] In 1966, the Court ruled that Quebec could not regulate the minimum wage in an interprovincial utility.[13] In the 1970s, the Court struck down Quebec's effort to licence cable television operators and attempts by Manitoba and Saskatchewan to regulate the trade and commerce of livestock, oil and potash.[14] On the other hand, the Court has upheld a number of new and controversial regulatory initiatives on nonresident ownership of land and Quebec's regulation of television advertising directed at children.[15]

Powers to spend have received relatively little consideration from the courts, but the Supreme Court in 1957 upheld the validity of federal spending on family allowances.[16] The provinces, as a leading constitutional law textbook aptly observes, "have never recognized any limits on their spending power and have often spent money for purposes outside their legislative competence."[17]

The courts have also had little to say about powers to provide services and have imposed few if any restrictions. It might be noted that several provinces have agencies providing railway or airline transportation, and that the federal government operates certain schools and hospitals as a by-product of its responsibilities for Indians and for national defence.

From 1949 on, and perhaps from even before then, the courts, on balance, do not seem to have had a decisive influence on the evolution of de facto division of powers. Some of their decisions dealt with relatively minor matters, while others were fairly obvious inferences from the division of powers as previously understood. Some of the more controversial decisions were circumvented by constitutional amendment, delegation or intergovernmental agreement, or simply by redrafting the legislation to achieve the same objective in a somewhat different way. The more fundamental cause of change must apparently be found in the reasons that lie behind the expanding activities of the state, a phenomenon obviously not confined to Canada, and in the reasons that explain why new kinds of state activity emerged in Canada at one level of government sooner than at the other.

Expanding State Activity

The impact of expanding state activity on Canadian federalism has been noted by various observers, including the Rowell-Sirois Commission in 1939 and F. R. Scott in 1945. Both noted that a formal division of powers, dating from an era of laissez-faire in the economic and especially in the social spheres of activity, had to be adapted to an era of much greater intervention by governmental authorities. Scott also noted the impact of Canada's then new international status as an independent actor on its federal system.[18] Yet the transformation since 1939—and especially since 1945—in the role of the state, and particularly in the amount of public expenditure, has been even more dramatic than in the first seven decades following Confederation.

At least seven major factors have contributed to the growth in the functions and activities of the state, all, with one possible exception, contributing to growth at both levels of government. The first factor, and the one that constitutes the possible exception, is the impact of the two world wars,

which accustomed Canadians to a more active, powerful and interventionist state than they might otherwise have accepted and at the same time accustomed politicians and public officials to the exercise of more power than they might otherwise have enjoyed.

It is arguable that this impact of the world wars was felt only at the federal level of government, but it is not impossible that there were some effects on the provincial level as well. The wartime activities of provincial governments have been ignored by Canadian historians, and the conventional wisdom that they were insignificant may require revision. In any event, the rising popular expectations concerning the appropriate level of state intervention (and of taxation) may ultimately have benefited the postwar provincial governments to some extent.

Even without war, most or all of the growth in state activities would probably have taken place, for six reasons.

1. Politicians have impelled the state to make expenditures and to provide services in an effort to gain the support of voters.
2. Bureaucracies have encouraged the expansion of state activities in an effort to maintain and enhance their own importance, power, prestige and access to funds.
3. Programs have been devised to reinforce the legitimacy of the state in the eyes of a population that is increasingly heterogeneous, rootless and uncertain in its loyalties.
4. Urbanization and related social changes have increased the dependence of the population on services and programs that only the state can provide.
5. The externalities created by modern capitalism, such as pollution, technological unemployment, or the sudden rise and fall of whole communities associated

with the extraction of non-renewable resources, have had to be dealt with by the state, since private enterprises accept no responsibility for the consequences of their own actions.

6. The increasing proliferation of special interest groups has caused a corresponding proliferation in the number of demands that the state intervene in support of particular group interests, whether or not this benefits, or is desired by, the society as a whole.

Electoral Politics

The first of these factors, state activities and expenditures designed to attract votes, has been a familiar Canadian phenomenon for nearly two centuries, and indeed was commented upon by Lord Durham in his report. The traditional "pork barrel" approach, for example improving the roads in a marginal constituency prior to an election, is by no means extinct, but it has been supplemented by more sophisticated and far-reaching programs directed toward whole sectors of the population, not necessarily defined in terms of location. The federal commitment to family allowances in 1942, Ontario's involvement in commercial aviation in 1971, and Alberta's program to subsidize interest payments on residential mortgages in 1982 are all good examples of buying votes with the taxpayers' money, whatever may be the merits of the programs concerned. Interestingly, the Canadian public's perception that the benefits must be paid for by the society, and are not a free gift from the politicians who promise them, appears to have made little or no progress since the days of "Duplessis donne à sa province." Part of the explanation, of course, is that the costs are spread thinly over the entire population while the benefits, in most cases, are concentrated and thus have more impact.

This factor has its chief impact on the spending and service-providing functions of the state. As discussed earlier, the formal division of powers between federal and provincial governments in relation to these functions is somewhat vague, and the courts have been permissive in their attitude toward initiatives by both levels of government. Both levels are in practice free to provide whatever expenditures and services appear to be dictated by electoral considerations, although the financial resources of a government in relation to its existing commitments may impose some constraints. Political circumstances might increase the probability that one level of government, rather than the other, will act. For example, a more competitive party system may produce a greater tendency to spend public funds for electoral gain.

Bureaucratic Self-Interest

Tendencies to self-expansion on the part of the bureaucracy have sometimes been cited as an explanation for the growth of the state, and the theory initially appears plausible. The reluctance of any bureaucracy to dissolve itself may well explain the persistence of state activities and programs once they have begun, and the resulting cumulative effect of expansionist pressures, but it is perhaps less convincing to argue that the bureaucracy generates the initial pressures that lead to state activities expanding in the first place. Robert Presthus in his empirical study of Canadian elites found that bureaucrats had distinctly less favourable attitudes toward state intervention (which he termed "economic liberalism") than did elected politicians or directors of interest groups.[19] The conservatism of bureaucrats in this regard, while particularly pronounced at the provincial level, was evident also at the federal. It may in fact be that bureaucracies are motivated less by a desire to expand than by a resistance to any change in their established routines, and a change that leads to expansion may be almost as threatening as one that leads to contraction. In any event, new programs or initiatives by government often lead to the creation of a new bureaucracy (whose personnel may be drawn in part from existing ones) rather than the expansion of bureaucratic structures already in place.

Insofar as bureaucratic tendencies to self-expansion are a factor, they will affect mainly the regulatory and service-providing powers of the state and, perhaps to some extent, the taxing powers. Spending programs, particularly if the money is provided with "no strings attached," do not typically require much bureaucratic manpower. The regulatory powers, and to a lesser extent the service-providing powers, are quite explicitly divided by Canada's formal Constitution, so there may be less randomness in determining which level of government will develop a new regulatory or service-providing function. Also, it is presumably the government that already operates similar or related programs, and thus has an existing bureaucracy with an interest in the field, which is likely to face bureaucratic pressures to provide a particular new program or service. It should also be noted that regulatory programs, and the bureaucracies that run them, are conducive to federal-provincial conflict; Christopher Armstrong's study of relations between the federal and Ontario governments over the regulation of insurance companies may be cited as an example.[20]

Legitimation

The desire to reinforce the legitimacy of the state in the eyes of the population is a very important factor that has led to the expansion of state activities in recent decades. In contrast to the situation at the time of Confederation, the population has largely been cut loose from the traditional attachments to the church, the extended family, the locality and the client-patron relationship with local notables, all of which gave stability to the Canada of Macdonald and Cartier. In addition, the population is far better educated and better informed than in the past, and is bombarded by influences from the printed and electronic media, many—or most—of which originate in a foreign country, the United States. In fact the permeability of Canada to ideological influences from an external source probably has no parallel in the world. Furthermore, the Canadian population is relatively heterogeneous, with two official and countless unofficial languages and with almost one-sixth of the population having been born outside of Canada. The problem of legitimation is reinforced by class conflicts that, contrary to the conventional wisdom, are at least as pronounced as those in other liberal democracies, judging by the length, duration and frequent bitterness of strikes in both the public and private sectors.

Efforts to promote legitimation will, like efforts to win elections, result mainly in the use of two types of powers: powers to spend and powers to provide services. Spending that contributes to legitimation may confer tangible benefits on a large proportion of the population (e.g., family allowances) or on a small and narrowly defined target group (e.g., support for amateur sport). It also includes spending on propaganda or on ceremonies designed to strengthen loyalty and attachment to the state. Legitimation may also be promoted by the use of powers to confer recognition or status (e.g., membership in the Order of Canada) and even, indirectly, by the use of some regulatory powers. The regulation of broadcasting to require a minimum quota of Canadian content is an example of an effort along these lines, although it is possibly counterproductive because of the resentment caused and the increased incentive to watch American channels that results.

Legitimation is an important activity for both the federal and provincial levels of government, and an important aspect of legitimation in Canada is the competition between the two levels. Each level seeks to mobilize support among the population for its battles against the other level and uses all the techniques of legitimation to this end. Louis St. Laurent was concerned as early as 1945 that the federal government become more "visible" in Quebec to counter the attraction of Quebec nationalism, represented at that time by the Union National.[21] Since 1968 this has been a major federal priority, and the Quebec government has responded in kind. Other provincial governments, particularly those engaged in conflicts with the federal government over natural resources, have also made legitimation a priority in recent years. Thus the total expenditure on legitimation in Canada is undoubtedly greater than it would be in a unitary state.

Competitive legitimation between levels of government is probably the best explanation for the recent plethora of government activities, programs and propaganda campaigns directed at specific target groups such as women, immigrants, ethnic minorities, artists, academics or fitness buffs. It also explains the existence of the Canadian Charter of Rights and Freedoms, and of the human rights codes in the provinces. It can even account for such apparently disparate phenomena as the televising of the House of Commons debates, Pope John Paul's visit to Canada in September 1984, and the massive celebrations of the seventy-fifth anniversaries of Alberta and Saskatchewan.

Urbanization and Industrialization

Another factor contributing to the expansion of state activity in recent decades is the social change associated with urbanization and industrialization. The main impact of this is the lessening of the independence of the individual and the family, and the resulting need for social insurance and income support programs, or what is generally known as the welfare state. This change has greatly increased the spending and service-providing functions of the state in all industrialized countries. In Canada it has af-fected mainly the federal level of government, which provides pensions, unemployment insurance and family allowances, and which subsidizes the provision of public assistance and health insurance by the provinces.[22] However, the provinces are the direct providers of some jointly funded services, and Quebec has its own contributory pension plan. Changes in the division of powers in this area have not been entirely informal, but have led to constitutional amendments in 1940, 1951 and 1964.

Corporate Capitalism

The externalities created by corporate capitalism are another, and according to some observers the most significant, factor contributing to the growth of the state. The profit-making activity of the private sector is possible only through extensive direct and indirect assistance from the state. This includes direct subsidies of various kinds; hidden subsidies built into the tax system; and the provision of services required by business—services that range from the training of the labour force and the conducting of research in government research establishments, to the provision of energy, transportation and other inputs whose costs are underwritten, to some degree, by the state. In turn, the profitable activities of the private sector have social costs such as environmental pollution, occupational threats to health and safety, and the stresses associated with the rise and fall of one-industry towns like Schefferville and Fort McMurray. These costs are largely assumed by the state as well. The total cost to the state of all this activity is staggering, even excluding the many "tax expenditures" that never appear on the expenditure side of the ledger. To take only one example, the 1982–83 estimates for the federal department of Energy, Mines and Resources approached eight billion dollars, more than the annual total of all federal expenditure only 20 years previously, and this did not include spending by the Crown corporation, Petro-Canada.[23]

Government activities that assist accumulation in the private sector are to be found among all four of the categories of powers discussed above, and are carried on by the federal and provincial, not to mention the municipal, levels of government. Tax expenditures are impossible without taxing powers; regulatory activities are frequently intended, in whole or in part, to assist the regulated industry (air carriers being a case in point); spending on direct subsidies is directed toward almost every sector of the economy; and a wide range of services is offered to business through government departments and Crown corporations.

In all federations this type of activity is shared by the different levels of government, but Canada is unusual, and perhaps unique, in the importance of the role played by the provincial level. Some unusual provisions of the Constitution Act, 1867, notably the provincial ownership of natural resources under section 109, contributed to this situation, and the thrust of judicial interpretation in the Haldane era (1912–28) should perhaps not be neglected. The main reasons for provincial prominence in accumulation related activities, however, are almost certainly of an informal nature, and are related to the economic and social underpinnings of the federal state. For example, the regional division of labour in Canada and the varying resource endowments of the provinces have produced specialized provincial economies: forestry in British Columbia, petroleum in Alberta, agriculture in Saskatchewan and so forth. A provincial government is likely to be more sensitive to the needs of an industry that plays a dominant role in its provincial economy than is a federal government which presides over a far more diversified economy. It is also possible that the historic preoccupation of the federal government with transportation and finance made it less sympathetic than provincial governments to the needs of other sectors of the economy. For example, it was the Ontario government, rather than the federal government, that took over hydro-electricity from the

private sector when manufacturing interests demanded such an initiative. In addition, the uneven development of the country makes federal economic policies an uneasy compromise between the needs of rapidly growing regions and those of stagnating or declining regions. Since in neither type of region are business interests fully satisfied with the results, businesses tend to turn to their provincial governments for policies more in tune with their own needs. Finally, it should be remembered that small or medium-sized firms with operations confined to a single province are still of very great importance in the Canadian economy, and such firms find it much easier to gain access to their provincial government than to the federal government.

Special Interest Groups

The final factor that may be called upon to explain the expansion of state activity is the demand by organized special interest groups for the state to act on their behalf. The vast majority of state activities and programs in all countries directly benefit only a specific target group of modest numerical size, but they are paid for by the entire population. Such activities are politically possible because the costs, being divided among a large population, are painless for each individual, while the benefits, being distributed among relatively few, are substantial enough for each participant that their loss would be resisted.[24] As society becomes richer, larger and more complex, organized groups and special interests of all kinds proliferate, each with its demands that the state do something on its behalf, and state activities proliferate accordingly. The empirical research of Robert Presthus, cited earlier in connection with the bureaucracy, may be cited again as evidence of the close link between organized group activity and the growth of the state. As Presthus describes it, "the larger outcome [of elite accommodation] is a relatively uncontrolled expansion of activities, without much qualitative differentiation among the competing claims of major social interests."[25]

One may hypothesize that most organized interests in Canada are relatively indifferent, at least to begin with, as to which level of government they would prefer to respond to their demands. Most of the major organized interest groups in fact operate at both levels and have a federal structure corresponding to that of the state itself. The choice of a level on which to concentrate their lobbying efforts is more likely to be influenced by pragmatic considerations than by respect for the supposedly watertight compartments of the Constitution. Certainly both the federal and provincial levels of government have been faced with numerous demands for intervention, and both have responded. It is probably impossible to quantify which has done so to the greatest extent, but one cannot doubt that untidiness in the de facto division of powers has resulted.

Some of the reasons why business interests often direct their attention to the provincial level have already been mentioned. For other types of organized interests—and Presthus has nine categories in addition to business—the reasons may be different. Physical proximity to the provincial capital may be a factor for groups with limited resources; the provincial capital is within four hours driving range for the vast majority of Canadians, while Ottawa may be half a continent away. Another factor is related to Canada's linguistic duality. The federal government must accommodate both anglophone and francophone interests, but it may as a result have difficulty in not falling between two stools. Many francophones have always perceived the federal government as too "English," and many anglophones, particularly in the West, increasingly perceive it as being too "French." Thus, unilingual interest groups and their leaders may feel more comfortable with a provincial government than with the federal government, and may direct their lobbying efforts accordingly.

CONSEQUENCES OF THE RECENT EVOLUTION

To summarize the argument of the preceding sections, the recent evolution of the division of powers has been characterized mainly by an increase in the number of fields of state activity not explicitly provided for in the formal Constitution, and by the involvement of both levels of government in the majority of the new fields—and in some of the more traditional fields as well. Thus, most fields of jurisdiction are now shared, and very few are exclusive to a single level of government. This section will explore the consequences of this situation from the viewpoint of governments and of private interests, and in relation to the normative criteria of effectiveness, efficiency and democracy.

From the perspective of governments, the expansion of state activity has had costs as well as benefits, a not surprising conclusion if one accepts the view that the factors conducive to expansion have been largely beyond the control of governments themselves. While some of the disadvantages associated with expansion would also exist in a unitary state, they are more pronounced in a federal state, in which several governments are expanding simultaneously on the same territory.

One problem that seems to be increasingly serious is the imbalance between the revenues and the commitments of governments. The federal government appears to have entered into a chronic position of being able to finance only about three-quarters of its expenditures out of current revenues, and must borrow to cover the rest. This cannot continue indefinitely. At the provincial level, even the most prosperous provinces have been forced into a combination of tax increases and draconian efforts to cut costs, particularly in the fields of health and education. Both levels rely increasingly on the personal income tax to finance their activities, but that form of taxation is clearly approaching a saturation point, and the economic and political consequences of further increases cannot be contemplated with equanimity. The problem is no longer merely one of vertical balance, which could be solved by transferring provincial functions to the federal government (as the Rowell-Sirois Report recommended) or by transferring federal revenues to the provinces (as the provinces demanded, with considerable success, in the Diefenbaker-Pearson era). The fiscal crisis of the state now afflicts both levels of government, and there may well be no easy solution. However, the duplication of effort by two levels of government with overlapping and ill-defined responsibilities certainly exacerbates the situation.

Another consequence of the recent evolution of the division of powers is that governments are increasingly frustrated by the inefficacy of their policies, so that both voters and governments are losing faith in the very possibility of achieving collective goals through political action. While there may be many causes for this phenomenon, not all of them related to federalism, one reason for it must be the deadlock between and the mutual frustration of governments pursuing their different objectives in the same functional area of jurisdiction, so that the actions of one government oppose, countervail and frustrate the actions of another. The situation appears to be a common one in fields as diverse as industrial policy, regional policy, energy policy, transportation policy, communications policy and health policy. Obstacles exist at the best of times to the successful achievement by public policies of the goals for which they are designed. The additional burden of having the policies of governments frustrated by the analogous policies of other governments is a serious matter.

This mutual frustration contributes in turn to another consequence, namely increased conflict between provincial governments and the federal government. The phenomenon is not a new one, of course, as the relations between Macdonald, Mowat and Mercier a century ago attest. In their era, however, such conflict involved only a few issues and a few governments at any one time, had little or no effect on the lives of ordinary Canadians, and was closely related to partisan conflict in a two-party system, so that the tension was periodically reduced by a change of government at one or the other level. In the last 20 years, by contrast, it has become endemic and almost continuous, with occasional "common fronts" involving most or all of the provinces, with vast bureaucracies and propaganda machines on both sides mobilized as though for war, with ordinary taxpayers and consumers turned into the pawns of intergovernmental struggles, and with the survival of the federation itself often called into question. Moreover, an increasingly fractured party system provides no possibility of relief. Faith in the federal government, respect for the Constitution and, except possibly in Ontario, the sense of a common identity as Canadians, have been so seriously eroded by these developments that it is uncertain whether they can ever be restored.

For private interests that are taxed, regulated, subsidized or provided with services by governments, the recent evolution of the division of powers has a number of other consequences. On the one hand, private interests have benefited in some ways from the competition between two levels of government with overlapping jurisdictions. For example, an entrepreneur wishing to incorporate a firm has a choice between seeking a federal or a provincial charter, and may select the jurisdiction whose rules and procedures are convenient. A cultural organization seeking a subsidy can apply to one level of government if refused by the other, or it may be fortunate enough to receive subsidies from both. It is for this reason that public choice theorists, who draw the analogy between voters in the political system and consumers in the market economy, view intergovernmental competition and overlapping jurisdictions in a federal system as beneficial.[26]

On the other hand, competition and overlapping have less attractive consequences for the private sector as well. Dealing with two levels of government is more costly and time-consuming than dealing with only one. There may be considerable confusion and uncertainty as to which level of government is actually responsible for performing a particular function and which has the administrative capability and the legal authority to do so. Difficulty may also arise if conflicting rules, regulations or directives come from federal and provincial governments, so that following those provided by one level of government leads to conflict with the other. For example, some oil companies have become embroiled in conflict between the federal government and the government of Newfoundland, both of which claim the right to regulate drilling activities and to issue permits on the continental shelf. There are more general adverse consequences as well. For example, the cost of duplication of effort between levels of government is ultimately borne by the private sector through higher taxes. Policies that are incoherent or ineffective because they are frustrated or counteracted by the policies of the other level of government will presumably not benefit the private interests that they were designed to benefit and that may have demanded them in the first place.

The balance between the good and bad consequences of overlapping and intergovernmental competition is likely to vary depending, among other things, on the type of powers that are being used by the governments in question. Duplication of taxing powers raises the spectre of "double taxation" or the "tax jungle" with which the Rowell-Sirois Commission was concerned. Since the Second World War this problem has largely been avoided by intergovernmental agreement and the partial integration of the personal and corporate income taxes, although the decision by Alberta in 1981 to follow the example of Quebec and Ontario in collecting its own corporation tax suggests the possibility of a trend back to the tax jungle of the prewar years. For the mining and petroleum industries, problems of double taxation have already appeared on some

occasions over the last ten or fifteen years, a difficulty exacerbated by different views among governments as to the relationship between royalties and taxes, insofar as the distinction still has any practical significance.

Duplication of regulatory powers, and uncertainty as to who can regulate what, are likely to pose even more serious problems. It is obviously not possible to adhere to the regulations of two governments attempting to regulate the same activity unless the regulations adopted by the two are identical, and in that unlikely event there would be little reason for both levels of government to remain in the field. Efforts by provincial governments to regulate portions of the broadcasting system, or by the federal government to bring caisses populaires under the legislative framework provided for the banks, have not made life easier for the private sector.

The consequences of duplication, overlapping and jurisdictional uncertainty in the spending and service-providing powers of governments are, however, much more likely to be benign, apart from their financial costs to the taxpayer. A symphony orchestra or a research laboratory that receives a million dollars from each of two governments is obviously no worse off than if it had received two million dollars from only one government—even if the administrative costs of subsidizing music or research in this way are somewhat higher—and the orchestra or the laboratory may even benefit from not putting all its eggs in one basket. In fact, the enthusiasm of public choice theorists for intergovernmental competition is largely a result of the fact that they seem to concentrate their attentions on the spending and service-providing functions of government and to ignore the less pleasant subjects of taxation and regulation.

Even here, however, some caveats are in order. Services are not quite as simple a case as are subsidies. Competition between a federal and a provincial air carrier probably does no harm, but for the federal government to set up a parallel school system within a province or for a province to establish an agency competing with the Canada Wheat Board or the National Harbours Board would make little sense. Even subsidies may be used to manipulate private interests or to force them to take sides in intergovernmental controversies, as when former Premier Maurice Duplessis ordered Quebec universities not to accept federal grants on pain of losing their provincial grants.

From the viewpoint of society as a whole, how can one assess the recent evolution of the division of powers in terms of efficiency, effectiveness and democracy? The last major effort to perform this task was that of the Rowell-Sirois Commission. Relying largely for its conclusions on a research monograph by Dr. J. A. Corry, the commission issued a stern warning against the evils of divided jurisdiction and a plea for the classic dual federalism of the 19th century, suitably brought up to date.[27] The warning was forgotten in the postwar enthusiasm for "cooperative federalism" and then in the almost continuous crisis that overtook the federal system from 1963 onward. Today, when the two levels of government are involved in a range of competing and overlapping activities that the commission could not possibly have imagined, the question perhaps poses itself with greater urgency than before.

Duplication of activities by two levels of government obviously has a financial cost related to the salaries and expenses of administrators performing parallel tasks, the upkeep of buildings in which to house these administrators, and so forth. Governments incur other costs in monitoring each others' activities or in coordinating their own activities with those of another government. Shared or cooperative activities may well depart from Weberian models of rational administration, as Corry argued, and competitive activities may simply duplicate each other to no purpose. Thus, the overall efficiency of the public sector has probably deteriorated as a result of the recent evolution of the division of powers.

Effectiveness is possibly more difficult to evaluate than efficiency, since the criteria are not self-evident. The symphony orchestra that receives two grants, to return to that example, will probably evaluate the effectiveness of public policy more positively than the financial institution or telephone company that faces two competing sets of regulations. For any type of public policy, more than one factor weighs in the balance. The policies of the federal government in most fields are probably more incoherent and slower to materialize than they would otherwise be because of the necessity to consult, inform or coordinate with the ten provincial governments. The complex contortions required to amend the Canada Pension Plan, as a result of provincial paramountcy in that field, provide an extreme example, but the snail's pace of policy-making with respect to taxation, the price of oil and natural gas, the financing of the health insurance system, the conservation of renewable resources, or the phasing out of the Crow's Nest freight rates suggests that the problem is a general one. Some federal initiatives, such as the guaranteed annual income, the restructuring of the Atlantic fisheries, or the proposed industrial strategy, were abandoned entirely as a result of provincial obstruction. Even the final version of the package of constitutional amendments that took effect in 1982, after the federal government decided to negotiate a compromise with the dissident provinces, recalls the familiar definition of a camel as a horse designed by a committee. Yet while all of this may be viewed by some observers as evidence of the ineffectiveness of the present informal division of powers, others will argue that responsiveness to varying provincial views and perspectives is itself a valuable component of "effectiveness," given the regional diversity which, in their eyes, the provincial governments represent. While the present writer is less sympathetic than most of his colleagues to this line of argument, its popularity is perhaps reason enough for a nod in its direction.

The discussion of the division of powers

from the standpoint of democracy can be brief, since most of the arguments resemble or parallel those that have already been discussed in some other connection. The measure of democracy is presumably the accuracy with which the wishes of the people are transformed into public policy. If one accepts the market model of the electoral process, overlapping and competing jurisdictions may increase the choices available to the voter-consumer—and the responsiveness to the voter's wishes of the governments that offer their wares in the political marketplace. Against this must be balanced the difficulty experienced by the voters in formulating their preferences and, above all, in organizing collectively to achieve them, if they are not certain about which level of government actually performs the function with which they are concerned. A government cannot easily be held responsible for its actions if it can

plausibly blame their consequences, or their lack of consequences, on another level of government that is either competitively or cooperatively involved in the same field of activity. A government that modifies its own policies in order to achieve a compromise with the policies of another government (a practice rather self-righteously described by former Premier Bill Bennett of British Columbia as "the Canadian way") cannot transform the wishes of its own electorate into policy as accurately as one that does not, unless the other government is more representative of the first government's electorate than is the first government itself. If the second government is in fact more representative, it can only be so by coincidence, and an unlikely one at that since it represents a different electorate, either larger or smaller as the case may be.

* * *

Notes

1. A.V. Dicey, *Introduction to the Study of the Law of the Constitution*, 10th ed. (London: Macmillan, 1961), 151.

2. K. C. Wheare, *Federal Government*, 4th ed. (New York: Oxford University Press, 1964), 10.

3. W. H. Riker, *Federalism: Origin, Operation, Significance* (Boston: Little, Brown, 1964), 5.

4. Jack Mintz and Richard Simeon, "Conflict of Taste and Conflict of Claim in Federal Countries," Discussion Paper #13 (Kingston: Queen's University, Institute of Intergovernmental Relations, 1982).

5. Federal data are from the Official Records of Parliamentary Debates. Alberta data are from Ernest Mardon, *The Guide to the Alberta Legislative Assembly, 1905–83* (Lethbridge, privately printed, 1983).

6. "Confederation as an instrument of steam power has been compelled to face the implications of hydro-electric power and petroleum," Harold Innis, *Essays in Canadian Economic History* (Toronto: University of Toronto Press, 1956), 368.

7. Dicey, *Introduction to the Study of the Law of the Constitution*, 171–80.

8. Frank R. Scott, *Essays on the Constitution* (Toronto: University of Toronto Press, 1977), passim. For a contrary view, see Alan C. Cairns, "The Judicial Committee and Its Critics," *Canadian Journal of Political Science* 4 (1971), 301–45.

9. *A.-G. Canada v. A.-G. Alberta* (1916), 1 A.C. 589; in re the Board of Commerce Act (1922), 1 A.C. 191: *Toronto Electric Commissioners v. Snider* (1925), A.C. 396; *A.-G. British Columbia v. A.-G. Canada* (1937), A.C. 377; *A.-G. Canada v. A.-G. Ontario* (1937), A.C. 327.

10. *John Deere Plow Company v. Wharton* (1915), A.C. 330.

11. *Proprietary Articles Trade Association v. A.-G. Canada* (1931), A.C. 310; in re Regulation and Control of Aeronautics in Canada (1932), A.C. 54; in re Regulations and Control of Radio Communication in Canada (1932), A.C. 304.

12. *Saumur v. Quebec and A.-G. Quebec* (1953), S.C.R. 299; *Birks and Sons v. Montreal* (1955), S.C.R. 799; *Switzman v. Elbling and A.-G. Quebec* (1957), S.C.R. 285.

13. *Minimum Wage Commission v. Bell Telephone Company* (1966), S.C.R. 767.

14. *Public Service Board v. Dionne* (1978), 2 S.C.R. 191; *Burns Foods v. A.-G. Manitoba* (1978) 1 S.C.R. 494; *Canadian Industrial Gas and Oil v. Government of Saskatchewan* (1978), 2 S.C.R. 545; *Central Canada Potash Company and A.-G. Canada v. Government of Saskatchewan* (1979), 1 S.C.R. 42.

15. *Morgan v. A.-G. Prince Edward Island* (1976), 2 S.C.R. 349, and *A.-G. Quebec v. Kelloggs's Company of Canada* (1978), 2 S.C.R. 211.

16. *Angers v. M.N.R.* (1957), Ex. C.R. 83.

17. Peter Hogg, *Constitutional Laws of Canada* (Toronto: Carswell, 1977), 72.

18. Frank R. Scott, "Constitutional Adaptations to Changing Functions of Government," in his *Essays on the Constitution*, 142–56.

19. Robert Presthus, *Elite Accommodation in Canadian Politics* (Toronto: Macmillan, 1973), 299.

20. Christopher Armstrong, *The Politics of Federalism* (Toronto: University of Toronto Press, 1981).

21. R. M. Burns, *The Acceptable Mean: The Tax Rental Agreements, 1941–1962* (Toronto: Canadian Tax Foundation, 1980), 46–7.

22. Keith Banting, *The Welfare State and Canadian Federalism* (Montreal: McGill-Queen's University Press, 1982).

23. Canadian Tax Foundation, *The National Finances, 1982–83* (Toronto: The Foundation, 1983), 217.

24. This is a major theme of Mancur Olson, *The Rise and Decline of Nations* (New Haven: Yale University Press, 1982). Olson attributes economic decline to the proliferation of special interest groups.

25. Presthus, *Elite Accommodation in Canadian Politics*, 348–9.

26. For example, M. H. Sproule-Jones, *Public Choice and Federalism in Australia and Canada* (Canberra: Centre for Research on Federal Financial Relations, 1975).

27. Donald V. Smiley, ed., *The Rowell-Sirois Report*, Book I (Toronto: McClelland and Stewart for the Carleton Library, 1963), 204–10.

Selected Readings

Chandler, Marsha A. "Constitutional Change and Public Policy: The Impact of the Resource Amendment (Section 92A)." *Canadian Journal of Political Science*, 19:1 (March 1986): 103–126.

Cheffins, R. I., and Johnson, P. A. *The Revised Canadian Constitution: Politics as Law.* Toronto: McGraw-Hill Ryerson, 1986.

Hogg, Peter. *Constitutional Law of Canada.* 2nd ed. Toronto: Carswell Company Ltd., 1985.

Meekison, J. P., Moull, W. D. and Romanow, R. J. *The Origin and Meaning of Section 92A.* Montreal: Institute for Research on Public Policy, 1985.

Smiley, D. V. *Canada in Question: Federalism in the Eighties.* 3rd ed. Toronto: McGraw-Hill Ryerson, 1980.

4. THE AMENDING FORMULA

J. Peter Meekison

On April 17, 1982, in a colourful ceremony in Ottawa, Queen Elizabeth II proclaimed the Constitution Act, 1982. For the first time since Canada became a nation Canadians could amend all parts of their own Constitution on their own soil without the consent of the British Parliament. Before patriation could be realized, it was essential to devise an agreed-upon means of amending the Constitution in Canada. Indeed, a central feature of the Constitution Act was the amending formula.

What factors must be taken into consideration when writing an amending formula for a constitution in a federal system? The role the constituent units or provinces are expected to play in securing amendments is a key factor in developing an amending formula. Should provinces have an equal say in the amending process or should there be some distinction among them based on criteria such as geographic size, population, linguistic differences and so on? What percentage of the provinces must agree before amendments can be approved? Alternatives here vary from no direct participation to unanimity. If the central legislature is bicameral and one house represents the constituent units, it could be argued that approval by that house affords sufficient protection to the provinces. The other extreme is agreement of all provinces on all amendments.

Should different parts of the Constitution be subject to different methods of amendment? Expressed another way, should the Constitution be compartmentalized? For example, to secure an amendment, certain parts, such as the amending formula itself, might be subject to unanimity of the provinces, while other parts might require only a simple majority. Some amendments might require the participation of the provinces while others might not. Thus, rather than speaking of an amending formula, it would be more accurate to speak of amending formulae. In Canada, from the beginning, it was recognized and accepted that the Constitution would have to be compartmentalized if an amending formula were to be agreed upon.

Another consideration in drafting an amending formula is what might be referred to as the influence of special issues. Governments have had to be sensitive to the position and concerns of Quebec in Confederation. Neither could the vast population differences between the most populous province, Ontario, and the least populous, Prince Edward Island, be ignored. The importance of these issues is particularly highlighted when a formula is being written more than one hundred years after Confederation. Before agreement is possible, these variables must be discussed and either dismissed, thus inviting failure, or integrated somehow into the formula, thus encouraging success. Accommodation of individual provincial concerns is perhaps the most notable distinction between the new Canadian amending formula and those found in other constitutions.

J. Peter Meekison, "The Amending Formula," *Queen's Law Journal* 8:1–2 (1982–1983): 99–122. Reprinted by permission of the author.

BACKGROUND

Efforts to establish an amending formula to the Constitution Act, 1867 (formerly the British North America Act, 1867) spanned slightly over half a century. It was first raised at the 1927 federal-provincial conference as one topic in a long list of subjects requiring intergovernmental negotiation. Fifty-four years later, agreement on an amending formula was finally secured, bringing to an end the longest debate on any specific change to the Canadian Constitution.[1]

This many years to develop and secure agreement on the amending formula appears to be an unusually long time. While it cannot be denied that over half a century of debate is excessive, concentrating solely on the length of time obscures the very real difficulty of writing an amending formula long after the Constitution has become operational.

Canada is the only country in the world which has had to resolve the constitutional dilemma of drafting an amending formula after its Constitution had evolved and the nation matured politically. Other countries tackle this problem at the time their constitutions are written. By and large, a constitution's amending formula receives less attention than other constitutional provisions like a Charter of Rights or the structure of the government. The reason is obvious. When a constitution is being written, the framers are usually more concerned with its initial content than with how to change it in the future. Nevertheless, an amending formula is included to accommodate change. In this regard, a key concern of the framers is the ease or difficulty of securing amendments. If the country is a federal state such as Canada, a second question is what say the constituent units should have in making amendments.

Canada found itself in a very different situation from other countries. Canada had a Constitution which did not contain a means for amendment by its own governments. Since it was a British statute, amendments to Canada's Constitution could be enacted only by the United Kingdom's Parliament. Over time, a series of constitutional conventions evolved governing the process by which amendments were made to the Constitution. Up to and including the Constitution Act, 1982, the United Kingdom Parliament had to participate in the amending process. This peculiar circumstance of history served as the most compelling force behind patriation and the search for an amending formula.

To say it took fifty-four years to agree on an amending formula is correct, but it is also equally fair to state that the subject was not discussed either intensively or continuously over that period of time. Indeed, it is more accurate to say that it was discussed periodically—on the average of once every ten years. Efforts to develop an amending formula were made in 1927, 1935–36, 1950, 1961 and 1964, 1968–71 and 1978–81.[2] Each attempt involved federal-provincial discussion and negotiation. On two occasions an intergovernmental agreement was briefly achieved, in 1964 and again in 1971.

In October 1964, First Ministers agreed on an amending formula known as the Fulton-Favreau formula. The key provision of the Fulton-Favreau formula was its requirement for unanimity before any amendments could be made affecting provincial legislative powers. In 1965, after some consideration of the implications of accepting an amending formula, the Quebec Government of Premier Lesage rejected the formula on the grounds that there were other more pressing subjects of constitutional reform than the amending formula. One reason was that Quebec was more concerned with substantive changes to the federal system than with the amending formula. Another reason for the change of mind was that Quebec, in the midst of the Quiet Revolution, was not anxious to see its constitutional aspirations subject to the rigours of the new amending formula. Thus the amending formula was destined to become only one of a number of items under review and not the sole object of constitutional discussions, which it had been up to that time.

During the period 1968–71, governments undertook what became the first of a series of comprehensive constitutional reviews.[3] One item of discussion was the amending formula. While the importance of establishing an amending formula was recognized, this topic received far less scrutiny than most of the other questions under consideration. When the subject was finally raised, a new formula was developed. This formula, which became known as the Victoria formula, was one of a series of provisions contained in a constitutional document called the Victoria Charter agreed to by all provinces and the federal government in June 1971.[4]

A few days after the conference, the Quebec Cabinet rejected the Victoria Charter. It should be understood that Quebec's objections were not with the amending formula but with other provisions in the Charter, specifically, the limited revisions to section 94A of the Constitution Act, 1867. Nevertheless, rejection of the Charter brought to an end this episode of constitutional negotiations.

THE AMENDING FORMULA EMERGES

After the failure of the Victoria Conference, a few years passed before governments once again tackled the question of constitutional reform. Some preliminary skirmishing took place in 1976 but it was the election of the Parti Québécois in the fall of 1976 which acted as the catalyst to bring governments back to the bargaining table in October 1978. One of the subjects to be discussed was the amending formula.

At the beginning of the negotiations, the only proposal on the table was the Victoria formula previously agreed to in 1971. Although the Fulton-Favreau formula was raised as an alterna-

tive it was never given serious consideration, partly because it had been superseded by the Victoria formula as the one most recently supported by all governments and partly because its requirement for unanimity would make the amending process too difficult. There were essentially three choices facing governments: accept the Victoria formula, modify the Victoria formula, or find an acceptable alternative.

Under the Victoria formula, amendments could be approved in the following manner:

> Amendments to the Constitution of Canada may from time to time be made by Proclamation issued by the Governor General under the Great Seal of Canada when so authorized by resolutions of the Senate and House of Commons and of the Legislative Assemblies of at least a majority of the Provinces that includes:
>
> 1. every Province that at any time before the issue of such Proclamation had, according to any previous general census, a population of at least twenty-five percent of the population of Canada;
>
> 2. at least two of the Atlantic Provinces;
>
> 3. at least two of the Western Provinces that have, according to the then latest general census, combined populations of at least fifty percent of the population of all the Western Provinces.

Provincial agreement was based on both population and region. Ontario and Quebec met the test of having twenty-five percent of the Canadian population, and thereby acquired a perpetual veto over constitutional amendments. The position of Ontario and Quebec was justified not only on the basis of their current population but also by the fact that they are considered regions. They were being treated no differently from the other two regions, Western Canada and Atlantic Canada.

The principal criticism of this formula was that some provinces were given a veto while others were not; Canada would be divided into first- and second-class provinces based upon population. It was argued that, in a federation, provinces—not regions—should be treated equally in the amending process. Also, since seats in the House of Commons are more or less distributed amongst the provinces according to population, the population principle was already recognized. For example, in 1982, Ontario and Quebec had 95 and 75 seats respectively out of a total of 282 seats in the House of Commons. The less populous provinces thought the size of the parliamentary contingent from Ontario and Quebec gave those two provinces adequate protection.

There was sufficient criticism of the Victoria formula that the first choice, agreeing to it as drafted in 1971, became unacceptable. That there should be a shift in the degree of support for the formula should not be surprising. Although all governments agreed to it in 1971, eight of the eleven governments had changed since then. Only the federal government, Ontario and New Brunswick had the same First Ministers in office. The commitment to the Victoria formula on the part of the others was not particularly strong because they had not participated in its development. Alberta and British Columbia had both expressed their disagreement with the formula during the 1976 constitutional discussions. The support that could be mustered was based primarily on the fact that the formula had been agreed to previously and there were no other serious alternatives.

Nevertheless, the strength of the criticism was such that either the formula had to be significantly modified or an alternative developed. For example, British Columbia sought to have its claim to a veto incorporated into the formula on the basis of its being the fifth region of Canada. Another modification suggested was the preparation of a short list of matters which would be subject to unanimity, giving every province a veto. Regardless of what might be included in the unanimity list, the main obstacle to be overcome continued to be the fact that two provinces had a veto over all amendments while the other eight provinces would have a veto only on those matters found in the unanimity list. Given this obstacle, governments attempted to develop a new formula.

One alternative which was given consideration became known as the "Toronto consensus." It was a variant of both the Fulton-Favreau and the Victoria formulae. It provided that amendments could be approved by Parliament and two-thirds of the provinces representing eighty-five percent of the population. In addition there would be a short list of items subject to a unanimity requirement. The only matter initially included in the unanimity list was natural resources. This subject was singled out in an effort to gain the support of Alberta.

The main criticism of the Toronto formula was the population requirement of eight-five percent. Given their large populations, both Quebec and Ontario would have a veto under this formula. The Atlantic provinces had less say under this formula than under the Victoria formula. Because of their small population it would take all four to defeat an amendment whereas under the Victoria formula it would take only three. The formula had little effect on the position of the western provinces. Given the population requirement, the opposition of any three would be sufficient to defeat an amendment while the combined opposition of British Columbia and Alberta would also be sufficient, as it was under the Victoria formula.

The figure of eighty-five percent was chosen because it was estimated that the population of Quebec would not go below fifteen percent of the total Canadian population. In short, the formula was designed to provide protection to Quebec. When suggestions were made to reduce the percentage requirement to some lower figure such as fifty or sixty percent, any support which the proposal might have secured from Quebec disappeared. Given these defects in design, the Toronto formula was set aside.

No significant progress on an amending formula had been made by the time the February 1979

Constitutional Conference was held. During the conference, Premier Lougheed of Alberta tabled a proposal for an amending formula which was fundamentally different from any alternative that had been thus far considered. The central element of the Alberta proposal was that provinces could "opt out" of any amendment which derogated from their existing legislative authority, proprietary rights or provincial privileges contained within the Constitution. The conference adjourned without resolving any of the constitutional questions on the agenda. While Canada was at that time no closer to settling the question of the amending formula, within three years the principles found in the Alberta proposal would form the key elements of the amending formula contained in the Constitution Act, 1982.

Constitutional discussions resumed immediately after the May 1980 Quebec referendum. Intensive negotiations took place throughout the summer, culminating in a Constitutional Conference in September 1980. Included on the agenda was the amending formula. While the Victoria formula started as the favourite, it finished a distant second to the Alberta formula which was presented to the conference as the "best efforts" draft. Although the Alberta proposal gradually gathered the support of the other provinces throughout the summer, it continued to receive a lukewarm reception from the federal government. Nevertheless, by the end of the negotiations, the federal negotiators were prepared to recommend it for the consideration of the Cabinet.

With the failure of the Constitutional Conference to reach agreement, the federal government decided to move unilaterally. In early October 1980, a Joint Resolution to amend the Constitution was tabled in Parliament. One of its provisions was an amending formula—the Victoria formula.[5] In addition to the Victoria amending formula, the Resolution contained a provision for referenda on constitutional amendments as a deadlock-breaking mechanism. Referenda could be initiated only by the federal government. Presumably they were to be used in instances where a federally-sponsored amendment had been defeated by the provinces, it being unlikely that the federal government would hold a referendum on a matter it had already rejected.

Eight provinces opposed the unilateral action of the federal government. In an effort to produce a compromise position on the Constitution, the eight provinces developed an amending formula and an alternative approach to constitutional reform. In principle, the formula proposed by the eight was identical to the 1980 "best efforts" draft, with one important exception. In instances where provinces opted out of an amendment which transferred legislative responsibility, they would be given full fiscal compensation by the federal government. This provision was inserted by Quebec and agreed to with varying degrees of enthusiasm by the other provinces.

The concept of fiscal compensation was not new. During the 1971 Victoria Conference a similar proposal was made by the Quebec Government with respect to the proposed amendment to section 94A. That amendment was to expand the scope of 94A to include family, youth and occupational training allowances. The federal government would not incorporate the fiscal compensation concept in 1971 and it was doubtful that its position had changed in the intervening decade. It should also be recalled that the failure to secure significant changes to section 94A was a key reason for the Quebec Government's rejection of the Victoria Charter.

Concurrent with their developing an alternative approach to constitutional reform, the provinces opposed to the federal government's unilateral action challenged that position in the courts. In the spring of 1981, the Supreme Court of Canada heard the case and in September 1981 gave its historic judgment. As a result of the Supreme Court decision, a Constitutional Conference was convened in Ottawa on November 2, 1981. The conference agenda consisted of three items: patriation, the Charter of Rights and Freedoms and the amending formula. Generally speaking, the compromise reached at the conference was acceptance of the provincial amending formula with the deletion of the compensation clause in return for provincial acceptance of the Charter of Rights. This meant that the formula was now almost identical to the 1980 "best efforts" draft. The deletion of the compensation clause was one of the main reasons the Government of Quebec opposed the Constitutional Accord.

A few days later, in an effort to gain the support of Quebec, the federal government proposed to the provinces that a limited compensation clause covering "education and other cultural matters" be incorporated in the amending formula. The provinces, other than Quebec, agreed to include this provision in the Joint Resolution passed by the House of Commons on December 2, 1981. Despite this change, Quebec continued to insist both on a full compensation clause and other items and continued to oppose the Resolution.

With the Proclamation of the Constitution Act, 1982, the search for an amending formula ended. Canadians now have the means to amend their Constitution without the necessity of resorting to the legislature of another country.

THE AMENDING FORMULA IN DETAIL

There are six different formulae or means by which the Constitution Act may be amended. The factors discussed at the beginning of this essay should be recalled because each of them is reflected, in one way or another, in the different provisions of the amending procedure. The six different means to secure amendment are

1. amendments under the general procedure (Section 38);
2. amendments by unanimous consent (Section 41);
3. amendments which apply to some but not all provinces (Section 43);
4. amendments by Parliament alone (Section 44);
5. amendments by individual Provincial Legislatures alone (Section 45);
6. amendments without Senate approval (Section 47).[6]

The critical variable found in the first five categories is the nature and degree of provincial participation. The sixth category is fundamentally different and addresses itself to the manner in which Parliament participates in constitutional amendments. Of these six categories, it is the first one, the general procedure, which distinguishes this amending formula from the Victoria formula, the Fulton-Favreau formula and all others which had been proposed over the years. The other five means are not unique to this formula. Nevertheless, there are certain differences between some of the specific provisions contained in this formula and other formulae which had been discussed in the past.

Amendments Under the General Procedure

The central element of the amending formula is the general procedure consisting of two components. The first component states how amendments are approved. The second component permits provinces to "opt out" of any amendment "that derogates from the legislative powers, the proprietary rights or any other rights or privileges of the legislature or government of a province."[7]

How Amendments are Approved

Under the general procedure, an amendment is approved by

(a) resolutions of the Senate and House of Commons; and

(b) resolutions of the legislative assemblies of at least two-thirds of the provinces that have, in the aggregate, according to the then latest general census, at least fifty percent of the population of all the provinces.[8]

Under this section both Houses of Parliament must approve all amendments to the Constitution. Expressed another way, Parliament has the only veto. The role of the Senate is, of course, modified by the requirements of section 47. In the event that the Senate opposes an amendment, that amendment would fail unless the House of Commons within 180 days "again adopts the resolution."[9] The principle of limiting the Senate's authority is found in the original 1971 Victoria formula. The rationale behind this provision is that the Senate, an appointed body, should not be in a position to block the will of the democratically-elected House of Commons and the requisite number of democratically-elected provincial legislatures. It also means that, should Senate reform eventually be initiated, the existing Senate could not veto any such reforms authorized by the House of Commons and the provincial legislatures.

Provincial approval under the amending formula is based on the premise of provincial equality. No single province has a veto. Nevertheless, the degree of provincial support required before an amendment takes effect is considerable. Two-thirds of the provinces must consent to the amendment and together they must represent fifty percent of the population of the ten provinces. This means that either Quebec or Ontario must support any amendment since their combined population exceeds fifty percent of the total provincial population. While this requirement is certainly not identical to the veto which Quebec and Ontario each had under the Victoria formula, it is a recognition of the significant population differences amongst the ten provinces.

At the moment agreement by two-thirds of the provinces means that seven out of the ten provinces must favour an amendment before it can take effect. While there are a number of potential combinations of provinces, the two-thirds requirement means that, at a minimum, one of the four western provinces and one of the four Atlantic provinces must support an amendment. In summary, before any amendment under the general formula is possible, as a minimum at least one western province, either Quebec or Ontario and one Atlantic province must be in favour.

Opting Out

If an amendment is one which "derogates from the legislative powers, the proprietary rights or any other rights or privileges of the legislature or government of a province" and a province dissents to the amendment, then that amendment "shall not have effect" in that province.[10] Expressed slightly differently, provinces may "opt out" of amendments which take away or reduce their existing responsibilities. The principle of opting out is the cornerstone of the new amending formula. It provides a guarantee to each and every province that constitutional amendments which derogate from their existing legislative powers, proprietary rights or other rights cannot be imposed upon them without their consent. The only other alternative which would have provided the same degree of protection is a unanimity requirement. The critical difference between the two alternatives, however, is that an individual province cannot veto or block an amendment agreed to by Parliament and the other provinces. Conversely, Parliament and the requisite number of provinces cannot force an unwelcome amendment on the dissenting provinces. While the idea of provinces or parts of the country ganging up on each other is remote, whenever the amending formula was discussed previously, guarantees for or protection of existing provincial rights were the focal points of negotiations. This is why, in the past, the principle of a unanimity rule was so readily agreed to. Quebec, for one, has consistently looked for such protection. Like unanimity, opting out gives every province an identical degree of protection, but unlike unanimity makes constitutional change more easily attainable.

The principle of opting out first appeared in 1936. At that time, a federal-provincial committee examining the issue of an amending formula recommended opting out for any amendment "in relation to matters coming within the classes of subjects enumerated in clauses (13) and (16) of section 92."¹¹ When Alberta tabled its proposal for an amending formula in February 1979, it expanded the scope of opting out to include those subjects requiring unanimity under the Fulton-Favreau formula.¹² To be sure that natural resource rights were protected under the amending formula the words "proprietary rights" were added.

The principle of opting out would apply to amendments to sections 92, 93, 94A and 95 of the Constitution Act, 1867, as amended, and now also to section 92A as found in the Constitution Act, 1982. These sections of the Constitution establish provincial legislative powers, and any amendment derogating from these legislative powers would be subject to opting out.

At Confederation there was a division of property between the provinces and the federal government. Section 109 of the Constitution Act, 1867 provides that "all lands, mines, minerals and royalties . . .shall belong to the several provinces . . . ." The 1930 Natural Resources Transfer Agreements place the western provinces in a similar position to the original provinces. Amendments to these proprietary rights would be subject to the opting out provisions. Other rights of a province found in the Constitution Act, 1867, which would be included under the opting out provisions are: section 60, salaries of Lieutenant Governors to be paid by Parliament; section 100, salaries of judges of superior, district and county courts to be paid by Parliament; and section 125, no lands or property belonging to Canada or any province shall be liable to taxation.

The major criticism of opting out was that it could eventually lead to a constitutional checkerboard and, ultimately, to political chaos. The lack of constitutional uniformity was of great concern to critics who often exaggerated the potential difficulties and overlooked the fact that, in

several important areas, constitutional uniformity does not exist today. A quick reading of the Constitution Act, 1867, as amended, reveals a number of significant constitutional differences amongst the provinces. Section 94 authorized Parliament to make uniform laws relative to property and civil rights for the three common law provinces of Ontario, New Brunswick and Nova Scotia. Quebec, with its civil law tradition, was excluded. That the section did not become operative does not change the fact that the different traditions of common and civil law were to co-exist side by side within the same political system. The language provisions in section 133 applied to Quebec and, in 1870, to Manitoba but not to the other founding provinces or to the other provinces as they joined Confederation. Throughout the original Act there are specific references to individual provinces which presumably preserved or protected a tradition or policy of importance to that province. As other provinces entered Confederation other differences were acknowledged. Section 93 is worded differently for the province of Newfoundland in recognition of its different denominational and common school system.

When the provinces of Manitoba, Saskatchewan and Alberta were established they were placed in a fundamentally different position from the original provinces with respect to ownership of natural resources. Not until the 1930 Natural Resource Transfer Agreements were the three prairie provinces "placed in a position of equality with the other provinces of Confederation." Even then the transfer agreements are not identical to section 109 of the Constitution Act, 1867. They are far more detailed and include, for example, references to matters such as unfulfilled Indian land claims, fisheries and national park boundaries.

The foregoing examples demonstrate that, for some matters, the Constitution differs or has differed in its application in individual provinces. These differences have not led to constitutional chaos but are a recognition of the principle that, in some circumstances, provinces have either sought to be treated individually or were treated differently.

Another provision of the Constitution which is similar in principle to opting out also requires consideration. Section 94A, included by amendment in 1951, authorizes Parliament to make laws governing old age pensions "but no such law shall affect the operation of any law present or future of a provincial legislature in relation to any such matter."[13] Without this clause permitting future provincial legislative action, it is doubtful that the 1951 amendment on pensions would ever have been approved. Provincial governments were willing to accept the amendment while at the same time maintaining and assuring for themselves a degree of protection against future considerations, whatever these might be. For example, in 1964 the Canada and Quebec Pension Plans were established. Because of section 94A, there was no legal impediment to prevent Quebec from developing its own pension plan; in effect, it opted out of a national plan. Since that time the two pension plans have evolved with governments working cooperatively to harmonize them. The pension plan example provides a further illustration that the principle of opting out will not automatically result in chaos and the disintegration of the federal system.

As previously mentioned, during the course of the discussions on the amending formula, Quebec insisted on a clause providing compensation to provincial governments choosing to opt out of an amendment. The rationale for compensation was that, in the event that some aspect of provincial legislative jurisdiction was transferred by amendment to the federal government, funds for any required expenditures would be raised through the system right across Canada. If a province opted out of an amendment, conceivably its residents could be taxed by both orders of government for the service or program. Some

form of fiscal compensation would overcome this problem. Section 40 of the amending formula authorizes "reasonable compensation" for amendments "relating to education and other cultural matters." While the scope of the section is limited, it nonetheless establishes within the Constitution the principle of compensation over certain types of amendments which presumably are of fundamental importance to Quebec. When amendments are considered, it will be necessary to determine whether they fall under the category of education and "other cultural matters." For example, would an amendment on family allowances be so defined? It is entirely possible that the courts could eventually give the phrase "other cultural matters" a broad interpretation and thereby permit compensation over a much wider range of subjects than was intended.

One further comment on the matter of opting out is necessary. A maximum of three provinces are eligible to opt out of an amendment to which the section applies. If there were a greater number of dissenting provinces, the amendment would be defeated and the status quo maintained. Nor can a province which has assented to an amendment alter its position and decide to opt out of an amendment once the amendment has been proclaimed. Of course, until proclamation, any legislature is free to change its position by revoking a resolution of assent.

Amendments by Unanimous Consent

The second method for amending the Constitution is under the unanimity requirement. During the course of 1981 interprovincial negotiations, it soon became apparent that a unanimity rule was necessary but that it should be very limited in scope. Section 41 of the Constitution Act, 1982, lists five subjects thought to be of such importance that the agreement of all provinces was necessary before an amendment could be approved. The five matters were as follows:

(a) the office of the Queen, the Governor General and the Lieutenant Governor of a province;

(b) the right of a province to a number of members in the House of Commons not less than the number of Senators by which the province is entitled to be represented at the time this Part comes into force;

(c) subject to section 43, the use of the English or the French language;

(d) the composition of the Supreme Court of Canada; and

(e) an amendment to this Part.

The principal reason for including "the office of the Queen, the Governor General and the Lieutenant Governor of a province" was that any changes to the office of the Lieutenant Governor should be uniform across the country and not subject to the opting out provisions. The alternative was to include this clause in section 42 which identifies a number of matters subject to the first part of the general amending formula. In weighing the two alternatives, uniformity was preferable to a situation where a province could see an amendment to a part of its own provincial constitution approved despite its opposition. The reason for including the reference to the office of the Queen and the Governor General was that it was felt that any changes to these offices were bound to have an effect on the office of the Lieutenant Governor. Given the fact that a debate over significant modifications to these offices such as their abolition or their strengthening could be extremely divisive, it was thought prudent to give all provinces an equal say with the federal government. That such a debate could be potentially divisive was demonstrated over some of the preliminary reactions to the provisions of Bill C-60, the 1978 federal proposal to redraft the British North America Act.[14] The sections of Bill C-60 which provided for the office of the Governor General gave some provinces sufficient cause to press for the inclusion of this clause in the unanimity provision, in order to ensure that they would have a say in any future amendments on this subject.

Section 51A of the Constitution Act, 1867 states, "notwithstanding anything in this Act a province shall always be entitled to a number of members in the House of Commons not less than the number of senators representing such province." This clause, the so-called "Senate floor," was incorporated in the Constitution by amendment in 1915. Since then (with the exception of the Victoria formula) it has been one provision of the Constitution which consistently has been thought of such importance that it should be subject to unanimity. The Senate floor is now established as of the date of the coming into force of the amending formula. Should Senate reform take place, any changes in provincial representation will not influence existing provincial representation in the House of Commons.

Amendments to the use of the English and French languages were one of a few matters specifically exempted from the 1949 amendment establishing Parliament's exclusive authority to amend parts of the Constitution. The Fulton-Favreau formula included this subject as one requiring the consent of Parliament and all provincial legislatures. The unanimity requirement gives the Province of Quebec the guarantee that Canada's linguistic duality, as outlined in section 133 of the Constitution Act, 1867 and the new Charter of Rights and Freedoms, cannot be amended without its consent.

A subject given serious consideration during the course of constitutional discussions over the past few years was the Supreme Court, including its composition, jurisdiction and the method of appointing members to the Court. At the moment, the size of the Supreme Court is provided by statute, Quebec being guaranteed three members.[15] Should there be a reference to the Supreme Court included in the Constitution, the only assurance the Province of Quebec has that its representation will either continue at the same level or meet its legitimate concerns that there always be a sufficient number of judges trained in the civil law is to include this matter as one requiring unanimous consent. Thus, reference to the composition of the Supreme Court of Canada in the amending formula may be termed an anticipatory provision.

The final matter requiring unanimity is an amendment to any provision in the amending formula. The amending formula and its specific provisions were thought to be of such fundamental importance that any change must require the consent of all partners in Confederation.

Specified Amendments Under the General Procedure

With the enactment of the British North America Act, 1949 (No. 2) Parliament was given authority to amend certain parts of "the Constitution of Canada." At the 1950 Constitutional Conference provinces expressed concern that the scope of Parliament's authority was too sweeping and insisted that it should be restricted. In the negotiations leading to the 1964 Fulton-Favreau formula, this issue was one which needed to be resolved. It was finally agreed that amendments to the Constitution which might alter those characteristics of the national government linked to or identified with the federal nature of Canada (e.g., the Senate) should not be passed by Parliament alone. As a result the idea of limiting the scope of Parliament's exclusive authority to amend parts of the Constitution was firmly established. This understanding was carried forward in later constitutional discussions and was reflected in the Victoria formula.

Section 42 of the amending formula is the direct result of these earlier negotiations. The list of matters contained in this section is a combination of the subjects excluded from Parliament's exclusive authority by previous agreements, anticipatory provisions, and new matters.

Those subjects excluded by previous agreements are

(a) the principle of proportionate representation of the provinces in the House of Commons prescribed by the Constitution of Canada;

(b) . . . the method of selecting Senators;

(c) the number of members by which a province is entitled to be represented in the Senate and the residence qualification of Senators.[16]

As can be seen, these three matters are linked with the federal nature of the central government. It was agreed at the 1964 Constitutional Conference ". . . that these were matters in which the provinces have a legitimate interest, and that therefore they should be expressly excluded from Parliament's unilateral amending authority."[17]

The next two matters, characterized as anticipatory provisions, are similar in principle to the first three:

(b) the powers of the Senate; and

(d) subject to paragraph 41(d), the Supreme Court of Canada.

Lengthy constitutional discussions had taken place on both institutions. Although constitutional reform or change to either the Senate or the Supreme Court is by no means a foregone conclusion, should discussions resume it is now clearly established that any amendment to the Constitution in these areas requires provincial participation.

The last two matters specifically referred to in section 42 are new in the context of ongoing constitutional discussions. They are

(e) the extension of existing provinces into the territories; and

(f) notwithstanding any other law or practice, the establishment of new provinces.

The first matter, "the extension of existing provinces into the territories," was included at the

suggestion of Nova Scotia and reflects a long-
standing historical concern of that province. A
quick comparison of the original four provinces
shows that they were approximately equal in area.
The northern boundaries of Ontario and Quebec,
and later Manitoba, were extended by Parliament.
There was no equivalent boundary extension of
the three Maritime provinces. The idea of a northern boundary extension of the four western provinces was raised as recently as 1968 by British
Columbia when Premier Bennett unveiled his
"Five-Province Plan."[18] The clause was definitely
not inserted to accommodate any expansionist
tendencies on the part of the western provinces.
Indeed, it was intended to have the opposite effect.
By making any northern boundary adjustments
subject to the amending formula as opposed to a
decision of Parliament alone, extension of provincial boundaries is much more difficult.

Provincial concerns over the establishment of
new provinces were raised in 1949 when Newfoundland became Canada's tenth province. This
subject was discussed during the 1976 interprovincial discussions on the Constitution. All provinces
agreed at that time to a proposal originally suggested by Quebec, that establishment of new provinces should be subject to the general amending
formula and not be the prerogative of Parliament
acting alone.[19] A change in the number of provinces has a direct impact on the Senate, the
amending formula and the regional balance in
Canada. During the 1980–81 interprovincial discussions on the amending formula, Quebec reminded the other provinces of their earlier
agreement and the provision was incorporated.
While it is possible, it is highly unlikely that
provinces would block the establishment of a new
province if Parliament had given its approval.

Amendments Which Apply to Some But Not All Provinces

The third category of amendments, found in section 43, is one which affects some but not all

provinces. Two matters are specifically referred
to in this section:

(a) any alteration to boundaries between provinces; and

(b) any amendment to any provision that relates
to the use of the English or French language
within a province.

The reference to boundaries ensures that any
existing provincial boundaries cannot be altered
without the consent of the provinces concerned.
The specific reference to language permits individual provinces to expand the use of English or
French in a similar fashion to what New Brunswick has done in the Charter of Rights. For
example, should the Province of Ontario choose
to extend the use of the French language, a constitutional amendment applying exclusively to
that province is possible. Other amendments
which fall into this limited category would be
amendments to the 1930 Natural Resources
Transfer Agreements or portions of the 1949
Terms of Union of Newfoundland with Canada.
It should be stressed that this section is limited to
those provisions of the Constitution which do not
apply to all provinces. Thus this section cannot
be used as a means of circumventing the general
amending procedure.

Amendments by Parliament Alone

Section 44 of the Constitution Act, 1982 reads as
follows:

> Subject to sections 41 and 42, Parliament may
> exclusively make laws amending the Constitution
> of Canada in relation to the executive government
> of Canada or the Senate and House of Commons.

This section carries forward the authority conferred on Parliament by the 1949 amendment
(No. 2) to the British North America Act. With
this specific reference and a general amending
formula, section 91(1) was no longer needed and
was repealed when the Constitution Act, 1982
was proclaimed. Two examples of amendments
Parliament has made to the Constitution under its

exclusive authority are the 1965 amendment setting the retirement age of Senators at 75 and the 1974 amendment on the size of the House of Commons.

Amendments by Individual Provincial Legislatures Alone

The only reference to constitutional amendment in the original British North America Act, 1867 was contained in the first clause of section 92. With the exception of the office of the Lieutenant Governor, provinces could amend their own constitutions. Section 45 incorporates this clause in the new amendment provisions. The repeal of 92(1) places the provinces in a position equivalent to that of the federal government.

PROCEDURAL REQUIREMENTS

The part of the Constitution Act, 1982 containing the amending formula also includes a number of sections which are best characterized as procedural, as opposed to substantive, elements of the formula. Specific sections are included on time requirements and initiation and proclamation of amendments.

Section 39 establishes minimum and maximum time limits under which constitutional amendments must be passed. The minimum time required to enact an amendment is one year. This time limit can be waived if all provincial legislatures have addressed the matter. The maximum time for securing a specific amendment is three years "from the adoption of the resolution initiating the amendment procedure thereunder."[20]

Introduction of a minimum time limit means that amendments do not automatically become effective or proclaimed whenever the Senate, House of Commons and two-thirds of the provinces representing fifty percent of the population have passed the necessary resolutions. When the required number of provinces have given ap-

proval, it is possible that as many as three provinces may not have expressed an opinion one way or the other on a particular amendment. The minimum time gives undecided provinces a reasonable length of time in which to make a decision. Depending upon when a particular amendment first surfaces and its content, individual provinces may choose to delay a decision for a variety of reasons. The government of a province may be close to an election and decide to make the amendment an election issue. Alternatively, it could call a snap election on the matter and ask the electorate for an expression of their opinion. This course of action may be adopted if the provincial government is considering opting out of an amendment. Alternatively, the provincial government could hold a referendum on the proposed amendment. Another reason for delay is that a provincial government could wait to assess the degree of support for an amendment before reaching a final position. In summary, the minimum time limit was designed to give all provinces sufficient time to make a reasonable decision. Parliament did not need equivalent protection because no amendment can become effective without parliamentary scrutiny and approval.

The maximum time limit provision was incorporated to ensure that the time limit on amendments was not open-ended. It is possible that at any given time there could be a number of proposed amendments which have achieved varying degrees of approval by legislative resolution. Without a maximum time limit the possibility always existed that an amendment initiated several years earlier, and later forgotten, could be approved. The United States Congress now incorporates a maximum time limit, ordinarily five years, in amendments referred to the states for their approval. The clause in the Canadian amending formula also ensures that proposed amendments will be debated while the circumstances surrounding their introduction remain current.

Constitutional amendments may originate in the Senate, the House of Commons or the

legislature of any province.[21] The significance of
this provision is considerable in that it could lead
to a large number of amendments under consideration at any given time. Recent Canadian experience has been that constitutional amendments
have been the subject of a constitutional conference where all governments participate. Presumably this practice will continue in the future.
Nevertheless, there is no reason to assume that
all future amendments will first be discussed at a
federal-provincial conference. The idea of a constitutional conference arose before an amending
formula had been established. With an amending
formula in place, new usages are likely to
emerge. One such development will probably be
the introduction into the Senate, House of Commons or ten provincial legislatures of many resolutions proposing constitutional amendments of
one kind or another. The amendment proposed
by British Columbia in September 1982 to include protection of property rights in the Charter
of Rights serves as an example.[22] Having adopted
the resolution itself, British Columbia then
mounted a campaign to seek the support of other
governments in the hope of securing the requisite
majority for approval.

In addition to provinces acting individually,
they may act collectively through forums such as
the Western Premiers' Conference, the Council
of Maritime Premiers or the Annual Premiers'
Conference. Conversely, there is nothing to prevent the federal government from initiating a
resolution in the House of Commons and then
proceeding to secure provincial consent through
a series of bilateral discussions with the provinces. In short, the potential political dynamics
behind constitutional amendment, now that there
is a clearly-defined amending procedure, may
have important implications for future federal-
provincial relations.

The final procedural matter is contained in
section 48. Amendments to the Constitution are
made by Proclamation issued by the Governor
General after necessary legislative resolutions

have been secured. The assumption has always
been that the Proclamation, subject to the minimum time limit, would immediately follow approval by the last legislative body. Nevertheless,
the possibility of delay always existed. This section requires that the "Queen's Privy Council for
Canada shall advise the Governor General to issue
a proclamation under this Part forthwith on the
adoption of the resolutions required for an amendment made by proclamation under this Part."

CONSTITUTIONAL CONFERENCE

The last provision of the amending formula is
section 49, which requires that the formula be
reviewed within the next fifteen years; that is,
some time before April 17, 1997. This section
was included to provide an opportunity to assess
the amending formula in a reasonable time after
it had become effective. Given the unanimity
requirement necessary to change the formula, it
is extremely doubtful that any significant
changes to its provisions will be forthcoming.

CONCLUSION

The search for an amending formula was long
and difficult. The foregoing analysis illustrates
the intricacies of the new formula. With different
requirements to amend different parts of the
Constitution, the Canadian formula is unques-
tionably the most complex and detailed procedure for constitutional amendment in any
federation. The rationale for each section is easy
to provide: specific guarantees and protection to
provinces individually and collectively were essential before agreement on any formula could be
achieved. While the formula finally agreed upon
is unique, it is still founded on a collective understanding dating from constitutional negotiations
initiated as early as 1927.

The problem of provincial participation and
consent was satisfactorily resolved only with ac-

ceptance of the concept of opting out, an idea based on the principle of provincial equality. Once this principle was entrenched special considerations or "compartmentalization" could be incorporated. The final product emerged section by section and reflects the political reality of Canadian federalism. Whether opting out will be used remains to be seen. Perhaps its threat will be sufficient to modify the wording of proposed amendments to accommodate provincial differences. There is no doubt that the dynamics of securing amendments will be different than they have been in the past when the convention of unanimity was thought to exist. Nevertheless, it is realistic to assume that proposed amendments will be structured in such a way that every effort will be made to avoid the exercise of opting out by individual provinces. Knowing that in the final analysis they are protected from certain amendments, the provinces may demonstrate a greater willingness to search for a consensus leading to a unanimous agreement.

One concluding observation is necessary. Agreement on an amending formula does not mean that either the frequency or number of constitutional amendments will necessarily increase. The amending formula only establishes the rules by which future changes to the Constitution can be made. Whether or not they will be made depends upon a demonstrated need for change and the political will to accomplish it. If previous amendments may be used as examples, that will has always existed in Canada. What was missing was an agreed-upon mechanism whereby the provinces were involved in making constitutional amendments. The mechanism is now in place and future constitutional changes will be incorporated through its provisions. The critical difference, however, between previous and future discussions on constitutional change is that the political means for securing agreement will be fundamentally altered by the establishment of an amending formula.

Notes

1. The formula agreed upon was accepted by the federal government and all provinces but Quebec.

2. For a discussion of constitutional amendments and the evolution of the process to 1949, see Paul Gerin-Lajoie, *Constitutional Amendment in Canada* (Toronto: University of Toronto Press, 1950) and G. Favreau, *The Amendment of the Constitution of Canada* (Ottawa: Queen's Printer, 1965).

3. See Canadian Intergovernmental Conference Secretariat, *The Constitutional Review, 1968–1971* (Ottawa: Information Canada, 1974).

4. For a copy of the Victoria Charter, see *The Constitutional Review, 1968–1971*, 373–96. The excerpt quoted in the next section is repoduced with permission of the Ministry of Supply and Services.

5. The formula originally contained in the proposed Joint Resolution was not completely identical to the 1971 Victoria formula but the basic principles remained the same. The key difference was the provision requiring the support of two Atlantic provinces representing fifty percent of the population. The effect of this modification was to eliminate a role for Prince Edward Island in the amending process because no matter which other Atlantic province it combined with, the fifty percent of the population requirement would not be met. During the parliamentary committee review of the Joint Resolution this provision was deleted. The parallel provision for the western provinces was also deleted in the later stages of the parliamentary process in the spring of 1981. Thus the

amending formula contained in the Resolution debated by Parliament in March 1981 was slightly different from the 1971 Victoria formula. The differences, however, were not seen to be fundamental.

6. All section references are to the Constitution Act, 1982.

7. Section 38(2).

8. Section 38(1). This provision was originally used in the 1964 Fulton-Favreau formula. The only difference is that the population requirement is based on the population contained in all the provinces whereas the Fulton-Favreau formula based it on the total Canadian population, i.e., including the territories.

9. Section 47.

10. Section 38(2) and (3).

11. Fulton-Favreau, p. 22.

12. The one omission is amendment to "the use of the English or French language," which is covered elsewhere in the formula.

13. Section 94A of The Constitution Act, 1867.

14. See Fulton-Favreau for a discussion of this question in greater detail. The scope of Section 91(1) was examined by the Supreme Court of Canada in the *Senate Reference* (1980) 1 S.C.R. 54. At that time the Court ruled that fundamental reform of the Senate was beyond the authority conferred on Parliament by Section 91(1).

15. Supreme Court Act, R.S.C. 1970, c. S-19, s. 6.

16. Section 42.

17. Fulton-Favreau, 38.

18. See British Columbia's submission to the 1969 Constitutional Conference.

19. The agreement is contained in the October 14, 1976 letter from Premier Peter Lougheed of Alberta, writing as Chairman of the Premiers' Conference, to Prime Minister Trudeau. A copy of the letter is reprinted in the Alberta Department of Federal and Intergovernmental Affairs, *Fifth Annual Report, 1976–77,* Edmonton, 1977.

20. Section 39(2).

21. Section 46.

22. The British Columbia example represents the first use of the amending formula by any legislature.

Selected Readings

Cheffins, R. "The Constitution Act, 1982 and the Amending Formula: Political and Legal Implications." *Supreme Court Law Review* 4 (1982): 43–54.

Dillinger, Walter. "The Amending Process in Canada and the United States: A Comparative Perspective." In Paul Davenport and R. H. Leach, eds., *Reshaping Confederation: The 1982 Reform of the Canadian Constitution.* Durham, North Carolina: Duke University Press, 1984.

Kilgour, D. M. "A Formal Analysis of the Amending Formula of Canada's Constitution Act." *Canadian Journal of Political Science* 16: 4 (December 1983): 771–7.

Romanow, R. J., Whyte, J. and Leeson, H. *Canada . . .Notwithstanding: The Making of the Constitution 1976–1982.* Toronto: Carswell, Methuen, 1984.

Scott, Stephen A. "The Canadian Constitutional Amendment Process: Mechanisms and Prospects." In Clare Beckton and A. W. MacKay, eds., *Recurring Issues in Canadian Federalism,* Research Studies prepared by the Royal Commission on the Economic Union and Development Prospects for Canada, vol. 57, Toronto: University of Toronto Press, 1985, 77–111.

5. Only in Canada: Federalism, *Non Obstante* and the Charter

Samuel V. LaSelva

We should entrench our fundamental rights in the Canadian constitution. . . .But we should include in the constitutional Bill of Rights the kind of *non obstante* provision now contained in our statutory bill, a provision which would allow Parliament to enact (or reenact) a statute which would then be legally valid irrespective of a judicial holding that is incompatible with the Bill of Rights. . . .In typically Canadian fashion, I propose a compromise, between the British version of full-fledged parliamentary sovereignty and the American version of full-fledged judicial authority over constitutional matters.[1]

So wrote Professor Paul Weiler before the enactment of the Canadian Charter of Rights and Freedoms, 1982. That the Charter contains a notwithstanding clause may be due, then, in no small part to Professor Weiler's essay in this *Review*. Moreover, the clause has since been defended by a number of constitutional scholars, and is thus well on its way to being viewed as the uniquely Canadian contribution to the theory of constitutionalism.[2] My purpose in this paper is to assess this constitutional optimism by subjecting the notwithstanding clause to a more systematic examination than it has yet received. Specifically, I shall outline four frameworks within which assessment of the clause must take place, and I shall suggest that it is with respect to the last framework—namely, that of federalism—that the clause encounters its greatest difficulties. That is

so, I shall suggest, because Professor Weiler and other defenders of the notwithstanding clause have given insufficient attention to the fact that Canada is a federal state.[3] In fact, their concern has not been federalism at all but the relationship between the legislature and the judiciary under a Bill of Rights, and their aim has been to secure and justify the ultimate supremacy of the legislature without depriving the judiciary of its most characteristic functions.[4] My objection is not that they have failed to justify the supremacy of the legislature or have deprived the judiciary of its role, for here they have been largely successful. It is, rather, that they have failed to secure the very supremacy that they have succeeded in justifying, largely because their argument has proceeded as if Canada were a unitary state. But Canada is, manifestly, a federal rather than a unitary state, and thus use of the notwithstanding clause—far from removing legislation from the judicial forum, as it would in a unitary state—brings into play the federal division of powers and its judicial construction. And Canadian experience with respect to that subject, I shall argue, suggests not only that a notwithstanding clause cannot secure the subordination of the judiciary to the legislatures, but also that use of the clause will entangle both the judges themselves and constitutional rights in the politics of federalism. But before elaborating this argument, I shall first outline the political objectives and concerns of the politicians who either advocated or opposed the notwithstanding clause; I shall then examine the clause from the perspective of constitutional theory, after which I shall

Samuel V. LaSelva, "Only in Canada: Reflections on the Charter's Notwithstanding Clause," *Dalhousie Review* 63:3 (1983): 383–398. Reprinted by permission of the *Dalhousie Review* and the author.

consider the role of the Supreme Court under both the Canadian Bill of Rights and the Charter of Rights and Freedoms.

POLITICIANS AND THE NOTWITHSTANDING CLAUSE

Entering politics with the belief that Canada needed a Bill of Rights binding upon both levels of government,[5] Prime Minister Trudeau also believed, together with Frank Scott, that though provincial consent had been difficult to obtain for other constitutional changes, "a Bill of Rights in theory should win acceptance more easily, since it does not disturb the balance of power."[6] No constitutional change, however, has been more difficult to secure than the Charter of Rights. It required two Supreme Court decisions and a series of concessions to the provinces, among them a notwithstanding clause. But that clause, it seemed to the Prime Minister, came dangerously close to defeating the very purpose of an entrenched Charter. Moreover, the government of Quebec refuses to recognize the legitimacy of the Charter and has already used the notwithstanding clause to override some of its major provisions. It was Quebec that the Prime Minister had hoped to please most by his constitutional initiative.

The Prime Minister based his argument for an entrenched Charter upon the idea of equal rights. Bills of Rights have not, traditionally, been justified upon that ground at all. Their justification has been either that they secure individual and minority rights by placing them beyond the reach of intolerant political majorities, or that, in federal states, the greatest threat to such rights comes from local rather than national government.[7] But the Prime Minister was not arguing that provincial governments failed to respect rights, or that rights were insecure in Canada. While an entrenched Charter would give greater security to rights, security of rights was not the issue. Rights can be reasonably secure

and yet unequal, and what primarily concerned the Prime Minister was the inequality of rights. "A constitutional bill of rights," he suggested, " . . .would well establish that all Canadians . . . have equal rights."[8] The federal Parliament could establish equal rights if it acquired additional legislative power, but the provinces would not consent to such a change in the division of powers. And individual action by the provinces would result in the diversity rather than the equality (or uniformity) of rights. Only the courts, operating under an entrenched Charter, could establish equal rights for all Canadians.

The Prime Minister linked equal rights not with egalitarianism but with unity. The Charter would promote some forms of equality: it would secure, for example, equal voting rights and equal freedom of conscience and the right to live and work anywhere in Canada. But the Charter would not diminish inequalities of wealth or political influence, nor did it even attempt to secure socioeconomic rights. Egalitarian objectives would have to be achieved by other means. However, the equal rights of the Charter would promote Canadian unity. "You will appreciate," the Prime Minister said of his proposal, "that . . .we will be testing—and, hopefully, establishing—the unity of Canada."[9] That hope draws upon two complementary ideas. It applies to Canadian federalism what Durkheim said of the division of labour: "[A]s a consequence of a more advanced division of labour . . .the contents of men's minds differ from one subject to another. One is gradually proceeding towards a state of affairs . . .in which members of a single social group will no longer have anything in common other than their humanity."[10] If federal diversity had deprived Canadians of everything but their humanity, then that status, expressed in terms of uniform constitutional rights, might unite them. This was reinforced by the American experience that equality of rights can serve to create a national identity and a unity that transcends the identification citizens have with states and regions.[11]

To many of the premiers, however, an en-

even this could be argued by way of ss. 1 & 33

Perhaps the reason why other provinces would be opposed to a Que Charter is that it would not be subject to debate by courts outside the province unlike what occurs with other provinces where an entrenched Charter transfers power from provinces to judiciary.

trenched Charter, equal rights, Canadian unity, political centralization, and the loss of provincial autonomy were much the same thing. The premiers did not oppose rights; they were not seeking to maintain, as Ottawa has sometimes suggested, parochialism and local intolerances. But the dispute over entrenchment, it was suggested in a paper prepared for the Government of Manitoba, "does not pertain solely, or mainly, to rights at all. It pertains, rather, to the transfer of power."[12] An entrenched Charter "would amount to a constitutional revolution," entailing the loss of provincial sovereignty and thus of provincial parliamentary democracy. It would transfer power from the provincial legislatures to the courts. And what that suggested to some of the premiers was the loss of provincial autonomy, for "[t]o judge by the American experience an entrenched Bill of Rights would tend to centralize authority, certainly if the federal government had a predominant say in appointments to the Supreme Court."[13]

But despite this claim, American experience does not in fact support the view that an "entrenched Bill of Rights would tend to centralize authority in any federation." Both that claim and the assertion of the Supreme Court—that the entrenched American Bill of Rights was of no value in the interpretation of the statutory Canadian Bill of Rights[14]—rest upon the same fallacy, namely that virtually everything depends upon constitutional status. The American Bill of Rights has centralized power not because it is entrenched, nor even because it is interpreted by a federally appointed Supreme Court. If those were sufficient conditions for centralization, then the process would have begun in 1791 and America might have avoided her Civil War. The original Bill of Rights could not centralize power because it limited only federal power. It was only after the Civil War, and as a result of it, that the Fourteenth Amendment was adopted. That amendment placed open-ended restrictions upon state power and conferred primary enforcement power upon Congress.[15] It should not be alto-

gether surprising that a provision designed to centralize power should do just that.

What American experience suggests, then, is that the actual provisions of a Bill of Rights are as important as its constitutional status. Critics of the proposed Charter could point, however, to no provision that resembled the Fourteenth Amendment of the American constitution. The Prime Minister had, in fact, insisted that his Charter "would not involve a transfer of legislative power from one government to another."[16] It would simply be a "common agreement to restrict the power of governments."[17] The latter statement was only partly true. Some rights, such as speech, are primarily restrictions upon governmental power and require little implementing legislation. But other rights, such as language, are effective only if supported by legislation. An entrenched Charter might well lead to more rather then less government. Yet it was precisely here that the Prime Minister showed his concern for federalism: "In order not to be inconsistent with the present constitutional division of powers, an entrenched bill of rights must recognize that any required legislation falls within the competence of Parliament in some respects and within the competence of the provincial legislatures in others."[18]

If the Charter of Rights is designed to promote unity rather than to centralize power, then a major *political* justification for the notwithstanding clause appears groundless: the provincial legislatures cannot use the clause to prevent a centralization of power that will not occur.[19] But frequent or extensive use of the clause could undermine the idea that Canadians have equal rights, and thus nullify the Prime Minister's goal of creating a Canadian unity based upon a Canadian identity. The provincial legislatures would be inclined to do just that if they believed, with Donald Smiley, that the Charter is "a device for strengthening national against provincial allegiances."[20] Legislative power is of little value to the provincial legislatures if voters identify with Ottawa rather than the provinces. Moreover,

Ottawa already possesses, under the Canadian constitution, far greater legislative power than do the provinces and has at its disposal the powers of reservation and disallowance, even though judicial interpretation and usage have restricted those powers. But if the Charter succeeded in changing the loyalties of voters, it is not inconceivable that the Supreme Court might abandon the Privy Council's decentralist interpretation of the Constitution for Macdonald's centralist interpretation, and that the powers of reservation and disallowance might be revived. Frequent or extensive use of the notwithstanding clause would nullify that possibility as well (providing of course that the courts upheld legislation enacted under the clause as within the legislative powers of the provinces).

I don't know if I can agree —

Can't force society to go in a direction that it was not already going.

CONSTITUTIONAL THEORY AND THE NOTWITHSTANDING CLAUSE

The Charter's notwithstanding clause is also an exercise in constitutional theory. According to orthodox theory, however, the clause encounters an immediate and insuperable difficulty. The purpose of the clause is to secure the ultimate supremacy of the legislatures; but legislative supremacy is thought to be the very antithesis of constitutionalism. The latter claim was given classic expression by Chief Justice John Marshall in the celebrated American case of *Marbury v. Madison*. The alleged difficulty is apparent in the Canadian Charter. The Charter purports to be paramount law. It is part of the Constitution of Canada which "is the supreme law of Canada, and any law that is inconsistent with the provisions of the Constitution is, to the extent of inconsistency, of no force or effect."[21] Yet the notwithstanding clause enables the legislatures to enact laws which conflict with the Charter. If *Marbury v. Madison* is sound, then

the notwithstanding clause defeats the very purpose of the Charter.

Marbury v. Madison is not based upon the view that federalism requires a judicial umpire; and it is not, primarily, an exposition of the law of the American constitution. It is, rather, an exercise in abstract political theory and its aim is to lay bare the very idea of a limited or constitutional government, of which the American is but one example. It sets out a series of alternatives between which "there is no middle ground"; and the alternatives are so constructed that Marshall's conclusion necessarily follows. A written constitution, the Chief Justice asserted, "is either paramount law...or it is on a level with ordinary legislative acts."[22] Since "all those who have framed written constitutions" contemplate them as forming paramount law, "an act of the legislature, repugnant to the constitution is void."[23] But should courts give effect to void acts of the legislature? Those who maintain that "courts must close their eyes on the constitution, and see only the law" would "subvert the very foundation of all written constitutions." They would give the legislature "a practical and real omnipotence," reducing to nothing the "greatest improvement on political institutions, a written constitution."[24]

Marbury v. Madison begins, then, by asserting the supremacy of the constitution; but it concludes by asserting a radically different kind of supremacy, namely that of the judicial version of the constitution. And it holds, even more radically, that the only alternative is legislative omnipotence. The heart of its argument is the equation of constitutional limitations and judicially imposed limitations, with the corollary that a written constitution is mere paper unless the courts defend it against the legislature. But the decision does not even attempt to establish these claims. Instead, it argues that courts ought to enforce the constitution rather than a statute which conflicts with it. And there are difficulties even here: for if courts were confined, as the Chief Justice implied, to preventing clear violations of the constitution by the legislature, judicial review would come to an end, since even a legislature bent on violating the constitution would not be foolish enough to do so clearly.[25]

Not only is the Chief Justice's principal argument a *non sequitur*, but his opinion overlooks the institutional incapacities of courts and ascribes to them functions that they do not and cannot perform. *Marbury v. Madison* implied that the most important task of the courts was to defend the constitution against the legislature. Yet it was not until 1857—more than fifty years after *Marbury v. Madison*—that the Court again asserted its power against an Act of Congress. Not only have American courts been hesitant to oppose Congress (concerning themselves far more with administrative and police action than legislation action[26]), but their power to gain compliance and their prestige have been lowest when they have sought to do so. "[T]he Court," Robert Dahl has written, "is least effective against a current law-making majority—and evidently least inclined to act."[27]

But what makes the Chief Justice's conception of constitutionalism altogether unworkable is his assumption that legislators are unconcerned with constitutionality. If that assumption were sound—if (as Ronald Dworkin has suggested)[28] legislators relied upon utilitarian and majoritarian considerations, while only judges based their decisions upon the constitution—then our constitutional polity would come to an end. For legislators, rather than judges, bear the exclusive responsibility for the enactment of laws, and most laws are either never tested in courts or receive limited judicial scrutiny only after being in force for a number of years. But a utilitarian and majoritarian legislature, unconcerned with constitutionality, would enact many unconstitutional laws and many of these would escape the judicial veto. Not only would such a legislature reduce to absurdity the presumption of constitutionality found in existing constitu-

tional systems, but the system itself could not be described as a constitutional system, since it would contain a significant number of unconstitutional laws. Yet *Marbury v. Madison* leads, logically, to such a system.

These difficulties both suggest that *Marbury v. Madison's* central assumptions are unsound and point to a more satisfactory theory of constitutionalism. If courts were the sole guardians of constitutionality, then *Marbury v. Madison* could not have implications which conflict with some of the most basic features of existing constitutional systems, nor would it lead to absurd results. It is not that courts are unimportant; but *Marbury v. Madison* attaches importance to the wrong judicial functions. And it mistakenly supposes that legislators are unconcerned with constitutionality. But if legislators—whose role in a constitutional system is crucial—are concerned with constitutionality, and if courts are important in different ways than *Marbury v. Madison* suggests, then constitutional theory should take account of these facts.

The Canadian Charter attempts to do that by means of a notwithstanding clause, a clause which attempts to secure the ultimate supremacy of the legislature without depriving the judiciary of its role. The Charter itself is supreme law, and it empowers the courts to review for constitutionality all matters within the authority of Parliament and the provincial legislatures. Thus Canadian courts possess virtually the same judicial powers that American courts have acquired as a result of *Marbury v. Madison*. And that is unaffected by the notwithstanding clause: for the supremacy of the Charter, so far as the courts are concerned, is no more undermined by the notwithstanding clause than it is by the power of formal amendment. The reverse may be nearer the truth since the clause, as Paul Weiler has suggested, may have a psychologically liberating effect upon judges, inclining them to be "adventurous . . .if only because the political process remains there as a backstop if they miscue badly enough."[29] But whether or not judges choose to be adventurous, their duty is to apply the Charter as supreme law.

That duty is important not because it prevents manifest violations of the constitution by the legislature, but because even a legislature which respects the constitution may violate it through inadvertence. And that suggests that talk of judicial deference and judicial activism—so common in American constitutional theory[30]—is often misleading, since those terms imply that courts must either exercise no independent judgment regarding constitutionality or must set themselves against the legislature. But in cases of legislative inadvertence courts uphold the constitution without opposing the legislature. In such cases the Charter's notwithstanding clause is of no consequence either: for a legislature is not likely to override a judicial decision which prevents it from doing what it never intended to do.

In other cases courts do not uphold the constitution so much as substitute judicial for legislative judgments of constitutionality. In those cases the judicial version of the Charter is supreme unless the legislatures decide otherwise. But the legislatures, if supported by public opinion,[31] may be more inclined to use the notwithstanding clause in such cases than some constitutional scholars suppose. And the Canadian Bill of Rights does not prove the contrary.[32] For though its notwithstanding clause was used only once and then only in a situation of apparent emergency, the Bill itself was never used to render inoperative laws of whose validity Parliament and the public were convinced. But if the legislatures should consistently fail to use the Charter's notwithstanding clause in situations in which its use is justified, then that failure would not only deprive the clause of its possible liberating effect upon the judiciary: it would also nullify the most important difference between the Charter and the American Bill of Rights.

In yet other cases Parliament and the legislatures are likely to use the notwithstanding clause to enact legislation designed to meet exceptional circumstances, if such legislation cannot be introduced otherwise. Thus Parliament would almost certainly use the clause to protect emergency legislation which failed to survive judicial scrutiny under the Charter's "reasonable limits test."[33] In such cases, however, the notwithstanding clause does not empower the legislatures to infringe constitutional rights so much as it acknowledges that Bills of Rights are framed for normal rather than exceptional circumstances. And that would remain true even if the Charter did not contain such a clause, for American experience with an entrenched Bill of Rights suggests that exceptional circumstances give rise to exceptional means.

All this supposes of course that legislators respect constitutional rights. But even if this were disputed, it would by no means follow that a notwithstanding clause makes infringement of constitutional rights easier or more likely. In the case of surreptitious infringements, for example, the clause may be of no consequence whatsoever. For if infringements are surreptitious because they would fail to receive wide public support if done openly, then a democratic legislature is not likely to override judicial decisions exposing such infringements. The notwithstanding clause would be used by a legislature whose infringements were supported by public opinion; but the clause does not enable such a legislature to infringe constitutional rights so much as it provides a new means of doing so. Even without such a clause, legislators can often undermine constitutional rights through the appointment and removal of judges, through manipulation of the jurisdiction of courts, through participation in the amending process, and by a variety of other means. But constitutionalism supposes that legislators respect rights, for otherwise a constitutional system could not exist. It supposes, as Holmes said in a different context, that "legislators are ultimate guardians of the liberties and welfare of the people in quite as great a degree as the courts."[34] And the Charter's notwithstanding clause supposes that too, for otherwise we can imagine no circumstances in which it would have relevant application.

THE CHARTER AND THE BILL OF RIGHTS

Although the notwithstanding clause owes its existence largely to the fear that the courts would supplant the legislatures as policy-makers under a Charter of Rights, that fear could not have been based upon Canadian experience. For judicial interpretation of the Canadian Bill of Rights, as Walter Tarnopolsky has observed, provides "no evidence . . .that any of the Canadian courts, and certainly not the Supreme Court of Canada, are declaring legislation inoperative because of excessive zeal to protect civil liberties against the legislators and administrators of Canada."[35] But the Charter differs from the Bill of Rights, and those differences may incline the courts to give it strong judicial application; and that in turn may incline the legislatures, as we have seen, to use the notwithstanding clause. What is crucial, then, is whether or not the Supreme Court will give the Charter overriding effect.

That question is obviously unanswerable since it presupposes knowledge of future judicial behaviour. But knowledge of judicial behaviour under the Canadian Bill of Rights is available. That the Supreme Court used the Bill (except in two cases[36]) as merely an interpretation statute came as no surprise to some academic lawyers. For they had insisted, even before the Bill became law, that it was an interpretation statute. Thus Frank Scott, writing in 1959, stated: "I regret that I don't think it means much as a matter of law. I just do not think it has amended all

the laws that now exist which are contrary to it—and there are many."[37] Bora Laskin, then a professor of law, concurred: his analysis of the Bill did "not portend any greater role for the proposed Canadian Bill of Rights than its operation as a political charter."[38] And W. R. Lederman—after adding (in 1967) his authority to the view that the Bill "contains only presumptions as to the construction of other federal statutes"—concluded that the Bill "is itself poorly drafted."[39]

When judges were asked to apply the Bill their reasons for refusing to use it as anything more than an interpretation statute bore a striking resemblance to the reasons given by the academic commentators. And most of their reasons related to the language of the Bill. Thus section 1 states: "it is hereby recognized and declared that . . .there have existed and shall continue to exist . . .the following human rights." Some of the judges took that to mean that the Bill created no new rights but merely enshrined the rights that Canadians already possessed; and that implied that if Canadians did not possess a right prior to the enactment of the Bill, then they did not possess the right as a result of it.[40] Section 2, which enacts that "Every law of Canada shall . . .be construed and applied," created difficulties as well. To some of the judges that phrase suggested that the courts were required to resolve conflicts between the Bill and other laws by interpretation; but if the conflict could not be so resolved, then the conflicting legislation must be applied.[41] If Parliament had intended otherwise, Chief Justice Cartwright reasoned, it would have added such words as "and if any law of Canada cannot be so construed and applied it shall be regarded as inoperative or *pro tanto* repealed."[42]

Parliament had intended otherwise. Parliament's intention became apparent when the Chief Parliamentary Draftsman explained the significance of the Bill in an essay published in 1968[43]—an explanation which appears to have convinced academic lawyers but not the judges.[44]

For though the Supreme Court used the Bill, shortly afterwards, to render inoperative a section of the Indian Act, *The Queen v. Drybones* was exceptional and the courts continued to use the Bill as an interpretation statute. At that point Parliament might have responded by simply amending the Bill along the lines suggested by Chief Justice Cartwright, thus reassuring the judges that the Bill (which has a statutory rather than a constitutional basis) was intended to have overriding effect. But Parliament, or at least the Prime Minister, seems to have thought otherwise, believing perhaps, with one constitutional scholar, that "the strongest argument for entrenching a Bill of Rights is the impotence of the present one."[45]

The suggestions of the judges were influential, however, in the framing of the Charter of Rights. Thus judicial interpretation of the Charter should be free of at least some of the difficulties encountered by the Bill of Rights.[46] The Charter, for example, does not speak of "recognizing rights" or of "existing rights," but confers rights. And laws which conflict with the Charter are not to be "construed and applied" but are "of no force or effect." Moreover, the Charter also possesses constitutional status, and thus avoids another alleged difficulty of the Bill of Rights, namely its statutory or at most quasi-constitutional basis.[47]

But there were other reasons for the difficulties encountered by the Bill of Rights, reasons whose force depended neither upon the language nor the status of the Bill. Thus, when the Supreme Court was asked to give overriding effect to the Bill, some of the judges expressed concern that the Court could do so only by performing functions which, in "the traditional British system that is our own by virtue of the B.N.A. Act,"[48] belonged exclusively to Parliament. For the courts were being asked to adapt the law to changing circumstances and thus to exercise, in effect, legislative power. Not only were the courts, some of the judges reasoned, ill-

equipped to perform these functions; but functions of this kind raised questions about legislative sovereignty and about the legitimacy of judicial review in a democracy.[49]

Although influential, such reasoning presupposes a fallacious view of the basis of judicial authority. It supposes, that is to say, that judicial action under a Bill of Rights is justified only if courts possess greater expertise than the legislature, or if the action in question is in fact "democratic." But to argue in this way is not only to require a standard of "proof" that may be impossible to attain: it is also to overlook the soundest basis for judicial action. "[W]e act in these matters," Justice Jackson held in a case concerning the American Bill of Rights, "not by authority of our competence but by force of our commissions."[50] That answer has never satisfied American constitutional scholars, but only because (as Justice Jackson himself recognized by invoking history) the American constitution does not confer a clear commission upon the judiciary.[51] The Canadian constitution, however, does confer such a commission, and thus Canadian Courts would be required to give overriding effect to the Charter of Rights even if it could be shown that the judiciary lacked the expertise of the legislature, or that judicial review was in fact undemocratic.

JUDICIAL FEDERALISM AND THE NOTWITHSTANDING CLAUSE

The Charter of Rights is, however, only part of the Canadian constitution. It presupposes the B.N.A. Act, and especially its division of legislative powers. That would be of little consequence if the Charter did not contain a notwithstanding clause, or if, though it contained such a clause, the B.N.A. Act allocated legislative jurisdiction over civil liberties in a precise manner. But the allocation of civil liberties jurisdiction is one of the most disputed features of the B.N.A. Act, so much so that Frank

Scott, for example, recommended entrenching a Bill of Rights on that ground alone: "It is hard to protect something by law when you do not know whom it belongs to. This is why my personal preference is for a bill of rights which is placed in the B.N.A. Act."[52] The Charter of Rights is of course part of the B.N.A. Act. But use of its notwithstanding clause requires courts to address logically prior and politically sensitive questions about which level of government has jurisdiction over civil liberties—the very question that, according to Scott and others, an entrenched Bill of Rights was to eliminate.

That civil liberties jurisdiction under the B.N.A. Act is radically uncertain is illustrated, though not exhausted,[53] by *Laurier Saumur v. The City of Quebec*—a case which raised the seemingly simple question of the validity of a municipal by-law prohibiting the distribution of pamphlets in the streets without the permission of the chief of police. The Supreme Court eventually decided that the by-law was *ultra vires*, but only by a majority of 5–4 and only after setting out at least three views of the constitutional position of civil liberties, none of which was accepted by a majority of the court. Thus Chief Justice Rinfret and Justices Kerwin and Taschereau, relying on provincial legislative power over property and civil rights and in relation to matters of a merely local or private nature, held that provincial legislative jurisdiction over civil liberties was unlimited.[54] But Justice Estey countered that federal jurisdiction was unlimited, given Parliament's power to make laws "for the peace, order and good government of Canada."[55] And Justices Cartwright and Fauteux insisted that some civil liberties (freedom of speech among them) fell partly under provincial and partly under federal jurisdiction.[56]

To some constitutional scholars, *Saumur* suggested more than that (in cases concerning the constitutional position of civil liberties) it was "not difficult to find some reason why a particular piece of legislation is invalid if the judges are so inclined."[57] *Saumur* also suggested, to Frank Scott at least, that the federal division of legislative powers could be used to protect what the judges understood to be the liberties of the subject. "For by saying that a particular statute exceeds the jurisdiction of Parliament or legislature, the courts remove the statute from the books and the liberties it destroyed are restored."[58] Such use of the division of powers was justified, Scott insisted, because it was the "function and duty [of judges] to act as guardians of our rights whether we have a Bill of Rights or not."[59]

But such use of the division of powers, as Scott himself acknowledged, also provided one of the most compelling justifications for entrenching a Bill of Rights. For not only was that approach to civil liberties jurisprudentially unsound, but it might turn out to be completely ineffective; and whether effective or not, it had serious implications for the structure of Canadian federalism. The approach was unsound because questions of civil liberties and questions of federalism were not coextensive in all cases.[60] And it might prove ineffective because the courts, using the federalism device, could find a statute *ultra vires* only by attributing jurisdiction over the liberties in question to the level of government that had not legislated. But that government, now secure in its constitutional jurisdiction, might choose to enact the very statute that the courts sought to remove from the books.

The question of effectiveness aside, such judicial tactics would not only have serious implications for the structure of Canadian federalism, but might even result in the diminution of provincial legislative power. The latter hinged upon the fact, as Walter Tarnopolsky observed in 1968, that "[t]here have been more civil liberties cases involving provincial governments than the federal government."[61] That fact, coupled with the uncertainty of legislative jurisdiction over civil liberties and the apparent determination of judges to uphold what they believed to be the liberties of the subject, would result in the courts "holding that the particular right . . .is beyond the jurisdiction of the province."[62] And that implied, Tarnopolsky reasoned, that "absence of an overriding Bill of Rights results in the diminution of provincial power."[63] An entrenched Bill of Rights would diminish provincial power too, but (unlike the device of judicial federalism) it would not transfer the relinquished power to the federal government. Those being the alternatives, it was, Tarnopolsky concluded, "all the more ironic that opposition to the proposed Charter of Human Rights should come from provincial spokesmen."[64]

It is even more ironic that provincial spokesmen should have demanded the inclusion of a notwithstanding clause in the Charter of Rights. For use of the clause—far from removing legislation from the judicial forum, and thus securing the supremacy of the provincial legislatures over the judiciary—requires the courts to address logically prior and radically uncertain questions about the allocation of legislative jurisdiction over civil liberties under the federal division of legislative powers.[65] And because that jurisdiction is uncertain, courts will be asked to hold legislation enacted under the clause *ultra vires* by attributing jurisdiction over the rights in question to the government that has not legislated. How these cases will be decided cannot of course be predicted. What can be said, however, is that the allocation of civil liberties jurisdiction is uncertain enough, contested enough, and sufficiently entangled in the politics of federalism to make judicial decisions with respect to it appear to have more of the

characteristics of judicial legislation than of judicial interpretation. And if those decisions, following the example of the 1950s, deal with provincial use of the notwithstanding clause by resorting to the device of judicial federalism, then use of the clause will bring about the very centralization of legislative power that it was intended to prevent. But even if the courts decide otherwise, their decisions will still have a profound effect upon the structure of Canadian federalism; and thus use of the notwithstanding clause will make judges more, rather than less, important.

Since these difficulties are rooted in federalism rather than in the relationship between the legislature and the judiciary under an entrenched constitution, they do not of course diminish the importance of the Charter's notwithstanding clause as a contribution to the theory of constitutionalism. But what they do suggest is that the notwithstanding clause is an advance primarily in the constitutional theory of the unitary state. For though it may be possible to construct a federal division of powers which is more precise than the Canadian, and thus to remove larger portions of it from the judicial forum, a characteristic feature of virtually all such divisions of powers is that they are both uncertain and contested. So long as this is the case, and so long as the courts are required to resolve the jurisdictional disputes which arise, a notwithstanding clause cannot ensure the supremacy of the legislature over the judiciary in a federal state. And this suggests that *Canadian* optimism concerning the notwithstanding clause is misplaced.

Notes

1. P. C. Weiler, "Of Judges and Rights, or Should Canada Have a Constitutional Bill of Rights?" *Dalhousie Review* 60 (1980/81): 231–2. The notwithstanding clause is set out in section 33 of the Canadian Charter of Rights and Freedoms.

2. See W. S. Tarnopolsky, "The Constitution and Human Rights," in K. Banting and R. Simeon, *And No One Cheered: Federalism, Democracy and the Constitution Act* (1983), 271; H. Marx, "Entrenchment, Limitations and Non-Obstante," in W. S. Tarnopolsky and G. Beaudoin, *The Canadian Charter of Rights and Freedoms* (1982), 70–3; J. Jaconelli, *Enacting a Bill of Rights: The Legal Problems* (1980) 61–91; and W. R. Lederman, "Concerning a Bill of Rights for Canada and Ontario," in *The Confederation Challenge* (1970), 61–91.

3. See Weiler, "Of Judges and Rights," 234–5: "I advance this proposal to define the relative responsiblity for, and ultimate authority over, fundamental rights only as between Parliament and the Supreme Court of Canada in Ottawa."

4. See note 2; and especially Weiler, "Of Judges and Rights," 231–5.

5. P. E. Trudeau, "A Constitutional Declaration of Rights," in his *Federalism and the French Canadians* (1968), 52.

6. F. R. Scott, *Civil Liberties and Canadian Federalism* (1959), 52. Compare Trudeau, "A Constitutional Declaration of Rights," 57.

7. The former justification is set out, for example, in the opinion of Justice Jackson in *Barnette v. West Virginia State Board of Education*, 319 U.S. 638 (1943). The latter justification is elaborated in Scott, *Civil Liberties and Canadian Federalism*, 23; and in W. H. Riker, *Federalism: Origin, Operation, Significance* (1964), 139–45.

8. P. E. Trudeau, *A Canadian Charter of Human Rights* (1968), 11. See P. H. Russell, "The Political Purposes of the Canadian Charter of Rights and Freedoms" *Canadian Bar Review* 61 (1983): 30–54.

9. Trudeau, "A Constitutional Declaration of Rights," 54.

10. S. Lukes, "Durkheim's 'Individualism and the Intellectuals' " *Political Studies* 17 (1969): 26.

11. See A. C. Cairns, "Recent Federalist Constitutional Proposals: A Review Essay" *Canadian Public Policy* 3 (1979): 354.

12. G. P. Browne, "On the Entrenchment of a Bill of Rights," mimeographed, Government of Manitoba, September, 1980, 1:1.

13. *Ibid.*, 13.

14. See, for example, Chief Justice Fauteux's remark in *Smythe v. The Queen* (1971) 19 D.L.R. 3d 480; and the discussion in W. S. Tarnopolsky, "The Historical and Constitutional Context of the Proposed Canadian Charter of Rights and Freedoms" *Law and Contemporary Problems* 44 (1981): 181.

15. See A. M. Bickel, "The Original Understanding and the Segregation Decisions" *Harvard Law Review* 69 (1955): 64; and R. Berger, *Government by Judiciary* (1977).

16. Trudeau, A Canadian Charter of Human Rights, 14.

17. *Ibid.*, 14.

18. *Ibid.*, 29.

19. Compare Browne, "On the Entrenchment of a Bill of Rights," 21.

20. D. Smiley, *The Canadian Charter of Rights and Freedoms, 1981* (1981), 12, 57.

21. See section 52 of the Constitution Act, 1982.

22. I. Cranch (1803), 177.

23. *Ibid.*, 177.

24. *Ibid.*, 178.

25. Marshall's opinion is criticized by J. B. Thayer, "The Origin and Scope of the American Doctrine of Constitutional Law," in L. W. Levy, *Judicial Review and the Supreme Court* (1967), 43–63; and by C. L. Black, *The People and the Court* (1960), 26–7.

26. W. S. Tarnopolsky, "Enacting a Bill of Rights: The Legal Problems" *Oxford Journal of Legal Studies* 2 (1982): 125.

27. R. A. Dahl, "Decision-Making in a Democracy: the Supreme Court as a National Policy-Maker," in L. W. Levy, *Judicial Review and the Supreme Court* (1967), 122.

28. R. Dworkin, *Taking Rights Seriously* (1977), 141: and especially his "Liberalism," in S. Hampshire, *Public and Private Morality* (1978), 134.

29. Weiler, "Of Judges and Rights," 227.

30. See, for example, M. Shapiro, *Freedom of Speech: The Supreme Court and Judicial Review* (1966), 5–45.

31. The five year limitation on legislation enacted under the notwithstanding seems to be designed to ensure that legislative opinion conforms to public opinion.

32. Compare Tarnopolsky, "Enacting a Bill of Rights," 124.

33. See Section 1 of the Canadian Charter, and the discussion in Marx, "Entrenchment, Limitation and Non-Obstante," 61.

34. *Missouri, Kansas and Texas Rwy. Co. v. May* (1904), 194 U.S. 270.

35. Tarnopolsky, "The Historical and Constitutional Context of the Proposed Canadian Charter of Rights and Freedoms," 192.

36. See *The Queen v. Drybones* (1970) S.C.R. 282; and *Hogan v. The Queen* (1974), 48 D.L.R. 3d 427.

37. Scott, *The Canadian Constitution and Human Rights*, 47.

38. B. Laskin, "An Inquiry Into the Diefenbaker Bill of Rights" *Canadian Bar Review* 37 (1959): 134.

39. Lederman, "Concerning a Bill of Rights for Canada and Ontario," 278.

40. See, for example, Justice Ritchie's opinion in *Robertson and Rosetanni v. The Queen* (1963), 41 D.L.R. 2d 485. Walter Tarnopolsky has called this the "frozen concepts" principle.

41. See Justice Pigeon's opinion in *The Queen v. Drybones* (1970) S.C.R. 282, 300.

42. *Ibid.*, 288.

43. E. A. Driedger, "The Canadian Bill of Rights," in O. E. Lang, *Contemporary Problems of Public Law in Canada* (1968), 40.

44. Lederman, "Concerning a Bill of Rights for Canada and Ontario," 286.

45. W. S. Tarnopolsky, "A Constitutionally Entrenched Charter of Human Rights—Why Now?" *Saskatchewan Law Review* 33 (1968): 247.

46. See Tarnopolsky, "The Constitution and Human Rights," 261; and P. W. Hogg, "Supremacy of the Canadian Charter of Rights and Freedoms" *Canadian Bar Review* 61 (1983): 69.

47. See, for example, Justice Martland's opinion in *Regina v. Burnshine* (1974), 44 D.L.R. 3d 584, 590.

48. See Justice Pigeon's opinion in *The Queen v. Drybones* (1970) S.C.R. 282, 306.

49. J. D. Whyte, "Civil Liberties and the Courts" *Queen's Quarterly* 83 (1976): 655.

50. *Barnette v. West Virginia State Board of Education* (1943), 319 U.S. 624, 640.

51. See L. Hand, *The Bill of Rights* (1963), 27–30; and H. Wechsler, *Principles, Politics and Fundamental Law* (1961), 4–15.

52. Scott, *The Canadian Constitution and Human Rights*, 50.

53. See also *Switzman v. Elbling and A. G. Quebec* (1957) 7 D.L.R. (2d) 337; D. A. Schmeiser, *Civil Liberties in Canada* (1964), 13–16; J. D. Whyte and W. R. Lederman, *Canadian Constitutional Law* (1977), 4–108; and W. S. Tarnopolsky, "A Constitutionally Entrenched Charter of Human Rights—Why Now?" 248, where it is suggested that "[t]here is a very deep disagreement with respect to the division of legislative jurisdiction over civil liberties."

54. *Laurier Saumur v. The City of Quebec* (1953), 2 S.C.R. 229, 301, 321.

55. *Ibid.*, 356.

56. *Ibid.*, 379.

57. Scott, *Civil Liberties and Canadian Federalism*, 27.

58. *Ibid.*, 27.

59. *Ibid.*, 27.

60. See P. Weiler, "The Supreme Court and the Law of Canadian Federalism" *University of Toronto Law Journal* 23 (1973): 342, and his *In The Last Resort* (1974), 192–6.

61. Tarnopolsky, "A Constitutionally Entrenched Charter of Human Rights—Why Now?", 249.
62. *Ibid.*, 249.
63. *Ibid.*, 249.
64. *Ibid.*, 249.

65. Section 31 of the Charter enacts: "Nothing in this Charter extends the legislative powers of any body or authority." Thus the Charter and especially the notwithstanding clause presuppose the legislative powers set out in the B.N.A. Act.

Selected Readings

Marx, H. "Entrenchment, Limitations and Non-Obstante." In W. S. Tarnopolsky and G. Beaudoin, *The Canadian Charter of Rights and Freedoms: Commentary*. Toronto: Carswell, 1980.

Morton, F. L. *Law, Politics and the Judicial Process in Canada*. Calgary: University of Calgary Press, 1985.

Slattery, Brian. "Legislation." *Canadian Bar Review* 61 (March 1983): 391–7.

Smiley, D. V. *The Canadian Charter of Rights and Freedoms, 1981*. Toronto: Ontario Economic Council, 1981.

Russell, Peter. "The Effect of the Charter of Rights on the Policy-Making Role of the Canadian Courts." *Canadian Public Administration* 25:1 (Spring 1982): 1–33.

Weiler, P. C. "Of Judges and Rights or Should Canada Have a Constitutional Bill of Rights?" *Dalhousie Review* 60 (1980/81): 205–37.

6. THE SUPREME COURT AND FEDERAL-PROVINCIAL RELATIONS: THE POLITICAL USE OF LEGAL RESOURCES

Peter H. Russell

From a purely quantitative point of view judicial decisions appear to be a significant factor in federal-provincial relations in Canada. Looking only at the Supreme Court of Canada and decisions reported in the *Supreme Court Reports*, I find that from 1950 (when the Supreme Court took over from the Privy Council as Canada's highest court) to the end of 1982, 158 cases concerned issues arising under Canada's original Constitution and its amendments. Nearly all of these concerned the division of powers between the two levels of government. The main exceptions were three cases dealing with entrenched language rights. The volume of constitutional litigation has increased in recent years: over half (80 out of 158) of all the Supreme Court's constitutional decisions since it became Canada's final court of appeal have been reported in the last eight years, 1975–82.

Not only has the Supreme Court rendered many decisions concerning federal issues but a number of them have involved issues of great political importance. Challenges to the Trudeau Government's anti-inflation program and to provincial energy policies, and questions relating to the conventions governing constitutional amendments readily come to mind. And this is only at the Supreme Court level. There were other cases relating to federal-provincial relations decided in the lower courts and not appealed to the Supreme Court. I doubt if the judiciary of any other federation is more active than Canada's in umpiring the federal system.[1]

A great many decisions is one thing. But what overall effect have they had on federal-provincial relations? Such a question is prompted by Canada's experience under the Judicial Committee of the Privy Council. The Judicial Committee as Canada's highest court clearly had a decentralizing effect on the federation. Canadians differ as to whether this was a good or bad thing. Scholars differ as to whether it was a correct interpretation of the Constitution. Conventional wisdom in English Canada is that the Judicial Committee reversed the intentions of the Fathers of Confederation, while French Canadians and a few maverick English Canadians, including the author, believe that the Confederation coalition harboured a very complex and somewhat contradictory amalgam of hopes and fears. Historians will never be able to agree on the weight to be attached to the Judicial Committee's decisions as compared with other political, economic and cultural factors in causing Canada to be one of the most decentralized federations. But surely everyone agrees that the overall impact of the Judicial Committee's decisions was decentralizing — and significantly decentralizing at that.

When we turn to an appraisal of the Supreme Court of Canada's influence on the federation it is important to distinguish two kinds of consequences that flow from its decisions. The

Peter H. Russell, "The Supreme Court and Federal-Provincial Relations: The Political Use of Legal Resources," *Canadian Public Policy* 11:2 (1985): 161–170. Reprinted by permission of *Canadian Public Policy* and the author.

most immediate results of court decisions are their effect on the legal powers of government. These legal results shape the constitutional capacity of government. But they do not determine how that capacity is used. Here we encounter the political as opposed to the legal consequences of judicial decisions. Government responses to judicial decisions contracting or expanding their powers — the changes they make in policy, the strategies they adopt for constitutional change — are not controlled by law. These political consequences are determined by the intentions and resources of politicians. Constitutional capacity is one of those resources and an important resource, particularly in a society that reveres the rule of law. But it is not the only resource. In a democratic federation it will often be less important than popularity or the general level of allegiance that a level of government enjoys. Thus the political significance of judicial decisions for federal-provincial relations may not be the same as the purely legal results.

LEGAL RESULTS

First let us briefly consider the main tenor of Supreme Court decisions in terms of their effect on Canada's constitutional law. A few years ago it could be said that the Supreme Court tended to favour the federal government.[2] Such a verdict was based primarily on decisions concerning peace, order and good government, property and civil rights and trade and commerce up to the early 1970s. Since then two scholars, Gilbert L'Ecuyer and Peter Hogg, writing in the late 1970s, have concluded that a review of the Supreme Court's decisions does not show a marked bias towards either level of government but an overall balance.

I think this verdict of balance is correct so far as constitutional jurisprudence is concerned. Indeed, writing now a few years after L'Ecuyer and Hogg, I would add that the Supreme Court's

overall record shows an uncanny balance. In so many areas the net outcome of its decision-making is to strike a balance between federal and provincial powers.

Quantitatively, there has been very little change in the federal victory ratio (federal laws upheld and provincial laws found unconstitutional as a percent of all constitutional cases). The federal victory ratio in constitutional decisions of the Supreme Court rose only slightly from 50.5 percent before 1949 to 54.7 percent for the two decades following 1949. For 1970 to 1982 the ratio fell a little to 53.9 percent. But these figures mean very little. One victory in a big case on a major point of constitutional interpretation may be worth many losses in relatively minor cases. It is when we look at the treatment of major points of doctrine that we can see how balanced the Court has been.

With regard to the most important federal powers — peace, order and good government, trade and commerce, taxation and criminal law — the Court has balanced what it has conceded to the central government with one hand by denying federal power or granting power to the provinces with the other. In the *Anti-Inflation* case, peace, order and good government for the first time served as the constitutional basis for a major, peace time federal economic policy.[3] But the Court's majority rejected the expansive national dimensions interpretation of this power which the Court had appeared to endorse in the 1950s and 1960s. The Court, as *Caloil*[4] and the 1978 *Agricultural Marketing Act Reference*[5] indicate, has been more willing than the Judicial Committee to use the trade and commerce power as a basis for federal regulation of economic activity which is essentially although not entirely international or interprovincial. But in *Vapor Canada*[6] and *Labatt*,[7] the Court, in vetoing federal economic regulations that were not tied to distinctively interprovincial or international commerce, indicated that it would be very cautious about opening up what sounds like the branch of trade and commerce with the greatest potential — "general regulation of trade affecting the whole Dominion." In *C.I.G.O.L.*[8] it restricted provincial power to tax natural resources, but then in the *Exported National Gas*[9] case it ruled that resources could be immunized from federal taxation if they are owned by the provincial government when they are exported from the province. While the Court in the *Canadian Indemnity Co.*[10] case upheld British Columbia's "nationalization" of the automobile insurance despite the interprovincial nature of the industry, in *Central Canada Potash*[11] it would not permit provincial management of a province's natural resources to embrace direct control of international trade in a resource. Overall, the Court's decisions affecting constitutional capacity for economic management have not tilted the balance of power decisively in one direction or another.

In the criminal justice field the timing has been different but the result the same. The Court's 1978 decisions in *McNeil*,[12] *Dupond*[13] and *Di Iorio*[14] capped a long developing tendency to dilute the exclusive federal jurisdiction over criminal law and procedure. These decisions eliminated the division of powers as a significant constitutional protection against provincial encroachments on civil liberties and, in that way, helped pave the way to the Charter. But in another series of cases beginning with *Hauser*,[15] *Cordes*,[16] and *Keable*[17] in 1979 and running through *Putnam*[18] to *Canadian Natural Transportation*[19] and *Wetmore*[20] decided in the fall of 1983, the Court has restricted provincial power in the area of prosecuting and policing. As a result, with regard to the enforcement of the criminal law, the Supreme Court appears to have given the central government precisely what it has denied that level with regard to the making of criminal law — namely exclusive constitutional power.

We can see the same kind of balance in the Supreme Court's treatment of the distribution of constitutional powers with respect to the judiciary. Some might regard this as a perverse balance for it is an even-handedness in the distribution of frustration. The Court has attempted to clarify earlier jurisprudence by formulating a test for determining whether provincial administrative tribunals or expansions of provincially appointed judges' functions run afoul of the guarantee of federally appointed provincial judges' jurisdiction based on section 96.[21] While this jurisprudence has enabled a number of provincial innovations in public administration to survive constitutional challenge, still it has not saved them all. Major provincial policies concerned with housing,[22] the unification of family courts,[23] and the regulation of professions[24] have recently foundered on the Supreme Court's enforcement of section 96. However the Court has balanced the books by restricting the federal power to establish courts under section 101. Its decisions in *McNamara Construction*[25] and *Quebec North Shore*[26] have reduced the jurisdiction of the Federal Court and in *Fuller*[27] destroyed the possibility of overcoming the inconveniences to litigants resulting from its interpretation of section 101. These decisions must reduce federal policy-makers' incentive to make further use of that constitutional power.

In the cultural field we find the same balance. The Court's decision in *Capital Cities*[28] confirmed hegemony in regulating the physical means of broadcasting and in *Dionne*[29] denied Quebec the power to develop local culture through the licensing of Cable TV outlets. But then in *Kellogg's*[30] the Court upheld provincial power to police advertising in the mass media. This decision together with the Court's rejection of federally-enforced product standards in *Labatt*[31] and *Dominion Stores*,[32] leave the provinces with considerably more constitutional clout than Ottawa in the general field of consumer protection.

Most dramatically, the balance can be seen in the Supreme Court's decision on constitutional amendment. In 1979, the Court denied the federal Parliament the power to change the Senate[33] and in 1982 it denied that Quebec had, as a matter of convention, a veto over amendments affecting its powers.[34] In between, in the 1981 *Patriation Reference*,[35] the outcome was the epitome of balance — half a loaf to each side. The Prime Minister could legally proceed to patriate the Constitution with an amending formula and Charter of Rights, but, if he did so without a substantial measure of provincial support, he would violate a convention of the constitution.

When we turn to explaining these decisions it is not easy to find evidence that the balance is the result of the conscious intentions of the justices. As Noel Lyon has pointed out, constitutional theory has not been the Court's long suit.[36] It is only a few judges who have occasionally put forward as a deep underlying premise the importance of maintaining a well-balanced federal system in Canada. There is a bit of this in Justice Beetz's reasons, in the *Anti-Inflation Reference*, for rejecting the national dimensions interpretation of peace, order and good government. The most carefully worked out and eloquent defence of balance that I am aware of is our new Chief Justice's opinion in the *Hauser* case. Ironically this was a dissent, and the historic balance Mr. Justice Dickson appealed to — a primary role for the federal Parliament in making criminal law balanced by a primary role for local authorities in the administration of criminal law — is the very opposite of the balance the Court has been moving towards in criminal justice.

One is tempted to adopt a more Hegelian style of explanation — an explanation in terms of the cunning of institutional history.[37] That is why I have referred to the balance as uncanny. While this will no doubt offend strict empiricists, is it really so mysterious? How often we have observed in other contexts — especially the sports arena — the pressure on umpires or referees to "even things up." Justices of Canada's Supreme Court must feel some of that pressure. After all, they are human too! They are umpiring a contest which the main protagonists — federal and provincial politicians — take very seriously. As um-

pires they know they have a credibility problem because one side, the federal government, appoints them and constitutionally controls their institution. It may, indeed, turn out that, if the Constitution is ever amended so that this federal control over appointments is modified and the Court becomes a creature of the Constitution, the Court will be under less pressure to retain its credibility.

Whatever the explanation of the balance achieved by the Court, one of its likely effects is to encourage constitutional litigation. Whatever side you are on in a constitutional dispute over the division of powers, the record of balance makes it reasonable to believe you might win. Most constitutional cases in recent years have been initiated by corporations resisting regulation or defence counsel in criminal cases. The frequency with which division of powers arguments have succeeded is an incentive to lawyers to raise constitutional issues at least as an auxiliary line of attack. Once private litigants have commenced constitutional litigation, governments tend to jump in as intervenants to make sure that their constitutional resources are adequately defended and that no opportunity is lost to whittle down the other side's. Governments themselves through the reference case procedure have initiated 16.5 percent of constitutional litigation since 1950.[38] While governments seldom turn to the Courts as the first arena of combat, a government is quite apt to do so when it is frustrated with political negotiations.

POLITICAL EFFECTS

Thus, one effect of judicial decision-making on Canada's federal system is simply that it has sustained litigation as a significant phase of federal-provincial relations. But beyond this what effects has it had on federal-provincial relations? One might be tempted to say that because its decisions have not tilted sharply in one direction it has had no significant effect on intergovernmental relations. But this would be a mistaken conclusion. Even though the decisions overall may not have altered the balance of power, many have had an important bearing on policy issues and on the bargaining resources of government.

Two kinds of policy or political effects of constitutional decisions can be distinguished. First, a decision on the division of powers usually means that a particular law stays on the books or is removed. This may have important implications for government policy. Of course, this is not always the case. Sometimes when a law is found *ultra vires*, government is able to achieve pretty much the same policy objective through a better drafted law or using some other constitutional power. Saskatchewan's recovery of oil revenues through an oil well income tax after having other taxes and royalties ruled unconstitutional in *C.I.G.O.L.* is a case in point. Some years ago Barry Strayer pointed out that "our constitution can sustain strong government at either level."[39] As recent initiatives of the federal government in the fields of medical insurance and higher education indicate, the level of a government's activity in a given field of policy depends less on its constitutional resources than on its will to use the resources it has.

But it would be a mistake to stretch this point too far. Court decisions on specific pieces of legislation may not exclude a level of government from a policy field but they will certainly influence the choice of instruments available to government in any given field. A classic example is the way in which the Privy Council's decisions forced the federal government to put its anticombines legislation in the form of criminal law.[40] This has had important policy ramifications: the criminal justice approach to competition policy has, to say the least, not been very effective. Here it is interesting to note that in the *Canadian National Transportation* case Justice Dickson, in a concurring opinion supported by two other judges, found that the Combines Inves

tigation Act could be supported as a general regulation of trade and commerce. Even if this position were to be adopted by a majority of the Court, the power of the big business lobby would seriously constrain the federal government's willingness to use its expanded constitutional resources as the basis for a more effective competition policy.

Besides their direct effect on the policy options of governments, constitutional decisions on the division of powers can have a second kind of effect which may be of more interest to the student of federal-provincial relations. This is the effect decisions have on the bargaining strength and position of governments in negotiating policy arrangements or constitutional change. From this perspective constitutional power should be viewed as a political resource just as popularity or a good international economic climate are resources for democratic politicians. Through constitutional litigation governments may gain or lose constitutional capacity in any given field. How governments use their constitutional gains or seek to overcome their losses depends on their political will and skill, and their other resources.

Recent Supreme Court cases provide some fascinating illustrations of court decisions as political resources. The *Patriation Reference* is a textbook example. The federal government was not willing to use the resource it gained in this case — namely the legal power to proceed unilaterally with its constitutional package — because it was apprehensive of the resource its provincial opponents had acquired in the same case — namely the Supreme Court's endorsement of the proposition that unilateralism violates a convention of the Canadian constitution. The provinces, on the other hand, realized that if they remained inflexible in opposition to Mr. Trudeau's package, legally he could and probably would "go it alone." As a consequence both sides went back to the bargaining table with reasonably equal constitutional resources and a compromise resulted.

More often in recent years, it is the federal

government that appears to have taken advantage of bargaining resources it has gained from judicial decisions. This is in a political context where the provinces have been on the offensive so far as changing the constitutional division of powers is concerned. For example, the Supreme Court's decision in the *C.I.G.O.L.* case provided the Trudeau Government with a very handy bargaining resource. The case did not have a significant effect on federal or provincial energy policies. However it gave Trudeau an exclusive power (the power to impose indirect taxes on non-renewable natural resources regardless of their destination) which he could offer to share with the provinces through a constitutional amendment "strengthening" provincial power over resources. Such an amendment was then used to meet the price Ed Broadbent set for obtaining the federal NDP's support for Trudeau's constitutional package.[41] The other major resource case the federal government won during this period, *Central Canada Potash*, was not nearly so useful, because here the federal government was not willing to modify its exclusive control over foreign trade. Section 92A limits provincial power over non-renewable natural resources exported from the province to interprovincial trade.

The federal victories in the cable television cases, *Capital Cities* and *Dionne*, may be useful, in much the same way, in dealing with Quebec. If a federalist party comes to power in Quebec and demands some constitutional changes in the division of powers, the federal government may be forced to take the renewal of this aspect of federalism half seriously. In such a situation, federal politicians may find that a constitutional amendment partially reversing these cases and giving the provinces, especially Quebec, a share of the regulatory power over cable TV is something they can give up without threatening major policy objectives. It is interesting that immediately following these decisions, the then federal Minister of Communications, Jeanne Sauve, offered to consider moving in that direction. In federal-provincial re-

lations it is nice to have goodies on the shelf that you can afford to give away if it becomes politically necessary to make concessions.

The Supreme Court's two decisions on off-shore mineral rights (BC in 1967[42] and Newfoundland in 1984[43]) illustrate both what politicians can and cannot do with a court decision favouring their level of government. The political strength of provincialism in Canada is such that federal politicians have not gone ahead and exercised the total and exclusive control over offshore mineral resources to which, by virtue of Court decisions, they are entitled. They have continued to try and negotiate a deal with the provinces over revenue sharing and regulatory control. The decisions, however, greatly increase the federal politicians' bargaining strength in these negotiations. While the federal Liberals are, no doubt, pleased with these judicial outcomes, federal Conservative leaders are in a somewhat different position. Some of them, especially Brian Mulroney's defeated rivals for the Conservative Party leadership, Joe Clark and John Crosbie, appear committed to giving back to Newfoundland by means of a constitutional amendment what the Supreme Court has denied that Province. Such undertakings may put an additional constraint on the extent to which a Conservative Government could take advantage of the court victory. For Mulroney that victory may almost be an embarrassment.

Indeed, it is possible that a government may win too much in a constitutional case. The Supreme Court's recent decision in *Canadian National Transportation* and *Wetmore* may be cases in point. Chief Justice Laskin's majority opinions in these cases are not entirely clear but they seem to give the federal government exclusive power to prosecute federal offences. If that is so, then the provinces may argue that the federal government should fiscally compensate them for their very substantial contribution to what is entirely a central government responsibility. Or, alternatively, the provinces might press for a constitutional amendment which will give them expressly what they believed to be implicitly theirs under their responsibility for the Administration of Justice in the province. Even though, at the level of popular opinion, there may have been some shift of allegiance to the central government in the 1980s, I doubt if an assertion by the federal government of exclusive power over the direction of criminal prosecutions would be politically acceptable in Canada today. Provincial demands resulting from these federal constitutional victories will be difficult to resist. From a political and fiscal point of view, the federal government may have been better off winning less — for example, paramountcy in a concurrent field.

Normally, I should think governments are happy to win as much as they can in constitutional cases, even though they may not be interested in making immediate use of what they have won. The Court's decisions in the *Chicken and Egg Reference*[44] and *Burns Food*[45] restricting the provinces' power to regulate commodities, a portion of which comes in from other provinces, is of assistance to a federal government that wishes to foster competition within the Canadian economic union. However, in agricultural marketing, interprovincial competition has not been an objective of federal policy. In fact, Ottawa, using the delegation device (a Court-created resource for getting around judicial decisions on the division of powers), gave provincial marketing boards the opportunity of setting provincial quotas.[46] Still, the Court decision enabled the federal Minister to orchestrate this structuring of the market — an opportunity which no doubt contributed to his political career.

Although for political reasons a government may not wish to make immediate use of a court victory, the very existence of a judicial decision containing a favourable doctrinal development might be a background factor in intergovernmental relations. Ottawa-Alberta negotiations over energy policy provide an example. No

doubt, the federal government would like to have come out of the *Anti-Inflation* case with a more expansive interpretation of peace, order and good government than the Court's majority gave it. Still, the deference the majority showed to federal use of emergency powers was significant. The Trudeau government for political reasons was not interested in using this power to combat continuing high inflation in the late 1970s and early 1980s. It even acted as if it could not on its own introduce a comprehensive system of controls. But in the fight with Alberta over energy pricing, when Premier Lougheed threatened to curtail drastically Alberta's petroleum supplies, the Supreme Court's willingness to attribute virtually unlimited power to Ottawa to deal with an emergency and its unwillingness to question the government's assessment of emergency conditions must have been a comfort to federal strategists. On the other hand, the Court's decision in the *Exported Natural Gas Tax* appeal seems to have set an outer limit on the extent to which Ottawa can control tax revenues from exports. However to use this constitutional resource against the federal government, a province would have to rearrange the legal ownership of developed resources in a manner that may be politically and ideologically unattractive. For the provinces, this diminishes the political value of the Court's holding in this case.

In certain contexts it is possible for governments to derive some value from losing constitutional cases. This is most likely to be the case for governments involved in agitating for constitutional change. A classic example is René Levesque's attack on the Supreme Court decision in the Quebec veto case as "the end of all illusions" about the possibility of Quebec achieving its proper status within the Canadian federation.[47] More subtle is the way in which provincial losses in section 96 cases have strengthened the provinces' case for an amendment to that section designed to remove the restrictions judicial interpretation have placed on the provinces' freedom to establish administrative tribunals. The Supreme Court's decision in *McEvoy*[48] indicates just how subtle are the political advantages which may result from losing section 96 cases. Here the Court indicated that the judicature sections of the Constitution prevent the federal Parliament as well as the provinces from unifying criminal jurisdiction in an "inferior" provincial court. This gives the federal government a constitutional excuse for not cooperating with provincial proposals to unify criminal or family jurisdiction under provincially-appointed judges.

So win, lose or draw, judicial decisions continue to affect the resources of the chief protagonists in the never-ending struggle for power that goes on within Canadian federalism. Viewed from this perspective we should not expect judicial decisions to tilt the balance of power decisively one way or the other. Instead the practical impact of decisions should be studied in terms of how they combine with the other resources of federal and provincial politicians within a particular political or policy context. In recent years, it is my assessment that despite a reasonable balance in terms of doctrine, as well as quantitatively, Supreme Court decisions on the division of powers have been more useful to federal than to provincial politicians in the struggle over constitutional change. This perhaps has had more to do with the skill and coherence of federal players in the constitutional game than with the inherent value of the resources the Supreme Court has given them.

THE FUTURE OF CONSTITUTIONAL LITIGATION

In 1958, J. A. Corry suggested that there was some ground for thinking that the Supreme Court of Canada was being retired from "its post as supervisor of the federal balance in Canada . . . by forces outside itself."[49] Corry thought that the effectiveness of federal-provincial conferences in resolving disputes and the open-ended nature of the federal government's fiscal powers were such that there should in the future be much less resort to the judicial forum to settle disputes about constitutional powers. However our federal history has not worked out this way. Corry was basking in the warm glow of a cooperative federalism that did not endure. The provinces became more constitutionally aggressive than he anticipated. As inflation increased federal policy-makers could not satisfy all of their ambitions through the spending power.

But if asked to explain why Corry's prediction turned out to be wrong, I would be inclined to give more weight to a factor that is extraneous to federal-provincial relations per se: a general increase in litigiousness. A few of the constitutional decisions handed down by the Supreme Court can be traced to a failure of politicians to resolve an issue through informal bargaining. The *Patriation Reference* and the offshore mineral cases are clear examples. But most cases, as has been pointed out, originated in the private sector when a lawyer representing a corporation, a trade union, or an individual raised a constitutional objection to a law or regulation that adversely affected his or her client. In the 25 years since Corry wrote a major expansion of the legal profession and the advent of legal aid have made legal advice much more accessible to Canadians.[50] Government legal departments have expanded, and may have become more independent of political control over litigation decisions. The Supreme Court of Canada's balanced response to federal and provincial claims has, as I have noted, not discouraged constitutional litigation. Indeed, the very sophistication of some of its jurisprudence — for instance its test for determining whether a provincial administrative body is performing a function appropriate for a section 96 superior court judge — sometimes creates new opportunities for resourceful, well-educated lawyers. In addition, the Supreme Court has made constitutional litigation more accessible by being far more generous in granting "standing" to individuals to raise constitutional issues in the courts.[51]

The addition of a constitutional charter of rights adds a whole new dimension to constitutional litigation. There can be no doubt that the Charter of Rights will generate many more cases than the division of powers. But it would be a serious mistake to think that division of powers cases will disappear. In 1983, for example, while the Supreme Court heard 25 requests for leave to appeal in cases involving the Charter of Rights it also heard 13 requests for leave to appeal in cases involving sections 91, 92 and 96 of the "old constitution."[52] Where legislation is challenged on both division of powers and charter of rights grounds, the Supreme Court will likely be inclined to treat the former as the threshold issue. If the legislation is found *ultra vires* in a division of powers sense, the court will not have to deal with the Charter issue.[53]

Those, like Paul Weiler who believe that the Canadian federal system might work better if there were no external judicial arbiter and the main political actors had to rely entirely on their capacity for negotiation and compromise to manage conflict, may be dismayed at the continuing significance of the Supreme Court as umpire of the Canadian federal system.[54] But so long as both political and legal power in the Canadian federation are so finely balanced between the two levels of government, disputes over jurisdiction are inescapable. Adjudication and informal negotiation in this context as in others should not be seen as mutually exclusive dispute settlement mechanisms.[55] In federal disputes as in family affairs negotiations in which the two parties work out mutually acceptable solutions is the preferable way of settling conflicts. But the negotiation process may be enhanced rather than impeded when it takes place in the shadow of a creditable and balanced adjudicator. The availability of such an adjudicator may in itself moderate extravagant claims of the protagonists. And when informal negotiations fail, as they often do between passionate and powerful adversaries, it is comforting to be able to turn to a body which can provide an authoritative determination of the legal points at issue. If the Supreme Court of Canada's record as constitutional umpire does nothing else, it at least establishes the Court's claim to legitimacy in this role.

Notes

1. The United States Supreme Court and West Germany's Constitutional Court settle more constitutional cases concerning fundamental rights but not more cases concerning federalism. For a survey of the role of the courts as constitutional arbiters in Australia, Canada, Ireland, Japan, the U.S.A., and West Germany, see Walter F. Murphy and Joseph Tanenhaus, *Comparative Constitutional Law* (New York: St. Martin's, 1977).

2. Peter H. Russell, "The Supreme Court's Interpretation of the Constitution from 1949 to 1960," and "The Supreme Court Since 1968," in Paul Fox, ed., *Politics: Canada*, 4th ed. (Toronto: McGraw-Hill Ryerson).

3. *Reference Re Anti-Inflation Act* (1976) 2 S.C.R. 373.

4. *Caloil Inc. v. A.-G. Canada* (1971) 1 S.C.R. 543.

5. *Reference Re Agriculture Products Marketing* (1978), 2 S.C.R. 1198.

6. *MacDonald v. Vapor Canada Ltd.* (1977) 2 S.C.R. 134.

7. *Labatt v. A.-G. Canada* (1980) 1 S.C.R. 914.

8. *Canadian Industrial Gas & Oil Ltd. v. Government of Saskatchewan* (1978) 2 S.C.R. 545.

9. *Re Exported Natural Gas Tax* (1982) 1 S.C.R. 1004.

10. *Canadian Indemnity Co. v. A.-G. B.C.* (1977) 2 S.C.R. 504.

11. *Central Canada Potash Co. Ltd. and A.-G. Canada v. Government of Saskatchewan* (1979) 1 S.C.R. 42.

12. *Nova Scotia Board of Censors v. McNeil* (1978) 2 S.C.R. 662.

13. *A.-G. Canada and Dupond v. Montreal* (1978) 2 S.C.R. 770.

14. *Di Iorio v. Wardens of the Montreal Jail* (1978) 1 S.C.R. 152.

15. *The Queen v. Hauser* (1979) 1 S.C.R. 984.

16. *Cordes v. The Queen* (1978) 1 S.C.R. 1062.

17. *A.-G. Quebec and Keable v. A.-G. Canada* (1979) 1 S.C.R. 218.

18. *A.-G. Alberta v. Putnam* (1981) 2 S.C.R. 267.

19. *A.-G. Canada v. Canadian National Transportation Ltd.* Released Oct. 13, 1983.

20. *The Queen v. Judge Wetmore, Kripps Pharmacy et al.* Released Oct. 13, 1983.

21. See J. Dickson's formulation of this test in *Re Residential Tenancies Act* (1981) 1 S.C.R. 714.

22. *Ibid.*

23. *Re B.C. Family Relations Act (1982) 1 S.C.R. 129.*

24. *Crevier v. A.-G. Quebec* (1981) 2 S.C.R. 220.

25. *McNamara Construction v. The Queen* (1977) 2 S.C.R. 655.

26. *Quebec North Shore Paper Co. v. C.P.R.* (1977) 2 S.C.R. 1054.

27. *The Queen v. Thomas Fuller Construction* (1980) 1 S.C.R. 695.

28. *Capital Cities Communications v. C.R.T.C.* (1978) 2 S.C.R. 141.

29. *Public Service Board v. Dionne* (1978) 2 S.C.R. 191.

30. *A.-G. Quebec v. Kellogg's Co.* (1978) 2 S.C.R. 211.

31. (1980) 1 S.C.R. 914.

32. *Dominion Stores Ltd. v. The Queen* (1980) 1 S.C.R. 139.

33. *Reference Re Legislative Authority of Parliament to Alter or Replace the Senate* (1980) 1 S.C.R. 54.

34. *Re Objection to a Resolution to Amend the Constitution* (1982) 2 S.C.R. 753.

35. (1981) 1 S.C.R. 753.

36. Noel Lyon, "Constitutional Theory and the Martland-Ritchie Dissent," in Peter H. Russell, Robert Decary et al., *The Court and the Constitution* (Kingston: Institute of Intergovernmental Relations, Queen's University, 1982).

37. A somewhat similar explanation of the Judicial Committee's decisions on the Canadian Constitution is offered in Murray Greenwood, "Lord Watson, Institutional Self-Interest, and the Decentralization in the 1980s," *UBC Law Review* 4 (1978).

38. Reference cases were most frequent at the beginning and end of the period. Of the 26 references between 1950 and 1982, 12 were in the 1950s and 7 in the 1980s. For a review of the use of reference cases see Barry L. Strayer, *The Canadian Constitution and the Courts* (Toronto: Butterworths, 1983).

39. Barry L. Strayer, "The Flexibility of the B.N.A. Act," in Trevor Lloyd and Jack McLeod, *Agenda 1970: Proposals for Creative Politics* (Toronto: University of Toronto Press, 1968).

40. *In Re Board of Commerce* (1922) 1 A.C. 191 and *Proprietary Articles Trade Association v. A.-G. Canada* (1931) 1 A.C. 310.

41. Section 92A(4) added by the *Constitution Act 1982* to the list of provincial legislative powers.

42. *Reference Re The Offshore Mineral Rights of British Columbia* (1967) 1 S.C.R. 792.

43. *Reference Re Property in and Legislative Jurisdiction Over the Seabed and Subsoil of the Continental Shelf Offshore Newfoundland.* Released March 8, 1984. The Supreme Court of Canada's third decision on offshore resources released on May 18, 1984, making a provincial lake out of the sea between Vancouver Island and mainland B.C. appears to be yet another chapter in the Supreme Court's balancing act.

44. *A.-G. Manitoba v. Manitoba Egg and Poultry Association et al.* (1971) 1 S.C.R. 689.

45. *Burns Food Ltd. v. A.-G. Manitoba* (1978) 1 S.C.R. 494.

46. With one minor qualification this was upheld by the Supreme Court in *Reference Re Agricultural Products Marketing* (1978) 2 S.C.R. 1198.

47. *Toronto Globe and Mail*, Dec. 7, 1982.

48. *McEvoy v. A.-G. N.B.* (1983) 1 S.C.R. 705.

49. J. A. Corry, "Constitutional Trends and Federalism," in A.R.M. Lower, F. R. Scott et al., *Evolving Canadian Federalism*, (Durham, N.C.: Duke University Press, 1958).

50. In Ontario, for instance, the ratio of lawyers to population has changed from 1:1142 in 1960 to 1:574 in 1981. See Law Society of Upper Canada, "Report of the Special Committee on the Number of Lawyers," *Gazette* 17: 2 (1983).

51. See Barry Strayer, *The Canadian Constitution and the Courts* (Toronto: Butterworths, 1983), chap. 6.

52. *Bulletin of Proceedings taken in the Supreme Court of Canada*, February 3, 1984.

53. In *Westendorp v. The Queen* (1983) 1 S.C.R. 43, Counsel of the appellant abandoned his Charter of Rights challenge to Calgary's by-law prohibiting street-soliciting by prostitutes and won the case on division of powers grounds. The Supreme Court ruled that the by-law encroached upon exclusive federal jurisdiction over criminal law.

54. Paul Weiler, *In the Last Resort: A Critical Study of the Supreme Court of Canada* (Toronto: Carswell, 1974).

55. For an analysis of the relationship between adjudication and informal methods of dispute settlement, see Jerold S. Auerbach, *Justice Without Law: Resolving Disputes Without Lawyers* (New York: Oxford University Press, 1983).

Selected Readings

Bernier, I., and Lajoie, A., research coordinators. *The Supreme Court of Canada as an Instrument of Political Change*. Research Studies prepared by the Royal Commission on the Economic Union and Development Prospects for Canada, vol. 46. Toronto: University of Toronto Press, 1985.

Cairns, Allan. "The Judicial Committee and Its Critics." *Canadian Journal of Political Science* 4:3 (September 1971): 301–45.

Hogg, Peter. "Is the Supreme Court of Canada Biased in Constitutional Cases?" *Canadian Bar Review* 57 (1979): 721–39.

Russell, Peter. "The Supreme Court's Interpretation of the Constitution." In Paul Fox, *Politics Canada*, 5th ed. Toronto: McGraw-Hill Ryerson, 1982, 592–621.

Snell, James G., and Vaughan, Frederick. *The Supreme Court of Canada: History of the Institution*. Toronto: University of Toronto Press, 1985.

Vaughan, Frederick. "Critics of the Judicial Committee of the Privy Council: The New Orthodoxy and an Alternative Explanation." *Canadian Journal of Political Science* 19:3 (September 1986): 495–519.

SECTION THREE

REGIONALISM AND PROVINCE-BUILDING

Regionalism is a multi-faceted concept and there is no consensus in the literature with regard to an appropriate definition. Despite this, one frequently cited definition is that of Rupert Vance, who defines a region as "a homogeneous area with physical and cultural characteristics distinct from those of neighbouring areas. As a part of a national domain, a region is sufficiently unified to have a consciousness of its customs and ideals and thus possesses a sense of identity distinct from the rest of the country."[1] Two of the themes found in Vance's definition are common to virtually all definitions of the term: the *existence* of territorially-based communities of people that are different from other communities on the basis of language, religion, economics, or ethnicity, and a *consciousness* on the part of the residents of the community that they do in fact constitute a separate and distinctive entity within a larger society.

There is no consensus within the academic literature as to the most salient variables that should be employed to demarcate the existence and the boundaries of a region. Geographers differentiate regions on the basis of physical features such as land forms, climate, and vegetation, while sociologists define a region by reference to linguistic and cultural communities. Economists often identify the existence of a region by reference to major "economic growth centres" within a nation-state.

In political science, regions are most often defined by the existence of political boundaries. The presence of a political boundary sets in motion a series of socialization processes that ultimately produce unique or distinctive subcultures within a society.

Canada has been characterized as a nation-state that is comprised of regionally based societies, a country of "limited identities." Furthermore, in comparison with other western societies, Canadians have retained strong attachments and loyalties to their local communities. As a consequence, the existence of a Canadian "national identity" continues to be a subject of debate.

Simeon and Elkins have identified distinguishable political subcultures in Canada, and empirical research over the past two decades has documented the strength of regional loyalties and attachments. For example, Québécois have traditionally viewed

---

1. Rupert Vance, "Region," *International Encyclopedia of the Social Sciences* 13 (New York: Macmillan Company and the Free Press, 1968), 377.

their provincial government as a critical instrument for the expression and protection of cultural dualism and as an important counterbalance to the power of the central government. With the exception of Ontario, the attachments of other Canadians to their provincial communities is no less strong.

Within English-speaking Canada, regional identities are fostered by formidable geographic barriers, differing historical experiences and patterns of settlement, distinctive regional economies, and the federal system itself. However, as Richard Vernon has argued, the "federal citizen" develops loyalties and a sense of attachment to both the nation and the region (province) in which one resides. In Canada, various research studies have confirmed that Canadians have developed a set of mutually reinforcing loyalties to both the Canadian nation-state and to regional (provincial) communities that will ensure the viability of the federal system in the future.

This section includes essays that document and assess the impact of socio-economic, linguistic, cultural, and institutional factors on the evolution of the Canadian federal state. Academic writings initially emphasized the importance of socio-economic, linguistic, and cultural factors; however, more recently, authors such as Donald Smiley and Allan Cairns have argued that these explanations are inadequate and that more emphasis should be placed on the impact of institutional factors on the evolution of Canadian federalism. Allan Cairns' article examines the interplay between political institutions and society. Provinces and provincial governments should be viewed as independent forces that, once established, act to shape their environment and mobilize political interests. Cairns' concept of "province-building" is often applied to explain the shift in power from the federal government to the provinces as well as the conflictual nature of federal-provincial relations.

Garth Stevenson's writings are strongly influenced by the concept of province-building. His essay attempts to place Canadian regionalism in a wider continental perspective. In doing so, Stevenson draws attention to some of the long-term implications of having provincial political elites be the primary vehicle for the articulation of regional interests.

The essay by Robert Young, Phillipe Faucher, and André Blais provides a useful counterbalance to the writings of Cairns and Stevenson. Its critical examination of the concept of province-building illustrates the limitations of a general explanatory framework such as province-building as an empirically accurate description and assessment of trends within the Canadian federal state.

7. THE GOVERNMENTS AND SOCIETIES OF CANADIAN FEDERALISM

Alan C. Cairns

The great mystery for students of Canadian federalism has been the survival and growth of provincial governments, particularly those of English Canada. Sociologically focused inquiries, with Quebec as an implicit model, have looked for vital, inward looking provincial societies on which governments could be based and, finding none, have been puzzled why these governmental superstructures, seemingly lacking a necessary foundation, have not faded away.

The sociological perspective pays inadequate attention to the possibility that the support for powerful, independent provincial governments is a product of the political system itself, that it is fostered and created by provincial government elites employing the policy-making apparatus of their jurisdictions, and that such support need not take the form of a distinct culture, society, or nation as these are conventionally understood. More specifically, the search for an underlying sociological base, whatever its nature and source as the necessary sustenance for viable provincial political systems, deflects us from considering the prior question of how much support is necessary. Passivity, indifference, or the absence of strong opposition from their environment may be all that provincial governments need in order to thrive and grow. The significant question, after all, is the survival of provincial governments, not of provincial soci-

eties, and it is not self-evident that the existence and support of the latter is necessary to the functioning and aggrandizement of the former. Their sources of survival, renewal, and vitality may well lie within themselves and in their capacity to mould their environment in accordance with their own governmental purposes.

In the analysis of contemporary party systems much has been made of the extent to which today's parties represent the historic residue of the cleavages of yesteryear. In the Canadian case the freezing of party alternatives fades into insignificance compared with the freezing by the federal system of initially five and now eleven constitutionally distinct and separate governments. The enduring stability of these governments contrasts sharply with the fluctuating fortunes of all parties and the disappearance of many. Governments, as persisting constellations of interests, constitute the permanent elements of the Canadian polity which, thus far, have ridden out the storms of social, economic, and political change.

The decision to establish a federal system in 1867 was a first-order macro decision concerning the basic institutional features of the new polity. It created competitive political and bureaucratic elites at two levels of government endowed with an impressive array of jurisdictional, financial, administrative, and political resources to deploy in the pursuit of their objectives. The post-Confederation history of Canadian federalism is little more than the record of the efforts of governing elites to pyramid their resources and of the uses to which they have put them. Possessed of tenacious instincts for their own preservation and growth, the governments of Canadian

Alan C. Cairns, "The Governments and Societies of Canadian Federalism," *Canadian Journal of Political Science* 10:4 (1977): 695-725. Reprinted by permission of the author. The essay has been abridged and edited to suit the needs of this volume.

federalism have endowed the cleavages between provinces, and between provinces and nation which attended their birth, with an ever more comprehensive political meaning.

The crucial, minimum prerequisites for provincial survival and growth have been the preservation of jurisdictional competence and territorial integrity. In terms of the former, it is notable that explicit change in the constitutional responsibilities of the two levels of government has been minimal, in spite of strong centralizing pressure on occasion. The division of powers has been altered to federal advantage only three times, in each of which unanimous provincial consent was obtained, and in two of which provincial paramountcy was respected. The paucity of amendments dealing with the division of power and the long-standing opposition of provincial governments to any formally agreed amendment procedures which might diminish their lawmaking authority without their express consent strikingly reveal an entrenched governmental conservatism where the constitutional base of provincial governing capacity is concerned.

Equally indicative of provincial tenacity in self-preservation is the integrity of provincial boundaries. No province has given up territory to which it had clear and undisputed possession. Where territorial "loss" has occurred, as in the 1872 case of the San Juan boundary settlement by the German Emperor which denied the claims of British Columbia, or in the case of Labrador decided by judicial determination in favour of Newfoundland in 1927, provincial frustrations have been pronounced and in the latter case, long-lived. Half a century later the claim of Quebec to Labrador remains a live issue to the Quebec government.[1] Disputed cases, such as offshore mineral resources caught between the counterclaim of federal and provincial governments, illustrate the vigour with which provincial positions are defended, even in the face of adverse court decisions. Where the possibility of territorial expansion has existed or still exists

with respect to contiguous territory outside provincial boundaries, the provinces have consistently manifested a revolution of rising expectations not yet dead. It has not only been the federal government assiduously extending the range of its jurisdiction from the limited Canada of 1867 to the ten-province Canada of 1949, and now extending its effective writ over Canada's Arctic frontiers, which displays a well-developed drive for territorial acquisition. The original boundaries of Quebec, Ontario, and Manitoba contained only a small portion of the land masses they now control. On occasion, inter-provincial controversy over disputed territory has even produced mini-border conflicts, as in the case of Manitoba and Ontario in the thirty-year period preceding the final determination of their boundary in 1912.[2]

The three Maritime provinces, doomed by location to be deprived of attainable territorial ambitions, have been tenacious in not giving up the political control over defined territories they individually possess. They resisted amalgamation in the 1860s, and in spite of the urgings of the Deutsch Report, they resist it today. "By any administrative logic," stated *The Economist*, "the three provinces should be bundled into one. But nobody will be crazy enough to try."[3] The hostile stance of Newfoundland to any possible reopening of the Labrador case by an independent Quebec further attests to the territorial conservatism of the provinces, tightly holding on to what they have won in the historical lottery of land acquisition. The provincial protection of, and search for *Lebensraum* is a relatively unexamined aspect of federal-provincial history deserving as much scholarly investigation as their better-known safeguarding of their formal jurisdictional authority. The protection of jurisdictional authority and the protection and expansion of provincial territory have been accompanied by an ever more vigorous employment of provincial legislative competence. Related to this as both cause and effect has been a concomitant increase in government personnel. A similar expansion of personnel, and a no less aggressive exploration of the limits of its constitutional responsibilities, have been displayed by the federal government.

It would be a serious mistake to view these governmental mountains as molehills. The several hundred political officeholders constitute only a trivial minority of those who wield government power and/or derive their income directly from public positions. The growth of one federal and ten provincial governments has produced large and powerful complexes of institutions and personnel with their own professional and personal interests and their own official purposes for the provincial and federal populations they govern.

The astute observation of Alexander Hamilton in *Federalist Paper* No. 1 two centuries ago has not declined in relevance: "Among the most formidable of the obstacles which the new Constitution will have to encounter may readily be distinguished the obvious interest of a certain class of men in every State to resist all changes which may hazard a diminution of the power, emolument, and consequence of the offices they hold under the State establishments."[4] Another certain class of men has attached itself to the central government.

It makes little sense to think of these impressive concentrations of power and personnel as superstructures whose existence and purposes are largely derivative of the electorate, the class structure, the pressure group system, or whatever. Even if we ignore their functions, the more than one million Canadians who work for federal and provincial governments, and their dependants, constitute an immense component of Canadian society directly tied to government. When we consider their functions of policy-making, service-provision, regulation, and protection, extending to the most specialized activities where government monopolizes the expertise in a given field, we are made aware that we live in a period of convulsive change in gov-

ernment-society relations. In the evolution of the divison of labour between those who govern, and those who are governed, the energizing, proselytizing, and entrepreneurial role increasingly rests with those civil servants and politicians with the capacity to influence policy and its administration.

While the sheer fact of large numbers directly dependent on government should not be underestimated as a crucial, if elementary, factor in government survival, that contribution is multiplied by the ramifying effects of the institutional and organizational complexes in which these employees work and have their being. The ministries, departments, agencies, bureaus, and field offices to which they daily report constitute partially self-contained entities, valued for their own sake, and possessed of their own life and interests. Their minimum desire is for a steady level of activity.

Typically, however, they seek to enlarge the scope of their functions. If the environment offers new opportunities for expansion in emergent problem areas they will compete with other bureaucracies for the prizes of status and growth offered by enhancement of their activity. If major challenges are made to their organizational identity, purpose, or cohesion they will fight back against unsympathetic political superiors and other menacing figures and forces in their environment.[5] If their functions decline in social utility or their expertise becomes obsolescent, they will scan the horizon of alternative possibilities in an aggressive search for new justifications for continued existence.[6] While they are subject to political control and direction they have impressive capacities to get their own way and to bend their political superiors to their will. Although their functions relate them to particular sectors of society, they are not puppets or simple reflections of interests of the groups they control, regulate, or service. "[B]oth the sector served and political leaders come to be forces in the environment which public servants must manage and manipulate so that they will demand or agree to expansion of the bureaucracy."[7] Their basic strength resides in the expertise which makes them indispensable to their political superiors and in the support of the external interests which have positively adapted to their policies. They represent a permanent, expansive aspect of government. They are the necessary instruments of an administered society which could not, without major disruption, survive their disappearance from the scene.

The presence in the Canadian federal system of eleven governments, each honeycombed with bureaucratic interests and desires of the nature just described, helps explain the expansion of each level of government, the frequent competition and duplication of activity between governments, and the growing impact of government on society. It is impossible to think clearly about Canadian federalism without devoting extensive attention to the one million Canadians parcelled out in eleven jurisdictions, and committed by loyalty, the terms of their employment, and self-interest to the particular government they serve.

These pyramids of bureaucratic power and ambition are capped by political authorities also possessed of protectionist and expansionist tendencies. The eleven governments of the federal system endow the incumbents of political office with the primary task of defending and advancing the basic interests of crucial sectors of the provincial or national economy and society. Each political office, particularly those of prime ministers and premiers, has a history which influences and constrains the succession of incumbents who briefly possess it. Thus, as André Bernard says: "No political leader in Quebec would ever dare voice a doubt about the sacrosanct objective of 'la survivance française en Amerique'. Survival of the French-Canadian people is an obligation, an article of faith. It has been so for 200 years. It is basic, fundamental."[8] Since 1871 the political leaders of British Columbia have consistently

pressed economic claims on Ottawa demanding compensation for the allegedly chronic financial maltreatment they have suffered from the federal government. The special needs and expenses associated with the harsh facts of geography and a primary resource based economy have been reiterated in countless briefs. Other provinces also have "fairly durable and persisting interests"[9] which reflect the relatively unchanging factors of society, economy, and basic position in the federal system. The claims derived from the preceding are nourished by the constantly refurbished memory of past grievances.

Provincial political elites not only seek to further the long-range interests of their society and economy, they also have "a vested interest in provincial status and power which the several provincial electorates perhaps do not share fully."[10] Their policy determinations reflect a varying mix of goals for their provincial citizenry and an institutional concern for the long-term survival of the political and bureaucratic power of government itself. On the other side of the bargaining table they encounter Ottawa, a larger version of their own expansionist tendencies, which in the slightly jaundiced words of Claude Morin, "is quite simply loyal to a solidly-rooted historical tradition, the unmistakable outlines of which could already be discerned in John A. Macdonald's remarks at the time the federation was put together."[11]

The inertia of the political and bureaucratic momentum of the governments they join inducts new recruits into prevailing definitions of the situation. This is instanced by the frequency with which staunch provincialists, from Joseph Howe onwards, become staunch federalists on entering the federal government. Thus, it is not surprising that the representatives of "French power" in Ottawa will seek solutions to French-English problems by policies which do not weaken the central government. They will try to make the federal government, and indeed the whole country a more congenial environment for francophones rather than opt for a solution which enhances the power of the government in Quebec City. It is also not surprising that such efforts are looked on with little favour by government elites in Quebec City. French Canadians in federal politics and in the federal civil service are conditioned to see the world through different eyes than their Quebec City counterparts.[12] What is attractive to the latter is often a direct threat to the political and bureaucratic needs of the former. Profound governmental constraints minimize the possibility of ethnic solidarity across jurisdictional boundaries.

Federal and provincial governments are not neutral containers or reflecting mirrors, but aggressive actors steadily extending their tentacles of control, regulation, and manipulation into society—playing, in Deutsch's terminology, a steering role—and thus fostering sets of integrated relationships between themselves and the various socio-economic forces and interests in their jurisdictions. Governing elites view their task as the injection of provincial or federal meaning into society, giving it a degree of coherence and a pattern of interdependence more suited for government purposes than what would emerge from the unhindered working of social and market forces. Each government's policies pull the affected interests into relations of dependence and attachment to the power centre which manipulates their existence. Each government seeks policy coherence in order to minimize contradictions leading to the frustration of its own policies. The inadequacies of the theory and advice on which decision-makers rely produce major discrepancies between governmental ambition and actual achievement. The byzantine complexity of internal government structures, and the sluggishness of the diffuse bureaucratic instrumentalities on which policy-makers depend, create additional obstacles to the coherence in policy and society that each government seeks. Nevertheless, given these limitations each government transmits cues and pressures to the environment tending to group the interests manipulated by its policies into webs of interdependence springing from the particular version of socio-economic integration it is pursuing. Provincial governments work toward the creation of limited versions of a politically created provincial society and economy, and the national government works toward the creation of a country-wide society and economy.

Federal policies are responses to nationwide considerations. From the perspective of Ottawa the provinces constitute concentrations of governmental power whose manipulation is difficult, but nevertheless must be attempted where necessary. In pursuing its mission as a national government from 1867 to the present, Ottawa has not hesitated to interfere with provincial policies by the disallowance of provincial legislation and more recently by the adroit and extensive employment of the spending power. The mission of provincial political elites is necessarily more restricted, being territorially confined by provincial boundaries, often restrained by weaknesses of financial capacity, and, formerly, hampered by administrative shortcomings. Nevertheless, the British North America Act gives the provinces jurisdictional authority in functional areas of expanding significance and, most important, gives them control of the natural resource base of their economy. While the jurisdiction of a province lacks the comprehensive coverage enjoyed by the government of a unitary state, it is a sufficiently impressive base of governmental power to elicit visions of futures to be pursued. It cannot be doubted, to cite only the more obvious examples, that Lesage, Smallwood, Douglas, W. A. C. Bennett, and Manning had coherent sets of public purposes for the provincial societies they governed. From their perspective the federal government and its policies constituted environmental uncertainties which had to be managed, exploited, or reduced, and in some cases bitterly attacked in the defence of the provincial futures whose creation they envisaged.

As they pursue their specific goals federal and provincial elites unwittingly serve the profound trend towards the increasing politicization of society. What Leon Dion calls the "political invasion of our daily lives . . . a new phenomenon in history,"[13] has a particular significance for a federal polity. In almost every conceivable aspect of our existence, from the workaday world of our daily occupation, to the private, intimate worlds of sex and love, our conduct is affected by the larger, pervasive world of federal and provincial competition and cooperation. We are light years away from the relatively apolitical, nongovernmentalized societies of 1867. No national society existed in 1867, and provincial societies were expected to be relatively free from extensive government controls by the newly-created provincial governments. A century later we have governmentalized societies, both federal and provincial, interwoven with each other in relations of competitive interdependence.

The institutionalization of government,[14] the construction of a sphere of political and bureaucratic existence differentiated from other spheres of collective life, automatically reduces the relative importance of non-government groups, interests and individuals in policy-making. There is impressive unanimity from students of Canadian government that members of the public are little more than spectators, mobilized by competing elites at three- to five-year intervals for electoral purposes, and then returned to their accustomed role as objects of government policy. "Canada," observes Richard Simeon, "combines the British tradition of a strong executive and centralized leadership with a relative freedom from mass pressure and popular constraint."[15] Even bitter and well-publicized intergovernmental conflict may take place in the face of almost complete public indifference or ignorance, as Claude Morin asserts was true of the recent Ottawa-Quebec hostilities over the latter's role at international conferences.[16]

Paradoxically, the institutionalization process which acts as a barrier to public influence on decision-making is the instrumentality for political and bureaucratic elites to bring society under ever more comprehensive government control and guidance. If socialism is about equality, contemporary Canadian federalism is about governments, governments that are possessed of massive human and financial resources, that are driven by purposes fashioned by elites, and that accord high priority to their own long-term institutional self-interest. We should not be surprised, therefore, to be told that in the early years of the Lesage regime "most governmental activity . . . was initiated by the government itself . . . ,"[17] to be reminded of the various federal government programs introduced by political and bureaucratic elites in the absence of strong demands,[18] and to read that the "demands on government have been in large part self-created."[19] It is abundantly clear that the massive impact of government on society at the output stage does not require a prior massive impact of society on government at the input stage.

By and large, the above analysis also applies to Quebec. The Quebec government, like the others, attempts to mould society in terms of its conception of a desirable future. Here too bureaucrats and politicians have the same disproportionate capacity to influence policy evident in other jurisdictions. But important differences exist. In recent years the political system they manage has been repeatedly shaken by social transformations, often government induced. Further, the society to which elites respond is not simply the provincial segment of an English-speaking North American culture which, with variations, dominates the rest of the country and the neighbour to the south. Although clusters of French culture exist elsewhere in Canada, its primary concentration in the province of Quebec necessarily involves the government of that province in a host of specific national questions. The government of Quebec is not in the business of controlling and directing the provincial segment of a larger society, but of fostering and stimulating a "full-blown society"[20] infused with nationalistic fervour by two centuries of minority status. This is a society in which the major groups, associations, and organizations increasingly "tend . . . to fall back on the Quebec government."[21]

The singular importance of provincial government in contemporary Quebec is partly a delayed compensation for the long era of negative government under Maurice Duplessis and his predecessors which bequeathed the modernizing governments of the past two decades a heritage of daunting problems. Also, the relative weakness of the francophone role in the private economic sector generates pressure to employ the majority-controlled provincial state to redress this no longer acceptable ethnic imbalance. Thus, although in contemporary Quebec, as elsewhere in Canada, the political debate centres on the precise nature of the leading role to be played by government, it is a debate with a difference. In recent years it has focussed with growing intensity on the fundamental question of the relationship of the people and government of Quebec with the rest of Canada. Specifically, the debate centres around the question of whether a sovereign Quebec government is the best instrument to satisfy the profound desire of francophone Quebeckers for a modern secure community. The existing system of political authorities is not taken for granted. The opponents of Confederation claim that it constitutes a mobilization of governmental bias hostile to national survival.

Our approach to the study of politics focusses disproportionately on the problems posed for governments by the transformation of society and too little on the problems posed for society by the escalating demands of government. Society, constantly challenged by new public policies ranging from education, economy, and welfare to the basic questions of life, death, and human meaning devotes more and more resources to the task of responding to government. In a narrow,

superficial sense this is most visible at the level of the taxpayer compelled to finance the numerous ill-conceived government ventures which litter the contemporary landscape of public choice. In recent years he has been burdened by the chaotic and unplanned introduction of automobile insurance in British Columbia, a system of railway passenger transportation whose escalating expenses produce less and less service, dramatic overruns on the Olympic installations in Montreal, and the burgeoning costs of the James Bay developments. Our Weberian conceptions of efficiency, economy, and rationality seem increasingly difficult to transfer from our lecture notes to the reality outside our window.[22]

These spectacular escapades, however, constitute only the tip of the governmental iceberg. In general, the ever more elaborate regulatory role of government greatly increases, "the overhead (compliance) costs of industry, trade unions and other groups in either protecting or extending their interests."[23]

To those affected by its actions contemporary government is correctly viewed as both a potential resource and a threat. It is always a powerful presence in the environment to be exploited, attacked, or evaded as self-interest and citizen duty dictate. In the complex contest between provincial governments seeking control, and individuals and organized interests seeking a favourable environment, the latter may respond by exit, taking advantage of the gap between the limited geographic reach of particular governments, and the area of free movement which constitutes the federal system, to move to more congenial jurisdictions.[24] Capital knows no loyalty. Its easy mobility across provincial and national boundaries exerts a strong pressure on each province not to deviate in its tax system from the other provincial systems with which it is in unavoidable competition, and on Canada not to impose a more burdensome or discriminatory system of taxes than exists in the United States.[25] In British Columbia, polarized by a free enterprise versus socialism rhetoric for half a century, the claim that investment would dry up if the CCF-NDP formed the government has been a standard election threat by big business and the various partisan opponents of the left.

The social and economic interests of Canadian society, seeking their own advantage, work the federal system in their search for the optimum relationship with its double layer of governments.[26] J. R. Mallory, writing of an earlier era, noted that powerful economic interests sought to stem collectivist inroads on their freedom by resort to extensive litigation to weaken the constitutional competence of the governments attempting to regulate them.[27] Conversely, as Trudeau observed and deprecated, those interests seeking advantage and/or protection knocked on any government door, hoping to benefit from the confusion of jurisdiction and elicit a positive reponse, "regardless of the constitution," from whichever level of government would listen.[28]

There is contemporary evidence that pressure groups attempt to influence the workings of the federal division of power by having the government closest to the centre of their organizational strength, and to which they have easiest access, handle the concerns affecting them.[29] Thus the Quebec-based Confederation of National Trade Unions "attempted to weaken the federal government in order to strengthen the provincial governments, the Quebec government in particular. The [Canadian Labour Congress], on the other hand, has striven mightily to restore or preserve the authority of the federal government and to cajole it into regaining the initiative."[30] In a period when the distribution of power was in flux, it "was found that the leadership of both groups made demands which, if adopted, would have resulted in the strengthening of 'their' level of government."[31] Yet another study reveals the success of the extractive industries in mobilizing provincial governments to fight the Carter Commission's proposal for higher taxes. The localization of the industries, their dominance of particular communities, and "their success in identifying their own prosperity with the prestige of particular regions,"[32] contributed to the intense and successful pressure they induced provincial governments to bring on their behalf at the federal level. The real victor, however, was the provinces whose success in thwarting Ottawa confirmed the dependent, client status of the extractive industries at the provincial level,[33] subsequently evidenced by heavy provincial tax and royalty increases.

There is, as just indicated, some manoeuverability in the relationship between organized pressure groups and the governments of the federal system. Nevertheless, the overriding tendency is for such groups to structure their associational life in accordance with the relatively stable jurisdictional location of the legislative authority which affects them. The increasing politicization and governmentalization of society elicits a proliferation of pressure groups struggling to fit the federal system's requirements for influencing policy. Canadian experience testifies to the basic astuteness of the observation of Roy C. Macridis that "wherever the political governmental organization is cohesive and power is concentrated in certain well-established centres, the pressure groups become well-organized with a similar concentration of power and vice versa."[34]

However, the working out of the process suggested by Macridis is often imperfect. Most groups affected by both federal and provincial governments, or where jurisdiction is unclear, have a federated group structure, but it is one in which the central, national executive is often made up of provincial or regional representatives and is dependent on provincial organizations. The latter reflect the local concerns of their members who often identify with the provincial agency which administers the provincial policies affecting them. As a result, the national executive is sometimes reduced to an aggregation of contradictory provincial particularisms unable to agree on a position towards proposed Ottawa policies. Further, the distrust of a distant government centre which, here as elsewhere, affects the workings of the Canadian polity, produces an antipathy to the national office and an occasional reluctance to staff and finance it at adequate levels.[35] In the party system, as is noted below, this federal tension is reduced by the increasing separation and independence of provincial and national parties from each other. Inadequate resources and low levels of institutionalization make it difficult for interest groups to develop and sustain a similar degree of federal-provincial organizational differentiation and specificity. As a consequence, their national efficacy, beset by the centrifugal pressures of divergent regional interests, is often weakened by internal contradictions.[36]

The impact of federalism is also evident in the workings of the party system.[37] The general tendency in federal regimes, as Carl Friedrich observes, is that "parties tend toward paralleling the government setup. . . . Political science has recognized for some time that the organizational structure of parties tends to correspond to the governmental pattern under constitutional democracy. This is only natural, since it is one of the purposes of parties to gain control of the government; therefore, if the government is federally structured, parties must adapt themselves to such a structure."[38]

In the contemporary era the structuring effect of federalism has generated a pronounced trend to the separation of federal and provincial party systems. This is manifested in tendencies towards distinct political careers at both levels, separate national and provincial organizations, and separate sources of party finance. Of particular significance is the development of public schemes of provincial election financing which reduce financial dependence on the national parties. The employment of the public resources of autonomous provincial governments to foster the autonomy of their party systems is an impressive illustration of federalism's capacity for self-reinforcement.

The federal system contributes to party system separation by its provision of discrete provincial arenas in which sectionally-based parties can capture power while weak in the country as a whole. The federal system also stimulates ideological differentiation between federal and provincial parties bearing the same name. This combines with divergent strategy requirements at the two levels to generate recurrent tensions between the federal and provincial branches of the party.[39] The parties at different levels of the federal system exist in different socio-economic environments, respond to different competitive situations, and are products of particular patterns of historical development and historical accidents. They fight elections under different leaders, at different times, and on different issues before different electorates in separate jurisdictions endowed with distinctive constitutional responsibilities. Numerous voters respond to this catalogue of differences by deliberately switching their votes as they move from one arena to another, particularly where a third party with a limited or nonexistent federal presence is provincially strong, as in British Columbia. The complicated translation of these differences into the strength or weaknesses of individual parties frequently results in striking dissimilarities between the federal and provincial party system in a particular province.

The circumstances in which provincial parties in power will support their federal counterparts almost entirely reflect strategic considerations.[40] From the federal perspective incumbent national parties of whatever persuasion recognize that the intergovernmental conflict and collaboration involved in the working of contemporary federalism are only minimally affected by purely partisan considerations.[41] "From the federal point of view, whatever parties are in power provincially will press provincial interests."[42] And from the provincial point of view the same holds true of power-holding parties at the federal level.

Given the unavoidable fact of different parties in office federally and provincially it would be damaging to the federal system for an incumbent national party to be integrally linked with and overtly supporting its provincial counterparts. In the case of the federal Liberal party in 1977 this would mean an intimate collaboration with eight opposition parties, mostly weak, and only two government parties, both in the Atlantic provinces. A hands-off policy and organizational structures separate from its own provincial namesakes are far more functional to a national governing party for that intimate collaboration with provincial governments which is required for the effective working of executive federalism. Party solidarity across jurisdictions is sacrificed for the greater good of intergovernmental agreement. Thus the knitting together of governments induces the federal-provincial separation of parties.[43]

The structuring effect of federalism on parties and interest groups has crucial consequences for the political system. The federal system was originally conceived as a layer of provincial governments representing territorial diversities and a central government with responsibilities for creating the national society it was to serve. It has become a system of powerful governments sustained by interest groups and parties which, with imperfections, mirror the governmental structure in which they exist. The chain of federal influence, commencing with the elemental fact of a federal constitutional system, has successfully exerted strong pressure to align parties, interest groups, and individual voters behind the distinct governments which are the essence of federalism. Federal and provincial governments, federal and provincial parties, and federal and provincial pressure groups reinforce each other, and they reinforce federalism.

The fleshing out of the governmental structure of federalism by interest groups and parties contributes to the vitality of the system by attaching powerful supports to each level of government which resist any diminution of its authority. "Groups organized on a local or regional basis will tend to strengthen local awareness, local loyalties and local particularism," while nationally-organized groups foster "national awareness . . . , feelings of identification with the national institutions of government . . . , [and] heighten feelings of efficacy and involvement with those institutions and thus promote national integration."[44] The symbiotic relationship between interest groups and the governments they interact with produces strong mutualities of interest in which each sustains and feeds on the other.[45]

Accordingly, the deliberate creation and fostering by governments of interest groups[46] to whose induced demands they wish to respond is a primary weapon for government survival in circumstances of aggressive intergovernmental competition. As already noted, however, special difficulties attend the organization of interest groups on a national level, raising the possibility that the expanding role of provincial governments and the more homogeneous environments they face may elicit a pressure group bias in favour of the provinces.

Systems of power-seeking parties have the same reinforcing effect for the level of government whose control they seek. Here too, however, there are powerful tendencies working on behalf of the provinces. The regionalization of the national party system with neither Liberals nor Conservatives capable of encompassing the sectional heterogeneity of the country, with the Conservatives suffering continuing weakness in Quebec, and the Liberals a like weakness on the prairies, complicates the party support base of federal authority.[47]

The national party system operates under a much more difficult set of constraints than the provincial in generating parties consonant with the needs of its level of government for support and legitimation. Governing provincial parties have a much smaller range of diversities to encompass than their federal counterpart. Further, a section or geographically concentrated interest left out of a provincial government party lacks the political force and focus which provincial governments can provide for sections unrepresented at

Ottawa. Finally, the provinces are protected by their numbers. A weak, minority, or unrepresentative government in a province is partially protected against federal competition by strong, aggressive provincial governments elsewhere in the system. No such safety in numbers was available to console the minority governments of John Diefenbaker and Lester B. Pearson or to protect the Trudeau Liberals from the consequences of their weakness on the prairies. Accordingly, the "absolutely critical latent function of the party system . . . the development and fostering of a national political culture . . . [and] generating support for the regime"[48] have been performed well below the optimum level in recent years.

*   *   *

A federal system of governments, supported by parties and pressure groups which parallel the governmental structure, and infused with conflicting federal and provincial visions of economy and society held by competing political and bureaucratic elites, requires a language of political debate appropriate to its fundamental political concerns.[49] Hence, the dominant political language since Confederation has been geared to the making of claims and counterclaims by the federal and provincial spokesmen for territorially-defined societies. In an indirect way, and with the passage of time, the federal language of political discourse became a vehicle for the standard normative controversies which concern modern political systems, questions dealing with equality, the socio-economic rights of citizens, and social justice. Inevitably, however, the pressure of existing language contributed to the clothing of new controversies in federal garments and their emergence in claims on behalf of provincial communities and governments, or charter members, or founding races, or the national interest as defined by Ottawa.[50]

Clearly, the political language of federalism, and the federal political system with which it is intertwined, have encouraged a politics in which provincial particularisms have been accorded special prominence. Provincial governments as the claimants for, and recipients of federal bounty have acted as surrogates for the communities they govern. In the dialectical process of federal-provincial controversies, the claims of provincial governments encounter the rival claims of the central government with its constitutional authority to speak for all Canadians, for the national community stretching from Bonavista to Vancouver Island. The political incentives for the federal government to couch its claims in the language of individual citizen rights and obligations[51] engender a direct conflict with provincial claims on behalf of territorially-based communities,[52] the reconciliation of which is worked out in the federal process.

Formerly, many of these conflicts derived sustenance from specific clauses in the British North America Act, from the terms of admission of individual provinces to the federal system, or from certain alleged intentions of the Fathers relating to the rights of particular provinces or communities. The resultant language of political debate was fundamentally stabilizing in its emphasis on rights and claims which presupposed continuing membership in an ongoing political system. Under the impact of the constitutional crisis of the past two decades, essentially precipitated by the changed objectives of Quebec political elites, and the concomitant allocation of the political decisions of 1867 to a distant and irrelevant past, the language of political debate has undergone a dramatic change. The historic, rooted language of the various versions of the compact theory has virtually disappeared, as have other backward-looking justifications which appealed to a common past. They have been replaced by a confusion of newly-developing political languages more nakedly power-seeking, which reflect the ambitions of some political elites to refashion their position, inside or outside the federal system, as the past fades into insignificance, and the induced obligation for other elites to respond in kind. In Quebec the forward-looking language of national self-determination has replaced the traditional elite emphasis on prescriptive rights derived from history and the constitution. The new attitude was graphically expressed by Claude Morin when he was deputy minister of federal-provincial affairs in the Lesage government. "Quebec's motto is: We're through fooling around! It seems ridiculous to me to invoke the Constitution. It is like invoking St. Thomas."[53]

The destruction of a customary, historical language was accelerated by the recent process of constitutional review which downgraded the Canadian constitutional heritage and promised new beginnings which it failed to deliver. The present language situation is clearly in flux[54] as disputants talk past each other, rather than to each other. No new linguistic paradigm in which debate can be couched has emerged.[55] Linguistic instability and federal instability reinforce each other.

The political language of federalism, a language for the conducting of political competition and cooperation between territorially-based groups and their governments, is necessarily hostile to the nation-wide politics of class. The politics and language of class assume that the conditioning effects of capitalism have washed out identities and political perspectives based on socialization into provincial frames of reference. This has not yet happened. In spite of the auspicious depression circumstances of its birth, its early antipathy to the provinces, and its long-standing attempts to create a new politics and language of class at the national level, the CCF and its successor the NDP have made only minor dents in the non-class language of federalism.

For nearly half a century left-wing academic analysis has stressed the allegedly inexorable logic of capitalist development in producing class polarization and a modern class-based politics, described as "creative politics" by its more recent exponents. Indeed, by constant repetition this perspective has become the time-honoured traditional language of a dissenting minority which updates the old arguments and the standard predictions decade after decade. Elections and surveys have been carefully monitored since the thirties in numerous attempts to detect the always imminent emergent trend of class mobilization and polarization, the assumed hallmarks of a maturing economy. The failure of reality to conform to the canons of this version of social science has evoked fulminations against federalism and an adroit use of the concept of false consciousness. These have had minimal impact on the non-class world view of elites and masses involved in the political world of federalism. The political language of territorially-based group competition derived from the federal system and socialized into the consciousness of political actors since Confederation has prevailed over the twentieth-century challenge from the weakly-developed language of class based on the economy.

*   *   *

Contrary to virtually all predictions, post-World War II Canadian politics has not displayed an irreversible trend to centralization, nor the manifestations of capitalist contradiction in polarized class politics, creative or otherwise. Instead, the provinces, aided by secular trends which have enhanced the practical significance of their constitutionally based legislative authority and by the deliberate improvement of their own bureaucratic power and capacity, have given a new salience to the politics of federalism and the territorially based diversities it encompasses, reflects, and fosters.

Canadian scholars have frequently noted, and almost as frequently regretted, that political elites have been unable to free themselves from the seemingly eternal burden of working the federal system and preventing the disintegration of the country. That burden continues to be our fate.

Success in grappling with the special burdens of governing a federal state does not come easily. The eleven governments of the provincial and country-wide societies of Canada require an effective coordinating capacity if each is not to frustrate the efforts of the others in their joint governing of the country.

The fact that the federal-provincial political arena is not restricted in scope to only a few matters of peripheral concern for society and economy enhances the importance of the task. Almost without exception, every crucial issue, including the constitutional framework of the country itself, eventually ends up at the conference table for resolution. "In few policy areas," according to Richard Simeon, "except perhaps defence, the post office or garbage collection, does one government act alone."[56]

Unfortunately, the contemporary search for intergovernmental coordination confronts a set of conditions inimical to conflict resolution. Reconciliation of federal and provincial objectives is facilitated when one or the other level of government is passive, when one level of government is clearly dominant, when the scope of government activity is minimal, or when the two levels deal with discrete, separable sectors of society and economy. Thus, in the early years of the federation there were few administrative conflicts related to jurisdictional divisions. "Both provinces and dominion, in the formative years, found quite enough to occupy their limited administrative resources without trespassing on the other's preserves."[57] This jurisdictional isolation is gone forever, and none of the other agreement-facilitating situations now prevails or is likely to do so in the future. Both levels of government are strong. Neither can dominate the other. Both pursue increasingly comprehensive and integrated goals with a consequent decline in their willingness to defer to the interests of external governments. Provincial willingness to defer to Ottawa has diminished with the development of administrative skills and professional competence in the provincial capitals.

This pessimistic appraisal is given extra weight by the developing integration of governments and societies in Canadian federalism. The competitive coexistence of provinces and central government has especially profound consequences in an era of expanded government bureaucracies, strong pressures for policy coherence by each government, and the massive extension of the tentacles of government regulation, control, and public ownership. The economy and society of each province are confronted with competing and sometimes opposing government directives emerging from separately conceived national and provincial plans for making sense of the same socio-economic order. The national and provincial perspectives, although they frequently encompass the same interests, inevitably take into account a different set and range of considerations. A coast-to-coast perspective based on the federal authority granted by the BNA Act, and especially sensitive to the existing relations between the federal government and Canadian society produced by past and continuing federal policies, confronts the provincial perspective, restricted in geographic coverage, based on a different assignment of constitutional authority, and responsive to the current relationships between the provincial government and provincial society.

In these circumstances, contemporary intergovernmental coordination is not a simple matter of agreement between a handful of political leaders and their staff advisers. It requires the coordination of powerful bureaucracies with deep policy roots in their societies and of "the publics that are implicated in their normal functioning."[58] It requires, therefore, the containment of ineradicable tendencies to conflict between the federal vision of a society and economy, and ten competing provincial visions, each building on the pervasive links between government and its environment forged by its predecessors.

The premises of 1867 were that federal and provincial governments could go their own separate ways with the provinces assuming only limited functions. Further, the then divergent French and English definitions of the good life minimized the possibility of fundamental French-English conflict between the governments of Quebec and Ottawa. This nineteenth-century recipe for intergovernmental and inter-ethnic harmony is gone.[59] In Quebec, according to Léon Dion, "culture, politics, and economic activity. . . will . . . have to develop new organic interrelationships," and federal policies will be judged by their contribution to this objective.[60] Contemporary federalism, consequently, is more than an arena for a debate between abstract ideas of the public good or for the conducting of competition between either governments or societies detached from each other. It is an arena in which the political and bureaucratic leaders of governmentalized societies and economies hammer out the next stage in the further evolution of the eleven distinct yet interdependent political economies and politicized societies which are the gifts of the past to the present. From this perspective it is no longer meaningful or appropriate to think of these economies and societies at the provincial and national levels as logically prior to governments. To an indeterminate, but undoubtedly significant extent they are the consequences of past government activity and will increasingly be so in the future.

Parliamentary government and federalism have contributed to a flexible, non-ideological, pragmatic style of politics which facilitates intergovernmental agreement. Federal politics, in particular, has always required political leaders with well-developed bargaining skills, capable of encompassing the profound diversities of the country in their appeals, politics, and leadership. One of Mackenzie King's "robust convictions," doubtless born of long experience, was "his belief that the really important people in the world were the conciliators."[61]

Formerly, pragmatism and expediency at the political levels of cabinets allowed a high degree of bureaucratic autonomy for specialists to work out agreements with counterpart civil servants in the other jurisdiction. Under this system of functional federalism, which was characteristic of the conditional grant era, federal-provincial relations were handled in discrete categories by specialists, guided by professional norms, and relatively independent of hierarchical superiors concerned with overall policy coherence and the opportunity costs of fifty-cent dollars. Under the new regime of political federalism, to employ Smiley's terminology, effective decision-making capacity has drifted upwards to politicians and bureaucrats, "with jurisdiction-wide concerns."[62] The desire of each level of government to put its own house in order by establishing central executive control over policy priorities and fiscal decisions has primarily focussed on the elimination of intragovernmental contradictions, incoherences, and uncontrolled spending. The inevitable side-effect, however, has been an attempt to manage the external environment in the interest of the same objectives. This has led Ottawa and most of the provinces to establish federal-provincial ministries, bureaus, or agencies to eliminate the uncertainty and disturbances of an ad hoc approach to intergovernmental relations.[63] The effort by each government to integrate its policy outputs is a reaction to the contradictions in the extensive existing policy grip of government on society, as well as a necessity for the many plans still germinating in myriad committees. The successful introduction of the latter requires deft manoeuvring through the minefield of existing policies.

Although societies can stand a great deal of chaos, the economic and social costs of contradictory policies generate pressures to minimize their incidence. Since this can be most effectively done within a single jurisdiction where only one overall political decision-making authority exists, there will be a tendency for intrajurisdictional clashes to be controlled or moderated at the expense of flexibility in handling inter-jurisdictional concerns. The playing out of this bias will result in a relative and absolute increase in irreconcilable policy clashes between governments.

The dynamics and weaknesses of political federalism are rendered more explicable if it is recognized that we have stumbled into a peculiar Canadian version of the American separation of powers. The reaching of agreement on the innumerable major issues which clog the federal-provincial agenda requires the approval of independent political authorities with distinct and separate bases of electoral, party, group, and bureaucratic support. They are not constitutionally beholden to each other, and they are aligned with large and powerful constituencies of interests that can be mobilized behind the evocative labels of provincial rights and the national interest. Indeed, the Canadian version of the separation of powers may be more difficult to work than its American counterpart, for it involves not just the separate legislative and executive strata of the policy-making process but governments, conscious of their historic position, jealous of their prerogatives, and aggressively enterprising in the performance of their managerial responsibilities for their societies.

Notes

1. See Luce Patenaude, *Le Labrador à l'heure de la contestation* (Montréal : Presses de l'Université de Montréal, 1972), and Jacques Brossard, et al., *Le Territoire Québécois* (Montréal : Presses de l'Université de Montréal, 1970), 17-9, for materials and analysis from a Quebec perspective on the Labrador dispute.

2. For an excellent technical description of boundary changes, see Norman L. Nicholson, *The Boundaries of Canada, its Provinces and Territories*, Canada, Department of Mines and Technical Surveys, Geographical Branch, Memoir no. 2 (Ottawa, 1964).

3. February 12, 1972, cited in Edgar Gallant, "Maritime Cooperation and Integration—A Progress Report," in O. J. Firestone, ed., *Regional Economic Development* (Ottawa, 1974), 167.

4. Roy P. Fairfield, ed., *The Federalist Papers*, 2nd ed. (Garden City, N.Y.: Doubleday, 1966), 2.

5. For a relevant case study, see A. Paul Pross, "Input versus Withinput: Pressure Group Demands and Administrative Survival," in A. Paul Pross, ed., *Pressure Group Behaviour in Cana-* *dian Politics* (Toronto: McGraw-Hill Ryerson, 1975).

6. "A classic case [of the survival capacity of public organizations] is the Halifax Disaster Relief Commission, established to handle claims arising from the Halifax explosion of 1917. In late 1975, the federal government introduced a bill to repeal the act respecting the Commission and to transfer authority for continuation of pensions and allowances to the Canadian Pension Commission. So long-lived was the commission that the bill winding it up had to make pension provisions for employees of the Commission itself." Donald Gow, "Rebuilding Canada's Bureaucracy," edited and revised by Edwin R. Black and Michael J. Prince (Kingston, 1976, Mimeographed), 40.

7. *Ibid.*, 40.

8. André Bernard, "The Quebec Perspective on Canada: The Last Quarter Century—Language Strife" (Paper for the University of Saskatchewan Conference on Political Change in Canada, March 17, 1977), 1. This leadership role is a response to the social and political fact that "No

power in the world can prevent francophone Quebeckers from perceiving themselves as a society and as a nation, original and distinct from the Canadian whole." Léon Dion, *Québec: The Unfinished Revolution* (Montreal and London: McGill-Queen's University Press, 1976), 45.

9. Donald V. Smiley, *Canada in Question: Federalism in the Seventies*, 2nd ed. (Toronto: McGraw-Hill Ryerson, 1976), 108.

10. Corry, "Constitutional Trends and Federalism," in A.R.M. Lower, et al., *Evolving Canadian Federalism* (Durham, N.C.: Duke University Press, 1958), 101.

11. Claude Morin, *Quebec versus Ottawa: The Struggle for Self-government 1960-1972*, trans. Richard Howard (Toronto: University of Toronto Press, 1976), 95.

12. *Ibid.*, chap. 13.

13. Dion, *Québec: The Unfinished Revolution*, 86.

14. For an extremely helpful general discussion of institutionalization see Samuel P. Huntington, "Political Development and Political Decay," in Norman J. Vig and Rodney S. Stiefbold, eds., *Politics in Advanced Nations* (Englewood Cliffs, N.J.: Prentice-Hall, 1974). "Institutionalization is the process by which organizations and procedures acquire value and stability. The level of institutionalization of any political system can be defined by the adaptability, complexity, autonomy, and coherence of its organizations and procedures" (115). In comparative terms, the Canadian political system is highly institutionalized.

15. Richard Simeon, "The 'Overload Thesis' and Canadian Government," *Canadian Public Policy* 2 (1976), 550, italics in original. Similar statements abound in the literature. "For today's citizens," states Dion, "as for their fathers, the State is still a distant 'they,' alien and almost inimical . . . ." (*Québec: The Unfinished Revolution*, 87). Smiley speculates that "elites are somewhat unresponsive to popular attitudes and that the citizenry for whatever reasons has a considerable tolerance for this unresponsiveness" (*Canada in Question*, 201). J. R. Mallory observes that "the mass of citizenry is perhaps as far away from the real decisions of government as they were two hundred years ago, and the cabinet system provides strong institutional barriers to the development of more democratic ways of doing things" ("Responsive and Responsible Government," *Transactions of the Royal Society of Canada*, Fourth Series, 12 [1974], 208). A recent volume on pressure groups documents instances in which government agencies withstood "considerable input pressure from the external environment, and that they may significantly influence that environment, if not dominate it" (A. Paul Pross, "Pressure Groups: Adaptive Instruments of Political Communication," in Pross, ed., *Pressure Group Behaviour in Canadian Politics*, 21). J. E. Anderson suggests that "in Canada the relations between civil servants and pressure groups are usually dominated by civil servants" ("Pressure Groups and the Canadian Bureaucracy," in W. D. K. Kernaghan, ed., *Bureaucracy in Canadian Government*, 2nd ed. [Toronto: Methuen, 1973], 99).

16. Morin, *Quebec versus Ottawa*, 43.

17. Dion, *Québec: The Unfinished Revolution*, 138.

18. John Meisel, "Citizen Demands and Government Response," *Canadian Public Policy* 2 (1976): 568.

19. Simeon, "The 'Overload Thesis' and Canadian Government," 546.

20. Bernard, "Quebec Perspective on Canada," 1.

21. Dion, *Québec: The Unfinished Revolution*, 156.

22. "I am deeply concerned that, on the evidence of the two-year examination carried out by the Audit Office, Parliament—and indeed the Government—has lost or is close to losing effective control of the public purse" (*Conspectus of the Report of the Auditor General of Canada to the House of Commons* [Ottawa, 1976], 3).

23. Ontario Economic Council, *The Ontario Economy to 1987* (Toronto, 1977), 38.

24. Geoffrey Young, "Federal-Provincial Grants and Equalization" in Ontario Economic Council, *Intergovernmental Relations* (Toronto, 1977), 43-4.

25. Donald R. Huggett, "Tax Base Harmonization," in Ontario Economic Council, *Intergovernmental Relations*, 56.

26. The appropriately cautious statement of Paul Pross should be kept in mind as a salutary check on some of the more speculative suggestions in the following paragraphs: "We know only enough to suggest that federalism is both an important influence on pressure group behaviour and that group

manipulation of intergovernmental relations may have a significant effect on the policy process" ("Pressure Groups: Adaptive Instruments of Political Communication," 23).

27. *Social Credit and the Federal Power in Canada* (Toronto: University of Toronto Press, 1967), 32, 37.

28. P. E. Trudeau, *Federalism and the French Canadians* (Toronto: Macmillan, 1968), 138.

29. Pross, "Pressure Groups: Adaptive Instruments of Political Communication," 22-3, and David Kwavnick, "Interest Group Demands and the Federal Political System: Two Canadian Case Studies," esp. 71-2, both from Pross, ed., *Pressure Group Behaviour in Canadian Politics*.

30. Kwavnick, "Interest Group Demands," 81.

31. *Ibid.*, 82.

32. M. W. Bucovetsky, "The Mining Industry and the Great Tax Reform Debate," in Pross, ed., *Pressure Group Behaviour in Canadian Politics*, 106.

33. Ibid., 108-9.

34. Roy C. Macridis, "Interest Groups in Comparative Analysis," *The Journal of Politics* 23 (1961): 38. He speculates that "this parallelism between the political system and the interest configuration is true everywhere." Compare Kwavnick's hypothesis: "The distribution of power between the central and provincial governments influences the structure, cohesion and even the existence of interest groups; that is, that the strength and cohesion of interest groups will tend to mirror the strength, in their particular area of concern, of the government to which they enjoy access. Interest groups which are provincially based and which enjoy access to the provincial governments will be strong compared with nationally-based groups enjoying access to the national government when the provincial governments enjoy a stronger position than the national government in the areas of concern to those interest groups, and vice-versa," and, "In short, the pressure goes where the power is—and takes its organization with it" ("Interest Group Demands," 72, 77). See in general David Truman, *The Governmental Process: Political Interests and Public Opinion*, 2nd ed. (New York: Knopf, 1971).

35. Helen Jones Dawson, "National Pressure Groups and the Federal Government," 30-5, in Pross, ed., *Pressure Group Behaviour in Canadian Politics*.

36. *Ibid.*, 31. In summary, Professor Dawson states: "Clearly Canadian federalism has had, and continues to have, a formidable impact upon the organization and behaviour of the pressure groups. It has complicated and confused their tasks while increasing their expenses and policy formulation problems," 35.

37. The next few pages are heavily dependent on Smiley, *Canada in Question*, chap. 4; and Edwin R. Black, "Federal Strains within a Canadian Party," in Hugh G. Thorburn, ed., *Party Politics in Canada*, 2nd ed. (Scarborough: Prentice-Hall, 1967). Black summarizes his interpretation with the statement: "Both the structure and the internal operation of a major party resemble that of the Canadian system of government. The sovereignty of provincial party units is as real and extensive as that of the provinces with respect to Ottawa," 139.

38. Carl J. Friedrich, *Limited Government: A Comparison* (Englewood Cliffs, N.J.: Prentice-Hall, 1974), 55.

39. See Black, "Federal Strains within a Canadian Party," for an instructive case study of the impact of federalism on federal-provincial party relationships.

40. Smiley, *Canada in Question*, 108-9.

41. *Ibid.*, 109-10.

42. *Ibid.*, 110.

43. See Reginald Whitaker, "The Liberal Party and the Canadian State: A Report on Research and a Speculation" (January 1977, Mimeographed), esp. 37.

44. Kwavnick, "Interest Group Demands," 71. Twenty years ago Corry identified the development of national associations and mammoth nation-wide corporations "compelled to think in nation-wide . . . terms," as crucial to the centralization of power in Ottawa ("Constitutional Trends and Federalism," 109, 111, 114).

45. Pross, "Pressure Groups: Adaptive Instruments of Political Communication," 6-9.

46. See J. E. Hodgetts, "Regional Interests and Policy in a Federal Structure," *Canadian Journal of Economics and Political Science* 32 (1966), 13-4, on the creation of regions for policy purposes by governments, and the attempts to generate re-

gional demands from those artificially-created administrative units.

47. See my "The Electoral System and the Party System in Canada, 1921-1965," *Canadian Journal of Political Science* 1 (1968), 55-80, for the contribution of the electoral system to the regionalization of the party system.

48. John Meisel, "Recent Changes in Canadian Parties," in Thorburn, ed., *Party Politics in Canada*: 34.

49. See William E. Connolly, *The Terms of Political Discourse* (Lexington, Mass.: Heath, 1974), for a stimulating discussion of political language highly relevant for the following few pages.

50. Edwin R. Black, *Divided Loyalties: Canadian Concepts of Federalism* (Montreal and London: McGill-Queen's University Press, 1975), 3.

51. This is particularly evident in Trudeau who, although committed to federalism, is basically an advocate of liberal individualism and a ferocious opponent of any move in the direction of basing political systems on nationalist criteria of ethnicity (Black, *Divided Loyalties*, 209-10; Smiley, *Canada in Question*, 175).

52. The group or community claims of the provinces are for external consumption. Within their own political spheres, provincial politicians speak of the rights of individual British Columbians, Newfoundlanders, etc.

53. Cited in Donald V. Smiley, *The Canadian Political Nationality* (Toronto: Methuen, 1967), 80.

54. See Black's discussion in *Divided Loyalties*, chap. 7, of the tortured and confused two-nations controversy of the late sixties.

55. Although resort to the past has lost relevance as a debating technique, the BNA Act remains as an uncertain arbiter of conflicting claims for policy-making authority. In circumstances of political competition, now as in the past, each government tends to attribute amplified meaning to its constitutional assignments of statutory authority, and restrictive definitions to the explicitly worded law-making authority of the other level of government. See Smiley's fascinating discussion of Quebec-Ottawa differences in interpreting provincial jurisdiction over education (*Canada in Question*, 30-4).

The contemporary federal strategy of linguistic manipulation, for which there are provincial counterparts, in described by Claude Morin as follows: "Confronting a Quebec government that was sensitive about its constitutional prerogative—more often the case with the Union nationale—Ottawa made sure to avoid the impression of a frontal assault on provincial sectors. 'Training' was the word used rather than 'education,' 'problems of urban growth' replaced 'municipal affairs,' the 'fight against unemployment' replaced 'social development,' 'community development' was the new expression for 'culture.' Ottawa could speak freely on any subject providing the terms it used did not ring suspiciously of those areas which Quebec, atavistically or otherwise, had come to regard as being within its own jurisdiction" (*Quebec versus Ottawa*, 78-9).

56. Richard Simeon, "The Federal-Provincial Decision Making Process," in Ontario Economic Council, *Intergovernmental Relations*, 26. See also John Meisel, "Cleavages, Parties, and Values in Canada" (Paper presented to the International Political Science Association, IXth World Congress, Montreal, 1973, Mimeographed), 3, 6-8, on the significant role of federal and provincial governments as the key protagonists for the expression of the three major political cleavages in Canada—ethnic, regional, and economic/regional.

57. J. E. Hodgetts, *The Canadian Public Service: A Physiology of Government 1867-1970* (Toronto: University of Toronto Press, 1974), 42.

58. Norton E. Long, "Power and Administration," *Public Administration Review* 9 (1949): 261.

59. Morin, *Quebec versus Ottawa*, 161.

60. Dion, *Québec: The Unfinished Revolution*, 102-3.

61. Cited in W. A. Matheson, *The Prime Minister and the Cabinet* (Toronto: Methuen, 1976), 150, italics in original. "No strong man in the emotionally satisfying sense has ever ruled this country—none will if it is to survive," stated Lester Pearson. "Attempting to reconcile what appears to be the irreconcilable will continue to be the task of Prime Ministers and in this take Prime Ministers tend to look uninspiring," ibid., 29.

62. Donald V. Smiley, "The Structural Problem of Canadian Federalism," *Canadian Public Administration* 14 (1971): 332.

63. See Simeon, "The Federal-Provincial Decision Making Process," 31-2, for a good brief discussion.

Selected Readings

Cairns, Allan. "The Other Crisis of Canadian Federalism." *Canadian Public Administration* 22: 2 (Summer, 1979): 175-95.

Clarke, H. D.; Jenson, J.; Le Duc, L.; and Pammett, J. *Political Choice in Canada*. Abridged edition. Toronto: McGraw-Hill Ryerson, 1980.

Elkins, David, and Simeon, Richard. *Small Worlds: Provinces and Parties in Canadian Political Life*. Toronto: Methuen, 1980.

Simeon, Richard. "Regionalism and Canadian Political Institutions." In J. P. Meekison, ed., *Canadian Federalism: Myth or Reality*. 3rd ed. Toronto: Methuen, 1977, 292-304.

Smiley, D. V. "Territorialism and Canadian Political Institutions." *Canadian Public Policy* 3: 4 (Autumn 1977): 449-57.

8. CANADIAN REGIONALISM IN CONTINENTAL PERSPECTIVE

Garth Stevenson

Few words have enjoyed such popularity among prominent Canadians in recent years as "region" and its various derivatives. A contributor to an influential volume of essays on the possible consequences of Quebec separatism expressed what has become the conventional wisdom when he asserted that "Canada is increasingly a collection of regionally based societies."[1] The Pepin-Roberts Task Force on Canadian Unity devoted six of its least impressive pages to an analysis of "regionalism," which it claimed was an important and growing force in the English-speaking parts of Canada, and the subject runs like a leitmotif through the remaining pages of its report. At the same time the Task Force admitted to a remarkable lack of conceptual clarity about the concept of "regionalism," considering how central it was to their analysis and conclusions:

> In this report, then, we will use the concept of regionalism in more than one way. Sometimes we will use it to mean economic and geographic regions transcending provincial boundaries. But more often we will use it to designate the provinces themselves. The provincial political institutions are the primary frameworks through which regional populations can organize and express themselves, and their existence serves in turn to develop the social networks and interests based on them, thus reinforcing the provincial focus of regionalism.[2]

Even earlier, in 1977, a student symposium on national unity had added its share to the confusion by reaching the apparently paradoxical conclusion that "the only challenge to the supremacy of regionalism is provincialism."[3]

The confusion is understandable, for the term "region" is commonly used in a number of different ways, most of which seem quite irrelevant to the phenomenon which Canadian scholars and writers are attempting to explain when they invoke the concept of "regionalism." Both the Quebec and Ontario governments use the term "region" for administrative entities of their own creation within the province, usually designed so as to integrate a number of neighbouring municipalities into a supposedly "rational" entity for planning purposes. In somewhat the same fashion the federal government has called into being a "Maritime region" in the hope of encouraging cooperation between a group of small neighbouring provinces. The concept of a five-region Canada (Atlantic, Quebec, Ontario, Prairie, and British Columbia) has been promoted by the government of British Columbia and is used by Statistics Canada for certain purposes but appears to have little meaning for the general public.[4] The amendment formula in the Victoria Charter, on the other hand, was based on the assumption of four regions, with British Columbia included in "western Canada." Railways, banks, and other institutions in the private sector divide the country into other arbitrary "regions" for their own administrative purposes. A geographer, an economist, a geologist, or a sociologist would define Canadian "re-

Garth Stevenson, "Canadian Regionalism in Continental Perspective," *Journal of Canadian Studies* 15:2 (1980): 16-28. Reprinted by permission of the *Journal of Canadian Studies*. The essay has been abridged to suit the needs of this volume.

gions" by different criteria and would undoubtedly arrive at different results.

Regionalism is not of course an exclusively Canadian preoccupation. Attempts have been made to divide the whole world into "regions" for either analytical or other purposes, as witness the large number of "regional" intergovernmental organizations and the widespread use of such terms as "Latin America" or "the Middle East." Like their Canadian counterparts these supranational "regions" seem to follow existing administrative boundaries rather closely and to reflect a rather confused mixture of ethno-cultural, geographic, and economic criteria. Even more directly comparable with Canadian thinking on the subject is the considerable attention that has been devoted recently to subnational regions in the larger unitary nation-states of Western Europe, a phenomenon that will be referred to again subsequently. Here there appears to be a more general consensus about the boundaries and identities of the relevant regions, if not about what administrative and institutional changes, if any, would be an appropriate response to their existence.

The country in which regionalism has been most extensively examined and written about over the longest period is, however, the United States. At least two contrasts may be noted between Canadian and American writing on this theme. In the first place, no individual American state is ever described as comprising a region by itself, even though as valid a claim might be made for Texas or California to enjoy this distinction as for Ontario or Quebec. In the second place, Americans make a distinction, which is entirely unknown in Canada, between regionalism and sectionalism. One standard work on the subject attempts to explain the difference as follows:

> . . . inherent in [sectionalism] is the idea of separatism and isolation; of separate units with separate interests. It must be clear that, since the very definition of regionalism implies a unifying function, it must be different from sectionalism as

everywhere defined by the historians. Here the distinctions are clear between the divisive power of self-seeking *sections* and the integrating power of co-ordinate *regions* fabricated into a unified whole.[5]

The same work goes on to assert, rather more obscurely, that

> Regionalism is organic, basic to the evolution of all culture. Sectionalism is mechanical and is basic to specialized and temporary ends.[6]

A more recent writer on American federalism, however, appears to make an almost contradictory distinction between the two terms:

> Sectionalism is not the same as regionalism. The latter is essentially a transient phenomenon that brings adjacent states together because of immediate and specific common interests . . . . Sectionalism involves arrangements of much greater permanence which persist despite the emergence of immediate conflicts or divergences among its components from time to time.[7]

At least implicit in some of the literature, however, is a more objective basis of distinction between regionalism and sectionalism. Regionalism in the American sense seems to be associated with the fact that adjacent areas of adjacent states often have an ecological unity and coherence transcending state boundaries, and not necessarily shared with other portions of the same states. This fact in turn is mainly attributable to the large number of navigable rivers which flow through two or more of the states or serve as interstate boundaries, and by the tendency of such rivers to attract a dense population. Residents of such areas tend to discover their common interests, or at least common problems, with respect to such matters as pollution, irrigation and flood control, as well as the urban problems of metropolitan areas that have developed astride artificial state boundaries. Those who are most aware of these common interests or problems seek remedial action by the state governments or, failing that, by the federal government.

Probably in some cases the state governments are motivated to act by their reluctance to see the federal government do so, a possibility which is very real given the nature of American political institutions. In any event both state-based regional instrumentalities, such as the Port of New York Authority, and federally-based ones, such as the Tennessee Valley Authority, are important phenomena of American life.

CANADIAN REGIONALISM

Despite its ambiguities, the American and European literature on regionalism seems generally to concur in a conclusion that appears essential if the term "region" is to retain any clear meaning or analytical usefulness. That conclusion is that a region is a territorial entity having some natural and organic unity or community of interest that is independent of political and administrative boundaries. Those boundaries may, like the river-based boundaries of many American states or the provincial boundary that bisects the Canadian city of Lloydminster, be maintained in defiance of a "natural" regionalism that contrasts with their own artificiality.

The usefulness of this conclusion, however, may be questioned on the grounds that it is difficult to separate what is natural from what is artificial, especially in the long term. Political and administrative boundaries exert such great influence under modern conditions that the state can reshape the underlying socio-economic realities in its own image. Over time the natural regions that may have existed before the boundaries were established will be obliterated, while the area within each set of boundaries will take on the appearance of a region, even if it was not one before. What the Task Force on Canadian Unity is apparently trying to say in the paragraph quoted above is that Canadian provinces have done this so successfully that for all practical purposes "province" and "region" are now synonymous. The same idea was expressed, al-

though far more clearly, by Alan Cairns in his 1977 presidential address to the Canadian Political Science Association.[8]

Clearly not all states, provinces, or administrative entities are equal in their boundary-maintaining abilities. Moreover, the ability of one entity to maintain or reinforce its boundaries may vary over time. Most would agree that Canadian provinces, perhaps because of their control over crown lands and resources, have much greater boundary-maintaining abilities than American states. Most would probably also argue, as the Task Force on Canadian Unity appears to do, that their boundary-maintaining abilities have increased in recent years. Thus while there still are some distinct regions cutting across provincial boundaries, such as the one that surrounds lakes Temiskaming and Abitibi, they are much less visible than their American counterparts.

A similar analysis of artificial boundaries in relation to natural regions can also be applied to the boundary between Canada and the United States. In fact an analysis of Canadian regionalism that fails to view it in its North American context is incomplete and seriously misleading. The definition of a boundary between British and American territories, and its subsequent reinforcement by Confederation and the transcontinental railways, divided a number of regions in the sense outlined above. Indeed the struggle to assert an east-west axis of communication against the pressure of a more natural regionalism is the major theme of Canadian history. The American historian Paul Sharp describes the process as it affected one of the regions along the international boundary:

> When the Canadian Pacific Railway reached Medicine Hat in 1883, the close ties between the American and Canadian areas were broken . . . .
>
> The regional divorce was as nearly complete as modern nationalism can devise and the surveyor's line across the plains took on the reality of an international boundary . . . .
>
> In a surprisingly short time, settlers on both sides lost the sense of regional unity so pro-

nounced during the preceding quarter-century. They remained good neighbours, but their economic and social contacts were increasingly casual.⁹

That the disruption of existing regionalisms was a difficult, artificial and by no means inevitable achievement was a fact apparent at the time both to those who supported and those who opposed the effort to build a Canadian nation. One of the latter group, Goldwin Smith, precisely described the situation only a few years after the C.P.R. was completed:

> Whether the four blocks of territory constituting the Dominion can for ever be kept by political agencies united among themselves and separate from their Continent, of which geographically, economically, and with the exception of Quebec ethnologically, they are parts, is the Canadian question.¹⁰

Smith, it will be noted, was among the first to play the game of attempting to determine how many regions, or parts of regions, could be found along the Canadian-American boundary. Like the drafters of the Victoria Charter, but unlike Statistics Canada, he apparently concluded that there were only four.

If one looks back at what might have been, and at what was urged by the opponents of Confederation and the National Policy, the outlines of the regional ties and interests that spanned the Canadian-American boundary can still be dimly seen. In the Maritimes opponents of Confederation, and later opponents of the protective tariff, saw a natural community between themselves and the New England states, just as New England itself had earlier opposed the War of 1812 because of its desire to trade with the Maritimes. The belief that Confederation had cut the Maritimes off from their natural hinterland and brought about their decline nourished an enduring tradition of political paranoia, despite the fact that New England experienced a similar decline within the American federal system.

Turning to Quebec, it is often assumed that the merchants and financiers of Montreal were the one group who clearly had a vested interest in the international boundary. Yet less than twenty years separated Confederation from the Annexation Manifesto of 1849, and the Montreal merchants of an earlier period had envisaged their western hinterland as lying south of the Great Lakes. The Grand Trunk was an international railway, with one terminus in Portland (Maine) and the other eventually in Chicago. Even the syndicate who built the C.P.R. really wanted to build their main line through Minnesota, which had been their first base of operations. Far from being the political outcome of their self-interest, the building of an all-Canadian line north of Lake Superior was a political choice imposed on them against their will by John A. Macdonald. George Stephen, the arch-typical Montreal capitalist and first president of the C.P.R., retained until his death a financial interest in the C.P.R.'s American rival, the Minnesota-based Great Northern Railway.¹¹

Ontario also had its transnational regionalism, particularly strong in the southwestern peninsula which John A. Macdonald distrusted as a hot-bed of "Yankees and Convenanters."¹² The Clear Grit opponents of Confederation, although few in number, testified to the existence of this regional sentiment. From their time to ours there runs a thin stream of tradition which sees Ontario's natural alliance as being with Michigan and New York rather than with what the old free-trader Richard Cartwright dismissed as "the shreds and patches" of Canada.¹³ Goldwin Smith, who despised Confederation, wrote that Ontario by itself had the potential to be a nation, and that it would benefit from free trade with the United States.¹⁴ A similar sentiment underlies the currently fashionable academic belief than an incipient industrial Ontario was stultified by wicked Montreal "merchants." Richard Cartwright is the real hero of Tom Naylor's two-volume attack on the National Policy.¹⁵

It is hardly necessary to comment on the existence of transnational regionalism in the Prairie provinces, where the arbitrary nature of the international boundary has always been most obvious. The strong support for Reciprocity in 1911, and the recent antics of former Saskatchewan Conservative leader Richard Collver, testify to an enduring, although by no means universal, sentiment. As for British Columbia, the belief that Washington State is less "foreign" than the other provinces of Canada is found there on every part of the political spectrum.[16]

After Confederation these assorted regionalisms were swept under the rug, if not entirely forgotten. A new coalition of political and economic interests, dominating the Conservative party and strongly influencing the Liberal party as well, emerged to reinforce and strengthen the international boundary. Its ideological underpinning was the belief that *British* North America represented a superior type of society to the violent, immoral, and anarchic United States. In Quebec the notion of an essentially Catholic society was likewise contrasted with the tarnished utopia to the south.

At the same time the economic and political nationalism of the United States itself reinforced the efforts of Canadian nationalists by creating additional obstacles to transborder trade and by making the contrast in ideological symbols between the two countries more conspicuous. The old balance of forces on the continent, which reached its high tide in the first third of the twentieth century, was compatible with the existence of two competing, but remarkably similar, well-integrated federal states, each with its own paraphernalia of railways, tariffs, and institutions. In a sense their rival nation-building strategies were mutually reinforcing.

More recently all the traditional devices and strategies that served to reinforce the international boundary have faltered and collapsed. The result has been the resurgence of regionalism and provincialism that the Task Force on Canadian Unity noticed, while singularly failing to appreciate its causes.

AMERICAN SECTIONALISM

While Canada has become more closely linked with the United States over the last generation, the United States has been changing. Historically that country was, like Canada, an artificial union of several British colonies in eastern North America, some of which had been taken by the British from other European powers while in others British influence was superimposed directly on the aboriginal society. While the traces of non-British European settlement in such states as New York and Louisiana admittedly did not amount to a cultural cleavage like that between French and English Canada, the United States was more deeply divided by the contrast between the plantation slave economy of the southern lowlands and the industrial economy that developed on a foundation of small scale independent commodity production in the north. As in Canada, expansion into the western half of the continent exacerbated the conflicts arising from the fundamental division in the older part of the country. Although the social base of southern separatism was destroyed by the outcome of the Civil War, the United States remained a heterogeneous entity. The South, like Quebec, became a backward hinterland embittered by military defeat and set apart by socio-cultural differences, while the American West, like its Canadian counterpart, chafed under the burden of tariffs, freight rates, and other alleged iniquities imposed on it by eastern capitalism.

American sectionalism, although never as extensively celebrated by the clerisy as provincialism has recently been by their Canadian counterparts, remained a latent force. The presidential election of 1896, like the Canadian general election of 1911, demonstrated that the discontented hinterland regions could not outvote the industrialized metropolitan core that controlled the federal state and dominated the country. After these defeats Western hinterland resentment in both countries turned to populist and even socialist third parties while older and poorer hinterlands—the South, the Maritimes, and Quebec—opted for a pork barrel strategy of exploiting their electoral influence within one of the major parties, to which they gave overwhelming support. Senatorial patronage and the "balanced ticket" in presidential elections served the same purpose as the rigid conventions governing "regional" representation in the Canadian federal cabinet. In both countries the hegemony of the industrialized metropolitan cores remained undisturbed in the early part of the twentieth century, and in both it was customary to conclude by mid-century that the centrifugal forces within the federal system had been permanently defeated.

Over the last generation, however, the United States has been transformed by the migration of economic power, wealth, and population away from the northeastern core of the country and towards the southern and western peripheries.[17] The process may have begun with the New Deal but was probably stimulated to a much greater extent by the massive military expenditure that became a permanent way of life from 1950 onwards, expenditure that for a mixture of economic and political reasons was disproportionately directed towards the West and South. The shift from coal to oil and gas, from wheat to fruits and vegetables, and from railways to airlines also contributed to the trend, as did the declining relative importance of Western Europe in American external trade. The social transformation of the South following the end of institutionalized racism in the sixties also contributed to the shift of economic activity in that direction. Finally the energy crisis of the seventies has greatly stimulated the economies of the Rocky Mountain states and other energy producing areas. New centres of economic power have recently emerged in Florida, Texas, California, Colorado, and other hinterland states to challenge traditional northeastern dominance.

These developments, like roughly parallel changes in Canada, have affected the political system. The three most recent elected Presidents have all been from what is now termed the "sunbelt," an area that had contributed no previous presidents in more than a century. In both countries the newly rich West, once the seedbed of political radicalism, has become the bastion of the right-wing (and traditionally protectionist) party in national elections. At the same time, and with the declining relevance of the protective tariff, what was traditionally the low-tariff party has grown stronger in the industrial heartland, a tendency reinforced by the migration of European Catholics into Ontario and of southern blacks into the adjacent states. The increasingly complex interplay of regional and ethnic politics may be illustrated by reference to a French Canadian Liberal Prime Minister with his political bastion in English Montreal and a white southern Democratic President who could not have carried his own state, let alone the country, without the black vote.

The traditional high-tariff parties, in whose halcyon days the Canadian-American boundary assumed its clearest definition, have fallen on harder times in both countries despite, or perhaps because of, the westward shift in their electoral base. The Nixonian "southern strategy" of appeasing racism parallels the pathetic efforts of Canada's Conservative party to gain a foothold in Quebec by flirting with Quebec nationalism. The regional power shift has been reflected in the bitter and to outsiders largely unintelligible struggles between so-called "liberal" and "conservative" Republicans, representing respectively the old northeastern and the new southwestern money. Even these struggles have had a pale echo in Canadian politics, where the so-called "Red Tories" who became the darlings of the media in the seventies look far more like Rockefeller Republicans than John A. Macdonald Conservatives.

Changes in the two North American political economies have had a reciprocal effect, although the effect of the larger country on the smaller has naturally been more pronounced than vice versa. The westward shift of economic power in the United States has contributed to the similar trend in Canada. Quebec and the Atlantic provinces, closely linked to New York and New England, have declined along with them. Ontario, having cast in its lot with the industrial states around the Great Lakes, is now in turn beginning to feel the effects of their decline. On the other hand British Columbia and Alberta are pulled upwards by the rapidly growing economies of the Pacific and Rocky Mountain states. Fainter effects may also be discerned in the opposite direction, as when Alberta's wealth spills over into neighbouring states or when capital fleeing from Quebec stimulates economic growth in Florida.

In the United States power has shifted south as well as west, and this fact has had another set of consequences for Canada. As labour and capital move elsewhere, the states along Canada's southern border are declining in relation to the rest of the United States. Between 1950 and 1975 the combined population of these ten states increased by only thirty percent, while the six southwestern states doubled in population and the eleven southeastern states (the former Confederacy) increased by fifty percent. Since 1975 the competitive position of the northern tier states has been further worsened by the energy crisis. Faced with declining prospects, these states seek solutions to their economic problems in closer ties with the neighbouring Canadian provinces. Canadian markets for their manufactures can replace the markets lost in the rapidly industrializing south. Canadian investment is avidly pursued, particularly by the State of New York. Above all, Canadian hydroelectricity, natural gas and oil, or even offshore oil processed in Canadian refineries, can help to overcome the energy deficit of the frostbelt. Minnesota and Washington in particular are already heavily dependent on Canadian sources of energy. Thus powerful economic interests in the United States have a vested interest in promoting transnational regionalism, which further strains the already fragile fabric of Canadian unity. Just as their ancestors terminated reciprocity once they had subjugated the South in 1865, so today's Yankees seek new forms of reciprocity to compensate for their loss of control over the South. As the Civil War produced Confederation, the resurgence of the sunbelt threatens to shatter it.

Rapid changes in any balance of power always produce conflict and upheaval. It is no accident that sectionalism, or as Canadians persist in calling it, "regionalism," has recently increased on both sides of the international boundary. The energy crisis of the 1970s has increased the tension by accelerating the long-term redistribution of wealth and power in both countries, even though the domestic prices of energy commodities are still artificially restrained in response to the exigencies of New England, New York and Ontario politics. The declining sections seek to reverse the inexorable trend through federal assistance and protection, relying on the fact that political power resulting from their previous economic hegemony has lingered on after the economic circumstances that gave it birth. The expanding areas of both countries prefer to "let the eastern bastards freeze in the dark," an expression that was coined in Texas but predictably appeared in Calgary almost immediately afterwards. The newly rich always resent their declining predecessors, whose privileged status no longer seems to correspond with their real importance.[18] This resentment is easily transferred onto the federal government, whose efforts to help the declining sections, for example by controlling energy prices, appear to confirm the long-standing suspicion that it represents the interests of the traditional metropolitan core. On the other hand the efforts of earlier federal governments on behalf of the hinterland regions which at one time required assistance have been conveniently ignored or forgotten. The federal government is now viewed as a restraint on the economic growth and prosperity of the expanding regions.

Because of the nature and extent of its economic ties with the United States, Canada is exposed to the impact of these continental shifts in wealth and power, which are far greater in magnitude than those which a self-contained Canada would have experienced by itself. Yet the Canadian political system is far less resilient in the face of these changes than the American. The collapse of the old metropolis-hinterland relationship between northeast and southwest is traumatic, but manageable, for the United States. The collapse of the Montreal-Toronto hegemony over Canada, on the other hand, may mean the disintegration of the federal system itself. The superior durability of the American system reflects the outcome of the Civil War. Industrial capital, which won that war, could not tolerate the barriers to labour mobility inherent in an ideology of states rights or its Canadian version, the compact theory of Confederation. Among other consequences this produced the fourteenth amendment, the broad interpretation of the commerce clause in the U.S. constitution, and refusal to surrender the public lands of the American west to the states at the time when their Canadian counterparts were being surrendered to the provinces. Yet despite all of this the resurgence of Western and Southern sectionalism in the United States today is not a negligible phenomenon. The organization of economic and political power on this continent is in a state of flux such as has not been seen since the 1860s, and the pattern which it will ultimately assume remains obscure.

CONTINENTAL INTEGRATION

Neither an assumption of inevitability nor a conspiracy theory is needed to explain Canada's descent into continentalism, nor did it result from a deliberate strategy on anyone's part. The National Policy had apparently run its course by 1930, so Western lands and resources were given to the provincial governments that would subsequently use them to tie their own economies to those of the northwestern United States. Tariffs were steadily reduced from 1935 onwards, dismantling the major barrier to north-south trade and leaving the provinces with apparently little choice but to conduct individual industrial strategies of their own. Meanwhile the other major component of the National Policy, transcontinental railways, was suddenly superseded by the airlines, which in less than thirty years constructed a veritable spiderweb of north-south ties linking each province or "region" of Canada with its American counterpart. Highway trucking, with its emphasis on short-distance movement, easily tied the major cities of southern Canada into the expanding networks of American expressways.

The United Kingdom had disappeared as an effective counterweight to American economic power by 1945. Ideologically its influence lingered somewhat longer, although as the United Kingdom declined the claim that "British" political institutions were somehow better than American began to lose its credibility. Anti-Americanism also became suspect in the ideological climate of the cold war. The final disappearance of the United Kingdom into a German-dominated "Europe," apparently reversing the outcome of two world wars, removed the last shreds of the ideological underpinnings of Confederation. Almost simultaneously French Canada's traditional ideology of Catholic nationalism collapsed as well. Canada was suddenly left to confront the United States without its traditional defences.

The collapse of the National Policy paved the way for a series of regional economic policies and strategies linking areas of Canada with contiguous areas of the United States, and largely conducted by provincial governments. The oil and gas of the western provinces linked them with markets along the St. Paul-Seattle corridor and with capital and expertise from Texas and

Oklahoma. A decade later the Columbia River
Treaty and the Autopact were two gigantic victories for north-south regionalism, each serving to
link a Canadian province with the neighbouring
states and to loosen its ties with the rest of Canada. The Columbia also provided Manitoba and
Quebec with a precedent to enter the power-
exporting business, to the benefit of Minneapolis
and New York respectively. Provinces borrow
American money to build power dams for American consumers, while Canadian consumers in
other provinces are forced to generate electricity
by burning scarce and expensive oil or by running the environmental risks of reliance on nu-
clear reactors.

From a provincial perspective, the natural
response to the decline of the National Policy,
whether or not it is viewed with regret, is to
revive the old north-south regional ties that Confederation and the National Policy temporarily
obliterated. With the international boundary losing both its economic and ideological significance, provincial governments increasingly see
themselves as operating a North American,
rather than exclusively Canadian, environment.
For a province like Alberta, blessed with large
supplies of scarce resources, this may be viewed
as an opportunity. For a province with fewer
assets it may be viewed with some anxiety, as
witness the constant references in contemporary
Quebec to the perils of being surrounded by
220,000,000 anglophones. But in either case it is
a perfectly rational response to seek allies where
they can be found in this new and unpredictable
environment. The natural place to look for them
is among the immediate neighbours to the south,
reviving half-forgotten regional alignments. The
immediate neighbours may share common interests and problems to some degree, and may reinforce one another's bargaining position. Boston
and New York capital can help Quebec in its
effort to catch up with Ontario. The Maritimes
and New England share common problems of
old, energy-deficient and slowly growing regions. The northwestern states feel almost as

remote from their federal capital as the western
provinces do from theirs. Canadian-American
ties have not only increased in number over the
last generation, but have tended to link areas that
are geographically proximate. This fact can be
illustrated with reference to almost any aspect of
the Canadian-American relationship.

American ownership in the Canadian economy, for example, is very unevenly distributed
among the provinces, with the heaviest concentrations in Ontario (manufacturing) and Alberta
(oil and gas).[19] Moreover, it shows a clear tendency to link the different provinces with nearby
areas of the United States. Quebec-based subsidiaries tend to be controlled from headquarters in
New York or New Jersey, Ontario-based subsidiaries from headquarters in New York, Michigan,
Pennsylvania or Illinois, British-Columbia-
based subsidiaries from headquarters in California, and Alberta-based subsidiaries from
headquarters scattered through the western half
of the United States.[20] In most cases these firms
conduct the same type of activity in similar environments on both sides of the border, with the
original U.S. operation having expanded into a
nearby part of Canada having similar characteristics.

The pattern of Canadian trade with the
United States is somewhat similar. British Columbia sends its lumber and natural gas to the
Pacific states and receives their food and manufactured goods in return. Alberta trades its oil
and gas for the products of the Midwest and the
western interior. Ontario's industrial economy is
heavily integrated with New York and Michigan
(Canada exports more to Michigan than to the
whole of Europe) and also depends on Appala-
chian coal. Quebec trades with New England
and the Middle Atlantic states, and the Atlantic
provinces are more closely linked with New England and to some extent with New York.

Similar observations could be made about
most of what are possibly the less important
aspects of the Canadian-American relationship.
Television stations in Burlington, Watertown,

Buffalo, Detroit, and Seattle have their Canadian spheres of influence. Tourist travel in both directions seems to link the provinces with states directly to the south of them, as do the exchanges of power between electric utilities and the route patterns of the commercial airlines. International unions tend to have their Canadian membership concentrated in one part of Canada (autoworkers in Ontario, woodworkers in British Columbia) with the U.S. headquarters and much of the U.S. membership often located in a nearby part of the United States. Historic patterns of migration and cultural diffusion can be discerned even today in certain ethnic and religious ties between nearby states and provinces (the Mormon connection between Utah and Alberta is a striking example). The general pattern, in short, appears to be one of a series of parallel but distinct north-south ties involving different provinces in different ways, rather than a generalized relationship between homogeneous entities called "Canada" and "United States."

This pattern may largely account for a phenomenon that appears to exist although it has not been rigorously measured or indeed, to my knowledge, identified: the tendency for Canadians in each province or "region" to believe that other parts of Canada are more Americanized in their culture and more continentalist in their preferences than their own. Plausible "evidence" can always be found to support prejudices of this kind, whether it is the efforts by the Maritime provinces to attract American investment, the fondness of Quebeckers for large cars and holidays at American beach resorts, the overwhelmingly American orientation of Ontario's external trade, the Prairie preference for lager beer and low tariffs, or the well-publicized allegations that some Vancouverites were buying groceries and real estate in Bellingham while Dave Barrett's government was in office. Although polling data suggest that attitudes concerning Canadian-American relations do not vary dramatically from one province to another, these prejudices encourage Canadians con-

cerned about excessive dependence on the United States to blame the country's plight on Canadians who happen to live somewhere else. Not only does this lessen the likelihood of any concerted national effort to reverse the tendency towards continentalism, but it reinforces artificial provincialism to which certain politicians are only too happy to respond. This provincialism and parochialism can be manipulated on behalf of American corporate interests in Canada, as it was when the governments of the Western provinces lobbied against the Carter Commission's proposals to reform the taxation of resource industries. Even the withdrawal of tax privileges from the Canadian edition of *Time* was portrayed in some quarters as a plot by Toronto against the Canadian hinterlands,[21] and several provincial governments intervened before the Supreme Court to contest the federal government's right to curtail the use of American border television channels by Canadian advertisers.[22] Many Western Canadians proudly regard the American firm which enjoys a virtual monopoly over the retail food market in the West as "Western," and thus as morally superior to the Canadian-owned "Eastern" firms that sell better food at lower prices in the competitive markets of Quebec and Ontario.

Transnational regionalism in North America is manifested in a variety of more or less formal relationships between state and provincial governments. Since the subject has been extensively explored elsewhere there is no need to describe it at length, except to point out that the greatest number of relationships are predictably between jurisdictions that are at least nearby if not actually contiguous.[23] The Ontario government has a variety of relationships with its neighbours around the Great Lakes, although none that appear to be of major political significance. There is a close bilateral relationship between British Columbia and the State of Washington. It is perhaps significant that on the night of his surprising election victory in 1972, Dave Barrett found it necessary to reassure the presumably anxious property owners of the coastal province, via the CBC, that he would do his best to cooperate with Governor Dan Evans.

The most conspicuous and interesting transnational relationships, however, are those that tend to revive the traditional Maritime-New England axis, with the significant difference that Quebec is also now involved. The decline of Montreal in relation to Toronto (itself a consequence of the collapse of the National Policy) has progressed to the point where Quebec now perceives itself as a disadvantaged hinterland like the Maritimes, rather than part of "Central Canada."[24]

Since 1973 there have been annual meetings of New England state governors and eastern provincial premiers, including the premier of Quebec. Although subjects discussed have included fisheries, tourism, and transportation, the major focus of attention has been energy, a fact that explains the timing of the first meeting. A permanent working group on energy has been established, and resolutions adopted at the conferences have dealt with such matters as jurisdiction over offshore oil, electricity exports from Quebec to New England, and the use of surplus oil refinery capacity in the eastern provinces to meet New England's needs. The general tone has been critical of the two federal governments for their alleged indifference to the needs of the states and provinces concerned. Most of the specific proposals, in relation both to energy and to other areas such as tariffs and transportation, have expressed an aspiration to promote regional integration without regard for the Canadian-American boundary, often combined with complaints that the two federal governments, particularly the Canadian, are standing in the way of this development.

In response to the increasing importance of their American ties, and the increasing conflict between their respective economic interests, the provinces have begun to demand a role in foreign policy, and one that would go far beyond the traditional efforts to attract investment or the functional relationships with border states re-

ferred to earlier. At the annual Premiers' Conference in 1977 the following statement was approved by all ten participants:

> While recognizing the primacy of the role of the federal government in international trade relations, the Premiers were of the opinion that the provinces also have legitimate interests and concerns in the international arena. Given these legitimate concerns and the large volume of Canadian trade with the United States, they agreed that it is entirely appropriate for the provinces to assume a more prominent role in Canada-U.S. relations.[25]

More recently the government of Alberta, in a position paper that bears the singularly inappropriate title of *Harmony in Diversity*, has recommended "that the Constitution include provisions that confirm the established legitimate role [sic] of the provinces in certain areas of international relations."[26]

Whatever this ambiguous expression is intended to include, there can be no doubt that Alberta is already deeply involved in Canadian-American relations. Soon after the Lougheed government took office it threatened to open a quasi-diplomatic mission in Washington, forcing the Canadian federal government to respond by adding an official to its own embassy with the sole responsibility of acting as a middleman between Edmonton and Washington. In 1976 Premier Lougheed suggested publicly that congressmen, senators, and governors from the northwestern United States should use their influence to bring about changes in Canadian, as well as American, commercial policy that would facilitate trade between Alberta and their region. Subsequently he suggested that Alberta would allow more natural gas to be exported to the neighbouring states if the Americans would also facilitate exports of beef and petrochemicals. The United States' administration has implied approval or at least acceptance of Alberta's international role through the well-publicized visit of Vice-President Walter Mondale to Edmonton at the end of 1977. Perhaps significantly, Mondale is from Minnesota, the historic spearhead of the American drive to the northwest.

Thus the uneven impact of continental integration on the different provinces of Canada is exposing the Canadian union to unmanageable strains. At the same time as it strengthens some of the provincial governments and encourages all to pursue their divergent interests independently, the process of continental integration seems to make the Canadian federal government increasingly superfluous. There is a parallel to this situation in Western Europe, where the process of continental integration represented by the community institutions in Brussels, and now by the elected European Parliament, has been accompanied by an apparent revival of "regionalism" in the peripheral areas of Italy, France and the United Kingdom, as well as an exacerbation of the sectional-ethnic conflict in Belgium. Both left-wing and right-wing supporters of the traditional centralized states see themselves, like their Canadian counterparts, as fighting a war on two fronts against continentalism and "regionalism." Peripheral separatists and romantic "Europeans," on the other hand, dream of a "Europe of the regions" which will dissolve the old nation-states with their tariffs, armies and frontiers, turn old peripheries into new centres of economic and cultural revival, and encourage contacts between artificially separated contiguous areas like Brittany and Cornwall.[27] Continental integration both weakens the old central governments and creates demands that they be weakened even further. Why should Scotland or Brittany not deal with Brussels, or with German businessmen, directly, rather than through London or Paris? Moreover, if Brussels assumes the old nation-state functions of foreign policy, defence, and macro-economic management, why should London or Paris exist at all? The parallel with recent developments in Quebec or Alberta hardly needs to be emphasized.[28]

CONCLUSION

Closely associated and mutually reinforcing, regionalism and continentalism have always threatened the survival of the Canadian state. The construction of that state was an act of political will in circumstances no less uncertain than those we face today. If in fact men make history, there is no reason to assume that the destruction of the Canadian federal state is inevitable. However, it can only be saved by policies based on a clear appreciation of present realities. . . .

Supporters of decentralization apparently assume that the formal constitution can be adjusted until it reaches some point of equilibrium with the centrifugal tendencies which they perceive in Canadian society, and that pressure for further decentralization will then cease. This ignores the fact that constitutional decentralization will contribute to further socio-economic decentralization, producing a vicious circle of national disintegration. It also fails to see Canadian regionalism in continental perspective. The weaker the Canadian federal state becomes, the more superfluous its few remaining functions will appear, given the fact that military defence and protection for the overseas interests of Canadian business are provided by the United States. The more autonomous the provinces become, the more they will be tempted, with varying degrees of enthusiasm, to pursue the option of north-south regionalism which is offered to them by their immediate neighbours, whose needs and interests appear so similar to their own. If Canadian interests are viewed as no more than the sum of provincial interests, and if provincial interests are defined in terms of east versus west or frost-belt versus sunbelt, the forty-ninth parallel will have no more practical significance than the Mason-Dixon Line or the boundaries of the Louisiana Purchase.

Notes

1. William P. Irvine in Richard Simeon, ed., *Must Canada Fail?* (Montreal: McGill-Queen's University Press, 1977), 170.

2. The Task Force on Canadian Unity, *A Future Together* (Ottawa, 1979), 27. Reproduced with the permission of the Minister of Supply and Services Canada.

3. Patricia J. Appavoo, ed., "Alternatives Canada: A Conference Report," *Behind the Headlines*, 26: 3 (1978): 12.

4. Jon H. Pammett, "Public Orientation to Regions and Provinces," in David J. Bellamy, Jon H. Pammett, and Donald C. Rowat, *The Provincial Political Systems* (Toronto: Methuen, 1976), table at 89.

5. H. W. Odum and H. E. Moore, *American Regionalism* (New York: Henry Holt, 1938), 39.

6. *Ibid.*, 43.

7. Daniel Elazar, *American Federalism: A View from the States*, 1st ed. (New York: Crowell, 1966), 112.

8. Alan C. Cairns, "The Governments and Societies of Canadian Federalism," *Canadian Journal of Political Science* 10: 4 (December 1977): 695-726.

9. Paul F. Sharp, *Whoop-up Country: The Canadian-American West* (Norman: University of Oklahoma Press, 1973), 313.

10. Goldwin Smith, *Canada and the Canadian Question*, new edition (Toronto: University of Toronto Press, 1971), 5.

11. Heather Gilbert, *The End of the Road: The Life of Lord Mountstephen*, vol. II (Aberdeen: Aberdeen University Press, 1977).

12. Quoted in Robert M. Hamilton, ed., *Canadian Quotations and Phrases* (Toronto: McClelland and Stewart, 1952), 154.

13. Quoted in J. Murray Beck, *Pendulum of Power* (Scarborough: Prentice-Hall, 1968), 67.

14. Smith, *Canada and the Canadian Question*, 204.

15. Tom Naylor, *The History of Canadian Business*, vols. I and II (Toronto: Lorimer, 1975).

16. At a Waffle caucus during the 1969 NDP convention, the present writer was astonished to hear a middle-aged British Columbia Waffler proclaim that he looked forward to a "Socialist United States of North America."

17. Kirkpatrick Sale, *Power Shift: The Rise of the Southern Rim and its Challenge to the Eastern Establishment* (New York: Vintage, 1976).

18. Alexis de Tocqueville, *The Old Regime and the French Revolution* (New York: Doubleday, 1955), 30 and *passim*.

19. *Foreign Direct Investment in Canada* (Ottawa: Information Canada, 1972), tables at 23 and 24.

20. See the data on head office locations in "The Financial Post 500," supplement to *The Financial Post*, 16 June 1979.

21. E.g. the comments by Simma Holt (Vancouver-Kingsway) in Canada, *House of Commons Debates*, 1st session, 30th Parliament, 6439-40.

22. *Capital Cities Communications Inc. vs CRTC* decided by the Supreme Court of Canada in 1977. The provinces involved were Alberta, British Columbia, Ontario, and Quebec. Saskatchewan's NDP government, to its credit, intervened on the opposing side.

23. Richard H. Leach, Donald E. Walker, and Thomas A. Levy, "Province-State Transborder Relations: A Preliminary Assessment," *Canadian Public Administration* 16: 3 (Fall 1973): 469-82.

24. E.g. Jacques Henri, "La Dépendence structurelle du Québec dans un Canada dominé par les Etats-Unis," *Choix* 7 (1975): 203-23.

25. Quoted in Government of Alberta, *Harmony in Diversity: A New Federalism for Canada* (Edmonton, 1978), 8.

26. *Ibid.*, 7.

27. E.g. Pierre Fougeyrollas, *Pour une France fédérale : vers l'unité européene par la révolution régionale* (Paris: Denoel, 1968). One might ponder the irony that those political forces in France who most bitterly oppose this point of view have devoted considerable effort over the last fifteen years to encouraging Quebec separatism.

28. For an interesting analysis by a left-wing Scottish

nationalist see Tom Nairn, *The Break-up of Britain: Crisis and Neo-Nationalism* (London: New Left Books, 1977). See also the critical review of the same work by Eric Hobsbawm, "Reflections on 'the Break-up of Britain,' "*New Left Review* 105 (September-October 1977).

Selected Readings

Bercuson, D. J., and Beeckner, P. A., eds. *Eastern and Western Perspectives*. Papers from the Joint Atlantic Canada/Western Canadian Studies Conference. Toronto: University of Toronto Press, 1982.

Gibbins, Roger. *Regionalism: Territorial Politics in Canada and the United States*. Toronto: Butterworths, 1982.

Gibbins, Roger. *Prairie Politics and Society: Regionalism in Decline*. Toronto: Butterworths, 1980.

Simeon, Richard, and Elkins, David. "Regional Political Cultures in Canada." *Canadian Journal of Political Science* 7: 3 (September 1974): 397-437.

Simeon, Richard, "Federalism and Free Trade." In Peter Leslie, ed. *Canada: The State of the Federation 1986*. Kingston: Queen's University, Institute of Intergovernmental Relations, 1987, 189-212.

9. THE CONCEPT OF PROVINCE-BUILDING: A CRITIQUE

R. A. Young, Philippe Faucher, and André Blais

Among political scientists, administrators, and teachers of politics in Canada, a picture of our changing federation has come to be shared widely. This image is labelled "province-building," a term coined by Black and Cairns in a seminal 1966 article.[1] The concept has since been incorporated into much academic and official writing on federal-provincial relations, and it occupies an unquestioned place in the background knowledge of many political analysts. Whether referring to "freewheeling decentralization," the "maximization of a regionally defined social welfare function," or "provincial administrative maturation," its meaning seems clear to most. No equivalent term exists in French, but in English Canada it appealingly comprehends the multifarious activities of provincial governments and, considered as a cause or goal, the concept even appears to offer some leverage in accounting for what provincial states do and for their intransigence in relations with the central government.

However, we think that the picture of province-building has become too vast and lurid. The concept is highly amorphous and complex, and

R. A. Young, Philippe Faucher, and André Blais, "The Concept of Province-Building: A Critique," *Canadian Journal of Political Science* 17:4 (1984): 783-818. Reprinted by permission of the Canadian Political Science Association and the authors. The essay has been edited to suit the needs of this volume.

The authors are grateful for the support of the Social Sciences and Humanities Research Council of Canada. They also benefited from discussions with many of their colleagues of the Canadian Political Science Association, especially Peter Leary.

different analysts emphasize different facets of the phenomenon to which it refers. But logically, "province-building" is just a tag applied to some generalizations about changes in the structure and activities of provincial states. Here we test these propositions, and find several to be inaccurate or overdrawn. Further, it appears that easy acceptance of the province-building image, which emphasizes uniformity and contemporaneity, has obscured interesting variations in provincial policy that deserve study. Since the concept is manifestly weak, its popularity demands explanation, so we briefly explore its functions in the conclusion.

PROVINCE-BUILDING: IMAGE AND PROCESS

The image of province-building is usually as follows. After the Second World War, the importance of provincial constitutional responsibilities increased with the rise of the welfare state. New social programs were sponsored by a powerful central government and provinces were generally willing to implement them with conditional-grant assistance. Around 1960, provincial docility with respect to taxation arrangements and shared-cost programs began to evaporate. Quebec's Lesage government took the lead in enunciating grievances, but all provinces increasingly resisted central government incursions into their jurisdiction and incessantly demanded more tax resources; they also sought influence in areas of Ottawa's jurisdiction. Provincial bureaucracies have grown enormously in size and competence; not only are they essential tools of provincialist politicians, but their own interests also favour expanded, activist states. Increased revenues and new capabilities of policy planning and co-ordination have enabled surer management of socio-economic change. Hence, provincial states have grown in capacity to serve provincial interests—or to shape them. While the provinces are especially concerned with primary industries because of their jurisdiction over increasingly valuable resources, they have also come to intervene more thoroughly in all sectors of provincial economies. These trends have two major effects: given the innate weakness of other integrative mechanisms in the Canadian federation, conflict between the central and provincial governments has increased, and, second, provincial economic policies seriously fragment the Canadian common market, so impeding a coherent response to international economic forces and reducing the surplus which integration produces.

This, then, is the image which the term "province-building" conveys. We expect it is familiar to most, though it must be presented as a composite because (as will be shown) formal definitions are both rare and diverse—and this is one reason why its currency is worth investigating. But analysts do always use the term to refer to a process. And they do tend to agree about two basic features of the changes which constitute it: province-building is considered to be a *recent* phenomenon and it is understood to be a *general* process which has occurred in all Canadian provinces. These key aspects deserve amplification.

Most analysts locate province-building in the post-1945 period, and especially in the 1960s and 1970s. Black and Cairns, unlike many of their successors, were careful to say that Canadians have been building provinces "since 1867," but their account emphasized the 1960-66 period, and they found remarkable the "occurrence of more important changes in Canadian federalism during the past quarter-century than those of the preceding seventy years." Stevenson's de-

scription of the interaction between provincial states and local interests has more historical sweep, but his analysis of state expansion centres on the 1960s and 1970s. Chandler and Chandler find that most significant change in provincial public administration has occurred over the last 25 years: "The maturation of the provinces, often referred to as province-building, is without doubt among the most far-reaching of the transformations." Maxwell and Pestieau say the provinces were content, until the 1960s, "to play a fairly passive role" in economic policy, while Bothwell, Drummond and English find in the past two decades a "pronounced tendency on the part of the provinces to conduct their own economies as far as possible in the narrowest interests of their own workforces or industries." Smiley, finally, finds Canadian federalism changing significantly from "the late 1950s onward": the story since then "is that of the relative weakening of the power of the national government and the strengthening of that of the provinces."[2]

How uniform has the process been? Quebec is considered by many to have led the provincial charge during the Lesage era, and to have been since then both more jealous of social jurisdiction and more aggressive in economic management. But still the underlying forces of fragmentation are claimed to be general: as Black and Cairns argued, "even if Quebec had remained quiescent, it is likely that pressures for change emanating elsewhere in the system would have had an almost similar impact." The Task Force on Canadian Unity agreed that the other provinces "have taken similar, if less drastic, initiatives to support and encourage what amounts to little less than the development of provincial societies." Stevenson writes that "the innovations associated with Manning in Alberta, with Roblin in Manitoba, with Robichaud in New Brunswick, and with Stanfield in Nova Scotia were no less 'revolutionary' than those presided over by Jean Lesage." Cairns takes the view that the "basic orientation" of provincial leaders has been alike, Maxwell and Pestieau

observe a competitive approach to economic policy "in all Canadian provinces during the 1970s,"
and Van Loon and Whittington, with stunning
simplicity, state that "all of the provinces began
to flex new political muscles and the Canadian
public was induced to look more and more to the
provinces for the satisfaction of their needs. The
responsibility for the establishment of governmental priorities in the country shifted from the
federal government to the provinces."[3]

THE LITERATURE ON PROVINCE-BUILDING: SIX PROPOSITIONS

What is the status of the concept? Logically,
"province-building" is a collective term which
subsumes a number of empirical generalizations. These are derived inductively: it is
perceived, for instance, that provincial administrations have increased in size, and this generalization forms part of the set which constitutes
province-building. So one can isolate several
propositions which collectively constitute
"province-building," and these will now be analyzed, and criticized on three main grounds.
First, generalizations often ignore important exceptions. Second, changes in the provinces may
not have affected either state operations or the
federal system in the way depicted in the province-building image. Third, inadequate account
is taken of pre-1960 events: discontinuity is often
described where none exists, and recent change
is magnified.

Proposition One

· The attitude of the provinces towards the central
government has changed: they have come to resist
federal incursions more staunchly and have increased their self-serving demands upon Ottawa.

The literature on province-building abounds with
contentions about qualities like the growing "self-

confidence and assertiveness of provincial governments."[4] Bothwell, Drummond and English
describe "the stampede of provincial politicians
for more power," and they discuss demands for
more fiscal resources with the heavy evaluative
overtones often applied by those writing for broad
consumption about federalism: "The provinces
saw the lush green grass of revenue and yearned to
graze in the federal field; like any good political
husbandman St. Laurent opened the gate before
the beasts kicked down the fence." More judi-
ciously, Simeon has summarized: "In seeking
mastery over the levers to promote their own
economic development the provinces 'intrude' on
Ottawa, seeking to limit federal discretionary
powers such as the power to spend, seeking a
greater provincial voice in federal decisions—
such as transportation and tariffs—which have
major regional effects, and calling for increased
provincial jurisdiction in some areas."[5] No one
could deny that in recent years there have been
important provincial demands made upon Ottawa,
most notably by Quebec, as well as instances of
determined resistance to central policies, especially by Alberta. But these attitudes have not been
uniform across provinces or policy fields, nor are
they unprecedented.

In several realms of social policy, federal
incursions have been accepted. Canadian federalism has accommodated itself to the spread of the
welfare state with an ease and lack of conflict—
and a continuing central predominance—that fails
to square with the endemic disagreement portrayed by the concept of province-building. In
income security, argues Banting, provinces other
than Quebec have not regarded jurisdictional matters as very important (though financing has been
a major issue).[6] In other social fields, jurisdictional docility is very evident, especially among
the weaker provinces. Under the Robichaud government, one of the most centralizing and techno-
cratic in Canada, New Brunswick was willing to
accept federal funding for, and influence over, the
construction of elementary and secondary
schools. When opting-out arrangements in the

1960s allowed provinces to reassert their jurisdictional prerogatives without penalty, only Quebec took advantage of them.

In the economic realm, provinces have objected to federal initiatives which counter established policies. But not all incursions are resisted. In the early 1970s, provincial administrations were concerned with unemployment and inflation, but wished Ottawa to be seen as responsible: they signalled in August 1975 that anti-inflationary moves by the central government would not be resisted. When the Anti-Inflation Board was created, eight provinces brought their public sectors directly under its purview, Saskatchewan and Quebec operating programs in parallel with national legislation.[7] Similarly, most provincial governments supported the Foreign Investment Review Agency in principle, and Saskatchewan, Manitoba and Ontario were strongly favourable: delay and high refusal rates appear to have irritated significantly only Quebec and Alberta. All provinces may find it advantageous to have Ottawa handle such issues which promise political losses or mutually destructive competition.[8] Finally, the provinces accepted a federal presence, through the Department of Regional Economic Expansion (DREE) in forestry, mining, road construction, and tourism. Where the financial position is weak—including Newfoundland, notwithstanding the rhetoric of the Peckford government on the Hibernia issue—this incursion has been welcome.

Demands for greater fiscal resources have generated more acrimony than in any substantive policy field. But the provinces (excepting, in theory, the Lévesque administration in Quebec) have recognized the legitimate role of the central government in stabilization policy, and this implies access to the necessary fields of taxation. The weaker provinces, while occasionally arguing for regionally varied taxation and monetary policies, have traditionally supported a central government with adequate fiscal capacity to exercise its redistributive functions. However strong have been Ontario's demands for more tax room, the province recently rejected a separate personal income

tax. Similarly, it concurred in changes to the equalization system to prevent itself becoming eligible for benefits. How does Ontario maximize autonomy and revenues?

Demands that the central government exercise its powers differently are common now, and some claim this is a recent development.[9] But surely pressure to allow gas exports or to redistribute the Crow benefit was no more extreme than western protests in the 1930s against tariff and exchange-rate policy. And in the East, there has been no recent agitation comparable to the Maritime Rights Movement of the 1920s, a united front of governments, business, labour, and commodity producers which protested the regional effects of national transportation policy and forced freight-rate concessions from Prime Minister Mackenzie King. More generally, there is a sense in which recent provincial efforts are trivial. If province-building means, in part, resistance to real or potential jurisdictional expansion by Ottawa, then the issue was largely settled by 1900 through the efforts of the Mowat administration to have its sovereignty recognized, to have provinces accepted not as mere administrative units but as entities coequal with Ottawa. This arduous struggle was conducted on many fronts, and the clear sense of provincial purpose and the tenacity with which it was pursued are at least as impressive as contemporary "province-building."[10] As for demands, what of the western provinces' efforts to wrest control of their resources from Ottawa, or the struggle by Maritimers to have fiscal need accepted as the ethical basis of federal-provincial finance, or the epic battle of Quebec and Ontario to extend their northern boundaries and escape confinement below the Shield? These early engagements determined the legal and territorial foundations of the state: late twentieth-century skirmishes are, in comparison, a matter of maintaining the edifice in reasonable repair.[11]

Provincial administrations are not manifestly more exigent than they have been in the past. Resistance to jurisdictional incursions varies across policy fields. A simple focus on intransigence obscures instances of slack defence, and questions about these may be very important in explaining what provincial governments do.[12] A simple emphasis on demands distracts us from considering how problems are defined provincially and what means are proposed to remedy them. Finally, belligerence towards Ottawa is not uniformly distributed across the provinces. Socialist governments have tended more than others to support central authority. Manitoba and the Atlantic provinces have often been jurisdictionally permeable. Most troublesome is Ontario, which has in many respects an interest in supporting central policy and a state powerful enough to carry it out; on different issues it must aim to assuage the grievances of other provinces either directly or through the central authority.[13] Either the concept of province-building applies to Ontario or it does not. If it does not, then its range of generality seems shrunken indeed. If it does, then it cannot include the propositions that extreme demands will be made on the central authorities and that all jurisdictional encroachments will be resisted with vigour. In that case it seems to mean that provincial behaviour towards the central government is a function of the societal interests at play and those of politicians and bureaucrats. This is reasonable and invites a search for explanatory factors and an attempt to understand how they combine (and have combined) to produce different policies. But the province-building label only impedes the search for variation and its cause.

Proposition Two

The provinces have greatly increased their financial and human resources, both absolutely and relative to the central government.

It is indisputable that the provinces have secured increased revenues. As Table 9-1 shows, gross general revenues grew from $3.1 billion in 1960, to $14.9 billion in 1970, and to $62.4 billion in 1980. Chandler and Chandler, who found that provincial revenues rose from 8.7 percent of GNP

in 1960 to 18 percent in 1976, make the logical link with provincial state activity: "Only as their revenue bases have been strengthened through tax arrangements, unconditional transfers, and natural resource revenues have the provinces become more autonomous and effective governments."[14]

But not all provinces have had such fortune. Neither has the rhythm of growth been consistent or uniform. Over this period, Alberta's revenues increased by a factor of 32 while New Brunswick's and Saskatchewan's rose by only 13. And disparities in rates of growth have widened over time: the highest rate (Ontario's) was only 1.5 times that of the laggard (British Columbia) over the 1951-1960 period, but in the 1970s Alberta's revenues grew 3.4 times as fast as Ontario's. Moreover, autonomy is best measured by discretionary, not total, revenue. When conditional transfers from the central government are excluded, the rates of revenue growth for the 1960-1970 period fall. Discretionary income growth rises over the 1970s, but conditional transfers still made up 13.7 percent of all provincial revenues in 1980.

Federal government revenues have increased as well. It is true that the rates of growth have been lower than for the provinces. But this difference has been moderating: provincial revenues grew at about 2.3 times the federal rate in the 1960s and 1.3 times in the 1970s (when revenue grew less rapidly for Manitoba and Ontario than for the central government). Further, increases in provincial revenues through the postwar period have not affected the central government's power to manage the economy. Federal tax revenues as a percentage of GNP have been remarkably constant in the postwar era, at 17.3 percent in 1948, 14.8 percent in 1958, 16.8 percent in 1968, and 16.3 percent in 1978.[15]

Is the provincial expansion unprecedented? Historical data in this area are not always reliable, but between 1913 and 1937, gross provincial revenues grew 2.0 times as fast as federal income, which is only slightly less than the rate for the whole 1960-1980 period. According to Perry, pro-

Table 9–1 Government Revenues and Expenditures ($000 000s)

	*1960***		*1970*		*1980*
		% *increase*		*%* *increase*	
Gross general revenue					
municipal governments	1 894	(306)	7 682	(219)	24 496
provincial governments*	3 127	(378)	14 935	(318)	62 359
central government	6 251	(166)	16 642	(251)	58 362
Gross general expenditure					
municipal governments	1 891	(358)	8 652	(223)	27 978
provincial governments*	3 506	(321)	14 752	(320)	62 009
central government	6 584	(139)	15 728	(332)	67 880

* Figures exclude the Yukon and the Northwest Territories.

** In a preliminary version of this article delivered at the annual meeting of the Canadian Political Science Association in 1983, an incorrect series was used for 1960 provincial expenditures. Consequently, percentages based on those figures are incorrect.

Source: Canada, Statistics Canada, cat. 68–203, *Municipal Government Finance* (Preliminary for 1980): cat. 68–207, *Provincial Government Finance*: cat. 68–211, *Federal Government Finance*. (Figures include debt retirement.) Reproduced with permission of the Minister of Supply and Services.

vincial own-source revenue increased 333 percent between 1874 and 1904, a rate 2.09 times that of the central government.[16] So, although the current magnitude of provincial income relative to GNP is unprecedented, the increase at the provincial level relative to Ottawa is not. Moreover, this gap in growth rates is narrowing, a trend which has been partly obscured by the exceptional revenue growth of Alberta.

With respect to the provincial public services, the evidence of province-building seems very strong, at least in so far as sheer numbers indicate greater capacity for action. Provincial civil service employment rose by over 400 percent between 1946 and 1971, the provincial public sector as a whole came very close to matching Ottawa's in size, and its quality may have increased as well: in the case of Quebec, for one, the ratio of professionals grew from 1:15 in 1959 to 1:3 in 1978.[17]

Assessing growth in the state is tricky because of changes and differences in classifications and structures, as well as the diversity of data

sources. But it is clear, first, that there has been important variation between provinces. Civil Service Commissions' figures show the public services increased, on average, 174 percent between 1960 and 1976, but the rates varied from 56 percent in Saskatchewan to 397 percent in Alberta.[18] Some of this growth represents the assumption of responsibilities formerly carried out by municipalities, such as welfare provision and hospital services. To avoid this distortion, one can lump all municipal and educational employees into the provincial public sector, excluding only those in nonprofit "institutions," and when this is done, it emerges that the overall provincial share of public employment was much the same in 1975 (54%) as in 1947 (52%).[19] Another qualification concerns various kinds of quasi-autonomous organizations beyond the normal departmental structures, which have been described as "major vehicles for expansion of the public service."[20] Such bodies are a rich area for study, but rapid rates of formation indicate nothing about their functions. The most significant growth seems to have been among agencies established to provide advice, and so their proliferation may reflect not an increased managerial capacity but rather a greater need for the state to secure information and consent for policy-making and implementation.[21]

Comparison with the central administration reveals faster growth in provincial bureaucracies, as the federal civil service grew only 115 percent between 1960 and 1976. But two qualifications need to be made. First, Ottawa's growth rates are somewhat depressed by the inclusion of an old and labour-intensive service, the post office. Second, central government expansion was very rapid in the late 1940s and 1950s. Growth between 1941 and 1961 was 350 percent, including the post office, and 467 percent when it is excluded—as opposed to the provincial rate of 198 percent. It was in the 1960s that growth in provincial civil services was most rapid, at a rate of 109 percent as compared with 51 percent in Ottawa.[22] The provinces were then catching up, not to an ever-dominant federal state, but to one which had expanded enormously in the preceding two decades. This trend now seems to have reversed. The federal civil service was larger than those of all the provinces combined until 1970; between then and 1976, the federal service grew 42.5 percent while the provincial total increased by only 30.9 percent. "Indeed, the *only* segment of public employment that has clearly expanded at a faster rate than 'normal' in the last few years appears to be the federal civil service."[23]

The quality of public servants is a more subjective area, but it is an important one. The contention that provincial bureaucracies have increased in competence is central to many accounts of province-building. Black and Cairns went so far as to say that "the traditional English-Canadian view of the federation as a pyramid or hierarchy becomes anachronistic with the location of superior administrative talent within the provincial rather than the federal functional departments."[24] But little evidence of this trend is produced; instead, many authors cite Simeon's

account of the Quebec delegation's superior pension scheme in 1964 or rely on anecdotal material.[25]

Some data are now available which bear on the competence of Canadian bureaucracies. Gunderson has found that 11.1 percent of the federal public service consists of professionals, as opposed to 21.5 percent in the provinces. But many provincial "professionals" are in social work and health, and the category is vague in any case. When one considers "highly qualified manpower" (HQM)—those employees with a university degree—the federal administration is far superior, with 6.3 percent of all HQM in Canada, as opposed to 3.9 percent at the provincial level.[26] Moreover, growth of the Ottawa civil service in the 1970s was more rapid than average (5%) among the scientific and professional (8.5%), administrative (12.9%) and executive (16%) components.[27]

In summary, the provinces have gained more financial resources. They have all, however, taken on new responsibilities, and conditional grants still make up significant proportions of revenues. Revenue increases have been very uneven across the provinces, and the strong position of Alberta is quite anomalous. The revenue balance has not tilted decisively against the central government, nor have the provincial battalions come to outweigh Ottawa's. More work is needed on the question of expertise—its growth, organization, and influence—but quantitative measures of quality do not show that Ottawa has lost dominance.

Proposition Three

The scope of provincial public policy has widened enormously, and state intervention, especially in the economic realm, has become deep and pervasive.

Cairns best makes the general case. Provincial states, like others, are "aggressive actors steadily extending their tentacles of control, regulation and manipulation into society"; a province seeks to form "webs of interdependence springing from the particular version of socio-economic integration it is pursuing"; hence, provincial governments "work toward the creation of limited versions of a politically created provincial society and economy, and the national government works toward the creation of a country-wide society and economy."[28]

The evidence most often cited concerns spending, which has grown very much at the provincial level. So, Chandler and Chandler show that the provincial share of government spending on goods and services rose from 18.6 percent in 1955 to 43 percent in 1975, and Simeon notes that in 1976, the provincial and municipal governments spent $52 billion as compared to Ottawa's $39 billion.[29] As Table 9-1 shows, gross provincial expenditure in 1980 was 17.7 times as large as it was in 1960, while federal spending grew only 10.3 times. Moreover, a large proportion of provincial spending consists of exhaustive expenditures, which have a more determinable economic impact than do the transfers which make up much of federal spending.

Such figures are impressive, but they can mislead. First, summary figures conceal very large interprovincial differences in spending growth. The rate of growth in Quebec between 1960 and 1980 was almost twice that in Manitoba and Saskatchewan. As well, the growth in gross general expenditure of Ottawa exceeded that of the provinces over the 1970s, which must reflect provincial restraint towards the end of the decade and Ottawa's large deficits. Finally, a significant part of provincial expenditure has been within the framework of conditional grants. This is especially true of the weaker provinces, but most find conditional programs impossible to refuse. And these grants do change provincial priorities: "If conditional grants did not significantly affect the independence of a provincial cabinet in at least some of its policy choices, the grant would have failed its basic rationale."[30] One can focus on discretionary expenditure by sub-

tracting 200 percent of conditional transfers from provincial spending and adding 100 percent of them to federal totals (while also subtracting unconditional transfers from the latter).[31] When this is done, interprovincial differences in growth rates swell, with the position of Alberta (and to a lesser extent of British Columbia) being extreme. Federal expenditure in 1980 emerges as 162 percent of combined provincial spending, rather than 109 percent. These corrections gloss over important structural changes in federal-provincial finance, some of which have been justified, in part, as a response to inexorable province-building. Nevertheless, they should give some pause to those who still see shrinking Ottawa besieged by provincial titans.

Sharp increases in provincial spending are, of course, nothing new. Total expenditure at the provincial level grew 1.6 times as fast as the central government's over the 1871-1901 period, and 2.8 times as fast between 1901 and 1931. "In all peacetime years except for 1896-1901, there has been a tendency for the share of the P-M [provincial-municipal] sector of total government expenditures to rise."[32]

Spending is not the only evidence of state activity. Regulation is at least as important, and its growth has become the object of much attention. At the provincial level, regulatory agencies remain little known, but examples abound of new initiatives in pollution control, industrial safety, agricultural marketing and consumer protection. As Chandler and Chandler observe: "Since 1945 there has been a remarkable expansion of such agencies in both provincial and federal politics."[33] But the greatest expansion of provincial regulatory activity took place in the early years of the century, as the provincial states established an initial presence in many policy fields, and particularly in economic regulation. By the 1930s, most provinces had established a framework of control over public health, consumer protection, produce grading and inspection, factory and mining conditions, securities, trust, loan and insurance firms, motor cars, trucking, utilities, resource conservation and liquor.[34] Of all existing provincial economic regulation statutes, 59 percent were passed by 1949. Priest and Wohl, who argue that the 19 percent of statutes passed in the 1970s are evidence of "particular rapid growth," could have written in 1919 that 33 percent had been passed in the preceding decade.[35] The 1910-1940 period was one of rapid expansion of state regulation. It is interesting to consider why regulation was the dominant instrument of the time, and to explore the conditions under which it is currently deployed. It is not true, though, that provincial regulatory activity has expanded exponentially.

Crown corporations are another matter. Here the evidence lends support to the view of new provincial activity. Fully 76 percent of provincial public enterprises have been established since 1960—as compared to 58 percent at the federal level.[36] Most of the present assets of these crown corporations were in place by 1960, but the rising numbers testify to more precise state intervention and greater direct involvement in production. The effects and causes of this development deserve close exploration, for here is one area where provincial activity has been markedly innovative, and where growth in expenditure has been much more rapid (3.5 times since 1958) than Ottawa's.[37] This might support Jenkin's claim that "the province-building phenomenon indicates an awareness on the part of certain provincial governments that economic and industrial restructuring demands initiatives that are far more sophisticated and *dirigiste* than the fiscal and regulatory policies so common at the federal level.[38]

But a number of considerations should shade the picture of *dirigisme* which the term "province-building" connotes. First, provincial spending on economic functions remains relatively small. Most of the great increase in expenditure has occurred within the traditional policy fields of debt service, protection, transportation and communications, health, social welfare, education, and unconditional transfers to municipalities. These accounted for 86 percent of total spending in 1960 and 80 percent in 1980. Relative spending on industrial development, transportation and communication, natural resources, and transfers to provincial enterprises has actually *declined* over the postwar period.[39] Spending on industrial development alone has increased from 0.4 percent of the total in 1960 to 1.0 percent in 1980, but spending of about $600 million in the latter year is not very impressive testimony that "most provinces are now seeking ways to restructure their economies in the direction of less specialization."[40]

If provinces were committed to such strategies, one would find substantial and increasing direct aid to manufacturing industries. Complete figures are available for Ontario and Quebec, where such aid did rise significantly over the 1960s and early 1970s. In Quebec, however, direct grants peaked at 1.0 percent of net government expenditure in 1976, and they have been less in Ontario. Total loans and loan guarantees outstanding have never exceeded 2 percent of current expenditures.[41] There has been, therefore, an increase in direct aid, but at least in these two provinces it was neither smooth nor ceaselessly expanding. Moreover, most direct assistance programs are open to any existing firm, and criteria of eligibility are broad. In Ontario and Quebec, there has been a close correspondence between the sectoral distribution of aid and the existing distribution of manufacturing value-added. More generally, where states have acted with discrimination, their intervention has been highly selective, addressing key growth areas (or revenue sources) or soft sectors (revenue drains), while leaving much else undisturbed. Alberta's initiatives in nonrenewable resources are exhaustively documented, but its forestry policy has been unexceptional. Newfoundland's efforts to control the offshore have attracted much attention, but its stance on minerals has been weak. Ontario has moved in food processing, but not in chemicals. The occasional highly visible provincial intervention, in short, does not equate with thorough and planned industrial restructuring.

Federal action has dwarfed provincial efforts. Ottawa has evolved comprehensive strategies in energy, communications and microelectronics, fisheries, and the soft sectors of textiles and footwear (through the Canadian Industrial Renewal Board). Such initiatives date from the early 1960s when the assault on inefficiency in the primary sector was spearheaded by the Agricultural and Rural Development Act. The General Development Agreement arrangements under DREE reinforced the capacity of Ottawa to modernize and rationalize or to prop up industrial sectors, as do the new Industrial Regional Development Agreements. Federal manipulation of corporate tax rates and bases has also grown enormously since 1960, as the system has become geared to the alleviation of (centrally defined) structural problems. The regional and sectoral effects of federal tax expenditures have not yet been closely calculated, but they are probably differential and very likely significant: tax expenditures for manufacturing alone rose from $88 million in 1960 to $540 million in 1979, in *constant* dollars.[42] In general, most provinces have had to react to spreading federal initiatives as the emphasis of Ottawa's policy shifted through the 1960s and 1970s from macroeconomic management to micro-level and structural concerns.[43]

Are provincial efforts to stimulate economic growth and to decrease the specialization of regional economies something new? Simply, the answer is no. Early provincial administrations, governing largely empty lands, were vitally concerned with development. All invested heavily in infrastructure, especially in railroads: consider Ontario's effort to build the Temiskaming and Northern Ontario or Quebec's support for the National Transcontinental.[44] H.V. Nelles has traced the deep involvement of Ontario governments in the resource sectors; while this is often cited to show the link between provincial states and resource industries, the calculated nature of the policies and the magnitude of intervention are neglected. Recent efforts are presumed to be more planned and sweeping, but the manufactur-

ing condition applied to timber and pulpwood is at least comparable with recent moves by the Ontario government to assist the automobile industry, and the application of the same condition to ores bears more than a passing resemblance to the new mineral taxation system of 1975 (which met a similar end). It is perhaps worth reflecting upon the $2 million loan guarantee extended to F. Clergue's Consolidated Lake Superior Corporation in 1904.[45] If that sum is taken as a proportion of total provincial liabilities, an equivalent guarantee today would be in the order of $5.2 billion. Provincial governments have aimed to attract manufacturing and to stimulate diversification since the time of the National Policy. Celebrated cases of interprovincial competition have occurred (and have been engendered too, recently, by federal efforts to implant industry on the periphery). But is there much novelty in Hydro-Quebec's cut-rate prices for the Pechiney aluminum smelter, or Alberta's initiatives in petrochemicals? Surely it is no innovation at all for provinces to "promote resource-related economic development; ensure a greater capture of economic rent by the provincial state than in the past; encourage related development through forward and backward linkages; promote greater participation by local capitalist enterprises; and use public enterprise as a last resource to protect provincial economic interests."[46]

What may be new is that provinces have a greater capacity to engage in these activities, that they may be more prepared than in the past to use direct measures, and especially public enterprises, to achieve them. Here the uniquely powerful position of Alberta must be reemphasized. It is not a province like the others, and one cannot generalize from the superb study by Richards and Pratt—as the authors themselves warned—to the weak (and Ottawa-led) spending in the Atlantic region, Ontario's strategic interest in the status quo, or Quebec's peculiar structural problems. The sweeping concept of province-building obscures the significant questions. What sectors have most preoccupied provincial governments? When? What instruments were deployed to foster them? Did this lead to conflict with Ottawa or not?

Finally, in the economic realm, it is clear that Ottawa's power and activity continues to dwarf the provinces: it is hard not to agree with Cairns that "in spite of the relative weakening of its position since the war and postwar years the federal government indisputably remains the strongest and most important government in the system."[47]

Proposition Four

> Provincial policy-making has changed profoundly, to become centralized, planned, and coherent.

This proposition is crucial to an image of the provincial state as the focus of political demands and the manager of provincial societies. Despite the weak evidence that intervention has increased significantly, the province-building picture may be preserved if state activity has become more purposive, incisive, and co-ordinated. Chandler and Chandler, for instance, define province-building largely in terms of administrative capacity: "All provinces have undergone substantial institutional maturation through the process of province-building. This has meant, above all, an expansion in the capacity of provincial systems to respond to and resolve social and economic issues." Pratt, similarly, describes the emergence in Edmonton of a "province-building administration committed to long-range economic planning, policy coordination, and a consistent strategy of economic development." The general argument is that the provinces have managed the problems of policy contradiction or overlap which arise when a state becomes active over more policy fields, that they now plan initiatives and so are less able to tolerate disruption, and that they aim, therefore, to direct coherently complex provincial societies with minimal federal interference.[48]

The principal mechanisms of coordination include central agencies, cabinet committees, and horizontal or field portfolios. But field portfolios have carried little coordinating power in Ontario, and in Quebec they appear to handle particular dossiers, but to be incapable of supervising the operations of line departments.[49] Cabinet committees are less developed than in Ottawa, though they do seem to have been effective in a negative fashion, as the well implanted envelope system has held down spending.[50] The record of central agencies is mixed. Studies of policy formation in Ottawa show the power to resist of determined and expert line departments, and there is obvious disillusionment with the elaborate central control and guidance systems established in the early 1970s.[51] At the provincial level the record is less clear, but the weight of policy expertise probably lies even more with large, technically oriented departments than it does in Ottawa. Tools to aid central agency managers, such as Management by Objectives, Program Planning, Budgeting Systems, and—especially—policy evaluations are less favoured and less common in the provinces: even in Quebec, little has been done to evaluate existing programs.[52]

Any central coordination must be impeded by the proliferation of special-purpose agencies in the provinces. All have some independence from normal departmental structures and from the executive, and this autonomy is maintained, presumably, by their specialized expertise and close links with clienteles. They are at least as likely as their federal counterparts to escape from financial and policy control.[53] The same holds for public enterprises. And, in general, the great departmental growth of recent years means that the task of coordination has become more difficult due to the multiplication of branches and the greater depth of the bureaucracy. Perhaps the beefed-up central agencies are only managing to keep abreast of these changes. While the growth and elaboration of provincial states must be tallied on one side of the province-building ledger, these same trends, in the absence of further evidence, must weigh against the argument that central control has increased. Coordination was perhaps greater when individual cabinet ministers were more firmly in command of their departments than they can be today, and when they could work out together a response to cross-portfolio problems. When ministers were part-timers and premiers finally decided most issues, central control may have reached a zenith from which it has since steadily declined.

Finally, centralization in a spatial sense has not occurred in most provinces. The image of the autonomous, *dirigiste* provincial administration makes little room for powerful subunits, yet municipalities in most provinces retain important revenue sources and discretionary powers, and they are active in both the social and economic fields. It is true that the level of provincial funding for municipal activities has risen and that an increasing proportion of transfers has come to consist of conditional grants.[54] But there are significant interprovincial variations in these figures, and transfers to municipalities overall form a smaller proportion of their budgets than do federal transfers to the Atlantic provinces, which have supposedly been able to engage in province-building. The discretion and veto power of municipalities and other junior authorities remains formidable in most provinces. The Ontario government, for instance, has had to work hard to cajole provincial hospitals to adopt its buy-Canadian purchasing policy, and it has not entirely succeeded. Arguably, the rise of metropolitan authorities has increased municipal power: the Toronto Islands dispute and the maintenance of control by Montreal over Olympic installations (until long after the damage was done) are instructive examples. In any case, efforts to centralize most functions for the purpose of coherent planning and economic efficiency have succeeded only in New Brunswick, and several attempts to integrate municipal authorities into comprehensive provincial development plans have come to little, most notably in the case of Ontario's Design for Development.[55]

Another much noted change in provincial public administration has been the creation of elaborate planning systems. Planning is undoubtedly a critical function, and its acceptance testifies to a shift in both popular and elite conceptions of the state's role, for it suggests the possible manipulation of previously unmanageable forces, and consequently a heightened responsibility of the state for the existing distribution of benefits—an imputed responsibility which provincial politicians have not always embraced with enthusiasm. Still, data-gathering facilities have been improved (though all provinces remain dependent on Ottawa in this domain), and planning and analysis groups are found within departments and central agencies, and also as distinct advisory bodies, like the recently abolished Office de planification et de développement du Québec.

To be effective in any case, planning groups and agencies must persuade other bureaucratic units to accept their formulations. In Ottawa, within departments, planning groups have had mixed results, as Prince and Chenier have shown.[56] Little comparative work has been done, but are such groups likely to have been more successful in the provinces, where an emphasis on pragmatic program delivery, a lack of commitment by senior managers to quantitative techniques, and overall financial restraint are all more pronounced than in Ottawa? Certainly the record of such units in Quebec has not been impressive.[57] The problem is more severe when departmental plans involve commissions, regulatory agencies, and public enterprises. Incorporating them, like exerting suasion over line departments, is a problem faced by central planning units.[58] Judging by the Ontario and Quebec experience, such units are also hindered by frequent reorganization of central structures, by the emergence of departmental or supra-departmental competitors, and by the inability to ensure that funds are allocated in accordance with prescribed patterns. This last is the critical planning stage which is rarely attained, because it constrains politicians in a way that publicizing vague objectives and choosing expediently from a smorgasbord of programs does not.[59]

Planning rhetoric should not be confused with reality. Case studies of provincial policy choices and of eventual outcomes remain very rare, and it is far easier to accept formal planning documents at face value than it is to find information about the realities of implementation. In the mid-1960s, for instance, the Quebec Department of Natural Resources, flush with enthusiasm to plan forest management from first principles, undertook a comprehensive planning process. Of particular concern were vast tracts of under-exploited land leased by the major firms. But it was not until 1975 that some reallocation of limits began, and this has been minor.[60] (In the meantime, mills have closed and changed hands, acid rain has confounded growth projections, and harvesting methods and cost structures have altered.) Similarly, Newfoundland's development strategy, as espoused in *Managing All Our Resources*, is comprehensive, thorough, and statist; but it remains a fond hope. The *Bâtir le Québec* document of 1979 laid out a comprehensive development strategy for the Quebec economy. But change in the program mix actually delivered was marginal at best, and the plan was explicitly indicative, designed only to orient the expectations of actors in the private sector.

Finally, policy implementation poses problems for provincial administrations. Planned change can be resisted by those called upon to modify their activities. It has been argued that provinces are highly capable of coordinating policy because they "have a much smaller range of diversities to encompass than their federal counterpart."[61] On the face of it, this is true of necessity, but intraprovincial schisms may be more salient and less amenable to complex trade-offs

than are regional differences at the national level. And particular interests may be relatively more powerful. Hence, an expanded capacity to manage socio-economic evolution could provoke an increased focus on the provincial state by more interested and demanding groups, so leading to decreased policy coherence. Such considerations concern the degree of autonomy of provincial states and their resources relative to major societal actors. *Within* the rubric of province-building, authors take very different positions upon the issue of whether stronger provincial states serve as instruments of local elites or whether they are capable ultimately of restructuring and reorienting provincial interests. But in either case, as Nordlinger has pointed out, the extent of state power cannot be simply inferred from financial and administrative resources:

> All other things being equal, a state with wide-ranging, penetrative capacities is confronted with markedly greater private demands and pressures, and is thus more susceptible to societal constraints than one whose capacities tend toward the other end of the continuum. And the dependence of private actors upon a highly developed mixed-economy welfare state is at least partly offset by the state's need for societal co-operation in formulating and implementing its ambitious social and economic policies.[62]

The realities of coordination and planning, therefore, may belie appearances. New structures and processes may not have substantially increased socio-economic control or produced the coherence ascribed to state policy in the province-building view. Indeed, given the paucity of studies of the normal functioning of provincial governments, policy coherence may have been noticed most when their projects have collided with those of the central government—but this will occur precisely *when* some coherence has been achieved. A massive effort, like Castonguay's in social services, may rock federal-provincial relations, but it may be entirely exceptional in the piecemeal and pragmatic world of provincial administration. Perhaps it would be useful to distinguish, then, between the occasional coherent policy thrust by a province, which must produce an aggressive stance towards Ottawa in relation to areas under central jurisdiction or influence, and more common instances when federal initiatives disrupt existing provincial programs (with effects more precisely measurable than in the past), provoking defensive reactions. With differences in policy formulation and outcomes carefully described, the search for causal factors can proceed.

Proposition Five

but it requires a bur. structure bur. can operate in conflict with resource industries

Provinces are most closely linked with the resource sectors, and so is province-building.

As Black and Cairns put it, "probably the most important aspect of province-building concerns the growth of influential elites in politics, administration, and resource-based industries."[63] The currency of such propositions owes much to the work of Nelles and of Richards and Pratt, but while widely generalized, they are rarely supported by systematic argument and evidence. Stevenson provides the most cogent exposition. He claims that after the National Policy took hold the economy could be broken down into secondary manufacturing (closest to the Ontario government), export-oriented agriculture (linked to the western provinces), and resource-exporting industries, predominant only in British Columbia but, of the three sectors, the one most "intimately associated with the provincial government, because the provinces owned most of the lands and resources." Manufacturers had some influence in Ottawa, but "only the banks, the life insurance companies, the steamship lines and the transcontinental railways were almost exclusively oriented towards the central government." After the Second World War, manufacturing fell under American dominance and

became more closely linked with the Ontario government, which fights for autonomy to support it. The massive expansion of the resource sectors is also geared to United States markets, and is firmly linked with the provincial states. In general, where the resource-exporting sector has grown most, provincial autonomy is most pronounced.[64]

But the straightforward association of provinces with resource industries poses some problems. First, these industries account for a very small percentage of revenues in most provinces, and this proportion has been declining steadily.[65] Low taxation of the resource industries could reflect a privileged position, but the trend of expenditures also began to decline early in the century, and resources, including agriculture, now account for only 4.9 percent of gross provincial expenditures. One could also argue that resource industries are basic to most provincial economies, so provincial administrations are vitally concerned with them (as manifested, perhaps, in favourable regulatory environments or tax holidays or supportive crown corporations). But primary industries now account for less than 10 percent of total output in every province except Saskatchewan (31%) and Alberta (19%).[66] More generally, the view that secondary manufacturing depends on (provincial) primary inputs, and that services to both similarly depend on a healthy primary base, was most persuasive in the early 1970s when raw material shortages emerged and when it appeared that this might reflect a permanent condition of global scarcity. Firms moved to secure supply, and governments enjoyed heightened bargaining power. But in recessionary times, it is not access to resources that counts, but access to markets, and this renders primary industries dependent on the fortunes of their downstream customers rather than vice versa.[67]

In general, analysts of province-building neglect the important federal role in resource development (in part because they neglect agriculture, an area of concurrent jurisdiction).[68] But the central government has a large presence in basic research, essential infrastructure, and support for investment and production. Its role is greatest in agriculture and the fisheries and frontier energy development, but DREE and its predecessors (and the Department of Finance) have figured in mining and forestry and oil and gas. Since 1871, the federal share of total state spending on resource development has ranged between 50 percent and 89 percent, and it was over 50 percent through the 1960s. Between 1956 and 1971, central government spending on natural resources and primary industries dropped as a percentage of the total in West Germany, Switzerland, the United Kingdom and the United States—but in Canada it rose.[69] The federal role in energy has increased since then, of course, notably with the National Energy Program, and involvement in other resource fields is unlikely to diminish with the new positive approach to regional development under the Department of Regional Industrial Expansion.[70]

Still, students of province-building tend to downplay the importance of the central government to the resource industries. In part, this may be because "resource" denotes primary extraction, and the focus is on sectors rather than companies. But few important firms are engaged solely in primary industry. Most are integrated forward into manufacturing and services. The model of the Alberta wildcatter, anxiously supporting Premier Lougheed against Ottawa's tax grabs, cannot be generalized very far.

Consider the forest sector—logging, lumber, and pulp and paper—which is the premier resource industry in Canada. The central players are the pulp and paper companies, which control most large logging operations and which have become increasingly dominant in the lumber industry. Of course these firms are interested in provincial governments. They set tax and royalty levels, provide infrastructure, and regulate or supply the vital factors of production—raw materials, labour, and electricity. Ultimately, the provinces control access to the resource and its price, and their power has been demonstrated in the past, most notably, perhaps, during the 1930s when they enforced cartelization. But if the provinces are not threatening access to the raw material, the companies must be most preoccupied with the central government. Transportation policy vitally concerns the industry. Ottawa sets tariff policies which affect the size of foreign markets, and it provides export assistance to reach them. Monetary policy shapes the rate of investment and affects the exchange rate, which is crucial to exports, operating ratios, and profitability: in 1977, for instance, 50 percent of Price's profits were attributable to the low Canadian dollar.[71] Taxation policies, and especially investment incentives, are most significant for the industry. When Abitibi-Price decided to acquire the Labrador linerboard mill in Newfoundland, the generous timber limits and the low rate of stumpage provided by the province were significant incentives; of compelling interest was the $200 million in unused capital cost allowance which the federal government agreed could accompany the purchase. In 1980, had all the provinces reduced the royalties extracted from the forest industries by one-half, firms would have saved about $79 million; yet the 3 percent inventory allowance introduced by Ottawa in 1977 was worth $108 million. The investment tax credit saved forestry firms $102 million in 1980—over twice what they paid the provinces in mining and logging taxes.[72]

Of course, one can generalize from pulp and paper no more satisfactorily than from fish or oil or iron ore. Much more research is needed on the precise relationships between different industries and both levels of government over time. But the simple assumption that jurisdiction over resources makes provincial states the principal focus of primary industries, and that these sectors must have a privileged spot in provincial plans, is insupportable on the evidence provided to date.[73]

Proposition Six

> Province-building conflicts with nation-building: in particular, provincial economic interventions fragment the common market and cause significant welfare losses.

There are three central ideas here. The first is that province-building has resulted in endemic conflict between the central government and the provinces: "Federal-provincial competition is not abnormal, or sporadic. It is frequent and widespread."[74] Second, there is the assumption that federalism has become a zero-sum game, in which goals achieved by one side represent losses for the other. As Stevenson puts it at the conceptual level, there "are really only two concepts of federalism, which may be viewed as opposite ends of a continuum . . . . Centripetal federalists prefer to strengthen the federal government's power at the expense of the provincial governments; centrifugal federalists prefer to do the reverse." Or, as Simeon put the fundamental polarity: "On the one hand there is a search for national community and national institutions capable of dealing effectively with common problems and achieving common purposes: this is the goal of nation-building. On the other hand is the desire to promote regional diversity, to permit locally defined communities to grow and pursue their own purposes: this is the goal of province-building."[75] The third theme is that destructive conflict surfaces most surely in the economic realm, as provincial efforts to build diversified economies must impair the overall common interest in the gains arising from interregional specialization. This problem defined the framework of Maxwell and Pestieau's treatment of the federation, and they concluded that, "in short, province-building and nation-building are not

compatible, at least in their present forms. They lead inevitably to federal-provincial clashes over national policy."[76]

Matters of jurisdiction are a zero-sum contest, and the long constitutional debates of the 1960s and 1970s threw open fundamental questions which affected all provinces. They also devalued the existing framework and encouraged unconstitutional raids of policy fields. Substantive matters became issues of constitutional principle. But not all incursions have been resisted, and not all provinces have acted aggressively; even at this basic level, conflict is not omnipresent. On questions of taxation, conflict can be even more intense since governments cannot occupy any area to their satisfaction without adequate revenues. But in establishing fiscal arrangements, the interests of the various provinces are highly diverse, and so non-zero-sum compromises have been possible. Indeed, as equalization spreads, the federal role is increasingly transparent; provincial leaders do not so much look to Ottawa now as through it, to their fellows.

As for substantive policy, much discord has been made evident. It may be that political scientists are prone to study conflict, or are inclined, perhaps, to focus on political actors, whose discussions must be conflictive since they concern matters irresolvable at the official level. In this way, federal institutions tend to expose policy disagreement; as Banting remarks, "federalism's primary contribution may be to the visibility of co-ordination failures."[77] The obverse is that co-ordination successes are not likely to be noticed. In any case, it is clear that on many important issues the attitudes of federal and provincial representatives are not fundamentally opposed. The central authorities have acted in Washington on behalf of British Columbia lumber producers in concert with the provincial administration, and even while disagreeing with Saskatchewan's potash policy Ottawa still protected the province from foreign pressure.[78] Particularly when spending is involved, there are many significant opportunities for fruitful collaboration, and a good number have been grasped by politicians and officials. While some are desperate efforts, like the alliance of the Cape Breton Development Corporation and the Sydney Steel Corporation, they can also be found in important sectors, as in the Ottawa-Ontario-Quebec programs to modernize the pulp and paper industry, or the mass transit initiatives involving the Department of Transport and the Urban Transportation Development Corporation and Bombardier. They can also be found in contentious fields like energy when one looks hard enough.[79] Province-building's presumption of conflict tends to sweep over the interesting question: where does cooperation exist and who benefits?

It is not clear why the zero-sum view of federalism should be presumed to pervade the entire central and provincial state apparatuses. Do politicians lack motivation to cooperate? Not always: spending opportunities, genuine policy achievements, and the image of effectiveness may all be realized, at times, through cooperative or at least coordinated activity. Some provincial politicians have run—and won—on the grounds that their party is most capable of cooperating with Ottawa, and some Conservative electoral appeal lay in their relatively conciliatory stance towards the provincial governments. But these instances, many would argue, are remarkable because they are unusual (and studies of co-operation and its motives are rare). So let us presume that politicians see most advantage, most of the time, in conflict. Must the same hold true for civil servants, who are ascribed much power by many analysts of province-building?

One possibility is that provincial program officials are more expert than before, and so are better equipped to resist the plans and prescriptions of their central counterparts. But this cannot hold if it is also true that a professional consensus between officials at both levels helped cooperative federalism to function in the 1950s and 1960s. Nor is it the case that officials

have been displaced from federal-provincial contact: in 1967, official-level meetings accounted for 89 percent of all encounters, and the figure in 1977 was 88 percent.[80]

Increased central control is the explanation favoured by many. The argument is that conflict has become more thoroughgoing in recent years because politicians and the new central agencies close to them made it clear to the lower echelons that new global priorities were operative and would dictate substantive policy stances: programmatic objectives were subordinated to power and prestige. "The previous practice of sectoral departments in one jurisdiction working out solutions to shared problems with their counterparts in another jurisdiction is being displaced by one which is dominated by federal and provincial commissars who oversee the totality of intergovernmental relations on behalf of their respective governments."[81]

There are some difficulties with this proposition. Not all provinces have established ministries of intergovernmental relations or well-staffed central units to control interactions. Where they are in place, it is not evident that such structures have been capable of coordinating line departments. Resistance is likely—the "commissars" reference is by a former deputy minister—and intergovernmental affairs agencies are only one among many central and control units.[82] How close is their purview of intergovernmental contacts? Do officials send along copies of correspondence or report telephone calls? Can intergovernmental affairs units routinely prevail when proposals involving collaboration are moving towards decision? Will their position remain tenable if they consistently frustrate the objectives of line departments? Much information is lacking here, but positive answers to such questions would be needed to substantiate the thesis that pervasive discord can be engendered by units specialized in intergovernmental affairs.

Most significantly, it is not clear that officials see their interest as lying in conflict. There are many policy fields where successful action is impossible without the collaboration or passive cooperation of the other level of government. Analysts of province-building tend to presume that officials have an interest in the growth of the provincial state because they seek to maximize personal benefits and departmental resources.[83] But in the federal system, provincial civil servants who wish to increase their resources, social impact, personal prestige and benefits must, in many departments, have an interest in ensuring that their projects are not frustrated by their federal counterparts. In some cases they seem to have maximized autonomy and budgets by tapping the federal treasury.[84] This is extreme, but there are situations in transportation, agriculture, forestry, consumer affairs, industrial development, culture, tourism, communications, and other policy fields where neither central nor provincial officials can act, let alone achieve their objectives, without the cooperation of their counterparts. There must be strong pressures towards mutually beneficial action. If the state apparatus has resources of expertise and resistance sufficient to allow it enough leverage over politicians that budgets inexorably increase (and in the view of some, to allow it to reorient provincial economies to ensure its own future revenue base), then it is hard to see how political acrimony could diffuse through provincial bureaucracies with sufficient thoroughness to dampen the fires of self-interest and to lead them to mutually destructive standoffs with their federal counterparts.

Finally, there remains the proposition that provincial economic policies have erected barriers to the mobility of productive factors, so fragmenting the internal common market and producing resource misallocations and important welfare losses. As the general case has been put, "Any lack of uniformity in government policies will have an impact on resource allocation by creating artificial advantage or disadvantage in one region compared to others."[85]

In a very useful analysis, however, Urquhart has criticized the notion that province-building and nation-building programs must be conflicting.[86] He shows that many initiatives are in fact complementary. Most obviously, nation-building policies like promoting energy self-sufficiency can accord with provincial priorities like developing heavy or residual oil extraction methods. Similarly, provincial initiatives designed to bolster or diversify regional economies can have important externalities which benefit Canada as a whole: the example of world-class health facilities in Alberta is instructive, as are Ontario's considerable efforts to increase exports of provincial manufactures. If such efforts do not lead to duplication and waste then overall social welfare is enhanced. Of course the opportunity costs of various investments could be such that the sum of provincial initiatives is not *optimal*, but this leads to a straightforward argument for a unitary state.

Even this would have grave weaknesses. A telling criticism of the market fragmentation case arises from the fact that many serious welfare losses are caused by Ottawa. Central policies which create distortions in regional price structures, and hence establish barriers, include regional investment tax credits and grants, Petroleum Incentives, Program Incentives, Unemployment Insurance Commission payments, the tariff, and regulated transport rates and energy prices. These measures erect *more* significant barriers than those created by provincial action.[87] There is no guarantee that increased central control over an undivided Canadian common market would produce a greater surplus from integration than currently exists. The potential to achieve gains from greater regional specialization would be there, but Ottawa also responds to regional or regionally concentrated demands, and greater centralization of power simply could result in larger welfare losses.[88]

CONCLUSIONS

The empirical evidence advanced in support of the trends which collectively constitute "province-building" is not very persuasive. The concept is over-general, and its users often find historical discontinuity where none exists, while merely presuming that certain dynamics are found in provincial states.

Staunch jurisdictional defence and exigent demands upon Ottawa are not new and are not uniform across policy fields or provinces. Provincial revenues have increased, as has occurred in the past, but they may not have conferred more autonomy on all provinces; as in civil service growth, Alberta stands out in this respect. There has been some shift in spending power to the provinces, and especially to the provinces and municipalities combined, and this interventionary capability has been matched by a new willingness to employ public enterprise and direct assistance to industry as tools of economic restructuring. But economic interventions are not obviously more deep or sweeping than in the past, and the principal focus of provincial activities remains service delivery in traditional policy fields. It is by no means evident that central policy guidance of a burgeoning state apparatus has been bolstered by new structures, or that policy has become more coherent and rational; planning documents proliferate but political commitment and implementation remain uncertain. Most important, power has not conclusively tilted towards the provincial capitals.

The concept of province-building obscures significant questions about which jurisdictional fields are defended against what forms of incursion, about which sectors and problems command provincial attention, and about which tools of intervention are used when and on behalf of whom. The concept inflates normal provincial efforts to preserve their areas of jurisdiction and to enhance their resources. It conflates the defensively expansionist deployment of windfall western revenues with Quebec's peculiar cultural and economic concerns, the Maritimes' blustering subordination, Newfoundland's desperate optimism, and Ontario's fundamentally ambivalent role in the federation.

Province-building, in short, does not constitute a recognizable whole, and its deployment as such impedes precise analysis of provincial and federal-provincial activity. For a concept to be useful scientifically, the elements which constitute it must be logically interrelated, and they must occur together empirically. Otherwise, the concept is merely a rhetorical device or a loose, albeit congenial, description. Concepts, after all, signify things. These things need not be elemental; on the contrary, complex phenomena are generally most interesting. But for complex concepts to have any validity, the elements which they subsume must be found together. If they are not, using such a concept is like having a category or syndrome called "measles" when sufferers sometimes get red spots and sometimes do not.

At first glance, the trends which make up province-building do seem to hang together logically. States which plan, for instance, are likely to resist incursions. But these elements do not necessarily hang together: it could be that outside "interference" in the affairs of *dirigiste* states would not be resisted were it filling critical gaps in planned economic or social change. Empirical study is essential, and it has been shown here that several of the individual components of province-building, such as that provinces increasingly defend their jurisdictions or that bureaucracies have grown fast, have met significant counter-examples. When those elements are considered in combination, discrepancies from the prescribed image are even more likely to be found. Quebec has sought to maximize fiscal resources, but the attitude of the Bourassa government towards Ottawa was not belligerent. Premier Peckford has taken a very firm line on the offshore, but his whole bureaucracy is relatively weak. British Columbia under the New Democratic party was a rapidly expanding state, but had little planning or central coordination.[89] New Brunswick has the most centralized administrative structure in Canada, but its economic development strategy is largely designed in Ottawa. Ontario has a superb administrative machine yet seeks to preserve the free movement of capital, goods, and labour throughout Canada. Saskatchewan was planning more coherently in 1945 than it is now, despite a substantial increase in its administrative apparatus. Where is the syndrome?

The weakness of the concept of province-building is revealed clearly when it is used in causal statements. There is nothing wrong with using complex concepts as causes, so long as the elements composing them are found together, like a syndrome. Measles, for example, often causes people to lie in bed for several days. But amorphous concepts easily lead to tautological explanations, like "measles causes red spots." The concepts are labels for a set of interrelated elements, and since it is possible to regard many trends as *manifestations* of province-building, so is it easy to slip into thinking of them as *consequences* of province-building. But this is invalid: the concept is said to cause or "explain" the elements which make it up. So a statement like "the process of province-building meant provincial leaders are no longer willing to be dictated to by the federal government," does not constitute an explanation at all; neither does the contention that neo-mercantilism "is the logical outcome of a confederation in which province-building has become a major force in economic-policy formation."[90] These are tautologies, and are like saying that someone gets angry because he is irascible or that opium makes people sleepy because of its "dormative qualities."[91]

Once more, the concept of province-building obscures more than it reveals. Changes in political stances, administrative structures, and state activities have occurred in the Canadian provinces, and while they do not fall into as coherent and uniform a pattern as the notion of province-building suggests, these changes must have causes and consequences. There has been, for instance, a proliferation of departmental planning agencies. This development might be associated with higher rates of interest-group formation or with more severe economic cycles; it may lead, where it has occurred, to more differentiated policy or to certain kinds of consultation with affected interests. Now greater planning capability is often considered a component of province-building, but province-building did not produce the consequences. Using it as a simple and convenient pseudo-explanation allows us to slide over the interesting questions: which elements of the "syndrome" are present where, when, and why, and which elements produce what effects?

The conceptual weakness of "province-building" has been made apparent recently in three ways. First, there is a tendency, when the term is defined at all, to use double-barreled definitions. McMillan and Norrie, for instance, say the term refers to "a policy of economic provincialism through which provincial government intervention is employed to establish an indigenous industrial base *and which* is intended to free the province from the domination of central Canadian economic and political interests under which it feels it has suffered as a hinterland economy."[92] Now if the first part is central to the concept, then it applies everywhere but is nothing new and need not engender conflict with Ottawa or other provinces. If the second part is crucial, then it cannot apply to Ontario and Quebec, but only to the hinterland (and probably not the eastern hinterland). If both parts apply, then it fits all cases (with the exception of a noneconomic dynamic in Quebec), but fits each incompletely. This is obviously unsatisfactory. A second manifestation of weakness is the tendency towards conceptual elaboration. Since all provinces do not make similar demands on Ottawa, we have "protest" and "entrepreneurial" regionalism: since strategies are not similar, we have "rentier" and "province-building" provincialism.[93] If Ontario must be in the same game, will we have "Ottawa-supportive province-building"? Perhaps for Newfoundland "immanent province-building" would do. The point is that to preserve the concept it must be ceaselessly elaborated to fit undeniable peculiarities.

This leads to the third, related, manifestation of explanatory weakness. Chandler and Chandler have attempted to use the concept as a central organizing framework for a comparative study of provincial politics and policy, using it to incorporate spending, regulation, changes in state structures and intergovernmental relations, and evolving social welfare and natural resources policy. Their account of these topics, and others, is groundbreaking: their work is comprehensive and illuminating. But the concept of province-building largely disappears from the substantive account. Its organizing and explanatory powers are obviously insufficient to comprehend and pattern the material, and the authors are led by their familiarity with the stuff of policy and politics in the various provinces to conclude that "there has been no single path of policy evolution and no common policy-making process."[94]

Province-building is a highly amorphous concept. The components do not hang together logically, nor do they occur together empirically. No one, to our knowledge, has tried to specify the conditions necessary and sufficient for province-building to be identified. The vagueness of the concept is clearly shown when one asks: what provincial policy would *not* qualify as province-building? The answers—inactivity, cooperation with Ottawa, and a shrinking of the state—provide some clues to the notion's latent appeal.

In light of its evident defects, one must ask why the concept of province-building has gained such wide currency. Why has it come to signify an image of the federation which so few question? One possibility is that its very lack of definition affords a comprehensive and readily applicable picture which helps us order and even explain complex and confusing events. But why *this* picture?

One clue to the latent functions of the concept is provided by the highly evaluative and emotive terms which often accompany it. Bothwell, Drummond and English write of "an assemblage of squalling mini-states," and of "jealous local sovereignties" which cling to "the full panoply of provincial pomp and power." Others, more anxious than scornful, describe the "unmanageable

strains caused by decentralization," and warn against the descent into a "vicious circle of national disintegration." Diabolical and apocalyptic themes are not uncommon: Pierre Lortie described the "unbridled forces that have been unleashed across the country and are presently embodied within the provincial governments," and Black and Cairns wrote of "powerful decentralizing pressures welling up from below," so threatening "that Canadian federalism is undergoing the greatest crisis since its inception."[95]

Such language is revealing. It is exaggerated, and coloured with an emotional shading which helps shape simple, archetypal images of the state. These images are politically significant, for leaders play upon them in seeking mass support. They are also shared widely at the elite level, and they define, ultimately, the parameters of acceptable action.

What are the symbolic implications, then, of "province-building"? First, the concept emphasizes conflict—pervasive, dangerous conflict. The thrust of the provincial governments' policies inevitably clashes with the goals of the central administration. This occurs on every important policy front (by definition), and preoccupies the whole state. There will be winners and losers, since conflict is nearing crisis. The concept thus embodies a tension which demands resolution. Since the central authority has been pushed to the limit of concession, the tension must be resolved, perhaps conclusively, by the reassertion of Ottawa's superior legitimacy. Implicit in province-building is a licence for nation-building. Second, the concept inherently diminishes the distinctiveness of the various provinces. Similar forces are at work in each: all are confrontational and all have an interest in divisiveness. Analytically, this obscures significant differences in policy outcomes and causes. Practically, its most noteworthy result is to deny any special dynamic in Quebec, so definitely rendering it a province like the others. This reinforces the legitimacy of a uniform federal counter-thrust to the general threat of province-building.

but what about the "distinct society" clause?

The implications of the concept are profoundly anti-federalist. It de-emphasizes the regional distinctiveness which is the basic justification for the establishment of federal as opposed to unitary states. It downplays cooperation and tolerance, and substitutes crude conflict for the fruitful tensions which may be amenable to creative resolution. It forces a hard choice—to be provincialist or federalist. Fortunately, most Canadians are able to live comfortably with the dual loyalties upon which a federal system ultimately reposes. But division at the elite level, of which the concept of province-building is a reflection and to which it contributes, is demonstrated by the misuse of the term "federalist" as a synonym of "centralist." Recently there have been few true federalists among Canadian elites. One cannot help suspecting that the central government will

yet reap a bitter harvest from its appropriation of the "federal" label. Perhaps the bias against the provincial state which the concept of province-building supports will find fuller expression in another term used by those whose aim is the dismantling of any strong state.

This is speculation. And perhaps analyzing the concept of province-building is now a sadly outdated enterprise, though useful for revealing problems neglected by easy acceptance of the concept. Canada has a new constitutional framework, new leaders have emerged, and new problems are imminent, to be managed by the state or not. If the concept has served some historical purpose, this has probably now run its course and the use of province-building will decline. We think it should.

Notes

1. Edwin R. Black and Alan C. Cairns. "A Different Perspective on Canadian Federalism," *Canadian Public Administration* 9 (March 1966): 27-44.

2. *Ibid.*, 40, 31; Garth Stevenson, "Federalism and the Political Economy of the Canadian State," in Leo Panitch, ed., *The Canadian State* (Toronto: University of Toronto Press, 1977), 71-100, and *Unfulfilled Union* (Toronto: Gage, 1979); Marsha Chandler and William Chandler, "Public Administration in the Provinces," *Canadian Public Administration* 25 (1982): 585; Judith Maxwell and Caroline Pestieau, *Economic Realities of Contemporary Confederation* (Montreal: C. D. Howe Research Institute, 1980), 78; Robert Bothwell, Ian Drummond and John English, *Canada Since 1945: Power, Politics and Provincialism* (Toronto: University of Toronto Press, 1981), 382; Donald V. Smiley, "Federal-Provincial Conflict in Canada," in J. P. Meekison, ed., *Canadian Federalism: Myth or Reality*, 3rd ed. (Toronto: Methuen, 1977), 3.

3. Black and Cairns, "A Different Perspective," 34; Canada, The Task Force on Canadian Unity, *A Future Together* (Ottawa: Supply and Services, 1979), 31; Stevenson, "Federalism and the Political Economy of the Canadian State," 83; Alan C. Cairns, "The Other Crisis of Canadian Federalism," *Canadian Public Administration* 22 (1979): 181; Maxwell and Pestieau, *Economic Realities*, 27; Richard J. Van Loon and Michael S. Whittington, *The Canadian Political System* (Toronto: McGraw-Hill, 1971), 227.

4. Richard Simeon, "Intergovernmental Relations and the Challenges to Canadian Federalism," *Canadian Public Administration* 23 (1980): 18.

5. Bothwell, Drummond, and English, *Canada Since 1945*, 406, 153; Richard Simeon, "Federalism and the Politics of a National Strategy," in Canada, Science Council, *The Politics of an Industrial Strategy: A Seminar* (Ottawa: Supply and Services, 1979), 22.

6. Keith G. Banting, *The Welfare State and Canadian Federalism* (Kingston: McGill-Queen's University Press, 1982), 139-40.

7. Alan M. Maslove and Gene Swimmer, *Wage Controls in Canada 1975-78* (Montreal: Institute for Research on Public Policy, 1980), 11, 32; Canada, Anti-Inflation Board, *Chronicles of the Anti-Inflation Board* (Ottawa: Supply and Services, 1979), 41-4.

8. Paul Rulison, "The Role of FIRA in Canadian Domestic Politics," paper delivered at the 1982 meeting of the Canadian Political Science Association, 6, 22-9; Rick Schultz, Frank Swedlove, and Katherine Swinton, "The Cabinet as a Regulatory Body: The Case of the Foreign Investment Review Act," Regulation Reference, Working Paper No. 16 (Ottawa: Economic Council, 1980): 123-4.

9. Gordon Robertson, "The Role of Interministerial Conferences in the Decision-Making Process," in Richard Simeon, ed., *Confrontation and Collaboration—Intergovernmental Relations in Canada Today* (Toronto: Institute of Public Administration of Canada, 1979): 80-3.

10. Christopher Armstrong, *The Politics of Federalism: Ontario's Relations with the Federal Government, 1867-1942* (Toronto: University of Toronto Press, 1981), 8-32.

11. It must be said, however, that the attitude of the government of the province of Quebec, on jurisdictional and constitutional issues, has reached new levels of intransigence since the election of the Parti Québécois. To the extent that this position is genuine and not a long-range bargaining strategy, the notion that its jurisdiction should be expanded to full sovereignty and that the central government could have no legitimate contact with Quebec citizens, represents a fundamental challenge to Ottawa. For theorists of province-building, however general the concept may appear, this may be the uncomfortable nub of the problem. It should be noted though that the extreme position of the Quebec government has reduced the belligerence towards Ottawa of other provincial administrations.

12. Banting, *The Welfare State and Canadian Federalism*, 50-1, 173.

13. This has been made quite clear by Simeon, despite his general contrasting of nation-building and province-building models. See his "Natural Resource Revenues and Canadian Federalism: A Survey of the Issues," *Canadian Public Policy* 6 (1980): 186: "A 'national policy' and 'Ontario regional policy' have, in most cases, been synonymous."

14. Marsha A. Chandler and William M. Chandler, *Public Policy and Provincial Politics* (Toronto: McGraw-Hill Ryerson, 1979), Table 1.2, 33.

15. Gérard Veilleux, "Intergovernmental Canada: Government by Conference? A Fiscal and Economic Perspective," *Canadian Public Administration* 23 (1980): 39.

16. M. C. Urquhart and K. A. H. Buckley, eds., *Historical Statistics of Canada* (Toronto: Macmillan, 1965), series G21 and G330; J. Harvey Perry, *Taxes, Tariffs and Subsidies*, vol. 2 (Toronto: University of Toronto Press, 1955), Table 1, 619.

17. Chandler and Chandler, *Public Policy and Provincial Politics*, 11; Roch Bolduc and James Iain Gow, "Environment and Administration. Quebec 1867-1980," in O. P. Dwivedi, ed., *The Administrative State in Canada* (Toronto: University of Toronto Press, 1982), 52.

18. Richard M. Bird, "The Growth of the Public Service in Canada," in David K. Foot, ed., *Public Employment and Compensation in Canada: Myths and Realities* (Montreal: Institute for Research on Public Policy, 1978), 42, Table A 2.5.

19. David Foot and Percy Thadaney, "The Growth of Public Employment in Canada: the Evidence from Taxation Statistics, 1946-75," in *ibid.*, Table 3.2.

20. Chandler and Chandler, "Public Administration in the Provinces," 586.

21. In Quebec in the early 1970s, 46 percent of 166 quasi-autonomous bodies were of a consultative nature (the comparable figure in Ontario being 45 percent), and a 1976 New Brunswick study found 440 consultative agencies attached to the bureaucracy, of which at least 60 percent had been set up in the preceding decade. See André Gélinas, *Les Organismes Autonomes et Centraux de l'Administration Québécoise* (Montréal : Les Presses de l'Université du Québec, 1975), 78-92; B. Bresner

et al., "Ontario's Agencies, Boards, Commissions, Advisory Bodies and other Pubic Institutions: An Inventory," in Ontario Economic Council, *Government Regulation* (Toronto: OEC, 1978), 207-75; New Brunswick, Cabinet Secretariat, "A (Second) Report on Citizen Participation in the Government of New Brunswick," (mimeographed report, May 1976), Appendix A, Table 3.

22. Bird, "Growth of the Public Service," Tables A 2.4 and A 2.5.

23. *Ibid.*, 31. At the nadir of Ottawa's relative strength in 1970, central-government employment as a proportion of total state employment was still higher in Canada than in West Germany, Switzerland and the United States. See Werner W. Pommerehne, "Quantitative Aspects of Federalism: A Study of Six Countries," in Wallace E. Oates, ed., *The Political Economy of Fiscal Federalism* (Toronto: D. C. Heath, 1977), Table 15-20.

24. Black and Cairns, "A Different Perspective," 41.

25. See Richard Simeon, *Federal-Provincial Diplomacy* (Toronto: University of Toronto Press, 1972). 54-6 and 213-6; and, for instance, David M. Cameron, "Whither Canadian Federalism? The Challenge of Regional Diversity and Maturity," in Meekison, ed., *Canadian Federalism*: 314-5.

26. Morley Gunderson, "Professionalization of the Canadian Public Sector," in Meyer W. Bucovetsky, ed., *Studies in Public Employment and Compensation in Canada* (Montreal: Institute for Research on Public Policy, 1979), Tables 4.2, 4.6.

27. David Foot, Edward Scicluna, and Percy Thadaney, "The Growth and Distribution of Federal, Provincial, and Local Government Employment in Canada," in Foot, ed., *Public Employment and Compensation in Canada*, Table 4.7 (years 1969-76).

28. Alan C. Cairns, "The Governments and Societies of Canadian Federalism," *Canadian Journal of Political Science* 10 (1977): 706.

29. Chandler and Chandler, *Public Policy and Provincial Politics*, 9; Simeon, "Federalism and the Politics of a National Strategy," 23-4.

30. Edwin R. Black, *Divided Loyalties* (Montreal: McGill-Queen's University Press, 1975), 81. Studies show that both closed and open-ended conditional-grant programs elicit spending, the first by approximately the amount of the grant, the second a little less. See Edward M. Gramlich,

"Intergovernmental Grants: A Review of the Empirical Literature," in Oates, ed., *Fiscal Federalism*: 219-39, and David K. Foot, *Provincial Public Finance in Ontario: An Empirical Analysis of the Last Twenty-Five Years* (Toronto: University of Toronto Press, 1977), 170-2, 189.

31. Black, *Divided Loyalties*, 81-4; Richard M. Bird, *The Growth of Government Spending in Canada* (Toronto: Canadian Tax Foundation, 1970), 33-8. These manipulations are probably less reasonable than they were when conditional grants were more strictly administered by Ottawa.

32. Barry D. Rosenfeld, "Canadian Government Expenditures, 1871-1966" (unpublished doctoral dissertation, University of Pennsylvania, 1972), 244, Table 5.1.

33. Chandler and Chandler, *Public Policy and Provincial Politics*, 129.

34. J. A. Corry, *The Growth of Government Activities Since Confederation* (Ottawa: King's Printer, 1939).

35. M. Priest and A. Wohl, "The Growth of Federal and Provincial Regulation of Economic Activity, 1867-1978," in W. T. Stanbury, ed., *Government Regulation: Scope, Growth, Process* (Montreal: Institute for Research on Public Policy, 1980), 111, Table 9.

36. Aidan R. Vining and R. Botterell, "An Overview of the Origins, Growth, Size, and Functions of Provincial Crown Corporations," in J. R. Pritchard, ed., *Crown Corporations in Canada* (Toronto: Butterworths, 1983), 320.

37. Marsha Gordon, *Government in Business* (Montreal: C. D. Howe Institute, 1981), Tables A 3 and A 4.

38. Michael Jenkin, "The Prospects for a New National Policy," *Journal of Canadian Studies* 14 (1979): 133.

39. Canada, Statistics Canada, cat. 68-207, *Provincial Government Finance*, various years, Table 2. These development functions took 32 percent of spending in 1951, 29 percent in 1960, and 14 percent in 1980.

40. Maxwell and Pestieau, *Economic Realities*, 20.

41. Philippe Faucher, André Blais and Robert Young, "L'Aide Financière Directe au Secteur Manufacturière au Québec et en Ontario, 1960-1980," *Revue d'études canadiennes* 18 (1983), Figure I.

42. André Blais, Philippe Faucher, Robert Young and Roger Poupart, "Les Avantages Fiscaux du Gouvernement Fédéral à l'Industrie Manufacturière Canadienne," (Note de Recherche, Université de Montréal, Départment de science politique, 1983), Tables 4 and 8.

43. Anthony Careless, *Initiative and Response* (Montreal: McGill-Queen's University Press, 1977).

44. Morris Zaslow, *The Opening of the Canadian North 1870-1914* (Toronto: McClelland and Stewart, 1971), 173-98.

45. H. V. Nelles, *The Politics of Development* (Toronto: Macmillan, 1974), 132-8.

46. J. D. House, "Premier Peckford, Petroleum Policy, and Popular Politics in Newfoundland and Labrador," *Journal of Canadian Studies* 17 (1982): 20-1.

47. Alan Cairns, "From Interstate to Intrastate Federalism in Canada," *Bulletin of Canadian Studies* 2 (1978): 31.

48. Chandler and Chandler, *Public Policy and Provincial Politics*, 98; Larry Pratt, "The State and Province-Building: Alberta's Development Strategy," in Panitch, ed., *The Canadian State*, 147; Donald V. Smiley, "An Outsider's Observations of Federal-Provincial Relations Among Consenting Adults," in Simeon, ed., *Confrontation and Collaboration*, 110.

49. Kenneth Bryden, "Cabinets," in David J. Bellamy, Jon H. Pammett and Donald C. Rowat, eds., *The Provincial Political Systems* (Toronto: Methuen, 1976), 315; Alain Baccigalupo, *Les Grands Rouages de la Machine Administrative Québécoise* (Montréal : les éditions agence d'arc, 1978), 195-203, 315. The Quebec Comité Ministériel Permanent de Développement Économique, for instance, had five staff members in 1978 and at best could arrange interdepartmental meetings.

50. R. M. Burns, "Budgeting and Finance," in Bellamy, Pammett and Rowat, eds., *Provincial Political Systems*, 322-40.

51. Richard French, *How Ottawa Decides* (Toronto: Lorimer, 1980); Rick Van Loon, "Reforming Welfare in Canada," *Public Policy* 27 (1979): 469-504; M. J. L. Kirby, H. V. Kroeker, and W. R. Teschke, "The Impact of Public Policy-Making Structures and Processes in Canada," *Canadian Public Administration* 21 (1978): 407-17.

52. Antoine Ambroise and Jocelyn Jacques, "L'appareil administrative," in G. Bergeron and Réjean Pelletier, eds., *L'État du Québec en devenir* (Montréal : Boréal Express, 1980), 128-9.

53. Gélinas, *Organismes Autonomes et Centraux*, 139-233, Table X.

54. T. J. Plunkett and Katherine A. Graham, "Whither Municipal Government?" *Canadian Public Administration* 25 (1982), Table 1.

55. Trevor Price, "The Philosophy of Local Government Reform in Ontario," paper delivered at the 1982 meeting of the Canadian Political Science Association.

56. Michael J. Prince and John A. Chenier, "The Rise and Fall of Policy Planning and Research Units: an Organizational Perspective," *Canadian Public Administration* 23 (1980): 519-41.

57. Baccigalupo, *La Machine Administrative Québécoise*, 375-6.

58. Jacques Benjamin, *Planification et Politique au Québec* (Montréal: Les Presses de l'Université de Montréal, 1974), 98-103.

59. N. H. Richardson, "Insubstantial Pageant: The Rise and Fall of Provincial Planning in Ontario," *Canadian Public Administration* 24 (1981): 582-3.

60. M. Duchesneau, "Éléments de la Politique Forestière au Québec," *Pulp and Paper Magazine of Canada*, 6 November 1970, 81-84; Pierre Lamy, *L'Industrie de Sciage au Québec 1960-1980* (Montréal: École des Hautes Études Commerciales de Montréal, 1981), Table 6.

61. Cairns, "Governments and Societies of Canadian Federalism," 717.

62. Eric A. Nordlinger, *On the Autonomy of the Democratic State* (Cambridge, Mass.: Harvard University Press, 1981), 21; see also 140-1, 193-4.

63. Black and Cairns, "A Different Perspective," 40.

64. Stevenson, *Unfulfilled Union*, 79-102, especially 90-1.

65. In 1980, resource revenues accounted for less than 3 percent of gross general revenue in all provinces except British Columbia (12.5%), Saskatchewan (28.6%), and Alberta (51.4%): Statistics Canada, *Provincial Government Finance*, text table I. See also Anthony Scott, "Who Should Get Natural

Resource Revenues?" in Anthony Scott, ed., *Natural Resource Revenues: A Test of Federalism* (Vancouver: University of British Columbia Press, 1976), 19, 41-2; and, for an historical view, Robin Neill, "The Politics and Economics of Development in Ontario," *Ontario History* 70 (1978): 281-90.

66. Maxwell and Pestieau, *Economic Realities*, Table 11.

67. The importance of market access in periods of slack demand may give some pause to enthusiastic nationalizers: see Michael Shafer, "Capturing the Mineral Multinationals: Advantage or Disadvantage?" *International Organization* 37 (1983): 93-119. In the present context it is interesting to note that the central government now more surely controls access to resource markets. Its power relative to the provinces, and perceived responsibility, should increase in recessionary times.

68. See, however, Grace Skogstad, "Supervising the Regulators: Producer-Controlled Marketing Boards," paper delivered at the 1983 meeting of the Atlantic Provinces Political Studies Association, for an interesting attempt to explain the formation and evolution of supply management boards according to federal-provincial dynamics.

69. Rosenfeld, "Canadian Government Expenditures," Table 4.2.6; Pommerehne, "Quantitative Aspects of Federalism," Table 15-17.

70. N. H. Lithwick, "Regional Policy: The Embodiment of Contradictions," in G. Bruce Doern, ed., *How Ottawa Spends Your Tax Dollars 1982* (Toronto: Lorimer, 1982), 131-46.

71. *Canadian Paper Analyst*, April 1978, 2: Values for other firms ranged between 25 percent and 45 percent.

72. Canada, Statistics Canada, cat. 61-207, *Corporation Financial Statistics 1980*, Table 2B and cat. 61-208, *Corporation Taxation Statistics 1980*, Table 2. The figures are for the primary forest industry, the wood industries, and the paper and allied products industry.

73. Where they are significant, resource revenues can allow lower taxation and easier borrowing, so providing less visible extraction by the state and giving civil servants and politicians more autonomy to make uneconomic investments and to dist-

ribute benefits to favoured individuals and classes: see M. L. McMillan and K. H. Norrie, "Province-Building vs. a Rentier Society," *Canadian Public Policy* 6 (1980): 213-20. This occurs in Alberta and arguably took place earlier in central Canada: see Neill, "Politics and Economics of Development in Ontario." It is easy to see the bureaucratic interest in such activity, but not the interest of the supposedly dominant resource bourgeoisie, and in this regard closer attention to the service and construction sectors may be warranted. The point remains, however, that even if some provincial governments are especially interested in resource firms, the converse is not necessarily true.

74. Cairns, "The Other Crisis of Canadian Federalism," 191.

75. Stevenson, *Unfulfilled Union*, 52-3; Simeon, "Current Constitutional Issues," in Ontario Economic Council, *Intergovernmental Relations* (Toronto: OEC, 1977), 18. It should be noted in fairness that Simeon, despite persistent portrayals of this fundamental opposition, has taken care usually to trace a distinct "Quebec nation-building" strand in Canadian federalism.

76. Maxwell and Pestieau, *Economic Realities*, 83.

77. Banting, *The Welfare State and Canadian Federalism*, 81.

78. Maureen Appel Molot and Jeanne Kirk Laux, "The Politics of Nationalization," *Canadian Journal of Political Science* 12 (1979): 248-50.

79. Ian T. Urquhart, "The Complexity of Community-Building in Canada: A Critique of Zero-Sum/Unitary Actor Interpretations of Nation-Building and Province-Building," paper delivered at the 1982 meeting of the Canadian Political Science Association, 7-14.

80. Gérard Veilleux, "L'Évolution des mécanismes de liaison intergouvernementale," in Simeon, ed., *Confrontation and Collaboration*, 37.

81. H. L. Laframboise, "The Future of Public Administration in Canada," *Canadian Public Administration* 25 (1982): 508. For the classic statement, see Donald V. Smiley, "Public Administration and Canadian Federalism," *Canadian Public Administration* 7 (1964): 371-88.

82. Laframboise, in a later piece on accountability, included the Federal-Provincial Relations Office among the other central agencies, which together made up one of the eight loci to which deputy ministers strained to be accountable: see "A Note on Accountability," *Optimum* 13 (1982):82-4.

83. See, for instance, Veilleux, "L'Évolution des mé-chanismes," 43-5; Stevenson, "Federalism and the Political Economy of the Canadian State," 83.

84. Donald J. Savoie, *Federal-Provincial Collaboration* (Montreal: McGill-Queen's University Press, 1981).

85. R. E. Haack, D. R. Hughes, and R. G. Shapiro, *The Splintered Market: Barriers to Interprovincial Trade in Canadian Agriculture* (Toronto: Lorimer, 1981), 57. See also Stevenson, *Unfulfilled Union*, 103-26, and Simeon, "Federalism and the Politics of a National Strategy," 12.

86. Urquhart, "The Complexity of Community-Building in Canada."

87. John Whalley, "The Impact of Federal and Provincial Policies on the Canadian Economic Union: A Theoretical and Empirical Overview," and "The Impact of Federal and Provincial Policies on the Canadian Economic Union: Federal Policies," papers delivered at the Workshop on Federalism and the Canadian Economic Union, London, Ontario, December 1981. There is room for debate about whether all central policies with differential regional effects create "barriers," or whether the policies must be overtly and intentionally discriminatory to count. This definitional question will affect the relative magnitude of the distortions found. Our view is that regional effects are measurable and are brought to national decision-makers' attention through a variety of mechanisms, so they have entered the policy calculus and all should be counted.

88. As Courchene has recognized, Ottawa can use any surplus generated through the removal of interprovincial trade barriers to attack regional disparities: "In effect it means that Ottawa will be able to do the very things that it wants to prevent the provinces from doing, namely to engage in policies that will alter relative prices across regions."

See his "Historical and Analytical Perspectives Relating to the Canadian Economic Union," paper delivered at the Workshop on Federalism and the Canadian Economic Union, London, Ontario, December 1981, 48.

89. Paul Tennant, "The NDP Government of British Columbia: Unaided Politicians in an Unaided Cabinet," *Canadian Public Policy* 3 (1977): 489-503.

90. Chandler and Chandler, *Public Policy and Provincial Politics*, 12; Maxwell and Pestieau, *Economic Realities*, 109.

91. Another causal fallacy occurs when the concept's evolutionary and developmental connotations stimulate anthropomorphisms, as when authors describe "the desire of provincial societies to develop unhindered" or the "maturation" of the provinces. See Jeff Evenson and Richard Simeon, "The Roots of Discontent," in Institute of Intergovernmental Relations and Economic Council of Canada, *Workshop on the Political Economy of Confederation* (Ottawa: Supply and Services, 1979), 176; Chandler and Chandler, *Public Policy and Provincial Politics*, 196. If understood as a shorthand for complex internal processes, such statements are not too misleading; but when provinces become people, change is easily misrepresented—to be inevitable or irreversible, for instance.

92. McMillan and Norrie, "Province-Building vs. A Rentier Society," 214 (emphasis added).

93. *Ibid.*; Raymond Breton, "Regionalism in Canada," in David M. Cameron, ed., *Regionalism and Supranationalism* (Montreal: Institute for Research on Public Policy and Policy Studies Institute, 1981), 57-79.

94. Chandler and Chandler, *Public Policy and Provincial Politics*, 292.

95. Bothwell, Drummond, and English, *Canada Since 1945*, 4, 147, 239; Garth Stevenson, "Canadian Regionalism in Continental Perspective," *Journal of Canadian Studies* 15 (1980): 26-7; Pierre Lortie, "Changing Strains of Federalism," *Policy Options* 1 (1980): 28; Black and Cairns, "A Different Perspective," 30, 44.

Selected Readings

Black, Edwin R., and Cairns, Alan. "A Different Perspective on Canadian Federalism." *Canadian Public Administration* 9 (March 1966): 27-44.

Bothwell, Robert, and Drummond, Ian, and English, John. *Canada Since 1945: Power, Politics and Provincialism*. Toronto: University of Toronto Press, 1981.

Richards, John, and Pratt, Larry. *Prairie Capitalism: Power and Influence in the New West*. Toronto: McClelland and Stewart, 1979.

Stevenson, Garth, *Unfulfilled Union: Canadian Federalism and National Unity*. Rev. ed. Toronto: Gage, 1982.

Vipond, R. C. V. "Constitutional Politics and the Legacy of the Provincial Rights Movement in Canada." *Canadian Journal of Political Science* 18 (June 1985): 267-295.

SECTION FOUR

FISCAL FEDERALISM

Federal constitutions must establish a clear division of executive and legislative authority and a sharing of revenue sources between the two levels of government. "Fiscal federalism" is the term used to denote more permanent, institutional arrangements relating to the financing of each component unit.

In Canada, because of the great variation in the population, the revenue base, and the economic activities of each province or region, fiscal federalism has been an issue of particular importance since 1867. For some provinces, the pressures of an accumulated debt, as well as the need to obtain aid in the financing of large-scale transportation and communication projects, provided the rationale for the acceptance of the original Confederation settlement. In the years following Confederation, the federal government has often used its unlimited access to all forms of taxation in order to offset the decentralist pull of unfavourable judicial rulings, particularly those of the Judicial Committee of the Privy Council. This has often produced intense and sustained political conflict between Ottawa and the provinces.

Because of this political conflict, a number of comprehensive studies have attempted to examine the general direction of fiscal federalism in Canada. These studies began with the landmark Rowell-Sirois Commission in the 1930s and continued with the 1981 Parliamentary Task Force on Federal-Provincial Fiscal Arrangements, the 1982 Economic Council of Canada report *Financing Confederation*, and more recently the Macdonald Royal Commission on the Economic Union and Development Prospects for Canada.

Central to fiscal federalism are three overriding issues. The first is *revenue-sharing*. This relates to whether each level of government possesses access to sufficient tax revenue in order to fulfill its constitutional obligations. The second major fiscal issue is *equalization*. This focuses on the federal government's efforts to compensate for disparities in the financial capacities of different provinces. Finally, there is the question of *financing programs of national interest*. This involves the federal government's attempts at managing the spillover effects of provincial programs and ensuring reasonable national standards in the social policy field. All three issues necessitate ongoing coordination of the fiscal and economic policies of the two levels of government. Coordination is necessary to ensure that the policy measures adopted by one government do not neutralize or offset initiatives taken by another.

Each of the essays included in this section attempts to outline a major issue of fiscal federalism. The excerpt from the Economic Council of Canada summarizes the nature of the Tax Collection Agreements which are negotiated between Ottawa and the provinces every five years. It reveals some potential problems as our tax system becomes more decentralized. Thomas Courchene has written more than any individual on Canada's unique system of equalization payments. Rather than focusing on the specifics of the present formula, his background study for the Macdonald Commission reviews the basic rationale for making equalization payments to our "have-not" provinces. Paul Barker provides an overview of the post-war evolution of shared-cost programs. He reveals how tax collection, equalization, and the use of the federal spending power are often interconnected and not easily separated in the actual operation of fiscal federalism.

10. TAX COLLECTION AGREEMENTS AND TAX AND FISCAL HARMONIZATION

Economic Council of Canada

THE TAX COLLECTION AGREEMENTS

Federal and provincial governments in Canada employ a variety of fiscal instruments, ranging from taxes on the incomes of persons and firms to broad-based sales taxes at the retail level and manufacturing sales level and specific excise levies on commodities like tobacco, alcohol, and gasoline. The relative importance of different instruments has varied over time. In Canada today, as in most other federal countries, income taxes have come to assume a predominant position both as sources of government tax revenue and as instruments of economic and social policy.

When several jurisdictions have the power to levy taxes, two types of potential problems arise. First, two different levels of government may exploit the same general tax base, as is the case in Canada with respect to corporate and personal income taxes. Coordination between governments with respect to the definition of the tax base, the achievement of economies in the collection of taxes, and administration of the system can enhance regional economic efficiency and taxpayer equity, but the very opposite may be the case if the degree of coordination is inadequate.

The second problem is that firms or persons undertaking economic activities in different jurisdictions may be liable to taxation by two or more provincial governments at the same level. For instance, firms can sell, provide services, have production facilities, and employ workers in more than one province. As for workers, their place of employment and their dwelling place may be in different provinces or they may change their province of employment or residence sometime during the year. It is not immediately clear which province or provinces should be entitled to tax the incomes of such workers or firms. Generally, allocation rules have been developed to determine whether, and to what extent, different jurisdications have a claim against taxable income.

The Tax Collection Agreements, among other things, provide a means of resolving these two potential problems with respect to taxes on personal incomes and on corporate profits. The federal government offers to collect either, or both, of these taxes for any province or territory, provided the jurisdiction establishes income tax legislation that meets certain conditions regarding the definition of the tax base, the allocation rules, and the rate structure.

Economic Council of Canada, "Tax Collection Agreements and Tax and Fiscal Harmonization," in *Financing Confederation: Today and Tomorrow* (Ottawa: Supply and Services Canada, 1982), chapter 9. Reproduced with permission of the Minister of Supply and Services Canada. The essay has been abridged and edited to suit the needs of this volume.

Personal Income Tax Provisions

The federal government collects and remits provincial personal income tax to any province that adopts the federal personal income tax base and sets a single rate of tax, expressed as a constant percentage of the basic federal tax payable. The federal government assumes all the cost of administration and collection and forwards the assessed amount of tax to the participating provinces. Currently, both of the territories and all provinces except Quebec have entered into an agreement with respect to the collection of personal income tax by the federal government. Moreover, all jurisdictions, including Quebec, have agreed that the taxpayer's place of residence on December 31 of the taxation year determines the province to which he or she is liable for income tax.[1]

Since 1972, the federal government has also undertaken to administer, subject to the conditions discussed below, certain provincial tax measures, for which it charges a fee based on a sliding scale. Under these arrangements, the federal government will make provisions for tax rebates and reductions and for tax surcharges, as stipulated by the provinces that are party to the Agreements. The intent of the conditions, which are not spelled out in any official or legal document, is to prevent the adoption of provisions that, in the opinion of the federal government, would discriminate against residents of the other provinces or that could have the potential to impede the proper functioning of the Canadian economic union. Currently, the majority of provinces take advantage of these provisions allowing personal income tax credits for, among other things, political contributions, property and sales taxes, cost of living, and mortgage interest. Tax rebates for royalties paid are offered by the four western provinces; these provinces and Ontario also offer selective tax reductions. New Brunswick has a negative surtax of 5.5 percent of provincial tax otherwise payable, and Saskatchewan and British Columbia have imposed surcharges on provincial tax otherwise payable in excess of a specified floor amount. Because it administers and collects its own personal income taxes, Quebec has complete autonomy in the

determination of the base, the rate structure, and credits and rebates for these taxes.

Corporate Income Tax Provisions

The centralized administration of corporate income tax is carried out in similar fashion, but the rules for determining the division of taxable corporate income among the provinces are more complex. Participating provinces use the federal definition of taxable profits and are allowed to set a dual rate structure, the lower rate of which applies to firms eligible for the federal small business deduction. Again, the federal government bears the costs of collection, and it forwards to the provinces the assessed amount of tax payable.

How and why a firm is subject to provincial corporate taxation is governed by two factors. First, the liability of a company for taxation in a province is determined by the so-called "permanent establishment" criterion. A company is deemed to have a permanent establishment in a province if it has a fixed place of business there or, alternatively, employs capital or labour above a given level in a province. Second, if a firm qualifies by having a permanent establishment in a province, the tax base against which the provincial corporation tax rate is applied is defined as the taxable income of that firm multiplied by a factor that gives equal weight to the proportion of the firm's payroll and its gross receipts in the province. Because of the nature of their activities, special rules exist for companies that operate in financial, insurance, and transportation industries.

The federal government collects the corporate tax of seven of the ten provinces under these rules. Alberta withdrew from the agreement in 1981 but currently maintains the same rules. A new provincial corporate tax structure may be legislated in Alberta following consultation with interested persons and firms. Ontario and Quebec, the other two provinces that run their own corporate tax systems, have traditionally maintained base definitions and allocation rules that broadly conform to those used by the other provinces.

In the case of the corporate tax, as in the case of the personal income tax, the federal government administers certain provincial tax credits and rebates for a nominal fee. Currently, Manitoba and British Columbia offer credits for political contributions. British Columbia also offers a credit for logging tax. Saskatchewan and British Columbia offer a tax rebate for royalties paid. In addition, all provinces party to the agreement, except Prince Edward Island, offer a small business rate reduction.

THE DEVELOPMENT OF TAX HARMONIZATION

The system of income taxation outlined above represents a higher degree of coordination than exists in many other federal states. It is useful to examine briefly the historical evolution of these arrangements in order to gain an understanding of the nature of the Tax Collection Agreements and the factors that helped to shape their development.

Section 92(2) of the British North America Act confers upon the provinces the power to levy "direct" taxes within their respective jurisdictions. As interpreted by the courts, this power includes, among other things, the right to impose personal and corporate income taxes and succession duties. Section 91(3) permits the federal government access to any field of taxation. The two sections together, therefore, establish the basis for joint occupancy of the income tax field by federal and provincial governments.

By the 1930s, both the federal government and the various provinces had in place taxes on personal income and corporate profits. The provisions governing these levies were uncoordinated in the sense that jurisdictions had different base definitions, rate structures, and allocation

rules. This was one of the factors—in addition to the serious financial problems facing all levels of government as a result of the Depression—that led the federal government (in 1937) to appoint a Royal Commission to review the entire fiscal system.[2]

The Commission was highly critical of the complete lack of uniformity in personal tax burdens across provinces and of the host of discriminatory provincial tax measures found to be in effect, such as exemptions for dividend income received from firms with headquarters in a province. In the corporate tax field, the Commission found that different tax rates were being imposed on different industries in the same province and on the same industry in different provinces. Because of different and conflicting allocation rules, interprovincial companies were often double-taxed on the same income.

The Commission felt that this lack of coordination and this discriminatory treatment seriously hampered the attainment of fiscal equity and economic efficiency. Moreover, it concluded in its Report that "duplication of services for the collection of taxes obviously increases costs both of government and of tax compliance" [Book II, p. 177]. Given this concern, it is understandable that the Commission recommended that the provinces withdraw completely from the personal and corporate income tax fields. Under its proposal, these taxes would have been levied only by the federal government, which would have imposed geographically uniform bases and rate structures. In return, provinces would have received from the federal government an annual national adjustment grant designed to enable them to meet a national average level of expenditure without the necessity of levying excessive tax rates in the fields they still continued to occupy. In addition to these grants, it was proposed that each province would receive 10 percent of the net income derived from mining, smelting, and the refining of ores and oil produced in the province.

The recommendations of the Royal Commission were rejected by the provinces of Alberta, British Columbia, and Ontario at a federal-provincial conference in 1941. The onset of the Second World War, however, had an important influence on federal and provincial attitudes, particularly as they related to the revenue needs of the federal government. The provinces temporarily withdrew from the income tax fields at the urging of the federal government, in exchange for which they received federal transfers—which later came to be known as tax rentals. The system of rentals remained unchanged until new agreements were reached in 1947, and it continued in modified form through the successive agreements of 1952 and 1957 . . . .

Beginning in 1947 and extending up to the final set of Tax Rental Agreements in 1957, participating provinces received a per capita payment from the federal government in exchange for withdrawing from the personal and corporate income tax fields.³ The per capita payments incorporated an element of implicit equalization. In 1957, explicit equalization payments were introduced, and a tax-sharing arrangement was negotiated whereby the tax rental was based solely on the source of the taxes collected. A prime motivation for this change of view on the part of the St. Laurent government was that the implicit subsidy for the poorer provinces contained in the tax rentals was unfair to Quebec, which on principle could not accept the loss of provincial autonomy involved in giving up its taxing powers. Another significant change from the previous Agreements was the opportunity for the provinces to split the tax fields and enter into an Agreement for either personal or corporate income taxes—instead of both or none—if they so wished.

The problem of determining where liability rests for the payment of taxes parallels the problem of the choice of allocation rules by a provincial jurisidiction. Two principles of taxation can be followed. The first is the residence principle, whereby taxes are levied on the basis of the province of residence of the wage-earner or the owner of an income-generating asset. The second is the source principle, under which taxes are levied on the basis of the province in which the income is earned.

In the development of uniform rules under the Tax Collection Agreements, first established in 1962, a number of considerations had to be taken into account in choosing between these two principles. Because it considers the taxpayer's income from all sources in determining tax liability, the residence principle is a more appropriate choice for a progressive tax structure based on ability to pay. For this reason, personal income tax is allocated on the basis of residence. The definition of residence is not perfectly unambiguous, however, especially when the taxpayer changes his or her province of residence sometime during the taxation year. As noted earlier, the test used by all provinces has for some time been the place of residence of the taxpayer on December 31 of the taxation year.

A residence-based corporate profits tax could allocate taxation power to the jurisdiction of incorporation or the place where the headquarters of a company is located. Provincial corporate taxes are usually justified, however, on the basis of the flow of services that a firm receives from the province in carrying on its business. This benefit criterion is more consistent with the source principle of taxation.

The problem remains, however, to determine the source of profit of a company operating in more than one province. Any allocation rules are essentially arbitrary. The compromise reached by the federal government and the provinces was, as indicated earlier, to weight sales and payroll equally. Sales were included because it was felt that payroll alone would allocate a disproportionate share of tax to the province where the firm's head office was located.⁴

To deal with the most important problem—avoiding double taxation of incomes—it is essential to have a uniform set of taxing rules. Provinces that are parties to the Tax Collection

Agreements are required to accept allocation rules established by the federal government, as outlined above. For provinces outside the agreements, taxing practices initially diverged from the federal standard, but by 1962 all provincial jurisdictions generally adhered to common allocation rules.

The 1962 Tax Collection Agreements established the system that essentially is in effect today. Provinces could set their own tax rate as a proportion of basic federal tax, but they had to maintain the federal tax base and rate structure. Participating provinces were also allowed to enter or reenter the corporation tax field.

In 1972, partial provincial control of the rate structure was achieved by the provision of federal administration of the tax credits against provincial income taxes. For personal income tax, at least, this was a significant departure from earlier policy. Prior to 1972, the progressivity of this tax was essentially determined by the federal rate structure.

PROVINCIAL AUTONOMY AND ECONOMIC EFFICIENCY

The evolution of the Tax Collection Agreements since 1941 has therefore been characterized by a progression of steps whereby the provincial governments have negotiated increased flexibility in employing income taxes as a means of achieving various provincial economic and social goals. The current arrangements have many desirable features. First, tax bases are relatively uniform across the country, making it possible to achieve economies in the administration and collection of tax revenue and also to minimize the compliance costs that taxpayers must bear. This is especially important for businesses operating in a number of provinces, which could well be required to keep eleven different sets of books if all governments had different tax systems.

A second notable feature is that allocation rules are uniform across all provinces with respect to both personal and corporate income tax. This is not completely the result of the agreements, however. It seems that all provincial governments appreciate the desirability of uniformity in these rules. Agreement on the assignment of bases to jurisdictions is sufficient to avoid the inequities of both double taxation and evasion of legitimate tax liabilities. The uniformity of taxing practices is laudable as well, because it avoids the economic inefficiencies that could otherwise result from the response of persons and firms to differences in tax rules that lead to significant differences in tax costs.

Even if tax bases are uniform and all jurisdictions employ the same allocation rules, however, problems relating to the allocation of resources can develop if there are significant differences in tax rates and tax burdens across the country that are not offset by differences in the flow of public service benefits financed by these taxes. The nominal tax rates applied to the basic federal tax on personal incomes by the nine provinces party to the Tax Collection Agreements as they pertain to personal income tax do differ markedly. . . . In addition, however, the effective tax rates also vary among provinces. This is partly because of the separate Quebec tax system and partly because of the varying abatements and credits applied by some of the provinces under the Tax Collection Agreements . . . .

The increased flexibility acquired by the provinces in establishing income tax rate structures led to a need to develop broad guidelines aimed at preventing the introduction of discriminatory measures that could reduce the efficiency of the Canadian economy. This goal is generally best served by treating residents and non-residents identically. To apply the principle of non-discrimination would involve, among other things, the prohibiting of differential treatment of resident and non-resident firms under the corporate income tax and the prohibiting of measures under the personal income tax that would create fiscal inducements to invest in one location over another.

Since provincial personal income tax is residence-based, differences in tax rates do not alter personal investment decisions.[5] An investor concerned with obtaining the best rate of return will allocate his portfolio across jurisdictions to maximize its gross return. But since personal income tax falls directly on personal income from property and employment earnings, the potential exists for migration of labour and capital to lower tax jurisdictions if the differences in tax burdens are not offset by benefits provided by government in the form of goods and services.

The provincial corporate tax, being source-based, falls on the capital income of all firms operating in a province regardless of whether the capital is owned by residents or non-residents. In a well-functioning capital market, profit-maximizing firms will allocate capital in such a way that after-tax returns are equalized across all jurisdictions in the long run. There will be a divergence between potential output and the actual output of the economy if this long-run allocation of resources between geographic areas differs from what it would be in the absence of any tax. This assumes, of course, that capital is relatively mobile. But if it is tied to a certain province because of locational advantages—such as proximity to markets or proximity to natural resources—then any favourable tax differentials available in another province must at least be sufficient to offset these advantages.

A great deal of the productive capital of the country is tied up in the way just described. There is, however, a large volume of "footloose" capital that, because of prevailing technology, can be located almost anywhere. In this situation, what is important is the relative cost of doing business in some locations as opposed to others. Such footloose capital would be expected to be responsive, among other things, to tax differentials in different jurisdictions. Some good examples would be the head offices of corporations or their research and development branches where activities are characterized by

the accumulation and processing of information. From the point of view of national economic efficiency, it is largely immaterial where such activities are located in Canada; hence the influence of differing provincial corporate taxes in determining location is not a matter of primary concern. To certain provinces, however, the resulting distribution of economic activity and of corporate tax revenues is obviously of considerable consequence.

Finally, it is important to note that the adverse effects of differentials in taxes on one factor of production depend in an intimate way on differentials in taxes on other factors. For example, since labour and capital are both needed in the production process, a personal income tax structure that attracts labour to one province will also tend to draw capital into that province, even if differentials in corporate taxes are non-existent.

Because fiscal power is centralized in a unitary state, the latter is in a position to institute taxation policies that can avoid misallocation of the economy's productive resources. Such a system, however, is usually taken to be constrained in its ability to respect differences in individual preferences for the mix and level of public sector outputs. A federal system of government that is able to accommodate these differences can enhance the level of well-being of the nation's citizens. This is the essential justification for provincial autonomy with respect to revenues and expenditures.

It needs to be acknowledged, however, that the efficient allocation of capital and labour may not be the only goal of public policy; it may also be shaped by other priorities.

The Tax Collection Agreements can be seen to be concerned with efficiency in the allocation of the nation's resources to the extent that they contribute to generating equal net fiscal benefits among the provinces and to minimizing impediments to the free flow of factors of production. The contribution of the agreements to keeping administration and compliance costs at a reasonable level is also important. They do not represent a constraint on provincial autonomy given the fact that all provinces have the option to withdraw from the Agreements.

Although the Tax Collection Agreements have served the country well over a period of many years, they have more recently become a source of contention. The challenge is to preserve their desirable aspects but only to the extent that they accommodate an acceptable level of provincial autonomy. The discussion in the next section attempts to outline certain aspects of this trade-off as it relates to several recent provincial fiscal initiatives.

RECENT PROVINCIAL INITIATIVES AND TAX COMPETITION

The increased flexibility that has been attained by the provinces in the field of income taxation has not prevented them from maintaining uniformity in important areas of taxation practice, whether or not they are parties to the Tax Collection Agreements. Indeed, it is easy to identify certain areas where provincial governments are well served by tax coordination. The reasons they agree to undertake such coordination are essentially the same as those which lead sovereign countries to enter into international tax treaties. At the very least, the latter incorporate principles of reciprocity and non-discrimination, the observance of which serves a common interest.

The provisions of the Tax Collection Agreements go far beyond those covered by typical international tax treaties, however—a fact that appears to have become a cause of growing dissatisfaction among the provinces with respect to certain provisions involving both personal and corporate income taxation. The main problem stems from the fact that some provinces, especially those with a large natural resource revenue

base, feel unduly constrained in their use of provincial income taxes as instruments for creating a more diversified and prosperous provincial economy.

* * *

The Promotion of Provincial Economic Development

The provinces generally consider that personal and corporate income taxes, both of which are covered by the Tax Collection Agreements, provide important instruments for encouraging economic development within their boundaries. Alberta, in particular, is concerned that the depletion of the resources upon which its current growth is based poses a serious threat for its future. To forestall economic decline, the province has decided to utilize a portion of its current resource revenues to build a diversified industrial structure—for example, by offering incentives to selected industrial sectors, including tax cuts, deductions, and refundable tax credits. The provincial government has indicated that one of its goals is to encourage companies to locate their head offices in Alberta and to carry on a greater proportion of their administrative and research and development activities there. Because the current agreements constrain the provinces in the use of such incentives or differential rates of taxation, Alberta has withdrawn from the corporation tax segment of the agreements and now administers its own corporate income tax system.

While the coordination of taxation under the agreements does not prevent the provinces from employing tax policy to promote economic development, the possible differentials in tax burdens between the provinces could have indirect implications for such coordination. Lower tax burdens on capital income in one jurisdiction can have several effects. First, by lowering the average tax on capital, they may induce further saving and investment. Second, the differential may entice capital to relocate from other jurisdictions—either other countries or other provinces. That is to say, provinces can manipulate the net fiscal benefits that accrue to the factors of production within their borders in an effort to increase the level of provincial economic activity. When such action is taken by one province, other provinces can be expected to react in the interests of preserving their own tax base. The general tendency, as recent examples illustrate, is for tax burdens to remain fairly uniform over time—the strength of this tendency depending upon the mobility of the factors of production that are subject to tax.

The status of estate taxation in Canada offers an interesting example. The Rowell-Sirois Commission found that multiple taxation of estates was common because provinces levied their taxes on the basis of both the prior residence of the decedent and the location of his assets. To overcome this problem, the Commission recommended that the provinces withdraw from the field of estate taxation. Under the Tax Rental Agreements that followed the Second World War, the provinces did withdraw from the succession duty field and were compensated, as in the case of income taxes, with per capita federal payments. The federal government entered the field of estate taxation at the same time. Under the 1957 agreements, 50 percent of federal collections of succession duties in each province was returned to that province as part of the movement towards tax sharing. In 1964, the provincial share was raised to 75 percent. Provinces outside the agreements pertaining to estate taxes received an abatement of the federal tax collected in their jurisdictions on the same percentage basis, or they received an equivalent cash transfer from the federal government.

Prior to 1972, British Columbia, Ontario, and Quebec levied their own estate taxes. As part of the overall federal tax reform of 1971, the federal government made capital gains that had accrued on assets taxable at death, but at the same time the government withdrew from the taxation of estates. Although six other provinces (all except Alberta) hastily entered the field, their use of the estate tax

steadily declined, until by 1980 only one province (Quebec) still levied a tax on estates. As one observer remarked, "given the high mobility of wealthy individuals, a set of uncoordinated and independent . . . provincial death taxes seems unlikely to be an important revenue source in any country."[6]

As mentioned earlier, Quebec and Ontario have maintained their own corporate tax systems for some years, consistent to a considerable degree with the federal definition of corporate taxable income, and have altered their own bases when the federal base changed. Moreover, corporate tax rates tend to exhibit significant uniformity across all jurisdictions and, again, tend to move together. Part of the explanation for the consistency of tax bases is found in each province's interest in minimizing the compliance costs of firms operating in two or more provinces. The explicit intention of tax rate uniformity is to avoid the loss of mobile capital to jurisdictions with lower tax burdens. If any province lowers the domestic tax burden on capital, it is in the interests of other provinces to follow suit.

The "tax competition" can thus result in reasonably harmonized tax burdens. Taxes, however, are not the only element that can be adjusted by provincial governments in an effort to attract capital investment by means of reducing costs. The provinces can also reduce costs to industry by undertaking expenditures for the purpose of providing a wide variety of supporting facilities and services for the benefit of business. The question that arises is whether competition of this sort is beneficial. With regard to the corporate tax in particular, does competition lead to a desirable sharing of the net burden of taxation between capital and labour?

There is no ready answer to this question.[7] On the one hand, it has been argued that mobility of capital—and the resulting demands on provincial resources to attract such capital—severely constrains the ability of the provinces to achieve the levels and distribution of services to the public that provincial governments would prefer. It has been contended by some that this competitive process among the provinces may result in a lack of sufficient revenues to fund the necessary public services. Each province would prefer to raise taxes to help finance needed expenditures, but each finds that its best interests lie in keeping its rates low no matter what the other provinces do. This argument contains a value judgment with respect to the appropriate size of the public sector. One could equally argue that provincial tax competition provides a beneficial constraint on the growth of the public sector. A proper evaluation of the question would likely require construction of a detailed model indicating how the magnitude of public sector expenditures is influenced by the preferences of citizens.

On the other hand, any harmonization of provincial taxes and expenditure benefits brought about by interprovincial competition can have desirable effects, as indicated earlier. Moreover, a healthy rivalry between jurisdictions can generate efficiency in the provision of public goods and services.[8] The results, again, depend on the objectives of the provincial decision makers.

The kind of competition we have outlined can occur to a considerable extent within the confines of the present fiscal arrangements, with provinces using tax rates and expenditure policies as their primary instruments. In fact, the recent history of provincial taxes and expenditures can be interpreted as the outcome of just such a process of tax competition among the more wealthy provinces to attract capital investment within their boundaries. For its part, the federal government has developed regional policies, including programs of conditional and unconditional grants, to help the "have-not" provinces meet this competition without being forced to cut back their level of public services severely. The recent increase in fiscal disparities among all provinces caused by the increase in natural resource revenues accruing to a few provinces has put a strain on the relative stability of this competitive process, most directly

because of the magnitude of equalization needed to maintain some reasonable balance in provincial fiscal capacity.

More indirectly, some of the provinces now see the corporate income tax in particular as being not just a source of revenue, but also an important tool for orchestrating the development of their provincial economies. They seek to do so by establishing different tax rates and other incentives for selected industrial sectors.

The above review is far from complete, of course, but it does serve to emphasize what is probably the most pressing problem facing the Tax Collection Agreements—the increased disparity in fiscal capacity among the provinces and the resulting implications for provincial development policies. The more richly endowed provinces may withdraw from the agreements if the latter do not provide the degree of flexibility required to enable them to pursue their development objectives. Moreover, this suggests that the withdrawal could become cumulative because other provinces may feel compelled to institute a separate tax system of their own in order to be free to establish comparable policies. Should such a development come to pass, many of the desirable features of the agreements would be sacrificed as well, including their contribution to economies in administration and compliance, as well as their influence on the maintenance of common allocation rules with respect to the taxation of income.

In this connection, the adoption of a "Code of Conduct," as suggested by some provincial governments, could serve a useful purpose. As proposed, it would complement the present agreements by defining acceptable behaviour in some, or all, of the areas of taxation or expenditure policy, regulatory activity, and procurement. Such a code should recognize the extent to which various policy instruments can be substituted for one another in order to achieve provincial objectives. Enforcement of the provisions of the code could take several forms, but the experience at the 1980 Constitutional Conference suggests that a constitutional provision that would be enforceable by the Courts would be unacceptable to many provinces. An alternative approach would be to entrust the policing of such an agreement to the provinces, with federal government support.

The above discussion has established two major points. The first is that a separate system of provincial taxes may well lead to significant differences in provincial tax structures with respect to the tax base, tax rates, and rules governing the allocation of taxable income. The second point is that the existence of different provincial tax systems could result in a misallocation of productive resources and a loss in economic efficiency.

With respect to the first point, it has been acknowledged that the provinces up to now have sought in certain important areas to coordinate tax policy either because they have had some incentive to do so or because they have been driven to that course by force of circumstances.

With respect to the second point, we earlier indicated some concern about the potential for fiscally induced migration and about the efficiency costs of such migration. There are several additional qualifications that should be noted. The first qualification relates to firms and their objectives. As a general rule, companies have an incentive to carry out their activities in those locations, and employing those technologies, which will result in the least cost to them after taking account of taxes. Even if there is a significant difference in the tax burden between two provinces that is not offset by other benefits, however, firms may seek ways to minimize the burden rather than relocate their production.

Through strategies such as incorporating in each province when tax rates differ and through choice of debt and equity financing, a firm can moderate the effects of the tax paid in each jurisdiction, as well as its overall tax burden. Moreover, if there is little cooperation between jurisdictions in the form of joint audits or other aspects of coordinated tax administration, the possibilities for tax avoidance and tax evasion are increased. Recent experience in the United States has shown that this avoidance or evasion can involve a significant amount of tax liabilities.[9]

Crown Corporations

Numerous Crown corporations are at present engaged in business activities in Canada, and more may be established in the future. Performing a variety of functions and operating in numerous industries, Crown corporations are important instruments of economic and social policy at both the federal and provincial levels. Without gainsaying their usefulness in the pursuit of policy objectives, there exist several issues with respect to these public enterprises that should concern policy makers and citizens. Many of these issues touch directly on the subject matter of this report. Included in this list would be the role of public enterprises in economic development, the implications of their taxation status, and the implications of the activities of Crown corporations for intergovernmental fiscal arrangements, especially the Equalization Program . . . .

Some provincial Crown enterprises, especially the electric utilities, have been explicit instruments of provincial development policy. Electric utilities were among the earliest provincial Crown corporations. By providing ample supplies of power at the lowest possible rates, provinces hoped to attract industry to their jurisdictions. To this end, most Crown corporations were established to undertake the production and distribution of electricity or to take over the operations of private owners. The utilities were aided in achieving the lowest possible financial costs by two provincial policies. First, the public owners, unlike private owners, did not demand a market rate of return—or, indeed, any return—on their equity investment; the corporations were simply required by legislation to recover their financial costs. Second, the cost of debt capital to the utilities was kept low through direct borrowing by the provinces or through provincial guarantees backing the debt of these utilities.

The tax treatment of Crown corporations engaged in business activities is also a serious concern. Section 125 of the BNA Act states that "no Lands or Property belonging to Canada or any province shall be liable to taxation." In practice this has meant that Crown corporations created at one level of government are exempt from paying taxes levied by the other level of government, or by other governments at the same level.

In reality, some payments are made. For instance, many federal and provincial departments and enterprises make grants in lieu of property taxes to municipal governments. In addition, Part VIII of the Fiscal Arrangements Act enables the federal government to enter into reciprocal taxation agreements with the provinces, under which both levels agree to pay each other's sales taxes. At present, the six provinces east of Manitoba have entered into such agreements with the federal government.

There are no intergovernmental agreements with regard to the payment of income taxes by Crown corporations. This tax exemption provides an incentive for governments at both levels to take over profitable private corporations. By following this course, the new public owners are able to appropriate the income tax revenue otherwise payable to the other level of government.

Although the potential exists for the erosion of the corporate tax revenue of each level of government, the problem is more acute for the federal government in view of the fact that it collects 70 percent of corporate income taxes.

The nature of these problems has been apparent for some time. In the debate surrounding the expropriation of several private electric utilities by the Quebec government in 1944, the province noted the apparent inequity in the fact that a portion of revenue from electricity sold by these companies was used to pay federal income tax, whereas in Ontario prices were lower because the provincially owned utility was exempt from federal taxes.

To encourage neutrality in the tax treatment of public and private utilities, in 1947 the federal government offered to transfer 50 percent of the federal corporate tax revenues collected from privately held utilities to the provinces. Currently, under the Public Utilities Income Tax Transfer Act, the federal government turns over to the provinces 95 percent of federal corporate income tax collected on private corporations involved in the distribution, or generation for distribution, of electricity, gas, and steam to the public. Estimated payments to the provinces under these provisions for the fiscal year 1980–81 were $72 million.[10]

Since it is not possible for the federal government to shield all private companies in this way if the expansion of provincial ownership is considered undesirable, one remedy would seem to be to make Crown corporations taxable either by agreement or by constitutional amendment.[11] It must be acknowledged, however, that defining the taxable income of Crown corporations would present difficult problems in view of the fact that, unlike private corporations, earning a return on investment may not be a primary concern in the operation of these businesses. Thus, as in the case of the provincial electric utilities, the federal tax could be avoided by charging prices to consumers that would not provide a reasonable rate of return on invested capital. Ironically, without a careful definition of the tax base, making these types of public enterprise liable for tax could actually generate increased takeover of private companies, after which a province could convert them to non-profit status by offering their services to residents at subsidized prices.[12] In addition, since the public enterprises may have preferential access to capital markets because provincial governments guarantee their debt, taxable profits could be reduced significantly by increases in the firm's debt / equity ratio. Alternatively, a province might be able to impose special taxes on these enterprises that (if deductible in the determination of taxable income) could also reduce their federal tax liability. All these considerations suggest that, if neutrality between public and private sector enterprises is the objective, it would be necessary to develop special rules to impute a tax base for Crown corporations if they are to be taxed on the same basis.[13]

Finally, interpretation of section 125 of the BNA Act has assumed considerable importance in the context of federal-provincial competition for the revenues derived from taxation of natural resources in the provinces. Of particular importance are the massive revenues from the production of oil and gas in the west.

Understandably the provinces involved consider the rents generated from the exploitation of the natural resource riches situated in their jurisdictions as their own property. The federal government has also been determined to capture some portion of these rents through the tax system by the use of two devices. The federal Petroleum and Gas Revenue Tax, and the Natural Gas and Gas Liquids Tax, under the National Energy Program, both of which were designed to raise revenues for the federal government, were viewed by the producing provinces as an actual or potential tax on their Crown property. A ruling by the courts in favour of the provinces with respect to either of these tax measures would imply that they could shelter their oil and gas revenues from federal taxation under the umbrella of Crown corporations.

To complicate matters, a province may wish to use the instrument of a Crown corporation for reasons other than merely to escape federal tax. Measuring rent is a complicated affair and given that the concept tends to possess the characteristics of a residual, a Crown corporation might be an efficient tool by which to collect these rents, either at the production stage or at some intermediary stage between the producer and the purchaser. Some provinces consider their taxation powers as insufficiently refined fiscal instruments for exercising their provincial rights over natural resources to best advantage. In addition

to this technical question, there are constitutional constraints on the use by provinces of potentially efficient tools—particularly the use of what have been interpreted by the Supreme Court as indirect taxes—that may favour the use of public enterprises. The point is that making provincial Crown corporations subject to federal tax may have the effect of confining the provinces to the use of inferior fiscal tools.

* * *

CONCLUSIONS

National economic efficiency is enhanced to the extent that the impact of the policies and programs of government is neutral in determining the allocation of resources across the country. It follows from this conclusion that equality of net fiscal benefits between provinces is one factor necessary to promote efficiency in the Canadian economy. The tax system, in turn, constitutes an important element in the determination of the net fiscal benefits that shall accrue to residents; consequently it also has important implications with respect to the goal of economic efficiency.

In a federal country, the income tax system should take account of the need to maintain neutrality in its impact on resource allocation by avoiding double taxation and other discriminatory measures. In addition, the tax system should also aim at achieving other subsidiary goals. When two levels of government in a federal country tax the same income and when individual persons and firms earn income in several provinces, it is desirable to devise a system that will minimize the cost of compliance for taxpayers and the cost of tax collection for governments and yet will enable the governments involved to maintain a high degree of individual autonomy.

Over the years, the Tax Collection Agreements have made an important contribution towards the realization of these goals. Since 1941, we have shifted from complete centralization of personal and corporate income taxes to a much more flexible sharing of income taxes between federal and provincial governments. The increased flexibility that has been attained by the provinces in designing their income tax systems has not prevented them from maintaining uniformity in important areas of taxation practice, whether or not they are parties to the Tax Collection Agreements. All provinces agree to rules governing the allocation of individual incomes and corporate profits for purposes of provincial levies, and these rules provide for the fair taxation of income. Broad conformity to the definition of the tax base helps prevent the sort of "tax jungle" problems that arose in the 1930s in Canada and that currently exist in other federal states.

Provinces that are party to the agreements have achieved significant flexibility in establishing tax rates and rate structures designed to achieve their provincial goals. The cost savings to the provinces as a result of the federal absorption of collection and administration expenses seem to compensate them adequately for their lack of autonomy with respect to their tax bases. Some provinces, however, have recently expressed concern about significant and unanticipated changes in the definition of the tax base by the federal government. Any negative impact of such changes on provincial tax revenues is partially offset by a federal guarantee. Some such guarantee seems to be desirable when tax bases are shared and when the federal government has unilateral control over the definition of those bases.

Although the agreements with respect to personal income tax appear stable, this is also the area where the economic costs of establishing separate systems are usually thought to be relatively small in terms of the potential impact on resource allocation. Increased provincial flexibility in the rate structure of personal income tax can probably also be accommodated at small cost. The introduction of discriminatory provisions, however, should not be condoned on either ethical or economic grounds.

Significant provincial coordination of taxation can coexist with an aggressive provincial development policy. The present agreement with respect to corporate income tax does not prevent provinces from using taxation rates as a primary tool for promoting economic development. In the case of some provinces, however, this is not a preferred instrument for economic development. In particular, it does not allow tax burdens to be differentiated by industrial sector.

Any province's development strategy, if it is to be effective, will operate to some extent at the expense of other provinces. In this respect, a Code of Conduct, agreed to by all provinces, would seem to be a desirable development. The virtue of such a code lies in its ability to address concerns outside the scope of the present Tax Collection Agreements, including the more volatile corporate tax rates, provincial expenditures aimed at attracting industry, and the entire range of regulatory measures enacted by provinces. Establishment of a Code of Conduct to govern these areas would serve the mutual self-interest of all provinces.

Notes

1. The income from non-incorporated businesses, such as income of the self-employed, and certain other income that is taxed under the personal income tax are allocated across the provinces according to the allocation rules used for corporate income tax.

2. The Rowell-Sirois Commission report.

3. The per capita payments attempted to recognize the fiscal needs of some provinces and the fiscal capacities of the more prosperous provinces. To this end, each agreeing province was usually offered a choice of transfer provisions. For example, in the 1947 Tax Rental Agreements, a province could choose an annual payment of $15 per capita or a payment of $12.75 per capita plus 50 percent of that province's tax receipts from the fields abandoned in 1940. Under the 1952 agreements, a province could choose per capita payments, as under the former agreements, or a formula offering specified percentages of federal tax yields in the province in the year 1948. In all cases the annual payment was to be subject to an escalation formula related to the growth in incomes and population. An interesting account of the evolution of the agreements is contained in R. M. Burns, *The Acceptable Mean: The Tax Rental Agreements, 1941–1962* (Toronto: Canadian Tax Foundation, 1980).

4. An extended discussion of the allocation rules can be found in E. H. Smith, "Allocating to Provinces the Taxable Income of Corporations: How the Federal-Provincial Allocation Rules Evolved," *Canadian Tax Journal* 24:5 (September-October 1976).

5. The allocation rules in note 1 apply here as well.

6. G. F. Break, *Financing Government in a Federal System* (Washington: Brookings, 1980), 50.

7. In order to answer this question, it is necessary to determine the influence on labour, capital, and consumers of the national average level of taxes and to reconcile possibly differing provincial preferences on the distribution of the burden among the various factors and consumers.

8. A forceful statement of the position that the desirable degree of fiscal harmonization will come about spontaneously through the action of forces, as here described, is contained in G. Bélanger, "Should Fiscal Harmonization Be Imposed?" a study prepared for the Economic Council of Canada, 1981.

9. See Break, *Financing Government*, p. 62, where he discusses the recent success of the Multistate Tax Commission in uncovering additional business tax revenue through joint audits conducted by the member states.

10. Canadian Tax Foundation, *The National Finances, 1980–81* (Toronto: Canadian Tax Foundation, 1981).

11. This, of course is controversial. Another suggestion, that of unilateral federal action, has been around for some time. In that case, the federal government would assign a tax liability to provincial Crown enterprises, and the amount of this liability would be deducted from the transfers that would otherwise have been payable to the provinces. Some such scheme was included in the federal budget proposals of 1946 (but there it was part of the Tax Rental Agreements). This provision did not appear in the final 1947 legislation. See Burns, *The Acceptable Mean*.

12. What distinguishes susceptible firms in this regard is the fact that a large proportion of their output is consumed by residents in the province. This is unlike public enterprises created in the resource industries, such as the Saskatchewan Potash Corporation, whose function is in part to collect rents. In these cases, a large proportion of output is exported outside the province.

13. Similar sorts of problems sometimes arise with private incomes. For example, since it is generally impossible to distinguish between the return to labour and the return to capital in the incomes of non-incorporated enterprises, such as proprietorships and partnerships, the compromise of taxing all income as personal income is used.

Selected Readings

Bird, R. M., ed. *Fiscal Dimensions of Canadian Federalism.* Toronto: Canadian Tax Foundation, 1980.

Canada, Parliamentary Task Force on Federal-Provincial Fiscal Arrangements. *Fiscal Federalism in Canada.* Ottawa: Minister of Supply and Services, 1981.

Canadian Tax Foundation, *The National Finances: An Analysis of the Revenues and Expenditures of the Government of Canada, 1985–86.* Toronto: Canadian Tax Foundation, 1986.

Courchene, T. J., Conklin, D. W., and Cook, Gail, eds. *Ottawa and the Provinces: The Distribution of Money and Power.* Vols. 1 and 2. Toronto: Ontario Economic Council, 1984.

Simeon, Richard. "Fiscal Federalism—A Review Essay." *Canadian Tax Journal* 30 (January–February 1982): 41–51.

11. EQUALIZATION PAYMENTS AND THE DIVISION OF POWERS

Thomas J. Courchene

*   *   *

The purpose of this chapter is not to focus in any detail on the precise nature of Canada's equalization program or on the manner in which the Canadian system of equalization has evolved since its inception in 1957. Rather, the purpose is to explore the variety of rationales for equalization and how they relate to the degree of decentralization we find in the Canadian federation, both in absolute terms and in terms of what we find in other federations.

*   *   *

HORIZONTAL AND VERTICAL BALANCE

Every federation has to grapple with the two perennial problems of intergovernmental finance—vertical and horizontal fiscal balance. Vertical fiscal balance relates to the allocation of revenues, relative to the allocation of expenditure responsibilities, between the provinces or states and the federal government. Horizontal balance relates to the relative fiscal capacities of

Thomas J. Courchene, "Equalization Payments and the Division of Powers," in his *Economic Management and the Division of Powers*, vol. 67 of *Research Studies for the Royal Commission on the Economic Union and Development Prospects for Canada* (Toronto: University of Toronto Press, 1986), 129-151. Reprinted by permission of University of Toronto Press. ©Minister of Supply and Services Canada, 1986. The essay has been abridged and edited to suit the needs of this volume.

the second tier of governments (i.e., provinces in Canada, states in the United States, cantons in Switzerland, laender in West Germany). In terms of vertical balance, the Canadian experience is probably typical of most federations. At the time of Confederation the importance of the expenditure responsibilities allocated to the provinces was minimal relative to those assigned to the federal government. Partly as a result, Ottawa was given the power to levy all manner of taxes and in particular was given exclusive jurisdiction over indirect taxes (including customs), the major source of revenues at the time. The march of economic and social events altered this balance. The expenditure functions allocated to the provinces under the Constitution—such as education, hospitals, welfare, highways—have become progressively more important over the years, a result of the transfer of responsibility to the state for functions previously undertaken by the family or church (welfare and to some extent education) and the advance of technology (e.g., the spread of the automobile and the corresponding need for highways). In any event, the provinces and their municipalities currently account for considerably more than 50 percent of total government spending. Accompanying this trend has been an ongoing problem relating to the vertical distribution of revenues in the federation: Ottawa's share of revenues has over much of the postwar period tended to exceed its share of expenditure responsibilities. Apart from requiring the provinces to stay within their own budget constraints (e.g., by borrowing, by increasing provincial taxes, or by paring expenditures), there are three ways to handle this problem of vertical balance:

1. to transfer some expenditure functions to the federal government;
2. to transfer funds or tax room to the provinces with conditions relating to the manner in which these funds can be spent;
3. to transfer funds or tax room to the provinces in a no-strings-attached (unconditional) manner.

All three avenues have been utilized in the Canadian federation.

Since unconditional transfers can be spent when and where the provinces please, they are more consistent with a decentralized federation than either conditional grants or the transfer upward of expenditure functions. As a theoretical matter, we might want to argue that a transfer of an expenditure function from the provincial to the federal arena is much more of a "centralist" solution than is the adoption of a conditional grant. But, as a practical matter, there may be little difference between the two since condition laden intergovernmental transfers can effectively emasculate provincial autonomy with respect to the expenditure category in question. However, this is not the place to elaborate on the interaction between centralization or decentralization and the design of intergovernmental transfers. Suffice it to say that in the Canadian federation, where judicial interpretation of the Constitution has assigned greater power to the lower levels of government than has been the case in the United States, intergovernmental grants have tended to be of the unconditional variety relative to those in the United States, thereby enhancing the more decentralist character of our federation. This relationship can go both ways. On the one hand, unconditional grants enhance provincial autonomy while, on the other, the greater autonomy of the provinces relative to the U.S. states may be the reason why intergovernmental transfers in our federation have tended to be unconditional.

Why is there this concern over vertical balance in a federalism when equalization payments are designed to correct horizontal imbalance? The reason is that the distinction between horizontal and vertical balance is not as clear-cut as we might expect. In correcting for vertical imbalance by means of intergovernmental grants, the federal government can follow two quite different routes. Anthony Scott refers to these two differing approaches as the "principle of derivation" and the "principle of equalization."[1] Under the former, intergovernmental grants are paid to the provinces in relation to the amounts of federal revenues generated in these provinces. Thus, if Ottawa transfers additional income tax points to the provinces according to the principle of derivation, the revenues received by the provinces are determined by the yield of the tax points within their respective jurisdictions. Almost invariably, this approach to rectifying a vertical imbalance in a federation will generate a substantial horizontal imbalance since, as Scott notes, the principle of derivation is "in essence . . . a negation of geographical redistribution."[2]

This negation does not apply if the "principle of equalization" underlies the solution to vertical balance. Scott defines the principle of equalization (not to be confused with Canada's formal equalization program) to mean that the vertical intergovernmental transfers are related not to the amounts of money derived from these provinces but are distributed to the provinces in a more equal fashion. One obvious example would be to transfer funds on an equal per capita basis (which, in essence, is what now occurs under the established programs). With the principle of equalization underlying vertical intergovernmental grants, it is less likely that a resulting horizontal imbalance will be generated.

Intergovernmental grants are, of course, not the only potential source of horizontal imbalance. More important in the Canadian federation are the provinces' own sources of revenues, particularly resource-related revenues. In some federations there exist formal programs, gener-

ally referred to as equalization programs, which
are designed specifically to offset this horizontal
imbalance in revenue across provinces or states.
I shall now turn to the various rationales for an
equalization program.

POLITICAL RATIONALES FOR EQUALIZATION

The Federalist/Constitutional Rationale

Since the first "official" proposal for an equalization program can be traced to the Rowell-Sirois
recommendation for a set of "national adjustment grants," it is not surprising that this report
is the source for some of the arguments for
equalization.[3] My interpretation of the Rowell-
Sirois Report with respect to these grants is that
they are argued for on two related grounds: one
of these I refer to as the "nationhood rationale,"
and it will be dealt with below; the other I have
called the "federalist or constitutional rationale." Essentially the argument here is that the
Constitution has assigned certain powers to the
provinces, and it is only by means of a set of
national adjustment grants (equalization payments) that these powers can be meaningfully
secured. From the Rowell-Sirois Report:

> They [the national adjustment grants] illustrate
> the Commission's conviction that the provincial
> autonomy in these fields must be respected and
> strengthened, and that the only true indepen-
> dence is financial security. . . . They are de-
> signed to make it possible for every province to
> provide for its people services of average Cana-
> dian standards . . . . They are the concrete ex-
> pression of the Commission's conception of a
> federal system which will preserve both a healthy
> local autonomy and build a stronger and more
> unified nation.[4]

The report goes on to say that the issue of horizontal fiscal imbalance was not a major concern
in 1867, particularly in the light of the specific

subsidies that were incorporated in the Constitution Act, 1867. However, over time, conditions
altered markedly and the initial conception of
subsidies had to be replaced by a more comprehensive and logical approach (i.e., the national
adjustments grants):

> The implications for public finance of the eco-
> nomic and social changes which have occurred in
> Canada are of far-reaching importance. As a result
> of the transcontinental economy which was delib-
> erately built up, with its notable concentration of
> surplus income, and later as a result of the disinte-
> gration of this economy [because of the depression
> and the ensuing tax jungle] no logical relationship
> exists between the local income of any province
> and the constitutional powers and responsibilities
> of the government of that province.[5]

One obvious solution would have been to recommend a transfer of these powers and responsibilities from the provinces to the federal
government. The report does not opt for this
alternative (except for unemployment insurance
and old-age pensions). Indeed, it mounts a
staunch argument for continued provincial control of the major expenditure functions. Moreover, it argues that in order to guarantee
provincial autonomy, the proposed national adjustment grants be unconditional in nature:

> It should be made clear that while the adjustment
> grant proposed is designed to enable a province
> to provide adequate services (at the average Ca-
> nadian standard) without excessive taxation (on
> the average Canadian basis) the freedom of action
> of a province is in no way impaired. If a province
> chooses to provide inferior services and impose
> lower taxation it is free to do so, or it may provide
> better service than the average if its people are
> willing to be taxed accordingly, or it may, for
> example, starve its roads and improve its educa-
> tion, or starve its education and improve its
> roads—exactly as it may do today. But no provin-
> cial government will be free from the pressure of
> the opinion of its own people . . . .[6]

As a final comment on the commission's emphasis on the role of equalization payments in pro-

viding the financial independence needed to ensure a province's ability to fulfil its constitutional responsibilities as well as the necessity for these payments to be unconditional in form, the following is particularly apt:

> The Commission's Plan [for national adjustment grants] seeks to ensure every province a real and not illusory autonomy by guaranteeing to it, free from conditions or control, the revenues necessary to perform those functions which relate closely to its social and cultural development.[7]

The Nationhood Rationale

Existing side by side with the federal or constitutional rationale for equalization payments is a national unity or nationhood rationale. Canadians, wherever they live, ought to have access to certain basic economic and social rights—rights which, as it were, ought to attend Canadian citizenship. The fact that some of these basic economic and social rights are assigned, constitutionally, to the provinces should not mean that individual Canadians should thereby be deprived of these services:

> The constitutional division of taxing powers, applied to the existing regional distribution of taxable income, has produced surpluses in some provincial budgets, and in others deficits which have inevitably been reflected in reductions of those community services which Canadians have come to look on as the minimum which their governments should supply. As a result, Canadian citizens in some provinces are receiving educational, health and other social services much inferior to those in other provinces and (quite apart from any question of governmental extravagance or the provision of unusually costly services). Canadian citizens in some provinces are required to contribute a much larger portion of their income to the government of the province than those in other provinces.[8]

Even more revealing is the following excerpt:

> In considering the relative fiscal needs of provincial governments, we are mainly concerned with a few divisions of their expenditures: on education, on social services, on development. It is of national interest that no provincial government should be unduly cramped in any of these respects. Education is basic to the quality of Canadian citizens of the future and it is highly undesirable that marked disparities in the financial resource available for education should exist as between Canadian provinces. Social services, like education, cannot be subjected to marked disparities without serious reactions on the general welfare and on national unity. An appropriate developmental policy is required in each province, and the only standard which can fairly be applied is the policy of the province itself . . . .[9]

A final quote from the report puts more emphasis still on the national unity issue:

> It is important to note that some of the provinces are quite unable to meet their obligations and at the same time provide the social and educational services which Canadians have come to look upon as essential. Such a situation cannot leave other provinces unconcerned. The investors in other provinces will suffer in the case of private or public insolvency among their neighbours. The producers in other provinces might suffer if markets are destroyed. Migrants must be admitted from depressed provinces, and it is not merely a nuisance and an expense but a positive danger to the more prosperous provinces if the migrants are illiterate or diseased or undernourished. Nor is the danger of competition from substandard labour in a distressed province a peril which can be disregarded. More important than all these considerations taken together is the danger to national unity if the citizens of distressed provinces come to feel that their interests are completely disregarded by their more prosperous neighbours, and that those who have been full partners in better times now tell them they must get along as best they can and accept inferior educational and social services.[10]

It is appropriate to note that while these two approaches are quite closely related, the implications for equalization are somewhat different. In particular, the nationhood rationale might be satisfied with conditional transfers related to the achievement of certain levels of basic services whereas the federalist or constitutional rationale would imply unconditional transfers. The transfers associated with the established programs would appear to satisfy the "nationhood" rationale. Although not formally viewed as an equalization program, the equal per capita transfer embodied in the Established Programs Financing (EPF) program does embody an equalization feature. Cast in terms of the previous section, the EPF transfers represent an approach to the vertical balance problem that is associated more with the principle of equalization than with the principle of derivation.

ECONOMIC RATIONALE FOR EQUALIZATION

Fiscal Equity

Economists have rationalized equalization on grounds of both equity and efficiency. The starting point for both these arguments is the recognition that the market income of Canadians living in different provinces does not reflect the additional benefits (or costs) that result from the operations of the provincial public sectors. This leads to both equity and efficiency concerns. I shall deal with the former first.

The Economic Council of Canada (1982) summarizes the equity case for equalization as follows:

[Consider the case where] the net fiscal benefits of most persons within a given province are not zero and there are interprovincial differences in net fiscal benefits between persons in similar financial circumstances. In this case, the requirements of equity would not be met by a federal tax and transfer system based solely on personal market incomes. Horizontal equity would not be achieved because persons with identical real incomes (including net fiscal benefits from provin-

cial budgets) would be treated differently under such a tax and transfer system. Nor would such a tax and transfer system produce vertical equity in the country as a whole. Provincial net fiscal benefits affect the real incomes or living standards of provincial residents (positively or negatively), but that impact is not taken into account by the federal income tax system (or the system of personal transfers). Hence, even if the federal tax system embodied in principle the desired amount of vertical equity, such equity would not be achieved because one important source of personal income is not taken into account by the federal tax system.

What is required to solve these problems is some form of transfer policy that takes account of these differences between provinces. The two main types of instruments that might be considered to achieve this goal are the personal transfer and income tax system and the intergovernmental transfer system.

The personal transfer and income tax system could be adjusted in several ways to achieve the desired goal. For example, each federal taxpayer could be required to adjust his taxable market income by adding or subtracting his amount of provincial net fiscal benefits. Alternatively, the federal tax rate could be adjusted for each province to take account of the effect of net fiscal benefits.

An alternative approach could involve the establishment of a system of intergovernmental grants that would provide transfers to provincial governments, the net value of which would be positive in provinces whose residents have relatively low per capita net fiscal benefits and negative in provinces with high net fiscal benefits. The latter approach, of course, is that embodied in the existing Equalization Program.[11]

As the council points out, to correct the problem with the personal tax transfer system might undermine the federal system. Hence, the appropriate route to follow is the intergovernmental transfer route, i.e., equalization.

Most economists would view the earlier nationhood rationale, and perhaps the constitutional rationale as well, as falling under the rubric of fiscal equity. In my opinion, however, they are conceptually distinct. Indeed, elsewhere I have challenged the notion that an equalization program follows directly from an argument based on horizontal equity—a system of mobility subsidies would appear to be equally consistent as a solution to equity concerns.[12]

Efficiency

Because equalization payments reduce the tax price of public goods and services in the recipient provinces they will also serve to inhibit outmigration from these provinces. Of this, there is little doubt, analytical or empirical. However, what is in some considerable doubt are the resulting implications for economic efficiency. One long-standing approach to this issue argues that equalization runs counter to efficiency because it inhibits the natural adjustment forces: labour is less inclined to seek higher rewards elsewhere because of the subsidy for public sector output provided by equalization.

The more recent argument is that equalization does serve to enhance efficiency.[13] Because of differential provincial fiscal capacities and, particularly, differential resource rents, net fiscal benefits (NFBs) vary considerably across provinces. As a result, prospective migrants will take account of both market income and NFBs in their calculus. Hence, it is possible that an individual or family would move to a province and accept a lower level of market income if this was more than offset by larger NFBs. This phenomenon has come to be referred to as "fiscal-induced" or "rent-seeking" migration. While this migration may be optimal behaviour for the individual or family, it runs counter to national efficiency. An equalization program which serves to "equalize" these NFBs across provinces would ensure that migration becomes dictated more by market than by fiscal considerations.

There is an important element of truth in both approaches. Were P.E.I.'s equalization payment reduced from its present near $1000 per capita level to zero it seems clear that the exodus of people would include some who, on productivity (efficiency) grounds, ought to remain in P.E.I. Similarly, the fact that P.E.I. and Newfoundland do receive $1000 per capita in equalization surely inhibits the migration of persons who, on efficiency grounds, ought to be located elsewhere.

What is clear, however, is that the recent Canadian equalization programs cannot be defended on grounds of efficiency. Consider the representative national average standard (RNAS) approach to equalization that prevailed over the 1977-82 period. The existence of massive resource rents in the western provinces led to the situation where Ontario qualified as a have-not province under the RNAS formula (even with only 50 percent of resource rents entering the equalization formula). The fact that Ontario was denied equalization implies, in terms of the notion of fiscal-induced migration, that too many Ontarians migrated to Alberta. Based on similar reasoning, too few Atlantic residents would have migrated to Ontario. Hence, it is difficult to make the case that the manner in which Canada has implemented equalization is motivated principally by efficiency concerns.

In this context, it is interesting to note that the United States does not have a formal equalization program. As Wallace Oates has remarked, there are no doubt differential net fiscal benefits across the U.S. states but just as likely these differential benefits will be capitalized so that there is no need for an equalization program on efficiency grounds. He concludes that equalization systems are basically a matter not of efficiency but of "taste."[14] It is true that to the extent that differential NFBs across provinces become reflected in differential land prices or rents, then the case for eliminating these NFBs on efficiency grounds (to prevent fiscal-induced migration) is correspondingly weakened.

Equalization and the Distribution-Allocation Trade-Off

There is one further efficiency aspect of equalization that merits discussion—the manner in which equalization relates to overall regional policy. As matters now stand, equalization is far from the only program designed to alter regional or provincial fortunes. The personal income tax system is frequently utilized to provide differential provincial incentives. For example, the incentives for research and development expenditures are more generous in the poorer provinces. There are regional benefits associated with the unemployment insurance program. The Department of Regional Economic Expansion (DREE) programs provide incentives for industry to locate in certain designated regions. There is pressure for Ottawa to provide an equalization feature to the Canada Assistance Plan since the incidence of welfare (on a per capita basis) varies across the provinces, and so on.

The issue that arises is whether the equalization program should be the principal policy avenue for regional or provincial distribution or whether there should be an equalization component in a wide variety of policy areas, including some that clearly alter the wage/rental ratio on a regional or provincial basis. . . .

Economists for the most part would argue for handling regional disparity concerns via distributional policies (such as a negative income taxation for individuals and an equalization program for provinces) and would shy away from utilizing government policy to distort the allocative process on a regional or provincial basis. No doubt there may have to be some exceptions to this principle, but in general I would support the proposition that equalization be the principal vehicle for regional or provincial distribution

and that the remainder of government policy refrain, wherever possible, from incorporating regional or provincial distortions with respect to resource allocation.

EQUALIZATION AND DECENTRALIZATION

It has become common to view the Rowell-Sirois recommendation for a system of national adjustment grants as the forerunner of the present system of equalization. There is a sense in which this is certainly true: equalization payments can be viewed as addressing the same issues as the national adjustment grants. Moreover, the wording of the new constitutional provision with respect to equalization is similar to the Rowell-Sirois phraseology.

However, there is also a sense in which equalization payments can be viewed as having taken on a life of their own, quite apart from Rowell-Sirois. One of the principal recommendations of the report was to centralize the collection of direct taxation. And under the exigencies of wartime economic management, personal and corporate income taxation were centralized at the federal level. In return, the provinces received "tax-rental" payments. . . . The history of the personal income tax arrangements in Canada, shows that the provinces were offered several options with respect to these tax rental payments. In terms of the phraseology employed earlier, it is correct to suggest that the vertical fiscal imbalance was addressed by transfers that followed the principle of equalization rather than the principle of derivation.

All this was changed dramatically when Quebec initiated its own personal income tax in 1954. In order to move toward more uniform treatment for all provinces, the federal government in 1957 offered all provinces given shares of the income taxes that arose within their boundaries. This system converted these transfers to the principle of derivation which, since it implied quite different per capita transfers across the provinces, generated a need for a program to restore horizontal balance. This was the rationale for the 1957 equalization program.

Whereas Rowell-Sirois recommended national adjustment grants as part of a package which would transfer all direct taxation to the federal level, the actual experience was such that Canada did not incorporate a separate equalization program as long as direct taxation remained under Ottawa's control (although it is true that the federal-provincial transfers under the aegis of tax rental payments did incorporate equalizing features); moreover, Canada embarked on a formal equalization program only when responsibility for direct taxation began to be returned to the provinces.

While the existence of an equalization scheme will in general enhance provincial autonomy and, therefore, lead to a decentralization of powers, the characteristics of the Canadian equalization program were and are such that they have contributed to a particular type of decentralization—decentralization of the power to tax. The poorer provinces could be enticed to accept decentralization via increased provincial tax room only to the extent that they would share "fairly" in the process. Indeed, this is one of the reasons why the equalization standard in the early years was defined in terms of the yield of the two richest provinces, rather than the national average. It was only after the program was broadened to include tax sources other than the direct taxes that the national average standard became generally accepted. Moreover, this way of viewing equalization also provides a rationale for the unconditional nature of equalization payments: the revenues accruing to the richer provinces from their enhanced tax room can obviously be spent as these provinces wish, so that it was only natural that the resulting equalization flows to the poorer provinces should also be unconditional.

There is a further implication relating to equalization and the division of powers—that it is far too narrow a conception of equalization to be viewed as a program only for the poor or recipient provinces. What equalization provides the richer provinces is the ability to increase their fiscal autonomy by flexing their power to tax. Indeed, the existence of an equalization program designed to equalize provincial tax revenues to the national average (now the five-province) standard probably provided the rationale for the substantial post-1957 transfer to the provinces of tax points for personal and corporate taxation. Even though there is still a large cash transfer component to the EPF payments, this cash transfer portion would no doubt be much larger without the existence of an equalization program.

In this sense, then, the equalization program is probably a major factor in determining the manner in which the fiscal system in our federation has been decentralized.

APPENDIX

Table 11–1   A Summary of Major Developments with Respect to Equalization

Date	Subject	Description of Amendments or Innovations	Comments
1867	BNA Act statutory subsidies	Payments to provinces in return for surrendering indirect taxes to Ottawa. The subsidies contained an element of equalization in that they were per capita grants up to a maximum population. They were revised on many occasions (e.g. Duncan Royal Commission, White Royal Commission) and were geared toward the notion of fiscal need. Still exist today, but are of no real financial significance now, whereas in 1867 they represented a substantial share of provincial revenues.	Important in that they allow the concept of equalization to be traced back to the BNA Act.
1940	National Adjustment Grants	Recommended in Rowell-Sirois Report. These grants were to be paid on the basis of fiscal need. Determined by evaluating provincial/local expenditure needs in relation to access to revenues.	Not implemented. However, the rationale for these grants—to enable provinces to provide national average levels of basic services at not unduly high tax rates—underlies the present-day formulations of equalization.
1957	First formal equalization program. Part of 1957–62 fiscal arrangements	Federal government agreed to bring per capita yields from the three standard taxes up to the average yield in the two wealthiest provinces. The revenue sources and tax rates were as follows: personal income taxes (10 percent), corporate income taxes (9 percent), succession duties (50 percent).	Equalization was restricted to the three "shared" taxes. The tax rates applied in calculating provincial revenues for equalization purposes were those that applied in the tax rental arrangements. Alberta fell into the category of a "have-not" province. Indeed, only the richest province (Ontario, at this time) did not receive payments. This was a necessary result of equalizing to the wealthiest two provinces.
1958	Increased equalization for personal income tax	The provincial share of personal income taxes paid to the provinces increased from 10 to 13 percent. This entered the equalization formula.	Equalization was tied in closely with the tax arrangements, as one might expect.

1958–61 Atlantic Provinces Adjustment Grants and Newfoundland Additional Grants Act	Additional unconditional grants to the Atlantic provinces, rationalized on the basis of their low fiscal capacity.	The additional grants appear to have been modelled after Rowell-Sirois adjustment grants.
1962 1962–67 fiscal arrangements agreement	Personal income tax share rose to 16 percent, in accordance with the tax arrangements. Introduction of 50 percent of three-year average of provincial revenues and taxes from natural resources. Equalization standard reduced to the national average level.	First initiative to expand equalization beyond shared taxes. As compensation for movement down to national average, the Atlantic Provinces Adjustment Grant was increased from $25 million to $35 million. Alberta and British Columbia become ''have'' provinces as a result of the resource provision.
1962–67 Provinces acquired an increasing share of personal income tax	The share of personal income taxes allocated rose from 16 percent at the outset of the arrangements to 24 percent by 1967. This increasing proportion automatically entered the formula.	Consistent linking of the equalization program with the tax arrangements.
1964–65 Natural resource changes	In fiscal year 1964–65, the equalization standard once again became the two top provinces. Resources were pulled out of the formula, and provinces could receive equalization only to the extent that their per capita entitlements exceeded 50 percent of the amount by which their per capita resource revenues (three-year average) exceeded the national average level.	Equalization payments increased because the impact of equalizing to the two top provinces was worth more than the pulling of resource revenues from the formula. Alberta and British Columbia had positive equalization entitlements, but these were reduced to zero by the resource deduction provision.
1967 Introduction of the representative tax system of equalization (RNAS)	Sixteen revenue categories, each with its own base, equalized to national average level. Revenues that were eligible for equalization were based on provincial total revenues. Entitlements were summed over all sixteen categories. This total, if positive, represented the province's equalization. Negative overall entitlements were set equal to zero (i.e., funding was a federal responsibility, no province paid money into the scheme).	Program was open-ended, driven by the degree of disparity in the revenue sources and by total provincial revenues. Underlying rationale cited for program was drawn from Rowell-Sirois Report. Attempted to be representative of taxing practices of provinces. Did not include revenues designated for local purposes.

(cont'd.)

Table 11–1 (cont'd.)

Date	Subject	Description of Amendments or Innovations	Comments
1972	Program extended	Addition of three new tax sources brought total to 19. Revenues from these three sources (race track revenues, medical premiums, hospital premiums) were previously equalized under miscellaneous revenues.	Part of the "housekeeping" involved in keeping the system "representative."
1973–74	School-purpose taxes included	That proportion of property taxes levied for school purposes was incorporated in the program.	Potentially a major modification in that property taxes are viewed as a local rather than as a provincial tax.
1974–75	Energy revenue modification	Two sorts of energy revenues, "basic" and "additional." Basic revenues refer to those derived in 1973–74. Additional revenues are those generated above this level and attributable to the rise in prices rather than to an increase in output. Basic revenues equalized in full. Additional revenues equalized to extent of one-third.	Abandonment of concept of "full" equalization. Financial implications of not enacting this measure would have been a tripling of total payments and the inclusion of Ontario in the have-not category.
1977	Equalization component of Fiscal Arrangements Act	Program expanded to 29 sources as a result of reclassification of revenues. Major changes in definitions of some tax bases. Only 50 percent of non-renewable resources eligible to enter the formula. Natural resources override provision meant that no more than one-third of total equalization could arise from resource revenues.	Postponed rather than solved problems created by mushrooming energy revenues. The 50 percent provision from 1977 onward was in fact a more generous treatment of energy resources than the "basic" and "additional" compromise devised in 1974. Federal government felt it was more consistent to treat all non-renewable resources in an identical fashion.
1981	Bill C-24	Two provisions: • withdrawal of sale of crown leases category from the program; • personal income override—no province eligible for equalization of its per capita personal income exceeded the national average level in the current and preceding two years.	The personal income override was made retroactive to fiscal year 1977–78, thereby confiscating over $1 billion of equalization due to Ontario. While one may agree with the spirit of the action, the personal income override is an arbitrary measure and does not fit well into the conceptual basis of the program, which has to do with fiscal

Date		
		capacities and not with personal incomes. This provision may lend support to a "macro" equalization program where the basis of fiscal deficiencies is calculated with respect to variables such as personal income.
1982	New tax source added	Under the National Energy Program, Ottawa returns half of oil export tax to the exporting provinces. It enters the formula.	Question becomes: should it enter as a separate category or be lumped in somewhere with existing revenues from energy? See conclusion.
1982	1982–87 fiscal arrangements. New Representative Five-Province Standard (RFPS) equalization program.	Five provisions: • New formula brings provincial revenues per capita up to the average per capita level of five provinces (Ont., Que., Man., Sask. and B.C.). Referred to as the representative five-province standard. • Coverage extended to include municipal revenues and 100 percent of resource revenues. • Beginning in 1983–84, equalization payments constrained by the rate of GNP growth. • Provision guaranteeing a minimum level of payment for recipient provinces. • A transitional payment incorporating minimums for a three-year period.	Removed the personal income override, the resource cap, the differential treatment of energy and non-energy resources, and extended the coverage to include all provincial and local revenues. Energy-related equalization will fall compared with the previous system because the five provinces comprising the RFPS are, on average, not energy rich. RFPS system replaces the original federal proposal for 1982—the "Ontario standard."
1982 (April 17)	Constitution Act, 1982	A provision ensuring equalization is enshrined in Canada's new Constitution.	"Parliament and the government of Canada are committed to the principle of making equalization payments to ensure that provincial governments have sufficient revenues to provide reasonably comparable levels of public services at reasonably comparable levels of taxation."

Source: Thomas J. Courchene, *Equalization Payments: Past, Present and Future* (Toronto: Ontario Economic Council, 1984), 65–7.

Notes

1. Anthony D. Scott, "The Economic Goals of Federal Finance," *Public Finance* 19:3 (1964): 252-3.

2. *Ibid.*, 252.

3. However, it should be recognized that features consistent with the notion of equalization can be traced back to the Constitution Act, 1867.

4. Canada, *Report of the Royal Commission on Dominion-Provincial Relations*, vol. 2 (Ottawa: King's Printer, 1939), 125.

5. *Ibid.*, 78.

6. *Ibid.*, 84.

7. *Ibid.*, 80.

8. *Ibid.*, 79.

9. *Ibid.*, 80.

10. *Ibid.*, 79.

11. The Economic Council of Canada, *Financing Confederation: Today and Tomorrow* (Ottawa: Supply and Services Canada, 1982), 27.

12. See Thomas R. Courchene, *Equalization Payments: Past, Present and Future*, (Toronto: Ontario Economic Council, 1984), chapter 3.

13. See Robin Boadway and Frank Flatters, *Equalization in a Federal State: An Economic Analysis* (Ottawa: Minister of Supply and Services Canada, 1982).

14. Wallace Oates, "Tax Effectiveness and Tax Equity in Federal Countries: Commentary," in C. E. McLure, Jr., ed., *Tax Assignment in Federal Countries* (Canberra: Australian National University, 1983), 94-7.

Selected Readings

Bird, R. M. *Federal Finance: An International Perspective*. Toronto: Canadian Tax Foundation, 1985.

Boadway, Robin, and Flatters, Frank. *Equalization in a Federal State: An Economic Analysis*. Ottawa: Economic Council of Canada, 1982.

Courchene, T. J. *Equalization Payments: Past, Present and Future*. Toronto: Ontario Economic Council, 1984.

Courchene, T. J. "Equalization Payments and Energy Royalties." In A. Scott, ed., *Natural Resource Revenues: A Test for Federalism*. Vancouver: University of British Columbia Press, 1975.

Humm, Derek, and Thomas, Paul. "Less Equal Than Others." *Policy Options* 6: 4 (May 1985): 14-16.

Watson, W. "Simpler Equalization." *Policy Options* 7: 8 (October 1986): 22-25.

12. THE DEVELOPMENT OF THE MAJOR SHARED-COST PROGRAMS IN CANADA

Paul Barker

INTRODUCTION

Federal-provincial fiscal arrangements in Canada are typically seen as being made up of three components.[1] The tax-sharing agreements, which involve the two senior levels of government coordinating their use of tax fields of concurrent jurisdiction, constitute one of the components. Equalization payments, which consist of unconditional transfers by the federal government to the poorer provinces, constitute a second component. And shared-cost programs, which entail the federal government paying for part of the cost of designated provincial programs, constitute a third component. Traditionally, payment under the shared-cost arrangement has been strictly conditional upon the provinces satisfying certain requirements, but this has recently changed.

The intent of this paper is to review the history of one of the components, namely, shared-cost programs. More specifically, the intent is to examine the development of the major shared-cost programs—medical care, hospital care, welfare assistance, and post-secondary education. The first part of the paper provides the necessary background. It discusses the aims of shared-cost programs and the fiscal mechanisms used by the federal government to finance these programs. The paper then outlines the basic stages of the history of the major shared-cost programs. The second part of the paper, the bulk of the paper, presents a detailed look at each of the stages.

An original essay written especially for this volume.

BACKGROUND

Aims of Shared-Cost Programs

Shared-cost programs are essentially fiscal arrangements whereby the federal government provides financial assistance to the provinces on condition that the assistance be used to help establish particular programs in areas under provincial jurisdiction. The federal government, in pursuing this kind of arrangement, has two immediate aims. One is to induce the provinces to introduce and maintain certain public programs. This is accomplished by offering to pay for part of the costs. The other aim is to influence the way in which the programs are operated. This is accomplished by attaching program conditions to the transfers. These conditions have the effect of ensuring that the programs satisfy specific national standards.

As for the ultimate aims of the federal government, it seems that Ottawa has at least two primary reasons for establishing shared-cost programs.[2] One is to deal with a mismatch of revenues and responsibilities. The federal government has the greater ability of the two levels of government to raise revenues. The provinces, on the other hand, have constitutional authority over important and costly responsibilities. The shared-cost arrangement brings together the revenues and the responsibilities. The other aim, the one that is most often associated with the shared-cost arrangement, is to establish programs that offer comparable benefits to all Canadians. Faced with provincial jursidiction over important areas of public policy, the federal government employs the shared-cost arrangement in order to guarantee the nationwide provision of essential services on a equitable basis.[3]

Fiscal Mechanisms

For the purpose of financing shared-cost programs, the federal government has used three types of fiscal mechanisms. One type is the conditional grant. There are in turn different kinds of conditional grants, but the one most relevant to the shared-cost arrangement involves the transfer of federal funds on condition that the provinces satisfy three requirements. First, the transferred funds must be spent on the program covered by the arrangement. Second, the provinces must participate financially in the arrangement. And third, the shared-cost program must operate according to certain program standards. The federal government ensures the fulfillment of the first two requirements by basing its payments on provincial expenditures on the program in question. In most cases, this "cost-matching" feature involves the federal government reimbursing the provinces 50 cents for every dollar they spend. As for the enforcement of the third requirement, Ottawa relies on the threat to withhold funds if program standards are not satisfactorily met.

This kind of conditional grant, the matching conditional grant, is the mechanism most closely identified with the shared-cost arrangement. Indeed, a shared-cost program is traditionally defined as a fiscal arrangement with a cost-matching feature and accompanying program conditions.

A second fiscal mechanism is the block grant. Roughly speaking, the block grant is a conditional grant with less stringent requirements. The block grant, or "block funding," is typically without both a cost-matching element and strictly defined program conditions. At times, it comes close to being an unconditional grant.

A third fiscal mechanism is the tax abatement or tax point transfer.[4] Instead of transferring funds, the federal government, using the tax abatement, transfers taxing rights by reducing or abating its taxes so that the provinces can increase their taxes without causing a rise in the total level of taxation in the country. Put differently, Ottawa makes room for the provinces in designated tax fields. As with the block grant, the term "block funding" is applied to this type of fiscal mechanism because cost-matching and strict program conditions are not usually part of fiscal arrangements involving tax point transfers.[5]

These latter two mechanisms, the block grant and the tax point transfer, are not always identified with the shared-cost arrangement. A case in point is the present arrangement for three of the four major shared-cost programs, which depends upon a combination of tax point transfers and block grants. Under this arrangement, there is no requirement that the provinces spend the tax revenue and the block grants on the three programs or take part financially in these programs. A defining characteristic of the shared-cost program, the explicit sharing of costs, is thus missing. However, some contend that the arrangement includes an understanding that the two will share in the costs of the programs, and there is a requirement that the provinces satisfy certain conditions relating to the operation of two of the three programs. For this paper, all arrangements will be called shared-cost programs with the recognition that some represent an extension of the shared-cost format.

Stages of the Major Shared-Cost Programs

The major shared-cost programs are to be found in the areas of health and social policy. In 1985-86, federal transfers of cash and abated tax room for medical care, hospital care, welfare assistance, and post-secondary education amounted to

$20.1 billion, representing 96 percent of federal spending on shared-cost programs.[6] The importance of these programs stems not only from the huge expenditures, but also from the impact of the programs on the daily lives of Canadians. Few days go by when individual Canadians are not affected by one or more of the major shared-cost programs.

The major shared-cost programs can be seen to have developed through a series of four stages. The first stage, from the end of World War II to the late 1950s, was the era of the conditional grant. Using the conditional grant, the federal government persuaded the provinces to establish shared-cost programs for public health services, various kinds of welfare assistance, and hospital care. The second stage, from 1960 to 1966, witnessed the emergence of new shared-cost programs for medical care and welfare assistance. Once again, the conditional grant was employed, but this time the conditions were less demanding—a result of provincial demands for greater flexibility. During this stage, Ottawa also established a special arrangement that allowed Quebec to receive tax points and supplementary cash payments instead of conditional grants.

The third stage, from 1966 to 1977, was a period of great change. The federal government first introduced a new shared-cost arrangement for post-secondary education, which involved tax point transfers and conditional grants. Later on, in 1977, the arrangements for medical care, hospital care, and post-secondary education were combined into one arrangement based on tax point transfers and block grants. The fourth stage, from 1980 to 1984, was a time in which the federal government tried to increase the conditionality of the major shared-cost programs. As well, it attempted to reduce its financial participation in these same programs. In these endeavours, Ottawa achieved only partial success. With the election of a new government at the federal level in

1984, the shared-cost programs now appear to be entering into a new stage of development.[7]

FIRST STAGE

Beginnings

The history of the major shared-cost programs begins with a series of proposals made by the federal government to the provinces immediately after World War II. The presence of "humanitarian sentiments," Ottawa's successful handling of the war effort, and the emergence of Keynesian economic analysis all suggested that government—more precisely, the federal government—assume an active role in postwar Canada.[8] The federal government responded to these and other factors with its package of interrelated proposals for the reconstruction of Canada. The package included, among other things, shared-cost programs in the areas of health and social policy.

Before this time, the two levels of government had entered into various shared-cost agreements relating to health and social policy. These agreements dealt with vocational training, control of venereal disease, unemployment relief, and old age pensions. However, aside from old age pensions, these programs were either temporary or funded at a relatively low level. The federal proposals of 1945 for health and social policy exceeded what had gone on before. The conditions of the moment, the need to face the challenges of peacetime, demanded such action.

In the area of social policy, the federal proposals revolved mainly around the matter of old-age pensions. The federal government proposed that it assume exclusive financial and administrative responsibility for the existing shared-cost program for old age pensions, which covered residents aged 70 and over who passed a means test. (The federal government would eliminate the means test.) It also proposed a new shared-cost program that would involve the federal government reimbursing the provinces for 50 percent of the cost of old-age pensions for residents aged 65-69 who passed a means test.

In addition, the federal government recommended that it take on the entire responsibility for welfare assistance for "unemployed employables" or individuals able to work but who were unemployed and had exhausted their unemployment insurance benefits. (Eventually, this proposal would form the basis of a shared-cost program.) Finally, Ottawa recommended an expansion of the projects funded under the shared-cost program for vocational education.

In the area of health policy, the federal government put forward an ambitious four-part proposal for a new shared-cost program. The major part provided for the establishment of provincial health insurance programs, offering medical care, hospital care, nursing services, and a host of other health services. The federal government, through conditional grants, would pay up to 60 percent of the estimated cost. A second part offered grants to the provinces so that the necessary staff could be recruited to plan and organize the proposed health insurance program. A third part made low interest loans available to the provinces and local hospital authorities in order to assist with the construction of hospitals. A fourth part, unrelated to the proposed health insurance program, provided grants to the provinces for the financing of a variety of public health services.

The use of the shared-cost arrangement at this time reflected certain constitutional and practical realities. The federal government, in response to various factors, wanted to introduce nation-wide programs in the areas of health and social policy. The introduction of such programs would lead, many believed, to beneficial developments—the maintenance of the purchasing power of consumers, the strengthening of Canadian unity and most important, the provision of a basic level of health and social services to all

Canadians. Unlike the provinces, the federal government had the financial resources necessary to carry out these plans. However, the federal government had little authority to legislate in these two policy areas. The British North America Act gave the provinces, not Ottawa, broad constitutional authority to pass legislation in respect to health and social policy. As the influential report of the Rowell-Sirois Commission noted in 1940, the constitution assigned responsibility for education to the provinces. As for health and social welfare matters, they were not expressly provided for in the constitution, the report said, but they nevertheless belonged primarily to the provinces by reason of provincial jurisdiction over such areas as hospitals, property and civil rights, municipal institutions, and matters of a local or private nature.[9]

One solution to these realities was for Ottawa to transfer a certain percentage of its taxes to the provinces. This would give the provinces the fiscal capacity to introduce new health and social programs. Ottawa, with its ambitious postwar plans, never considered such a solution. In any case, there was no guarantee that the transferred tax revenues would be spent appropriately. A second solution was to transfer responsibilities from the provinces to the federal government. As shown, the federal government had used this solution in some of its proposals in the area of social policy. However, Ottawa recognized that the provinces would be unsympathetic towards a series of proposals that entailed the provinces giving up major responsibilities. As a result, the federal government turned to a third solution—the shared-cost program. The federal government would make grants to the provinces with the stipulation that the provinces satisfy certain conditions. The money involved would provide the provinces with the financial means and incentive to take actions in the areas of health and social policy. The conditions would ensure that the funds would be used to establish programs that would effectively give Canada a nation-wide system of health and social programs. The conditional grant would allow the federal government to do indirectly what it could not do directly.

There was a further aspect to the shared-cost solution, namely the authority to make grants. The federal government had little legislative authority in the areas of health and social policy, but it had the authority to spend in these areas. This authority, the federal spending power, was inferred largely from two provisions in the British North America Act: "Raising of money by any mode of Taxation" and "Public Debt and Property." The two provisions read together meant that the federal government, having raised funds through its power to tax, could spend its revenues or property on any government, institution, or individual. As well, it could attach any conditions to the use of the funds so long as they fell short of an attempt to legislate or regulate in an area of provincial jurisdiction. In short, federal involvement in fields of provincial jursidiction had a constitutional basis.

In 1945 and 1946, the federal and provincial governments met to discuss the package of federal proposals. Many provinces, though critical of some aspects of the proposals, appeared willing to accept the package. But Ontario and Quebec strongly criticized the proposals, largely because they felt that the proposals placed the provinces in a subordinate position. The premier of Quebec said, for example, that the health proposal contained principles "incompatible with the autonomy of the province," and added that the plan for health care, if accepted, would lead to further federal intrusions into this area of provincial jurisdiction.[10]

Quebec and Ontario correctly perceived the nature of the federal proposals. The proposals allowed for aggressive federal action in areas under provincial jurisdiction. But Ottawa's plans only mirrored the centralized nature of Canadian federalism at the time. The same factors that led the federal government to present the proposals—

the nation-wide presence of humanitarian sentiments, the perceived capabilities of Ottawa, and the influence of Keynesian ideas—also gave the country a strong federal government. The pendulum of power, its movement signifying the relative strength of the two levels of government, had swung far over to the federal side.

The final federal-provincial conference on the proposals, held in May 1946, adjourned without agreement. Ottawa and the provinces had been unable to come to an understanding. However, this was hardly the end of Ottawa's plans. The federal government, now at the height of its powers, would pursue the proposals over the next decade. As it turns out, the proposals had provided the federal government with a blueprint. And the blueprint included shared-cost arrangements in the areas of health and social policy.

Initial Developments

The first of these arrangements to be developed dealt with health care. In 1948, the federal government established the National Health Program. Under this program, Ottawa would make grants available to provinces so as to assist in the financing of a number of activities, including care of crippled children, control of cancer, general public health, health surveys, professional training, public health research, control of tuberculosis, mental health, and construction of hospitals. In essence, the grants represented the health proposal of 1945 without the health insurance program.

Basically, the payments took the form of conditional grants. The payments had to be spent on the specified health services. Also important, the grants were closed-ended, meaning that Ottawa would only spend up to a certain limit. (Later, when establishing the major programs, the federal government would make the grants open-ended.) A further feature of the arrangement was that most of the payments were allocated on the basis of a flat grant and population. So, for example, the payment for mental health provided each province with a flat grant of $25 000 and additional sum of money based on population.

Finally, two of the grants were matching conditional grants. These would be allocated on the basis of provincial expenditures on areas covered by the grant arrangement. The federal government would reimburse the provinces for half of their expenditures or, to put it differently, return to the provinces 50 cents of each dollar they spent. The matching grant thus required the provinces to share explicitly with the federal government the cost of the health services. It also provided the provinces with an incentive to spend on these services. Given that the arrangement reduced the cost of each provincial dollar to 50 cents, health services funded by matching grants came at half price. Not surprisingly, Ottawa would use matching conditional grants to induce the provinces to set up the major shared-cost programs.

The health grants were significant in two respects. First, they provided the basis for the emergence of the major health insurance programs. As the prime minister, Mackenzie King, said in 1948, the grants represented "the fundamental prerequisites of a nation-wide system of health insurance."[11] Second, the grants launched the era of the conditional grant.

The next development, strictly speaking, was not a shared-cost program. It constituted a federal initiative directed at an area of provincial jurisdiction, post-secondary education, without the direct participation of the provinces. However, it set the grounds for the emergence of shared-cost arrangements in the field of post-secondary education.

In 1941, the federal government, by order-in-council, began making grants directly to universities. The goal of the grants was to pay for the education of war veterans. In 1945, Parliament passed legislation that gave further support to the making of grants to universities for war veterans. These two actions did not represent the first instance of federal involvement in the area of education, since conditional grant programs for vocational and technical education had been in existence since 1912, but they did represent the first instance of federal involvement in university education.

Six years later, in 1951, a royal commission, set up by the federal government to look into matters relating to the arts, letters, and sciences, found universities badly in need of additional funding. Accordingly, the commission recommended that the federal government make per capita grants of 50 cents to universities. Ottawa accepted the recommendation and began the system of per capita grants in 1951. Under the arrangement, the grants would be allocated to each province according to its share of the total population of the country; within the individual provinces, the funds would be allocated to each university according to its share of the total enrollment of full-time students.[12]

At first, all of the provinces accepted the arrangement. However, provincial enthusiasm for the grants was decidedly mixed. On the one hand, the universities needed the funds and the provinces were unprepared to offer them much aid. On the other hand, education was a provincial responsibility. The federal government had, using its spending power, once again entered into an area of provincial jurisdiction. Worse, the federal government, in doing so, had not properly consulted with the provinces. And worse still, the payments would be made directly to the universities and not through provincial governments.

One year after the introduction of the program, in 1952, the premier of Quebec, Maurice Duplessis, ordered the universities of Quebec to refuse the per capita grants. He argued, as he had about the federal health proposal of 1945, that the arrangement trespassed onto provincial territory and that it could lead to further intrusions. The universities complied with the order. The new federal program for post-secondary education, one that would later be made into a shared-cost arrangement, had a serious failing.[13]

Further Developments

Federal-provincial activities in the fields of health and social policy during the 1950s went beyond education and public health care. With the provinces, the federal government introduced new shared-cost programs in the general area of social welfare. This time, Ottawa relied on open-ended, matching conditional grants. In 1952, it began to offer to pay 50 percent of the cost of provincial pensions for persons aged 65-69 who passed a means test—a proposal from the federal package of 1945. (At the same time, the federal government assumed full financial and administrative responsibility for old-age pensions for persons aged 70 and over—another proposal from 1945.) In the same year, the federal government made arrangements for the continuation of the existing shared-cost program for blind persons, which had started in 1937. The program involved the federal government paying 75 percent of the cost of provincial allowances to blind persons who passed a means test. Two years later, in 1954, Parliament passed legislation enabling the federal government to pay 50 percent of the cost of provincial allowances for disabled persons in need.

These arrangements involved strict conditions. For example, to receive funds under the new arrangements, the provinces had to establish extensive eligibility criteria and place ceilings on monthly payouts to beneficiaries. In addition, each province had to sign a contract or "agreement" with the federal government. These agreements outlined the details of the arrangements, including the conditions, the shareable costs, the procedures of reimbursement, and the grounds for termination of federal payments.

In 1956, a further development occurred in the field of social policy. The two levels agreed to an arrangement whereby the federal government would reimburse the provinces for 50 percent of the cost of provincial allowances for unemployment assistance. Initially, the arrangement covered only "unemployed employables," but a year later the arrangement was changed to include "unemployed unemployables" or individuals who were unemployed and who were not expected to gain employment. The social welfare programs established earlier in the decade had been programs for persons who fell into very narrow categories. Now, the categories had been widened to include all those in need by reason of being unemployed.[14]

In terms of expenditures, the biggest development in the history of shared-cost programs took place one year later with the emergence of an arrangement for hospital care insurance. In 1945, the federal government had proposed the setting up of a health insurance program that included hospital care. Now, in 1957, the federal government and the provinces were proceeding with that part of the proposal dealing with hospital care. The new arrangement followed a familiar pattern. The federal government would reimburse the provinces for approximately 50 percent of their expenditures on hospital care. The payments would be conditional upon the provinces satisfying certain requirements. And all provinces would be required to sign individual agreements with the federal government.

There were, however, some noteworthy variations in the arrangement. With the other shared-cost programs involving open-ended, matching conditional grants, the federal government paid 50 percent of the cost of each of the provincial programs. With hospital care, it paid 25 percent of the per capita cost of the provincial program and 25 percent of the national average per capita cost of insured hospital services, multiplied by the insured population of the province. As a result, for provinces with costs below the national average—mostly the poorer provinces—the federal contribution amounted to more than 50 percent; for those above, the contribution amounted to less than 50 percent. In other words, the federal government with this arrangement took notice of the differing capacities of the provinces to raise revenues. In 1957, the federal government had also established a program that provided unconditional transfers—equaliza-tion payments—to the poorer provinces. The hospital arrangement showed that the attempt to equalize the fiscal capacities of the provinces was not limited to the formal equalization pro-gram.

Also relevant, the financing arrangement stipulated that provincial hospital costs eligible for cost-sharing had to be reduced by the amount collected by hospitals through "authorized charges." These charges, set by the provinces, were fees that patients would have to pay at the point of service. The purpose of this provision was to discourage the setting of such fees. The federal government feared that a preponderance of authorized charges could either deter some from seeking hospital care or create a financial burden for some families or both. Nearly thirty years later, similar federal fears would lead to major federal-provincial conflict over fiscal ar-rangements for health care.

Finally, the conditions relating to the opera-tion of the hospital plans were especially de-manding. All services included in the arrangement had to be available to all residents on uniform terms and conditions. Only services specified in the agreements were to be eligible for cost-sharing, and the provinces had to ensure that high operating standards were maintained in the hospitals. Lastly, adequate records had to be kept and made available to Ottawa for auditing. The rigorous review of financial statements would determine which expenditures were shareable and which were not. As Taylor says, "the degree of control was extraordinary."[15]

Despite the federal controls, by 1961 all provinces had signed hospital agreements with the federal government. However, this was the last time the provinces acceded to such strong federal control.[16] The shared-cost program for hospital care represented the end of the first stage. The era of the conditional grant was fin-ished and with it went the dominance of the federal government.

SECOND STAGE

Quebec and Contracting Out

The first stage had indeed been a period of fed-eral dominance. The extent and nature of the shared-cost programs established during this time revealed a strong federal government. Ot-tawa had managed to establish its presence in the largely provincial fields of health and social pol-icy. And it had done so largely on its own terms, using the conditional grant.

A number of factors contributed to the dom-inance of the federal government. These factors included those mentioned earlier and others, such as the expertise of the federal bureaucracy and fear of a serious economic downturn. But in the late 1950s a number of factors conspired to push the pendulum toward the provincial side. These factors included the failure of the federal government to solve major postwar economic problems, the increased administrative compe-tence at the provincial level, the emergence of aggressive provincial leaders willing to use the levers of the state, and the growing importance of matters under provincial jurisdiction.[17]

A final factor was the transformation taking place in Quebec. Like the other provinces, Que-bec was undergoing changes associated with the term "province-building"—increased adminis-trative skills, more conscious use of the state, formulation of explicit provincial objectives, and so on. But Quebec was doing more than just establishing the presence of a province. It was trying to preserve and modernize the French culture in Canada. This extra dimension gave a certain zeal to the activities of Quebec and pushed it ahead of the other provinces in chal-lenging the federal government.

This last factor triggered the start of the second stage. Under Duplessis, Quebec had ar-gued against the use of conditional grant ar-rangements and had consequently refused to take part in some of them. However, this had had little

↳ dominance of fed gov't diminished.

effect on the extent and nature of the shared-cost programs. Quebec had accepted some of the arrangements. As for the others, Duplessis, with his belief in limited government, made little effort to secure the lost funds through some other type of fiscal mechanism. All in all, Ottawa could still proceed with the shared-cost programs and do so with the preferred course of action—the conditional grant.

In 1960, with the emergence of the Quiet Revolution and the election of a new premier, Jean Lesage, Quebec's position on the conditional grant programs began to change. No longer was it willing to lose federal funds by refusing to participate in the major shared-cost arrangements. Unlike Duplessis, Lesage and his ministers subscribed to a belief in active government. Indeed, the provincial government would be the major means by which to modernize Quebec. However, like Duplessis, Lesage was unwilling to countenance federal involvement in areas of provincial jurisdiction.

Not surprisingly, Quebec's new position produced a new demand. The province indicated that it would "opt-in" to all shared-cost programs that it had until now refused to participate in. This, though, would only be temporary. The federal government, Quebec said, had to end its involvement in the shared-cost programs. The premier provided the official rationale: " . . . these programmes are now sufficiently well established on the provincial scale to enable the Federal government to cease taking part in them and to vacate these fields."[18] In other words, the federal presence was not needed to ensure a nationwide system of health and social programs. Public support would prevent the provinces from dismantling the "established programs."

Equally important, the federal withdrawal had to be accompanied by a federal tax abatement whose yield equalled the amount of funds transferred under the conditional grant programs. The abatement, or "fiscal equivalence"

of the grants, would permit the provinces to finance the shared-cost programs at present levels. In the past, Quebec had suffered the cost of refusing conditional grants—loss of federal dollars. Now, the province refused to accept the cost.

For Quebec, there was a precedent for this proposed arrangement. In 1959, the federal government and Quebec had finally resolved the matter of university funding in Quebec. The federal government agreed to transfer one percentage point of corporate taxable income to Quebec in lieu of federal payments to Quebec universities. In addition, adjustments (increases or decreases in equalization payments) would occur to make certain that the yield of the tax point was equal to what Quebec would have received if it had accepted the per capita funding arrangement. The province believed that the same arrangement, the transfer of tax points, could be used for the conditional grant programs.

In 1965, the federal government responded to Quebec's demand. Parliament passed legislation which permitted provinces to "contract out" of one or more shared-cost programs. Under this arrangement, the provinces would be granted a tax abatement in place of federal grants. Moreover, the abated taxes would be equalized to the average yield of the same number of tax points in the two richest provinces; in other words, any difference between the yield of the abated taxes and the average yield of the same number of taxes in the two richest provinces would be made up in equalization payments. Also, the appropriate cash adjustment would be made to ensure that the yield of the equalized tax abatement equalled the amount the provinces would have received under the old arrangement. The programs included in the contracting-out arrangement were hospital care, vocational and technical training, the health grants, and the four social welfare arrangements—all the conditional grant programs set up in the first stage and more.

The legislation also required provinces

which contracted out to respect all conditions and requirements specified in the shared-cost agreements for an interim period of two or five years (depending on the program). As a result, the programs had to be operated as if they were still conditional grant programs. However, after the interim period the two levels of government would sign an agreement that would make the arrangement unconditional. This would signify Ottawa's acceptance of the truly established nature of the programs.[19]

Only Quebec accepted the arrangement. It contracted out of all the major shared-cost programs. The other provinces felt that the arrangement provided insufficient funding. They feared that they would be given full financial responsibility without the necessary financial means. As well, some provinces largely approved of the shared-cost arrangements. For now, then, the English-speaking provinces believed that it was best to stay with the present shared-cost arrangements. The new contracting-out arrangement was thus recognition of the special nature of Quebec.

The Canada Assistance Plan and Medicare

The contracting-out arrangement was not the only sign of increasing provincial influence. With contracting out, the federal government had addressed the specific concerns of Quebec. But the other provinces, though unwilling to go as far as Quebec, also had some concerns about the shared-cost programs. The poorer provinces claimed, correctly, that the richer provinces were better able to match federal funds, with the result that payments were considerably higher in the richer provinces. Consequently, the poorer provinces felt that Ottawa should assume more than 50 percent of their costs. For their part, the richer provinces focused on the availability of federal funds. They said that the federal funds distorted the priorities of the provinces because they created an irresistible incentive to spend on

shared-cost activities even though they might not be of the highest priority. And all provinces disliked the conditions, especially those that limited coverage to very specific services.

The federal reaction to these and other criticisms was to lessen the conditionality of the new shared-cost programs. In 1966, the federal government introduced the Canada Assistance Plan (CAP). CAP provided for the consolidation of the four existing shared-cost programs in the area of social welfare and for the inclusion of certain social services as a shareable cost. More relevant, the conditions were "conspicuously few."[20] The grants used to finance the new program were essentially matching grants. There were few program conditions. (Also important, Quebec was permitted to contract out of the agreement.)

The shift to less stringent conditional grant programs was in evidence later on in 1966. In December, the federal government passed legislation authorizing the introduction of a new shared-cost program for medical care insurance ("medicare"). In presenting the new arrangement, the federal government revealed its sensitivity to provincial concerns about conditional grants: the prime minister announced the new arrangement as a "general Federal-Provincial *understanding*" and denied that it was a conditional grant program.[21] Strictly speaking, this was untrue, for the financing formula contained a cost-matching feature and there were program conditions. Nonetheless, the program did have features that suggested a move away from the old form of conditional grants. For example, no individual agreements had to be signed. As the prime minister said, the arrangement was to be an understanding.

More important, the provinces would only have to satisfy fairly broad "criteria" and not carefully specified conditions. These criteria, which came to be known as the principles of medicare, included portability of benefits, comprehensive coverage of services, public administration, universal coverage, and access to services unimpeded by excessive patient charges. Similar criteria could also be found in the arrangement for hospital care. However, the arrangement for medical care excluded the tight federal controls found in the one for hospital care—the careful specification of insured services, the agreements, and the detailed federal audits.

The financing formula was also relevant. The federal government would pay to each province that participated in the arrangement 50 percent of the national average per capita cost of insured services, multiplied by the insured population of the province. This went further than the formula for hospital care in recognizing the different fiscal capacities of the provinces.

The passage of the legislation for medical care signaled the end of the second stage. During this stage, the provinces had forced the federal government to assume a defensive posture. The result had been the contracting-out arrangement and conditional grant programs with less confining conditions. To some at the federal level, these developments were regretable, especially the special arrangement for Quebec. And this sentiment, it seems, was shared by many throughout the country.[22] All in all, it was time for Ottawa to adopt a new position. Indeed, by 1966 the new position had already been articulated.

THIRD STAGE

A Renewed Federal Government

The new position of the federal government had various elements (some of which related to the tax-sharing agreements). One of the major elements entailed giving greater respect to the line between federal and provincial responsibilities. Ottawa would henceforth try to entice the English-speaking provinces to accept the contracting-out arrangement. This would limit federal involvement in areas of provincial jurisdiction. As well, Ottawa would be much more reluctant to set up new conditional grant programs. This element and others revealed Ottawa's belief that

the only way to halt provincial advances was to stress the importance of the constitution and the federal responsibilities contained within the constitution.

However, the most immediate federal concern at the moment was not the general provincial offensive, but rather Quebec. Something, the federal government believed, had to be done about the special status of Quebec in the shared-cost arrangements. With the arrival of Pierre Trudeau in Ottawa, the federal government now thought more than ever that any special status for Quebec encouraged separatist tendencies in the province. Some elements of the new position reflected this concern. For instance, federal-provincial arrangements had to "lead to uniform intergovernmental agreements." As well, the position on new shared-cost programs would give Quebec little opportunity to contract out of the programs and hence further enhance its special status.

The solution to the problem of Quebec, Ottawa decided, was to make the other provinces like Quebec. "In essence, the special status which had been gained by Quebec would become a general status, to be enjoyed by all of the provinces," one of the architects of the solution later wrote.[23] And this would be consistent with the attempt of the federal government to adhere more strictly to the provisions of the constitution.

The solution became evident in 1966. At this time, the federal government proposed a new contracting-out arrangement. Under the arrangement, provinces would contract out of the conditional grant programs for hospital care, social welfare, and public health and receive in return seventeen points of federal personal income tax. The yield of the abated taxes would be equalized to the national average yield of these taxes. Cash adjustments would be made to equate the yield of the equalized taxes with the funds available under the existing arrangements.

As with the contracting-out arrangement for Quebec, provinces who accepted this arrangement would be required to respect program conditions until 1970. Also, the cash adjustments, the third part of the proposed arrangement, would after 1970 no longer be equal to the difference between the yield of the equalized taxes and the old amount. Instead, they would increase annually by a factor of one and a half times the growth in provincial personal income. Federal payments would thus cease to be based on provincial expenditures. The matching element was to disappear. With this severing of the link between federal transfers and program costs, the provinces would be truly on their own.

All of the relevant provinces rejected the proposal. Again, the focus of provincial concern was the financing formula and its ability to keep up with actual program costs. Some of the provinces put forward an alternative to the federal proposal. They recommended an arrangement whereby the federal government would continue to pay its share of the costs but limit the conditions to the requirement that the funds be spent in the general area of health and social policy. These provinces accepted the principle of cost-sharing, that of both levels assuming roughly equal responsibility for financing, but they rejected the strict conditions that accompanied the transfers. What was required, they said, was just a more flexible cost-sharing arrangement.

The provincial reaction to the federal proposal uncovered the determination of the provinces to achieve their objectives with respect to the shared-cost programs. The reaction also uncovered the continuing influence of the provinces. With the resurgence of the federal government, the pendulum of power had not swung back to the federal side, but rather now found itself somewhere in the middle. Its location indicated the existence of two strong levels of government.

The proposed contracting-out arrangement was not the only sign of the new federal position. It could also be seen in the new shared-cost arrangement for post-secondary education. To assist the provinces with the financing of post-secondary education, the federal government an-

nounced, in 1966, that it would transfer four equalized points of personal income tax and one equalized point of corporate income to the provinces. Further, cash payments would be made to ensure that the entire federal contribution to any one province amounted to either 50 percent of the operating costs of post-secondary institutions or $15 per capita, whichever was greater. The provinces accepted the arrangement. They badly needed the transfers to deal with the increasing enrollments in post-secondary institutions.[24]

As a consequence of the new arrangement, the federal grants to the universities—and Quebec's special arrangement for post-secondary education—would end. As well, the new arrangement would cover all federal financial involvement in education. As a result, some of the conditional grants for technical and vocational training—and Quebec's special arrangement for contracting out of these grant arrangements—would end too.[25]

In one move, then, the federal government had satisfied some of its newly articulated aims. First, it had reduced Quebec's special status in two important areas. Now, more of the arrangements were uniform. In addition, Ottawa had shown respect for the constitution by ending its program of per capita grants for universities. And it had done the latter without totally eliminating federal influence. The agreement contained no conditions relating to the operation of post-secondary institutions, but the grants made under the agreement were essentially matching grants. Ottawa could be assured that the provinces would direct substantial amounts of provincial funds into this area in order to receive federal dollars.

Federal Concern over Cost

In the years immediately following 1966, the federal government continued with its counter-offensive against the provinces. The motive, though, of the federal government changed. In the mid-1960s, Quebec's special status and the prospect of provincial advances worried Ottawa.

But with the coming of the new decade, another concern developed: the cost of federal participation in the shared-cost programs. In 1960, federal expenditures on shared-cost programs equalled $385.7 million. Ten years later, federal expenditures had risen to $1896 million, representing an almost five-fold increase in federal spending. The major culprits, of course, were the shared-cost programs in the areas of health and social policy. In 1961, the first year in which all provinces and territories participated in the hospital care arrangement, federal expenditures on hospital care equalled $284 million. By 1970, the figure had increased to $919 million.[26] To Ottawa, the expenditures on shared-cost programs were out of control.

This is not to say that cost became the exclusive concern of the federal government. The old concerns, especially the special status of Quebec, still greatly occupied Ottawa. Indeed, in the early 1970s the federal government had acted on its concern about Quebec. It effectively refused to end the interim nature of Quebec's contracting out arrangement for the major shared-cost programs. But the concern about Quebec and the provinces now had to be seen alongside the problem of the high and uncontrollable costs of the shared-cost programs.

The reasons for the uncontrolled growth in costs were easy to detect. One was the open-endedness of the arrangements. The only limit was the ability of the provinces to spend. Another was the matching element, which provided an incentive for provinces to spend on shared-cost programs. A further reason was that the federal government often shared with the provinces only the costs of the most expensive services. Under this kind of arrangement, the provinces had little incentive to develop more efficient ways of delivering services. The most obvious example of this was health care. The federal government shared only in the cost of expensive hospital and medical care, which in turn inhibited the development of less expensive but equally effective forms of health care.

Federal concerns about the cost of the shared-cost programs led to various proposals and changes relating to the financing of medical care, hospital care, and post-secondary education. (CAP, the other major shared-cost program, escaped this process largely because it had become part of an extensive review of social security programs.) In 1971, the federal government announced that there would be a 15 percent limit on the annual growth of federal transfers for post-secondary education beginning in 1972. In 1971, the federal government also put forward a new arrangement for hospital and medical care. It proposed that the federal transfers for the programs be paid in the form of per capita block grants, escalated annually by growth in GNP and population. The proposal also included a "thrust fund" that would provide for a $30 per capita payment on a one-time basis to the provinces. The purpose of the fund would be to assist the provinces with the development of new and efficient health services.[27]

For Ottawa, the attraction of the proposal was its closed-ended nature. With the arrangement, the federal transfers would have a reasonable and predictable limit. Increases in transfers would be based on GNP growth and not provincial spending decisions. Also, the proposal included provisions that would make federal payments for health care equal across the provinces. This development, the federal government believed, would address the criticisms of the poorer provinces and contribute to Ottawa's attempt to equalize provincial revenues. Ottawa felt that the attraction of the proposal for the provinces was its flexibility. Under this arrangement, the provinces would be largely free to develop and operate their health systems. They only had to respect the principles of medicare. As well, the thrust fund provided them with a good start toward developing new health services.

Strangely, Ottawa, it seems, took little notice of the failings of the proposal from a federal perspective. To be sure, the proposal (and like ones) facilitated control of costs, but it also gave the provinces full responsibility for significant and, more important, highly visible programs. Ironically, the federal government, with its proposals, was effectively pushing the pendulum towards the provincial side.

The provinces varied in their reaction. The arrangement for the most part pleased Quebec and Ontario. For these two provinces, a transfer of tax points was preferable, but the block grant was a step in the right direction. It meant less federal involvement. As before, the other provinces felt that Ottawa was abandoning its responsibility for these increasingly expensive programs. And all the provinces charged that the formula for escalating annually the block grant—GNP and population growth—would yield insufficient revenues. The proposal was not acted upon.

Two years later, the federal government made another proposal for changing the health care financing arrangements. This time, it proposed a transfer of six equalized points of personal income tax and all federal taxes on alcoholic beverages and tobacco. Also, a small cash payment would be made, if necessary, to make up the difference between the yield of the transferred taxes and the total federal contribution to health care. The latter equalled the federal contribution in 1972-73 escalated yearly by growth in GNP and population. The provinces said "no" to the proposed arrangement on the now familiar grounds that the transfers would not keep pace with actual program costs.

With its proposals rejected, the federal government once again acted unilaterally. In 1975, it announced that increases in federal transfers for medical care would be limited to 13 percent in 1976, 10 percent in 1977, and to 8 percent in the following years. Also, it gave the required five-year notice of its intention to renegotiate the arrangements for hospital care.

CAP and the Social Security Review

In 1973, CAP became part of a federal-provincial review of social security programs. Initially, the review achieved some successes. Ottawa announced increases in federal family allowances ("baby bonuses") and agreed to a provincial role in the family allowance program. The federal government also increased benefits under the federal pension plans. But the review soon experienced problems when it tried to achieve a major goal: to harmonize and combine a series of social security programs. Consequently, the review centered on what was essentially a reform of CAP. The major reform proposal, forwarded by Ottawa, concerned a new system of cash payments for welfare recipients. Specifically, Ottawa proposed a two-part system, with one part providing cash payments to the unemployed and the other providing cash payments to those employed, but whose income from employment was not enough to meet their needs. The innovative aspect of the proposal was the provision of social assistance to the latter group—the "working poor."

All the provinces, and eventually the federal government itself, had reservations about the proposal. Predictably, no action was taken on it. With this development, the review shifted its attention to social services funded under CAP (for example, day care). Some progress was recorded here. In fact, new legislation was introduced into Parliament in 1977. Broadly speaking, the legislation enriched the package of social services and made them available to all on either a universal or a means-tested basis. But the bill was withdrawn later in 1977 and a new piece of legislation was put in its place. The new bill changed the fiscal mechanism used to finance social services, replacing the conditional grants with block grants. The change was largely a result of a similar development in the areas of health and post-secondary education. But this legislation, too, was withdrawn, an action that again reflected developments relating to health care and post-secondary education. Clearly, something was happening to the other major shared-cost programs.[28]

Established Programs Financing

In 1976, the two levels of government conducted a series of negotiations over the financing of health care and post-secondary education. This was, of course, a continuation of the process that had started in 1971. (It might even be said that the process had started in 1966.) But these negotiations appear to have had a special intensity, partly because all governments were under pressure from the electorate to address the problem of high government expenditures.

During the negotiations, the participants presented their now familiar positions. Ontario, for example, came to the bargaining table with its indictment of conditional grants. The availability of federal dollars, it said, distorted provincial priorities. Also, the arrangements shared only in the cost of the most expensive forms of care. And unilateral actions by the federal government—placing limits on federal transfers and ending arrangements—left provinces with unexpected financial burdens. The grants and their requirements, the province concluded, produced excessive bureaucracy.

At a federal-provincial conference held in June 1976, the prime minister reiterated the concerns of the federal government: the high cost of the arrangements, the uncertainty at the federal level caused by the fact that federal transfers were based on provincial spending, and the unequal transfers to provinces under the arrangements for hospital care and post-secondary education. The prime minister also laid out the provincial concerns, an indication that the federal government was now ready for major change in this area.

Not all the provinces, as noted earlier, objected to the shared-cost programs as then structured. The majority of them seemingly supported Saskatchewan's position: "The problems that exist . . . are not inherent in the cost-sharing mechanism itself; they are defects in the program design, and they can be corrected."[29]

Basically, this was a call for matching grants with fewer conditions. But the major players, the federal government, Quebec, and Ontario, wished for an end to the current arrangements for medical care, hospital care, and post-secondary education. The new arrangement, Established Programs Financing (EPF), was announced early in 1977 and made effective on April 1, 1977.

Under the new arrangement, the federal payment was based on the national average per capita contribution of the federal government to the programs for the fiscal year 1975-76. This payment would be increased each year by growth in population and by the average annual rate of nominal GNP growth in the three preceding years. Essentially, the arrangement had established a benchmark or base figure which would be adjusted annually by population and GNP growth.

The federal contribution was split into two parts—tax points and block grants—and each part represented about one-half of the total contribution. The transfer of tax points consisted of 13.5 equalized points of personal income tax and one equalized point of corporate income. In reality, the net transfer amounted to only 9.143 points of personal income tax, since the provinces already possessed the remaining tax points under the old arrangement for post-secondary education. Also, one of the 9.143 points constituted partial compensation for the termination of the "revenue guarantee." (The revenue guarantee was a federal transfer to the provinces made as a result of federal tax reforms.) At this time, it was unclear whether the compensation was part of EPF.

The other part consisted of a number of block grants or cash payments. First, and most important, there was the "basic" cash payment, which amounted to about 50 percent of federal contributions in 1975-76 and which would be increased annually. Second, there was a "transitional" cash payment, equal to the difference between the yield of the transferred tax points and the basic cash payment. This payment was made to soothe provinces which feared that the transferred tax points might not yield enough revenue. Third, there were "levelling" payments, which would eventually lead to equal per capita cash grants to the provinces and thus eliminate existing differences in federal payments to the provinces. Finally, a cash payment, equal to one equalized point of personal income tax, was made to further compensate the provinces for the termination of the revenue guarantee.

The only conditions attached to the arrangement related to the health care programs. The provinces would have to respect the principles of medicare and similar criteria outlined in the hospital care legislation. Other conditions traditionally associated with health care, including the requirement that the transferred funds be spent on the programs and the penalty for permitting authorized charges, were discarded. As for post-secondary education, there were no conditions.

The new arrangement also included a new block grant program called Extended Health Care. Under this program, the federal government would pay a per capita grant of $20 to the provinces, escalated annually in the same way as the basic cash payment. One of the primary goals of the program was to reorient the health care system towards more efficient health services—the same goal as the "thrust fund" proposed six years earlier.[30]

On the surface, the new block-funding arrangement appeared to meet the many criticisms of the old arrangements for the three programs. For the federal government, a lid had been placed on its contributions. As well, federal payments would be the same across the provinces. And the federal government would no longer be accused of intruding into areas of provincial jursidiction. The provinces, of course, still had to observe the principles of medicare, but for Ottawa this represented only a minor intrusion. In any case, the "established" nature of the programs, Ottawa believed, would make it unnecessary to enforce these conditions.

For the provinces, the arrangement provided greater flexibility. The long list of complaints about conditional grants, which Ontario had articulated during the negotiations, had been addressed. To be sure, the arrangement had a negative side for some of the provinces. By eliminating cost-matching, EPF had cut the connection between program costs and federal contributions. However, there seemed to be provisions in the arrangement that ensured that the provinces would not be caught financially short.

Altogether, it appeared that EPF marked an end to serious federal-provincial conflict over shared-cost programs. The arrangement had "disentangled" the two levels of government, eliminating the basis of much conflict. The history of the major shared-cost programs, for all intents and purposes, was at an end. It soon became clear, though, that the end had not come. The EPF arrangement had only provided the impetus for a new stage of development.

FOURTH STAGE

Problems with EPF

The federal government quickly became disenchanted with the EPF arrangement. (CAP, once again, was to escape the turmoil.) At first, two matters concerned the federal government. One was the high level of federal contributions made under EPF, the other the failure of the provinces to respect what the federal government saw as the essential conditionality of the arrangement. Shortly thereafter, in 1980, a third concern, the lack of federal "visibility" in the EPF arrangement, would emerge.

The first of the concerns to become evident was the one over federal spending on EPF. In 1978, a year after the introduction of EPF, the federal government proposed a change in the arrangement that would reduce the rate of increase of federal transfers. The proposal was part of a hastily designed federal program of spending reductions. The change required provincial consent, given that the legislation covering EPF effectively stipulated that no unilateral action could be taken before 1982. The provinces rejected the federal proposal, and the federal government responded in part by withdrawing the new block funding legislation for social services.

Federal concerns about contributions to EPF continued into the early 1980s. By this time, it had become clear that Ottawa had overestimated the yield of the transferred tax points. Consequently, the transitional payment, the cash grant that ensured that the yield of the points equalled the basic cash payment, became large and seemingly quite permanent. The new arrangement was supposed to result in greater control of federal contributions. This was not happening.

In 1979, the other initial concern, the conditionality of the arrangement, came to the fore. Extra-billing, the practice by which doctors charge over and above the insured amount, had increased in some provinces. Also, hospital user fees (authorized charges) had been either raised or introduced in a few of the provinces. In reaction, the federal government claimed that these developments could lead to patients being denied medically-required care—at a minimum, a violation of the principle of "reasonable access" to care. The federal government intimated that one of the reasons for the charges was that provinces were diverting federal funds for health care into other areas (or alternatively, failing to match federal funds) and relying on patients to make up the shortfall through the payment of direct charges for hospital and medical care.

At about the same time, there were concerns about the commitment of the provinces to the funding of post-secondary education. As with health care, the provinces appeared to be limiting their expenditures for higher education. In 1975, federal transfers represented about 45 percent of provincial expenditures on post-secondary education. By 1979, the percentage had risen to 57 percent.[31] The net effect was insufficient funding for post-secondary education and a consequent decline, many said, in the quality of education.

Federal concerns about conditionality uncovered the differing interpretations of the EPF arrangement. For the provinces, the arrangement, fundamentally speaking, was unconditional. This view had at least two important implications. First, the federal funds transferred under the arrangement could be used for any purpose. The notion of dividing expenditures on health and post-secondary education into federal and provincial shares was wrong-headed. The federal transfer simply went into the consolidated revenue funds of the provinces, to be allocated to any program. Second, the only conditions in the arrangement, the principles of medicare, were to be interpreted in light of the basically unconditional nature of EPF. In short, the provinces would determine whether the conditions were being satisfied. And they had determined, at this time, that the level of direct charges did not constitute a violation of the principles of medicare.

The federal government saw the arrangement differently. For Ottawa, the arrangement was a means of achieving two seemingly conflicting goals. On one side, it wanted to deal with all the problems associated with old shared-cost arrangements—the open-endedness, the matching grants, the unequal transfers, the inflexibility, the claims of federal intrusion. The use of tax points and block grants reflected this goal. The federal government, using the two fiscal mechanisms, would pass to the provinces an amount of money with few, if any, conditions. As stated earlier, Ottawa played down the inclusion of the principles of medicare in EPF. The arrangement was sold as an unconditional arrangement.

On the other side, the federal government wanted to maintain the integrity and national character of the established programs. Ottawa thought that this would be ensured by the established nature of the programs. Also, the federal government had split the transfer into two sections, partly so that it could use the threat to withhold the cash payment if the provinces reduced the programs in any serious way. (Tax point transfers are more difficult to take back than cash transfers.) Finally, Ottawa had made it clear that it expected to have a say in the operation of the programs.

All in all, the federal government seems to have wanted the arrangement to be both conditional and unconditional. To use Gunther and Van Loon's aptly awkward term, Ottawa seems to have desired a "circumscribed unconditionality."[32]

The confusion in the position of the federal government led to hesitation on Ottawa's part. This could be seen in Ottawa's initial reaction to extra-billing. It noted the negative implications of the development, but appeared unwilling to do anything substantial about it. With the election of the Progressive Conservatives at the federal level in 1979, the federal government did begin to inch towards more assertive action with regards to direct patient charges. It asked Emmett Hall, an important figure during the introduction of medicare, to review the matter of direct charges and other health issues. One year later, in 1980, Hall reported and recommended among other things that extra-billing be banned.

The Hall report was important. The federal government eventually would follow quite closely the major recommendations. But at least as important was the government to whom the report was presented. In early 1980, the federal Liberals had unseated the Conservatives and regained power. And they were determined to take decisive action on many matters, including the EPF arrangement.

A Stronger Federal Government

Back in power, the Liberal government of Pierre Trudeau formulated a strategy to raise the visibility of the federal government. From now on federal policies would be designed to increase the direct contact between Ottawa and individual Canadians. This meant that the federal government would no longer be satisfied dealing with Canadians indirectly through the provinces. This indirect contact, Ottawa believed, had lead to a type of federalism, a highly decentralized type of federalism, that threatened the very unity of the nation.

The new strategy had implications for the EPF arrangement. Ottawa would try to limit its contributions under the arrangement. In part, this reflected growing concern with the federal deficit, but it also reflected the new strategy: savings garnered from EPF could be used for wholly federal programs. Further, the federal government would try to carve out a role for itself in the operation of the established programs. This would ensure the maintenance of the programs and give the federal government a higher profile. Lastly, the federal government would insist upon the provinces acknowledging Ottawa's contribution to the established programs in their publications and elsewhere.

In a sense, these goals were the ones already articulated in the previous two years. The only new element concerned the desire to see federal contributions explicitly acknowledged. But these goals were now stated with much greater certainty and purpose. Gone was the hesitation born of Ottawa's conflicting views on EPF. Ottawa's position was now clear: EPF was conditional (and too expensive).

The federal budget of November 1981 formalized Ottawa's position on EPF. To start with, the federal fiscal transfer for EPF would be reduced. A change in the calculation of the transfer would lessen the increase in cash payments to the richer provinces. More important in terms of dollars, the compensation for the revenue guarantee would end. Ottawa denied a link between the compensation and EPF and consequently claimed that this action could not be considered a reduction in EPF payments. The provinces saw the matter differently. There was a link.

The federal budget also indicated that the national standards for health care—the principles of medicare—would be clarified and a mechanism developed to ensure the maintenance of the standards. Ottawa's major concern here was to address the matter of direct charges. As for post-secondary education, new federal-provincial arrangements would be devised. Though unstated, the purpose behind the development of new arrangements was, it seems, to attach conditions to the federal transfer (for example, "reasonable access to education"). Ottawa said that the proposed actions for both areas would be undertaken in consultation with the provinces and result in new legislation.[33]

Failure and Success

Over the next three years, to the end of the fourth stage, there occurred some developments in the area of post-secondary education. Most of them related to amendments made to the EPF legislation in 1984. The amendments were important, especially one that placed a temporary ceiling on the transfer for post-secondary education, but they fell short of new legislation outlining federal conditions for post-secondary education. There had been discussions on the matter of conditions, . but the provinces had mostly refused to consider an increased federal role in this area. In any case, provincial education ministers, representing the provinces in these discussions, found themselves overshadowed by provincial finance ministers who were unsympathetic to any additional federal involvement in post-secondary education. Also important, there was a lack of consensus at the federal level. Some federal representatives wanted to forego any new federal role in post-secondary education and instead concentrate on reducing the federal contribution; others wanted to end the federal contribution totally and use the savings on a system of direct grants to post-secondary students; and still others wanted to pursue what they felt to be the goal of the budget announcement of November 1981—the establishment of federal conditions for post-secondary education.

There emerged therefore no new legislation for post-secondary education. The federal government had failed to accomplish its goal in respect to higher education. Fortunately for Ottawa, it fared much better with health care.

In July 1983, the federal government, following unproductive talks with the provinces over direct charges, released a position paper on health care.[34] The paper showed a federal government determined to ban direct charges. Ottawa had thus heeded its budget statement and clarified the national standards: direct charges represented a violation of the principles of medicare. But it was also necessary, as the 1981 budget said, to find a way to preserve the principles—to find a way to ban extra-billing and hospital user fees. The authors of the paper recognized that the federal government lacked the authority to ban direct charges itself. It would have to be done indirectly through funding. Already, Ottawa had the authority to withhold all cash transfers for health care, but this would be an overreaction to the problem. What was required, the paper effectively said, was a mechanism that would produce reductions in federal contributions small enough not to cripple provincial health systems, but large enough to make the provinces want to eliminate the practices. The paper failed to state the mechanism explicitly, but it was implied: for every dollar of direct charges paid by residents, the federal government would decrease its transfer by one dollar.

Also left unstated was the federal belief that the incentive in the proposed arrangement would not be solely financial. There was a political aspect to the penalty. With the penalty, Ottawa could clearly label provinces that permitted direct charges—an unwelcome label. Moreover, the money lost, though insignificant in terms of total provincial revenues, would appear large to the public and to interest groups attempting to secure funds from provincial governments.

The provinces reacted strongly to the paper. The provinces claimed that the federal government had already seriously damaged provincial health systems by reducing federal funding. Now

Ottawa was proposing, the provinces said, to do further damage by restricting the way in which the provinces operated their health systems. The federal government, in response, essentially ignored the provinces. It felt, with some reason, that it had given the provinces every chance to discuss direct charges in the preceding year. Further, it felt that some of the provinces, especially Alberta, had made matters worse by announcing its intention to introduce new hospital user fees in 1983. This is not to say that Ottawa was solely motivated by provincial actions. The proposed penalty, which was to be part of a new piece of federal legislation, was clearly part of Ottawa's strategy to heighten the visibility of the federal government. Also, a federal election was in the offing, and some federal Liberals hoped that the matter of direct charges would become an election issue.

In December 1983, the federal government introduced the Canada Health Act into Parliament. The bill contained a number of important provisions, but the essential one dealt with direct patient charges. According to the bill, the provinces could not permit extra-billing and user fees if they wished to qualify for the full federal cash transfer. If a province failed to satisfy this condition, the cash transfer would be reduced automatically by the amount charged through extra-billing and user fees. The bill also made provision for the return of all withheld funds if a province eliminated or banned the two practices before April 1, 1987. Four months after its introduction into the House of Commons, the Canada Health Act became law.

With the passage of the Canada Health Act, the fourth stage came to an end. The federal government had finished with its attempt to restructure EPF, and to change the balance of power between the two levels of government. The power and inspiration behind this attempt, Pierre Trudeau, had announced his intention to leave politics. Equally important, public support for aggressive federal action had dissipated and now cooperation between the two levels of government was wanted.

CAP

During the fourth stage, CAP was subject to many of the same forces that impinged upon the health and post-secondary education programs. The federal government had its criticisms of CAP—the high level of federal funding, the lack of national standards, and the absence of any real federal presence in the program. The provinces, for their part, dismissed the federal criticisms and recommended the inclusion of new services under CAP. Despite the presence of these forces, the program emerged unchanged at the end of the fourth stage. The reasons for this are unclear, but they might include federal reluctance to limit welfare contributions in the bad economic times of the early 1980s and the concentration on the EPF arrangement. Whatever the reasons, CAP remained the last of the old-style major shared-cost programs, the ones involving open-ended, matching conditional grants. CAP had, as Banting states, "quietly outlasted the convulsions that . . . reshaped fiscal federalism."[35]

The Present

The major shared-cost programs now appear to have entered into a new stage of development. The apparent transition largely reflects the position of the new Progressive Conservative government in Ottawa. It has promised to "breathe a new spirit into federalism" and to establish "a constant process of consultation and cooperation."[36] The federal unilateralism of the 1980s is to end. The result of all this, the new government says, will be more harmonious federal-provincial relations or "national reconciliation."

In the area of shared-cost programs, there are definite signs of the new spirit. The federal government has so far foregone the introduction of the equivalent of the Canada Health Act for post-secondary education. (There were fears, largely provincial, of such action.) As well, the Mulroney government has conducted studies, such as those of the Neilson Task Force, that emphasize the need for greater federal-provincial cooperation in the areas of health and social policy.[37] And it has even developed new shared-cost agreements with the provinces. In September 1985, the federal government announced that the two senior levels of government had entered into an arrangement that focuses on finding employment for the "unemployed employables" who receive cash payments under CAP.[38] Further, it appears that Ottawa and the provinces may soon come to an agreement on a new program for child care.

The provinces have also contributed to the perception that the shared-cost programs have entered into a new stage. Of interest here is the provincial reaction to the Canada Health Act. The provinces had threatened to continue to challenge the act after its passage, but this has not occurred. Instead, the provinces have seemingly accepted the act. A number of provinces have banned the practice of extra-billing, with the result that there is now little or no extra-billing for insured health services in Canada. Also, hospital user fees subject to penalties under the Canada Health Act have all been eliminated.

Admittedly, there are also signs that national reconciliation may yet remain elusive. The Neilson Task Force said that Ottawa would have to look seriously at establishing a greater presence for the federal government in post-secondary education. This might include attaching conditions to the federal transfer: there might still be a Canada Post-Secondary Education Act. In fact, the federal Department of Secretary of State has been pursuing discussions with the provinces on this matter, and the federal Throne Speech of October 1986 contained a proposal for a national forum on post-secondary education. Also relevant, the federal government is now engaged in a full-scale analysis of social policy, which is in part a response to the recommendations of the Macdonald Commission. The intent is to direct more of the funds spent on income maintenance and the like to those truly in need. This review, with its wide reach, could lead to some disagreements between Ottawa and the provinces.

Most important, the federal government, facing a large budget deficit, has reduced its financial commitment to the established programs. In June 1986, Parliament passed an amendment to the EPF lesgislation that will reduce the annual rate of growth of federal transfers. Now, the annual rate of growth will be determined by calculating average nominal GNP growth in the preceding three years, which is the old way of determining the rate, and then subtracting two percent from this figure. So, for example, a rate of 8 percent calculated under the old arrangement would now be 6 percent (or the inflation rate. The amendment ensures that the rate of increase will not fall below the inflation rate except in times of high inflation).[39]

Seven months before the passage of the amendment, at a first ministers' conference, the provinces urged Ottawa not to pass the amendment in 1986. The provinces recognized that the transfers for the established programs would have to be reviewed, but they wanted this done as part of the renegotiation of other major federal-provincial fiscal arrangements which was to be carried out during 1986. Ontario was particularly disturbed about the then proposed amendment, saying that the federal government was transferring the deficit problem to the provinces. More fundamentally, Ontario stated that Ottawa had failed to consult with the provinces on the matter, and as a result the federal government was "contaminating the federal-provincial relationship in this country."[40] Perhaps it is premature to conclude that the shared-cost programs have passed into a new stage. The programs may still be in the conflict-ridden fourth stage.

CONCLUSION

"The financial relations between Ottawa and the provincial governments," the late F. R. Scott wrote, "form one of the most complex and changing aspects of Canadian federalism."[41] Although written over thirty years ago, and mostly in relation to the tax rental agreements, the comment accurately summarizes the history of the

major shared-cost programs. The programs and
their attendant relationships have been complex.
The programs, with their reliance on various
types of fiscal devices, are truly familiar to only
the most dedicated students of fiscal federalism.
Moreover, it seems that the arrangements have
become more complex. Even the authors of recent arrangements are unsure of the meaning of
their creations. If he were writing today, Scott
doubtless would emphasize the complexity of
federal-provincial fiscal arrangements.

The complexity, of course, goes beyond the
programs themselves. It is tempting, and not
altogether wrong, to see the history of the major
shared-cost programs as a struggle between two
monolithic forces—the federal government on
the one side, the provinces on the other. Indeed,
this paper has constantly referred to the pendulum of power, whose movement signifies shifts
towards a more centralized or decentralized form
of federalism. Nevertheless, the relationships
surrounding the shared-cost programs are richer
and more intricate than a battle between the
forces of "nation-building" and "province-
building." The relationships, to borrow a term,
amount to "multi-faceted federalism," a federalism in which the different provinces hold differ-

ent positions and thus have different relationships with Ottawa.[42] What Saskatchewan wants,
for example, with respect to the operation and
financing of shared-cost programs will be different from what Ontario wants. This awareness
makes the complex structure of the shared-cost
programs more understandable and perhaps
more acceptable: the programs represent an attempt to satisfy the demands of multi-faceted
federalism.

The programs have also been constantly
changing. The shared-cost programs started out
as a series of conditional grants. Then a new kind
of arrangement emerged: contracting out. After
this, many new proposals for reforming and developing shared-cost arrangements appeared.
Eventually, one of the proposals, involving block
grants and tax point transfers, replaced all but
one of the major conditional grant programs.
Now, this new arrangement itself has been challenged. All of these changes are, of course, to be
expected because of the continuing evolution of
federalism in Canada. As Scott says, federal-
provincial fiscal arrangements are an aspect of
Canadian federalism. And so long as the nature
of Canadian federalism remains in flux, the
shared-cost programs will know only change.

Notes

1. For example, see Perrin Lewis, "The Tangled
Tale of Taxes and Transfers," in Michael Walker,
ed., *Canadian Confederation at the Crossroads*
(Vancouver: Fraser Institute, 1978).

2. The issue of federal aims with respect to shared-
cost programs has generated a number of studies
and perspectives. For a perspective similar to the
one presented here, see D. V. Smiley, *Constitutional Adaptation and Canadian Federalism Since
1945* (Ottawa: Information Canada, 1970), 9-10.
For a more complex perspective, see Robin Boad-

way, "Federal-Provincial Transfers in Canada: A
Critical Review of the Existing Arrangements," in
Mark Krasnick, ed., *Fiscal Federalism*, a study
prepared for the Royal Commission on the Eco-
nomic Union and Development Prospects for
Canada, vol. 65 (Toronto: University of Toronto
Press, 1986), 1-22.

3. Richard Bastien, *Federalism and Decentralization: Where Do We Stand?* (Ottawa: Government
of Canada, 1981), 28.

4. The term "tax point" comes from defining each

percentage point of the federal tax on personal income and each percentage point of federally-taxable corporate income as a tax point. So, for example, a transfer of 10% of the federal tax on personal income would represent a tax point transfer of 10 points. Also, there is a difference between the tax point transfer and the tax abatement, but it is of minor importance for this paper.

5. There are other ways of examining federal financing of shared-cost programs. See, for example, Canada, *Report of the Royal Commission on the Economic Union and Development Prospects for Canada*, vol. 3 (Ottawa: Supply and Services, 1985), 238-40.

6. Canada, *Federal-Provincial Programs and Activities, 1985-1986* (Ottawa: Federal-Provincial Relations Office, 1986), iii.

7. For a different view of the stages of development of the shared-cost programs, see Allan M. Maslove and Bohodar Rubashewsky, "Cooperation and Confrontation: The Challenges of Fiscal Federalism," in Michael J. Prince, ed., *How Ottawa Spends: 1986-87. Tracking the Tories* (Toronto: Methuen, 1986).

8. Smiley, *Constitutional Adaptation and Canadian Federalism Since 1945*, 9-10.

9. Canada, *Report of the Royal Commission on Dominion-Provincial Relations*, book 2 (Ottawa: Queen's Printer, 1940), 15, 33, and 50.

10. Malcolm Taylor, *Health Insurance and Canadian Public Policy* (Montreal: McGill-Queen's Press, 1978), 62.

11. *Ibid.*, 164. For a comprehensive review of the health grants, see Canada, Department of National Health and Welfare, *Annual Report, 1948-9* (Ottawa: Queen's Printer, 1949), 77-88.

12. For more on this development, see George E. Carter, "Financing Post-Secondary Education Under the Federal-Provincial Fiscal Arrangements Act: An Appraisal," *Canadian Tax Journal* 24:5 (September-October 1976): 505.

13. For an examination of the developments surrounding the introduction of the per capita grant arrangement, see J. Stefan Dupré, " 'Contracting Out': A Funny Thing Happened on the Way to the Centennial," in Canadian Tax Foundation, *Proceedings of the Eighteenth Tax Conference, 1964* (Toronto: Canadian Tax Foundation, 1965).

14. Donald Smiley provides further details on these developments in his monograph, *Conditional Grants and Canadian Federalism* (Toronto: Canadian Tax Foundation, 1963), 9-10.

15. Taylor, *Health Insurance and Canadian Public Policy*, 230. For further details on this arrangement, see chapter 4 of Taylor's book.

16. In 1960, the federal government introduced a new arrangement for vocational and technical training. However, unlike the arrangement for hospital care, it involved few controls. See Anthony G. S. Careless, *Initiative and Response: The Adaptation of Canadian Federalism to Regional Economic Development*. (Montreal: McGill-Queen's University Press, 1977), 55.

17. A number of scholars have examined the shift in influence toward the provinces. For example, see Alan Cairns, "The Other Crisis of Canadian Federalism," *Canadian Public Administration* 22: 2 (Summer 1979), 180-1.

18. George Carter, *Canadian Conditional Grants Since World War II* (Toronto: Canadian Tax Foundation, 1971), 89.

19. For further details, see *ibid.*, chapter 5.

20. *Ibid.*, 40. For a discussion of the formulation and implementation of CAP, see Rand Dyck, "The Canada Assistance Plan: The Ultimate in Cooperative Federalism," *Canadian Public Administration* 19:4 (Winter 1976).

21. Taylor, *Health Insurance and Canadian Public Policy*, 364. For more on the medicare arrangement, see chapter 6 of Taylor's book.

22. Richard Simeon, *Federal-Provincial Diplomacy: The Making of Recent Policy in Canada* (Toronto: University of Toronto Press, 1972), 66.

23. A.W. Johnson, "Federal-Provincial Fiscal Relations: An Historical Perspective," in Thomas Courchene et al., *Ottawa and the Provinces: The Distribution of Money and Power*, vol. 2 (Toronto: Ontario Economic Council, 1985), 129.

24. For more on this arrangement, see Carter, "Financing Post-Secondary Education Under the Federal-Provincial Fiscal Arrangements Act: An Appraisal."

25. J. Stefan Dupré, et al., *Federalism and Policy Development: The Case of Adult Occupational*

Training in Ontario (Toronto: University of Toronto Press, 1973), 25-6. At the same time, Ottawa ended all remaining conditional grants for vocational and technical training and assumed exclusive responsibility for those covered by these grants—the unemployed and the employed who required retraining.

26. Grant, *Canadian Conditional Grants Since World War II*, 24 and 30. Canadian Tax Foundation, *The National Finances, 1967-68* (Toronto: Canadian Tax Foundation, 1968), 92.

27. For further details on the arrangement, see Maurice LeClair, "The Canadian Health Care System," in Spyros Andreopoulos, ed., *National Health Insurance* (New York: J. Wiley and Sons, 1975): 81-3.

28. The Social Security Review has received considerable attention from scholars. See, for example, Christopher Leman, *The Collapse of Welfare Reform: Political Institutions, Policy, and the Poor in Canada and the United States* (Cambridge: MIT Press, 1980).

29. George E. Carter, "Financing Health and Post-Secondary Education: A New and Complex Fiscal Arrangement," *Canadian Tax Journal* 25:5 (September-October 1977), 544.

30. For a good, clear discussion of EPF, see Lewis, "The Tangled Tale of Taxes and Transfers," 81-4.

31. Magnus Gunther and Richard J. Van Loon, "Federal Contributions to Post-Secondary Education: Trends and Issues," in David Nowlan and Richard Bellaire, eds., *Financing Canadian Universities: For Whom and By Whom?* (Toronto: OISE Press, 1981), 164.

32. *Ibid.*, 162.

33. For more on the 1981 proposals for EPF, see Canada, Allan J. MacEachen, *Fiscal Arrangements in the Eighties, Proposals of the Government of Canada* (Ottawa: Department of Finance, 1981).

34. Health and Welfare Canada, *Preserving Universal Medicare: A Government of Canada Position Paper* (Ottawa: Minister of Supply and Services, 1983).

35. Keith Banting, "Federalism and Income Security: Themes and Variations," in Thomas Courchene et al., eds., *Ottawa and the Provinces: The Distribution of Money and Power,* vol. 1 (Toronto: Ontario Economic Council, 1985), 269.

36. Canada, House of Commons, *Debates*, November 5, 1984, 6.

37. The relevant reports of the Ministerial Task Force on Program Review (the formal name for the Neilson Task Force) are *Education and Research*, *Health and Sports*, and *Service to the Public: Canada Assistance Plan*.

38. Canada, House of Commons, *Debates*, September 19, 1985, 6790-2.

39. The amendment is even more complicated than outlined here. See Canada, House of Commons, *Debates*, April 25, 1986, 12666-8.

40. David Peterson, "Notes for a Statement on Restoring Cooperative Federalism for Health and Education," address to the Annual First Ministers' Conference, Halifax, Nova Scotia, November 28-29, 1985, 7.

41. F. R. Scott, *Essays on the Constitution* (Toronto: University of Toronto Press, 1977), 291.

42. J. Stefan Dupré, " 'Contracting Out': A Funny Thing Happened on the Way to the Centennial," 217-8.

Selected Readings

Banting, Keith. *The Welfare State and Canadian Federalism*. Kingston: McGill-Queen's University Press, 1982.

Bird, Richard. "Federal-Provincial Fiscal Transfers in Canada: Retrospect and Prospect." *Canadian Tax Journal* 35:1 (January-February 1987): 118-33.

Brown, M. *Established Program Financing: Evolution or Regression in Canadian Fiscal Federalism*. Canberra: Australian National University, 1984.

Carter, Frank. "How to Tame the Spending Power." *Policy Options* 7:8 (October 1986): 3-7.

Hawkes, David C., and Pollard, Bruce G. "The Medicare Debate in Canada: The Politics of New Federalism." *Publius: The Journal of Federalism* 14 (Summer 1984): 183-98.

EXECUTIVE FEDERALISM

A federal constitution attempts to provide the framework for a clear-cut division of authority between component governments. However, in reality, jurisdictional interdependence is a characteristic of all mature federal states. Canada proves to be no exception to this trend. Over the past four decades, federal and provincial governments have become increasingly engaged in a complex process of joint decision-making and policy coordination in an attempt to reconcile and accommodate diverse and conflicting political goals, objectives, and strategies. The term "executive federalism" describes the sophisticated network of relationships and interactions between the representatives of Ottawa and the provinces.

Few studies have documented the full extent of federal-provincial interaction in Canada. It is estimated that at least one thousand federal-provincial meetings (bilateral, regional, or multilateral) take place during the course of a year. Several hundred more interprovincial contacts may be added to the list. The central institution of executive federalism is the Conference of First Ministers and Premiers. Because the deliberations are widely reported, and sometimes televised, the Conference stands as the most visible forum for federal-provincial discussion. Even more important is the fact that the leaders of the eleven governments possess the ultimate authority to make fundamental public policy choices and to commit their governments to federal-provincial agreements.

Immediately below the First Ministers' Conference lies a labyrinth of functional or "sectoral" policy committees of cabinet ministers, permanent intergovernmental secretariats, and technical committees of non-elected public servants. The overwhelming majority of these contacts occur in confidential deliberations among bureaucrats. Unique to Canada is the emergence of specialized staff agencies (departments of intergovernmental affairs) which plan long-range bargaining strategies and direct the conduct of intergovernmental negotiations. These bodies represent an attempt by governments to "rationalize" the policy process and "professionalize" the conduct of intergovernmental relations.

So critical is executive federalism to the workings of the Canadian federal state that many scholars have defined the essence of Canadian federalism almost solely in terms of federal-provincial interaction. Writing for the Royal Commission on Dominion-Provincial Relations (the Rowell-Sirois Commission), J. A. Corry envisaged an increasingly interdependent Canadian federal state in which both administrative cooperation and conflict would become essential ingredients. In the 1950s, A. R. M. Lower described the emergence of a new governmental form—a "government of governments"—that would ultimately shift political power from the Parliament of Canada and the provincial legislatures to federal and provincial political elites (cabinet ministers) meeting at formal intergovernmental conferences. In the 1960s, J. R. Mallory popularized the term "cooperative federalism" to describe the changing character of the Canadian federal state. This conception of federalism envisaged public policy as a "pragmatic and piecemeal" response to circumstances of mutual interdependence.

During the 1970s, Richard Simeon developed the concept of "federal-provincial diplomacy" to characterize a unique combination of social, institutional, and behavioural variables that produced a pattern of intergovernmental relations quite distinct from other federations. Within the Canadian context, the interactions of federal and provincial governments were considered similar to those between sovereign states bargaining and negotiating within the international community. Recently scholars such as Alan Cairns and Donald Smiley have focused on the "normative" consequences of the decision-making process, arguing that participants often enhance intergovernmental conflict, rather than political harmony.

The initial essay contained in this section provides an overview of the evolution of the machinery of intergovernmental liaison and an explanation of the role and function of interministerial conferences. As a former senior advisor to the federal government, Gordon Robertson documents the continuing frustrations of Ottawa in its attempts to establish a meaningful form of integrated consultation with the provinces.

Stefan Dupré focuses on the process as well as the structure of executive federalism. This essay, written as a background study for the Royal Commission on the Economic Union and Development Prospects for Canada (the MacDonald Commission), examines the dynamics of "summit diplomacy" in several policy fields. Dupré's study demonstrates how interpersonal contacts and different forms of cabinet organization influence the degree of intergovernmental collaboration and confrontation.

Elliot and Lily Feldman examine an often ignored, but increasingly important aspect of executive federalism—the interaction between Ottawa and the provinces in the conduct of foreign policy. The essay points to a growing provincial bureaucratic establishment concerned with matters that were once considered beyond both the interest and the competence of the provinces. In the past two decades, several of the provinces (Ontario, Quebec, Alberta, and British Columbia) have become international actors in policy areas that bear directly on the health and well-being of provincial economies or the cultural integrity of the province (as in the case of Quebec). Where federal unilateralism once prevailed, intergovernmental consultation has become a practical necessity.

The article by Donald Smiley explores the consequences of "government by conference." Smiley argues that the present process of defining national priorities distorts political debate, weakens the accountability of governments to their electorates, and enhances the possibility of intergovernmental conflict by placing the status and prestige of governments above specific program objectives. Basic to his argument is a belief that federal-provincial conflict is disruptive or "dysfunctional" to the operation of the federal system.

A partial counterpoint to Smiley is provided by Albert Breton in his "Commissioner's Statement," issued as a supplementary commentary to the final report of the MacDonald Commission. Breton challenges the traditional view that intergovernmental conflict is a destabilizing influence within a federal state. In contrast, he views intergovernmental conflict as a means of promoting policy innovation and as an assurance that the political system will be responsive to the wants and needs of the public. Future explanations and evaluations of executive federalism will be influenced by this application of public choice theory.

13. THE ROLE OF INTERMINISTERIAL CONFERENCES IN THE DECISION-MAKING PROCESS

Gordon Robertson

INTRODUCTION

Interministerial conferences are not a new feature of Canadian federalism—Confederation was a youthful twenty years old when the Premiers of some of the provinces first met in conference in 1887. Dominion-provincial conferences, at the highest level of representation, were a later development; the first was held in 1906, nearly forty years after Confederation. In the last ten years or so, however, as our federalism entered its second century we have witnessed a proliferation of interministerial conferences, particularly of the federal-provincial variety where representatives from the eleven "senior" governments join in multilateral meetings with formal agendas. Such federal-provincial conferences have a growing public profile.

This paper will contend that, while the traditional roles of federal-provincial conferences continue, in recent years—especially at First Ministers' meetings—a particular role has received increasing emphasis, that is, the conference's role as a forum for the articulation by provincial premiers of regional or provincial perspectives on matters which are substantially within the legislative authority of the Parliament of Canada. Other roles and attributes of interministerial conferences will be touched upon, including the influence of "open" conferences, which have facilitated the development of the regional advocacy role and which have other ramifications for the decision-making process.

CONTRIBUTING FACTORS IN THE PROLIFERATION OF FEDERAL-PROVINCIAL MINISTERIAL CONFERENCES

A federal system of government was adopted in 1867 which permitted citizens direct representation in a central Parliament as well as in one or other of the provincial legislatures. Both orders of government would function within distinct and fairly well-defined areas of legislative authority, and each would be sovereign within its own sphere of competence—except that the federal authority would be more sovereign than the others. Although a relatively neat compartmentalization of powers was possible in the 19th century—because government at all levels intervened little in the economic and social lives of citizens—there was recognition of the potential conflict of policies, programs, and activities of the two orders of government. When the Consti-

Gordon Robertson, "The Role of Interministerial Conferences in the Decision-making Process," in *Confrontation and Collaboration—Intergovernmental Relations in Canada Today*, ed., Richard Simeon (Toronto: The Institute of Public Administration of Canada, 1979), 78-88. Reprinted by permission of The Institute of Public Administration of Canada and the author.

tution Act was drafted the solution was not to provide for mechanisms for consultation and co-ordination. It was rather, to provide for the possibility of hierarchical control from the centre. This was clear in the role assigned to Lieutenant-Governors—as agents for the Governor General-in-Council most notably in exercising the power to reserve provincial bills for the pleasure of the Governor General-in-Council. It was also apparent in the federal power of disallowance and federal paramountcy in the two areas of concurrent jurisdiction: agriculture and immigration. These were not, in concept or in the facts of that day, mere symbolic gestures. They were intended to be real, and they were.

Thus, particularly in the first forty years, our federalism was characterized by

— compartmentalization of powers—even as late as the 1930s governments could consider that "relief" was a provincial problem and that the only federal role was to consider how to provide special interim financing;
— federal government supremacy, best exemplified by its extensive use of the powers of reservation and disallowance (149 times during the first 40 years after 1867).

Under these circumstances, there was little need for federal-provincial ministerial conferences; as noted earlier, the first conference of the prime minister and the premiers was not held until 1906. One did not need to consult to avoid or to remedy conflicting actions when more direct means were available!

In contrast, during the last decade federal and provincial ministers and senior officials have come together at formal meetings an average of 500 times a year.

Several factors which have contributed to the proliferation of federal-provincial conferences can be isolated:

— To start with, judicial interpretation, particularly towards the end of the 19th century, gave larger meaning and substance to the powers of provincial legislatures under Section 92 of the Constitution Act and thus reduced the scope of authority in Parliament.
— Then, government at each level has burgeoned and increased in complexity as its role in society has expanded. New activities have given a very different meaning to the old words and inflated the effect of the powers for all.
— And in particular, the federal spending power has been used extensively, in some cases to counter the imbalance between enhanced provincial legislative authority and limited tax access created as a result of (1) above, or to meet the new demands on the public sector noted in (2).

Meanwhile, changing public attitudes towards the two orders of government made reservation and disallowance by the federal government increasingly unacceptable for use as an instrument of policy in resolving conflicts. Thus, although these powers were exercised on 149 occasions during the first 40 years after Confederation, they have been used only 32 times in the seventy-one years since. The last use of disallowance was in 1943 and of reservation in 1961.

These developments have combined to alter dramatically the relationships of the federal and provincial governments. Although the text of the Constitution Act itself has not substantially changed, judicial interpretation and the practice of government have combined to modify greatly the meaning of the powers it allocates. In some areas the demarcation lines between the sources of authority for new or expanded activities have become so unclear as to be blurred in the most objective attempt at delineation. The result of this, and of other cases of failure to pay due regard to the remote sources of constitutional authority, is claims of territorial encroachment—not always in one direction—and persistent boundary disputes. Reflecting the increased complexity and integration of society at large, where what one party does almost always affects the actions of others, the activities of the two orders of government have become much more interdependent than they used to be. This has given rise to the frequent need for collective exercise of powers, even where there is no formal, constitutional recognition of shared or concurrent jurisdiction. Individual initiatives often have to be harmonized or reinforced for full effect, and joint financing may be required, especially for certain programs undertaken at federal initiative. In short, the evolution of the Canadian society and of Canadian federalism has brought us to the point where governments must now work together and make deals constantly or else markedly increase the risk of conflict and ineffectiveness.

Intergovernmental business in Canada is conducted by governments, of course, not by legislatures. More specifically it is conducted by cabinet members, notably by first ministers. This works because a cabinet in our parliamentary system can normally "deliver" legislative support on virtually any matter, save possibly in minority situations. Interministerial conferences are thus an adjunct to executive power, a demonstration of where power actually resides, and the centrepiece of what Professor Smiley has called "executive federalism."

The proliferation of federal-provincial ministerial conferences can, then, be viewed as a perfectly natural outcome of the great expansion in government's role and of the continuing need of governments to cope with the interdependence of their activities. Nevertheless, one role for federal-provincial conferences in the decision-making process has remained constant throughout: to provide an opportunity to ascertain and to adjust or accommodate the spillover effects on provincial government policies and programs of federal government initiatives.

This proposition contains within it a focus of decision-making that deserves to be traced more explicitly. The usual subjects for discussion at federal-provincial ministerial conferences are the policies and programs, in preparation or in operation, of the federal government—rarely of the provincial governments. One obvious reason for this is that federal actions are much more likely to concern all parties at the conference table. There is greater potential for the business of all ten provincial governments to be affected when the federal government makes a move, than when one, or even more than one, province takes action within its sphere of authority. In performance of this constant role, federal-provincial conferences serve as the meeting ground for the separate decision-making processes of the federal government and the provincial governments. Provincial ministers participate because their own decisions in their own governments could be altered or affected as a direct result of the federal initiatives under discussion, not just because of a general interest in the subjects on the agenda. Interministerial conferences, then, provide a forum where the principals gather to transact the business that derives from the interdependence of their activities—although not from fully reciprocal interdependence for the agenda does not normally include provincial initiatives. The effect on the federal government of initiatives of individual provinces tends to be dealt with in bilateral exchanges.

In this sense, the familiar role of interministerial conferences has remained constant, though exercise of the role has increased greatly. But that is by no means the whole story. More recently, another role of federal-provincial conferences has been given considerable emphasis. This role, which is not new but is now greatly enhanced, is an important aspect of first ministers' conferences and has added further complexity to intergovernmental dealings. This is the evolution of provincial premiers and ministers as regional spokesmen on national issues, or, more accurately, perhaps, their increased use of federal-provincial conferences as a forum for the expression of regional interests in matters substantially within the federal authority that affect the residents of each province or region but not necessarily the decisions of provincial governments.

INTERMINISTERIAL CONFERENCES IN THE DECISION-MAKING PROCESS

The sorts of decisions, agreements, and understandings which are now sought through federal-provincial ministerial conferences pertain to

— the familiar role of accommodating the direct impacts, financial or otherwise, which federal initiatives may have on the priorities, policies and programs of provincial governments; and

— the newly emphasized role of identifying and reconciling regional points of view in the design of federal actions where intergovernmental linkages are not necessarily a central factor.

With hindsight, it is easy enough to see why the second role gained prominence. Federal-provincial conferences were a ready forum with no automatic mechanism to differentiate between the items that would call for co-operative arrangements between governments and those in which the federal government would have the capacity and the jurisdiction to act on behalf of the country as a whole, and where any effects on provincial governments as such would be uncertain and indirect.

The Western Economic Opportunities conference of 1973 was, perhaps, a milestone in the expansion of this second role of interministerial conferences. On that occasion discussions were directed almost entirely to westerners' grievances and aspirations in respect of federal policies—freight rates, tariffs, federal agricultural policy, etc. The federal government accepted the four provincial premiers as valid interlocutors on these matters, even though it was recognized on all sides that they did not share in the decision-making responsibility and that the activities of their governments were not directly affected.

It is partly because we have lacked an effective forum for open regional advocacy and brokerage within our institutions at the federal level

of government that provincial premiers and ministers have been assuming more and more the role of regional commentators and critics in areas of federal jurisdiction. Started by Quebec long ago, this regional advocacy by the provincial governments has in recent years become more widespread as the western governments have increasingly taken a similar tack. Governments in the Atlantic provinces in their own way also seek out and utilize opportunities to draw attention to the particular points of view of their areas in respect of federal policies. It is not clear whether Ontario has yet perceived itself as a "region" in the same sense, although the time may come. There are thus many reasons why, in a federal-provincial conference setting, the premiers and their cabinet colleagues frequently act as spokesmen for the people and the interests of provinces, as social or geographical entities, on matters where the Parliament of Canada has primary legislative authority and where the federal executive has the decision-making responsibility. One could mention here grain marketing, ocean fisheries, national transportation, and exploitation of uranium.

We might ask ourselves whether, in emphasizing this particular role of federal-provincial conferences, we may have created a situation in which the public at large gain a wrong impression, or become quite confused, about who is in charge of what.

To clarify this point one must distinguish between consultations and negotiations. Where federal-provincial conferences discuss matters within federal jurisdictions they help the federal government choose courses of action for which it has full authority. The viewpoints and wisdom of provincial governments and ministers are solicited but the decisions rest with the federal government, as does the responsibility. In this sense a conference is a consultation. Only where there are interdependencies of authority and responsibility, where harmonization requires quid pro quo on both sides, does true negotiation occur.

Nevertheless the dynamics of conferences

can leave the impression that the participants are in the midst of bargaining sessions when the federal government is, in reality, consulting the leaders of provincial governments on a decision that is its own to make. This can occur in situations where the recommendations made by provincial interlocutors may be cast, or could be interpreted by observers, as demands which must be met, even though the federal government is technically and constitutionally free to act as it thinks best and must carry the responsibility for whatever decision it finally takes, whether the provincial governments concur or not. If the subsequent federal decision does not incorporate or reflect the views expressed by provincial ministers, then the federal government can be reproached for having seemingly disregarded the positions of individuals who may be taken by some to be full partners in the decision itself. If this occurs frequently enough the result could be to undermine the apparent authority of the federal government to take decisions of its own where it will be and must be held responsible. The provincial advocates and the public at large may become misled about respective responsibilities. Another consequence could be that the federal government would become less inclined to engage in consultations at the conference table because of the misunderstandings and criticism that can accompany them, especially if the views of provincial governments are not followed in some or all respects. All of these eventualities, I believe, merit recognition and serious consideration.

Each of the central institutions of our federation is to some degree flawed as a forum for the fullest expression and reconciliation of regional interests. Constraints are imposed by "rep. by pop.," strict party discipline, the need to maintain "confidence" in the House of Commons, and by cabinet solidarity. If the central institutions, where much of the responsibility for this advocacy and brokerage function lies, could be overhauled to be more effective in this sense, there would be less need for federal-provincial conferences to fulfill this function. But limita-

tions are inherent in our parliamentary system and in our collective executive. It is in relation to the consequences in our central institutions, and the frustrations they create, that one can note the concern expressed from time to time by various members of the House of Commons about federal-provincial conferences. Such conferences provide a national platform where leaders elected at the provincial level perform the role of spokesmen for all interests of their province. In this role they sometimes substitute for, sometimes complement—and often overshadow—members of Parliament elected to the federal forum for discussion and also federal ministers who can properly consider that they have a role as regional spokesmen for federal affairs. Sometimes the issues, which are later presented to Parliament in the form of bills or appropriations, are more fully aired at federal-provincial meetings than in the House of Commons. Federal-provincial conferences do not in fact reduce the accountability as such of governments to Parliament and to legislatures. Parliament is the locus of responsibility and accountability for our national government, but, because of the nature of our system, it is not the public and apparent locus of regional argument and compromise.

Our federation was structured to allow the voter direct representation in both orders of government, not to create a competitive situation. It was to establish a division and specialization of responsibilities, not to afford the voter two voices on any single issue. The situation that has emerged in federal-provincial ministerial conferences, however, is one in which the voters' provincial representatives proffer advice and recommendations to the voters' federal representatives on how the latter should exercise their constitutional authority even where impacts on provincial government policies and programs may not be chiefly at issue. Sometimes the advice constrains the federal government, which, on occasion, is as it should be. On other occasions the advice provides support to the federal government to take action that would be politically hazardous or unacceptable to the public at large without provincial government support. How the advice is given, and received, can itself affect federal-provincial relations.

Federal-provincial conferences have, thus, come to be viewed by some as an institution that provides checks and balances in the federal system. Some analysts regard this as a healthy development, and in some respects it is. However, it might be worth asking whether, at conferences, the checks operate only in one direction—to constrain the federal government. There appears to be no corresponding check on provincial policies or actions.

Obviously, however, there are some matters under provincial jurisdiction which are of national interest and as such might justify comment from the federal government. An example could be found in the very broad field that education has become since 1867. However, provinces have, shall we say, protective instincts in this regard and they seem not to welcome federal comment or advice even on matters where it is clear that there is a broad national interest in the total result of provincial policies and actions about education.

In contrast, the federal government has invited the views of provincial premiers and ministers in respect of matters in fields wholly or primarily within federal jurisdiction, such as international affairs, foreign trade, and transportation. It is worth noting that it was the federal government that suggested these sorts of items for the agendas of federal-provincial conferences. But in the end the provincial governments have an interest in these matters, not ultimate or even partial authority—just as the federal government has a clear interest in some aspects of education and the results of policy there, but not authority. Dare I suggest that, were the federal government to express concern about, say, the level of literacy in Canada, the provinces ought not to regard this as an "intrusion"?

Why in spite of the problems posed has the federal government nevertheless engaged the provinces in consultations on these "federal" matters?

— In the first place, it recognizes that better federal legislation, policies or programs can result if its proposals are exposed to constructive criticism, often in the crucial early stages of development.

— Secondly, federal-provincial conferences do partially compensate for deficiencies in the functioning of regional advocacy and brokerage within central institutions. More importantly, they facilitate the *visible* introduction of regional and provincial viewpoints into the federal decision-making process whereas in Cabinet and in caucus there is no such visibility.

— Thirdly, when these conferences are open, they heighten the public's awareness of the range of regional perspectives and, perhaps most important, of the complexity of reconciling these perspectives.

This feature, visibility, has an important influence on the role of interministerial conferences. The foremost purpose of federal-provincial ministerial conferences remains to secure agreements, understandings and sometimes binding, precisely-defined decisions, affecting intergovernmental business, to arrive cooperatively at solutions to practical problems posed by the acknowledged interdependency of governmental activities. Experience of public affairs, and also of ordinary human affairs in all spheres, argues that to achieve this purpose, conferences should not be entirely open.

There are several reasons:

— Open conferences hamper the process of reaching decisions, because of reluctance on the part of the participants to make concessions that might cause problems with the audience back home. If this forces the necessary bargaining "underground", the role of officials may be magnified.

— For bargaining to begin, political and partisan rhetoric must give way to straight talk. This usually requires closed doors, since the public stance of contest between leaders of opposing parties is essential to the political process.

— Openness can be a divisive influence in that the debate, under the compulsion of the confrontational quality of the bargaining process, can highlight differences of opinion and viewpoint rather than the common ground.

— Individual, practical problems can become hostages to a public relations exercise that may be necessary for broader political or other purposes.

This is not to say that privacy is a sufficient condition for effective cooperation and compromise but it is probably a necessary one. Management and labour, even in the newspaper or communications fields, do not do their bargaining and make their deals on camera.

On the other hand, federal-provincial conferences serve other purposes, in addition to the regional advocacy considerations already noted, that argue for open doors and for a high public profile:

— to permit legislators to observe the proceedings and thereby the conduct of intergovernmental business carried out at the executive level;

— to show to a wide audience the degree of collective sensitivity and responsiveness to issues of national concern, such as building economic confidence;

— to enhance public understanding of the subjects under discussion and to demonstrate federalism in practice.

There may be a price to be paid whether a conference is open or closed to public view, depending on what has to be achieved. These considerations need to be carefully weighed and assessed for each conference in light of its particular purposes. Per-

haps some combination of open and closed sessions is generally to be preferred. Certainly as the participants get closer to decisions the pressure mounts for closed door sessions. Even though the steps by which ultimate decisions are arrived at may not therefore be public, conference communiqués tell the results and can be used to infer much of what took place—especially if the initial bargaining positions are known, and communiqués are supported by reports and explanations by participants after the event.

Interestingly, the question of closed versus open conferences has not been raised much with regard to multilateral ministerial conferences held among provincial governments. Why not? One wonders whether the practice of federalism is enhanced when the provinces meet behind closed doors to form a common front against the federal government. It would be interesting to have the question discussed since there appears to be a growing pattern of this kind as a part of the process of interministerial discussion.

Although in recent years the federal government has not been invited as an observer, it is apparent that these interprovincial meetings frequently do serve to prepare the provinces for conferences with the federal government. The federal side—and the public—can only speculate what the impact has been on subsequent federal-provincial conferences. Obviously it helps to have a thorough airing of a subject beforehand. Obviously, too, provincial bargaining power is greater if the provinces can reach a united stance in response to a federal proposal. But to the extent that, for example, regional and interprovincial differences are squared away in camera, at a stage preliminary to a federal-provincial meeting, interprovincial conferences weaken the very arguments which are now advanced in favour of open conferences. There is a danger that interprovincial consensus may be only a lowest common denominator which masks major issues, conflicts and choices. One might also ask whether equality of representation in interprovincial meetings enhances, replaces or countervails "rep. by pop." in the determination of national interest, and whether on balance this is good for the federation or not.

FUTURE PROSPECTS

In general, the prospect is for interministerial conferences to remain a vital and heavily-used mechanism for federal-provincial relations. While some of the developments that caused the proliferation, such as the expanded role of government, may be slowed or even halted, others almost certainly will not. New circumstances, such as more use of concurrent powers, may induce even greater reliance on the conference forum. In any case, the underlying problems posed by a complex world and interdependence of government activities will not change. Governments will need to continue to adapt the practice of federalism to the demands placed upon them.

In terms of the institutions of federalism, a new second chamber of Parliament . . . may affect the situation somewhat. However, the premiers and their ministers will continue to be the legitimate voices and decision-makers as regards the impact of federal initiatives on provincial governments. Only a Bundesrat consisting of provincial ministers sitting as a second chamber could conceivably replace them in this role. The intention of the federal government is, of course, that the proposed chamber should add to the ability of central institutions to identify and reconcile in an effective manner the differing regional and provincial interests that can be affected by federal action. If this were to occur it might lessen the corresponding role now played by federal-provincial conferences, but several factors connected with a reformed upper house will ensure that such conferences remain an important feature of our system.

— Provincial premiers would be free to speak out even if appointees of provincial legislatures or governments were making all the "right" arguments in a new upper house. Federal-provincial conferences will continue to be a convenient forum for them to do that.

— Federal legislation, which would be the business of the upper house, is a relatively small part of government action which includes as well policies, programs and regulations.

— Consultation at federal-provincial conferences usually relates to intended legislation, not legislation already introduced in Parliament. To this extent, federal-provincial discussion would still precede debate in the House of the Federation.

CONCLUSIONS

I have discussed the increased use of interministerial conferences in the decision-making process in Canada. They are an institution that was not foreseen in 1867 and did not constitute a part of the plan for our federal system. I have suggested that they have become increasingly important, in recent years, because of three factors: first, the increase in the power of the provincial governments; secondly, the increased role of all governments and the increasing complexity of their action in our society; and, thirdly, the extensive use of the federal spending power in promoting a variety of shared-cost programs. With these developments, a mechanism for cooperation between the two levels of government, in decisions and in actions, was clearly needed. The interministerial conference has performed that role. I have suggested, however, that the conferences have had other effects that we should not ignore. As the importance of shared-cost programs of the old design has diminished with mechanisms of financing that do not involve "conditions" attached to the federal spending, the substance of conferences has increasingly turned to provincial participation in the consideration of matters within federal responsibility. Provincial premiers and ministers have increasingly assumed the role of regional spokesmen on "federal" as well as on "provincial" matters.

If these propositions are correct, we should enquire about the consequences for our federalism and for our sense of common purpose. We have seen an increasing tendency . . . to use inter-ministerial meetings at the provincial level, with no federal participation, to arrive at "common fronts." Is there not a danger that, if it becomes the general practice for inter-provincial differences to be worked out in private, with the concerted voice of the ten provinces then being expressed against the federal view in public, an impression will be created of a federal government that represents no one, of a federal government that is opposed by all provincial governments, and of a government whose action is apparently adverse to the interests of all regions?

I exaggerate in order to make a point. Our processes have moved, without anyone intending it, in a direction that reinforces the tendency to regional difference that is already so strong in Canada and that regrettably makes it more difficult for us to maintain a firm sense of national purpose and of common interest. I think we must consider with some care whether these are tendencies we want to encourage in the best interests of this country. The proliferation and functioning of federal-provincial interministerial conferences have, I think, been a mixed blessing for our federal system and for our country. They have served real and necessary purposes but there are at this time reasons to consider just where they may be taking us.

Selected Readings

Meekison, J. P. "First Ministers Conferences in the Canadian Federal System." In T. J. Courchene, D. W. Conklin, and G. Cook, eds., *Ottawa and the Provinces: The Distribution of Money and Power.* Vol. 2. Toronto: Ontario Economic Council, 1985, 162-183.

Pollard, B. G. *Managing the Interface: Intergovernmental Affairs Agencies in Canada.* Kingston: Institute of Intergovernmental Relations, Queen's University, 1984.

Simeon, R., ed. *Confrontation and Collaboration: Intergovernmental Relations in Canada Today.* Toronto: Institute of Public Administration of Canada, 1979.

Simeon, R. *Federal-Provincial Diplomacy: The Making of Recent Policy in Canada.* Toronto: University of Toronto Press, 1971.

Spector, N. "Federal-Provincial Professionalism." *Policy Options* 5:6 (November 1984): 44-6.

Woolstencroft, T. B. *Organizing Intergovernmental Relations.* Kingston: Institute of Intergovernmental Relations, Queen's University, 1982.

14. REFLECTIONS ON THE WORKABILITY OF EXECUTIVE FEDERALISM

J. Stefan Dupré

In recent years, interaction among federal and provincial first ministers has fallen into a state of disarray. At the level of ministers and officials, federal-provincial relations have become so varied and so complex that they defy generalization. As a long-time national sport, executive federalism, like the post-expansion NHL, has become the subject of anxious hand wringing by many of its practitioners and much of its audience. This essay, written by one of the latter, but enriched by the insights of a small number of experienced practitioners,[1] probes the workability of executive federalism. By workability, I do not mean the capacity of executive federalism, on any given issue or at any given time, to produce federal-provincial accord as opposed to discord. Because executive federalism is rooted in what Richard Simeon has labelled succinctly the "political independence" and the "policy interdependence"[2] of our federal and provincial governments, it is these governments that make the fundamental choices to agree or disagree. Whether executive federalism works involves not whether governments agree or disagree, but whether it provides a forum (or more accurately a set of forums) that is conducive, and perceived to be conducive, as the case may be, to negotiation, consultation, or simply an exchange of information.

A major theme of this essay is that the workability of executive federalism is to an important

degree a function of the manner in which the executives of our federal and provincial governments operate. This is explored in an introductory way under the heading Executive Federalism and Intragovernmental Relations, and probed further in the next two sections, one entitled Federal-Provincial Functional Relations, the other Federal-Provincial Summit Relations. These sections probe selective circumstances under which executive federalism has been a more or less workable mechanism of federal-provincial adjustment. The final section of this essay, titled Prescriptions for Workable Executive Federalism, proposes procedural and substantive directions that executive federalism might seek to follow for the balance of this century.

EXECUTIVE FEDERALISM AND INTRAGOVERNMENTAL RELATIONS

The fundamental facts of Canadian constitutionalism are federalism and the cabinet-parliamentary form of government. The first means that the Canadian territorial division of power takes the form of two constitutionally ordained levels of government, each endowed with distinct yet often overlapping jurisdiction. The second means that executive and legislative institutions, through the constitutional conventions of responsible government, are fused in such a manner that what Thomas Hockin calls "the collective central energizing executive" (cabinet) is the "key engine of the state"[3] within each of the federal and provincial levels of government.

The Canadian version of the rise of the modern administrative state yields progressively larger and more potent federal and provincial bu-

J. Stefan Dupré, "Reflections on the Workability of Executive Federalism," in *Intergovernmental Relations*, ed., Richard Simeon, vol. 63 of *Research Studies for the Royal Commission on the Economic Union and Development Prospects for Canada* (Toronto: University of Toronto Press, 1985), 1-32. Reprinted by permission of University of Toronto Press. © Minister of Supply and Services Canada. The essay has been edited to suit the needs of this volume.

reaucracies, formally subordinated to their respective cabinets, and growing federal-provincial interdependence as each of these levels of government, driven by its energizing executive, actualizes the jurisdictional potential conferred upon it by the Constitution. With almost Sophoclean inevitability, the resulting need for a non-judicial mechanism of adjustment is met by what Donald Smiley so aptly calls executive federalism, "which may be defined as the relations between elected and appointed officials of the two orders of government in federal-provincial interactions . . . ."[4] Smiley includes relations among the elected and appointed officials of provincial governments under the umbrella of executive federalism, but this essay will refer to such purely interprovincial relations as "executive interprovincialism." This is in part to stress the fact that relations between governments that share identical jurisdiction are different from relations between governments that share divided jurisdiction, in part to acknowledge that executive interprovincialism has not infrequently been a provincial response to executive federalism.

"The relations between elected and appointed officials of the two levels of government" are taken as the constant that defines executive federalism. Executive federalism has been categorized in the literature from the standpoint of outcomes, as cooperative or conflictual federalism. From the standpoint of actors, it has been called summit federalism (relations among first ministers and/or their designated ministerial or bureaucratic entourage) and functional federalism (relations among ministers and/or their officials). From the standpoint of participating governments, it has been labelled multilateral (the federal and all ten provincial governments), multilateral-regional (the federal government and the governments of some, normally contiguous, provinces), and bilateral (the federal government and a single province). These labels—and others—will be used where appropriate in the text of this essay; all, however, are

deemed conceptually secondary to the notion of executive federalism as embodying the relations between the elected and appointed officials of the energizing executives of our federal and provincial levels of government.

It is this simple notion that permits me to observe that executive federalism, as a mechanism of federal-provincial adjustment, cannot be divorced from intragovernmental considerations, i.e., from the structure and functioning of the "collective central energizing executives" with which the conventions of the Constitution endow Ottawa and each of the provinces. Without altering one iota of the constitutional conventions that give them their central energizing force, cabinets can operate in vastly different ways. Thus, for example, at any given point in time, there will be differences in the manner in which cabinets operate in Ottawa, as distinct from large provinces, and as distinct from small provinces. Such differences, which may be accentuated by the role of political, especially prime ministerial, personalities and by the complexion of different governing parties, will be acknowledged as this essay proceeds. More important to a general consideration of executive federalism are historically distinguishable modes of cabinet operation. I shall distinguish three such modes of cabinet operation. The first, which I choose to label the "traditional" mode, is one in which cabinets can be said to operate primarily in what Jean Hamelin calls "chamber(s) of political compensation."[5] This mode of cabinet operation antedates the rise of the modern administrative state and, for that matter, of executive federalism. Here, cabinet ministers, given the limited scope of their respective governments, pre-eminently articulate and aggregate matters of regional or local political concern, and are primarily in the business of dispensing patronage. The extent to which the federal cabinet, in this mode of operation, can itself provide a mechanism of federal-provincial adjustment has been sketched aptly by Donald

Smiley.[6] The second and third modes of cabinet operation, which respectively accompany the rise and then the maturation of the modern administrative state, are the ones that are material to executive federalism. I shall call the second the "departmentalized cabinet" and the third the "institutionalized cabinet."

The "departmentalized" cabinet at once reflects and abets the rise of the modern administrative state. Government departments, allocated among ministers as their respective portfolio responsibilities, are the prime depositories of public sector expansion and of the special expertise which fuels and responds to expansion. The functions assigned to a department make it the natural focus of discrete client interests, and the inputs of these departmentally oriented clientele groups interact synergistically with the "within-puts" of the department's expert bureaucrats. For ministers, this interaction breeds "portfolio loyalty" both because they perceive that their effectiveness is judged by their departmental clienteles and because they depend on departmental expertise for policy formulation and implementation. Subject to greater or lesser degrees of prime ministerial direction, ministers are endowed with a substantial measure of decision-making autonomy which redounds to the benefit of their departmental clienteles and bureaucracies. In the departmentalized cabinet, a minister is of course always a member of what by constitutional design is a collectively responsible executive but, as James Gillies puts it so well, "the principle of Cabinet collective responsibility [is] based on the commonsense notion of confidence in one's colleagues, rather than on the concept of sharing of knowledge or decision-making."[7]

In the "institutionalized" cabinet, by contrast, various combinations of formal committee structures, established central agencies, and budgeting and management techniques combine to emphasize shared knowledge, collegial decision making, and the formulation of government-wide priorities and objectives. "The major thrust," Smiley writes, "is to decrease the relative autonomy of ministers and the departments working under their direction."[8] More than this, the institutionalized cabinet generates distinguishable categories of ministers; what Douglas Hartle calls the "central agency" ministers and the "special interest" ministers.[9] The portfolios of the former, in Hartle's words, "cut across special interest lines for they reflect the several dimensions of the *collective* concerns of the Cabinet."[10] Meantime, the ministers in the second category continue to pursue, "as they are expected to pursue, the special interest of special interest portfolios."[11] In this setting, intragovernmental decision making becomes not only collegial, but acquires a competitive, adversarial flavour.

The original Canadian home of the institutionalized cabinet is the Saskatchewan of Premier T. C. Douglas, and its best documented manifestations are those of the Pearson-Trudeau-Clark-Trudeau era in Ottawa. With substantial variations, both spatially and temporally, the institutionalized cabinet has as its theme the quest to make contemporary government decision-making manageable. It arises initially as the response to the perceived defects of the departmentalized cabinet in the face of the range, complexity, and interdependence of the decisions that contemporary governments are called on to make. Once in place, it can be adjusted into a variety of configurations as the quest to make contemporary decision-making manageable continues to be pursued with all the intensity of the quest for the Holy Grail. From one perspective, effectively articulated by Peter Aucoin, the institutionalized cabinet subjects special interests to the welcome challenge of greater scrutiny and increased competition.[12] From a contrary perspective, articulated with similar effectiveness by James Gillies, the institutionalized cabinet can so dissipate the input of special interests into the policies which affect them that it threatens to undermine the doctrine of government by consent.[13]

Which perspective is more nearly correct (and both may have enormous elements of validity) is less important for an essay on the workability of executive federalism than the stark fact that the intergovernmental relations between elected and appointed officials of our two levels of government are bound to be affected by the very different intragovernmental relations that characterize the departmentalized and institutionalized modes of cabinet operation. To expound, let us consider federal-provincial functional relations and federal-provincial summit relations. In each instance, the transition from the departmentalized to the institutionalized cabinet has fundamental implications, as do the various configurations which institutionalized cabinets can acquire.

FEDERAL-PROVINCIAL FUNCTIONAL RELATIONS

From the 1920s into the 1960s, the Canadian story of income security, social services, health care, vocational education, transportation infrastructure, and resource development is a tale in which federal-provincial functional relations play a starring role. True to the operation at each level of government of the departmentalized cabinet, executive federalism rests upon relations between program officials, deputy ministers, and ministers from federal and provincial departments with overlapping or complementary missions. The relations are financially lubricated by numerous conditional grants which apply the federal spending power to individual programs that frequently, but not invariably, aspire to national standards. When categorized in terms of outcomes, federal-provincial relations are justifiably labelled as cooperative federalism.[14] The ingredients of these relations can be readily enumerated to yield what I choose to call the "functional relations model" of executive federalism. Each element in the model is remarkably conducive to the formation and maintenance of what Albert Breton and Ronald Wintrobe call "net-

works," that is to say, "trust relationships or trust ties,"[15] along intergovernmental lines.

— The appointed federal and provincial program officials involved in functional relations share common values and speak a similar vocabulary as a result of common training in a particular profession or discipline, e.g., public health, social work, or education.

— Departmentalized cabinets make it likely that the commonalities of functional relations at the level of program officials will percolate to the deputy ministerial and ministerial levels. In the departmentalized setting, deputy ministers often will have risen through the ranks of their departments, thus sharing the outlooks of their program subordinates. As for ministers, the relatively uninhibited portfolio loyalties bred by the departmentalized cabinet induce a coincidence of views, notwithstanding their diverse political and professional backgrounds. Furthermore, the measure of decision-making autonomy which ministers enjoy as members of their departmentalized cabinets means that there is minimal likelihood that federal-provincial accord at the ministerial level will be questioned or reversed by first ministers or cabinets.

— The trust relationships generated by the above two elements draw ongoing sustenance from the longevity of the federal-provincial structures within which functional relations are conducted. Enhancing as they do the likelihood of repeated transactions over long periods of time, these stable structures, to borrow the words of Breton and Wintrobe, "increase the future return to investments in trust."[16] They ensure that federal and provincial ministers, deputy ministers, and program officials, at any given point in time, have a stake in their future relationships.

— The financial lubricant supplied by conditional grants serves to aid and abet trust relationships in that the resulting program activity at the donating and recipient levels of government enhances bureaucratic careers and ministerial reputations. Such grants also insulate program activity from budgetary competition to the extent that they generate the familiar lock-in effect ("we are locked in by promises made to the provinces") at the federal level, and the equally familiar carrot effect ("50-cent dollars") at the provincial level.

— Special interests (e.g., those focused upon public health, welfare or education) achieve virtual representation in the processes of executive federalism through the associational ties of department officials and the loyalty of ministers to their clientele-oriented portfolios.

If the four decades of federal-provincial functional relations, from which the above model is derived, can indeed be labelled an era of cooperative federalism, the evident exception is Quebec. But this exception supports rather than undermines the importance of the model's components. To the extent that Quebec officials shared professional backgrounds similar to those of their counterparts from Ottawa and the anglophone provinces, their distinctive academic formation was anything but tantamount to the common school ties (corresponding to the restricted number of professional faculties then found in English-speaking universities) worn by anglophone program officials. Moreover, in the Quebec version of the departmentalized cabinet, ministerial autonomy was severely circumscribed by the prime ministerial style of Maurice Duplessis and by the government-wide objective, founded on widely shared respect for classical as opposed to cooperative federalism, of protecting provincial jurisdiction and indigenous institutions. Again, in that Quebec did not uniformly exclude itself from functional arrangements it is to be noted that the temporal longitude of federal-provincial structures, coupled with the open-ended availability of conditional grants, permitted selected shopping by the Quebec government and accommodated its acquiescence to programs of its choosing, normally in the domain of income maintenance. Finally, with respect to special interests, the extent to which Quebec's self-imposed exclusion from federal-provincial functional relations enjoyed societal support is testimony to the segmentalist orientation,[17] driven by linguistic barriers, of this province's elites.

As the decade of the 1960s unfolded, federal-provincial functional relations underwent a significant metamorphosis. This metamorphosis paralleled and reflected the transition within governments from the departmentalized to the institutionalized cabinet. The budgetary distortions which conditional grants generated through their "lock-in" and "carrot" effects, once discovered by rational budgetary processes, spelled the demise of these grants on a grand scale. Equally consequential was the extent to which functional relations had to adapt to broader governmental considerations, acquired bilateral dimensions, and were forced to accommodate sudden shifts in personnel and structures. A few sketches, culled from the realms of social assistance, manpower training, and regional development are illustrative.

Social Assistance

The successful negotiation of the Canada Assistance Plan (CAP), in the period 1963-66, wrought the termination of several categorical conditional grant programs in favour of a broad shared-cost approach to income security and social services for persons in need. Rand Dyck's instructive account of the negotiations makes it abundantly clear that the long-standing relations among federal and provincial deputy ministers of welfare enveloped the emergence of CAP in a cooperative atmosphere.[18] However, Dyck notes that federal welfare officials, along with a number of their provincial counterparts, were oriented on professional grounds to favour a shared-cost design that would stimulate the achievement of high national standards. These views were over-ridden in favour of flexibility by federal central agencies sensitive to broader federal-provincial issues. (Dyck names the Department of Finance, Treasury Board, the Privy Council Office, and the Prime Minister's Office.[19]) The outcome was a CAP which relegated the matter of interprovincial discrepancies to the unconditional, fiscal capacity-related equalization payments of the Fiscal Arrangements Act, left welfare standards to the budgetary processes of provincial governments, and accommodated Quebec demands to the point where its opted-out position in the realm of social assistance became largely symbolic. What the CAP episode illustrates is

— the continuing importance of long-standing trust ties among functional officials;
— a new central agency presence in federal-provincial functional relations; and
— the capacity of central agency influence to contribute to a harmonious federal-provincial outcome linked to considerations that lie beyond specialized professional norms.

The Social Security Review, launched in 1973, yields a different sketch of functional relations coloured by a different manifestation of the institutionalized cabinet. The origins of the Social Security Review lay partly in the Ottawa-Quebec jurisdictional discord (which eventually aborted the Victoria Charter in 1971), and partly in the capacity of policy analysis (epitomized by Quebec's landmark Castonguay-Nepveu report) to articulate the attractiveness of sweeping welfare reform, which, through a guaranteed annual income, would reconcile income maintenance with equitable work incentives for low-wage earners. The Review is distinctive because a significant number of its participants were by design individuals without social welfare backgrounds. This was visibly symbolized in the person of the then newly appointed federal deputy minister of welfare, A. W. Johnson, previously secretary of the Treasury Board (Johnson's

minister, Marc Lalonde, had been principal secretary in the Prime Minister's Office prior to his entry into electoral politics); and it was tangibly manifest in the involvement, in both federal and provincial delegations, of economists and manpower officials, as well as of social welfare specialists. According to Johnson's account of the first two years of the Review, the diverse backgrounds of the participants eventually yielded a degree of mutual education. This was preceded, however, by time-consuming discord, bred by the extent to which "those concerned with employment and employment services were inclined to be suspicious of (social work) phrases like 'fullest functional potential' and the social workers tended to regard the manpower people as being excessively preoccupied with employment rather than the 'whole person'."[20]

Once federal-provincial functional relations are called upon not only to accommodate central agency influence, but to open their channels to individuals who articulate their positions from the standpoint of diverse professional backgrounds, there is reason to temper one's expectations of what they are capable of producing. And in the result, the failure of the Social Security Review to produce a guaranteed annual income invites the further consideration that, as it proceeded, this exercise unravelled an agenda item whose ramifications were simply too broad to be accommodated at any level of federal-provincial relations short of the summit. The government-wide concerns that can be injected into functional relations by central agency personnel do not obviate the competitive features of collegial decision-making within the institutionalized cabinets of individual governments. Programs with an intimate bearing on the guranteed annual income, like federal and provincial minimum wage laws, federal unemployment insurance, and provincial workers' compensation, are the preserve of agencies other than welfare departments. This being so, Keith Banting's verdict that the Social Security Review "was doomed from the outset by interdepartmental barriers at both levels"[21] has great weight. The institutionalized cabinet reduces departmental autonomy in a quest to make contemporary decision-making manageable. However, pursuing this quest in the framework of competitive collegiality and finding the Holy Grail remain two quite different things. The sources of the failure of the Social Security Review include interdepartmental tensions within each of the respective levels of government. And incidentally, to those who criticize executive federalism as an essentially closed process, Banting offers a telling rejoinder when he writes: "The politics of executive federalism focus the full glare of government and public attention on *intergovernmental* coordination failure. In comparison, *intragovernmental* failures languish in the twilight of cabinet discretion."[22]

This triggers a final observation with respect to the Social Security Review. Its one strong note of federal-provincial accord was sounded early in its existence, and produced a new source of asymmetric federalism: provincial configuration, i.e., provincial capacity to alter, within limits, the rates of benefits paid by the federal family allowance program. The point is that this achievement involved a program entirely within the portfolio of Health and Welfare Canada. A few years after the termination of the Review, the provincial gratification with which configuration had been received, particularly by Quebec, was undone by a unilateral federal measure—in the realm of taxation. Quebec had chosen a provincial configuration of family allowances that increased the rate of allowances with the rank of a child in the family. However, the Child Tax Credit, initiated in 1979, took no account of child ranking and was accordingly incongruent with Quebec social assistance benefits that had been integrated with the provincially configurated family allowances.[23] The resulting discord over federal unilateralism was quite as real as the fact that the source of federal unilateralism lay outside the welfare portfolio. In the circumstances, tax policy takes on the guise of an external event that impinged negatively on trust ties between federal and provincial welfare ministers.

Manpower Training

The design of the federal Adult Occupational Training Act of 1967 was in part the product of the major retreat from conditional grants sounded by summit federal-provincial fiscal concerns. It was also in part the outcome, at the highest level of federal economic policy-making, of a unilateral decision to transform the vocational training of adults into an adjunct of employment policy.[24] Unveiled by Prime Minister Pearson at the federal-provincial summit conference of 1966, adult occupational training terminated almost 50 years of conditional grants in the realm of vocational education and assigned the use of training as an employment policy tool to the newly created Department of Manpower and Immigration. This initiative ended the functional relations long articulated by the vocational education divisions of provincial departments of Education and the Training Branch of the federal Department of Labour. The Branch's practice of recruiting its personnel from the ranks of provincial vocational education specialists had ensured the prevalence, across divided jurisdiction, of shared professional norms. The Technical and Vocational Training Advisory Council, the structure within which federal-provincial trust ties had flourished during its 25 years of existence, was dissolved. Henceforth, through what was couched simultaneously as a constitutional claim and an effort to disentangle federal-provincial relations, the federal government would purchase, at full cost, training courses for adults, selected by its employment placement counsellors on the basis of these counsellors' assessments of their clients' aptitudes and future employment prospects. The desired training could be purchased either from public institutions under provincial control or from private sources.

That the federal manpower design of the mid-1960s never became reality is poignantly apparent from the fact, almost 20 years later, that this Commission listed as an unmet challenge the provision of "timely opportunities for retraining in order to enable working Canadians to adapt to changes resulting from technological innovation and competition."[25] The fate of the federal design was sealed within months of its unveiling by a provincial victory which stands as an early exhibit in the annals of competitive, as distinct from cooperative, federalism.[26] In brief, what happened was that provincial departments of education successfully interposed themselves between federal adult training and public post-secondary institutions, forced federal officials to deal with them as "exclusive brokers" of training courses, and used their exclusive brokerage to eliminate private-sector training programs as potential competitors. The ingredients of the provincial educationists' success included

— support from the highest levels of their governments in a setting where the establishment of new postsecondary institutions (CAATs, CEGEPs, community colleges) enjoyed province-wide priority, and the task of orderly institutional development brooked no outside interference;

— their own close relations with college administrators who, in turn, possessed strong local and community ties; and

— federal inexperience with training programs and institutions, coupled with an incapacity to assess, let alone forecast, manpower needs.

Early on, the federal manpower initiative stimulated vigorous recourse to executive interprovincialism. It gave impetus to the formation of the Council of Ministers of Education in the summer of 1967, and to the initial prominence of the CME's Manpower Programs Committee as an inter-provincial *cum* educationist counterstructure in the realm of adult training. As for federal-provincial relations, the federal design had been based on little by way of formal structure: the federal aim was to substitute buyer-seller relations for those of executive federalism. A multilateral body, known first as the Federal-Provincial Meeting of Officials on Occupational Training for Adults, and subsequently as the

Canada Manpower Training Program (CMTP) committee, was intended originally to ease exchange of information; but it immediately became a forum where federal and provincial officials divided themselves along professional lines, between federal economists bent on training as an adjunct of employment and provincial educationists wedded to the development of the "whole person." In short order, provincial insistence upon exclusive brokerage forced the formation, along increasingly structured lines, of bilateral federal-provincial committees. It was in these committees that the "purchase" and "sale" of training became a negotiated, shared-cost planning process subservient, most especially in the case of Ontario, to provincial institutional and enrollment strategies.

In that bilateralism is a fount of asymmetry in federal-provincial relations, it permits more or less cooperative or conflictual atmospheres to prevail in different provincial contexts. Significantly, it appears that the Ottawa-Quebec relationship in adult training proved at least a partial exception to otherwise conflictual relations at the functional level. In this instance, the provincial side of the bilateral relationship was articulated not by educationists, but by officials of the Quebec Department of Manpower and Immigration, whose professional backgrounds parallelled those of their federal counterparts. Recalling the times, a senior Quebec Manpower official noted that the conflict between economists and educationists, which elsewhere plagued federal-provincial functional relations, had instead emerged in Quebec as an intragovernmental conflict around the provincial cabinet table.[27] This invites the observation that cabinets are endowed with means of conflict resolution which federal-provincial bodies can never possess.

Regional Development

Thanks to the scholarship of Anthony Careless and Donald Savoie, there exists a relative wealth of information of the nexus between federal-provincial functional relations in the realm of regional development and the emergence of institutionalized cabinets at each of these levels of government. Careless concentrates on the years 1960-73 and traces regional development from its genesis in the ARDA of Diefenbaker and Hamilton, through the first era of the Department of Regional Economic Expansion (DREE).[28] Savoie, focusing exclusively on New Brunswick, takes up where Careless leaves off and sketches the course of regional development under what, in 1973, became a radically reorganized and deconcentrated DREE.[29] While a few paragraphs cannot do justice to the richness of the Careless and Savoie accounts, it is illuminating to highlight the essential thrust of what their works uncover.

ARDA (which stood initially for the Agricultural Rehabilitation and Development Act passed in 1961) was basically farm-oriented and spawned projects which "concentrated upon dealing with land and resources in order to improve the farmer's well-being."[30] Operated with the provinces on a shared-cost basis, ARDA involved intergovernmental transactions conducted on a bilateral basis by the federal Department of Agriculture and its provincial counterparts along the lines of the traditional federal-provincial functional relations model.

The initial ARDA lasted only until 1964 when, with only the acronym retained, the Agricultural and Rural Development Act was legislated into being, along with a special Fund for Rural Economic Development (FRED). As their names suggest, ARDA-FRED moved beyond farming to the much more encompassing realms of rural poverty and thus embraced a planned approach to regional development. ARDA-FRED was made the responsibility of a new federal department, Forestry and Rural Development, and launched a very different set of federal-provincial functional relations. These relations were to be articulated not by agriculture officials, but by planning specialists. And because the scope of ARDA-FRED was such that it embraced numerous provincial departments, it called for a government-wide planning capacity at the provincial level. Accordingly, the federal government under

ARDA-FRED assisted especially the smaller and poorer Maritime Provinces in developing their own initial versions of the institutionalized cabinet. The resulting program agencies, planning secretariats, or improvement corporations were linked to premiers' offices, cabinet committees, or both. The consequent provincial planning capacity was viewed by federal personnel as a positive step which they had helped to induce and signalled the emergence of new bilateral networks of like-minded federal and provincial officials.

As these networks formed, however, the institutionalization of the federal cabinet was unfolding apace. The advent of PPBS (Program Planning Budgeting System), with its emphasis on program objectives, and the 1966 reorganization that yielded a separate Treasury Board Secretariat and Department of Finance, each with its own minister, gradually impinged upon the Department of Forestry and Rural Development. The mission of Treasury Board officials focused upon efficiency and effectiveness in the pursuit of defined objectives, while Finance acquired direct influence over the priority to be accorded to such objectives, notably in the striking "of a balance between economic proposals for maximizing 'welfare' (regional aid) and those for 'efficiency' (national productivity)."[31] Then came the new decision-making cabinet committees launched by Prime Minister Trudeau in 1968, and the enhanced role of the Privy Council Office as the manager of the committee system and the PCO's intolerance for "lack of effective interdepartmental relations in the federal government."[32] In the face of this configuration of events, structures and concerns, the Department of Forestry and Rural Development gave way, in 1969, to the new Department of Regional Economic Expansion.

Geared to the insistence that federal spending must effectively and visibly pursue federally designed objectives and federally determined priorities, the Department of Regional Economic Expansion (DREE) shifted the focus of regional development away from rural poverty and toward industrial and urban growth, with emphasis on

public works and jobs. At this juncture, the officials of the provincial planning agencies found at
one and the same time that their Forestry and
Rural Development network had disappeared and
that their planning premises no longer coincided
with those of Ottawa. As bilateral relations degenerated into an atmosphere of proposal and
counter-proposal, it became increasingly clear
that DREE's preferred style would be to bypass
provincial central agents altogether in favour of
direct dealings with individual provincial departments. As a result, DREE succeeded in imposing
this style to varying degrees in different provinces
(indeed to the point where, in Nova Scotia, the
provincial planning secretariat was dissolved).
Lying behind DREE's success was not only the
fiscal leverage of federal spending, but the impatience of provincial cabinet ministers with the
planning agents of their own institutionalized cabinets.

Within a decade, regional development had
moved from bilateral networks of federal and provincial agriculture officials to bilateral networks
of planning officials to a setting in which a new
centrally oriented federal department was pene-
trating provincial departments and writing off
province-wide concerns. Then in 1973, the
grounds shifted once again. In the wake of ministerial and deputy ministerial shuffles, and of the
Liberal minority government produced by the
1972 election, DREE suddenly perceived itself as
excessively insensitive to the provinces. It also
discerned, through internal review, that regional
development, whose focus had already shifted
from farming to rural poverty, and thence to industrial and urban growth, should again acquire a
new orientation. This time the orientation would
be "the identification and pursuit of development
opportunities."[33] The quest that this implied was to
be shared with provincial governments and, to
ensure on-site federal involvement, DREE was
deconcentrated into provincial offices, each
headed by a Director-General with substantial
decision-making authority. Operating under the
umbrella of a ministerial General Development

Agreement with a ten-year lifespan, each provincially based DREE Director-General was designated the prime negotiator of subsidiary
agreements with the provinces, these agreements
being the "action pacts"[34] pursuant to which spatial or sectoral development projects would be
undertaken.

Savoie's detailed study of federal-provincial
relations under the Canada-New Brunswick
General Development Agreement sketches an
original portrait precisely because DREE's deconcentration was without parallel in Canadian
administrative history. Launched on their shared
quest to identify and pursue economic opportunities (whatever they might be), DREE's field
personnel, headed by its Director General in
Fredericton, and their provincial counterparts,
headed by the Secretary of the New Brunswick
Cabinet Committee on Economic Development,
formed trust ties based upon "being purpose- or
result-oriented."[35] However, an alliance between
federal field personnel, who are remote from
Ottawa headquarters, and provincial officials,
who are proximate to provincial politicians and
senior bureaucrats, exposed a gap between slow
decision-making at the federal level and quick
decision-making at the provincial level. In addition to their proximity to the cabinet of a small
province, provincial officials possessed "carrot
effect" leverage from the shared-cost nature of
development projects (in the New Brunswick
case, a leverage which could be as high as 20-
cent dollars). Faced with the consequent ease
with which provincial decisions could be extracted, the federal government could only compromise its own decision-making apparatus. At
DREE headquarters, officials often found their
involvement "limited to reviewing subsidiary
agreements and this only after the agreements
[had] been fully developed and agreed upon by
provincial DREE and provincial government officials."[36] As for the federal Treasury Board, it
was left in a position where rejection or revision
"would in fact not only be rejecting or revising a
proposal from a federal government, but also one

that [had] been approved by a province, in the case of New Brunswick, by the Cabinet."[37] Meanwhile, federal operating departments, on whose economic missions DREE-New Brunswick agreements impinged, found that they were not infrequently by-passed or compromised.

Early in 1982, the DREE of the General Development Agreements fell before one more federal attempt to make the decision-making this department had circumvented manageable. DREE's reincarnation, merged with elements of the former Department of Industry, Trade and Commerce into the Department of Regional Industrial Expansion (DRIE), was accompanied by the deconcentration of a central agency called the Ministry of State for Economic and Regional Development (MSERD). This central agency, itself created a scant four years earlier to serve the conflict-ridden cabinet committee on economic development, was in turn slated for dissolution upon John Turner's accession to the office of prime minister in the summer of 1984. As for the General Development Agreements, they were allowed to die a natural death upon the expiration of their ten-year terms. Their replacement, named Economic and Regional Development Agreements, called upon the field officials of MSERD to play a key role (this role was made moot by the intended abolition of MSERD). About the only thing that could be said with certainty, as of mid-1984, was that the federal-provincial networks formed under the deconcentrated DREE had been destroyed.

Executive federalism, during the era of that deconcentrated DREE, displayed elements strongly reminiscent of the tradition-derived model of federal-provincial functional relations. Federal and provincial officials found common ground in the imperative to produce results out of their vague mandate to identify and pursue economic opportunities. The nine-year life of the bilateral structure, in which they articulated their relationship, reinforced trust relations. The financial lubricant of cost-sharing was copiously available. However, at least in the New Brunswick

case, the provincial officials were central agents, not departmental personnel, and the federal DREE officials, given the wide scope of regional development, did not represent a department upon which clienteles with clear-cut functional interests focused. The result was, particularly in the negotiation of sectoral sub-agreements (e.g., agriculture, forestry),[38] that the societal interests most directly affected had neither direct nor virtual representation. The capacity of DREE officials to circumvent the federal decision-making process, coupled with the carrot-effect leverage, which the provincial central agents could deploy vis-à-vis provincial departments, only reinforced this outcome. It appears that it was only when regional development projects were more spatial than sectoral that active consideration of affected societal interests entered into federal-provincial negotiation. In New Brunswick, there were the spatially defined interests of the Acadian northeast, with their partisan links to the Liberal cabinet in Ottawa, and of the anglophone southwest, with their partisan links to the Conservative cabinet in Fredericton.[39]

FEDERAL-PROVINCIAL SUMMIT RELATIONS

Federal-provincial summit relations are epitomized in the media-haunted conferences of the 11 first ministers, but they have come to encompass also a variety of central agency ministers and officials. This being the case, they are also strongly conditioned by the extent to which, within governments, the quest to make decision-making manageable is eminently prime ministerial. In this regard, it is to be noted both that first ministers are the chief architects of their own institutionalized cabinets, and that they alone can elect to change or bypass the decision-making structures and processes of these cabinets at any given time, and on any particular matter.

Federal-provincial summitry has fallen into a state of disarray. The starring role in how this came about must be assigned to the all-too-familiar conflicting forces that first ministers have so audibly articulated: Quebec nationalism/independentism, post-OPEC western Canada assertiveness, Ontario's defence of its economic pre-eminence, Atlantic province resentments, and federal counteroffensives to perceived excesses of provincialism. All these forces roosted at the federal-provincial summit table during the constitutional review exercise of 1980-81. Their continuing saliency, exacerbated by the fact that the outcome of the constitutional review was declared illegitimate by the Government and Legislature of Quebec, finds expression in the extent to which first ministers have become prone to talk past each other from their respective capitals, rather than with each other on the basis of their policy interdependence. It is tempting to conclude that federal-provincial summit relations, having fallen into such disarray, can be rescued, if at all, only by new political personalities and governing parties with new orientations. After due reflection, I have personally succumbed to this temptation. My confession openly made, I shall probe summit relations, for the purpose of this section, principally in the context of their longest-standing agenda item, fiscal arrangements. The lengthy history of these particular relations enables us to discern how summitry can be workable; the present condition of these once workable relations aptly demonstrates the recent magnitude of summit disarray.

The taxing, spending, and borrowing activities of government have always given a special status to departments of finance (or treasury). Long before the rise of the institutionalized cabinet and the coining of the term "central agency," finance departments stood out as horizontal portfolios whose government-wide scope made them readily available adjuncts of first ministers. The war-conditioned initiation of tax rental agreements in 1940 gave to fiscal matters what turned out to be a regular quinquennial place on the agenda of federal-provincial summitry. By 1955, once the financial exigencies of recent and antici-

pated public-sector growth were apparent, the first ministers naturally turned to their finance officials in order to equip their fiscal conferences with an expert infrastructure. Thus was born the Continuing Committee on Fiscal and Economic Matters, to which was added a Tax Structure Committee of finance ministers in 1964 and then, beginning in the late 1960s, the still ongoing practice of pre-budget formulation meetings of ministers of finance.[40]

With these underpinnings, federal-provincial summit relations, through the devising of the 1977-82 Fiscal Arrangements, achieved results that are well-known: divorce of tax collection agreements from intergovernmental transfers and tax sharing; orderly reallocations of income tax room between the federal government and the provinces; unconditional equalization payments geared to provincial fiscal capacity, as measured by a representative tax system; curtailment of conditional grants, and the development, initially, of a shared-cost and then, of a block-funding approach to health and post-secondary education; and accommodation of income tax reform through federal revenue guarantees to the provinces.[41] The path to these achievements was often acrimonious. Thus, for example, the 1967-72 Fiscal Arrangements, while they did not provoke united provincial opposition, were never endorsed by a summit meeting.[42] The 1977-82 Arrangements, which did receive summit endorsement in December 1976, previously had provoked a provincial common front.[43] What remains constant is that first ministers, whether or not they endorsed a particular set of Arrangements and however heated their periodic disagreements, had come to perceive their relations, underpinned as they were by finance ministers and officials, to be workable. The elements of this workability can be readily enumerated so as to comprise a "fiscal relations model" of federal-provincial summitry.

— Financial issues are inherently tangible and quantifiable. Accordingly, the parameters within which they are discussed can often be delimited within the bounds of common-sense bookkeeping (e.g., the question of tax room for the provinces is constrained by the fiscal capacity required to make federal equalization payments; and the extent to which provincial natural resource revenues can enter into an equalization formulation is confined by reference to what constitutes a tolerable growth rate in the size of the federal equalization bill). Also, the bounds of any particular issue can be narrowed and even resolved through easily measured saw-offs (e.g., the provincial common front, which formed in 1976 around a revenue guarantee termination payment of four personal income tax points, was bargained down to one point in tax room and one point in cash).[44]

— Finance officials share not only the common vocabulary of macroeconomic analysis, but also the common outlook (the "treasury mentality") bred by their roles as governmental fiscal managers. These characteristics, once situated under the umbrella of the long-lived Continuing Committee on Fiscal and Economic Matters, are conducive to the formulation of trust ties.

— Network formation among finance ministers is facilitated by the trust ties among their officials and abetted by their common preoccupations with revenue, and with managing the spending ambitions of their cabinet colleagues.

— From first ministers down to finance officials, the fixed maximum five-year term of fiscal arrangements means that any particular configuration of issues, however disputed, must once again be opened to review. This simultaneously eases the climate of consultation ("nothing is forever") and invites reinvestment in trust ties.

What happens to this "fiscal relations model"? Its effective operation remains abundantly apparent in the design of the 1977-82 Fiscal Arrangements and, most particularly, the Established Programs Financing (EPF) feature of these arrangements. The block funding of health and post-secondary education disentangled federal rates of spending from provincial rates of spending, and vice versa. As such, EPF contributed to the quest to make the spending of each order of government manageable. It is precisely what might be expected to emerge from an intergovernmental network of finance ministers and officials. The summit consensus of December 1976 testifies to the continuing influence of this network on first ministers, not least when two circumstances are recalled. First, the Parti Québécois had come to power in the autumn of 1976. Second, in the preceding summer, outright provincial rejection of Prime Minister Trudeau's minimalist constitutional patriation package had signalled the full awakening of western provincial governments to constitutional issues and their consequent rejection of the Victoria amendment formula.

But December 1976 marked the last hurrah of the fiscal relations model. Its outline is barely discernible in the fashioning of the 1982-87 Fiscal Arrangements. From David Perry's account, it is apparent that negotiation among finance ministers and officials had little impact on any component of these arrangements other than equalization.[45] Here, the main result was a five-province representative average standard in lieu of the initial federal proposal for an Ontario average. For the rest, the fiscal relations model was inoperative. This is due in part to the weakening of the position of the Department of Finance within the federal government. It is more especially due to the fact (perhaps because of this weakness?) that the government of Canada chose to pursue its counteroffensive against provincialism beyond the constitutional review and into the fiscal domain.

By the mid-1970s in Ottawa, the institutionalization of the federal cabinet had attenuated the hegemony of Finance as the key horizontal portfolio in fiscal and economic management. Indeed, competition among central agencies, notably Finance, the Treasury Board Secretariat, and the Privy Council Office, was a documented reality.[46] The emergence, as the 1970s blended into the 1980s, of yet two more central agencies, the Ministry of State for Economic (later, Economic and Regional) Development and the Ministry of State for Social Development, engendered further competition for the Department of Finance in the decision-making processes of the Government of Canada. As Douglas Hartle asked pointedly in noting these developments, "Is it credible that Finance has as much impact on federal-provincial fiscal relations and on economic and social development policies as it had when it was the over-all 'economic manager' of the federal government?"[47]

The relative waning of the Department of Finance (and with it the fiscal relations model) in the devising of the 1982-87 Fiscal Arrangements was signalled with the appointment of the Parliamentary Task Force on Federal-Provincial Fiscal Arrangements (the Breau Task Force) in 1981. This innovation could be viewed—and justified— as a positive step because it involved members of Parliament in the pre-legislative process and opened the fiscal arrangements to interest group involvement. But it also unleashed an Ottawa-centred view of the fiscal arrangements, in particular of its EPF (Established Programs Financing) component. The EPF block cash payment was perceived as lacking an acceptable basis in accountability to Parliament. Moreover, the Breau Task Force proved to be a federal magnet for interest groups dissatisfied with provincial spending and policies in health care and post-secondary education. It met, as Rod Dobell has noted, "the desire of provincially based interest groups operating in areas falling within provincial jurisdiction to appeal to the federal government for action [standards, criteria, rules, whatever] to offset the impacts of provincial government spending [and legislative] priorities."[48]

At this juncture, it became apparent at the highest political levels of the federal government that the abandonment of block funding could be pursued in the name of parliamentary accountability and responsiveness to interest group demands—demands whose allure was enhanced in turn by polls demonstrating public antipathy to-

ward user charges and extra billing by physicians for insured services. The upshot, after a stopgap extension of EPF for the first two years of the 1982-87 Fiscal Arrangements, was the Canada Health Act of 1984. And the potent appeal, especially in an election year, of the values of accountability and responsiveness, was dramatically underlined by the all-party support given to the passage of this act in the House of Commons.

A starkly unilateral federal initiative endorsed by the prime minister, the Canada Health Act emerged not from the Department of Finance, but from the collegial processes of cabinet decision-making, served now not only by the Privy Council Office and its offshoot, the Federal-Provincial Relations Office, but by the Ministry of State for Social Development as well. In essence, the act lays down a code of provincial government conduct toward insured hospital and medical services. User charges and extra billing by physicians are deemed a violation of the code and are henceforth subject to measured reductions in the EPF cash transfer to the offending provinces. Furthermore, compliance with the code requires a province to enter into a formal agreement with medical practitioners and dentists with respect to their compensation and to the resolution of compensation disputes through conciliation or arbitration. Failure to comply entails reductions in the cash transfer, that are left for the federal cabinet to determine.[49]

These details starkly spell the demise of block funding and with it the disentanglement of provincial from federal spending. Beyond spending, the very manner in which provinces choose to deal with health care practitioners becomes subject to federal fiscal intervention. What emerges is a fundamental reorientation of federal-provincial fiscal arrangements that has completely circumvented summit consultation and its underlying networks of finance officials and ministers. Thus does the disarray in federal-provincial summitry, exacerbated by the conflicting forces so apparent in the constitutional review, now embrace the fiscal arrangements that stood for decades as the staple agenda item of first ministers' conferences. One more point needs to be made.

The Canada Health Act fits the mould of federal counter-offensives to perceived excesses of provincialism. In this instance, however, the perceived excess at which the counter-offensive takes aim lies outside the mainstream of those which the Government of Canada sought to counter in the constitutional review. There, the perceived excesses converged around matters of economic policy. The slogan "Securing the Canadian Economic Union" was the subtitle of the federal position paper on economic powers.[50] The economic union is to be secured from what are deemed to have been, for about a decade, balkanizing and unilateral provincial incursions into the economic realm in the form of a wide variety of protectionist measures and province-centred industrial and resource development policies. The Canada Health Act, for its part, has nothing to do with countering such provincial economic incursions. It constitutes a federal counter-offensive to provincial policies in the social realm of health care, policies which are a mixture of fiscal, cost-control, and professional compensation considerations. As such, the act is defensible in the name of accountability and responsiveness to interest group demands for equity. Meantime, however, the provincial incursions that have been perceived to affect the economic union are themselves defensible on the same grounds. Are not protectionism and province-centred development policies a reflection of provincial responsiveness to interest group demands, and of the ultimate accountability of provincial governments to their electorates? Viewed in this light, the condition that leaves the 11 ministers with their summit interaction in disarray is, if nothing else, deliciously ironic. And the irony will be compounded if post-secondary education comes to join health care as the subject of a code of provincial conduct, a matter under active internal consideration in Ottawa both before and after the 1984 election campaign.

The present condition of summit disarray casts a shadow over all manifestations of executive federalism. Nonetheless, I persist in holding the view, especially under favourable assumptions regarding personalities and governing parties, that this condition is not intractable. I insist, however, on stressing that the path to renewed workability, especially where interaction among the first ministers is concerned, does not lie in one more comprehensive attempt to "get the constitution right." This is because I consider that any summit process called upon to devise the "right" constitution is too likely to fail in the attempt, even allowing for sweeping changes in the *dramatis personae* of first ministers. When we include the 1968-71 route to the aborted Victoria Charter along with the 1980-81 exercise that yielded (only after Supreme Court assistance) the Constitution Act of 1982, it is apparent that multilateral summitry has failed twice to achieve central institution reform, disentangle the division of jurisdiction, and recognize the historical mission of Quebec in the cultural domain. Setting aside whether or not these reforms were desirable in principle, I find a straightforward explanation for this double failure in what I call a "constitutional review model" of federal-provincial summitry. It is, in all respects, the diametrical opposite of my fiscal relations model.

— Constitutional issues, being symbolic and abstract rather than tangible and quantifiable, are not amenable to readily measurable trade-offs.

— The officials who underpin constitutional review deliberations include law officers who, to the extent that they view their respective governments as legal clients, may tend to magnify jurisdictional jealousies rather than reduce them on the basis of shared professional values.

— The horizontal portfolio ministers most closely involved are federal and provincial Ministers of Justice and Attorneys-General whose portfolios include recourse to adversarial processes before the courts, and who are therefore prone to examine constitutional proposals in this light.

— The whole process of a comprehensive constitutional review exercise focuses the attention of all participants, from first ministers down, on the "one last play" that will be the constitutional engineering feat of comprehensive change. The anticipated proximity of this last play depreciates investment in long-term trust.

— Because it is known that the "one last play" yields a quasi-permanent end result, given the rigidity of the amendment process, negotiations are inherently more tension ridden than when "nothing is forever."

My "constitutional review model" demonstrates all the reasons why the last thing I would prescribe for the current disarray in federal-provincial summitry is another comprehensive attempt at constitutional review. In the vocabulary of economics, the transaction costs are enormous, and the opportunity costs are likely to engulf all other matters that should occupy the summit agenda.

*   *   *

PRESCRIPTIONS FOR WORKABLE EXECUTIVE FEDERALISM

Having turned my back on the constitutional domain, where shall I look for workability in executive federalism? First, I will extract what I consider to be the moral of my stories of functional and summit relations, and on this basis formulate a number of propositions for first ministers in their roles as the heads of our "central energizing executives." I will then outline a prescription addressed to summit relations as such, one which has found favour with the experienced practitioners of executive federalism, who have given me the benefit of their insights. Finally, I will make a few observations concerning the potential of executive federalism in coming to grips with substantive economic and fiscal issues.

Two Tales of Executive Federalism

I have told a story of federal-provincial functional relations according to which there was a time, lasting until the mid-1960s, when these relations had sufficient commonality to be explained by a simple conceptual model. Thereafter, functional relations galloped off in several directions, as witnessed by examples which, though restricted in number, suffice to convey that wide variability in such relations has become a matter of fact. My tale of summit interaction, for its part, was about relations which, when fiscal arrangements were on the agenda, could be explained by another model, valid as late as the mid-1970s. These relations then bogged down in a state of disarray.

So much for my tales; what is their moral? When all is said and done, the moral of my stories is that the formation and maintenance of networks (i.e., trust ties) between the appointed officials of the two orders of government play a fundamental role in the workability of federal-provincial interaction. Trust ties can be a function of shared professional training and norms, as in the functional relations model; they can be a function of geographical proximity and of shared desire to extract results from a vague mandate, as in the case of the deconcentrated DREE of 1973-82, and they can be a function of the shared vocabulary of macroeconomic analysis and a common interest in managing the spending ambitions of operating departments, as in the fiscal relations model.

Trust ties are communicable to ministers; even more so when ministers possess a measure of independent decision-making autonomy in their portfolios instead of being oriented to collegial decision-making processes within their cabinets. Finance ministers are a special case. Presiding as they do over the original and historically most potent central agency, they are in a position to capitalize on the trust ties among their officials to the extent that they have primary access to first ministers. Once this primacy is hedged by competing central agencies (especially by central agencies under other central agency ministers, who vie for their own access to their first ministers) finance ministers are in danger of becoming "central agency ministers like the others." The utility of finance officer networks thus will be dissipated.

The moral of my stories is simple enough. If it evokes a sense of nostalgia for the "good old days" of departmentalized cabinets, when operating department ministers enjoyed decision-making latitude and finance ministers presided over a horizontal portfolio unchallenged by insurgent central agencies, so be it. I happen to believe that future cabinet reorganizations, especially in Ottawa, can well afford a touch of nostalgia. I also believe, however, that in one form or another institutionalized cabinets are here to stay. The multiplicity, complexity, and interdependence of the decisions which contemporary governments are called upon to make demand both cabinet committees and central agencies. They ensure that the quest to make decision-making manageable will remain ongoing and will lead to continuing experimentation with forms and processes, and this will extend beyond the executive and into legislative assemblies, if only because institutionalized cabinets, in attenuating the autonomy of "special interest" departments and ministers, generate a need for new channels of interest group consultation, new adjustments designed to accommodate the desideratum of government by consent. All of this has implications for the workability of executive federalism to which first ministers especially should be sensitive and which I choose to address by means of a handful of practical propositions.

— Central agencies per se are not inimical to the conduct of federal-provincial functional relations among ministers and officials. The case of the Canada Assistance Plan demonstrates that central agents can constructively inject government-wide concerns into functional relations. The key distinction to be observed is between occasional appearances to communicate or clarify general policy and ongoing participation in the process of consultation or negotiation. The latter is to be reserved for departmental ministers and officials.

— Once central agents (and for that matter officials from different departments with different professional backgrounds) enter a domain that has hitherto been the preserve of functional interaction among particular operating ministers and departments, as in the Social Security Review, then first ministers have reason to be concerned that the agenda item involved is too broad to be handled short of summit processes. Such an item is better placed before the first ministers themselves or before central agency ministers, who have been given a specific prime ministerial mandate to coordinate the departments involved with the item concerned (e.g., a guaranteed annual income).

— First ministers can virtually guarantee unworkable federal-provincial relations if, by design or inadvertence, the officials charged with articulating the positions of the two orders of government do so on the basis of the clashing norms of different professions. Manpower training is an excellent case in point. If professional norms clash and the matter cannot be confined to one professional group, intergovernmental consultation or negotiation by administrative generalists is to be preferred. Outstanding interprofessional differences are best left to fester or be resolved around each government's cabinet table. In line with this thought, I cannot resist the parenthetical insertion that I have long found incomprehensible the federal government's occasional plaintive request for an entrée into the Council of Ministers of Education. More than an interprovincial club, the CME is a club of professional educationists and fated to remain so for as long as primary and secondary education continue to dominate provincial education portfolios, which they will. Professional faculties of education stand in splendid isolation from the universities in which they are located. This fact speaks eloquently about containing one's expectations of what an educationist club could usefully contribute to manpower economics or scientific research and development.

— When the possibility of internal governmental reorganization appears on a first minister's agenda, he should actively consider its potential implications for workable federal-provincial relations. An internal reorganization that destroys an established federal-provincial network (e.g., the dismantling of the deconcentrated DREE in 1982), or that nips an incipient intergovernmental network in the bud (e.g., the replacement of the Department of Forestry and Rural Development by the centralized DREE of 1969), involves costs in foregone trust ties. These costs might have been avoided if the desiderata prompting the proposed change (visibility, closer adherence to Treasury Board guidelines, whatever) had first been communicated clearly to the federal-provincial networks as criteria to which their interactions should adapt. On the other hand, a reorganization might yield a new agency in order to enhance the internal priority that a government wishes to accord to a particular function. If that government's position in a particular federal-provincial interaction is currently less than constructively articulated, consideration should be given to assigning that role to the new agency (e.g., the new Ontario Manpower Commission in the Ministry of Labour might logically assume the key role in federal-Ontario training relations).

— The institutionalization of cabinets means that departmental ministers and officials are less effective conduits for the claims of client interest groups than was once the case. By the same token, the capacity of special interests to achieve a degree of virtual representation in many forums of federal-provincial interaction has gone the way of the functional relations model. An enhanced use of parliamentary committees to ventilate group interests beckons on both counts. If recourse to such

committees poses a particular problem in matters of federal-provincial interaction, this is because interest groups are not necessarily prone to follow the jurisdictional flag when the opportunity of open hearings presents itself. The more impressive problem that lurks behind parliamentary committees is asymmetry in group presentations. The Breau Task Force, implicated as it is in the current federal-provincial fiscal disarray, was a magnet for public spending coalitions; on the other hand its companion Task Force on Pension Reform, another inherently federal-provincial matter, attracted groups closely identified with the case for fiscal restraint.[51] First ministers should consider, and indeed might well consult on, the manner in which legislative committees examining matters of federal-provincial import could be equipped with terms of reference that attract the widest appropriate spectrum of contending views. So that parliamentarians might themselves have the opportunity to view federal-provincial relations writ large, rather than through the terms of any particular committee assignment, there might be merit as well in making an annual federal-provincial relations debate a set feature of each legislature's agenda, as with the Throne Speech and the Budget.

The above propositions can be considered as easily by first ministers in their respective capitals, as they can be at a summit conference. There is much to executive federalism below the formal interaction of first ministers themselves. My propositions are meant to sensitize the heads of our governments to what can be done with respect to federal-provincial interaction generally. What of their own interaction?

Toward Routinized Federal-Provincial Summitry

The good news about the recent disarray in federal-provincial summit relations is that the contending party leaders in the 1984 federal election campaign all promised to do something about it. While anyone who is familiar with the value of Canadian electoral promises has reason to call for the proverbial grain of salt, the prospect that this low-cost promise will be fulfilled by the landslide victor of the 1984 election is enhanced by the honeymoon he has been accorded by his provincial counterparts. The accompanying fact that Prime Minister Mulroney is engaged in producing, at an apparently measured pace, his own version of the institutionalized cabinet yields a situation that is brimming with potential. Given the recent disarray in federal-provincial summitry, I have been inspired by those experienced in the practice of executive federalism to advance the view that the most portentous outcome of an early post-election summit would be agreement to hold annual first ministers' conferences as routine events each year. Such routinized conferences are as laden with potential as they are devoid of glamour. Their attractiveness lies precisely in being both.

Where being devoid of glamour is concerned, routine annual summits would not supplant any first ministers' meetings that must take place (e.g., on the constitutional matter of native rights) or that might take place on any momentous agenda item (e.g., fiscal arrangements). Their explicit purpose would be to make summit interaction a commonplace event. Their potential agenda would extend to any matters that already involve, or should involve, federal-provincial interaction at any level, from that of officials to that of first ministers. Their informal atmosphere would stress consultation and exchange, not negotiation. Emphasis on the fundamentally routine nature of the events would contain public and media expectations. It should involve an undertaking among first ministers that routine meetings do not include televised proceedings or invite pre- or post-conference posturing by the participants.

As for the potential of routine annual summits, several considerations are worth highlighting.

— Because the matters that could appear on the agenda of routinized meetings potentially em-

brace anything of federal and provincial concern, preparation for each such meeting will necessitate close and ongoing interaction on the part of senior central agency officials situated in first ministers' offices or cabinet offices. The pressure on these officials to "show results" by extracting manageable annual agendas from their vague mandate should abet the formation of trust ties and promote workable proceedings.

— The nexus between federal-provincial interaction and intragovernmental organization, illustrated by the propositions I addressed to first ministers earlier in this essay, provides a practical if not invariably palatable menu for interchanges among the very individuals who, at the apex of their respective cabinets, share incentives to make manageable their own decision-making, and the formal powers of organizing and reorganizing their governments.

— Regularly recurring events have the capacity to gather their own momentum and to evoke constructive patterns of behaviour. The latter range from mutual sensitivity, in areas where governmental actions unavoidably overlap, to identifying opportunities for disentanglement, which might in time become the subject of individual constitutional amendments. Supremely, I dare to hope that routinized summitry would breed and nurture among first ministers what J. A. Corry calls "constitutional morality,"[52] a behaviour pattern that focuses on the norms, as distinct from the mere legalities, of federalism; a pattern that seeks simultaneously to capitalize on the socio-economic forces that bind a federation and on those that demand decentralization.

Economic and Fiscal Issues

A prescription which calls for routinized summitry is one which focuses on a process that is incremental and that takes a long-run view of federalism. If it finds favour in the eyes of some experienced practitioners of federal-provincial diplomacy and selected political scientists, is this not because it is so congruent with the shared background and norms of what—let's face it—is just another professional group (if indeed the adjective "professional" is even applicable)? What about the urgency of economic issues in a Canada which, with its double-digit unemployment rate at the head of a long list of alarming symptoms, has its abundant share of the end-of-the-century problems besetting all advanced capitalist and social democratic systems?

Executive federalism must indeed come to grips with economic issues. It is hardly within my purview, and even less within my competence, to analyze the substance of these issues. Nonetheless, I do not hesitate to venture two sets of observations concerning the potential of executive federalism in coming to grips with substance. The first involves the importance of containing one's expectations of what might be called "multilateral economic summitry," and of searching out agenda items that hold at least some promise of early success. The second, whose relative urgency is easily measured by the face that the next set of fiscal arrangements spans the years 1987-92, seeks to galvanize fiscal summitry into renewed and reoriented coherence.

I have several reasons to contain my own expectations of what multilateral summit relations can achieve with respect to economic issues writ large. For one thing, there is the track record of summitry with respect to the regionally most divisive economic issue in recent years: energy. Here, the intractable manner in which Premier William Davis of Ontario chose to present the position of energy consumers (not least during the Clark government interlude) guaranteed that summit negotiations must be confined to bilateral interaction between Ottawa and the producing provinces, rather than pursued on the agenda of the 11 first ministers.[53] For another, there is the elaborate exercise in multilateral economic summitry of 1978, complete with ministerial and other working groups. In Michael Jenkin's words, "The results of the conferences tended to

be either agreements on general principles that later turned out to hide very real differences, or agreements on isolated issues which did not, in themselves, add up to a coherent program of political action."[54] More generally, it is a fact that provincial premiers have been prone to use economic conferences as vehicles for charging the federal government with economic mismanagement, while the Government of Canada has perceived many provincial economic positions as an affront to its primacy in the economic realm. Once again, personality changes might rectify this situation, but it should be borne in mind that any summit conferences called in the near term to deal with "the economy" are bound to be major media events, replete with opportunities for political posturing. Such conferences, if they are to have any chance of meeting public expectations, will be in need of restricted agenda items, selected with an eye to their potential for eliciting consensus and demonstrating movement.

One possibility lies in regional development, now perhaps even more disoriented than after DREE's demise in 1982, because the Ministry of State for Economic and Regional Development has been dissolved. Federal-provincial interaction in regional development necessarily hinges in the main on bilateral relations, but a multilateral economic summit might well address in principle the future orientation of bilateral agreements. Michael Trebilcock, in a recent address to the Ontario Economic Council, suggestively raised the possibility that the thrust of future agreements might concentrate preferably on economic adjustment rather than development.[55] What he calls "General Adjustment Agreements" would focus upon adjustment costs arising from freer international trade and reduced barriers to internal trade.

Then there is the possibility of seeking summit approbation of Michael Jenkin's proposal for a continuing structure at the level of ministers and officials, which he calls the Canadian Council of Industry and Technology Ministers.[56] Bearing in mind that within governments (notably within the federal government) tensions among economic portfolios have been painfully apparent, I do not foresee that a CCIT has the same potential for trust ties as the long-standing Continuing Committee on Fiscal and Economic Matters. It beckons nonetheless, especially to screen what might or might not provide workable agenda items for future economic summits, and to assist in staffing the more informal, routinized summit meetings.

My own favourite, subject to a heavy discount for this very reason, is the possibility of economic summit deliberations on manpower training. What could be sought here is what is within the capacity of first ministers as heads of government to grant: federal-provincial interaction by ministers and officials concerned not with education, but with training as an employment placement and economic adjustment tool. The functional conflict, which reverberated some 20 years ago when the federal government attempted a serious initiative in this regard, arose in what I established earlier in this essay was a context peculiar to the times. In the mid-1960s, employment and training for employment had not acquired the overtones of the moral and ethical imperative that they possess today. And now that non-university post-secondary institutions are firmly established and mature, they no longer justify provincial insulation from outside influence—be these called "federal," "economic," or "labour market" influences. If I discern a problem with placing manpower training on the agenda of an early economic summit, it is because this restricted agenda item may be swept up in the controversy of a Canada Health Act approach to post-secondary education. Having prescribed, in a suggestive vein, possibilities for workable economic summitry in the near term, I conclude by addressing what I consider to be the most pressing matter of substance for the processes of executive federalism: the fiscal arrangements for 1987-92.

The Canada Health Act, as I have already pointed out, leaves executive federalism in a position that is nothing if not deliciously ironic. Here is a federally devised code of provincial conduct to be implemented through the application of the federal spending power in the realm of social policy. This initiative came on the heels of a quite different federal thrust, one which, in the context of the constitutional review, sought to establish greater federal primacy in the realm of economic policy. Having largely failed in the latter, the Government of Canada successfully undermined provincial primacy in the realm of social policy. Here, surely, is Corry's principle of constitutional morality turned on its head. And it has its own economic downside. As Thomas Courchene observes:

> With health costs already representing over 30 percent of some provincial budgets and escalating rapidly, with the likelihood of even more cost increases arising from the combination of increasingly expensive diagnostic treatment and an aging population, and with a concerted effort by numerous health-related associations to be covered under the universal health plan, it would appear that increased innovation and experimentation is essential in order that more efficient ways of delivering health care can be found. Already much in the way of provincial experimentation is ongoing . . . . To the extent that the Canada Health Act serves to promote uniformity rather than flexibility and to favour conformity rather than innovation, it is clearly a move in the wrong direction.[57]

Putting Corry and Courchene together, the Canada Health Act is a *massive thrust* in the wrong direction. To be sure, it can be justified on grounds of accountability and responsiveness to interest group pressures. But so can any of a number of provincial interventions in the economic realm, including protectionist interventions, which generate costs that are not simply imposed on provincial electorates, but are externalized (i.e., borne elsewhere in the country). As Robert Prichard puts it so well, the externalities that flow from such interventions "are affected by a fundamental illegitimacy that does not apply, at least in theory, to federal intervention."[58] The parallel illegitimacy of the Canada Health Act is that health costs are largely internalized within provinces and yet will be driven by a federal code. Thus a code applies where it has no basis in constitutional morality or economic rationality and is non-existent with respect to matters where it is warranted.

It is this precarious and anomalous situation which, in my view, cries out for rectification in the fiscal arrangements of 1987-92. The outcome that is earnestly to be desired is one in which a code of provincial conduct is withdrawn from the realm of social policy and applied instead in the realm of protectionist economic policies. The long-standing network of finance officials and ministers must be galvanized to probe once again the relative roles of tax sharing and fiscal transfers in matters of social expenditure. If the federal spending power is to be used to secure adherence to codes of provincial conduct, let this be examined in the realm of conduct that has perverse economic consequences, not where decentralized experiments in cost control are to be desired.

I fully appreciate that to transpose codes of conduct from social to economic policy will be a matter of the utmost political delicacy. The toothpaste, so to speak, is well out of the tube on two counts: any federal prime minister knows that the Canada Health Act enjoys significant support, and any provincial first minister knows equally well the forceful stake of special interests in provincial economic protectionism. What will be central is nothing more or less than the extent to which first ministers, jointly and severally, can discern that grand abstraction, the public interest, as distinct from particular interests. The test I pose to executive federalism, from the level of finance officials to the summit, involves 1987-92 fiscal arrangements that will at least move in the direction of constitutional morality and economic rationality. The movement, as distinct from the outright resolution, is what is of supreme importance. Because in fiscal arrangements, as distinct from constitutional reform, "nothing is forever," the 1992-97 arrangements will present a further opportunity. What should be accomplished between now and 1987 is the movement, not without difficulty or even acrimony, as testimony to the reactivated workability of executive federalism.

Notes

1. Richard Simeon, on behalf of the Royal Commission on the Economic Union and Development Prospects for Canada, assembled a Working Group on the Mechanisms, Process, and Politics of Intergovernmental Relations whose members were David R. Cameron, J. Peter Meekison, Claude Morin, and Donald Stevenson. The author served as the group's *animateur* and Karen Jackson as its *rapporteur*.

2. Richard Simeon, "Intergovernmental Relations and the Challenges to Canadian Federalism," *Canadian Public Administration* 23 (1980): 21.

3. Thomas A. Hockin, *Government in Canada* (Toronto: McGraw-Hill Ryerson, 1976), 7.

4. Donald V. Smiley, *Canada in Question: Federalism in the Eighties*, 3d ed. (Toronto: McGraw-Hill Ryerson, 1980), 91.

5. Jean Hamelin, *The First Years of Confederation* (Ottawa: Centennial Commission, 1967) cited in Donald V. Smiley, "Central Institutions," in *Canada and the New Constitution: The Unfinished Agenda*, vol. 1, edited by Stanley M. Beck and Ivan Bernier (Montreal: Institute for Research on Public Policy, 1983), 36.

6. Smiley, "Central Institutions," 28-9 and 34-5.

7. James Gillies, *Where Business Fails* (Montreal: Institute for Research on Public Policy, 1981), 84.

8. Smiley, *Canada in Question*, 277.

9. Douglas Hartle, *Public Policy Decision Making and Regulation* (Montreal: Institute for Research on Public Policy, 1979), 72.

10. *Ibid.*

11. *Ibid.*

12. Peter Aucoin, "Pressure Groups and Recent Changes in the Policy-Making Process," in *Pressure Group Behaviour in Canadian Politics*, edited by A. Paul Pross (Toronto: McGraw-Hill Ryerson, 1975), 174-92.

13. Gillies, *Where Business Fails*, 137.

14. Donald V. Smiley, *Constitutional Adaptation and Canadian Federalism Since 1945*, Document 4, Royal Commission on Bilingualism and Biculturalism (Ottawa: Queen's Printer, 1974), chap. 8.

15. Albert Breton and Ronald Wintrobe, *The Logic of Bureaucratic Conduct* (Cambridge: Cambridge University Press, 1982), 78.

16. *Ibid.*, 75.

17. Albert Breton and Raymond Breton, *Why Disunity? An Analysis of Linguistic and Regional Cleavages in Canada* (Montreal: Institute for Research on Public Policy, 1980), especially 58-60.

18. Rand Dyck, "The Canada Assistance Plan: The Ultimate in Cooperative Federalism," *Canadian Public Administration* 19 (1976): 587-602.

19. *Ibid.*, 592.

20. A. W. Johnson, "Canada's Social Security Review 1973-75: The Central Issues," *Canadian Public Policy* 1 (1975): 471.

21. Keith Banting, *The Welfare State and Canadian Federalism* (Kingston and Montreal: McGill-Queen's University Press, 1982), 80.

22. *Ibid.*, 82.

23. Louis Bernard, "La conjoncture actuelle des relations intergouvernementales," in *Confrontation and Collaboration: Intergovernmental Relations in Canada Today*, edited by Richard Simeon (Toronto: Institute of Public Administration of Canada, 1979), 103.

24. J. Stefan Dupré et al., *Federalism and Policy Development: The Case of Adult Occupational Training in Ontario* (Toronto: University of Toronto Press, 1973). Save where otherwise noted, the account of manpower training is drawn from this book.

25. Royal Commission on the Economic Union and Development Prospects for Canada, *Challenges and Choices* (Ottawa: Minister of Supply and Services Canada, 1984), 47.

26. Alan C. Cairns, "The Other Crisis of Canadian Federalism," *Canadian Public Administration* 22 (1980): 175-95.

27. Claude Mérineau, Assistant Deputy Minister of Manpower, Government of Quebec, oral commentary at a seminar on adult occupational training given by J. Stefan Dupré at the Centre for Industrial Relations, McGill University, January 29, 1974.

28. Anthony G. S. Careless, *Initiative and Response: The Adaptation of Canadian Federalism to Regional Economic Development* (Montreal: McGill-Queen's University Press, 1977).

29. Donald J. Savoie, *Federal-Provincial Collaboration: The Canada-New Brunswick General Development Agreement* (Montreal: McGill-Queen's University Press, 1981).

30. Careless, *Initiative and Response*, 72.

31. *Ibid.*, 131.

32. *Ibid.*, 164.

33. Savoie, *Federal-Provincial Collaboration*, 28.

34. *Ibid.*, 30.

35. *Ibid.*, 155.

36. *Ibid.*, 134.

37. *Ibid.*

38. *Ibid.*, 48-57.

39. *Ibid.*, 55-7 and 70-85.

40. Smiley, *Canada in Question* 95-6.

41. Perrin Lewis, "The Tangled Tale of Taxes and Transfers," in *Canadian Confederation at the Crossroads*, edited by Michael Walker (Vancouver: Fraser Institute, 1978), 39-102.

42. Richard Simeon, *Federal-Provincial Diplomacy: The Making of Recent Policy in Canada* (Toronto: University of Toronto Press, 1972), 259-62.

43. A. S. Rubinoff, "Federal-Provincial Relations: Is Our Conduct Changing?" paper presented to the annual conference of the Institute of Public Administration of Canada, Victoria, B.C., September 17-18, 1977.

44. *Ibid.*, 22.

45. David B. Perry, "The Federal-Provincial Fiscal Arrangements for 1982-87," *Canadian Tax Journal* 31 (1983): 30-4.

46. Richard D. French, *How Ottawa Decides: Planning and Industrial Policy-Making 1968-1980* (Ottawa: Canadian Institute for Economic Policy, 1980).

47. Douglas G. Hartle, *The Revenue Budget Process of the Government of Canada: Description, Appraisal and Proposals* (Toronto: Canadian Tax Foundation, 1982), 66-7.

48. Rod Dobell, "Alternative Consultation Processes: Prospect for 1987 and Beyond," notes prepared for discussion at the Ontario Economic Council conference, "Ottawa and the Provinces: The Distribution of Money and Power," Toronto, May 14-15, 1984, 13.

49. *Ibid.*, 7-11.

50. Jean Chrétien, Minister of Justice, *Securing the Canadian Economic Union in the Constitution* (Ottawa: Minister of Supply and Services Canada, 1980).

51. Dobell, "Alternative Consultation Processes," 2.

52. J. A. Corry, "The Uses of a Constitution," in Law Society of Upper Canada, Special Lectures, *The Constitution and the Future of Canada* (Toronto: Richard De Boo, 1978), 1-15.

53. Jeffrey Simpson, *Discipline of Power* (Toronto: Personal Library, 1980), 179-203.

54. Michael Jenkin, *The Challenge of Diversity: Industrial Policy in the Canadian Federation*, Science Council of Canada Background Study 50 (Ottawa: Minister of Supply and Services Canada, 1983), 128.

55. Michael J. Trebilcock, "The Politics of Positive Sum," notes prepared for discussion at the Ontario Economic Council conference, "Ottawa and the Provinces: The Distribution of Money and Power," Toronto, May 14-15, 1984.

56. Jenkin, *The Challenge of Diversity*, 175.

57. Thomas J. Courchene, "The Fi ' Arrangements: Focus on 1987," notes for an address to the Ontario Economic Council conference, "Ottawa and the Provinces: The Distribution of Money and Power," Toronto, May 14-15, 1984.

58. J. Robert S. Prichard, with Jamie Benedickson, "Securing the Canadian Economic Union: Federalism and Internal Barriers to Trade," in *Federalism and the Canadian Economic Union*, edited by Michael J. Trebilcock et al., Ontario Economic Council Research Studies (Toronto: University of Toronto Press, 1983), 49.

Selected Readings

Dupré, J. S., Cameron, D. M., Kechnie, G. H., and Rotenberg, T. B. *Federalism and Policy Development: The Case of Adult Occupational Training in Ontario*. Toronto: University of Toronto Press, 1973.

Dyck, R. "The Canada Assistance Plan: The Ultimate in Cooperative Federalism." *Canadian Public Administration* 19: 4 (Winter 1976): 587-602.

Milne, D. *Tug of War: Ottawa and the Provinces under Trudeau and Mulroney*. Toronto: Lorimer, 1986.

Savoie, D. *Federal-Provincial Collaboration: The Canada-New Brunswick General Development Agreement*. Montreal and Kingston: McGill-Queen's University Press, 1981.

Shultz, R. J. *Federalism, Bureaucracy and Public Policy: The Politics of Highway Transport Regulation*. Montreal and Kingston: McGill-Queen's University Press, 1980.

Veilleux, G., "Intergovernmental Canada: Government by Conference? A Fiscal and Economic Perspective." *Canadian Public Administration* 23: 1 (Spring 1980): 33-53.

15. THE IMPACT OF FEDERALISM ON THE ORGANIZATION OF CANADIAN FOREIGN POLICY

Elliot J. Feldman
and
Lily Gardner Feldman

Since 1978, the Premier of Quebec has been invested as a Grand Officier (usually conferred only on heads of state) of *Légion d'Honneur* in France, and Quebec's delegation to Paris has continued to enjoy diplomatic status.[1] The Premier of British Columbia has been received in Tokyo as a head of state. Quebec, Alberta, and Ontario all maintain important political and economic offices in Europe and in the United States. The governments of Quebec and Ontario sell hydroelectric power to New York and the New England States; the government of British Columbia sells coal to Japan.

These four Canadian provinces are international actors. They design and implement international trade policies, conduct negotiations for economic and cultural exchanges with the governments of foreign countries, independently monitor domestic activities in other countries, and lobby foreign governments. Their bureaucracies and budgets devoted to international affairs are in three cases very substantial and growing. Although they sometimes act internationally in concert with the government of Canada, they frequently act alone. Their firm commitments to defend provincial interests beyond Canadian borders challenge conventional

concepts of sovereignty and the federal view of a national monopoly in the field of foreign policy.

Elements of this challenge to Ottawa have long precedent in Canadian history, but the political content and circumstance of developments in the 1970s and 1980s make the overall direction and thrust a new dimension in the international system. Students of international relations in general and most observers of Canadian politics and foreign policy in particular have not yet appreciated the potential significance of these trends and have not provided an adequate theory to explain their emergence, categorize their present condition, or predict their future direction. The Canadian example, however, is not unique, and a theoretical understanding consistent with empirical findings is essential for comprehension of an international system in which national or central control over foreign policy is fragmenting, and definitions of both the physical and metaphysical boundaries of the nation-state are demanding modification.

TRANSGOVERNMENTALISM IN THEORY

Transgovernmentalism—activity abroad conducted by the constituent governments of a federal union or subunits of a central government—is widespread and not particularly new. The principal question raised by such activity is whether it is important. We will give "im-

Elliot J. Feldman and Lily Gardner Feldman, "The Impact of Federalism on the Organization of Canadian Foreign Policy," *Publius: The Journal of Federalism* 14:4 (1984): 33-59. Reprinted by permission of *Publius*.

portance" two meanings here: (1) whether such activity changes the outcomes of international relations from what may have been expected had contact been confined to traditional central government international actors, and (2) whether the sovereignty of the traditional nation-state is eroded by such activity. Robert Keohane and Joseph Nye have suggested that transgovernmentalism is important because it influences the business of international organizations and, in turn, domestic policies.[2] Although Keohane and Nye correctly recognize that foreign policy is not the exclusive domain of central government foreign ministries, they underestimate the scope, magnitude, and significance of transgovernmentalism for three main reasons: (1) their focus on international organizations pays insufficient attention to the bilateral governmental activities of subunits; (2) their reliance on random examples exposes no pattern and reveals only ambiguous motivations for subunit foreign activity; (3) their implicit adoption of an American pluralist model for international political penetration fails to embrace the most remarkable dimension of transgovernmentalism, the ever-expanding foreign activity of territorial subunits in federal systems. A careful explanation of foreign policy formulation and activity in the Canadian federal system will refine and expand on the primarily functional, non-territorial concerns of the Keohane/Nye argument.[3]

Keohane and Nye were concerned with exposing the presence of international actors in addition to traditional central government agents. They were justly criticized by Samuel P. Huntington for subordinating the significance of activity and policy to the identification of actors,[4] but Huntington, too, did not include the full range of actors and, hence, the growing impact of their activity. Keohane and Nye offer a universal definition for transgovernmental actors as "refer[ring] to sub-units of government on the occasions when they act relatively autonomously from higher authority in international politics," but they recognize only competitive agencies

within central governments.[5] The greatest growth in activity, in Canada at least, has been in the provinces.[6]

Keohane and Nye centered much of their analysis on the proposition that greater conflict among central government agencies leads to greater transgovernmentalism, and in a 2x2 table they argued that the greatest transgovernmentalism follows when such conflict is combined with weak centralizing authority over the bureaucracy.[7] Hence, the two main causes for transgovernmentalism appear to be bureaucratic rivalry and weak centralizing authority.

Keohane and Nye's description of activity is confined to "transgovernmental policy coordination" and "transgovernmental coalition building" within international organizations. Activity, however, is far more complex and warrants more refined categorization according to strategy, scope and magnitude, type, participants, and style.[8] Empirical evidence of the Canadian provincial experience will be used to assess international activity in these categories.

Canadian experience reveals that in the case of territorial transgovernmentalism, only some international activity of subunits is attributable to conflict, and that federal authority may belie political reality in the determination of whether a subunit can or will act independently. Hence, the next section of this article, focusing on the reasons why Canadian provinces are involved internationally, will demonstrate the need for alternative causal explanations.

REASONS FOR TERRITORIAL TRANSGOVERNMENTALISM

Provincial governments engage in international relations because (1) they have the bureaucratic and fiscal wherewithal, the formal opportunity, the jurisdictional obligation, or the political necessity (internal reasons) to do so; and (2) the international system beckons them or foreign partners look directly to them (external reasons).

Richard Leach (citing Thomas Levy) and Roff Johannson have emphasized the postwar emergence of economic issues on the international agenda as a new opportunity for provincial governments to improve their economies,[9] but there are many other external stimuli. For example, Ontario is obliged to deal with neighboring New York and Michigan because of fourteen international bridges which the federal government has no interest in administering or maintaining. The government of Japan chose the British Columbia government as a negotiating partner for the mining and sale of coal. The government of France, albeit not without encouragement, frequently has invited the government of Quebec to participate in conferences with representation separate from the government of Canada. And the vice president of the European Commission of the European Community toured Canada in 1982, encouraging the provinces to confer directly with Brussels on European issues that concern them.

As Keohane and Nye, Leach, Johannson, and Garth Stevenson all have recognized,[10] the "low politics" of economics and commerce have been elevated to loftier international consideration during the last decade, highlighting longstanding provincial international activity. However, changes in the international environment do not provide a complete account for the reasons that provinces engage in foreign policy. Even the most traditional foreign policy domain of defense and security has not entirely escaped provincial interest, and in all spheres there are important domestic motivations.[11]

Conflict with Ottawa does account for much of Quebec's foreign activity. In many instances, Quebec is motivated politically and empowered constitutionally to seek non-Canadian partners in trade, commerce, scientific and student exchange, and pollution control; but Quebec's motives are often economic, and its activities compatible with the federal government. A confidential study of the federal Department of External Affairs, surveying the activities of provincial foreign delegations, concluded that

with the possible exception of Quebec's delegation in Paris, provincial foreign offices complemented Canada's foreign missions.[12] Moreover, whatever conflictual explanations suit the case of Quebec, even in Paris, they may be wholly inappropriate in reference to the other provinces. It would be unreasonable to argue that Ontario will engage in international activity the more it is in conflict with Ottawa, or the weaker Ottawa appears vis-à-vis Ontario. Indeed, Ontario upgraded its presence in Paris to a political office partly at the behest of the federal government, to help offset the Quebec presence in Paris.

Central governments may ask subunits to engage in foreign activity (e.g., the Ontario office in Paris), and subunits sometimes enlist the foreign policy apparatus of central governments that willingly help. When British Columbia decided it wanted to expand markets in Japan, the Canadian embassy in Tokyo provided full support and arranged appointments for the province's emissaries with leading Japanese officials. The federal government may have perceived a political advantage in providing a western province with such service; but the important point is that the foreign activity was designed, initiated, and defined by a province, with the federal government then providing willing assistance.

Central governments may be expected to mobilize support for foreign policy among interested subunits, including provincial governments, but assistance to independent foreign initiatives is not explained by extant theory. Furthermore, central governments may have both the authority and the political desire to thwart provincial activity, yet may countenance acts of independence out of political necessity. Canada's National Energy Board, a creature of the federal government, could prevent Quebec from striking independent deals with New England for the sale of hydroelectricity, and the government of Canada has made plain its desire to curtail all Quebec pretenses for international recognition and independence. However, the government of Canada cannot afford politically the appearance of damaging Quebec's economy by preventing the sale of a renewable resource. In this instance, Quebec negotiates directly with elected officials in New England, more out of economic interest than out of political ambition, but the political symbols are never forgotten.

Canadian bureaucrats may complain about the independence of a crown corporation, the Canadian Wheat Board, but politicians can be relieved that the Wheat Board can defy declarations of the Canadian national interest and sell wheat abroad. The corporation's headquarters are in Winnipeg, and its policies are certainly shaped by the wheat farmers of the prairies. Politically the arrangement is ideal for a federal government that wants to appear in control but can also plead captive. Although the Board is not formally provincial, it surely reflects the interests of the prairies more reliably than the foreign policy interests of Ottawa.

According to Canada's constitution, the provinces share with the federal government responsibility for their own economic welfare and growth. Most provincial governments appreciate the international implications of such a role.[13] Moreover, provincial bureaucracies have grown steadily in the past two decades and, in many ways, some are a match for their federal counterparts. This development has given some provinces ever greater confidence in their ability to promote their own interests, first within Canada but increasingly abroad.[14]

Most analysts of Canadian federalism refer to a continuous pendulum, balancing federal and provincial authority, which swung to the provinces during Quebec's Quiet Revolution. The simultaneous rise in consciousness about international economic interdependence has provoked more foreign initiatives. In some instances, provincial leaders simply do not think they can rely on the federal government to defend provincial interests abroad. Alberta, for example, initially chagrined by Canada's National Energy Program and the probable impact of any American retaliation, established a Washington listening post in New York. (Ottawa's clout has

kept provincial political offices physically out of the American capital.) Manitoba's threat to set up a Washington office over dissatisfaction with federal representation on the Garrison Diversion project induced Ottawa to organize an all-party federal-provincial special mission to lobby the U.S. Congress. Officials in British Columbia and Alberta, moreover, acknowledge that Quebec has thrown light on an international path that could benefit their own provinces, and they have followed accordingly.

The motivations for Canadian provinces to engage in foreign policy range from a quest for independence to an inducement of special federal assistance. Relations with federal officials can be antagonistic or fully cooperative, and the federal government may prohibit provincial foreign activity or provoke it. The federal government may possess the authority to prevent a foreign activity but not use it (e.g., the National Energy Board on hydroelectricity), or it may lack appropriate formal power but may achieve fixed goals by other means (e.g., keeping provincial political offices out of Washington, D.C.). Provinces may have political or economic objectives, and as an assessment of the range of provincial activity will show, politics may not be limited to the contest over federal or provincial supremacy. Once bureaucratic competence and fiscal means are present, perceived jurisdictional responsibility may predict which provinces will enter the international arena, on what occasions, and in reference to which issues. However, the kind of simple typology proposed by Keohane and Nye about degrees of conflict and authority cannot make sense out of the Canadian reality.

TRANSGOVERNMENTAL STRATEGIES

Each of the provinces of Quebec, Ontario, Alberta, and British Columbia pursues international relations differently, even when their purposes often are the same. Their different strategies reflect different attitudes toward Ottawa and different perspectives on the nature of federalism. Thus, domestic political considerations shape the mechanisms for the conduct of provincial foreign policy.

Quebec is by far the most independent-minded of the provinces, concentrating strategy on the performance of elaborate bureaucracies in the Ministry of Intergovernmental Affairs and in official permanent delegations in ten countries stretching from Tokyo to Brussels and from Boston to Caracas. Of the twenty-five offices posting representatives outside Quebec, only three are elsewhere in Canada (Moncton, Toronto, Edmonton) compared to eight in the United States. Although cooperation with the federal government to bolster tourism and the economy has grown, even these foreign efforts are complemented by formal activities (as in cultural or educational exchanges) and symbolic gestures designed to highlight Quebec's independent identity. Representation abroad is integral to Quebec's claim for separateness at home.

With thirteen foreign delegations in seven countries (and one more planned for the U.S.), Ontario's international profile may not appear so much more modest than Quebec's; however, Ontario is self-conscious about being at the center of the Canadian federal system. Ontario officials frequently doubt that their interests abroad are pursued adequately by the federal government, but consultation between provincial and federal officials on foreign questions is constant. There are no Ontario international initiatives taken without federal knowledge or sanction, and Ontario tries to utilize federal resources as much as possible. Ontario especially wants to avoid any suggestion that the province's independent international activity could be interpreted as a challenge to federal sovereignty.

Although Alberta's international efforts are not nearly as elaborate as those of Quebec or Ontario, the province's essential attitude oscillates between dissatisfaction with the federal government and a desire for an independent voice (and eyes and ears) on the one hand, and a

desire not to upset Confederation on the other. On some issues, such as immigration, concrete influence is preferred to formal power, and in multilateral trade negotiations of the GATT, Alberta settled for a policy of influencing Ottawa. Whereas in the United States, a state's foreign policy interest is often expressed through a congressional delegation,[15] Canadian federalism requires different channels of influence. Not a single member of Parliament from Alberta sat in the majority Liberal caucus in Ottawa; consequently, the provincial government had to deal directly with appropriate Ottawa officials. In part because of the political composition of the federal parliament, Alberta in fact sought unsuccessfully its own representation to the GATT ministerial meetings in 1982. Ottawa has conceded direct provincial participation in the subcommittees of Canada's joint commissions with the European Community and Japan, but continues to resist Alberta's pressure for a direct role in international economic conferences.

Alberta cedes some activities, such as trade regulation, to the federal government; but in trade promotion, Albertan officials claim that the federal government has not done its job well. As a result, the province has appropriated independent responsibility. In tourism the province tries to coordinate efforts with the federal government and does not work entirely on its own. Five of Alberta's six offices abroad (in four different countries) are designed to complement the federal government, although the two-person office opened in New York in 1982 is a response to dissatisfaction with the federal defense of Albertan interests in Washington; its purpose is to assure that "the Alberta Government is fully informed of United States energy developments as well as political, economic, and financial policies."[16]

Alberta chooses independence in some international activity, including the monitoring of foreign events, but prefers coordination and cooperation with the federal government in others. Strategy ranges from an independent political office in New York to provincial consultation with appropriate federal departments. Alberta's international interests range well beyond trade and commerce, and the domestic political pressures of a multi-ethnic population can be considerable. But Alberta's international strategy is designed neither for the independence pursued by Quebec nor the image of compliance cultivated by Ontario.

British Columbia's international activities are the least developed of these four provinces, and current strategy is again a fair reflection of the province's attitude toward confederation. Provincial officials believe that general compliance with Ottawa maximizes British Columbia's claim to special help when it is most needed and is the most cost-effective strategy; the province seeks above all to mobilize the federal government. However, British Columbia's history in international affairs has been quixotic, frequently reflecting completely independent initiatives in defiance of Ottawa. Moreover, the elaborate international activities of the Department of Industry and Small Business Development (ISBD) follow a philosophy of dependence on federal help that is not always shared in the Ministry of Intergovernmental Relations where a first serious, comprehensive look at British Columbia's international interests began in 1982. British Columbia maintains but two tourism offices abroad, the policy preferred by ISBD, but before the recent austerity period, the Ministry of Intergovernmental Relations was studying whether to locate delegations in cities as distant as Tokyo and Paris.

Above all, British Columbia wants to influence the federal government to pursue foreign policies protective of provincial interests. Officials have feared that confrontations between Canada and the United States, stimulated by Ontario-based issues (e.g., acid rain), could precipitate American retaliation harmful to the innocent western provinces, as in the 1982 disputes over softwood lumber. In issues of this kind British Columbia wants to dissuade Ottawa from generating anti-Canadian feeling in Washington; but provincial ministers and officials also have been

aware of the potential value of persuading Washington directly that disputes over acid rain do not warrant an ill will that could harm the friendly Canadian west. Provincial and federal spokesmen lobbied successfully in Washington to avert threatened American legislation that would have damaged the province's forest industry.

British Columbia has taken considerable independent initiative in promoting trade and commerce, and in some branches of the government there is hard thinking about alternative strategies for promoting the province's international profile. British Columbia, like Ontario, is devoted to confederation; but the provincial bureaucracy is decidedly less experienced in shaping sophisticated strategies that do not appear to threaten national unity while serving provincial interests.

The efforts of all four provincial governments have been abetted by Ottawa's view that international initiatives in "low politics" are non-threatening. All the provinces accept the shared jursidictional responsibility for economic development, and all therefore seek to promote commerce, trade, and tourism. All want to influence international tariff and trade agreements, although the interests of the manufacturing heartland diverge from the interests of the resource-producing west. Each still is determining the most effective approach to economic self-interest in terms of the delicate condition of national unity, but none will permit unity to stand in its way. Even the cooperative British Columbia approach exploits the fragile union by emphasizing that a price of provincial compliance is federal devotion of resources to foreign provincial ambitions.

The spectrum of strategies arrayed by these four provinces stretches from more transgovernmentalism due to conflict (Quebec) to more thorough cooperation and coordination (Ontario). Nevertheless, the federal government has ceased to acknowledge most of this activity as supportive of a strong center. When provinces make independent forays into foreign capitals to argue their case, the federal government fears foreign exploitation of Canadian disunity.[17] As the magnitude and scope of provincial initiatives have grown, the federal government has been more inclined to discard the low-high politics dichotomy and to seek greater control. The reaction may well be, as the federal government defines its own international interests, too little and too late.

TRANSGOVERNMENTAL ACTIVITY

Scope and Magnitude

Roger Swanson has referred to the "scope" of transgovernmentalism in Canadian-United States relations by counting the sheer number of transactions.[18] A great quantity of such activity may of itself threaten a central government (and Swanson cited 766 interactions between U.S. states and Canadian provinces in 1974 alone, before several provincial bureaucracies had even geared up for such activity[19]); but the resources devoted may be a more reliable indication of how serious constituent governments are about independent foreign activity. Although many transactions are inexpensive, the maintenance of a bureaucracy and foreign offices for foreign relations can require genuine commitment.

The scope and magnitude of transgovernmentalism involve the number of foreign activities, the range of functional areas they include, their expense, and the foreign and domestic bureaucracies needed to operate and support them. Provincial reporting of such information is not yet consistent. Most international activity is uncoordinated, but some measures can be taken. In Alberta, the Department of Federal and Intergovernmental Affairs maintains an International Division of eleven full-time staff members, including six officers and an executive director. In addition, Alberta's six offices abroad absorb about 50 percent of the entire department's budget ($5.4 million for fiscal year 1984). Approximately one-third of the remaining 50 percent of

the department's budget is devoted to the International Division.[20] Of course, this formal structuring of a bureaucracy to shape coherent policy and to monitor social, economic, and political affairs in other areas of the world only begins to reveal Alberta's international interests. In 1981, for example, 23 percent of the province's gross domestic product, representing $9.88 billion, was exported out of Canada. The Alberta cabinet includes a Minister of State for Economic Development—International Trade to promote such foreign activity, and many other government departments conduct foreign relations.

The government of Alberta gives foreign aid ($7 million in 1981-82) and sends advisers to Indonesia and Nigeria. It has signed an agreement for "Friendship and Affiliation" with Hokkaido, Japan, that fosters exchanges in culture, education, recreation, agriculture, science and technology; it has a "special relationship" in similar areas with the Chinese province of Heilong-jiang; and it is involved in cultural, scientific, and educational activities with a range of other countries. Government missions in 1981-82 went to the Middle East, Western and Eastern Europe, Africa, Latin America, and the Asian Pacific Rim as well as the Soviet Union and the United States. With the latter, regional relations increase constantly and include Premier Lougheed's attendance at the June 1983 Western Governors' meeting, the presence of the Minister for Federal and Intergovernmental Affairs at the September 1983 Western States Legislators' meeting, visits by several western governors to Alberta, and planned institutional links with the Western Governors' Association. The agricultural committees of Alberta and Montana met for the first time in Spring 1984. In 1983, as in 1981, Premier Lougheed visited Washington to meet directly with U.S. officials and politicians. Various foreign missions from over twenty foreign countries came to Alberta.

Trade continues to be Alberta's primary international emphasis. Following his month-long trip to China and Japan in August-September

1983, Premier Lougheed proposed various ways to improve Alberta's competitiveness in world markets, especially in the Pacific Rim; he called for "full partnership" among the federal government, the private sector, and the provinces rather than the mere "consultation" referred to by Ottawa's *A Discussion Paper*, the federal statement on trade policy for the 1980s.[21] He personally has pressured the prime minister to pursue more open trade for Japanese automobiles and Chinese textiles, signaling a revival of Canada's geographic cleavage over trade and tariffs.

British Columbia's foreign activities have been conducted primarily by a small staff in the Department of Industry and Small Business Development (ISBD). However, as with Alberta, British Columbia's transgovernmentalism cannot be measured solely by the commitment of full-time staff in the official bureaucracy. In 1980, British Columbia exports were valued at more than $9.4 billion, with more headed for Asia and the Pacific Rim than for the United States. The northeast coal megaproject, which contracts for the mining and shipment of enough coal to Japan to cover 30 percent of that country's need for twenty years at a total investment of nearly $3 billion, is the product of provincial initiative and persistence.[22] The federal government was a full partner in the study phase, and the embassy in Tokyo helped throughout the project into the early 1980s. From the beginning, however, it has been up to British Columbia to execute plans and contracts. The project in early 1984 is on schedule, and shipments of coal began at the end of 1983. This international project may mean 10,000 jobs for the province,[23] and large-scale celebrations were planned for the summer of 1984 at the site for the new town.[24]

After a period of self-reflection, austerity, and bureaucratic reorganization in 1983, the British Columbia government again is thinking internationally. In May 1984, Premier Bennett reciprocated the visit of the premier of the People's Republic of China. Annual meetings focusing on transboundary environmental and energy

issues have continued with the State of Washington and in the trilateral arrangement among the Yukon, British Columbia, and Alaska. They may now increase. The main objective of British Columbia's 1984 bilateral agenda is increased sales of oil and gas.

In addition to the nine full-time members of the International Relations Branch of the Ontario Ministry of Intergovernmental Affairs (some seventy total personnel), the ministry staffs and controls directly the province's agencies general in Paris and Brussels. These agencies also have personnel working for the Ministry of Industry and Trade, which itself controls ten other overseas offices. The Agent General's office in London, with thirty-five full-time staff, is responsible in parts to the premier, the Ministry of Industry and Trade and the Ministry of Agriculture and Food. In June 1983, Ontario opened an agency general in New York "in recognition of the importance of that location and the fact that such offices help build Ontario's profile and reinforce its image."[25] The office is administratively responsible to the Ministry of Industry and Trade. During 1983 two "satellite" offices (reporting to New York and Los Angeles respectively) were launched in Boston and San Francisco. Another is planned for Philadelphia. Unlike Alberta, Ontario does not see its New York office as a window on Washington, D.C.; such monitoring is done from Ontario.

Intergovernmental Affairs' share alone for overseas offices in 1982 and in 1983 was estimated at $1 million, more than 14 percent of the entire intergovernmental relations budget. In all, Ontario spends more than $6 million on its offices outside Canada. In addition to the $1 million for overseas offices, the International Relations Branch accounts for $500,000 of the total $7 million Intergovernmental Affairs budget. Counting Protocol Services for visitors to Ontario, half the total Intergovernmental Affairs staff is involved in international affairs.[26]

The United States inevitably is a major focus for Ontario. Ontario has signed protocols with

Michigan and Ohio, sells quantities of hydro-
electric power on contracts between the province
and New York and New Jersey, and lobbies directly in Washington, D.C. over acid rain with
the full support and sympathy of the federal
government. Ontario's premier has meetings, arranged by the Canadian Embassy, with senior
members of the U.S. government to discuss On-
tario-U.S. issues. Although the Great Lakes Water Quality Agreement is an executive agreement
between Canada and the United States, the Province of Ontario is the primary Canadian actor
(with substantial federal funds) through the Can-
ada-Ontario Agreement on Great Lakes Water
Quality. On a host of other transborder issues,
there are regular contacts between several Ontario government ministries and agencies and the
United States.

Ontario attaches considerable importance to
personal discussions with high-level officials.
During 1981-83, Premier Davis or his ministers
visited the U.S., Australia, New Zealand, and
Western Europe. During 1983, Ontario hosted
senior government officials from Asia, the Middle East, Eastern and Western Europe, and Africa and concluded its first "twinning"
agreement with the Chinese province of Jiang
Gsu. The provincial government has developed
close relations with the foreign consular corps in
Toronto.

Although "the search for markets and investment" is Ontario's principal international
concern, much attention is also paid to the composition of the province's population, thus involving the provincial government in
immigration policy. Various forms of foreign aid
have been extended through disaster relief and
through specific grants to Commonwealth island
nations in the Caribbean. The Ministry of Education runs a program in the Caribbean, organizes student and teacher exchanges with several
countries (including the United States), and sec-
onds personnel to international organizations,
including UNESCO, WHO, FAO, and the ILO.

International relations have greater priority

for Quebec than for any other province. At least
one-half of the staff in the Ministry of Intergovernmental Affairs alone is committed full-time
to international relations (of a total of more than
400 positions). The International Division spent
$36.3 million (including $13.89 million for overseas offices) in 1981-82, some 76 percent of the
entire ministry's budget; this allocation increased in 1982-83, even as government spending declined generally. As in other provinces,
there is expenditure and manpower commitment
to consider for foreign affairs in ministries responsible for international trade, commerce,
tourism, immigration, culture, and agriculture,
all of which have foreign representation of their
own. Education, too, supports various international activities without posting representatives
abroad. Quebec exports outside Canada over 40
percent of its gross domestic product, at a value
in 1980 of $15.2 billion. There can be no doubt,
by the sheer magnitude and scope of commitment, that Quebec fashions itself an independent
international actor.

In addition to its historical relationship with
France, Quebec has extensive relations with other
European countries. Under the leadership of Intergovernmental Affairs Minister Jacques-Yvan
Morin, Quebec placed increased emphasis on the
United States. The U.S., France, Europe, Africa,
Latin America, and Asia have their own bureaus
in the Intergovernmental Affairs Ministry. In all
cases, visits to and from Quebec at the highest
levels are countless. With the transformation of its
Office québécois du commerce exterieur into a
separate ministry, Quebec is aggressively pursuing trade promotion and investment to complement its political and cultural activities.

Roger Swanson identified ten functional areas in which provincial international activity
could be classified: agriculture, commerce and
industry, education and culture, energy, environmental protection, human services, military and
civil defense, natural resources, public safety,
and transportation.[27] Levy, Stevenson, and Leach
add "administrative interactions" and "political

relationships."[28] All four provinces discussed here engage internationally in almost all these activities, which cover most of the range of international relations.

The distribution of activity of course varies among provinces. Quebec's transgovernmentalism is generally more political, cultural, and educational; that of the other provinces is more economic. The Swanson, Levy, Stevenson, and Leach studies all focused on provincial relations with the United States; but as Johannson observed, the range of activity has extended even beyond these categories into foreign economic aid, investment, technical advising, and scientific and technological exchange.[29] As the categories have multiplied with the greater internationalism of the provinces, even the general distinction between economics and politics has begun to fade. Although Alberta's concerns are predominantly in industrial development and investment, energy, natural resources, trade promotion, and agriculture, greater attention is being paid in the 1980s to cultural, educational, scientific, and technological exchanges. Furthermore, Alberta House in London was deeply involved in the constitutional patriation debates, bridging domestic to foreign policy in a purely political activity.

Although British Columbia's foreign activities have been primarily economic, as demonstrated by the staffing distribution in ISBD, Intergovernmental Relations is concerned with the gamut of international endeavors less expressly economic. Scientific agreements have been signed with Alaska, for example, to study the development of hydroelectric power, and there is considerable interaction with the State of Washington over environmental issues.

Ontario's focus is political and cultural in Paris, Brussels, and London, but economic in most other areas. Nevertheless, special aid to Italian earthquake victims, educational grants for Canadian studies in the United Kingdom, legal proceedings against foreign corporate polluters on the Great Lakes, and the provincial airlifting of 35,000 British subjects to increase Ontario's Anglo-Saxon population (in 1938; the contemporary counterpart is a full-time immigration officer at Ontario House in London) demonstrate that Ontario certainly does not confine itself to a narrow definition of legitimate international intervention.

Type

Although the provinces do not sign international treaties, they do sign "agreements," "arrangements," and "accords," the contents of which often seem like treaties.[30] Furthermore, they can be involved centrally in international treaties that affect them, the most celebrated instance perhaps being British Columbia's effective veto over the initial Columbia River Treaty between Canada and the United States. Provincial crown corporations sign contracts with foreign public authorities and governments, as in the hydroelectric agreements between Quebec Hydro and New England, and Ontario Hydro and New York. Although the respective federal governments accept these international contracts, they resemble in most aspects commercial treaties.

Most international relations, for the provinces as for the federal government, are more informal. British Columbia has informal firefighting agreements with the State of Washington, informal agricultural exchanges with New Zealand, and civil defense agreements with both Washington and Montana. Alberta has entered into international economic cooperation agreements jointly with the federal government and foreign partners, and maintains informal agricultural exchanges with Japan. A plethora of formal and informal agreements link Ontario to the bordering American states. A similar array ties Quebec to New England.

Given the range of joint understandings, agreements, activities, and even direct treaty involvement, it is difficult to discern the precise differences between the type of international activity pursued by the provinces and the type pursued by the federal government. However, the provinces do generally avoid security and defense issues, do not bind other provinces in their foreign agreements, remain subject to federal authority for the export of commodities (e.g., wheat and energy), and usually remain excluded from sending independent representatives to multilateral forums, such as the GATT. Still, Quebec enjoys considerable independent representation in francophone conferences, and provincial spokesmen frequently are members of Canadian delegations to international organizations and negotiations.

Participants

All levels of provincial governments engage in foreign relations. The premiers of Alberta, British Columbia, Ontario, and Quebec have all led official missions to Europe, the Far East, and the United States. Some have gone to Mexico, Central America, the Caribbean, and South America. Alberta's Minister of State for Economic Development—International Trade has visited more than fifty countries officially, and ministerial missions are more frequent and far-flung than the forays of premiers. British Columbia's Education Minister has travelled officially to the Far East, Australia, and New Zealand.

It is apparent that the foreign missions of provincial politicians enjoy popular resonance. Nevertheless, lower level civil servants also travel frequently. Of course, all this activity is in addition to the foreign offices, and often the travel is directed to countries where the provinces have no permanent representation.

The Canadian government looks upon provincial travel abroad with a benign cynicism, imposing no restrictions but often implying that it is frivolous and redundant of federal activity already supporting provincial interests. However, the federal government takes a more serious look at the foreign interlocutors. Offices with any political content are actively opposed for Washington, D.C. (Quebec has a tourism office)

and seriously discouraged for other national capitals. Ottawa wants to guarantee but one political voice for Canada.

The federal government's attitude on foreign partners for the provinces has met with mixed results. In response to Ontario's desire in 1971 to create an independent office, Ottawa created a position of "Counsellor (Provincial Interests)" in the Canadian Embassy in Washington, filled by a federal official responding to provincial inquiries and concerns. An Ontario Ministry of Intergovernmental Affairs official was seconded to the Embassy for two six-week periods in 1981 and 1982 to assist in lobbying the U.S. Congress on acid rain. In the summer of 1982 a Manitoba official was accepted by the Embassy to assist in lobbying on the Garrison Diversion project. The United States Department of State met twice in 1974 with representatives from all ten provinces, over Ottawa's strenuous objections. The Alberta and Quebec offices in New York openly work the Washington corridors.

The United States government usually has respected Ottawa's anxieties and not encouraged senior level contact between the White House and provincial leaders. Other countries, including especially Japan and France, have not shared this attitude, however, and provincial premiers have conferred officially with prime ministers. Because of Commonwealth tradition, most provinces have long maintained large missions in London, while Paris and Tokyo are the centers of economic as well as political activity. All the provinces, nevertheless, have stayed out of Bonn and Rome (although Quebec has an immigration officer), presumably in some deference to Ottawa. Of course, Ontario has an office in Frankfurt, and Quebec has offices in Dusseldorf and Milan. These cities were viewed as more important sites in the early 1980s for the promotion of trade and tourism than the German and Italian capitals.

In the threat sometimes perceived by the federal government from provincial foreign activity, nothing creates greater anxiety than Quebec's relations with France and *la francophonie*.

The federal government is concerned that the French-speaking world may extend Quebec independent international recognition, implicitly denying Ottawa's claim to represent all Canadians. Hence, assessment of importance for foreign activity among Canadian provinces necessarily includes the foreign interlocutor according to status and rank, and according to geographic location, with particular sensitivity attached to Quebec's relations with the French-speaking world.

Different participants, then, operate in a variety of settings. There are examples among all four provinces of the conduct of foreign affairs in international organizations, in institutionalized offices abroad, in highly structured foreign missions, in summit meetings (as between the premier of British Columbia and the prime minister of Japan), and in international conferences in Canada and elsewhere.

Style

Quebec's foreign activities are well known to most Canadians, not merely because of their scope and magnitude, but also because Quebec actively wants Canadians—and citizens of other countries—to take notice. Quebec wants to make an international impression as an independent actor, both to satisfy its calculated requirements for economic health and well-being, cultural continuity and educational development, and to fulfill the mission of the Parti Québécois government of making Canada give in to *le fait français*. Hence, Quebec deliberately challenges the government of Canada, especially in the francophone world, demanding to represent internationally the francophones of North America.

Quebec's international style is contrasted most by Ontario. Ontario is also very active internationally, but self-consciously seeks a low profile for these activities in Canada. Highly conscious of image, Ontario chose bilingual personnel to staff its Paris office, emphasizing to the French that francophones in large numbers come from Ontario as they do from Quebec, and that the French world in Canada therefore is not wholly separatist. Within Canada, however, Ontario hopes its international efforts will be inconspicuous. Indeed, in 1977 the Ontario government closed down eleven foreign offices, partly due to fiscal restraints, but also because of the fear that Ontario's international activities would lend themselves to an image of a fragmented Canada. Above all, Ontario wants to pursue its own best interests without detracting in any way from the image of sovereignty lodged in a united Canada governed not from Toronto, but from Ottawa.

The Ontario style is shared in attitude by British Columbia, which goes even farther in choosing not to maintain any foreign offices (although that policy may be changing). Alberta is more undecided, sometimes wanting to reassure an image of unity, but sometimes wanting to assert Alberta's independent view.

In determining the importance of international activity, style plainly counts. It is significant in the federal government's own sense of sovereignty, and in deciding whether other countries will take foreign initiatives seriously. The government of Canada would like to believe that no country will deal with a province unless there is federal support and sanction; however, Quebec has demonstrated on several occasions that not all countries share Ottawa's anxiety or think it necessarily in their own best interest to defend Ottawa's claim to decide the weightier issues affecting relations beyond Canada's borders.

THE INTERNATIONAL ACTIVITIES OF OTHER PROVINCES: A COUNTRY-WIDE TREND?

This study has concentrated on the international relations of Alberta, British Columbia, Ontario, and Quebec because they are the most active provinces abroad. In structure, content, and purpose, the remaining provinces are much less visible and conform most to the British Columbia variant of uncoordinated and somewhat spasmodic activity. However, whereas British Columbia may not have the structural or financial wherewithal to pursue external relations with the intensity of Alberta, Ontario, or Quebec, it wants an international profile and pursues it with help from the Department of External Affairs and Canadian consulates and embassies. The remaining provinces engage in some international activity but do not share British Columbia's grander purpose.

Nova Scotia and Saskatchewan retain their historic Houses in London, primarily for the pursuit of trade opportunities. Saskatchewan is reorganizing its Department of Economic Development to reflect more the coordination of international economic activity. Premiers and ministers of Economic Development from Saskatchewan have traveled abroad promoting trade.

Although the office of Secretary of the Cabinet for Federal-Provincial Relations coordinates some international activity in Manitoba, most external relations are *ad hoc*.[31] The Executive Council and Department of Finance, and Energy and Mines have gone to international financial markets in the United States, Western Europe, and Japan for major capital projects such as hydroelectric development. On specific issues, such as the Garrison Diversion, Manitoba has involved itself directly in arguing Canada's case to the United States. Manitoba has frequent bureaucratic contacts with U.S. border states (Minnesota and North Dakota) on commodity taxation, river drainage, and exchanges of agricultural information—activities that have flourished especially when there have been good personal relations between the leadership in the province and the states. But Manitoba traditionally has deferred to Ottawa's foreign policy establishment, citing both the cost of international activity and the jurisdiction of the federal government.

Newfoundland, too, is sensitive to federal jurisdiction. For financial and political reasons, Newfoundland relies on the Department of External Affairs for the pursuit of its international concerns.[32] Senior Newfoundland officials believe that relations are better with External on matters pertaining to the leasing of military bases to the U.S., Law of the Sea, fisheries, pulp and paper, forestry, offshore oil and gas, and the status of St. Pierre and Miquelon than with a number of federal line ministries of utmost importance to the province, including Fisheries. Newfoundland has been included directly in international negotiations or has made representations to Ottawa on these concerns. Occasionally the federal government also invites the province to join the Canadian delegation to international forums, such as UNESCO or the ILO, that are of no particular relevance to Newfoundland.

New Brunswick's Cabinet Secretariat for Intergovernmental Affairs also deals with international questions, such as various links with New England; but like Newfoundland's Secretariat, its primary concern is federal-provincial relations.[33] Cultural agreements with France are handled by the Department of Historical and Cultural Resources, while trade issues are the responsibility of the Department of Commerce and Development; however, both departments channel their international activity through the Department of External Affairs in Ottawa.

Prince Edward Island is the province with the fewest international activities. Its dependence on federal auspices is total.[34] Trade promotion is limited largely to the export of potatoes and canned milk, initiated by line agencies such as the Department of Agriculture or by the Potato Marketing Board. As other provinces, Prince Edward Island has been invited by the federal government to participate in Canadian delegations to international meetings, and sometimes it has accepted. There is no central agency mechanism for international affairs, although the Secretary to the Cabinet monitors activities.

In sum, movement among Canada's six poorer and smaller provinces toward independent international initiatives has been modest and disorganized. Generally, they believe that Ottawa has represented them well (although exceptions, such as Manitoba's dissatisfaction over Garrison, do arise), and they are happy to have the federal government expend resources on their behalf beyond Canada's borders. Above all, they are aware that, were they more frequently dissatisfied, the price of lobbying Ottawa would be far more manageable than the price of international recognition.

REORGANIZING CANADA'S FOREIGN POLICY ESTABLISHMENT

The government of Canada has acknowledged the importance of provincial activity by increasing dramatically its effort to cooperate, co-opt, and pre-empt provincial initiatives.[35] The centerpiece of the federal response is the reorganization of the Department of External Affairs, begun in January 1982.

Three main principles animated the decision to restructure the government of Canada's foreign policy-making apparatus: (1) low politics could no longer be given secondary importance; (2) too many agencies within the federal government were conducting foreign policy without coordination; and (3) the provinces were appropriating to themselves foreign activity that rightly should be controlled more by the federal government.

Three main provisions of the reorganization address these three principles. First, the trade functions of the Department of Industry, Trade and Commerce were transferred totally into the Department of External Affairs. Trade commissioners in Canadian embassies and consulates would begin reporting through a new structure where the Secretary of State for External Affairs would ultimately be responsible. In this transfer, the trade functions were given formal equivalence to the traditional diplomatic functions of the department, and in the long-range planning

and budgetary commitments, the trade side has reason to expect superior treatment.[36]

Recognition of international trade as of equal or greater importance to Canada in foreign affairs than the traditional diplomacy for which Canada had earned a remarkable international reputation was not unrelated to the other two principles and main provisions of the reorganization. In addition to the absorption of international trade, the Department of External Affairs gained the functions of a central agency. Foreign policy had always been a line function, and the Department of External Affairs maintained its own responsibilities free of other ministries and agencies. With the reorganization, all agencies and departments of the federal government would be required to report any activity with international implication to the Department of External Affairs. Thus a new coordination and coherence was to be achieved through the foreign ministry.

Most of the activity competing with External Affairs had been economic in character or implication. Issues of border broadcasting, for example, might have appeared appropriately within a mandate on communications; but the reorganization recognized the considerable financial investments involved in these issues. The greater importance attached to low politics made the central agency responsibilities inevitable.

When the Department of External Affairs had neglected economic affairs, and the provinces enjoyed a jurisdictional responsibility to assure economic growth and development, the provinces discovered that they could fulfill their mandate best by engaging in foreign commerce. Thus, the provinces captured much of the international activity affecting the Canadian economy. Consequently, the reorganization sought to improve the mechanisms for control and information flow while increasing provincial reporting of foreign activities to the federal Department of External Affairs. At the time of the reorganization, the department already had identified more than thirty-five formal mechanisms for the provinces to participate in Canada's foreign relations and for provincial international economic relations to be coordinated through the federal government;[37] but the mandate under reorganization was to make these mechanisms more effective and to develop new ones if necessary.

The reorganization of the Department of External Affairs began with the conviction that the federal government was losing its grip on international economic activity because various Ottawa agencies operated at will and the provinces had become increasingly active. Furthermore, the prime minister's closest advisers had concluded that Canada's future foreign relations must give greater emphasis to trade and commerce, the very areas in which the federal government had previously adopted a benign view of provincial initiatives.

IMPORTANCE

Alberta, British Columbia, Ontario, and Quebec are all very active internationally. In addition to their coordinated efforts through intergovernmental affairs ministries and offices abroad, many other departments conduct foreign relations. All of them have formal bureaucratic commitments to world trade, including a minister specifically responsible for international economic activity in Alberta, Ontario, and Quebec. Three of the provinces actively try to influence the foreign policies of the federal government. Interactions between provincial governments and governments of the several states are beyond counting, and the provinces have diversified relations beyond North America.

Is all this activity important? Does it alter expected outcomes in international relations, and does it erode traditional sovereignty? By both these standards, measurement is as difficult as it would be for the foreign policy of any nation-state. The interminable debates over the value of foreign aid, consular offices, trade fairs,

and academic and cultural exchanges, cannot be settled here. Nevertheless, there are some major developments affecting Canada that likely would not have occurred without provincial government initiative.

Although Alberta hardly is reproducing the federal Department of External Affairs, it is establishing institutional apparatus for the ongoing management of rapidly increasing international relations. Alberta has developed an international trade expertise that qualitatively appears a fair match for the federal government. Without Alberta's independent efforts, exports certainly would be fewer. It is difficult, of course, to measure the impact of foreign diplomacy on economic prosperity, but no more so for the provinces than for the federal government. It is impossible to establish whether Alberta's foreign aid and technical advisory programs have made a difference in the Third World. They have resulted from Third World requests and presumably, therefore, are perceived by recipients as valuable.

Even as Ontario's international endeavours are strictly in cooperation with the federal government, repeated internal studies have pointed to the direct value of independent foreign activity for the province. With some site changes, the office closures in 1977 proved very temporary because new studies persuaded the provincial government that activities more than justified their costs. Foreign office commitments are growing in the early 1980s, despite austere provincial budgets, because provincial officials are convinced that the risk to Canada's unified image has receded and Ontario's interests can be protected best by independent international relations.

Ontario would not sell hydroelectric power to New York without the initiative of its crown corporation any more than British Columbia would sell coal to Japan without the efforts of ISBD and the premier. Such arrangements reverberate throughout the international system. Japan will be buying 30 percent of its coal from British Columbia beyond the year 2000, and New York will reduce its dependence on foreign oil through the hydro power generated in Ontario.

Quebec would not have committed $15 billion to the James Bay hydroelectric project if it did not intend to sell the inevitable surplus of this renewable resource to New England. New England, in turn, may reduce the pollution of coal-generated electricity and the expense and risk of oil from overseas. Such essential measures increasing the economic interdependence of Canada and the United States are coming about through territorial transgovernmentalism, not through the traditional international contacts of national governments.

Quebec has been trying to establish a benign sympathy in the United States for its ambitions for sovereignty. Causal relations in the area of international affairs are impossible to discern, but Washington's apparent sympathy for a unified Canada has not contributed to active opposition to Quebec's initiatives in the United States. Although Washington may have decided that neutrality with some preference is best, it is also possible that Quebec's active lobby in the American media, cultural establishments, and the academy have blunted to some extent official inclinations to fear the implicit instability of Quebec's aspirations.

Whether political or economic, the foreign activities of the provinces have yielded outcomes that would not have occurred otherwise. In some instances, those outcomes translate into many jobs and dollars. In other instances, they can be found in greater understanding and in efficiency (as in various tourism agreements which have emerged transborder across the continent). They have increased Canadian-American interdependence and thereby reduced North American dependence on other areas of the world. Certainly by these measures, territorial transgovernmentalism as pursued by the Canadian provinces is important.

As long as international economic activity was not considered foreign policy, most of the international endeavours of the provinces were not considered threatening by the government of Canada. Some federal officials still regard the annual meeting of the eastern premiers and the New England governors as a clambake and party, even though this setting has spawned a variety of agreements increasing the convenience of moving goods and services between the two countries and fostered the energy discussions that have been cited here. However, the reorganization of the Department of External Affairs is a clear signal that low politics are central to Canada's foreign policy and that the activities of the provinces, like the activities of other federal departments and agencies, must be monitored and perhaps controlled.

The federal-provincial office within the Department of External Affairs was created originally to monitor the political activities of Quebec abroad. In the 1980s, the essential mandate of this office is growing. The office is expected to keep each province abreast of Canadian foreign policy that may affect the interest of a given province. It is expected to coordinate provincial interests and initiatives with federal policy. It is expected, when asked, to assist provincial foreign missions. Its mandate, however, is not to curtail provincial initiative. In many instances the office is expected to encourage the provinces to be more involved internationally. Under the auspices of this office, provincial representatives in Ottawa have been invited to constant meetings with foreign visitors on all manner of subjects, from cultural and educational exchange to economic opportunity. In some cases, this effort has suggested internationalizing the activities of provinces that maintain Ottawa offices for primarily domestic purposes.[38] Hence, the federal government is actually expanding the international involvement of the provincial governments, while trying to carry the provinces under a federal umbrella to protect sovereignty.

The government of Canada openly has feared a challenge to sovereignty from the foreign political initiatives of Quebec. International conferences have become the setting for a great contest of will. In at least one instance, the federal government made substantial financial contributions to an international organization as a pay-off to exclude separate representation from Quebec.[39]

The actual threat to sovereignty is impossible to measure, but the perception of threat is unmistakable and far more important. Until the reorganization of External Affairs, the government of Canada perceived a threat from Quebec alone. The reorganization suggests that the threat will no longer be perceived exclusively from Quebec, or exclusively from foreign political initiatives. If economic issues are central to Canada's foreign policy, then the uncoordinated economic endeavours of the provinces are potentially as threatening as Quebec's search for political recognition.

The federal government of course does not characterize the reorganization of External Affairs in the terms described here. Incoherence among federal agents is acknowledged, but the challenge from the provinces is discounted. The steps to improve monitoring and control of provincial activity are called progress in cooperative federalism. However, in no other arena has the federal government declared an activity federal business and then encouraged the provinces to do more. Foreign policy is not likely to prove an exception.

PREDICTION AND DIRECTION IN TRANSGOVERNMENTALISM

Keohane and Nye predicted a direct relationship between increased conflict among subunits of government and increased transgovernmentalism. This relationship does not stand the test for Canadian territorial transgovernmentalism and may in some examples, such as Ontario, be reversed. Indeed, Keohane and Nye have taken the consequence for the cause. An increase in conflict between Ottawa and the provinces may result from provincial transgovernmentalism, but the source of provincial behaviour is altogether different, with the lone and only partial exception of Quebec.

Although provincial behaviour may derive chiefly from economic motivation, objectives generally are consonant with the federal government. However, it would be reasonable to hypothesize that the provinces have forced a reordering of federal priorities. Ottawa's apparent desire and need to represent all Canadians in all foreign affairs can oblige the federal government to outdo the provinces where they have placed priority or taken initiative. Ottawa agrees with the objective of aid to *la francophonie*, but gives the objective greater priority (and more money) because of Quebec. Ontario, by suing American power utilities in U.S. courts, forced a new federal emphasis on disputes over acid rain. By playing the "Washington card," Manitoba instigated a greater devotion of federal resources to Garrison. While these instances do not involve traditional conflict, they do suggest provincial leverage over the federal agenda. Typically, in the Canadian experience, Ottawa's style is to co-opt, not to compete or conquer.

According to Huntington, the operations of non-central government units beyond national borders depend upon the organization having means of communication and transportation, and technological and organizational capability "to operate across vast distances and in differing cultures."[40] This emphasis on sophisticated organization helps explain the differences in the amount of transgovernmental activity pursued by different provinces. Quebec and Ontario are certainly the largest provincial government organizations in Canada, and they are the most engaged in international affairs. Of the four provinces considered here, British Columbia certainly is the least articulated of governments and is the least internationally involved.

Capability alone of course is not sufficient to stimulate international activity. It is also necessary to have a clear jurisdictional responsibility, mandate, or goal. In Canada the provinces share responsibility constitutionally for economic development, and that jurisdiction has demanded transgovernmental relations in a country profoundly dependent upon exports and trade. Levy and Munton argue that as provincial bureaucracies become more capable, they interpreted their constitutional mandate in terms that pushed them onto the international scene.[41] Furthermore, the government of Canada posed no serious obstacle to this activity because it had relegated such international economic activity to secondary importance in foreign affairs. Quebec, of course, also perceived a political goal, and the federal government therefore responded early to the notion of a provincial challenge to federal government prerogative.

The federal government has decided that international economic activity also may question central authority; therefore, it seeks a realignment of the foreign policy apparatus. However, as Feldman and Milch have argued, perhaps the most irreversible Canadian development of the 1970s has been the growth of provincial bureaucracy, in both size and sophistication. Levy and Munton have made a similar argument about the evolution of Canadian foreign policy.[42] The federal government, recognizing that it probably cannot alter the chosen international path of most provinces, therefore seeks greater cooperation and co-optation. The provinces are likely to cooperate only as much as it suits them.

In all but Quebec, central agency functions for foreign policy within intergovernmental affairs ministries have arisen in reaction to political and bureaucratic discovery that substantial international activity has been underway for some time without coordination or coherence. Indeed, Ontario began studying and inventorying its own transgovernmentalism in the 1960s, which induced a restructuring of the ministry and the creation of an international division. The formation of such central agency bureaucracies in the provinces presaged the similar federal initiative. Provincial experience may therefore be suggestive of Ottawa's own future.

In Ontario, the central agency function is not particularly effective. Most departments and agencies continue to operate in the international arena independently of any reporting or coordinating function in the Ministry of Intergovernmental Affairs. In Quebec, a struggle developed in 1982 between Intergovernmental Affairs and the newly organized Ministry for International Trade. The economic functions which had been within Quebec's equivalent of a foreign ministry appear to have been separated, the opposite of Ottawa's reorganization. The reactive bureaucratic reorganizations to impose coordination on the conduct of foreign business do not reveal much success.

Feldman and Milch predicted that provincial bureaucracies would develop in the 1980s as mirror images of the federal government, in part because they are designed to deal with federal counterparts. They argued that the same lack of coordination bedevilling the federal government would likely befall the provinces.[43] In the arena of transgovernmentalism, the cycle of bureaucratic reorganization seems to be justifying that prediction.

The constitutional division of responsibilities in Canada seems to guarantee increased transgovernmentalism of ever greater consequence in the 1980s. To the extent that the federal government chooses to perceive such activity as an intrusion on federal prerogative, the provinces will be threatening Canadian sovereignty, both in political and in economic spheres. As long as the federal government seeks to co-opt the provinces, it will also be giving the provinces a free ride into international affairs, which moreover is in the very nature of federalism. With the shifts in the international agenda and in the international priorities of the government of Canada, with the entrenchment of able and committed provincial bureaucracies, and with their own increasing difficulty in coordinating provincial activity, a segmentation of foreign policy is likely to grow, to multiply Canadian voices internationally, and to increase the uncertainty about who speaks for Canada. Canada's foreign policy will have been domesticated,[44] not because it fully reflects a consensus on Canada's domestic character, but because it will give an international presence, in both form and function, to the complexities and contradictions of Canada's mosaic.

Notes

1. Annemarie Jacomy-Millette, "Aspects juridiques des activités internationales du Québec," *Le Canada et le Québec sur la Scène Internationale*, ed. Paul Painchaud (Montréal : Université du Québec, 1977), 543. The Paris delegation was opened in 1961. Although there are full privileges and diplomatic immunities, it is not on the diplomatic list. Delegations in Mexico and Venezuela, however, are accorded full diplomatic status without such qualification.

2. Robert Keohane and Joseph Nye, "Transgovernmental Relations and International Organizations," *World Politics* 27 (October 1974): 39-62.

3. Nye coedited a volume on U.S.-Canada relations, and Keohane coauthored with him an introductory essay, "Introduction: The Complex Politics of Canadian-American Interdependence." Although the volume includes Kal J. Holsti and Thomas Allen Levy, "Bilateral Institutions and Transgovernmental Relations between Canada and the United States," which deals specifically with the transgovernmental activities of Canadian provinces, Keohane and Nye ignore this content in their introduction and in Nye's concluding essay. See Annette Baker Fox, Alfred O. Hero, Jr., and Joseph S. Nye, Jr., eds., *Canada and the United States: Transnational and Transgovernmental Relations*, Special Issue of *International Organization* 28 (Autumn 1974). For other discussions of territorial transgovernmentalism and the foreign activities of Canadian provinces, see Ronald G. Atkey, "The Role of Provinces in International Affairs," *International Journal* 26 (Winter 1970/71): 249-273; Ronald G. Atkey, "Provincial Transnational Activity: An Approach to a Current Issue in Canadian Federalism," in Ontario Advisory Committee on Confederation, *Background Papers and Reports*, Volume 2 (Toronto: Queen's Printer of Ontario, 1970); Earl H. Fry, "The International Relations of Sub-National Governments: Coping with the 'Many Voices' Phenomenon in an Interdependent World," paper prepared for presentation at the Roundtable on Pluralism and International Relations, International Political Science Association, Corfu, September 1980; P. R. Johannson, "Provincial International Activities," *International Journal* 33 (Spring 1978): 357-78; Richard Leach, "Central Versus Provincial Authority in Making Foreign Policy for Canada," paper presented to the Seminar on Canadian-United States Relations of the University Consortium for Research on North America, Harvard University, October 1981; Thomas Allen Levy, "Le role des provinces," *Le Canada et le Québec sur la Scène Internationale*, ed. Paul Painchaud, 109-45; Thomas Allen Levy and Don Munton, "Federal-provincial dimensions of state-provincial relations," *International Perspectives* (March/April 1976): 23-7; Garth Stevenson, "The Distribution of Foreign Policy Making Power Between the Federal Government and the Provinces," paper prepared for the Seminar on Canadian-United States Relations of the University Consortium for Research on North America,

Harvard University, April 1980; Roger Frank Swanson, "The Range of Direct Relations Between States and Provinces," *International Perspectives* (March/April 1976): 18-23; Roger Frank Swanson, *Intergovernmental Perspectives on the Canada-U.S. Relationship* (New York: New York University Press, 1978); Michael Tucker, *Canadian Foreign Policy: Contemporary Issues and Themes* (Toronto: McGraw Hill Ryerson, 1980), especially 52-72. On the activities of particular provinces, see the Special Issue of *Le Canada dans le Monde, Les Provinces Canadiennes : Importance et Orientations de Leurs Relations Internationales, Choix*, report of the XIIIe Congress of the Centre Québécois des Relations Internationales, Montréal, 8-9 October 1981, with articles by Claude Roquet on Quebec, Raymond Daigle on the Atlantic provinces, Denis Massicotte on Ontario, Wayne Clifford on the western provinces, and a comment by Christopher Leman; also, P. R. Johannson, "British Columbia's Relations with the United States," *Canadian Public Administration*, Summer 1978; Bernard Bonin, "A Foreign Economic Policy for Quebec?" paper prepared for the Seminar on Canadian-United States Relations of the University Consortium for Research on North America, Harvard University, February 1982; Painchaud, *Le Canada et le Québec sur la Scène Internationale*, Part 4, pp. 441-544; Department of Federal and Intergovernmental Affairs Alberta, *Ninth Annual Report, March 31, 1982* (Edmonton: Department of Federal and Intergovernmental Affairs, October 1982); Ministry of Intergovernmental Affairs Ontario, *Ontario's International Relations: A Perspective, 1982-1983* (Toronto: Ministry of Intergovernmental Affairs, September 1983); Ministère des Affaires Intergouvernementales, *Rapport annuel 1981-1982* (Québec City, Ministère des Affaires Intergouvernementales, November 1982).

4. Samuel P. Huntington, "Transnational Organizations in World Politics," *World Politics* 25 (April 1973): 333-68.

5. Keohane and Nye, "Transgovernmental Relations," 41.

6. Even though their emphasis in examples falls exclusively on the foreign contacts of subunits within the central level, the universal nature of the Keohane/ Nye definition of transgovernmentalism legitimizes the application of their framework to territorial subunits such as the Canadian provinces.

7. Keohane and Nye, "Transgovernmental Relations," 49.

8. These categories or variations on them are proposed in the two articles by Johannson, "Provincial International Activities" and "British Columbia's Relations with the United States"; and by Swanson, *Intergovernmental Perspectives*.

9. Leach, "Central Versus Provincial Authority," 16; Johannson, *ibid.*, 358; also, Levy and Munton, "Federal-Provincial Dimensions of State-Provincial Relations," 23.

10. Leach, ibid.; Keohane and Nye, "Transgovernmental Relations," 42; Johannson, ibid., 362-3; Stevenson, "The Distribution of Foreign Policy Making," 5, 9-10.

11. Leach, *ibid.*, says provincial protest affected the federal decision on the BOMARC missile under Diefenbaker, 18.

12. Interview with Gilles Mathieu, Office for Federal-Provincial Relations, Department of External Affairs, Ottawa, 10 June 1982.

13. On the impact of jurisdictional responsibilities on international activity, see Leach, "Central Versus Provincial Authority," 1-3; Stevenson, "The Distribution of Foreign Policy Making," 11-5; both articles cited of Atkey, Johannson, "Provincial International Activities," 361-2 and "British Columbia's Relations with the United States;" Levy and Munton, "Federal-Provincial Dimensions."

14. Levy and Munton, *ibid.*, specifically link bureaucratic growth to the increased international activity of the provinces.

15. Norman Ornstein, "American States, Canadian Provinces, and Foreign Policy Decisions" (Paper prepared for the Seminar on Canadian-United States Relations of the University Consortium for Research on North America, Harvard University, April 1980).

16. Department of Federal and Intergovernmental Affairs Alberta, *Ninth Annual Report*, 35.

17. Interview with senior official, Canadian Embassy, Washington, D.C., 13 February 1984. For a discussion of this argument and the lobbying efforts

of provinces in the U.S., see Charles F. Doran and Joel J. Sokolsky, *Canada and the Congress: Lobbying in Washington* (Washington, D.C.: Center of Canadian Studies, 1983), 37-9, 44-5, 91-5, 135, 138, 152-4.

18. Swanson, *Intergovernmental Perspectives*, 222.

19. Swanson, "The Range of Direct Relations," 18.

20. Telephone interview with Wayne Clifford, Executive Director of the International Division, Edmonton, 15 February 1984. The $2.7 million spent by the Department of Federal and Intergovernmental Affairs on offices abroad does not represent the total cost of maintenance. Renting of the offices is covered by Public Works and Economic Development and probably adds another 60-100 percent to the figure borne by FIGA. In response to a question from the Legislative Assembly, FIGA is calculating the precise overall cost of maintaining offices abroad.

21. Federal and Intergovernmental Affairs Alberta, Excerpts from Premier Lougheed's speech at the Canadian Pacific Rim Opportunities Conference, Calgary, 7 October 1983.

22. Interview with Lorne Sivertson, ISBD, Victoria, 17 June 1982; interview with Jack McKeown, ISBD, Vancouver, 18 June 1982. The overall investment includes $350 million for a 130 kilometer rail spur; $150 million for a new coal port at Prince Rupert; construction of a new town, access roads, and development of the coal fields.

23. Much skepticism has been expressed about the project, especially by the provincial New Democratic Party in opposition. British Columbia's investment should not be recovered until close to the end of the twenty year contract, and Japan's direct investment is modest. The province itself has had to put up $.5 billion, and none of the coal extracted will be for domestic use. Hence, the entire development is designed to make British Columbia a resource extracting and importing province to a foreign buyer unwilling to post the necessary capital.

24. Telephone interview with Peter Heap, whose Federal-Provincial relations section of the British Columbia Ministry of Intergovernmental Relations deals with international questions, 13 February 1984.

25. Ministry of Intergovernmental Affairs Ontario, *Ontario's International Relations*, 18-9.

26. Telephone interview with John Carson, head of the International Relations Branch, Ontario, 16 February 1984.

27. Swanson, *Intergovernmental Perspectives*, 240.

28. Holsti and Levy, "Bilateral Institutions," 888; Stevenson, "The Distribution of Foreign Policy Making," 17-8.

29. Johannson, "Provincial International Activities," 370-4.

30. Two articles prepared for the *Background Papers* of the Ontario Advisory Committee on Confederation are useful: Mr. Justice Bora Laskin, "The Provinces and International Agreements" (Spring 1965); R. J. Delisle, "Treaty-Making Power in Canada" (July 1966). See also Atkey, "The Role of Provinces," and Jacomy-Millette, "Aspects juridiques."

31. Telephone interview with Jim Eldridge, Deputy Secretary to the Cabinet for Federal-Provincial Relations, Winnipeg, 16 February 1984.

32. Telephone interview with Cyril Abery, Deputy Minister, Intergovernmental Affairs Secretariat, St. John's, 16 February 1984.

33. Telephone interview with Arthur Parks, Deputy Minister, Office of the Premier, Fredericton, 16 February 1984.

34. Telephone interview with Doug Boylan, Secretary to the Cabinet, Executive Council Office, Charlottetown, 17 February 1984.

35. There is a long history of provincial activity and an equally long history of federal reaction. A celebrated early study introduced by Lester B. Pearson in 1968 was prepared by the Secretary of State for External Affairs, Paul Martin, "Federalism and International Relations." This government document (long out of print) made comparisons to ten other federal systems and emphasized the ways in which the federal government cooperated with the provinces. Other discussion on federal mechanisms may be found in Leach, "Central Versus Provincial Authority," 4-13, 23-8; Stevenson, "The Distribution of Foreign Policy Making," 27-9; and Atkey, "Provincial Transnational Activity."

36. Confidential interview with senior official in Department of External Affairs, November 1982.

37. "Mechanisms for Federal/Provincial Coordination in International Economic Relations" (Internal memorandum of Federal Coordination Office, Department of External Affairs, Ottawa, January 1982, Mimeo).

38. Saskatchewan officials, for example, found themselves invited to various meetings in the Department of External Affairs during the first year of the reorganization.

39. Tucker, *Canadian Foreign Policy*, 54-5, details Ottawa's financial contributions to the Agency for Cultural and Technical Cooperation in 1977.

40. Huntington, "Transnational Organizations in World Politics," 342.

41. Levy and Munton, "Federal-Provincial Dimensions of State-Provincial Relations."

42. Elliot J. Feldman and Jerome E. Milch, "Organizing Disunity: Rational Planning in Canadian Administration," *Encounter with Canada: Essays in the Social Sciences*, ed. Wayne Reilly (Durham: Duke University Center for International Studies, 1980), especially 95-9; Levy and Munton, ibid.

43. *Ibid.*, and at greater length in Elliot J. Feldman and Jerome E. Milch, *The Politics of Canadian Airport Development: Lessons for Federalism* (Durham: Duke University Press, 1983).

44. The term "domestication," referring to the formulation of Canadian foreign policy as an extension of domestic politics, is used by Peyton Lyon, "The Trudeau Doctrine," *International Journal* 26 (Winter 1970/71).

Selected Readings

Keating, T., ed. *The Provinces and Canadian Foreign Policy*. Toronto: Canadian Institute for International Affairs, 1986.

Meekison, J. P. "Provincial Activity Adds New Dimension to Federalism: A Western View." *International Perspectives* (March/April, 1977): 8-11.

Morris, G. L. "The Treaty-Making Power: A Canadian Dilemma." *Canadian Bar Review* 45 (1967): 497-503.

Stairs, Denis. "Foreign Policy." In S. M. Beck and I. Bernier, eds. *Canada and the New Constitution, The Unfinished Agenda*. Vol. I. Montreal: Institute for Research in Public Policy, 1983, 155-87.

Swanson, R. F. *State/Provincial Interaction: A Study of Relations between U.S. States and Canadian Provinces*. Washington, D.C.: United States State Department, 1974.

16. AN OUTSIDER'S OBSERVATIONS OF FEDERAL-PROVINCIAL RELATIONS AMONG CONSENTING ADULTS

Donald V. Smiley

These are an outsider's observations of what I have come to call executive federalism. My credentials as an outsider if not an observer are outstanding. I have never attended a federal-provincial conference and my ignominious career as a minor functionary of the federal and then the Saskatchewan governments did not involve me in these relations. And I can assure Gordon Robertson and other guardians of official secrecy in the conduct of public business that since leaving government employment about 20 years ago I have never read a classified document—except of course those published by the media. I am a law-abiding man and I would not want to disobey the Official Secrets Act or provincial variants thereof or to connive that others should do so. Beyond that, I hold to another principle to the effect that I *will* sound off about governmental matters based on a reading of the public record alone and if my judgements are for that reason superficial and perverse the fault is with those who withhold the necessary information from me and other private citizens.

I am not totally an outsider of course because as a university teacher of Canadian gov-

ernment I "live off" federalism. Perhaps I can be accused of gross ingratitude for being as critical of it as I am in this paper. In a sense I should regard myself as did a senior scholar of American law who responded in the 1950s to a query by saying that he would not have the slightest objection to taking an oath to support the Constitution of the United States because for over 40 years the Constitution had supported *him*. I have sometimes written as if the complex and mysterious system of executive federalism in Canada was one of the most distinguished achievements of the mind and heart of man and in this connection I have now and again quoted John Porter's contrary assessment with some derision: " . . . it may be speculated that (Canadian) federalism as such has meaning only for politicians and senior civil servants who work the complex machinery they have set up, as well as for scholars who provide a continuing commentary on it, but that it has very little meaning for the bulk of the population."[1] I am no longer as sure as I once was that Porter was totally wrong.

My charges against executive federalism are these:

— First, it contributes to undue secrecy in the conduct of the public's business.

— Second, it contributes to an unduly low level of citizen-participation in public affairs.

— Third, it weakens and dilutes the accountability of governments to their respective legislatures and to the wider public.

Donald V. Smiley, "An Outsider's Observations of Federal-Provincial Relations Among Consenting Adults," in *Confrontation and Collaboration: Intergovernmental Relations in Canada Today*, ed. Richard Simeon (Toronto: The Institute of Public Administration of Canada, 1979), 105-113. Reprinted by permission of The Institute of Public Administration of Canada. The essay has been abridged to suit the needs of this volume.

— Fourth, it frustrates a number of matters of crucial public concern from coming on the public agenda and being dealt with by the public authorities.
— Fifth, it has been a contributing factor to the indiscriminate growth of government activities.
— Sixth, it leads to continuous and often unresolved conflicts among governments, conflicts which serve no purpose broader than the political and bureaucratic interests of those involved with them.

First to secrecy. It is I believe undeniable that executive federalism contributes to the undue secrecy by which public affairs are conducted in Canada. This secrecy is not very profound—there is a great deal of information about federal-provincial affairs on the public record and journalists and even scholars can penetrate what confidentiality there is in many cases. However, we are likely to have a federal freedom of information act and corresponding legislation in most if not all of the provinces in the next five years or so and it is almost inevitable that these enactments will confer on governments the power to withhold from public scrutiny documents involving federal-provincial relations.

The second charge is that executive federalism contributes to an unduly low level of citizen-participation in public affairs. In part this is a result of the secrecy to which I have already referred. In larger part it is a result of the extraordinary complexity of the process. For example, how can one reasonably expect intelligent public or even parliamentary debate on the Federal-Provincial Fiscal Arrangements and Established Programs Financing Act of 1977—perhaps one of the most important enactments of the Canadian Parliament in recent decades? And I would also defy anyone without specialized training to make sense of the national dimension and emergency doctrines as these were argued in the Anti-Inflation reference of 1976. But apart from secrecy

and complexity, executive federalism discourages citizen participation by contributing to a very minimal role for political parties in the formulation of public policy and in the articulation and aggregation of public demands. Political parties—and I am speaking here of the extra-parliamentary components of parties rather than caucuses and cabinets—are not very influential in matters related to policy, although they of course play a vital role in the nomination of candidates for public office and strive to elect such persons. So far as governments themselves are concerned, partisan complexions are not very important in federal-provincial relations and it would be a most extraordinary event if any intergovernmental conference divided on partisan lines. Executive federalism thus restricts the role of parties in public policy and the constructive participation of citizens in the formulation of policy by party activity.

Federalism in its Canadian variant weakens the accountability of governments to their respective legislatures and the wider public. As participation was the cause of a decade ago, so is the accountability of those who act in the name of governments today. In a formal sense the British-type parliamentary system meets the accountability criterion well—ministers are responsible for the acts carried out under the legal authority conferred upon them and the cabinet is collectively responsible for its policies to the legislature. It is almost trite to say that these traditional doctrines of ministerial and cabinet responsibility are now under question as being misleading or inoperative or impossible to attain. My own views on the matter are confused. The pristine doctrines of ministerial and cabinet responsibility cannot be applied without some significant modifications to governments with the scope of activity which prevails today. Yet to reject these doctrines completely is surely indefensible for without them we appear to have no guides to the most fundamental of political relations—between governments and legislatures, among members of the political executive, between elected politicians and bureaucrats, between governments and those whom they govern. At any rate, federalism contributes to the weakening of the responsibility of the executive to the legislature and Thomas Courchene has rightly judged this of the 1977 legislation concerning federal-provincial financial relations:

> " . . . the entire negotiation process with respect to the new fiscal arrangements essentially bypassed the Parliament of Canada. It is true that the Fiscal Arrangements Act is an act of Parliament. But our federal representatives were effectively presented with a *fait accompli*, hammered out between representatives of Ottawa and the ten provincial governments. The bulk of the Commons debate on the bill was directed toward sorting out the details of the various provisions. There was no debate in the traditional sense of the term . . . . Public opinion was not brought to bear on the new arrangements. This is in marked contrast to the information that has been available in the print and electronic media relating to the upcoming revision of the new Bank Act, for example. Yet the Bank Act revision pales in comparison with renegotiating the financial bases of the federation in terms of the impact on the Canada of tomorrow."[2]

To the extent then that the actual locus of decision-making in respect to an increasing number of public matters has shifted from individual governments to intergovernmental groupings the effective accountability of executives both to their respective legislatures and to those whom they govern is weakened.

My argument then is that executive federalism contributes to secret, non-participatory, and non-accountable processes of government.

But in an even more crucial sense federalism puts some issues permanently or almost permanently on the public agenda and keeps others off. The American political scientist E. E. Schattschneider wrote: "All forms of political organization have a bias in favor of the exploitation of some kinds of conflict and the suppression of others . . . . Some issues are organized into politics while others are organized out."[3] There *are* important regional and provincial differences in Canada—Simeon and Elkins have demonstrated variations in basic orientations to government as one goes from province to province,[4] the provincial and regional economics differ in the levels of income they provide to their citizens and their kinds of development, most French-speaking Canadians live in Quebec and in areas contiguous to Quebec and Ontario and New Brunswick. But as Simeon has cogently argued, these differences do not in themselves explain why Canadian politics is almost monopolized by territorially-based conflicts to the neglect of other issues which divide Canadians along other cleavages[5]—for example, rich as against poor, authoritarians as against liberals, the upwardly-mobile as against those with stable or declining status and so on. Why is Ottawa so much more preoccupied with the reduction of regional economic disparities than with redistributive measures on an interpersonal basis? How was it that the crucial debate over public retirement pensions of the mid-1960s involved hardly at all the intergenerational distribution of burdens and benefits? I think I could argue that the continuing competition for tax points in respect to levies on individual incomes pales in significance with the circumstance that the existing system by any coherent standards of equity confers indefensible benefits on some citizens and imposes indefensible burdens on others but there is little or no debate on these latter lines. Let us be frank about it. Executive federalism "organizes into politics" the interests of governments and of those private groupings which are territorially concentrated. The system almost by its inherent nature weakens the influence of other interests.

Federalism is thus an important influence in perpetuating inequalities among Canadians. This is so despite countervailing efforts of the central government to narrow regional economic disparities and to sustain national minimum standards of public expenditures and services by the provincial and local governments.

One of the results of the continuing conflicts between Ottawa and the provinces is to displace other conflicts among Canadians, particularly those between the relatively advantaged and those who are less so. So long as the major cleavages are between governments, inequalities *within* the provinces are buttressed. I would also argue but in a tentative way that the processes of executive federalism have contributed to the somewhat indiscriminate growth of government activity in the past two decades. I am very much aware here of Richard Bird's caution in his distinguished study that " . . . the ratio of total government expenditure to GNP is not a meaningful subject for analysis . . . ."[6] and that in order to understand this general phenomenon we must look at the factors determining the levels of public expenditure on particular functions. Yet the expansion of the public sector seems not to have led and seems not to be leading in the direction of social and economic equality and in itself has created new forms of privilege. The relation between federalism and the increases in public expenditure is complex. I have the impression that the dynamics are somewhat different in the Atlantic region from those prevailing elsewhere in Canada. In a recent essay on Prince Edward Island where government and politics are the dominant industries Frank MacKinnon argues that "individual and community effort decrease as large government takes over an increasing proportion of the activities of the society."[7] The historian T. W. Acheson has said this of the recent involvement of the national authorities in the Maritime provinces:

> Another side effect of the federal intervention was the creation of a new bourgeoisie elite composed of professional civil servants, medical doctors and academics who joined the lawyer-politician-businessman leadership of the community and gave to it a distinctly professional flavour. Indeed, with its emphasis upon place and sinecures, and with the patron-client relationship which the monopolistic hierarchies of provincial

governments and institutions of higher learning encouraged, Maritime society began more closely to resemble an eighteenth- than a nineteenth-century society . . . . It was a captive elite largely dependent for opportunity, position, and status on federal resources and ultimately subject to the will of the federal government. Most important, it was an elite with no resource base, one incapable of generating anything more than services, producers of primary or secondary goods played little role in its ranks.[8]

While governmental and political activity is less dominant in the larger provinces there has arisen a competitiveness between the federal and provincial authorities that has resulted in a costly duplication of effort.

My last charge against executive federalism which I shall discuss in somewhat more detail than the others is that it leads to continuing conflicts among governments and that, to borrow a horrible item from the sociologists, these conflicts are in large part dysfunctional. I should not for a moment deny that in public affairs and elsewhere there are useful conflicts among people—for example, students of the institution of marriage tell us that the most loving and long-lasting unions are of couples who fight a good deal. So far as our governmental system is concerned, both courts and legislatures proceed by adversarial methods, parties compete vigorously with one another for votes and there may be creative conflicts within individual governments such as those between functional departments and central agencies. And if we were to come to a situation where there were no differences between Ottawa and the provinces some of us would be uneasy because that would mean that one order of government was able to dominate the other completely.

One of the crucial elements in contemporary executive federalism is the increasing importance of intergovernmental affairs specialists, of officials and agencies not responsible for particular programs but rather the relations between jurisdictions. In the context of American federalism Samuel Beer of Harvard University has variously designated this complex of interests as the "topocracy" and the "intergovernmental lobby" and has analyzed its continuing conflicts with those responsible for specific functional activities of government.[9] Claude Morin and the able group of young people he gathered around him in the Quebec Department of Federal-Provincial Affairs in the 1960s were the harbingers of this new breed in Canada. The role of the intergovernmental affairs specialist is to protect and extend the powers of the jurisdiction for which he works, and an important element of this power adheres in its financial resources. Despite the high-flown justifications that such persons make for their occupations, this is in fact their only important role. The game is at least as intricate as international diplomacy, with which it shares many similarities, and the players have the satisfaction that no one has as yet been killed because of their activities. The context is clubby and when new members join they soon discover that they can't be very influential unless and until they accept the almost wholly implicit rules of the club. In his stance toward other governments the federal-provincial relations specialist has a single-minded devotion to the power of his jurisdiction. And because his counterparts in other governments have the same motivations, conflict is inevitable. In his relations with elements of his own government the objective of the federal-provincial specialist is to ensure that operating agencies will not by collaborative intergovernmental interactions weaken the power of federal or provincial jurisdictions as such.

I have come to the pessimistic conclusion that as governments become more sophisticated in their operations conflict among these governments will increase in scope and intensity.[10] Almost by definition, sophistication in this sense means that jurisdictions will rank and make more explicit their objectives and will be concerned with increasingly precise measures of

evaluation of actual and projected policies. And as governments are disposed to conduct their operations in a less fragmented and haphazard way it is inevitable that they will strive to control their environments and to make these less uncertain. It is almost trite to say that an important part of these environments are composed of other governments. In general then, the related factors of the increasing influence of intergovernmental specialists and the increasing maturity of governments leads directly to continuous and unresolved conflicts between Ottawa and the provinces. My impression is that on both sides the power of one level or the other has become an important value independent of the objectives towards which the exercise of such powers are or could be directed.[11] Further, it seems that many of these actual and emergent conflicts are not susceptible to authoritative resolution. So far as such matters as the provision of costly health, welfare, and educational services are concerned the characteristic situation is that the provinces have the jurisdiction while Ottawa has superior fiscal resources. In A. D. Scott's terms the federal government will in such circumstances "buy jurisdiction" at a mutually-agreed "price" between the two levels, although under the Canadian ground-rules the federal authorities will in perpetuity pay for jurisdiction they bought in the past and subsequently relinquished. The circumstances in respect to the regulatory activities of government—telecommunications, consumer protection, transportation, environmental control, and so on—are less susceptible to authoritative resolution. Here jurisdiction is often divided—and in many cases in dispute—and Ottawa's superior fiscal resources cannot be used to secure provincial compliance. And it is in respect to the regulatory activities of government, along with the new disputes about the administration of justice, where federal-provincial conflicts have become most intense.

*   *   *

Notes

1. John Porter, *The Vertical Mosaic* (Toronto: University of Toronto Press, 1965), 384.

2. Thomas Courchene, "The New Fiscal Arrangements and the Economics of Federalism," *Options*, Proceedings of the Conference on the Future of the Canadian Federation (Toronto: University of Toronto, 1977), 345.

3. E.E. Schattschneider, *The Semi-Sovereign People* (New York: Holt, Rinehart and Winston, 1966), 71.

4. Richard Simeon and David Elkins, "Regional Political Cultures in Canada" *Canadian Journal of Political Science 7* (September 1974): 394-437.

5. Richard Simeon, "Regionalism and Canadian Political Institutions," in J. Peter Meekison, ed., *Canadian Federalism: Myth or Reality*, third edition (Toronto: Methuen of Canada, 1977), 292-304.

6. Richard Bird, *The Growth of Government Spending in Canada* (Toronto: Canadian Tax Foundation, 1970), 189.

7. Frank MacKinnon, "Prince Edward Island: Big Engine, Little Body" in Martin Robin, ed., *Canadian Provincial Politics*, second edition (Scarborough: Prentice-Hall of Canada, 1978), 242.

8. T.W. Acheson, "The Maritimes and 'Empire Canada'" in David Jay Bercuson, ed., *Canada and the Burden of Unity* (Toronto: Macmillan of Canada, 1977), 104-5.

9. See Samuel Beer, "Federalism, Nationalism and Democracy in America" *American Political Science Review* 72 (March 1978): 9-21; and his "The Adoption of General Revenue-Sharing: A Case Study in Public Sector Politics," *Public Policy* 24 (Spring 1976): 127-95.

10. I have argued this in more detail in *Canada in Question: Federalism in the Seventies*, second edition (Toronto: McGraw-Hill Ryerson of Canada, 1976), 76-9.

11. A recent example of this is the way that the governments and various interest groups defended their constitutional preferences on the anti-inflation reference of 1976. The stakes as here perceived were not entirely or even mainly the 1975 legislation but rather the implications of the Supreme Court decision for future jurisdictional disputes. See Peter H. Russell, "The Anti-Inflation Case: The Anatomy of a Constitutional Decision," *Canadian Public Administration* 20 (Winter 1977): 632-65.

Selected Readings

Cairns, A. C. "The Other Crisis of Canadian Federalism." *Canadian Public Administration* 22:2 (Summer 1979): 175-95.

Kernaghan, K. "Intergovernmental Administrative Relations in Canada." In K. Kernaghan, ed. *Public Administration in Canada*. 5th edition. Toronto: Methuen, 1985, 152-65.

Reid, J. "Federal-Provincial Conferences: Their Implications for Legislators and Political Parties." *Canadian Parliamentary Review* 4:3 (Autumn 1981): 2-5.

Smiley, D. V. "Federalism and the Legislative Process in Canada." In W. A. W. Neilson and J. C. MacPherson, eds. *The Legislative Process in Canada: The Need for Reform*. Montreal: Institute for Research on Public Policy, 1978, 73-113.

Smiley, D. V. "The Structural Problem of Canadian Federalism." *Canadian Public Administration* 14:3 (Fall 1971): 326-43.

17. COMPETITION AND COOPERATION IN THE CANADIAN FEDERAL SYSTEM

Albert Breton

At its simplest, a federal state can be formally defined as a type of political organization in which there are at least two levels of jurisdiction—in Canada, national and provincial—between which the entire set of constitutional powers is divided. The assignment of these powers between the governmental levels is not made by one level alone. That distinguishes federalism from confederalism, a system in which the assignment of powers is made by the provinces alone, and from unitary states, structures in which powers are assigned by senior governments acting in isolation. According to that definition, Canada is and has been a federation and never a confederation. The Canadian provinces, on the other hand, in their relationship with their municipalities, are unitary states.

The division of powers and the mode through which it is effected define federalism well, albeit in a way that is too formal to be very useful in understanding how such a system actually works. From that point of view, what is much more important are the implications of any division of powers for the operations of, and relationships between, the governments of the federation, all of which are responsible governments. The central and most important implication is that in the search for popular support—something that is as needed for the

effectiveness of governing parties as revenue is essential for the effectiveness of business firms—the governments of a federation will find themselves competing with each other. Federalism thus adds more competition to that already present in responsible or party government.

One point needs emphasis. Political competition is not something that politicians choose or want, whatever their commitment to federalism and, more broadly, to liberty and to democracy. In that respect, they are exactly like business entrepreneurs who do not want competition either. Competition arises from the necessity to respond to the actions of others; it is "forced" on people by the environment. One does not even have to be aware that one is competing to be competitive. A business firm that adopts a new technology to reduce its costs is acting competitively; one that advertises and places some of its output on sale is acting in a competitive fashion; someone who supports a particular social movement or a particular lobby is competing; as is the politician who seeks harmony with provincial governments by removing the contentious questions from the agenda of federal-provincial encounters.

There is so much mystification about this that I must dwell on two corollary points at the risk of seeming to insist on the obvious for those who have seen their way clear on the subject. First, there is the whole bag of issues that are best summarized by the words "cooperative federalism." What is cooperative federalism and how is it to be distinguished from other types of federalisms? To my knowledge, the expression has never been formally defined. That may not be a lacuna because we all have, from practical exper-

Albert Breton, "Supplementary Statement," in *Report of the Royal Commission on the Economic Union and Development Prospects for Canada*, vol. 3 (Ottawa: Supply and Services Canada, 1985), 486-526. Reproduced with permission of the Minister of Supply and Services Canada. The essay has been abridged and edited to suit the needs of this volume.

ience and observation, a good intuitive idea of what is meant by these two words. Two or more persons working together to lift a heavy object; two or more persons engaged in a search for something lost; two or more persons removing snow from a road; these are examples of the kind of behaviour we have in mind when we think of cooperation. In other words, someone helping someone else achieve a certain goal or objective.

Cooperative federalism by analogy would exist if all the politicians of a federation worked together to achieve some collective end. Instead of working on their own for their citizens, governments would work together for the betterment of all "the people." Before examining what is meant by cooperative federalism in more detail, I would like the reader to ask him or herself why it is that we do not, as societies, organize the search for justice on a cooperative basis, but instead set defence against prosecuting attorneys in courts of law? Why do we not organize the working of party politics on a cooperative basis, but instead pit political parties against each other in grand electoral contests? Why do we not organize the search for truth on a cooperative basis, but instead require scholars and scientists to compete for research funds and for limited space in research publications? And, finally—though the list could go on—why do we not organize the production of goods and services on a cooperative basis, but instead implement laws that make cooperation an offence?

These examples underline the fact that in some areas, cooperation is *not* an efficient principle of social organization and that it is less efficient than competition, essentially because cooperation can easily degenerate into collusion, conspiracy, and connivance, and that this is not necessarily good! In the case of federalism, would cooperation be a better principle of social organization than competition? To answer the question, it must be recognized that cooperative federalism is aimed at removing the competition which is a natural by-product of federal organization.

Consequently, to be able to answer the question, it is necessary to know whether competition is a "good" feature of political organizations.

I have posed the question here, however, because I wish to stress that the notion of cooperative federalism is part and parcel of the politics of "elite accommodation" which plays such an important role in the dynamics of party governments. Indeed, in practice, cooperative federalism is nothing but executive federalism. This has been defined by Smiley "as the relations between elected and appointed officials of the two orders of government in federal-provincial interactions and among the executives of the provinces in interprovincial interactions."[1] The executive federalism contemplated by cooperative federalists, however, effectively extends to all the areas of federal-provincial contact. It transfers to executive and bureaucratic bargaining and negotiation what properly belongs to the realm of the political.

Cooperative federalism does not necessarily eliminate federalist competition, but by moving it into executive and bureaucratic offices and corridors, it mutes its public manifestations and its effectiveness. The heart of cooperative federalism is secret deals, not the stuff on which a lively democracy thrives! There are other implications of the doctrine of cooperative federalism; I mention two.

A first is a by-product of drumming into the psyche of Canadians the belief that federalism is or should be cooperative. Once that is achieved, it provides a fruitful background for the arguments of those, sometimes in one province, sometimes in another, who wish to promote and foster separatism. Indeed, a process that is inherently competitive, even if it is called cooperative, is bound to throw up incidents which separatists—themselves competitive individuals—will use to argue that "the system does not work," because on a particular matter the politicians of a province have been rebuffed or have simply lost in the competitive game. It would be relatively easy to document that the rhetoric of Canadian separatists is often based on the notion that federalism is not as cooperative as one had been led to believe it should be. I cannot undertake that documentation task here. I simply note that if Canadians had been helped to understand that federalist politics, like all politics, is inherently competitive, the propaganda of separatism would have fallen on more barren ground.

A second implication of the doctrine of cooperative federalism relates to the condemnation, by those who adhere to it, of unilateralism, that is, of independent action by any one government of the federation. Unilateral action by one government is, of course, a derogation from cooperation, since when one is acting alone one is not cooperating. Consequently, those who espouse cooperative federalism decry unilateral action on the part of any government in the federation. Although in principle, the condemnation applies to all, in practice it strikes much harder at the federal government, simply because the provinces, if they want to act in unison, have to come to an agreement—something that is not easy to do for essentially competitive entities. To put it differently, in the normal course of affairs, the central government is likely to act unilaterally more often than the provinces, to the extent that these wish to act as one, because the costs of coordination are positive. A condemnation of unilateralism, if enforced, would therefore affect the central government more than the provinces.

Cooperative federalism, because it proscribes unilateral action, is therefore a disguised ploy to shackle the federal government, to prevent it from addressing the problems it alone can resolve and is constitutionally responsible for resolving. Indeed, condemning federal unilateralism is condemning the federal government for acting constitutionally! This is so true that if one takes the trouble to go behind the language of cooperative federalism, to the reality of the arguments which it seeks to convey, one discovers either confederalism or a conservative view which seeks to reduce the role of the federal

government and, indeed, of all governments in society.

In concluding this argument, I note that the condemnation of unilateralism is also a denial that the division of powers between orders of government is essential to federalism. That indeed is the crux of the matter. Cooperative federalism, if it came to pass, would deny federalism itself. Those who seek cooperative federalism and labour for its realization, seek and labour for a unitary state disguised in the trappings of federalism, but from which competition would have been reduced to a minimum or even eliminated.

The second corollary point related to the mystification surrounding the notion of political competition pertains to the language of competition and of federalism. Competition in the marketplace, in courtrooms, in parliaments, on hustings, in university seminars, and wherever it takes place is sometimes smooth, so smooth that one could be led into believing that it is not there. But at other times, it is rough, so rough that outsiders are often at a loss in trying to understand why so much energy and effort are displayed, why opponents are characterized in such vile fashion, why the parties become uncouth and impolite in the process of competing. In describing this second circumstance, it is not uncommon for the outsiders, who would have no problem with "well-behaved" competition, to describe the situation in terms of conflict, rancour, combat, suspicion, disharmony, and so on, and to attach to these expressions a negative connotation. The stage is then set for appeals to cooperation and for a rhetoric that praises the virtues of cooperative federalism.

Words have emotional content. For that reason, debates and disagreements are sometimes resolved by using a different language. It is important, however, that the change in vocabulary be only that, not the occasion for unnecessary changes in institutions. When competition is acrimonious one may wish to reduce its acrimoniousness; that can be a legitimate objective. But it is not because we choose to relabel a competitive process by some other name, such as conflict, disharmony, or rivalry, that we will have improved things. Indeed, if relabelling leads to the search for unwarranted institutional changes, we may have worsened the situation. Prosecuting and defence attorneys may be uncouth and antagonistic to each other; things could possibly be better if such behaviour did not exist, but surely justice would not be well served, if, to remove such behaviour, courtroom procedures were transformed from competitive into cooperative ones!

Many a time I have been struck by the fact that those who resist the notion of competition and its reality in fact take offence at the language of competition. The question of how a language can be made more genteel and gracious is an interesting and difficult one. It may be possible to have a genteel and graceful competitive federalism, but whether it is or not has little bearing on whether competitive federalism is desirable or not.

*   *   *

Notes

1. D. V. Smiley, *Canada in Question: Federalism in the Eighties*, 3d edition (Toronto: McGraw-Hill Ryerson, 1980), 91.

Selected Readings

Fletcher, F. J., and Wallace, D. C. "Federal-Provincial Relations and the Making of Public Policy in Canada: A Review of Case Studies." In R. Simeon, ed. *Division of Powers and Public Policy*, Research Studies of the Royal Commission on the Economic Union and Development Prospects for Canada. Vol. 61. Toronto: University of Toronto Press, 1985, 125-205.

McRoberts, K. "Unilateralism, Bilateralism and Multilateralism: Approaches to Canadian Federalism." In R. Simeon, ed. *Intergovernmental Relations*, Research Studies of the Royal Commission on the Economic Union and Development Prospects for Canada. Vol. 63. Toronto: University of Toronto Press, 1985, 71-130.

Norrie, K., Simeon, R., and Krasnick, M. *Federalism and Economic Union in Canada*. Research Studies of the Royal Commission on the Economic Union and Development Prospects for Canada. Vol. 59. Toronto: University Press, 1985.

Sproule-Jones, M. *Public Choice and Federalism in Canada and Australia*. Canberra: Australian National University Press, 1975.

INTERGOVERNMENTAL RELATIONS

What issues emerge in Canada as continuing matters of federal-provincial dispute? Who are the major intergovernmental "actors" and what negotiating strategies do they employ in their dealings with the federal government? This section includes four essays that focus on the relationship between Ottawa and a particular province (Ontario and Quebec) or a regionally based grouping of provinces (Atlantic Canada and western Canada).

Donald Savoie has written extensively on the subject of regional development. Working within the framework of "dependency theory," he concludes that the economic dependency of the Atlantic region on federal fiscal transfers and regional economic development programs have seriously undermined the autonomy of each of the Atlantic provinces. As a consequence, feelings of regional alienation emerge when important decisions relating to the development of the Atlantic economy are imposed on the population by Ottawa. While the three Maritime provinces have traditionally adopted a "cautious" and "pragmatic" stance in their relationships with Ottawa, the Government of Newfoundland has, during the past decade, assumed a more assertive posture and has openly challenged the authority of the federal government in a number of policy areas, such as offshore resources and the management of the fishery.

No issue has preoccupied Canadians more in the last three decades than the relationship between the federal government and the Province of Quebec. The provincial election of 1960 was a pivotal event in the history of the province. With the defeat of the Union Nationale and the assumption of power by a reform-oriented Liberal Party led by Jean Lesage, the defensive, conservative nationalism that had characterized the regime of Maurice Duplessis was replaced by a positive nationalism of growth. The "Quiet Revolution" strained patterns of elite accommodation that had been reasonably successful in managing conflict between Canada's two linguistic communities. Alain Gagnon and Joseph Garcea document the strategies employed by successive provincial governments to enhance Quebec's cultural, fiscal, and political autonomy and thereby achieve a form of special status within the federation. The authors conclude that the concept of "sovereignty-association" advocated by the Parti Québécois from 1976 to 1985 can be traced directly to the constitutional positions and priorities defined by Quebec premiers since 1960.

Rand Dyck's essay assesses Ontario's role in the Canadian federation and concludes that intergovernmental relations between Ottawa and Queen's Park have been a paradox—at times harmonious and conciliatory and at other times confrontational and competitive. To illustrate this unique relationship, Dyck documents the policy issues that have been a source of intergovernmental conflict and cooperation. His analysis reveals that virtually every provincial administration since Confederation, regardless of political persuasion, has attempted to safeguard and, on occasion, to expand the power and influence of Ontario within the federation. More than any other intergovernmental actor, Ontario has maximized its interests through the skillful use of political resources.

During the 1970s the increasingly aggressive stance taken by western provinces (most notably Alberta) added a new dimension to intergovernmental relations. In many respects, the perennial question of Canadian politics, "What does Quebec want?", was replaced with a concern for the long-term implications of "western alienation." David Elton's essay reviews those shared historical experiences which have contributed to widespread western dissatisfaction with the distribution of economic and political power within the Canadian federal system. In Elton's view, past federal-provincial disputes over energy pricing and the constitution have served to erode Ottawa's legitimacy in the region, increase cooperation among western governments, and hasten the search for new forms of provincial input into national decision-making, most recently expressed in demands for a reformed Senate.

18. THE ATLANTIC REGION: THE POLITICS OF DEPENDENCY

Donald J. Savoie

Harvard economist John K. Galbraith, on a recent visit to Atlantic Canada, compared the region to the land that God gave to Cain. How could it lag economically, he wondered, given its strategic location? "The Maritime provinces," he explained, "are on the main path from Europe to the United States—right on the greatest seaway . . . how in the world did it happen that development jumped right over them?"[1] The underdevelopment of Atlantic Canada has, of course, also been a source of puzzlement to many social scientists in Canada and to governments at all three levels. A variety of theories have been developed to explain the phenomenon and many costly government initiatives have been put in place in an attempt to spur Atlantic Canada's economic growth.[2]

The purpose of this chapter is to consider the most important theories put forward to explain the region's underdevelopment, to examine its continuing struggle for economic development, and to view this struggle from a federal-provincial perspective. The underlying theme of the chapter is that the failure of the Atlantic provinces to thrive has and continues to shape federal-provincial relations in the region. The economic weakness of the four Atlantic provinces and their struggle for economic development has served to condition their response to federal government initiatives and also their approach to federal-provincial relations. This is true both for provinces which pride themselves on effective but quiet collaboration with the fed-

eral government, such as New Brunswick, and also for those which have adopted a more aggressive posture towards Ottawa, as in the case of Newfoundland.

THE DEPENDENCY DEBATE

Much has already been written about the dependent economy of Atlantic Canada. This issue has dominated not only political and policy debates in the region itself, but also those in Ottawa on the Atlantic economy in recent years. When the federal government launched its major federal-provincial efforts for regional development through the former Department of Regional Economic Expansion in the late 1960s, hardly anything was said about the dependency of the Atlantic economy. But now, some twenty years later, a great deal is being said about it and there is general agreement, even among Maritimers, that their economy is highly dependent and that it is in the long-term interest of the region to reverse the pattern. This is where the agreement ends, however. There are conflicting views not only on the most appropriate measures to deal with the dependency problem, but also on its exact nature and cause.[3]

The term "dependency" is employed by economists, sociologists, political leaders, and observers to explain the region's underdevelopment. Unfortunately, as Ralph Matthews has observed, "complications and misunderstandings [have arisen] because different theories used the same technical terms in different ways and with different meanings . . . especially in the use of the term dependency."[4] Radical political econo-

An original essay written especially for this volume.

mists at one end of the spectrum and neo-classi-cal economists at the other all employ the term, and all with substantially different meanings.

The diversity of ideas stemming from the radical political economists and the dependency theorists means that the summary which follows will not suffice to give the reader a full appreciation of this school of thought. A much more thorough review of the literature would be required for that purpose. But since its framework of analysis has been so widely applied to the economy of Atlantic Canada, the ideas which have emerged are much too important to ignore. The school also now has a good number of adherents, including some in Atlantic Canada.[5]

A recent and typical example of the application of the dependency theory to development within space is found in Neil Smith's book on *Uneven Development*, where he writes: "capital is like a plague of locusts. It settles in one place, devours it, moves on to plague another place. Better, in the process of restoring itself after one plague, the region makes itself ripe for another. At the very least, uneven development is the geographical expression of the contradictions of capital."[6] The process of capitalistic accumulation, he argues, leads to a concentration of wealth, not only in the hands of a particular social class, but in particular places as well, leading to polarization of development. Underdevelopment in some regions and cities is the opposite side of the coin to development in others.

Dependency theorists have pointed to a systematic draining of capital and resources from the Atlantic economy by other regions. Ralph Matthews contends that "dependency theorists can legitimately argue that the eastern regions of Canada would not need today's transfer payments if they had not earlier been drained of their wealth."[7] Today's out-migration, dependency theorists insist, is simply a continuation of the systematic draining of a valuable resource from the region. They can hardly accept, as the neo-classical economists readily do, that such migration will assist in promoting long-term development, and self-

sustaining growth in the region. It is functional, according to the dependency theorists, to have regional disparities in a capitalistic economy. For one thing, slow-growth regions can provide a pool of labour that can be tapped by developed regions and then dismissed whenever economic circumstances require it. Slow-growth regions will thus lose an important segment of their human resources during periods of economic growth, but recapture it when economic conditions are weak. This serves to make the social overhead costs a tremendous burden for slow-growth regions and ensures that they will never break away from a vicious circle of regional poverty and dependency. Added to this is the fact that capital will also invariably be drained from slow-growth regions by the policies and procedures of a capitalist banking system to finance new industrial investments in the developed regions.[8]

Dependency theorists even suggest that Ottawa's regional development policy increases the region's dependency on the developed regions rather than effectively reducing it. The policy, it has been suggested, operates in the interest of the dominant regions and the dominant class in both the developed and underdeveloped regions. When industries are lured to the Atlantic region with federal cash grants, their basic purpose is to maximize profits and "to remove wealth from the area rather than to increase the wealth and benefit the living conditions of those who live there."[9] In cases where local firms are awarded regional development grants, many such firms are engaged in resource exploitation so that the federal cash grants actually "subsidize the export of resources from the region rather than encouraging local development."[10]

The neo-classical economists also write of dependency in the Atlantic region, but, of course, they do not share the same perspective as the dependency theorists. The strength of the neo-classical view lies in its roots in the mainstream of economic thought.

In the simplest terms, neo-classicists believe that transfer payments and continuing regional programs make slow-growth regions dependent on government. This is the opposite effect to what is intended. They point out that regional disparities in Canada have not narrowed over the years—indeed, if one looks at standard indicators of employment and earned income per capita—it is apparent that Atlantic Canada now counts on government transfer payments to sustain its level of consumption.[11] As James Cannon observed, "Conventional indicators or regional disparity [i.e., in Atlantic Canada] have shown remarkable resistance to regional development policies."[12]

The solution, according to the neo-classicists, is to let market forces resolve the disparities. Regional unemployment, they insist, results from a failure to equilibrate labour supply and demand.

In the neo-classical theory, regional disparities cannot persist. If wages are lower in one region than in another, capital will flow to that region, thus raising labour productivity and wages. Labour, on the other hand, will flow from the poor to the rich regions, reducing wages there. If returns to capital are higher in one region than another, capital will flow from the low-return to the high-return region, making it more scarce, raising its returns in the low-return region, and making it more abundant and lowering returns in the high-return region. If surplus labour is reduced by lowering wages, the market can take advantage of lower production costs. New economic activity should follow and employment be created, albeit with lower wages than may be available elsewhere in the country. If either the entrepreneurs or the workers want to stay in a particular region, despite a lower level of capital or labour productivity, or higher transport costs, a free market will reduce wages and returns to capital will be enough to permit the disadvantaged region to compete, thus maintaining full employment of both labour and capital.

The neo-classical view has gained support in recent years. One can easily appreciate that senior finance officials in Ottawa would embrace this theory more readily than that of the radical political economists. But there are other rea-

sons. Concern over growing government deficits, and a preoccupation with our ability to compete on international markets have led policy makers and observers to concentrate on efficiency rather than equity in public policy. The view that government activities on behalf of regional development ought to be retrenched and market forces set free to create the necessary equilibrium obviously appeals to all those who insist on efficiency as the guiding principle in defining new policies, and to those who are calling for cuts in federal spending to control the federal deficit.

DEVELOPING THE REGION: A CENTRAL PROBLEM

How is the dependency debate viewed in Atlantic Canada? Political leaders in the region readily acknowledge that there is a problem, though they have not considered which theory of dependency best explains the reasons for the region's underdevelopment. But, as David Alexander noted, there is among politicians in the region and Atlantic Canada generally "certainly a longing to shed the humiliation of dependence and charity."[13]

Public policy specialists and economic development planners in Atlantic Canada have attempted to come forward with measures to lessen the region's dependency. The great majority of these measures have been supported through federal-provincial programming. We have now reached the point where virtually the entire discretionary economic development budget of the four Atlantic provinces falls under federal-provincial programs. By and large, the economics and politics of pragmatism have shaped regional development programming and by extension federal-provincial relations in the region for the last twenty years. The reasons for this are varied. Certainly provincial governments have found the theoretical models explaining the region's underdevelopment to be of little value. For one thing, the dependency and neo-classical models exude an aura of other-worldliness to government planners. Both models are largely non-operational in that they have few acceptable prescriptions for specific times and places. Consequently, they have had very little effect. One keen student of regional development has remarked wryly: "There is no manual for dependency theory planning."[14]

The few policy makers who have turned to these two models have found important shortcomings in both. Anyone even remotely familiar with actual regional development programs in the Atlantic region, for instance, will find that the dependency theorists have conveniently overlooked some important facts. For instance, contrary to popular belief, the cornerstone of Ottawa's regional development policy over the past twenty years has not been cash grants to lure outside investors to Atlantic Canada. Something like 80 percent of Ottawa's regional development budget has been spent on federal-provincial programming for regional development. For the most part, these programs have provided new infrastructure facilities, such as roads, schools and new port facilities. In addition, Ottawa's regional development cash grants program has been essentially limited to new or expanded manufacturing and processing facilities and not to resource extraction.[15] As well, over 80 percent of the federal grants in the Atlantic region has been to locally-owned businesses.[16]

The neo-classical approach also has important shortcomings. These have been well documented elsewhere and there is no need to go over all of them here. Suffice to note that neo-classicists do not even attempt to deal with Atlantic Canada's historical grievances.[17] Although admittedly too much is made in the region over the negative impact national policies have had on the local economy, it remains that the Maritimes have not shared equally with other regions in the benefits of confederation. Maritime industrial development suffered from the reorganization of the railways and from the national policy, with Ontario and Quebec acquiring the protected industries. The market was certainly not free of

distortions in the past in shaping Canada's current economic structure. To suggest that it ought now be set free to deal with our regional problems would strike some as analogous to the home team changing the rules of the game in the bottom of the ninth inning.

The neo-classical paradigm also runs into difficulty when confronted with the real world of politics. Neo-classicists favour, for example, "people prosperity" over "place prosperity"; that is, they emphasize the welfare of individual Canadians more than that of geographical collectivities. There are obvious practical difficulties with this approach. In a federation, it is hardly possible to expect that all regional or provincial governments will subscribe fully to the view of people prosperity over place prosperity. The Nova Scotia government, for example, may well be primarily concerned with the well-being of all residents within its jurisdiction. Viewed from the perspective of the country as a whole, however, this constitutes an emphasis on place, not people. Province-building—that is, the establishment of measures designed to stimulate growth within provincial boundaries—has become an inevitable fact of life for Canadian policy-makers. For the federal government to wash its hands of any regional development responsibility could well give rise to all kinds of additional "me first" provincial economic initiatives. In the end, provinces would "sabotage" the neo-classical approach and costly competition would surface.

In the absence of a widely accepted theoretical framework from which the underdevelopment of the region can be explained, political leaders in Atlantic Canada have sought their own explanation. They quickly arrived at a consensus as to why they lag behind nationally in economic development. There is also strong evidence to suggest that there is widespread support for this consensus among the population in the region.

Every Atlantic premier holding office during the past fifteen years has pinned the blame for the region's underdevelopment on federal government policies and programs. They have all gone beyond historical grievances, such as the reorganization of the railways, the national policy, and the terms of Confederation, to argue that current federal policies retard development in Atlantic Canada.

Premier Richard Hatfield summed up the general view when he declared before a Senate Standing Committee that "there is an attitude here in Ottawa . . . that there are certain things that we cannot do down there because we are not so capable of doing them, that there are only certain things that we can do and we should stick with them."[18] Others from the region insist that national policies are in reality designed for the more developed and populous areas of southern Ontario and Quebec. This is particularly true in the case of economic development. Regional programs, they insist, are simply compensation for the slow-growth region because it does not benefit from national programs. But, they also argue, the compensation has not been nearly enough.

It would appear that at least some Ottawa-based senior public servants involved in regional development programming tend to agree with this view. One of these has remarked that promoting "real" regional development (i.e., something beyond transfer payments) in Ottawa "was like pulling against gravity."[19] Observers from outside government have also come to the same conclusion. David Alexander, for example, has argued that Atlantic Canada is the only region which did not benefit economically from Confederation. He then added that the very basis and structure of the Atlantic economy—for example, ocean-related resources—requires a national government with a "genuinely international orientation." This, he reported, "is precisely what Upper Canada is not and never has been."[20]

It is true that the region has benefited substantially over the past twenty years or so from federal regional policies and programs. But many firmly believe that had it not been for the political and economic troubles of Quebec, Ottawa would never have introduced special regional development policies at all.[21] Moreover, they now report that the federal regional development budget has gradually shifted its focus away from Atlantic Canada. Ontario, they reveal, is now receiving as much federal financial resources annually for federal-provincial regional development agreements as are New Brunswick and Newfoundland. And this precisely at a time when the Ontario economy is buoyant and that of Atlantic Canada is stagnant. Thus, the one area of federal government programming which should by definition favour the Atlantic provinces has become national in scope, with the budget about evenly split among all the provinces with the exception of Quebec which gets a major share of Ottawa's regional development budget. Current federal spending patterns for regional development actually support this view.[22]

DEVELOPING THE REGION: DEALING WITH OTTAWA

It is easy for the region's policy makers to conclude that the Atlantic economy is dependent on other regions, particularly on federal transfer payments, and that federal policies and programs are largely responsible for the region's underdevelopment. It is quite another matter for them to come up with solutions and also to strike an appropriate approach to federal-provincial relations. Other than requesting more federal funds for still more cost-shared agreements and projects, the four Atlantic premiers have not been forthcoming with suggestions for Ottawa to consider in revising federal government economic policies so as to benefit the Atlantic region.

The point is often made in the region that the structure of national political institutions is such that the more populous central provinces have effective political control over national policies. Restructuring national political institutions to give more weight to peripheral regions in national policy is one possibility. But this in turn could well attenuate the role of the four Atlantic premiers in defending the interests of the region and particularly in being seen doing so. Lashing out at national policies before television cameras at federal-provincial conferences always makes for good politics at home for provincial premiers though in the end it may have very little actual impact on national policy.

The dilemma for Atlantic Canada is clear: assuming that federal policies discriminate against their economic interests, they should naturally favour a greater degree of decentralization and decision-making to the provincial level. Yet, because of historical and economic forces, the Atlantic provinces are probably the least capable of designing and implementing economic policies autonomously.

The fiscal capacity of the Atlantic provinces is particularly weak by national standards and a greater proportion of equalization payments on a per capita basis are directed to this region than elsewhere. In addition, though Ottawa's regional development has been shifting westward, it remains that the Atlantic provinces still finance virtually all their economic development initiatives through federal-provincial development agreements. There are currently fewer and fewer new initiatives being accepted for cost-sharing but, as in the past, what is being accepted represents almost the entire new economic development budget in the region. Over 40 percent of their provincial revenues comes from federal transfer payments. By comparison, for example, Ontario and Saskatchewan receive between 20 to 25 percent of its revenues from federal transfer payments, and Quebec receives about 30 percent.

The impact of federal transfers on policy-making in the Atlantic provinces is manifold. For one thing, it means that virtually all new government initiatives in the region are designed with potential federal cost-sharing in mind. New initiatives, however desirable they may be from a provincial government perspective, are often scrapped for others which are less desirable but which stand a better chance for federal cost-sharing.[23]

This provides the federal government with an opportunity not only to shape the interventions but also to influence the pace they might take. All the provinces are of course subject to proposed federal cost-sharing in areas of provincial jurisdiction. As is well known, Ottawa took the lead in introducing major social programs through its spending powers and all ten provinces responded so that such programs as medicare, though falling under provincial jurisdiction, are national in scope.[24]

In the case of the Atlantic provinces, however, federal cost-sharing permeates *every* policy field, and *every* government department and agency concerned with both social and economic development. Federal cost-sharing schemes in the region are present in both long-established programs as well as in newly-established programs.

Nova Scotia, for example, several years ago, saw potential economic development opportunities in ocean-related industries. It put together a development package, submitted it to Ottawa and waited for federal cost-sharing approval. Approval came a few years afterwards and the programs were then put in place by the province.[25] It is highly unlikely that on its own Nova Scotia would have introduced the programs.

Other similar examples can be found in all four Atlantic provinces. New Brunswick, for instance, identified some time ago a forestry complex involving a forest ranger school and research facilities, among other things, as a key feature of its provincial economic development strategy. It submitted the proposal to Ottawa, waited several years before it obtained federal cost-sharing approval, and then proceeded to implement the project.[26] Other provinces are not nearly so dependent on federal cost-sharing for new initiatives. Ontario, Quebec, and Saskatchewan, for example, have recently put together important new economic development packages without federal cost-sharing.[27]

There is yet another factor which inhibits the four Atlantic provinces from either occupying their own fields of jurisdiction more energetically or even staking out different policy positions in their dealings with Ottawa. The fiscal weakness as well as the size of the four provinces have prevented them from gaining the expertise in their bureaucracies to rival Ottawa or even other provinces in all policy fields. There are many instances in policy debates where this has been obvious. Provincial government officials in the Atlantic provinces also readily admit that their governments cannot compete with the expertise of federal officials in all policy fields. In the case of the pension plan, for instance, one senior New Brunswick official observed: "We just went neutral on the Canada Pension Plan, we just eased right out of it. We just didn't have the capacity to tackle it. What did interest New Brunswick was the financial aspect. My main interest as a Treasury Board Type was how much money would be available to New Brunswick. We didn't contribute many ideas. The two questions I was supposed to ask were the size of the fund and what were the strings going to be."[28]

CONFLICTS OR COMPROMISE: BARGAINING FROM WEAKNESS

Though there is widespread agreement among the Atlantic provinces that federal policies are largely responsible for the region's underdevelopment, they have been remarkably restrained in their relations with Ottawa since the Second World War. The one exception is Newfoundland, and this only since the mid-1970s.

One might assume that the Atlantic region would be ideal for the development of radical politics, given its structural economic problems and high unemployment levels. Radical politics in turn, one might also assume, would give rise to confrontation with the federal government over appropriate national and regional economic politics.

The fact that we have seen neither is likely a result of the region's political culture and the strong presence of the federal government in the decision-making process of its provincial governments. The political values of Atlantic Canada, suggests David J. Bellamy, are rooted in the legacy of the Loyalists, the prerevolutionary French traditions, and ingrained conservatism.[29] He has also observed that political values are conditioned by a preference for the status quo and by a "fondness for an ordered hierarchical society."[30] Moreover, he adds that patterns of action in the Atlantic region are "resistant to change and respond to subtle moods of tradition and past experiences. Innovation is regarded with suspicion, if not with open hostility."[31]

To be sure, a number of important studies of Canada's political culture have singled out differences between Atlantic Canadians and other Canadians.[32] Richard Simeon and David Elkins suggest, for example, "that the low level of immigration may mean little importation of new ideas; the high level of emigration may mean that some of the most 'modern' individuals . . . have left."[33]

But the region's political culture can only explain part of why governments do what they do. If one looks to find examples of innovative thinking in either social or economic policies, one would have to look to Ottawa and to the larger provinces, such as Quebec and Ontario. The one exception, of course, is New Brunswick's program of Equal Opportunities launched in the mid-1960s. Robert Young suggests that "one might explain the relative absence of social policy innovation in the Maritimes as a function, in part, of the relatively low average income and the weak tax bases accessible to provincial governments."[34] The same, of course, could be said about economic policy.

The provincial bureaucracies in Atlantic Canada simply do not have the human resources to devote their attention to more than a handful of major policy issues. What personnel is available is invariably earmarked for the operational side of government. Since the implementation of federal-provincial cost-sharing schemes frequently rests with the provinces, their government departments are far more oriented towards program delivery than is the federal government. It is worthwhile to note, for example, that the total staff complement of the economic policy section of the Cabinet secretariat in the Government of New Brunswick amounts to four.

The paucity of policy and research capacity in the Atlantic provincial governments prompted Ottawa at one point to offer to share the cost of salaries of provincial public servants engaged in economic policy planning.[35] The federal government has also established numerous joint economic planning and implementation committees with the four provinces in order to come up with new initiatives. Seeing that the Atlantic provinces were weak on policy, research, and analysis, Ottawa moved to strengthen this capacity, if only to ensure a greater chance of success for joint planning. What is important to underline is that the federal government has been present at nearly all levels, in provincial bureaucracies in Atlantic Canada, in planning and, albeit to a lesser extent, in implementing economic policies and programs.

The above, combined with generous federal cost-sharing on programs, has obvious implications for federal-provincial relations and more broadly for the way Atlantic Canada perceives itself in the Canadian federation. For the region, the present scheme of things is akin to a "catch 22" situation. Much of Atlantic Canada is convinced that Ottawa's national policies are in large measure responsible for the region's underdevelopment. Attempts to become less dependent, however, have been through federal-provincial programming, managed by federal-provincial committees staffed at least in part, by federal public servants. The region's dependency, it can be argued, is not limited to transfer payments to individuals and to the provinces. It extends even to the provincial policy and decision-making processes, though here the dependency is less visible.

More than any other provinces, the Atlantic provinces have to be particularly cautious in their approach to federal-provincial relations. So much of their economic structure and planning is dependent on federal programming that the region is constantly aware of Ottawa's important presence. At any given time, there can always be found major economic projects waiting for Ottawa's approval for cost-sharing.

Many remain convinced that the last time the region adopted a particularly aggressive stance towards a specific federal policy, it paid a high price. This happened in the early 1980s when three of the four Atlantic provinces vigorously opposed Ottawa's constitutional proposals. The government of Prince Edward Island, in a speech from the throne, labelled Prime Minister Pierre Trudeau "un-Canadian" for attempting to move unilaterally on the constitution in the speech from the throne. Shortly after that the federal government moved to restructure substantially the province's comprehensive economic plan. No longer would the federal government cost-share all projects under the plan and no longer would the province deliver all the initiatives. Henceforth, the plan would be divided into two parts—one a federal-provincial component, to be cost-shared by Ottawa and delivered by the province and a second to be delivered by the federal government.[36] The economic weakness of the region is a constant reminder to its political leadership that you bite the proverbial hand that feeds you at your own peril.

This economic weakness explains certainly in part the pragmatic approach the Atlantic provinces have taken to federal-provincial relations. Because of the region's underdevelopment, the provinces, whether governed by a Liberal or Progressive Conservative government, reject out of hand neo-conservative ideology. Government intervention in the economy is favoured by all four provinces who have, over the past fifteen years, put in place a mind-boggling variety of measures designed to spur economic development.[37] The basis for approving these measures, however, often has had more to do with the availability of federal cost-sharing than with the economic viability of the measures themselves.

Virtually every provincial government policy

and every provincial government department in the region is susceptible to change and even minor adjustments in federal policy. This has prompted some observers to remark that at least three of the four Atlantic provinces are essentially centralist. That is, they prefer a strong central government with the necessary policy tools and financial resources to alleviate regional disparities in public services and economic opportunities.

There is plenty of evidence to suggest that the region has not fully sorted out the inherent contradictions in its position. On the one hand, political leaders in Atlantic Canada argue that a major reason—perhaps the most important reason—for the region's underdevelopment is discriminatory federal policies and national programs. The region has often pointed out that it does not carry much political weight on the national scene. Representations in the House of Commons, in the federal Cabinet, and in federal bureaucracy heavily favour central Canada. Yet, on the other hand, the region's provincial premiers by and large prefer a strong central government and have said so publicly on many occasions.

NEWFOUNDLAND

The one exception, of course, is Newfoundland. Premier Peckford startled the Canadian political establishment in the early 1980s when he boldly declared before a constitutional conference that the concept of Canada as put forward by Premier Lévesque of the Parti Québécois was much closer to his own view than the one presented by the Canadian Prime Minister, Pierre Trudeau.

The provincial identity in Newfoundland is strong, perhaps stronger than any other province except Quebec. Newfoundland perceives itself as a distinct society, and Newfoundlanders are quick to draw the parallel with Quebec that both are old societies on this continent and that both evolved in isolation from the North American mainstream. During most of the province's 400-year history, Newfoundland's primary cultural ties were with

Britain, and its primary economic ties were with the United States. Association with Canada represents less than a tenth of that history.

Newfoundland shares one important common characteristic with the other three Atlantic provinces: it is underdeveloped and highly dependent on federal transfer payments. As in the other Atlantic provinces, there is a "longing to shed the humiliation of dependence and charity." An advisor to Premier Peckford explained Newfoundland's relations with Ottawa in this fashion: "They'll never let us drown, but under no circumstances would they ever send us a swimming instructor."[38]

For Premier Peckford, the way ahead for Newfoundland is clear. The federation must be decentralized, and Newfoundland must control its offshore resources and the fishery. In Peckford's view, every time Newfoundland has turned to outsiders for development, the province has either had bad investors, as in the case of the oil refinery at Come-by-Chance, or it has become dependent, as in the case with Ottawa.

Thus, the Newfoundland government's strong position for greater provincial control of policy is ineluctably linked to a desire to extricate the province from a position of economic dependence. The province explained in a five year development plan that "never again would it trade its ownership birthright" and made it clear that taking advantage of new opportunities in oil, gas, and the fisheries could be the province's last chance to develop the province properly.[39]

Premier Peckford stood firm in his dealings with Ottawa and would not compromise on the offshore resources issue. It should be remembered, however, that his disinclination to compromise was largely restricted to this issue and that of the fisheries, both of which he regarded as essential. During the constitutional talks of the early 1980s, he showed himself willing to give way or go along with a consensus on matters he saw as unessential to the economic interests of the province, such as the Charter of Rights. It should also be noted that past successes had reinforced Peckford's faith in non-compromise as a valid political course. The most notable was the battle over the 1977 provincial oil and gas regulations, when Peckford was provincial minister of Mines and Energy. The companies boycotted the Newfoundland offshore for a year before acceding to Newfoundland's (i.e., Peckford's) terms. The premier had already played David to Goliath—and won. He had taken a position he considered just, stuck to it despite wavering on the part of the provincial Cabinet, and oil companies eventually gave in and came back. In short, the issue of economic independence was much too important to Newfoundland's future to allow for compromise.[40]

As is well known, Premier Peckford refused several Ottawa proposals to compromise on the offshore issue. Even pressure resulting from a signed agreement between Ottawa and Nova Scotia on the province's offshore did not force his hand. Heading into a provincial election, Peckford campaigned almost exclusively on the offshore issue and won the 1982 election with a bigger mandate than he had received in 1979. He waited for a change of government in Ottawa before signing an offshore agreement. Terms were settled with the newly elected federal Progressive Conservatives and the Atlantic Accord was signed in February 1985. The terms of the Accord recognized Newfoundland and Labrador to be the principal beneficiary of the wealth of oil and gas off its shores. It also gave Newfoundland equal say with the federal government in managing the resources.[41]

For much of the late 1970s and early 1980s, Newfoundland was *un cas à part* from the other Atlantic provinces. Much has been said about the distinct historical and cultural features of the province to explain its defiant approach to Ottawa, an approach uncharacteristic of the other three Atlantic provinces. However, an equally, if not more important explanation, was the opportunity Newfoundland saw to put its economy on a strong, independent footing.

The desire to pull the regional economy away from its dependency status is strong in all four Atlantic provinces. Newfoundland saw offshore resources as the one opportunity to do so. For the other three provinces, New Brunswick and Prince Edward Island in particular, opportunities for a more self-reliant economy are still tied to federal-provincial programming. Thus, they consider the best solution to be a strong central government willing to cost-share programs in both the social and economic policy fields. But, in the words of a senior government official from the region, "put a Hibernia oil field in the Northumberland Straight, and you could well see New Brunswick and Prince Edward Island adopt a different approach to federal-provincial relations."[42] The current pragmatic approach seen in the region during the past twenty years would likely give way to a more independent position, should such an opportunity arise, and a firm call for a more decentralized form of federalism could be expected.

Notes

1. See "Legacy of Achievement," *Dimension* (Moncton, Winter 1986): 12.

2. See, among others, Donald J. Savoie, *Regional Economic Development: Canada's Search for Solutions* (Toronto: University of Toronto Press, 1986).

3. See Donald J. Savoie, "Some Theoretical Considerations," in Donald J. Savoie, ed., *The Canadian Economy: A Regional Perspective* (Toronto: Methuen, 1986).

4. Ralph Matthews, *The Creation of Regional Dependency* (Toronto: University of Toronto Press, 1983), 56.

5. See, among others, R. J. Sacouman, "The Peripheral Maritimes and Canada-Wide Marxist Political Economy," *Studies in Political Economy* 6 (1981): 135–50, and Henry C. Veltmeyer, "A Central Issue in Dependency Theory," *Canadian Review of Sociology and Anthropology* 17: 3 (1980): 198–213.

6. Neil Smith, *Uneven Development* (New York: Basil Blackwell, 1984), 52.

7. Matthews, *The Creation of Regional Dependency*, 75.

8. Savoie, "Some Theoretical Considerations," 19.

9. Matthews, 114.

10. *Ibid.*

11. See, among many others, Thomas J. Courchene, "Avenues of Adjustment: The Transfer System and Regional Disparities," in Michael Walker, ed., *Canadian Confederation at the Crossroads: The Search for a Federal-Provincial Balance* (Vancouver: The Fraser Institute, 1978), 145–86.

12. James B. Cannon, "Explaining Regional Development in Atlantic Canada: A Review Essay," *Journal of Canadian Studies* 19: 3 (1984): 65–86.

13. David G. Alexander, "New Notions of Happiness: Nationalism, Regionalism, and Atlantic Canada," in David Alexander, *Atlantic Canada and Confederation* (Toronto: University of Toronto Press, 1983), 91.

14. Benjamin Higgins, "The Task Ahead: The Search for a New Local and Regional Development Strategy in the 1980s," (Nagoya: United Nations Centre for Regional Development, undated), 12.

15. Savoie, *Regional Economic Development*, chapters 3, 4, 5, and 8.

16. Interview with a former senior DREE official. See also Government of Canada, DREE, Reports on Regional Development Incentives, various dates.

17. See, among others, Alexander, "New Notions of Happiness," 91.

18. Canada, *Proceedings of the Standing Senate Committee on National Finance* (4 December 1980), issues no. 18, 19, and 22.

19. Quoted in Donald J. Savoie, "The Toppling of DREE and Prospects for Regional Economic Development," *Canada Public Policy* 10:3 (1984): 334.

20. David G. Alexander, "Canadian Regionalism: A Central Problem," in David Alexander, *Atlantic Canada and Confederation* (Toronto: University of Toronto Press, 1983), 46.

21. Alexander, "Economic Growth in the Atlantic Region," ibid., p. 75.

22. As of May 14, 1986, the federal government had committed the following amounts to the ten Economic and Regional Development Agreements:

Quebec	$600,000
British Columbia	$287,500
Newfoundland	$268,700
Nova Scotia	$257,045
Manitoba	$255,550
New Brunswick	$215,717
Saskatchewan	$118,790
Ontario	$113,000
Prince Edward Island	$103,078
Alberta	$ 84,800

23. See Donald J. Savoie, *Federal-Provincial Collaboration: The Canada-New Brunswick General Development Agreement* (Montreal: McGill-Queen's University Press, 1981), chapters 8 and 9.

24. See, among many others, Richard Simeon, *Federal-Provincial Diplomacy: The Making of Recent Policy in Canada* (Toronto: University of Toronto Press, 1972), chapters 3, 4 and 7.

25. See, Government of Canada, Department of Regional Economic Expansion, *The Canada-Nova Scotia Ocean Industry Subsidiary Agreement*, 24 July 1981.

26. See Government of Canada, Department of Regional Industrial Expansion, *Forestry II.*

27. See, for example, Government of Ontario, Notes for Remarks by the Honourable David Peterson, Premier of Ontario and Minister Responsible for Northern Development and Mines, Sault Ste. Marie, 8 July 1986.

28. Simeon, *Federal-Provincial Diplomacy*, 187.

29. David J. Bellamy, "The Atlantic Provinces," in David J. Bellamy et al., eds., *The Provincial Political Systems: Comparative Essays* (Toronto: Methuen, 1976), 3–18.

30. *Ibid.*, 10.

31. *Ibid.*

32. See, for example, Stephen H. Ullman, "Regional Political Cultures in Canada: A Theoretical and Conceptual Introduction," in Richard Schultz et al., eds., The *Canadian Political Process*, 3rd edition, (Toronto: Holt, Rinehart and Winston, 1979), 3–14.

33. Richard Simeon and David J. Elkins, "Provincial Political Cultures in Canada," in David Elkins and Richard Simeon, eds., *Small Worlds: Provinces and Parties in Canadian Political Life* (Toronto: Methuen, 1980), 69.

34. Robert A. Young, "Teaching and Research in Maritime Politics: Old Stereotypes and New Directions," *Journal of Canadian Studies* (forthcoming): 26.

35. See Savoie, *Federal-Provincial Collaboration.* Salaries of provincial public servants in the Atlantic region were cost-shared under the Prince Edward Island Comprehensive Development Plan and Planning Subsidiary Agreements, under the General Development Agreements in the other Atlantic provinces.

36. "Federal Activity to Remain Strong," *The Guardian* (Charlottetown), 8 October 1981, 3. See also "P.E.I. Legislature Opens with Accusation Ottawa Acting in 'Un-Canadian Manner'," *Halifax Chronicle Herald*, 20 February 1981, 1.

37. See, among others, Savoie, *Regional Economic Development*, and Government of Canada, Department of Regional Economic Expansion, *Annual Report* (various dates).

38. Quoted in Bruce Little, *An Approach to Newfoundland* (Ottawa, unpublished manuscript, 1982), 7.

39. Government of Newfoundland and Labrador, *Managing All Our Resources* (St. John's, Spring 1982).

40. Little, 26.

41. See Bruce G. Pollard, "Newfoundland: Resisting Dependency," in Peter M. Leslie, ed., *Canada: The State of the Federation* (Kingston: Institute of Intergovernmental Relations, Queen's University, 1985), 83–117. See also, Government of Newfoundland and Labrador, *The Offshore: We've Been Fair* (brochure, 1984).

42. Interview with a deputy minister, Government of New Brunswick, August 1986.

Selected Readings

Alexander, David G. *Atlantic Canada and Confederation: Essays in Canadian Political Economy.* Toronto: University of Toronto Press, 1983.

Forbes, Ernest R. *Maritime Rights: The Maritime Rights Movement, 1919–1927.* Montreal: McGill-Queen's University Press, 1979.

MacNutt, W. S. *The Atlantic Provinces: The Emergence of Colonial Society.* Toronto: McClelland and Stewart Limited, 1965.

Matthews, Ralph. *The Creation of Regional Dependency.* Toronto: University of Toronto Press, 1983.

Pollard, Bruce G. "Newfoundland: Resisting Dependence." In Peter M. Leslie, ed. *Canada: The State of the Federation 1985.* Kingston: Institute of Intergovernmental Relations, Queen's University, 1985, 83–117.

Rawlyk, G. A., ed. *The Atlantic Provinces and the Problems of Confederation.* St. John's: Breakwater, 1979.

Savoie, Donald J. *Regional Economic Development: Canada's Search for Solutions.* Toronto: University of Toronto Press, 1986.

19. QUEBEC AND THE PURSUIT OF SPECIAL STATUS

Alain G. Gagnon and Joseph Garcea

Since 1960 successive Quebec governments, in sharp contrast with most other provincial governments, have consistently pursued special constitutional, fiscal, and program objectives. They have sought and in some instances succeeded in attaining special powers, resources, roles, and ultimately some forms of special status within the Canadian federation. The signing of the Meech Lake and Langevin Block accords in 1987, in which the Quebec government attained considerable concessions on constitutional reform from the others governments within the federal system, is the product, though by no means the final product, of persistent demands made by successive Quebec governments during the past quarter century.

This article provides an overview of those governments' objectives and achievements in the realm of *de jure* and *de facto* constitutional reform and, to a lesser extent, in fiscal and program matters which invariably relate to constitutional issues.[1] It concludes both that their overarching objective has been to maximize that province's cultural, fiscal, and political autonomy, and that successive Quebec governments have been a powerful force at the forefront of the provincial rights movement, both in blocking or precluding federal intrusions into areas of provincial jurisdiction and also in expanding the scope of provincial powers and roles in several policy sectors. Finally, it concludes that Quebec does have some form of special status within the

Canadian federation, though not always to the extent or for the reasons generally assumed.

LESAGE (1960–1966): FROM EQUALITY TO SPECIAL STATUS

The transition from the Duplessis to the Lesage era entailed a shift from "isolationist" to "non-isolationist" autonomy rooted in a new, proactive, rather than reactionary, nationalism.[2] Lesage supplanted Duplessis's penchant for dual federalism, in which each level of government operates only within its jurisdictional boundaries, with cooperative federalism, which at least in part undoubtedly stemmed from his political experience at the federal level. However, as evidenced by Lesage's 1962 campaign slogan "maîtres chez nous" (which echoed Duplessis's slogan "maître chez soi") what did not change was a commitment to maximize the Quebec government's autonomy vis-a-vis the federal government.[3]

Duplessis maintained that Québécois culture could best survive and thrive in isolation from the federal government and the rest of Canada.[4] His strategy revolved around two related axes: the disintegration of existing constitutional, fiscal, and program links with the federal government through disuse, and minimizing the development of additional links irrespective of their economic appeal.[5] The notable deviation from the strategy of non-cooperation irrespective of the economic benefits was the acceptance of the unconditional equalization program initiated in 1957. Manifestations of that strategy include, for example, the persistent refusal of the Duplessis regime to con-

An original essay written especially for this volume.

sent to constitutional reforms proposed by Prime Minister St. Laurent in 1950 or to participate either in federal-provincial tax-sharing agreements in 1947, 1952, and 1957, or cost-sharing programs in fields such as health, welfare, and post-secondary education.[6] Only after his death in 1959 did the Quebec provincial government sign the federal-provincial agreement on financing post-secondary education, the first "contracting-out" arrangement in Canada, which in subsequent years has been used more by Quebec than any other province.[7]

In reaction to the philosophy of the Duplessis era, the Lesage administration assumed power with a disposition toward reform, both within Quebec and in its relations with the federal and provincial governments. Its strategy basically entailed an active involvement in intergovernmental relations in an effort to recoup lost political power, prestige, and fiscal resources needed for the development of the Quebec state and society. This strategy was evident in its pursuit of various objectives during its six years in power—years which began with a call for equality, though not necessarily uniformity, among the provinces and ended with a call for special status for Quebec. The overarching objective throughout was, as another of its slogans suggests, a strong Quebec in a new Confederation.[8]

During its two terms in power the Lesage administration failed to develop a consistent position on constitutional reform. This resulted from divisions both in the National Assembly and, more importantly perhaps, within the Quebec Liberal Party itself. Such divisions constrained Lesage to reject both the Fulton formula in 1961 and the Fulton-Favreau formula in 1966, largely because they did not guarantee Quebec the requisite powers to participate in the development of national policies and programs, the reform of national institutions, and the development of French-Canadian language and culture, and ultimately to maximize its autonomy. More specifically, he rejected the Fulton formula because the federal government refused to delimit its powers,

gained in 1949, to unilaterally amend those parts of the constitution concerning exclusive federal jurisdiction and certain aspects of national institutions, such as the Monarchy, the Senate, and the Supreme Court. He rejected the Fulton-Favreau formula because changes to the division of powers required unanimous federal and provincial consent.[9] The unanimity principle was strongly opposed in Quebec, ostensibly because it could preclude bilateral agreements regarding the delegation of powers between the provincial and the federal governments in areas such as language policy—at the time, being investigated by the federal Royal Commission on Bilingualism and Biculturalism. Concerned about a negative impact on its electoral fortunes, the Lesage government succumbed to the wishes of strong provincialist and nationalist forces in Quebec. In rejecting the formula Lesage asserted that Quebec would endorse neither patriation nor any amending formula until issues such as Quebec's powers and role, as well as safeguards for minority rights were settled to Quebec's satisfaction. This became the official position of subsequent Quebec governments, with very limited and temporary deviations.

Having rejected the Fulton-Favreau formula, and faced with the prospect of losing votes to Daniel Johnson in the 1966 election, the Lesage government tried to consolidate any support that had waned in the battle over the amending formula by assuming a more nationalist and provincialist posture. The most significant effort in this regard was a shift from its earlier position of "equality" for all the provinces, to "special status" for Quebec. Such a shift was evident as early as 1964 when, upon concluding the pension negotiations, Lesage declared that he had attained a "statut spécial" for Quebec.[10] Internal divisions within the Quebec Liberal cabinet, caucus, and party however made even this shift a highly contentious and divisive issue. The strongest critics, of course, were René Lévesque and his followers, who embraced the doctrine of "états-associés", the precursor of "souveraineté-association", and left the Quebec Liberal Party. During its last year in power, the Lesage government's doctrine of special status was enunciated both in a policy paper ("A Strong Quebec Within A New Confederation") and in speeches by Premier Lesage and Gérin-Lajoie, the Minister of Education. The latter presented his government's new position in the form of a rhetorical question in which an incipient "dual alliance" conception of Confederation is evident: "Up to the present, Quebec has asked nothing for itself which it would not be willing to recognize for the other provinces. But one may wonder whether this is the correct attitude to take! . . . What objection would there be if Canada were to adopt a constitutional regime which would take into account the existence of the two 'nations' or 'societies' within one Canada?"[11]

During its six years in power, the Lesage administration also made special efforts to give Quebec a larger role in interprovincial, federal-provincial, and international relations. Its most significant initiative in interprovincial relations was convening a Premiers' Conference in 1960, which has been institutionalized into an annual event. Lesage's ostensible purpose for such conferences was interprovincial cooperation among equals to harmonize their respective activities and to present a common front in their negotiations with the federal government. Within the federal-provincial relations sphere it was instrumental in convening more frequent and formal conferences of first ministers and ministers and in the establishment of an intergovernmental conference secretariat financed and managed by the two levels of government.

In international relations it asserted the right to participate directly and without federal control in matters which, either in whole or in part, were within the legislative jurisdiction of the provinces. Of particular interest for Quebec at that time was to attend the conferences of the Francophonie and to conclude agreements with member countries in order to develop vital cultural and economic links. Towards that end, with the permission of federal and French authorities, Quebec in 1961 posted a provincial Consul Géné-

ral in Paris and concluded agreements between 1964 and 1966 with the French government regarding youth and cultural exchanges. Such agreements constituted an unprecedented provincial initiative at that time.[12]

The Lesage administration also sought to maximize provincial program and fiscal authority. Basically its efforts revolved around three interrelated axes: the right to opt-out of federal-provincial shared-cost programs; the right to establish provincial welfare and development programs independently from the federal government; and greater fiscal authority through a larger share of taxation, the elimination of unconditional grants, and increased unconditional equalization grants.[13] A major part of the rationale for such a strategy was the symbolic and electoral value of Quebecers perceiving the provincial, rather than the federal, government as their principal benefactor. Towards that end, it opted-out of several federal-provincial shared-cost programs, also established provincial social programs such as the Quebec Pension Plan, and laid the foundation for others. Perhaps its most significant achievement in this area was to constrain the Pearson government to pass legislation granting Quebec and all other provinces the right to opt-out, with some form of compensation, of all social programs. In 1965, when the legislation came into effect, Quebec opted-out of all major programs in exchange for a substantial increase in its share of personal income tax.[14] At that time no other province expressed an interest in this arrangement, despite the federal government's enticements to prompt their participation and thereby eliminate any semblance of special status for Quebec.[15]

Finally, the Lesage administration attempted to influence federal policies and programs deemed to affect the province either directly or indirectly. It was particularly interested in influencing the nature and scope of the Canada Assistance Plan, family allowances, regional development, language policy, foreign policy, immigration policy, and even national economic policies. In its 1966 Budget Speech, for example, it advocated a formal role for Quebec, and to some extent also for the other provinces, in the formulation and implementation of Canada's fiscal, monetary and trade policies.[16] Subsequent Quebec provincial governments have demanded a similar role in those and other policy areas that traditionally had been considered under the aegis of the federal government.[17]

In sum, the Lesage administration was influential in initiating changes in Quebec's powers, resources, roles, and status and also set the broad parameters for most of the objectives and demands of subsequent Quebec governments. The concessions it extracted from Ottawa have been characterized by some analysts as an incipient de facto special status for Quebec.[18]

JOHNSON & BERTRAND (1966–1970): "ÉGALITÉ OU INDÉPENDANCE"

The transition from the Lesage to the Johnson and Bertrand administration involved elements both of continuity and change. The continuity in their respective demands on Ottawa for constitutional and fiscal reform, and also for greater powers, roles, and status in domestic and international relations was a function both of the policy convergence which occurred between the provincial Liberal and Union Nationale parties as the 1966 election approached, and the presence of several key intergovernmental affairs advisors who worked for both governments.[19] Nevertheless, the Union Nationale's 1966 election victory resulted in important changes in perspective, strategy, and to some extent even objectives.

Such changes were embodied in Johnson's campaign slogan "Égalité ou Indépendance." This slogan captures two major differences between the Johnson-Bertrand and Lesage administrations. First, unlike the former, the latter did not threaten Ottawa with independence as a feasible or desirable option. Second, whereas for Johnson and Bertrand the term "equality" meant equality between the representatives of the two founding linguistic groups, for Lesage it had

generally meant equality among the provinces, despite the incipient "binational" and special status perspective which, to reiterate, was evident during his last year in power. Johnson's position constituted a strong reassertion of the "dual alliance" perspective, with Quebec as the protectorate of the rights and interests of the Québécois and, to some extent, also Francophones outside Quebec. This perspective, which reflected the position of Quebec's Tremblay Commission, led Johnson to demand, both in his first Speech from the Throne and at various federal-provincial conferences, constitutional reforms congruent with what he perceived as the binational character of the Canadian polity.[20] He asserted that Quebec was no longer willing to accept the restrictions resulting from the powers accorded to it in 1867.[21] Johnson's call for constitutional reform was a significant departure from the traditional constitutional conservatism of the Union Nationale regarding the inviolability of, and the federal government's obligation to operate in accordance with, the original compact. Yet, it was cautious in its approach and, like the Lesage government, would not consent either to an amending formula or patriation until an agreement had been reached on the division of constitutional powers.

Those demands did not change with Jean-Jacques Bertrand at the helm, who echoed his predecessor's binational autonomist theme. During negotiations on the constitution in 1969 he stressed that a constitutionally entrenched special status for Quebec should be considered and that reform should focus on collective, rather than individual, rights, including the right of nations to self-determination.[22] All of this, of course, was antithetical to Prime Minister Trudeau's longstanding position regarding the general thrust of constitutional reform, Quebec's status in the constitution, and the role of Quebec governments within Confederation.[23]

Fiscal and program autonomy was the second major objective of the Johnson-Bertrand regime and one in which it seemed to be much more adamant, but perhaps no more successful, than the Lesage administration. Whereas the Lesage administration was content to "opt-out" of federal-provincial initiatives that were national in scope, the Johnson-Bertrand administration indicated that it wanted the federal government to "get out". Suggestions that Johnson's rhetoric for public consumption was often tougher than his demands in the negotiating process, however, indicate that differences between him and Lesage were less than is generally assumed.[24] Johnson and Bertrand reiterated the demands of the previous administration for, among other things, the right to 100 percent of all major direct taxes collected in the province, restriction on Ottawa's role in distributing funds to individuals via various national social programs funded either by the federal government alone or on a shared-cost basis, and full provincial responsibility for programs such as pensions, manpower training, family allowances, health, and welfare. Johnson asserted that in all of these areas, special status for Quebec was desirable. He added that Ottawa's arrangements with Quebec should not be contingent upon the former's arrangements with the other provinces; after all, Quebec was not a province like the others. The Trudeau government reiterated its position that it would not enter into agreements with Quebec which might add to the semblance of special status for that province, as had resulted from the opting-out provision both in the 1959 agreement on the post-secondary education grants and the 1964 agreement on pensions.[25] Despite such pronouncements, however, evidence suggests that the Trudeau government made certain concessions to the Johnson-Bertrand regime, as well as subsequent Quebec governments, in areas such as international relations and immigration that are tantamount to some form of *de facto*, though not necessarily *de jure*, special status.

An increased role in international relations and immigration was the third major objective of the Johnson-Bertrand regime. In these areas it also seemed more assertive and ambitious than its predecessor and gained significant concessions from both the Pearson and Trudeau governments. Its principal objective was to broaden the role which had been conceded to the Lesage administration in the Francophonie.[26] In its efforts to increase its role in the field of immigration, the Johnson-Bertrand administration upgraded a small immigration bureau established by its predecessor into a full fledged department and concluded a verbal agreement with the federal government giving Quebec greater powers and a more direct role in that policy sector.[27] That verbal agreement was followed by a series of written bilateral Quebec-Ottawa agreements under the Bourassa regime in 1971 and 1975 and under the Lévesque regime in 1978, which in an incrementalist fashion have broadened Quebec's powers and roles in the recruitment and selection of certain classes of immigrants. In the absence of similar powers and roles for other provinces, that is tantamount to what some consider a form of special status for Quebec in this policy sector.[28]

BOURASSA (1970–1976): CULTURAL AUTONOMY AND PROFITABLE FEDERALISM

Bourassa, like his predecessors, sought a decentralized but financially "profitable federalism" in which Quebec could attain the requisite powers and financial resources to maximize its autonomy in the social and cultural spheres within the context of the Canadian federal system, even if it entailed some form of special status. Indeed, both for Bourassa and his strongly provincialist social services minister, Claude Castonguay, this was the key objective in negotiations with Ottawa. In 1973, for example, they concluded a Quebec-Ottawa agreement on the establishment of a provincially administered family allowances program which could vary the federal benefits rate.[29] Ottawa extended the offer to all other provinces but, to date, Quebec has been the only province to establish and operate its own plan and, except for Alberta, to vary the federal rate.[30] This is another example of Quebec gaining a concession from the federal government which, for various political reasons, the latter has felt compelled to extend to all other provinces in order to avoid the semblance of, and possible criticism for, granting Quebec special status.

The overarching objective of the Bourassa regime in the area of constitutional reform was, unlike the Johnson-Bertrand regime, not the entrenchment of a binational state per se, but a reformed federal system designed to give Quebec special powers and resources to facilitate the "preservation and development of the bicultural character of the Canadian federation."[31] In other words, its objective was to devise a constitution more cognizant of the cultural needs of the Québécois rather than the political emancipation of the "French-Canadian nation" via constitutional reform based on the "dual alliance" perspective of Confederation. Among other changes sought by the Bourassa government during the negotiations on the Victoria Charter was an amendment to section 94A of the constitution to grant the provinces paramountcy in the field of pensions and other fields of social policy. The federal government's refusal to accommodate Quebec in this matter angered nationalist and provincialist factions both inside and outside the provincial Liberal Party. Those factions pressured Bourassa to reject the Victoria Charter after he had initially agreed to it in principle, ostensibly because neither the constitution nor the proposed amending formula provided adequate scope and safeguards for Quebec's cultural sovereignty. Thus, once again as in 1961 and 1966, it was opposition from the strong provincialist and nationalist forces inside and outside the governing party combined with the prospect of losing electoral support that led a Quebec government to reject a constitutional amending formula.

In 1975, the federal government reopened the constitutional negotiations with a discussion paper which proposed that the focus be limited to patriation and an amending formula. The exercise of powers in social policy, communication, and immigration would be clarified in subsequent negotiations through bilateral and multilateral federal-provincial agreements rather than formal constitutional reform. That discussion paper also contained a revised version of the Victoria Charter which reflected Bourassa's views from 1971 that the preservation and full development of the French language and Québécois culture was a fundamental purpose of the Canadian federation. According to Garth Stevenson, therein also "lurked the spectre of unilateral delegation of powers, and indeed of 'special status for Quebec'."[32] The Bourassa regime reluctantly agreed to consider patriation with an amending formula without prior agreement on the division of powers, provided there were significant "constitutional guarantees" for the French language and culture.[33] Perhaps it did so in search of an issue which might detract from criticism on its general performance during its mandate. In seeking a new mandate it made constitutional reform one of the major components of its platform. Bourassa's campaign literature stated that patriation would be supported provided that a new constitution included Quebec's traditional demands which, among other things, included a Quebec veto over constitutional amendments; participation in Supreme Court appointments; provincial paramountcy in cultural and educational matters; the right to opt-out of federal programs with compensation; provincial participation in the recruitment and selection of immigrants and paramountcy in their integration in Quebec society and placement in the labour market; and severe limitations on Ottawa's declaratory and spending powers in areas of provincial jurisdiction, though not in other areas.[34] These proposals, which clearly reflect Bourassa's provincialist posture and his dual objective of cultural autonomy and profitable federalism, were not enough to garner an electoral victory. In November 1976, the Liberal government was replaced by Parti Québécois and would not return to power until 1985. In the interim the Parti Québécois confronted Ottawa with its own objectives and demands.

LÉVESQUE & JOHNSON (1976–1985): SOVEREIGNTY-ASSOCIATION VIA SPECIAL STATUS

The Parti Québécois regime, under the leadership of René Lévesque and briefly Pierre-Marc Johnson's in 1985, accepted special status only as an interim measure en route to its stated objective of sovereignty-association, embodying the dual principle of political sovereignty and economic association.[35] In this regard it differed from both the Lesage and Bourassa Liberal governments, for whom sovereignty-association and independence were not feasible or desirable options and also Daniel Johnson's Union Nationale, for whom independence was an alternative or final option only if all else failed. Ironically perhaps, while sovereignty-association remained a cornerstone of the Parti Québécois's platform throughout its stay in power it was subordinated during each of its election campaigns from 1976–85 to avoid alienating certain parts of the electorate that balked at the idea. Indeed, it was probably the realization that it was a risky venture to hold an election on the issue that led the Lévesque government to permit Quebecers to express a preference through a referendum rather than an election.

The Parti Québécois and its objective of sovereignty-association added new imperatives and dimensions to Quebec-Ottawa relations, particularly during the three major phases of constitutional negotiation between 1976 and 1985: pre-referendum, post-referendum/patriation, and post-patriation.[36]

During the pre-referendum constitutional negotiating process the Parti Québécois regime was more reactive than proactive. Basically, it reacted against federal initiatives for constitutional patriation and reform outlined in the federal white paper ("A Time for Action") and the corresponding legislation (Bill C-60), which contained many of the provisions of the Victoria Charter. During this phase, however, the Parti Québécois government refused to consider the renewal of Confederation. Its stated objective was to exercise the Québécois nation's right to self-determination pursuant to the United Nations Declaration of Human Rights in order to attain full political sovereignty and possibly sovereignty-association for Quebec through democratic means.[37]

In this phase and, to a varying extent, in some of the subsequent phases the Lévesque government opposed at least four major aspects of the federal constitutional patriation and reform plan.

First, in keeping with the traditional position of all Quebec governments since 1960, it opposed the federal government's proposed approach of postponing negotiations on comprehensive reforms in the division of powers until agreement had been reached on patriation with an amending formula and possibly also a charter of rights and freedoms. It did so based on the calculation that by accepting the federal approach Quebec would lose a key bargaining chip in the negotiations over the division of powers because the federal government, after it had achieved its principal goals, would be less inclined to make concessions. This was also the rationale for the strong opposition to the alternate federal approach of unilateral patriation that Quebec, along with other provinces, challenged in the courts with mixed results. Towards the end of the second and during the third phases of constitutional negotiations Premier Lévesque moved away from this traditional position.[38] To a large extent, perhaps, he was constrained to do so by the federal government's legal and political victories during those phases.

Second, the Lévesque government opposed any amending formula which did not grant it both broad veto and opting-out powers deemed essential to protect the interests and character of Quebec.

Third, it opposed the entrenchment of a charter of rights and freedoms that was national in scope. It felt that without the necessary limitations with respect to its applicability in Quebec, such a charter would not only preclude provincial variations in rights and freedoms but also circumscribe provincial powers, impinge on provincial laws such as Quebec's language law (Bill 101), and ultimately strengthen the role of the courts at the expense of the legislatures, thereby moving Canada toward "judicial federalism" and away from executive and administrative federalism. Its fears were not unfounded. In 1986 the Quebec Court of Appeal ruled that Quebec's language law restricting the use of languages other than French on public signs is unconstitutional under the Canadian Charter of Rights and Freedoms.[39]

Fourth, the Lévesque government opposed federal proposals for very limited adjustment to the division of powers prior to patriation. Again in keeping with the position of its precursors, it argued that Ottawa's proposed adjustments did not meet Quebec's objectives for a significant decentralization of powers and resources, a broader role in decisions regarding national institutions and policies/programs affecting that province, a constitutionally recognized special status, and in general maximized provincial autonomy.

In 1979 the Quebec government received support for its objectives of a more decentralized federation, a greater provincial role in determining minority language rights, and de facto and possibly even de jure special status for that province in the recommendations of the federal Task Force on Canadian Unity.[40] The federal government, however, did not accept the thrust of those recommendations and continued to work with its own agenda.

The lack of positive results during the first phase of constitutional negotiations led the Lévesque administration to pursue the sovereignty-association option in a more direct and vigorous fashion in the referendum phase. In June 1979, one month after the election of Clark's Conservative government with its "community of communities" depiction of Canada, Premier Lévesque announced that a referendum on sovereignty-association would be held the following spring. In the interim, he tabled the white paper

on sovereignty-association ("Quebec-Canada: A New Deal") and the referendum question, both of which were strongly debated within his cabinet, caucus and party, as well as in the National Assembly and the media.[41] By the time the preliminary planning for the referendum was completed, the Lévesque government was faced with the surprising return to power of Pierre Elliott Trudeau, who not only proved instrumental in the referendum win by the "NON" forces, but was more determined than ever to implement his constitutional plan with or without the support of the Parti Québécois government.

The post-referendum/patriation phase of the constitutional negotiations was premised on the widespread view that the referendum result (60% NON, 40% OUI) reflected a desire in Quebec for a new constitutional order which the federalist forces had promised during the referendum campaign. Shortly after the referendum, the Lévesque administration was again reacting to federal initiatives for constitutional patriation and reform. The federal government was motivated by what it considered a mandate or moral imperative from the Québécois to achieve constitutional reform. It was also motivated by two additional and related considerations. First, the fact that it would not be confronting a Liberal provincial government in Quebec minimized the possibility of a schism between the provincial and federal wing of the Liberal party. Second, the fact that the government in power was avowedly separatist and had incurred a loss of political support and party unity in the course of the referendum campaign strengthened Ottawa's hand both in Quebec and in the rest of the country.

From June 1980 to the historic federal-provincial conference of first ministers in November 1981, where it was alone in refusing to sign the constitutional accord, the Quebec government, with the express support of all parties in the National Assembly, reiterated its complaints about the federal approach. Lévesque's efforts to form and maintain a united provincial front among the "gang of eight" (all provinces except Ontario and

New Brunswick) against the federal government's constitutional package proved futile. In the eleventh hour the other seven premiers abandoned Premier Lévesque despite their "common positions" agreement, which included several major, albeit contradictory, concessions both by Quebec and the other provinces. The Quebec Premier conceded the equality of all provinces principle and, contrary to his earlier position, consented to patriation with an amending formula without first either revising the division of powers or securing a Quebec veto. The other provincial premiers conceded that Quebec is a distinct linguistic and cultural society with a special role and status, including the right to maintain or sever ties with the Canadian federation.[42] The latter part of that concession was deemed particularly important by the Lévesque government because not only would it justify increased autonomy within the context of Canadian federalism, but such recognition also constituted a significant step toward sovereignty under international law. Trudeau's refusal to assign Quebec special roles and status in the Constitution Act of 1982 was based on his traditional reluctance to heighten Quebec's status either under international law or in the constitution. Indeed, even when accommodating Quebec at the de facto level he made considerable efforts to preclude any semblance of special status. Trudeau's efforts to encourage all provinces to sign immigration agreements comparable, though not identical, to that signed by Quebec in 1978 is a case in point.[43]

The post-patriation phase of constitutional negotiation essentially commenced after the 1984 federal election when the Conservatives replaced the Liberals in Ottawa. Premier Lévesque declared the negotiations with the new government a "beau risque" both for the Parti Québécois and for the province of Quebec. In May 1985 he presented the Mulroney government with its "Draft Agreement on the Constitution" containing Quebec's twenty-two conditions for signing a constitutional accord.[44] The introductory remarks in the "Draft Agreement" suggest that the Quebec government's strategy was to pressure the Mulroney government to live up to its 1984 campaign statements regarding the importance of Quebec signing the constitutional accord and its pledge to facilitate that process. The thrust of proposals in the Parti Québécois' "Draft Agreement" was a reiteration of positions advocated since 1960 to maximize Quebec's powers, resources, roles, status, and autonomy within Confederation. Toward that end it proposed the following:

1. Constitutional recognition of Quebec as a distinct society and its provincial government as the principal authority in social, cultural, linguistic, educational, and health matters;

2. Limited applicability of the Canadian Charter of Rights and Freedoms in Quebec to include only democratic rights (Sections 3–5);

3. Recognition of Quebec's primary responsibility over employment, economic, and regional development policies and programs;

4. Significantly increased powers for Quebec in the field of communications, exclusive jurisdiction in marriage and divorce, paramount jurisdiction in the selection and settlement of immigrants, and a greater role and status in international relations "in all that relates to its jurisdictions and its identity, particularly within the framework of the 'Francophonie'";

5. Recognition of Quebec's right to veto not only constitutional amendments, but also the creation of new provinces and the reform of certain national institutions;

6. The right to appoint both the three judges trained in Civil Law to the Supreme Court of Canada, and also Quebec Superior Court judges;

7. Recognition of Quebec's right to opt-out of both certain constitutional

amendments as well as conditional-grant programs, with compensation;

8. Abolishing the federal government's powers of reservation and disallowance and severely limiting the scope of its spending power by making conditional grants subject to the will of the majority of provinces.

The contents of that document, and particularly the proposals to grant Quebec a veto and expand its powers, suggest the Parti Québécois government had temporarily settled for special status, something which only six years earlier it had criticized as a dangerous illusion both for Quebec and the rest of Canada.[45] According to one analyst it effectively opens the door to [*de jure*] special status which would confirm the actual situation of Quebec."[46] Conspicuous by its absence in those proposals, of course, is "sovereignty-association," the traditionally distinguishing objective of the Parti Québécois which, despite considerable opposition within the party was temporarily subordinated, as it was in its election platforms of 1976, 1981, and 1985.

Despite the subordination of that irritant in his government's relations with Ottawa, however, Premier Lévesque again was unable to conclude a constitutional accord with the federal government and the other provinces. Deep divisions within the Parti Québécois and Premier Lévesque's Cabinet both over the issue of constitutional reform and whether sovereignty would be included in the next election platform precluded concerted efforts at negotiation. Such divisions were not new for the Parti Québécois. In 1979, 1981, and 1984, for example, Premier Lévesque had to convince his party to settle for sovereignty-association rather than seek a mandate on the more sensitive issue of full independence because the latter option posed serious electoral risks. In 1981 it required a special vote dubbed the "Renérendum," prompted by Lévesque's threat to resign, for the party to rescind an earlier vote calling for full independence.

Eventually, in 1985 this and related issues precipitated both the resignation of several prominent cabinet ministers from the Lévesque government and, in turn, the Premier's own resignation.[47] Ironically, some of the disgruntled ministers who resigned that year joined a coalition for independence, just as Lévesque himself had done nearly two decades earlier.

The tasks of negotiating a constitutional accord and uniting the Parti Québécois's general membership, caucus, and cabinet were left to Lévesque's successor, Pierre Marc Johnson, who led the party into a provincial election shortly after he assumed the premiership. In an effort to find the middle ground between various factions both within his party and the province he declared that the sovereignty-association option had not been abandoned, but his immediate goal was to gain concessions from Ottawa that maximized Quebec's status and autonomy within the Canadian federation. For that purpose, both during the 1985 election campaign and his short term as premier, he endorsed the thrust of the proposals contained in the "Draft Agreement," which constituted the core of his policy of "national affirmation."

Some of those proposals were also endorsed by the Quebec Liberal Party both during and after the 1985 provincial election. Consequently, as of the 1985 election the two major parties adopted very similar positions on constitutional reform and other federal-provincial matters.

The major difference between them has been the future prospect of sovereignty-association, which remains a central albeit temporarily subordinated objective of the Parti Québécois, but not of the Quebec Liberal Party which, according to one of its policy papers, prefers to retain existing ties with the rest of Canada and engage in a "pragmatic and positive approach" to federal-provincial relations.[48] The principal differences in the area of constitutional reform relate primarily to the applicability of the Canadian Charter of Rights and Freedoms in the province of Quebec and the scope of Quebec's powers in a revised constitution.[49]

BOURASSA: RETURN TO CULTURAL AUTONOMY AND PROFITABLE FEDERALISM

The election of the Bourassa government on December 2, 1985, marked a reassertion of the cultural autonomy and profitable federalism objectives advocated both by the Lesage and Bourassa governments in previous decades.

The pursuit of those objectives was evident at the First Ministers' Conference on the Economy in November 1986, where Premier Bourassa demanded a greater transfer of fiscal resources from Ottawa as a means to increase Quebec's cultural autonomy, roles, and status within Confederation, as well as in the constitutional negotiations leading to the Meech Lake Accord on April 30, 1987, and the more detailed Langevin Block Accord of June 3, 1987.

Before engaging in negotiations with the federal government on constitutional reform, however, the Bourassa regime modified at least two major policies relating to constitutional matters enacted by the Parti Québécois government. First, it relented on the enforcement of the French-only sign law; and second, it terminated the blanket application of the "notwithstanding clause" of the Constitution (section 33) to all provincial laws, ostensibly because, according to Gil Rémillard, Minister of Intergovernmental Affairs, it amounted to little more than an empty symbolic gesture which deprived Quebecers of fundamental constitutional rights. "The Quebec government," he said, "does not have the right to take Quebecers hostage for the purpose of constitutional talks."[50] Upon reforming these provincial policies on constitutional matters, the Bourassa government turned its attention to constitutional negotiations with Ottawa and the other provinces.

The Bourassa government's principal objectives for constitutional reform emanated from various policy papers of the Quebec Liberal Party produced during the late seventies and early eighties.[51] Of particular significance is the 1985 policy paper ("Mastering Our Future") which echoed the perspectives and broad objectives of previous Quebec Liberal governments, criticized the Parti Québécois' approach to intergovernmental relations and constitutional negotiations, and outlined the following five major conditions for constitutional reform which served as the basis of negotiations leading to the Meech Lake and Langevin Block accords:

1. the explicit constitutional recognition of Quebec as a "distinct society," homeland of the francophone element of Canada's duality;
2. solid guarantees for Quebec's cultural security by increasing Quebec's constitutional right to a critical role in the recruitment and selection of immigrants to that province;
3. granting Quebec the key role in the appointment of the three Supreme Court Judges with expertise in Quebec civil law;
4. limiting the federal government's spending power in areas of provincial jurisdiction; and
5. a full veto on constitutional reform, entrenched in the amending formula.[52]

Both at Meech Lake and at the follow-up constitutional conference in the Langevin Block in Ottawa, Premier Bourassa convinced all other first ministers to accept those five conditions for signing the constitutional accord even though, in some cases, he made some compromises on the wording of the text. Ultimately, however, the Langevin Block accord requires a constitutional amendment providing Quebec with

— constitutional recognition as "a distinct society" which is to be preserved by the federal government and preserved and promoted by the Quebec government;
— the right to require the federal government to select the three "Quebec" judges for the Supreme Court of Canada from a list of candi-

dates submitted by the Quebec provincial government;

— the right to require the federal government to select Senators from Quebec from a list of candidates submitted by the Quebec provincial government, at least until more extensive State reform is achieved;

— a veto over constitutional amendments to all matters outlined in section 42 of the Constitution Act, 1982, which previously required the support of only ⅔ of the provinces with 50% of the population for matters regarding the number of Senators and M.P.s from each province, the powers and methods of selecting Senators, changes to the Supreme Court, the establishment of new provinces, and the extension of existing provinces into the territories;

— the right to opt-out of national shared-cost programs in areas of exclusive provincial jurisdiction with compensation, provided the province initiates a comparable program "that is compatible with the national objectives";

— power over the selection of immigrants and a guarantee of "reasonable" compensation for costs incurred in the settlement of "foreign nationals" within Quebec.[53]

Several key observations are in order regarding these provisions in the proposed constitutional amendment flowing from the Meech Lake and Langevin Block accords. First, some sections of the proposed amendment simply give *de jure* recognition to de facto developments in federal-provincial relations since the early sixties. The principle of opting-out with compensation, for example, had been utilized in certain limited cases in previous decades in some fields of jurisdiction, and as noted in the Meech Lake accord, Quebec's role in the selection of independent immigrants had been granted in 1978 under the Cullen-Couture agreement. Second, the thrust of section 40 of the Constitution Act,

1982, regarding opting-out with compensation would be broadened if the proposed amendment is adopted. Whereas in the Constitution Act, 1982, compensation was limited to provincial powers relating to "education and cultural matters," the proposed amendment would extend compensation to all fields of provincial jurisdiction. Third, the proposed veto on constitutional amendments is not exclusive to Quebec. The unanimity principle which previously applied only to section 41, has been extended to include all matters in section 42. The requirement for seven provinces with 50% of the population, however, still applies to other constitutional amendments.

In 1987, the opposition parties and various provincialists and nationalists in Quebec adopted the traditional posture of criticizing the government for compromising on demands related to Quebec's autonomy and cultural integrity. Parti Québécois leader Pierre-Marc Johnson charged that the agreement was "a leap backwards for Quebec," and NDP leader Jean-Paul Harney charged that it would "mortgage the province's future" and leave it weaker.[54]

Johnson and Harney were particularly critical of the ambiguities surrounding the "distinct society" clause and the limited and mitigated scope of the veto power. They criticized the Bourassa regime for its inability to gain an exclusive veto. They maintained that Quebec's veto had been compromised because it was also granted to other provinces. With such a veto power other provinces could frustrate future constitutional and institutional reforms advocated by Quebec, the federal government, and a majority of the provinces. Bourassa, however, insisted that this concession to the other provinces did not detract from his province's gains. They also charged that the "distinct society" clause fails to secure Quebec full power over language matters because it is unduly ambiguous and could be subject to counter-productive interpretation by the courts. Johnson argued that the wording of that particular section of the accords merely served to entrench the status quo and reaffirmed the primacy of the federal Charter of Rights and Freedoms. Premier Bourassa and his Minister of Intergovernmental Affairs responded that they had "won absolute protection for the French culture" and that the power of the provincial legislature to make laws on language matters was "100 percent watertight." Premier Bourassa added that if the courts failed to agree with the Quebec government on this point, the latter could invoke the notwithstanding clause (section 33) of the constitution, allowing it to override the federal Charter of Rights and Freedoms. He also insisted that once this accord is entrenched there would be other opportunities for future gains.[55]

The opposition parties were also critical of the process utilized by the Quebec government during the constitutional negotiations, especially the lack of opportunity for public input during the early stages. The leader of the Quebec NDP proposed a provincial referendum for the ratification of the constitutional amendment as a means to ensure public input and consent.

Pierre-Marc Johnson's criticism of the details of the accord was not fully based on differences in substance. After all, the key elements of Bourassa's demands were very similar to the conditions outlined in the Parti Québécois' 1985 "Draft Agreement on the Constitution" and its policy of "national affirmation," endorsed at the June 1987 P.Q. convention, which entails a backing away from the party's separatist policies in favour of a gradual accumulation of powers for the province within the federation.[56]

The signing of the Meech Lake and the Langevin Block accords is significant in several regards. First, it is indicative of Quebec's role as a major provincial force in federal-provincial relations. Second, most of the contents of those accords provides further evidence of the federal government's traditional tendency to grant all other provinces almost everything it grants Quebec. It does so for the dual purpose of gaining the

support of the other provinces and minimizing or precluding criticisms of granting special status to Quebec. Third, there was a departure from the traditional federal government position not to explicitly recognize Quebec as a unique or "distinct society" within the constitution even though in certain instances it did so in practice. Similarly, it marked a departure from the federal practice of widening the scope of its spending power, in favour of a limitation of the same in areas of provincial jurisdiction. Fourth, it is evidence of the success of Quebec's strategy of étapisme, whereby after making incremental gains at the *de facto* level for several years, it is poised at this stage in history to make significant gains at the de jure level. Fifth, it provides further evidence of the persistent criticism faced by Quebec provincial governments from the opposition parties and various provincialist and nationalist factions within Quebec for in any way compromising Quebec's ability to retain or to augment its powers, status, autonomy, and fiscal resources. This persistent criticism results in a process of inflating demands towards Ottawa, a long-established tradition of Quebec politics which is fuelled by the parties' fears of being outflanked.

Still, the question remains: Why could a constitutional agreement which included Quebec be reached in 1987, but not in 1982? The major reason is that there were key changes in political imperatives and personalities in Quebec, Ottawa, and to some extent in other provinces.

For Bourassa and Mulroney there was an electoral imperative for Quebec to sign the constitution. Both had made strong commitments during their respective electoral campaigns to get Quebec's signature on the constitution. Failure on their part to do so could be interpreted as an unkept election promise and have a negative impact on the electoral fortunes of their parties within Quebec. Moreover, philosophical differ-

ences between the Bourassa and Mulroney regimes were not as great as they had been between
the Trudeau and Lévesque regimes. Unlike
Lévesque, whose separatist goals clashed in
principle with constitutional reform to maintain
the federal system, either in its existing or marginally modified form, Bourassa was committed
to increasing Quebec's powers and status within
the existing federal framework. Similarly, unlike
Trudeau, who held a vision of a federal system
with a constitutionally powerful national government in which Quebec could expect special concessions and accommodations primarily at the
de facto but not *de jure* level, the Meech Lake
and Langevin Block accords suggest that Mulroney is quite prepared to accommodate Quebec at
the *de jure* level by, among other things, granting
that province constitutional recognition as a distinct society. In fact, Trudeau's intervention during the negotiations on the Meech Lake accord
was largely based on fundamental objections to
the constitutional entrenchment of certain common practices in federal-provincial relations
which, in his view, did more than simply give de
jure recognition to developments at the *de facto*
level; rather, entrenchment transformed "federal
concessions" at the *de facto* level into "provincial rights" at the *de jure* level.[57]

Agreement was also reached because the other
provincial governments had their own expedient
reasons for supporting the Quebec initiative. By
supporting Quebec's demands, they obtained concessions on constitutional and institutional reforms
from the federal government which they may have
not been able to secure on their own. Unlike 1982,
unanimity was required in 1987 for amendment,
hence the other provinces could not achieve their
objectives if Quebec did not endorse the final accord. Finally, the first ministers' willingness to
endorse this accord was undoubtedly facilitated by
the lack of strong opposition across the country.

All of these imperatives, personalities, and
expedient considerations coalesced in 1987 to
produce a propitious moment for a constitutional
accord. Nevertheless, it is noteworthy that unlike
1982 when the Constitution Act was given royal
assent, as of June 1987 the Langevin Block accord is still at the preliminary stages of the entrenchment process and its entrenchment in its
present form is not assured. It may still be subject
to a metamorphosis and possibly even outright
rejection by one or more of the signatories as it is
debated in the national and provincial legislatures. Quebec's last minute rejection of the Victoria Charter in 1971 and the Constitution Act of
1982 suggests that the closer governments get to
entrenchment, the more difficult it becomes to
achieve unanimity.

Even if constitutional entrenchment is
achieved, however, it does not represent the final
stage in demands for constitutional reform from
Quebec. Indeed, the entrenchment of the
Langevin Block accord may constitute only the
first, albeit an important round for Bourassa in the
area of constitutional negotiations. The second
round, according to Quebec's Minister of Intergovernmental Affairs, will entail negotiations on
further constitutional and institutional reforms.[58]
In fact, the agenda for the second round, as outlined in the Meech Lake and Langevin Block
accords, includes: Senate reform; roles and responsibilities of the various levels of government
in fisheries; entrenchment of annual First Ministers' conferences both on the Constitution and on
the economy; and any "other agreed upon matters" that first ministers consider important for
negotiations.

The willingness of the various governments
to engage in the second round of negotiations will
undoubtedly depend on how they fare in this first
round. After all, constitutional reform is not only
a dangerous endeavour, it is usually taxing on both
the principal combatants and their parties.
Bourassa's government, even if it is successful in
this round of negotiations, will probably not engage in a second round until it obtains another

electoral mandate. Cultural autonomy and profitable federalism will undoubtedly remain the key coordinates for the Bourassa regime in federal-provincial relations and constitutional reform.

THE PURSUIT OF SPECIAL STATUS: AN ASSESSMENT

This overview underscores several important perspectives on the nature of the Quebec polity and the dynamics of its politics in the past quarter-century. First, Quebec is a highly heterogeneous, fragmented, and dynamic polity, perhaps more so than any other provincial polity in Canada.[59] The duality (francophone-anglophone) that characterizes Canada as a whole is replicated in Quebec, albeit in reverse numerical proportions. The two linguistic groups are divided into at least four, by no means mutually exclusive camps (i.e. federalists, provincialists, nationalists, and separatists) which in turn are themselves divided into factions between and within parties, each with its own objectives, priorities, and strategies.[60] Second, Quebec politics do not simply revolve around questions of distribution and redistribution, but also entail fundamental questions about the nature, composition, and organization of both the Quebec and Canadian polities. Third, there have been frequent changes of political parties in power. Finally, agreements between these governments and the federal government at the constitutional, fiscal, and programmatic level are contingent on political conditions and considerations at any given point in time.

There are several striking features of the constitutional, fiscal, and policy/program objectives of Quebec governments since 1960. First, there are similarities and differences in their respective objectives related to Quebec's powers, rights, and status within the Canadian federation. All Quebec governments agree that Quebec must have maximum political autonomy to safeguard its unique linguistic and cultural heritage. In their efforts to maximize that province's autonomy in the federation they have generally demanded the following:

1. recognition of Quebec as a distinct society;

2. *de jure* and *de facto* constitutional reform that not only guarantees Quebec a veto power, but also maximizes the scope of Quebec's jurisdiction and, concomitantly, minimizes federal jurisdiction in most policy fields;

3. a division of federal-provincial fiscal resources that is more advantageous for Quebec;

4. a reduced federal role in the development, delivery, and financing of provincial policies/programs; and

5. an increased Quebec role both in determining the composition and operation of federal institutions, and also in decisions regarding the development, delivery, and financing of federal policies/programs.

In short, within the existing federal system, successive Quebec governments have generally sought to move towards a "dual federalism" in matters of provincial jurisdiction and concern, and towards both "cooperative federalism" and "intrastate federalism" in matters traditionally of federal jurisdiction and concern.

Not all Quebec governments, however, agreed either on marginal adjustments to the terms of Confederation or even Quebec's full membership within the Canadian federation. The Parti Québécois administration, for example, claimed that Quebec could not realize all of its aspirations under either existing or marginally modified terms of Confederation. Its demands for changes to those terms in Quebec's favour constituted only an interim measure until they could be supplanted with sovereignty-association or even full independence. Towards that end, it adopted a stage by stage strategy that would neither jeopardize its position as the governing party nor give rise to radical conflict within the Quebec polity. This is what is commonly referred to as its strategy of étapisme.

Second, in terms of Quebec's roles within the Canadian federation there is an ascriptive and a substantive dimension to consider. In the ascriptive dimension, for Quebec governments it does not make a significant difference whether Confederation is depicted either as a compact between provinces or an alliance between two language group; in both cases they ascribe to themselves important, powers, roles, and status either as founding signatories of the "provincial compact" or legitimate representatives of the French-speaking group in the "linguistic alliance."[61] Differences between them on this point tend to be on the precise nature of Quebec's relations with the rest of the country as reflected in slogans such as "égalité," "statut particulier," "états associés," "souveraineté culturelle," "souveraineté association," and "indépendance."

In the substantive dimension, since the early sixties and even earlier, Quebec provincial governments have been a powerful force at the forefront of the provincial rights movement. They have been instrumental not only in expanding both the scope of provincial responsibility in most policy sectors and the provincial share of fiscal resources, but also in blocking or precluding federal intrusions into areas of provincial jurisdiction. Thus, although successive Quebec governments have not been able to attain all of their objectives, there is no doubt that, both individually and collectively, they have had a significant impact on both Quebec's powers, resources, roles, and status within the federation and ultimately the structure of the Canadian federation and the dynamics of intergovernmental relations therein.

Third, several analysts agree that Quebec has attained a form of special status in some, if not all, policy sectors.[62] They do so despite acknowledgement of conceptual problems related to special status. Beckton and Mackay, for example, concede that "one reason that the Quebec status issue is so perplexing is that it encompasses many different components. The use of the term 'status' begs the question: status in what sense? Legal status, political status, cultural status and eco-nomic status all suggest different considerations." Nevertheless, they conclude that "Quebec does have a *de facto* special status in Canada. The question is how much *de jure* special status Quebec should have."[63]

The conceptual problems associated with special status lead us to be cautious in our assessment of Quebec's case. Special status should not be confused with the rightful assertion of a province in fields of jurisdiction, including those that are constitutionally unchartered or judicially unexplored, provided such fields are equally available to all provinces who wish to assert themselves therein. By the same token, however, the fact that either one or even several, though not all other provinces enjoy the same special rights or privileges does not in itself deny that Quebec has a special status; rather, it might be that several provinces share a special status in some or all policy sectors. For this reason it might be useful to distinguish between exclusive versus shared special status. Similarly, it may be useful to distinguish between initiatory and permanent special status. Unlike the latter, which implies permanence, the former refers to a province's capacity to initiate and attain changes either in its powers, resources, or roles vis-à-vis the federal government, which Ottawa then concedes to all other provinces.[64]

Thus, insofar as one may infer an element of special status in Quebec's case, our analysis suggests that generally (the special provisions for Quebec in the Constitution Act of 1867 regarding the Civil Code aside) Quebec's special status has been limited in the past quarter-century to certain policy sectors related to social and cultural matters; it is *de facto* rather than *de jure* and "initiatory" rather than permanent. Quebec-Ottawa agreements in the fields of pensions, immigration, and family allowances are cases in point. Recommendations both of the Task Force on Canadian Unity and most recently of the Macdonald Royal Commission to grant Quebec some form of *de facto* and even *de jure* special status suggest that many of Quebec's demands are increasingly being recognized as legitimate and plausible by prominent figures linked to the federal level.[65] This is bound to help Quebec's search for constitutionally entrenched special status. Indeed, the recognition of Quebec as a "distinct society" in the Meech Lake and Langevin Block accords is a significant step in that direction which, if entrenched in the constitution, would be tantamount to de jure special status for that province.

The developments of the past quarter-century suggest that while we can expect changes of players it is unlikely that, at least in the short term, there will be significant changes either in the objectives of Quebec governments or in the dynamics both within Quebec and in its relations with the rest of Canada. While there is little consensus on probable or even desirable developments in Quebec's relations with the rest of Canada, most would agree that something needs to be done soon to rectify the anomalous situation whereby the province representing over one-quarter of the country's population is subject to a major part of a written constitution that it has not officially endorsed.[66]

Recent efforts by the federal government to get Quebec's signature on the 1982 Constitution Act suggest it is cognizant that Quebec's objectives cannot be overlooked or frustrated indefinitely. After all, secession either with or without some limited form of economic association is no longer considered a radical option. The Parti Québécois has made most people realize that, even though its costs and benefits for Quebec and Canada remains a moot point, it is a plausible option.

Indeed, perhaps this "secessionist potential," presently much stronger in Quebec than in any other province, makes it a province unlike the others and partly facilitates its ability to attain special powers, resources, roles, and status within the Canadian federation. That ability, of course, is also facilitated by the nature and electoral significance of its population given the dynamics of the federal electoral and party systems. Ironically,

while the nature and dynamics of the Quebec political system provide the impetus and momentum for the Quebec provincial governments to negotiate a better deal, those same factors traditionally have also generated forces which divide Quebec and weaken its government in the intergovernmental bargaining process. Even on the issue of greater autonomy on which, in principle at least, there has been a high degree of consensus among Quebecers, some differences persist between and even within parties about the exact nature of such autonomy, as well as the most feasible and desirable means and timetable to achieve it.

Nevertheless, since 1985 there has been a growing consensus among the major parties within Quebec on the issue of constitutional reform. In addition to the convergence which occurred in the position of the Liberal Party and Parti Québécois during the 1985 electoral campaign, in January 1987 the Quebec New Democratic Party embraced the autonomist position of those two parties. In its efforts to establish itself as a major party in that province the NDPQ adopted several proposals which, in terms of the right to self-determination at least, surpass those of the current Liberal government. Among its major proposals were a veto power in all areas that impinge on provincial jurisdiction, the right to opt-out of national programs with compensation, exclusive jurisdiction on linguistic matters, and the right to self-determination.[67] Such proposals reflect the political imperatives that impinge on the electoral success of all parties in Quebec and are consistent with the objective of successive governments to maximize that province's autonomy. No government or major provincial party in Quebec can afford to accept a constitutional settlement that restricts this autonomy. The political events of the past quarter-century in Quebec certainly offer no indications of a significant departure.

Notes

1. The socio-cultural, socio-economic, and ideological bases of their objectives are analyzed in several works. See, for example, Alain G. Gagnon, ed., *Quebec: State and Society* (Toronto: Methuen, 1984); Kenneth McRoberts and Dale Posgate, *Quebec: Social Change and Political Crisis* (Toronto: McClelland and Stewart, 1980); William D. Coleman, *The Independence Movement in Quebec: 1945–1980* (Toronto: University of Toronto Press, 1984), 3–19; Michael D. Behiels, *Prelude to Quebec's Quiet Revolution: Liberalism Versus Neo-Nationalism, 1945–1960* (Kingston: McGill-Queen's University Press, 1985); and Denis Monière, *Ideologies in Quebec: the Historical Development* (Toronto: University of Toronto Press, 1981).

2. For a good primary source which contrasts the position of the Lesage Liberals with that of the Union Nationale just prior to the 1960 election, see Jean Lesage, *Lesage s'engage: liberalisme québécois d'aujourd'hui* (Montréal: Les Editions Politiques du Québec, 1959); for a discussion on various forms of Quebec nationalism and their perspectives on federalism in that era, see Behiels, *Prelude*, 37–60, 185–219.

3. Duplessis verbalized the "maître chez soi" slogan as early as the 1945 election campaign; see Herbert F. Quinn, *The Union Nationale: A Study in Quebec Nationalism* (Toronto: University of Toronto Press, 1963), 191. For excerpts from speeches by Jean Lesage (Lib.), René Lévesque (Lib.), Pierre Laporte (Lib.), Daniel Johnson (U.N.), and Jean-Jacques Bertrand (U.N.), all made in the early sixties and all advocating greater autonomy for Quebec, see Frank Scott and Michael Oliver, eds., *Quebec States Her Case* (Toronto: Macmillan, 1964).

4. See excerpts from speeches by Duplessis to this effect in Kaye Holloway, *Le Canada, pourquoi l'impasse?* (Montreal: Editions Nouvelle Optique, 1983), 361.

5. For analyses of the social, economic, and political developments in Quebec in the Duplessis era see Quinn, *The Union Nationale*, and also works cited in note 3.

6. Ironically, in the case of funding for post-secondary education, Duplessis was supported by Pierre Elliott Trudeau, who characterized the federal proposals as undemocratic and unconstitutional. See Behiels, *Prelude*, 210, and Alain G. Gagnon, "The Development and Nationalization of Social Sciences in Quebec," *Quebec Studies* (forthcoming).

7. Donald V. Smiley, *Constitutional Adaptation and Canadian Federalism Since 1954* (Ottawa: Information Canada, 1970), 69–80.

8. Jean Lesage, *Un Québec fort dans une nouvelle confédération* (Québec, 1965).

9. Edward McWhinney, *Quebec and the Constitution 1960–1978* (Toronto: University of Toronto Press, 1979), 47. In 1978 the Supreme Court ruled that major Senate reform which impinges on provincial rights regarding representation therein requires the consent of the provinces.

10. Lesage's statement in the National Assembly cited by Richard Simeon, *Federal-Provincial Diplomacy: The Making of Recent Policy in Canada* (Toronto: University of Toronto Press, 1972), 59.

11. Paul Gérin-Lajoie, Convocation Address at Carleton University, April 1965, cited by Smiley, *Constitutional Adaptation*, 124, 158; see also, Paul Gérin-Lajoie, "Canadian Federalism and the Future," in *Concepts of Federalism*, ed. Gordon Hawkins (Toronto: Canadian Institute of Public Administration, 1965), 62–8, and Speech by Premier Lesage to the Ste-Foy Chamber of Commerce, December 14, 1965, reproduced in *Le Devoir*, December 23-24, 1965.

12. Claude Morin, *Quebec Versus Ottawa: The Struggle For Self-Government 1960–1972* (Toronto: University of Toronto Press, 1972), 35–40; see also John Fitzmaurice, *Quebec and Canada: Past, Present and Future* (London: Hurst & Co., 1985). For an argument to grant Quebec special status in international relations, see Howard A. Leeson, "Foreign Relations and Quebec," in *Canadian Federalism: Myth or Reality*, ed. Peter J. Meekison (Toronto: Methuen, 1977), 510–25.

13. Smiley, *Constitutional Adaptation*, 69–80, 103–9; and Smiley, *The Canadian Political Nationality* (Toronto: Methuen, 1967), 59–78.

14. Garth Stevenson, *Unfulfilled Union: Canadian Federalism and National Unity* (Toronto: Gage Publishing, 1982), 163–4.

15. Simeon, *Federal-Provincial Diplomacy*, 76–7.

16. Cited by Smiley, *The Canadian Political Nationality*, 68–70.

17. For a discussion of Quebec's influence on the formulation and implementation of federal policies and programs, see Morin, *Quebec Versus Ottawa*, chapter 8.

18. See, for example, Smiley, *Constitutional Adaptation*, 125; and McRoberts and Posgate, *Quebec*, 113.

19. Vincent Lemieux, "Quebec: 'Heaven is Blue and Hell is Red'," in *Canadian Provincial Politics: The Party System of the Ten Provinces*, ed. Martin Robin (Scarborough: Prentice-Hall, 1978), 257.

20. See David Kwavnick, ed., *The Tremblay Report: The Report of the Royal Commission of Inquiry on Constitutional Problems*, (Toronto: McClelland and Stewart, 1973), 45.

21. See Daniel Johnson, *Égalité ou indépendance* (Montréal: Les Editions de l'Homme, 1965), 120. He reiterated that position both at the 1967 Confederation for Tomorrow Conference and at the 1968 Federal-Provincial First Ministers' Constitutional Conference just a few months before his death.

22. For a concise statement which captures Premier Bertrand's autonomist sentiments, particularly in the area of social and cultural policy, see excerpts of his speech at the Constitutional Conference of December 8–10, 1969 in J. M. Beck, ed., *The Shaping of Canadian Federalism: Central Authority or Provincial Right?* (Toronto: Copp Clark Publishing, 1971), 227–9. For a review of the constitutional negotiations in the late sixties, see Simeon, op. cit., chapter 5.

23. Pierre Elliott Trudeau, *Federalism and the French Canadians* (Toronto: Macmillan of Canada, 1968).

24. Simeon, *Federal-Provincial Diplomacy*, 235 and Peter Hopkins, "Daniel Johnson and the Quiet Revolution," unpublished M.A. Thesis, Simon Fraser University, 1977, 38–40.

25. For references to Trudeau's concern with granting Quebec special status, see Simeon, *Federal-Provincial Diplomacy*, 90, 96, 99, 261, 284. For a discussion of the fiscal negotiations and the objectives of Quebec and Ottawa, see Simeon, *Federal-Provincial Diplomacy*, 66–87, 111–5; and Morin, *Quebec Versus Ottawa*, 7–28.

26. For an analysis of the disputes which ensued over substantive policy issues and related symbolic matters of protocol, such as seating arrangements and the display of flags at international conferences, see Louis Sabourin, *Canadian Federalism and International Organizations: A Focus on Quebec* (Ottawa: Institute for International Cooperation, 1971).

27. See Freda Hawkins, *Canada and Immigration: Public Policy and Public Concern* (Montreal: McGill-Queen's University Press, 1972), 213–34; and for an analysis of the constitutional powers of Quebec and the federal government in the field of immigration, see Jacques Brossard, *L'Immigration: les droits et pouvoirs du Canada et du Québec* (Montréal: Les Presses de l'Université de Montréal, 1967).

28. See Joseph Garcea, "Provincial Initiatives in Immigration (1966–1986); Asymmetry and Special Status," paper presented at the Canadian Political Science Association, Winnipeg, June, 1986; and also Ph.D. dissertation in progress on this topic by the same author.

29. For an excellent summary of Quebec-Ottawa negotiations on this issue, see John Saywell, *1972 Canadian Annual Review of Politics and Public Affairs* (Toronto: University of Toronto Press, 1974), 88–119.

30. Canada, Health and Welfare, *Basic Facts on Social Security Programs* (Ottawa: Ministry of Supply and Services, 1986), 17–9.

31. Premier Robert Bourassa, speech at the First Ministers' Constitutional Conference in Ottawa, September 14–15, 1970, cited by Jean-Louis Roy, *Le choix d'un pays: Le débat constitutionnel Québec-Ottawa 1960–1976* (Ottawa: Leméac, 1978), 205.

32. Stevenson, *Unfulfilled Union*, 210.

33. See Prime Minister P. E. Trudeau, "1976 Correspondence to all Provincial Premiers," in Meekison, ed., *Canadian Federalism*, 140–69.

34. See John Saywell, *1976 Canadian Annual Review of Politics and Public Affairs* (Toronto: University of Toronto Press, 1977), 43, 93–4.

35. For an excellent explanation of the sovereignty-association option, see Jean Pierre Charbonneau and Gilbert Paquette, *L'option* (Montréal: Les Éditions de l'Homme, 1978).

36. For a cogent account of constitutional negotiations during the first two phases, see Edward McWhinney, *Canada and the Constitution 1979–1982* (Toronto: University of Toronto Press, 1982).

37. Parti Québécois, *Official Program of the Parti Québécois*, 1978 edition, 7–8; an abridged version of the P.Q.'s 1979 official program is included in Paul Fox, ed., *Politics: Canada*, fifth edition, (Toronto: McGraw-Hill Ryerson, 1982), 197–202. For an excellent discussion on the political and legal aspects of Quebec's right to self-determination, see Donald V. Smiley, *Canada in Question: Federalism in the Eighties* (Toronto: McGraw-Hill Ryerson, 1980), 297–300; and also Pierre De Bané and Martial Asselin, "Quebec's Right to Secede," *Canadian Forum* 52 (May 1972): 6–11.

38. See Gérard Boismenu, "Backing Down or Compromising the Future: Quebec's Constitutional Proposals," in *Canada: The State of the Federation (1985)*, ed. Peter M. Leslie (Kingston: Institute of Intergovernmental Relations, 1985), 59–60.

39. Aileen McCabe, "Court Victory for Bilingualism Puts Bourassa on the Spot," *The Ottawa Citizen*, December 22, 1986, A3.

40. Canada, The Task Force on Canadian Unity, *A Future Together: Observations and Recommendations* (Ottawa: Ministry of Supply and Services, 1979), 86–7.

41. Quebec, *Canada-Quebec: A New Deal* (June, 1979); see also the policy paper of the Parti Québécois, *d'Égal à Égal* (February, 1979).

42. Gil Rémillard, *Le fédéralisme canadien: Le rapatriement de la constitution* (Montréal: Québec/Amérique, 1985), 115–7.

43. Garcea, "Provincial Initiatives," 10.

44. Quebec, *Draft Agreement on the Constitution: Proposals by the Government of Quebec*, May 1985.

45. Government of Québec, *Québec-Canada: A New Deal* (Québec: Service des publications officielles, 1979), 45.

46. Boismenu, "Backing Down," 54.

47. For a review of these and other episodes of the Lévesque era see Graham Fraser, *PQ: René Lévesque & the Parti Québécois in Power* (Toronto: Macmillan of Canada, 1984); and Boismenu, "Backing Down," 48–50.

48. Liberal Party of Quebec, *Mastering our Future*, 45.

49. Boismenu, "Backing Down," 57.

50. Gil Rémillard, Quebec Minister of Intergovernmental Affairs, Speech to a seminar at Mont Gabriel co-sponsored by the Institute of Intergovernmental Relations and the Ecole d'administration publique du Québec, May 9, 1986, mimeographed, 6.

51. Quebec Liberal Party, *A New Canadian Federation*, 1980; idem, *A New Political Leadership For Quebec*, January 1983; and idem, *Mastering Our Future*, 1985. For a summary of some of these and other policy papers, see Fitzmaurice, *Quebec and Canada*, 235–41.

52. See, Quebec Liberal Party, *Mastering Our Future*, 1985.

53. See text of "Meech Lake Communiqué" of the First Ministers' meeting on the Constitution, April 30, 1987, mimeographed; reprinted in "Meech Lake Accord: The details to be still worked out," in *The Ottawa Citizen*, May 7, 1987, A9; see also "1987 Constitutional Accord" [Langevin Block Accord], June 3, 1987, mimeographed (reproduced in the appendix at the end of this volume).

54. Ken MacQueen, "Quebec NDP Leader Condemns Meech Accord," *The Ottawa Citizen*, May 20, 1987, A4; "PQ Attacks Bourassa Over Accord," *The Ottawa Citizen*, June 5, 1987; and

"Meech Lake Dangerous To Quebec, warns Parti Québécois," *The Ottawa Citizen*, June 2, 1987.

55. "PQ Attacks Bourassa Over Accord," *The Ottawa Citizen*, June 5, 1987; and "Meech Lake Dangerous to Quebec, warns Parti-Québécois," *The Ottawa Citizen*, June 2, 1987.

56. See "Johnson Seeks PQ Delegates' Support for His Policy of National Affirmation," *The Ottawa Citizen*, June 13, 1987, A14; and Michael Rose, "What Bourassa Won," *Maclean's*, May 11, 1987, 11.

57. See the essay by Pierre Elliott Trudeau, reprinted in *The Ottawa Citizen*, May 27, 1987, A9.

58. See "Quebec House Leader Denies New Constitutional Demand," *The Ottawa Citizen*, November 20, 1986, A10.

59. For a discussion of the fractionalized elite and populace in Quebec, see Paul-André Linteau et al., *Le Québec depuis 1930* (Montréal: Boréal Express, 1986); Donald V. Smiley, "French-English Relations In Canada and Consociational Democracy," *Ethnic Conflict in the Western World*, ed. Milton Esman, (Ithaca: Cornell University Press, 1977), 179–203; and Reginald A. Whitaker, "The Quebec Cauldron: A Recent Account," in Gagnon, *Quebec: State and Society*, 70–91.

60. Whereas the term "provincialists" refers to those who have an affinity to the Quebec state, "nationalists" refers to those who have an affinity to the Québécois nation. The argument that it is more appropriate to speak of a French-Canadian nation than a Québécois nation because membership extends beyond Quebec's borders is made by the Special Joint Committee of the Senate and the House of Commons on the Constitution *Final Report*, 4th Session 28th Parliament, 1972, 13–4. A counter argument is made by two members of that Special Committee who issued a minority report; see Pierre De Bané and Martial Asselin, "Quebec's Right to Secede," *Canadian Forum* 52 (May 1972): 6–11.

61. For a concise discussion of the compact and alliance theories of Confederation respectively, see

chapters 5 and 6 in Edwin R. Black, *Divided Loyalties: Canadian Concepts of Federalism* (Montreal: McGill-Queen's University Press, 1975), 149–202. On bicommunalism or the "two nations principle" in Quebec, see Peter Leslie, "Canada as a Bicommunal Polity," *Recurring Issues in Canadian Federalism*, Clare Beckton and Wayne Mackay, research coordinators, vol. 57 of Macdonald Royal Commission Background Studies (Toronto: University of Toronto Press, 1986), 113–44.

62. For example see the Task Force on Canadian Unity, *A Future Together*, 86–7; Smiley, *Constitutional Adaptation*, 125; McRoberts and Posgate, *Quebec*, 290. For a discussion on federalism and special status with Quebec as the focus, see J. Brossard, "Fédéralisme et statut particulier," *Problèmes de droit contemporain (Mélanges Louis Baudouin)*, ed. A. Popovici (Montréal: Presses de l'université de Montréal, 1974), 425–46.

63. Wayne Mackay and Clare Beckton, "Institutional and Constitutional Arrangements: An Overview," *Recurring Issues in Canadian Federalism*, 3–4.

64. For a discussion of various forms of special status (i.e. initiatory, perennial, *de facto*, and *de jure*), see Garcea, "Provincial Initiatives".

65. See Canada Royal Commission on the Economic Union and Development Prospects for Canada, *Final Report*, vol. 3 (Ottawa: Minister of Supply and Services, 1985), 240–1, 477–9; and Task Force on Canadian Unity, *A Future Together*.

66. For discussions of alternative scenarios for the future, see Smiley, *The Canadian Political Nationality*, 102–6; Stevenson, *Unfulfilled Union*, 126–238; and Daniel Latouche, *Canada and Quebec, Past and Future: An Essay*, vol. 70 of the Macdonald Royal Commission Studies (Toronto: University of Toronto Press, 1986), 86, 121–52.

67. "Provincial NDP Seeks Special Role For Quebec," *The Ottawa Citizen*, January 12, 1987, A5; and "Vive La Différence . . . ," *Le Droit*, January 12, 1987, 4.

Selected Readings

Fraser, Graham. *P.Q.: René Lévesque and the Parti Québécois in Power*. Toronto: Macmillan of Canada, 1984.

Latouche, D. *Canada and Quebec, Past and Future: An Essay*. Research Study Prepared for the Royal Commission on the Economic Union and Development Prospects for Canada. Vol. 70. Toronto: University of Toronto Press, 1986.

Lévesque, R. *Memoirs*. Toronto: McClelland and Stewart, 1986.

McRoberts, K. "The Sources of Neo-Nationalism in Quebec." *Ethnic and Racial Studies* 7: 1 (January 1984): 55–85.

McRoberts, K., and Postgate, D. *Quebec: Social Change and Political Crisis*. Rev. ed., Toronto: McClelland and Stewart, 1980.

Morin, C. *Quebec Versus Ottawa: The Struggle for Self-Government, 1960–1972*. Toronto: University of Toronto Press, 1976.

20. THE POSITION OF ONTARIO IN THE CANADIAN FEDERATION

Rand Dyck

One of the paradoxes of Canadian federalism is the relationship between the province of Ontario and the national government. The crux of the conundrum is that Ontario has appeared to be the most consistent beneficiary of federal economic policies since 1867, while at the same time it has often been engaged in fierce disputes with Ottawa. On other occasions, however, relations between the federal and Ontario governments have exhibited considerable harmony. In this chapter an attempt will be made to account for such fluctuations in friendliness as well as for the frequent coincidence of simultaneous provincial influence in, and dissatisfaction with, the federal government.

Before examining specific issues which have gained prominence in Ottawa-Ontario relations, some of the possible factors which colour the relationship should be discussed. The first is the numerical strength of Ontario within the policy-making apparatus in the national capital. Ontario has furnished five Canadian prime ministers—Macdonald, Mackenzie, Bowell, King, and Pearson—who collectively held office for 53 out of 120 years, or 44 percent of the time, as of 1987.[1] In addition, Ontario has almost always had the largest contingent of federal cabinet ministers, with an average of about 35 percent.[2] Similarly, because it has been the largest province in terms of population, Ontario has always had the

most numerous group of MPs, declining from about 45 percent at the time of Confederation to just under 35 percent today.[3] But its numerical superiority has been greatest in the ranks of the public service, and given the degree of bureaucratic influence in the policy-making process, this numerical predominance might actually be most significant of all. While the geographic origins of federal bureaucrats is infrequently measured, it was noted in 1965 that 48.3 percent of the middle and upper ranks of the federal public service was born in Ontario.[4] Thus Ontario has never been able to complain that it does not have adequate representation in Ottawa. Since numbers are the most consistently persuasive factor in the making of public policy in a democracy, federal policies are generally tilted in its favour. Where this was occasionally not the case, Ottawa must have been pursuing priorities based on non-numerical considerations.

If Ontario has been well represented in Ottawa throughout, we must look further to explain variations in federal-Ontario relations and for the cause of the frequent hostility between the two levels of government. A second factor to note, then, is the extent to which different parties formed the the federal and provincial governments. In fact, this has been the norm: for 76 out of 120 years or 63 percent of the time, different parties held power in the two capitals. This split result could have happened even if the Ontario electorate had voted consistently for the same party at both levels. What is more striking, therefore, is how frequently the Ontario electorate has contributed to that divided result by electing a

An original essay written especially for this volume. The author wishes to acknowledge the research assistance of Michael Marion, the financial support of SSHRCC, and the insights of officials of the Ontario Ministry of Intergovernmental Affairs.

majority of its own members in the two legislatures from different parties.[5]

This phenomenon has been investigated at
great length and various explanations have been
offered. Perhaps Ontario voters either deliberately or unconsciously try to create a balance
between their federal and provincial representatives. On the other hand, there may be greater
similarities in ideology, policy, or orientation
between the federal level of one party and the
provincial wing of another than between the federal and provincial branches of the same party. A
third suggestion is that the split is more a question of voter abstention than vote switching—that
federal Liberals, for example, abstain in provincial elections. A final theory is that in the absence of strong party identification, the
phenomenon can simply be explained as the ac-
cidental result of different leaders, different issues, and different circumstances.[6]

This raises another important point with respect to the Ontario electorate. It has generally
been less provincially oriented and more federally minded than that of any other province.
Studies of such differential loyalties have consistently found that at least 90 percent of Ontarians
think of themselves as Canadians first.[7] Thus to
speak of disputes between Ontario and Ottawa is
imprecise.[8] Where there has been conflict, it has
usually been between the government of Ontario
and the government of Canada, and a majority of
the Ontario electorate often support the federal
point of view. But if the Ontario electorate is
federally oriented, and if federal policies are
generally designed in the interests of Ontario, we
are no further ahead in our search for explanations of the hostility.

The government of Ontario could primarily
be opposed to the federal government for reasons
of money, power, and status. Ontario politicians
might wish to expand the provincial share of joint
tax fields and limit federal taxation within the
province or alternatively demand more federal
subsidies. Joe Martin writes, for example, that to
Ontario "the key aspect of federal-provincial re-

lations is finance, not constitutional or jurisdictional matters."[9] Power politics could involve
expanding provincial jurisdiction, defending it
from federal interference, or minimizing the
conditions attached to federal subsidies. Differences of approach or simply a desire to enhance
personal importance and prestige would be possible motives behind such political or bureaucratic quests for provincial autonomy, and other
means of increasing or maintaining provincial
status can also be imagined.

Another factor here could be little more than
simple personality conflicts between first ministers or other leading officials. Politicians in particular are noted for their need for
ego-nourishment, and it would come as no surprise if a premier of a large province like Ontario
found it difficult to get along with an equally big
ego in Ottawa. If not entirely a question of self-
importance, then it may be that some personalities have not "hit it off" as well as others.

It is not likely, however, that all Ontario-
Ottawa conflict over the years can be reduced to
questions of provincial status or personality.
Genuine policy differences are apt to be at the
heart of many such difficulties. In this case, it
might be useful to categorize such differences in
terms of the major cleavages which are commonly identified at the national level.[10] First,
relating to the regional economic cleavage, federal-Ontario conflict could be the result of Ottawa's pursuing a policy which favoured one or
more regions at Ontario's expense. This would
typically involve, directly or indirectly, raising
money in Ontario and spending it somewhere
else. Second, concerning the ethnic cleavage, the
government of Ontario might object to federal
policies because they were more sympathetic to
francophone interests than Ontario would like
them to be. A class cleavage or ideological split
might also lead to federal-provincial conflict if
Ottawa should, for example, take a more left-or
right-wing approach in social or economic policy than was supported at Queen's Park. Finally,
Ontario might object to a federal policy regard-

ing the United States, whether Ottawa was more or less continentalist in its thinking than was the case in the province.

It can therefore be hypothesized that the main reasons for disputes between Ontario and the federal government are as follows: different government parties; money, power, and status; leader personalities; and policy differences based on regional economic, ethnic, or class cleavages, or relations with the United States. Conversely, warmer periods in federal-Ontario relations result from the absence of such factors, leaving Ontario's influence in the national government to prevail. Let us review federal-Ontario relations since 1867, and in more detail since 1948, looking especially at prominent disputes, and relate these interactions to the seven factors outlined.

THE PRE-WAR PERIOD

The Mowat-Macdonald period from 1871 to 1896 was replete with conflict, and many observers have taken this era to represent the normal state of affairs between the two levels of government. While there is no doubt that partisan differences and personal bitterness were also involved in the contest, Mowat's main motive was to enhance provincial status and power on such issues as the Ontario boundary, the power of the Lieutenant-Governor, and the federal power of disallowance.[11] As a result, the two levels began to exist in a truly federal relationship, where neither was subordinate to the other.

There was less difficulty during the subsequent 10-year period of Liberal rule in both Ottawa and Queen's Park, where the main intergovernmental problem had to do with resource development (the "manufacturing condition") as it related to the United States.[12] When the Conservatives came to power in Ontario in 1905, the pace of federal-provincial conflict increased again. These disputes centred on the nationalization of private power companies, the use of the

federal declaratory power with respect to railways, and Premier Whitney's opposition to a reciprocity treaty with the United States.[13] The following 10 years of partisan congruity were marred only by power struggles between federal and provincial bureaucrats over such issues as conditional grants and the regulation of the insurance industry.[14] A number of federal-Ontario disputes arose during the 1920s between the provincial Conservative government of Howard Ferguson and the federal liberal regime of Mackenzie King.[15] One of these was a provincial demand for unemployment relief from Ottawa, leading King to assert that he would not give any provincial Tory government a "five-cent piece." On this issue money and partisanship generated the dispute, but on a variety of discordant hydro questions, intergovernmental problems were more centred on competing jurisdiction and the U.S. connection. A relatively peaceful period of Conservative rule at both levels followed from 1930 to 1934.

The next decade constituted the nadir of federal-Ontario relations, and even though both levels had Liberal governments, they fought over every imaginable issue.[16] These included taxation at the 1935 dominion-provincial conference, hydro production and exports, RCMP reinforcements in connection with the 1937 Oshawa strike, relief funds, and the appointment of a new Lieutenant-Governor. Hepburn ultimately agreed to the constitutional amendment on unemployment insurance, but was critical from the start of the Rowell-Sirois Royal Commission on Dominion-Provincial Relations, especially of any federal encroachment on provincial taxation powers. It was in this context that Hepburn declared that Ontario would no longer be the "milch cow" for the rest of the country. Hepburn's opposition to the Wartime Taxation Agreements was somewhat ironic, for they were designed to meet federal obligations in World War II, an operation in which Hepburn took a particular interest. The climax of his hostility against Mackenzie King was reached in Hepburn's repeated criticism of federal handling of the war and his sudden introduction of a motion in the

Ontario legislature in January 1940 which condemned the federal government for not prosecuting the war with greater vigour. The bases of this most difficult decade of federal-Ontario relations were thus a defence of Ontario's own powers and revenues and a bitter personality feud which affected all intergovernmental contact. The common Liberal party label of the two governments and leaders did nothing at all to salve the sore; indeed, it probably made the situation worse.

George Drew, as the Conservative opposition leader in Ontario, had been a close ally of Mitch Hepburn in criticizing Mackenzie King's conduct of World War II. Assuming the premiership in 1943, Drew continued to pursue a basically antagonistic relationship toward King for the next five years, even after the War was over.[17] Drew opposed the federal Family Allowance scheme of 1944, for example, partly because he saw that the bulk of federal taxes levied to pay for it would fall upon Ontarians and partly because the benefits would go largely to Quebec, an ethnic consideration.

The post-war plans of the federal government were so comprehensive in scope that they were sometimes regarded as a "New National Policy" replacing that of 1878-79.[18] Those aspects which directly affected federal-provincial relations included taxation agreements, a national shared-cost public health insurance plan, and federal assumption of complete responsibility for the employable unemployed. In these and other ways, the New National Policy took advantage of the wartime predominance of the national government and the birth of Keynesian economics to give the provinces a subordinate role in the federal system.[19] At the 1945-46 federal-provincial Reconstruction Conference, at which these federal Green Book proposals were discussed, Drew strenuously opposed federal plans to retain Ottawa's wartime taxation powers while simultaneously embarking on such unilateral or joint social programs as hospital insurance and old age pensions. Instead, he unveiled his own counterproposal, which included sharing income and corporate taxes, provincial control of succession duties, and an interprovincial adjustment fund to assist the poorer provinces. Drew felt that the provinces would need more not less revenue for their own post-war social programs, as had been outlined in his famous 22-point program of 1943. Leading the provincial attack on Ottawa's invasion of direct tax fields, he denounced federal centralization, and the conference adjourned without success. Bilateral federal-provincial negotiation continued over the next few years, but neither Ontario nor Quebec was ever satisfied. In refusing to sign tax rental agreements with Ottawa, they continued to levy their own corporate and succession taxes.

Drew's conflict with Ottawa was primarily based on provincial rights and money, it is true, but several other factors were also involved. These included the difference in government party, opposition to Keynesian economics and to the redistributive aspects of federal proposals, a certain ethnic prejudice, and a personal bitterness toward Mackenzie King.

THE FROST ERA

With a change of first ministers in both capitals in 1948-49, a new era of cooperation emerged between Ottawa and Toronto. A warm personal relationship between Leslie Frost and Louis St. Laurent overcame any conflict that might have been expected because they belonged to different parties, but it was also the case that Frost, unlike Hepburn and Drew, "had no ambition to promote Ontario's local concerns into full-dress constitutional battles."[20] In fact, the congeniality between Frost and St. Laurent contrasted with the coolness between the new premier and his predecessor, George Drew, who was now the federal Tory leader.

There was little Ontario reaction, for example, when the federal government cut off court appeals to the British Privy Council and also adopted a partial constitutional amending formula in 1949. After an agreeable federal-provincial conference in 1950, Ontario signed a tax-sharing agreement with Ottawa in 1952, and Frost supported the federal proposal for a Trans-Canada Pipeline and the shared-cost Trans-Canada Highway. On the social side, a new conditional grant Unemployment Assistance Act was adopted without difficulty, fulfilling one of the Green Book proposals. Then Frost helped push the federal government into a national hospital insurance scheme. While neither leader was personally enthusiastic about the idea, health insurance had been promised in the 1945 Green Book, and Frost and St. Laurent both saw it as a political necessity. According to Malcolm Taylor, Ontario's assumption of the leadership of those pressing the federal government to fulfill this part of its 1945 proposals was "clearly the determinative force that brought about the nation-wide system we now have."[21]

When Frost began his battle for new hydroelectric developments to cope with Ontario's urgent need for additional power supplies in 1951, St. Laurent was completely sympathetic. The federal prime minister repeatedly threatened American authorities that Canada was about to proceed unilaterally with the St. Lawrence Seaway and power project. Such pressure finally persuaded the U.S. to enter into the joint construction and ownership of the project in 1954.

Not counting the push which Frost had to give the federal government on health insurance, there was only one major conflict between Ottawa and Ontario during this period—federal-provincial financial relations. In 1955 St. Laurent unveiled a new approach for the 1957–62 period which included equalization payments for have-not provinces and a new taxation scheme under which the provinces would receive a percentage of the provincial yield from three federal taxes: 10 percent of personal income taxes, 9 percent of corporation taxes, and 50 percent of succession duties. Frost's counterproposal was to leave Ontario a larger share than other provinces of the two first tax fields, to give the provinces complete control of succession du-

ties, and to make provincial natural resource taxes deductible from the federal tax. For the first time, St. Laurent felt that Frost was putting provincial and partisan considerations before the national interest,[22] and while the proposals were later somewhat revised, Ontario continued to express its displeasure. Frost asserted, for example, that Ottawa's "whole psychology is to squeeze Ontario down as far as it can go and be as generous to the other provinces as possible."[23] Even so, he was much more moderate in his demands than certain other voices in the province, such as *The Globe and Mail.* Probably because of this dispute with the federal Liberal government and his affection for the new national Tory leader, John Diefenbaker, Frost campaigned vigorously for the PC party in the 1957 federal election.

If Frost had had such good relations with the federal Liberal government until the mid-1950s, it is not surprising that Ontario and the new Conservative government were extremely friendly, at least until the premier's retirement in 1961. Diefenbaker had been greatly moved by Frost's efforts in the 1957 federal election campaign, and the increase in Tory seats in Ontario substantially contributed to the overall result.[24]

In fact, there were several monetary issues in which, primarily because of this electoral assistance, Diefenbaker seemed to be responding to Frost's requests. A change made in the formula used to calculate provincial Unemployment Assistance grants in 1957, for example, was attributed to pressure from Ontario.[25] The immediate increase in the provincial share of personal income tax from 10 percent to 13 percent was also of most benefit to Ontario, and that province later claimed the largest share of federal funds in connection with the new technical and vocational education program.

During the Diefenbaker period it became necessary again to discuss the federal-provincial taxation system for 1962–67. Although the prime minister was usually considered to be generous to hinterland areas in such programs as ARDA and Atlantic Provinces Adjustment Grants, the

1962–67 taxation agreement was seen by some as meeting the demands of Ontario at the expense of the other provinces. At the first ministers' conferences in 1960 and 1961, Frost first demanded 50 percent of personal and corporate income taxes as well as succession duties, and while accepting the principle of equalization, argued that the formula was unfair. The federal government responded that it would vacate the three tax fields to the extent they were now returned to the provinces (10 percent of personal income taxes, 9 percent of corporate taxes, and 50 percent of succession duties). Thereafter, if provinces wished to raise their share, they would be free to do so, and Ottawa would continue to collect them. Furthermore, the provincial share of income tax would rise from 16 percent to 20 percent over a five-year period. Thus, although the federal response was quite a departure from Frost's original demands, Ontario was due to gain most from the changes adopted.[26] They were not sufficient for Ontario to avoid introducing a retail sales tax, however, but Frost expressed a willingness to delay its implementation as well as his own retirement if Diefenbaker thought such actions would harm the federal party.[27]

Thus, Frost's term of office was characterized by a tranquility in federal-provincial relations, largely influenced by the personality of the man and his lack of obsession with provincial status. Moreover, he interacted with Liberal and Conservative federal prime ministers with almost equal congeniality, and partisanship was not an important element in this period. There was a congruity in federal-provincial ideology toward social programs as well as in policy toward the U.S., but the one issue that did create federal-provincial friction on two occasions was the renegotiation of taxation agreements.

ROBARTS AND PEARSON

In contrast to the preceding period, the next five years, during which Robarts and Pearson overlapped in office, was one of intense federal-pro-

vincial activity, and much of it quite antagonistic.

The new era of "cooperative federalism" was characterized by almost continual federal-provincial conferences during 1963 and 1964. The first issue, the Municipal Loan Fund, was designed to enable municipalities to alleviate unemployment with capital works projects. The provinces would have to approve the projects, but the funds would come directly from Ottawa. Quebec led the fight against this alleged interference with provincial control over municipal government, but Ontario joined in to argue that a preferable approach would be to increase the share of taxes received by the provinces so that they could pass on the funds to their municipalities. As a result, at a first ministers' conference in July 1963 Pearson altered the scheme on the spot, even to the extent of allowing provincial administration of the program.

The pensions issue was not settled so quickly or easily. In this case, both Ontario and Quebec had previously started work to develop their own provincial plans.[28] Unlike Quebec, "Robarts favoured a national pension plan in principle, but it had to fit with Ontario's approach to the problem;" otherwise, Ontario would go it alone.[29] The issue was complicated by its intrusion into the 1963 provincial election campaign in which federal Health and Welfare Minister Judy LaMarsh blamed Robarts for blocking the federal plan and portrayed him as a captive of the private insurance industry. This was because he had favoured a more restricted public plan that could be integrated with private plans, rather than one that would displace them.[30] Lesage unveiled the detailed Quebec proposal at the first minister's conference of April 1964, which was followed by two weeks of secret feverish negotiation between Ottawa and Quebec. Much to the chagrin of Judy LaMarsh, Pearson then announced a compromise agreement which was closer to the Quebec plan than to Ottawa's. There remained a good possibility that dissatisfied Ontario would still develop its own, but after seeking changes in the package until

January 1965, Robarts finally announced that Ontario would participate in the national plan.[31]

The concentrated federal-provincial discussions of 1963–64 also centred on taxation agreements, conditional grants, and equalization. Robarts' general position on these issues was to obtain more tax room but to restrict any liberalization of equalization payments. Once again, though, Ontario was overshadowed by Quebec, as Lesage claimed a minimum of 25 percent of personal and corporate income taxes and 100 percent of succession duties. Robarts had mixed feelings about a Quebec demand to opt-out of conditional grant programs. He acknowledged the value of many of these programs, but was somewhat concerned about the rigid federal conditions imposed. A resolution of these problems was attached to the Ottawa-Quebec pension plan compromise of April 1964. Provinces could opt-out of joint programs, there would be an accelerated increase in their share of personal and corporate income taxes, equalization payments would be increased, and the provincial share of succession duties would be raised to 75 percent— a mixed bag, as far as Ontario was concerned.

A more peaceful period of federal-provincial relations followed, during which Ottawa announced its "War on Poverty." Out of extensive federal-provincial consultation at both the political and bureaucratic levels, the Canada Assistance Plan emerged, for example, as a measure to increase federal subsidization of provincial and municipal social assistance programs and services.[32] Along with other provinces, Ontario welcomed the monetary aspects and flexibility of this program as well as the process through which it was developed. Meanwhile, Robarts, who had sometimes cooperated with Quebec in opposition to Ottawa, seemed to be moving closer to the federal government as Lesage increased his demands for greater provincial autonomy and claimed to represent the interests of all French-speaking Canadians.

More difficult federal-provincial financial issues soon arose again, however, and the fall of 1966 saw the culmination of several such problems, largely in connection with a renegotiation of fiscal arrangements for the 1967–72 period. Ottawa announced its preference to disentangle federal and provincial finances by urging all provinces to opt-out of conditional grant programs with the incentive of a large personal income tax abatement. Apart from that, the federal government would not reduce its share of the three standard taxes any further, but the provinces were encouraged to raise their own taxes beyond the level of the federal abatement. All of this seemed at odds with the recently released report of the Tax Structure Committee, and Robarts was opposed to the whole thrust of the federal position—independent federal and provincial taxation, an end to shared-cost programs, and an insufficient increase in taxation abatements. At the same time, Ottawa responded to Robarts' repeated plea for additional federal funding for post-secondary education, but only in connection with the stunning announcement of an "abrupt termination of a long-standing conditional grant relationship with the provinces in the domain of technical and vocational education."[33] There were annual accusations over federal-provincial financial arrangements throughout the rest of the decade, first in 1968 when Ottawa reiterated its 1966 proposal and imposed a unilateral social development tax, in 1969 when Ontario threatened to introduce its own provincial income tax, and again in 1970 in response to the federal white paper on tax reform. On this subject, Ontario countered Ottawa with a critical analysis of the federal white paper as well as with its own proposal.

The other major confrontation between the federal and Ontario governments was over medicare. This major new shared-cost program came at a peculiar time, 1965–66, just as Ottawa was trying to extract itself from such intertwined arrangements. Unlike Frost on hospital insurance, Robarts led the provincial attack against the federal medicare program in what some saw as Ontario's toughest anti-Ottawa stance since 1940.[34] He was upset at the process involved—the contradiction between the philosophy of cooperative federalism and the lack of provincial consultation on such a large program. Like other premiers, he objected to being pressured into increasing the provincial budget to pay for its share of the cost, especially when he had other financial priorities. As in the pensions debate, Robarts also preferred a private sector role in medical insurance, feeling that Ontario had already struck the right balance—private plans for those who could afford them and a recently enacted partial public program for those who could not. While there was some hesitation within the Pearson cabinet itself, the legislation finally went into effect on July 1, 1968. It was a "major, bitter setback" for Robarts and one of the greatest disappointments of his political career, but at least a role for private carriers had temporarily been salvaged.[35] At first he refused to join the program, but eventually capitulated in October 1969, lashing out with the following famous criticism:

> Medicare is a glowing example of a Machiavellian scheme that is in my humble opinion one of the greatest political frauds that has been perpetrated on the people of this country.[36]

It was partly his unpleasant experience with Ottawa on these various issues—pensions, finances, and medicare—which convinced Robarts that the whole future of the country should be examined. The other factor, of course, was the Quiet Revolution in Quebec, of which Robarts was one of the most knowledgeable observers. As the decade wore on, the work of the Royal Commission on Bilingualism and Biculturalism had sensitized most thoughtful Canadians to the danger to national unity which was at hand. In 1965, Robarts himself established the Ontario Advisory Committee on Confederation, and in August 1967 announced that the government would implement its recommendation for bilingual and French secondary schools in the province. The federal government still believed that ad hoc arrangements would be sufficient to solve the problem, however, and in these circum-

stances Robarts took the initiative to convene the Confederation of Tomorrow Conference in Toronto in November 1967.[37] Pearson was opposed to a province calling a federal-provincial conference on any subject, and the two leaders argued about the issue for some months. Finally, Ottawa acquiesced in the idea of an interprovincial conference to discuss confederation, and to which it would send only public servant observers.

Beyond the discussion of current federal-provincial problems, the conference gave Premier Daniel Johnson an opportunity on national television to set forth the Quebec government's case. Robarts "appealed to English Canadians through the television cameras to recognize the need for change and to attempt to understand the feelings of French Canada and French Canadians."[38] Even Pearson was pleased with the results, and before long the federal government took up the challenge of constitutional reform.

That issue dominated Robarts' last three years in office as far as federal-provincial relations were concerned. In a series of first ministers' conferences interspersed with ministerial and bureaucratic meetings, many difficult subjects were addressed. In the end, however, Quebec vetoed the Victoria Charter which incorporated a national consensus on several such issues.

The vast amount of federal-Ontario interaction during the Robarts years cannot be easily summarized, but we can identify the major sources of the frequent conflict. The two governments were of different political stripes, but this did not appear to be of great significance because two provincial Liberal governments of the day—Quebec and Saskatchewan—actually caused Pearson more anguish than Conservative Ontario. Neither was personality a major factor, with Pearson generally exhibiting considerable diplomatic skill, and both men being of a reasonably congenial nature.[39] Instead, the main problem was one of provincial money, power, and status. Almost every initiative undertaken by the Pearson government had provincial implications, and despite his efforts in most instances to cooperate with the provinces, the latter resented such federal interference. On pensions and medicare, Ontario simply had a different approach; in the case of the municipal loan fund, Ontario resented federal encroachment on a provincial field; and before the Confederation of Tomorrow Conference, Ontario thought Ottawa was proceeding too slowly. Many of the problems centred on taxation, where Ontario always wanted more revenue. Still, behind all these disputes was a desire for more effective federal-provincial consultation, and when he felt that Quebec's demands for more power were becoming unreasonable, Robarts spoke up for a strong federal government. There were some ideological differences between the Pearson and Robarts governments, at least in the sense that the latter was less wedded to public sector programs in medicare and pensions.[40] On the other hand, Canada-U.S. issues did not provoke any federal-Ontario problems, and Ontario was one of the few provinces that rarely if ever objected to the bilingualism policies of the federal government.

DAVIS AND TRUDEAU

Federal-provincial relations did not dominate the Ontario political agenda so completely during the 13-year premiership of Bill Davis which coincided with the Trudeau era in Ottawa. Nevertheless, many issues had an intergovernmental dimension and three in particular affected Ontario—finances, energy, and the constitution.

First, there was the ever present problem of federal-provincial fiscal arrangements. On the taxation side, in the early 1970s, Ontario repeatedly led the provincial charge for a transfer of sufficient tax room to cover the costs of joint programs with no strings attached. By 1973 the federal government itself wanted to be relieved of its 50% commitment in most conditional grant programs, especially when it had no control over escalating provincial costs. After several years of

discord on specific cost-sharing formulas and revenue guarantees, a basic federal-provincial consensus was incorporated into the 1977 Established Programs Financing Act. Health insurance and post-secondary education were made block grant programs in which specific federal conditions were removed, and federal support consisted of a complicated mix of cash and tax transfers.

Ontario also called for a study of the costs and benefits of the equalization payment program, but there was no response except for minor adjustments in the formula used. In 1978, when Ontario itself would have qualified, the province readily agreed to a formula change to preserve its ineligibility, and a few years later it was a voice in the wilderness in suggesting that western provinces use their resource revenues to help finance equalization directly.

In 1982 another five-year fiscal arrangement was required. In this case, after a good deal of discordant and fruitless discussion, Ottawa unilaterally imposed a financial regime on the provinces. The federal government ended the revenue guarantee system and cut back on the increase in transfer payments, actions which naturally evoked the ire of the provinces. Thus, on this recurrent issue, Ontario and Ottawa were leading antagonists.

Concerning the energy issue, on the other hand, Ontario and the federal government started out with major differences but ended up as allies. In the 1973–80 period, Ontario stood almost alone in opposing Alberta's regular demands for petroleum price increases, as Ottawa generally sided with the western provinces. Ontario presented several arguments in favour of keeping oil and natural gas prices below the international price. It had previously paid higher prices than necessary in order to support the petroleum industry in western Canada; higher prices would fuel inflation, which in turn would make Ontario industry less competitive in the international marketplace and contribute to more unemployment; and price increases were only fattening company profits and the coffers of a few governments, rather than being poured back into increased production. The province's unstated concern was that the wealthier the west became, the more it would challenge Ontario's influence in national policy-making.[41] In addition, as the west prospered, a certain amount of industry and finance would likely migrate there from Ontario. Davis and his government used every possible device to bolster their case: meetings with Alberta Premier Peter Lougheed and other authorities, speeches, federal-provincial negotiations, legal threats, an investment of $100 million in the Syncrude project (and later, the purchase of 25 percent of the shares in Suncor), a Royal Commission on Petroleum Pricing, and a 90-day freeze on gasoline and fuel prices just prior to the 1975 provincial election—but it had little overall impact.

During his short tenure in office, Joe Clark had negligible success in mediating between the Davis and Lougheed positions. As the Tory Prime Minister was increasingly perceived to be leaning in Alberta's direction, Davis stepped up the rhetoric against him.[42] When the Trudeau Liberals returned to power in 1980, largely because of a sweep of Ontario (using Davis's anti-Clark quotes in their commercials), they took a position on energy policy that was much closer to that of the Davis government.[43] Ontario was happy, for example, that the unilateral federal National Energy Program of October 1980 continued to restrain price increases. Davis was also satisfied that the provincial and corporate shares of such increases were reduced in favour of the central government, in contrast to the outrage generally expressed in the west on this point. Ottawa made adjustments in NEP in September 1981, May 1982, and June 1983, basically to obtain Alberta's approval, but even so, Ontario could only applaud the thrust of the post-1980 federal policy.

The third major federal-provincial problem of the Davis-Trudeau period concerned the constitution, but here Ontario and Ottawa saw eye-to-eye on almost every aspect of the question.[44] Ontario generally favoured the federal position at the first ministers' conferences of 1978 and 1979. Even more striking than Ontario's support of the substance of the proposal, was its endorsement of Ottawa's approach—its declaration that it planned to proceed unilaterally with patriation after federal-provincial discussions collapsed in 1980.

Then, at the fateful first ministers' conference of November 1981, Ontario played a vital conciliatory role between the other provinces and the federal government. Two of its bargaining chips included changes to the amending formula (voluntarily relinquishing its veto) and introducing the notwithstanding clause. Ontario's Attorney General Roy McMurtry received much attention at the time, but it now appears that it was Davis himself along with Saskatchewan's Allan Blakeney who deserve much of the credit for the ultimate success of the venture. The delicate chain of communication, especially in the overnight negotiations, consisted of Blakeney interacting with the dissident provinces on one side and with Davis on the other, while Davis would alternatively use his persuasive talents on Blakeney and Trudeau.[45]

Why did the Ontario government take such a dramatically pro-Ottawa position on the constitutional issue when other Conservative provincial governments and the federal Conservative party were so adamantly opposed? First, it seems that the energy issue had left Davis with little feeling of affinity for Joe Clark or the other provinces. It had forced him to take a "national" perspective and to support Ottawa against any further threat of decentralization in the federation. Mobility rights would similarly help remove restrictions which other provinces had imposed on the free movement of Ontario's people, goods, and capital. Second, Davis had long favoured patriation, had now been attracted to the Charter as a "statement of nationhood," and acted from a fear of letting the country down.[46] The idea of the Charter became fundamental to the province's position, even though he was not overly concerned about its specific content.[47] Third, French language education rights, the part of the package so dear to

Trudeau's heart, were already established in Ontario, so that they would pose no problem as long
as the province could withstand pressure to become officially bilingual.

Three less significant federal-provincial issues in this period should also be mentioned
briefly. First, Ontario lined up squarely behind
Ottawa in its wage and price control program of
1975. The Trudeau government went far beyond
normal federal jurisdiction in imposing this
emergency legislation, and there was no consultation with the provinces beforehand. They were,
however, exhorted to apply the program to their
own public services, and Ontario did so with
such rapidity (by order-in-council rather than by
legislation) that its action was subject to a constitutional challenge along with one to the federal
Anti-Inflation Act itself. Ontario was also more
than happy to go along with another federal restraint program—the "6 and 5" program of
1982-83—as it again put a ceiling on wage increases in the provincial public sector.

In the second place, there were many secondary economic issues.[48] Davis repeatedly
called for first ministers' conferences on the
economy to discuss such issues, and several
meetings were held. They rarely resolved any
problems, however, and Ottawa soon grew weary
of listening to provincial complaints. At one such
conference in 1982, Davis lamented to the prime
minister as follows:

> I guess my frustration really stems from what is
> more an attitudinal approach on the part of you,
> sir, and the government of Canada, an approach
> where I sense that minds were made up prior to
> our arrival. . . .I sense that [federal] points were
> not only inflexible and intransigent, but . . .cast
> in stone.[49]

It was at the same meeting that Trudeau
declared that "cooperative federalism is dead
. . .in the sense that the federal government is
expected to hand money over to the provinces for
them to spend in any which way."[50] Although he

had never been very cooperative with the provinces, this post-1982 policy is sometimes called
"new federalism." It was said to involve unilateral action rather than provincial consultation,
greater federal visibility and control over funds
transferred to the provinces, a disentangling of
federal and provincial programs, and a bilateral
rather than multilateral approach to such provincial negotiation as did take place.[51]

Another aspect of the "new federalism"
could be seen in connection with medicare. After
numerous federal threats, the Canada Health Act
was unveiled in 1983 to penalize provinces which
allowed extra-billing by doctors and hospital user
fees. Although Alberta was probably the main
target of the federal initiative, Ontario also allowed doctors to extra-bill, and it therefore reacted angrily to the legislation.[52] At the same
time, legislation was introduced by which the
federal government unilaterally separated its
EPF funds between health care and post-secondary education and set the level of contributions to
each. In both cases, Ottawa changed the terms of
Established Programs Financing in mid-stream
without provincial consent.

If the Frost period was generally a harmonious one in federal-Ontario relations, and if the
Roberts era was mostly one of conflict, the years
during which Bill Davis was premier were an
almost even mix of cooperation and discord.
Some of the conflict could be explained by a
partisan difference from the Trudeau Liberals,
but Ontario's relations with the short-lived Clark
Conservative government were no less antagonistic.[53] Some of the difficulty might be attributed to the personality of the prime minister and
his general condescension towards provincial
premiers. On the other hand, the fact that Davis
himself was usually seen as a moderate, likeable
leader partially explains why Ontario got along
better with Ottawa than most other provinces
during this period.[54] The lack of federal respect
for the provinces in the Trudeau era undoubtedly
contributed to much of the problem. Ottawa's

frequent resort to unilateral measures or apparent lack of interest when provincial viewpoints were being articulated, especially on fiscal arrangements and other economic issues, was a denial of the status provinces had come to expect. This attitude was neatly embodied in the "new federalism" philosophy of the early 1980s.

To distinguish other cases of harmony from instances of conflict, it is necessary to examine the nature of the issue involved. On regional economic issues such as energy policy and the mobility clause of the constitution, where the new economic nationalism of the west caused a threat to national unity, Ontario moved to support the federal government. It was in the economic interest of almost all Ontarians, to say nothing of their political sentiments, to keep the country together with a strong central government. Furthermore, Ontario reasoned, it would continue to have substantial influence on national policies since the province still had the largest number of seats at stake in a federal election. Somewhat similarly, it was to Ontario's economic benefit to keep Quebec in Confederation, especially by means of new constitutional arrangements which did not weaken the national government.

On ethnic issues, Ontario also supported the federal position, both because it endorsed the specifics of that approach and also because it would help sustain the Canadian economic union. Ontario parted company with Ottawa only on the issue of "official bilingualism" within the province, and here internal electoral considerations—the fear of an anglophone backlash—overrode the imperatives of national unity. For practical purposes, however, Ontario was probably as bilingual as any other province even without a declaration of official bilingualism, and Davis somehow hoped that Quebecers would realize that, while certain Ontario anglophones would not.[55]

In the two other instances—wage controls and medicare—ideology was the major factor, although in different ways. On the two occasions

when the federal government introduced wage controls, Ontario immediately followed suit, demonstrating a similar disregard for the interests of the working class. On the other hand, Ottawa's concern about extra-billing indicated a more left-wing approach than did Ontario's defence of the medical profession, and this difference resulted in conflict.

PETERSON AND MULRONEY

Brian Mulroney had already taken over as prime minister when Frank Miller succeeded Bill Davis as premier, but despite the fact that they were both Conservatives, relations between them were not the best. Miller was treated with little respect when he tried to make the province's case in connection with federal gasoline pricing, while Mulroney made a brief and ineffective appearance in the provincial election campaign that resulted in the formation of a Liberal government under David Peterson.[56]

Peterson assumed the position of Minister of Intergovernmental Affairs as well as Premier, and during the first two years of his regime, the most significant intergovernmental issue was that of "free trade." The Ontario position was not the knee-jerk opposition that some expected, nor as strong as in 1911. Instead, the new government basically urged Ottawa to proceed with caution and with provincial cooperation. In such discussions, Ontario was "open-minded, fair-minded, but tough-minded."[57] It was anxious to secure and enhance its access to the American market, but only if mutual improvements in job opportunities and living standards resulted.

In appearances at First Ministers Conferences in Halifax in November 1985 and Vancouver in November 1986, at premiers conferences, and in several public speeches, many to American audiences, Peterson developed a consistent, sceptical theme. In Halifax, for example, he suggested three steps to improve the Canadian position in the negotiations: the creation of a task force to pool the intelligence resources of the federal and provincial governments; a commitment to reduce all barriers to the free movement of people, goods and services within Canada; and a meaningful involvement of the provinces in the negotiating process. Peterson continued to worry that Ottawa was mesmerized by the free trade issue, that it did not understand the full implications, and that it was proceeding on the basis of hopes, guesses, and assumptions. He also raised questions about the impact of free trade on Alberta, Quebec, and other provinces, and suggested that other markets such as the Pacific Rim should be exploited as well. Later he led an Ontario trade mission to the Far East. Although the federal-provincial task force to gather information did not materialize, Ontario came to the 1986 FMC with several reports of studies which it had already undertaken on its own.[58]

Peterson also stated repeatedly that Ontario was not prepared to bargain away certain essentials. Canada must "maintain the ability to preserve our unique values, and our unique ways of solving our own problems."[59] He emphasized the reduction of regional disparities through regional development grants and equalization payments, the commitment to economic and social justice through medicare and unemployment insurance, and the maintenance of cultural sovereignty through support of Canadian cultural industries. In addition, the Auto Pact was frequently mentioned. Peterson explained to American audiences that it provided the economic backbone of Ontario and Michigan, and was crucial to the economic growth of both Canada and the U.S. Based neither on protectionism nor unfettered free trade, it was "a managed trade approach that is by and large fair to both countries."[60] To Canadian listeners he argued that the safeguards in the Auto Pact must remain intact because they also safeguarded "Ontario's ability to contribute to Canadian economic growth."[61]

On the third point raised in Halifax, the provincial role in the talks, Ontario put much effort into the question of process and appeared to have considerable impact. The first ministers adopted the principle of "full provincial participation" in the negotiations, and Peterson later held Mulroney to his commitment when some apparent federal backtracking developed.[62] Although Ontario's relations with the new federalist and Liberal Bourassa government in Quebec were strengthened with considerable fanfare, and although Quebec also had its reservations about free trade, there was no attempt to gang up on Ottawa on the substance of the issue.

Peterson was also concerned to resolve certain immediate trade problems with the U.S. rather than await a long-term agreement. On the softwood lumber dispute, for example, he had strong reservations regarding the federal-B.C. approach, preferring to fight the countervailing duty in the courts. Ontario then acquiesced in the majority view, not wanting to weaken the Canadian case any further, but Peterson was highly upset at the eventual result.

There were several other federal-Ontario issues of a lesser magnitude in the 1985-87 period. Not surprisingly, the problem of federal transfer payments to the provinces was raised again, as the Mulroney government sought to reduce the federal deficit in any way it could. At the Halifax meeting Peterson and Mulroney engaged in a uncharacteristically heated exchange on this subject, accusing each other of "unbecoming temerity."[63] On another recurrent issue, natural gas pricing, Ontario objected strongly to a federal-Alberta deal in October 1985 which did not result in an immediate price cut.

At least four new issues on the agenda also had potential for federal-Ontario conflict. On child care, Ontario repeatedly urged the federal government to take up the challenge in spite of the financial and administrative problems which it was likely to present.[64] On financial institutions, Ontario was upset that a federal proposal to establish international banking centres focused on Montreal and Vancouver and left Toronto out. The Peterson government was also wary of Ottawa's plans for deregulation of the banking and financial industries, looking out for the consumer interest after the recent Ontario experience with trust company failures. On the question of aboriginal rights, the two governments were generally allied, but the province pressed Ottawa for greater financial commitment, especially with respect to the non-status category. Finally, Ontario was concerned about federal plans for tax reform.

The general atmosphere surrounding federal-provincial relations in Canada obviously improved after the election of the Mulroney government, as evidenced by increased multilateral and bilateral consultation. As for Ontario, none of the issues just discussed, at least until 1987, led to serious intergovernmental antagonism. This can be explained in part by two agreeable personalities at the top who were not particularly bothered by their partisan differences.[65] A strong Ontario contingent on the government side in Ottawa also ensured that its basic macro-economic policy served Ontario well, even if the province's relative prosperity left it on the sidelines as federal largesse was distributed to other regions. In fact, there was a general absence of regional economic, ethnic, or ideological differences between the two capitals. Another reason was the Peterson government's lack of obsession with provincial power; indeed, if there was any concern at Queen's Park, it was probably over Mulroney's consensus-orientation, combined with his government's strapped financial condition. These characteristics might prevent it from taking the initiative that Ontario felt a national government should. On the other hand, even though Ottawa's role was further weakened by the 1987 constitutional accord under which Ontario gained additional powers along with the

other provinces, Peterson played a major conciliatory role in bringing the various sides together. The greater issue was to persuade Quebec to join the constitutional regime, and Ontario accepted additional provincial influence in the federal system largely as a means to that end. The most likely factor to upset the harmony in the future was U.S. relations, namely the prospect of too many federal concessions on free trade.

CONCLUSION

This review of federal-Ontario relations indicates that the government of Ontario has rarely been oppposed to basic national economic policies. The main exceptions are Drew's antagonism toward the "New National Policy" of 1945–46, and Davis's criticism of the national energy policy prior to 1980. Similarly, it was rare for the Ontario government to object to federal policies because of their ethnic orientation. The leading exceptions were Hepburn and Drew's complaints about the federal war effort, which was presumably constrained so as not to offend French Canada, a suspicion Drew later extended to certain domestic policies. Given the small percentage of francophones in the province, however, Robarts, Davis, and Peterson supported the recognition of French language rights as much as Ottawa could reasonably have wished, stopping just short of a declaration of official bilingualism. A certain amount of ideological conflict has arisen between Ottawa and various Ontario governments, particularly during the Hepburn, Drew, and Robarts eras, and in almost every case it was Ottawa that could be said to be further to the left. Relations with the U.S. were also a source of federal-provincial tension, especially in the earlier period where Ottawa was more continentalist than the province. A similar pattern has characterized the re-emergence of the issue in the Peterson era.

It can therefore be concluded that while the

four major cleavages that are said to confront federal policy-makers have precipitated Ontario-Ottawa conflicts from time to time, they have generally not been very significant. This assessment is consistent with the strong Ontario representation in Ottawa, usually including the government side of the Commons.

Personalities and partisanships are another category of factors that might have contributed to federal-Ontario discord. There were the classic personality conflicts between King on the one hand and Hepburn and Drew on the other, and a slightly less serious personal antagonism between Mowat and Macdonald. Otherwise, Ontario premiers have generally interacted agreeably with federal prime ministers, and Frost in particular had a very close relationship with two of them. Neither is the partisan factor as prominent as one might expect, given the proportion of time that different parties were in power in the two capitals. It can be said, however, that partisan differences often complicated relations, and made them especially difficult in the Mowat and Drew periods. Nevertheless, a common party tie did nothing positive for Hepburn and King, and a partisan difference was no problem at all for Frost and St. Laurent. These two factors have sometimes been significant, then, but they still leave much of the discord unexplained.

Ultimately, the most common conflicts between the Ontario and federal governments have related to the question of provincial autonomy and problems of money, power, and status.[66] Almost from the start, Ontario demanded increased provincial revenues, and this even explains much of the difficulty in the Hepburn and Drew periods. Since World War II, such battles have climaxed at least every five years with the renewal of federal-provincial fiscal arrangements. Because Ontario is the largest single source of individual and corporate income in the country, it is only logical that this province repeatedly led the fight for greater tax room.[67] Ontario has not taken such a consistent stance on conditional grants,

and while it generally supported equalization, it often tried to make the formula less generous to have-not provinces. At the same time, once Mowat and the courts established a truly federal intergovernmental relationship, Ontario has not been a leader in seeking to increase its legislative jurisdiction at Ottawa's expense. At most, Hepburn and Drew (along with Duplessis in Quebec) led the fight against increased federal jurisdiction in the 1940s. Most other Ontario premiers have been content to object to the way Ottawa behaved in areas of shared jurisdiction. For example, Ontario protested against certain conditions attached to federal subsidies, the lack of consultation in developing or later discontinuing shared-cost programs, and the distortion of provincial priorities in order to take advantage of federal cash. Other status questions that arose, especially in the early years, concerned boundaries and the use of federal disallowance and declaratory powers.

In short, it is not popular or even governmental concern over national policies so much as the provincial government's desire for autonomy and dissatisfaction with the mechanics of the federal system—Ontario's finances, power, and status— that have aroused most of the discord. It is hardly surprising, however, that two large political systems frequently interacting in the bosom of a single state would have their share of disagreements.

What is striking, in fact, is that Ontario's attempts to restructure the federation, or to prevent its restructuring by Ottawa, were primarily restricted to the Mowat, Hepburn, and Drew eras, when several factors favouring a provincial-rights stance coincided. Since 1948 there has been a fairly consistent Ontario government view that the national government must remain strong. Robarts had more difficulty with Ottawa over specific issues than his fellow Ontario premiers in this period, but even he was forced to defend the federal government on occasion in the face of seemingly endless demands for greater autonomy by Quebec.[68] Such an attitude is not only based on Ontario's trust that Ottawa will normally do what is in the province's interest. It is also a defence of Ontario's economic interest in the Canadian common market, the economic union, that has been threatened by decentralizing forces in Quebec and in the west. In addition, it is fully in keeping with the Ontario political culture which is not overly oriented to the province. Moreover, it may be the only way Ontario can influence certain vital developments in other provinces. The crucial energy issue was certainly a catalyst to Davis's thinking on this question, as no amount of interprovincial Ontario pressure seemed to have any impact on Alberta. From that point, Ontario saw Ottawa as an ally in its concern about the vulnerability of its own economy, and Davis joined the federal side in the constitutional debate. Even though the province has since regained its economic pre-eminence, this perspective continues to be held.

Thus David Peterson, in the tradition of Leslie Frost, John Robarts, and especially Bill Davis, recognizes Ontario's stake in keeping Canada together with a central government that can act in the "national" interest. Of course, he may seek to maximize the province's tax room and federal transfers or disagree with Ottawa on other specific points, usually related to shared programs. But otherwise Ontario is likely to continue to play the honest broker role among the provinces and between them and Ottawa, as it did in dealing with Quebec's new constitutional demands. This is the role made famous by Robarts at the time of the Quiet Revolution and by Bill Davis in the 1981–82 constitutional debate. Indeed, similar to Robarts in some respects, Peterson may try to push the federal government into a more assertive national leadership role, rather than seek a consensus on every issue, something Davis did not have to worry about with Trudeau. The paradox of Ontario's role in the federation is surely resolved by taking such a stance.

Notes

1. King did represent a Saskatchewan constituency between 1926 and 1945, and Macdonald a B.C. riding from 1878 to 1882; nevertheless, they are usually classified as Ontarians. In addition, both Meighen and Diefenbaker were born in Ontario, and Turner might be classed as an Ontarian in his brief period as Prime Minister without a seat. See R. M. Punnett, *The Prime Minister in Canadian Government and Politics* (Toronto: Macmillan, 1977), 10.

2. If the actual number of cabinet ministers from each province is calculated, Quebec comes out ahead, but this is because of greater turnover. In terms of "person-years" it is closer to the proportion of the population of each province, namely 28 percent for Quebec and 36 percent for Ontario. See Richard Van Loon and Michael Whittington,

The Canadian Political System, third ed. (Toronto: McGraw-Hill Ryerson, 1981), 454–5. Another method of classification which overcomes the shorter tenure of Quebec ministers is to calculate the percentage of Ontario ministers at the time each federal cabinet was formed, as presented by W. A. Matheson, *The Prime Minister and the Cabinet* (Toronto: Methuen, 1976), 26. These figures also average about 35 percent and are as follows:

1867	5 of 13	38%
1873	6 of 14	43%
1878	4 of 14	29%
1896	4 of 14	29%
1911	7 of 18	39%
1917	9 of 22	41%

1920	6 of 17	35%	
1921	6 of 19	32%	
1930	7 of 19	37%	
1935	4 of 16	25%	
1948	7 of 20	35%	
1957	6 of 21	29%	
1963	10 of 25	40%	
1968	10 of 29	34%	
1979	11 of 30	37%	
1980	13 of 33	39%	
1984	12 of 28	43%	(Turner)
1984	11 of 40	28%	(Mulroney)

3. Ontario's percentage of seats in the House of Commons since 1867 has been as follows:

1867–1872	45%
1872–1874	44%
1874–1882	43%
1882–1887	44%
1887–1904	43%
1904–1908	40%
1908–1917	39%
1917–1925	35%
1925–1949	33%
1949–1968	32%
1968–1979	33%
1979–1988	34%

On 10 occasions since 1878 the majority of Ontario MPs returned in a federal election were on the opposition side, but on the other 20 occasions, and in most recent years, the majority of Ontario MPs were on the government side.

4. It is strange that so little data is available on this point and that not more controversy has arisen about it. Van Loon and Whittington give the one rare statistic mentioned, see *The Canadian Political System*, 3d ed., 467.

5. The numbers on this phenomenon vary according to the method of calculation. In 24 of 33 Ontario provincial elections, the winning party was different from the party in office in Ottawa. Alternatively, in 16 of 30 federal elections since 1878 the party taking the most seats in Ontario was different from the party in office in the province.

6. On this point, see John Wilson and David Hoffman, "The Liberal Party in Contemporary Ontario Politics," *Canadian Journal of Political Science* 3 (1970); Ian Stewart, "Friends at Court:

Federalism and Provincial Elections on Prince Edward Island," *Canadian Journal of Political Science* 1 (1986); and Robert J. Williams, "Ontario's Party Systems: Federal and Provincial," in H. G. Thorburn, ed., *Party Politics in Canada*, fifth ed. (Scarborough: Prentice-Hall, 1985).

7. See Roger Gibbons, *Conflict and Unity: An Introduction to Canadian Political Life* (Toronto: Methuen, 1985), 115. Gibbons' own survey, conducted in April 1983, found that 93 percent of Ontarians thought of themselves as Canadians first. When Harold H. Clark, Jane Jenson, Lawrence LeDuc, and Jon H. Pammett surveyed voter opinion in the 1974 federal election, they found 51 percent of Ontarians identified with the federal government. Federal identification did not exceed 25 percent in any other province. See Harold D. Clark et al., *Political Choice in Canada*, abridged ed. (Toronto: McGraw-Hill Ryerson, 1980), 51, 55.

8. Richard Simeon makes this point, as well as many others, in his article, "Ontario in Confederation," in D. C. MacDonald, ed., *The Government and Politics of Ontario*, 3d ed. (Toronto: Nelson, 1985). He also notes that the private corporate interests in the province, the economic elite, have played a part in raising federal-provincial disputes.

9. Joe Martin, *The Role and Place of Ontario in the Canadian Confederation* (Toronto: Ontario Economic Council, 1974), 2.

10. Van Loon and Whittington stress these four environmental factors, as does Gibbins in his *Conflict and Unity*.

11. J. C. Morrison, "Oliver Mowat and the Development of Provincial Rights in Ontario: A Study in Dominion-Provincial Relations, 1867–1896," in *Three History Theses* (Toronto: Ontario Department of Public Records and Archives, 1961), and Christopher Armstrong, *The Politics of Federalism: Ontario's Relations with the Federal Government, 1867–1942* (Toronto: University of Toronto Press, 1981).

12. H. V. Nelles, *The Politics of Development, Forests, Mines and Hydro-electric Power in Ontario, 1849–1941* (Toronto: Macmillan, 1974), and Armstrong, *The Politics of Federalism*, chap. 2.

13. C. W. Humphries, *'Honest Enough to Be Bold':The Life and Times of Sir James Pliny Whitney* (Toronto: University of Toronto Press, 1985), 191-2.

14. Armstrong, *The Politics of Federalism*, 127.

15. Peter Oliver, *Howard Ferguson, Ontario Tory* (Toronto: University of Toronto Press, 1977); Joseph Schull, *Ontario Since 1867* (Toronto: McClelland and Stewart, 1978), 268; Armstrong, 175.

16. Reginald Whitaker, *The Government Party* (Toronto: University of Toronto Press, 1977), chap. 8; Neil McKenty, *Mitch Hepburn* (Toronto: McClelland and Stewart, 1967); and Armstrong, *The Politics of Federalism*, chaps. 9 and 10.

17. On this period, see Marc J. Gotlieb, "George Drew and the Dominion-Provincial Conference on Reconstruction of 1945-6," *Canadian Historical Review* 66: 1 (1985); Schull, *Ontario Since 1867*, 318-20; Garth Stevenson, *Unfulfilled Union*, 2d ed. (Toronto: Macmillan, 1982), 134-7; Robert Bothwell et al., *Canada since 1945: Power, Politics, and Provincialism* (Toronto: University of Toronto Press, 1981), 91-8. King's diary frequently revealed his antipathy toward Drew, and he congratulated himself repeatedly on retiring before Drew took over as leader of the federal Conservative party so he would not have to deal with him on a daily basis. J. W. Pickersgill and D. F. Forster, *The Mackenzie King Record*, vol. 4, 1947-48 (Toronto: University of Toronto Press, 1970). Drew expressed similar feelings in return, Gotlieb, 45.

18. D. V. Smiley, *Constitutional Adaptation and Canadian Federalism Since 1945* (Ottawa: Royal Commission on Bilingualism and Biculturalism, 1970), 9.

19. *Ibid.*, 18.

20. Robert Bothwell, *Canada since 1945*, 150.

21. Malcolm Taylor, *Health Insurance and Canadian Public Policy* (Montreal: McGill-Queen's University Press, 1978), 158.

22. Dale Thomson, *Louis St. Laurent: Canadian* (Toronto: Macmillan, 1967), 412.

23. Schull, *Ontario Since 1867*, 346.

24. John Diefenbaker, *One Canada*, vol. 2 (Toronto: Macmillan, 1976), 7, 29.

25. Rand Dyck, "Poverty and Policy-Making in the 1960s: The Canada Assistance Plan" (Queen's University Ph.D. thesis, 1973), 60. Frost wrote to the author that "from my standpoint I was anxious to strengthen my own negotiating position and I felt I could best do this by increasing the representation of my own Party in the Federal Parliament."

26. John Saywell, ed., *The Canadian Annual Review*, 1961 (Toronto: University of Toronto Press, 1963), 24.

27. John Diefenbaker, *One Canada*, vol. 3 (Toronto: Macmillan, 1977), 97.

28. See, for example, Kenneth Bryden, *Old Age Pensions and Policy-Making in Canada* (Montreal: McGill-Queen's University Press, 1974), 166; Richard Simeon, *Federal-Provincial Diplomacy* (Toronto: University of Toronto Press, 1972), 150.

29. A. K. McDougall, *John P. Robarts: His Life and Government* (Toronto: University of Toronto Press, 1986), 102.

30. Simeon, *Federal-Provincial Diplomacy*, 281-2. See also Judy LaMarsh, *Memoirs of a Bird in a Gilded Cage* (Toronto: McClelland and Stewart, 1968), chap. 5.

31. "Ontario had no influence on the final shape of the plan except to limit the federal government's freedom of action in amending it;" Bryden, *Old Age Pensions*, 175. Simeon, *Federal-Provincial Diplomacy*, 61, says much the same thing.

32. Rand Dyck, "The Canada Assistance Plan: the Ultimate in Cooperative Federalism," *Canadian Public Administration* 19 (Winter 1976).

33. J. Stefan Dupré et al., *Federalism and Policy Development: The Case of Adult Occupational Training in Ontario* (Toronto: University of Toronto Press), 11.

34. McDougall, *Robarts*, 217.

35. *Ibid.*, 226, 259. See also Taylor, *Health Insurance and Canadian Public Policy*, 369.

36. Quoted in Taylor, *Health Insurance*, 375.

37. Simeon, *Federal-Provincial Diplomacy*, 91-4. Robarts' concern for national unity was articulated in a pamphlet published in 1968 called "Ontario in Confederation."

38. McDougall, *Robarts*, 199.

39. Simeon, *Federal-Provincial Diplomacy*, 239-42. Pearson and even Judy LaMarsh wrote of their

personal affection for Robarts. See Lester B. Pearson, *Mike* vol. 3 (Toronto: University of Toronto Press, 1975), 256; Judy LaMarsh, *Memoirs of a Bird*, 85.

40. Simeon, *Federal-Provincial Diplomacy*, 169.

41. Davis said in 1980, for example, that "Regional dissatisfactions must not be allowed to constrain the capacity of this province, its people, and its government to speak out for Canada through the force of our numbers [*sic*] and political strength, advance and sustain our nation's progress and fundamental strength." *Canadian Annual Review of Politics and Public Affairs*, 1980, 76.

42. Jeffrey Simpson, *Discipline of Power* (Toronto: Personal Library, 1980), 171–205.

43. *Ibid.*, 280 and 350.

44. Their only significant difference on constitutional issues was over official bilingualism for Ontario. Trudeau repeatedly pressured Davis on this point. See, for example, Claire Hoy, *Bill Davis* (Toronto: Methuen, 1985), 306–8, 330; Bruce Pollard, *The Year in Review 1983: Intergovernmental Relations in Canada* (Kingston: Institute of Intergovernmental Relations, 1984), 18, 39–41, 228; and Ronald Zukowsky, *Struggle over the Constitution from the Quebec Referendum to the Supreme Court* (Kingston: Institute of Intergovernmental Relations, 1980), 64.

45. Roy Romanow et al., *Canada. . .Notwithstanding* (Toronto: Carswell/Methuen, 1984), 98, 191–2, 204–5; Hoy, *Bill Davis*, 349–51 and 366–8; Sheilagh Dunn, *The Year in Review 1981: Intergovernmental Relations in Canada* (Kingston: Institute of Intergovernmental Relations, 1982), 20–34; and Edward McWhinney, *Canada and the Constitution 1979-1982* (Toronto: University of Toronto Press, 1982) 94.

46. Romanow, *Canada. . .Notwithstanding*, 107, 200; Nathan Nurgitz and Hugh Segal, *No Small Measure* (Ottawa: Deneau, 1983), 106–10.

47. Hoy, *Bill Davis*, 355–7, 359–60, 363, 376; Ronald Zukowsky, *Struggle over the Constitution*, 2, 64. Hoy writes that Davis never addressed the need for the Charter, but saw it as a "sexy political move, a trendy reform."

48. *Canadian Annual Review of Politics and Public Affairs* (1978), 114, 121, 123; *Canadian Annual Re-*view (1981), 355; *Canadian Annual Review* (1982), 52, 54; Sheilagh Dunn, *The Year in Review 1981*, 175.

49. *Canadian Annual Review*, 1982, 56; Sheilagh Dunn, *The Year in Review 1982: Intergovernmental Relations in Canada*, 3, 82.

50. Bruce Pollard, *The Year in Review 1983*, 5.

51. Sheilagh Dunn, *The Year in Review 1982*, 7–8; Pollard, *The Year in Review 1983*, 2–7, 86.

52. *Canadian Annual Review* (1983), 56, 228.

53. On the partisanship issue, Davis said, "Nothing would be easier for me during the course of these constitutional discussions than to retreat behind my partisan affiliations and oppose what is being put forward from Ottawa because it has been put forward by a Liberal." *Canadian Annual Review* (1980), 76.

54. On the role of personality, see Hoy, *Bill Davis*, 321, 356, 364.

55. Ontario actually tried to manage the dissemination of information on this issue so that this would happen. Hoy, *Bill Davis*, 297, 307–8.

56. Rosemary Spiers, *Out of the Blue: the Fall of the Tory Dynasty in Ontario* (Toronto: Macmillan, 1986), 108–9, 117–8. Perhaps Mulroney did not like Miller's treatment of Norman Atkins.

57. David Peterson, "Notes for Remarks to the Americas Society," November 6, 1986, New York, 5. See also Robert Nixon's May 13, 1986 budget speech, 3. In terms of public opinion, Ontario was the major source of opposition to free trade. See Duncan Cameron, ed., *The Free Trade Papers* (Toronto: Lorimer, 1986), 29.

58. Cameron, *The Free Trade Papers*, chaps. 8, 14, and 16.

59. Peterson, "Remarks to the Americas Society," 17.

60. David Peterson, "Notes for Remarks to the Economic Club of Detroit," September 15, 1986, Detroit, 5 and 18. The brewing industry was another chief concern.

61. David Peterson, "Opening Statement to the First Ministers Conference," Vancouver, November 20, 1986, 6.

62. On the role of the provinces in the free trade issue, see Richard Simeon, "Federalism and Free

Trade," in Cameron, *The Free Trade Papers*. In June 1986, the premiers persuaded Ottawa that "full provincial consultation" required a first ministers conference every three months to review and set the direction of the talks.

63. Rosemary Spiers, *Out of the Blue*, 193. By taking on Mulroney on national televison, Peterson quickly established himself as a premier to be reckoned with. He also complained about federal cuts to training and employment development, and about the lack of consultation on the EPF cuts, saying: "That action put an enormous strain not just on our ability to meet important commitments, but also on the goal of restoring harmony and civility in federal-provincial relations," Peterson's Opening Statement to the First Ministers Conference, Halifax, 8. Many thought that Peterson outperformed Mulroney at the Vancouver meeting as well.

64. Peterson, Opening Statement in Vancouver, 2 and separate statement on equality of women, 2–3.

65. Mulroney defended Peterson against some of Miller's charges when the latter's government was defeated. See Spiers, *Out of the Blue*, 176.

66. Bothwell et al. write that "Drew represented an Ontario tradition of assertive provincial rights . . . which was deeply embedded in the province's political and adminstrative history," *Canada since 1945*, 93. Stevenson (perhaps forgetting Quebec) says that "Ontario remained until very recent times the most militant in resisting the federal government and waving the banner of provincial rights," *Unfulfilled Union*, 71.

67. Simeon, "Ontario in Confederation," 142, writes that "While poorer provinces have tended to emphasize the need for federal financial assistance, and for a greater level of federal redistribution of wealth, Ontario has emphasized the need for fiscal autonomy—for a smaller federal tax burden which would allow the province room to expand its own taxes."

68. Stevenson surely overstates the case in writing that the early 1970s represented "a dramatic reversal" of Ontario's characteristic position "under every Premier from Oliver Mowat to John Robarts," *Unfulfilled Union*, 106.

Selected Readings

Armstrong, Christopher. *The Politics of Federalism: Ontario's Relations with the Federal Government, 1867–1942*. Toronto: University of Toronto Press, 1981.

Gotlieb, Marc J. "George Drew and the Dominion-Provincial Conference on Reconstruction of 1945-6." *Canadian Historical Review* 66:1 (1985): 27–47.

Hoy, Clair. *Bill Davis*. Toronto: Methuen, 1985.

Martin, Joe. *The Role and Place of Ontario in the Canadian Confederation*. Toronto: Ontario Economic Council, 1974.

McDougall, A. K. *John P. Robarts: His Life and Government*. Toronto: University of Toronto Press, 1986.

Simeon, Richard. "Ontario in Confederation." In D. C. MacDonald, ed. *The Government and Politics of Ontario*, 3d ed. Toronto: Nelson, 1985, 133–58.

21. FEDERALISM AND THE CANADIAN WEST

David Elton

While many western Canadians undoubtedly live out their lives without ever seeking to understand the concept of federalism, they live in a political environment in which Canada's federal system of government permeates almost every aspect. Indeed, federal-provincial relations is the heartbeat of Canadian politics and relevant to one's daily life be he a resident of Brandon, Manitoba; Moose Jaw, Saskatchewan; Medicine Hat, Alberta; or Vancouver, British Columbia. For example, farmers fighting grasshoppers in the fields surrounding Brandon and Moose Jaw are influenced by federal-provincial relations because both governments share responsibility for agriculture and would probably negotiate a coordinated program to combat the problem. Similarly, a secretary's job at an oil drilling company located in Medicine Hat may well be dependent upon federal-provincial agreements concerning everything from resource production grants to personal taxation. The same is true of the university professor in Vancouver seeking research funds to determine the economic viability of fish farming. In sum, relations between provincial governments and Ottawa and between the provinces play an important role in determining whether, how, and when the needs and demands of citizens will be met.

The objective of this essay is to describe and explain federal-provincial relations between the four western provinces and Ottawa by examining the social, economic, and political factors that shape interactions between these provinces and Canada's national government. First, the process often referred to as "province-building" by political scientists will be examined. Second the development and maintenance of a strong national identity among western Canadians will be discussed. The third section will deal with the development of a regional political culture, which has at its core western alienation. The fourth section will examine the extent of regional governmental cooperation. The fifth section will deal with federal-provincial conflicts, focusing on the conflicts which arose over the regulation of natural resource development and taxation during the volatile 1970-85 period. The sixth section will discuss the western provinces' position on constitutional change during the 1967-82 period. The seventh and final section will examine events leading up to the 1987 Meech Lake Accord as a paradigm of the relations between the western provinces and Ottawa.

PROVINCE-BUILDING

Although political commentators often talk of the Canadian west as a meaningful political entity, and government departments and agencies often lump data from Canada's four western provinces into one category labelled "western Canada," the individual provinces are more more significant as social, economic, and political entities than this often used regional designation would suggest. Admittedly Manitoba, Saskatchewan, Alberta, and to a lesser extent British Columbia were originally nothing more than political artifacts created on the basis of

An original essay written especially for this volume.

geometric design, with often vague references to natural geographic features. For example, in 1905 the establishment of the Saskatchewan-Alberta boundary on the fourth meridian, was arrived at in much the same way as one might divide a pie into equal parts: an arbitrary line is drawn to ensure that each portion is approximately the same size. The northern boundary of the three "prairie provinces" (a designation that relates to a relatively small portion of the three provinces' topography) was established by simply extending the original arbitrary northern boundary of the 1871 British Columbia eastwardly along the sixtieth parallel. The rationale for these boundaries did not take into consideration geographic, economic, or sociological considerations. Instead the provinces were created according to geometry and the political imperatives of the day.[1] As is often the case with artificially created political boundaries, provincial boundaries rapidly came to have important economic and social relevance. As provincial political institutions began to make decisions, impose regulations, and champion causes on behalf of their electorates, their residents began to develop provincial identities.

One of the key factors influencing the development of western provincial political identities was the exercise of provincial jurisdictional responsibilities. From the date of their creation, provincial governments, often deliberately, at other times unintentionally, encouraged the development and strengthening of provincial loyalties. Activities ranging from the seemingly mundane but significant development of provincial hospital care, agriculture research, and the regulation of intraprovincial trucking to the creation of symbols such as provincial flags, provincial flowers, and special events related to provincial history, encouraged western Canadians to identify with their respective provincial governments. The creation of educational policy programs and associations is a good case in point.

Separate school systems in the four western provinces have resulted in the creation of unique training and staffing procedures, differences in curriculum and performance criteria, and the creation of professional and other related associations on a province-wide basis. As a result, the school system of Medicine Hat, Alberta is similar to, and more closely affiliated with, the school system of Edmonton rather than that of the neighboring community of Swift Current, Saskatchewan. The same is true of the school system in Dawson Creek, British Columbia and Grande Prairie, Alberta. Dawson Creek school teachers, students, and parents are required to interact with the educational bureaucracy in distant Victoria and have nothing to do with the much closer educational bureaucracy in Edmonton.

While provincial regulations over working conditions, medical services, professional services, municipal government, etc., were fostering a sense of provincial identity among western Canadians, provincial identities were being further strengthened by another force inherent in the province-building phenomenon: the relative isolation of large population centres from one another. In most instances large communities in western Canada are located at a considerable distance from provincial boundaries. This spatial reality has created a social, economic, and political situation where the people of one province are largely isolated from those of the other provinces. As a consequence there is little need or incentive for extensive cooperation between local residents of different provinces. The notable exception which proves this rule is Lloydminster, now a community of 15 000, which is divided almost evenly by the Saskatchewan-Alberta border.

The organization of communication networks, particularly the media, on a local community basis has also contributed to the province-building phenomenon. Newspapers, magazines, and even radio and television tend to serve local communities within a single province, sometimes the province as a whole, but seldom the region. There have been some publications, such as the *Western Producer*, the *Grain*

Growers Guide, and since 1986 a public affairs weekly, the *Western Report*, which have had a regional readership, but these publications make up a relatively small part of the media presence in western Canada.

The location of print and electronic media audiences primarily within a particular community (e.g., Vancouver's daily, *The Province*, or Winnipeg's *Free Press*) ensures that a large portion of their public affairs news and commentary will focus upon local and provincial news. The radio station in Brandon, for example, carries news about Manitoba provincial affairs affecting communities such as Churchill, located hundreds of miles away on the James Bay, more often than it does Saskatchewan provincial affairs affecting the nearby community of Estevan, Saskatchewan. Whether it be the initiation and delivery of provincial government programs, the provincial nature of electronic and print media, or the development of professional sports franchises such as the Saskatchewan Roughriders football team, western Canadians have developed strong provincial identities. Simultaneously, however, national identities have also been developed.

NATION-BUILDING

The building of the Canadian Pacific and Canadian National railways, the creation of the Canadian Broadcast Corporation (CBC), and the implementation of unemployment insurance, family allowances, old age pensions, and even athletic leagues such as the Canadian Football League (CFL) all played a part in the entrenchment of a strong national identity and attachment to Canada among western Canadians. Of particular relevance to the west was the creation of uniquely western Canadian organizations such as the Canadian Wheat Board and regionally beneficial programs such as the Crowsnest Pass freight rate and its contemporary equivalent the Western Grain Transportation Act. The strength

of westerners' national ties are evidenced by the extent to which the residents of all four western provinces support national causes, be it serving their country in war, or simply distinguishing themselves from their southern American neighbours, many of whom are physically much closer than are central or Atlantic Canadians.

An examination of values and attitudes towards a wide range of economic, social, and political issues relevant to Canadians also indicates the extent to which the mindset of western Canadians is similar to that of other Canadians. The data collected by national polling organizations indicate not only that western Canadians share many national attitudes and values, but also that differences of opinion within western Canada are often greater than differences of opinion between residents of Canada's west and the rest of the country.

In addition to the development of strong provincial and national ties, a set of regional attitudes and values have also developed that clearly distinguish western Canadians from other Canadians.

A REGIONAL IDENTITY

At the same time western Canadians were developing the strong provincial and national identities referred to above, a common regional identity was being forged. This sense of regional identity is not based upon a positive reaction to government actions or symbols such as flags and logos, rather it is based upon recurring problems westerners have experienced in seeking to find practical political and economic solutions for dealing with property and natural resource development, the cost of supplies, and the sale of their products.

From early settlement days up to the present, westerners have run up against politically constructed barriers which limit their growth and development with regards to resource utilization, consumption, and the marketing of their products. A brief elaboration of each in turn provides an insight into the national policies which have influenced the development and direction of western Canada's political culture and approach to federal-provincial relations.

Property and Natural Resources

When British Columbia entered Confederation in 1871, the province was given the same powers as those extended the four original provinces of Ontario, Quebec, Nova Scotia and New Brunswick; yet the three prairie provinces were denied control over crown lands on the grounds that the national government needed to retain control over crown lands to ensure the orderly flow of immigration into the region. This unequal constitutional treatment of Manitoba, Saskatchewan, and Alberta created considerable friction between the three provincial governments and Ottawa from the outset.[2]

The federal government's decision to retain control over property and natural resources for "the purpose of Canada" (a 19th century equivalent of the "national interest") was contentious not simply because it smacked of colonialism, but also because it had a direct impact upon the daily lives of residents in the three provinces. Prairie settlers were required to provide roads, schools, and other services commensurate with development without provincial control over land allocations or access to revenues from the sale of crown land. Unlike Canadians in other provinces, who had direct control over the orderly development in their communities, this power rested with the distant bureaucrats of the national government. And to add insult to injury, the massive grants of land made by the federal government to the CPR further hampered the provincial government's ability to deal effectively with local land-use issues.[3]

During most of the first three decades of this century, and particularly during the decade following the First World War, demand for control over property and natural resources was the controversial centerpiece of federal-provincial relations between the three prairie provinces and Ottawa. While the federal government's decision in 1930 to transfer control over property and natural resources to Alberta, Saskatchewan, and Manitoba placed them on an equal footing with British Columbia and the other provinces, Ottawa's unwillingness to treat the three provinces equally was one of the key factors in the development of a legacy of distrust and animosity which has never dissipated.

The contemporary equivalent of the struggle for constitutional control over property is the ongoing controversy over the production and sale of oil and gas. Beginning with the federal government's decision to set a ceiling on oil and gas prices in 1973, and culminating with the 1980 National Energy Policy, federal regulation of this industry has become a vivid symbol of Ottawa's colonial mentality towards western Canada.

Tariff Policies

A second national policy which discriminates against residents of all four western provinces is the national government's tariff policy, set up to protect the domestic market for Canadian manufacturers from American and European competition. Most of these manufacturers are located in Ontario and Quebec. In effect, western Canadians are coerced into buying manufactured goods ranging from tools and clothing to household necessities at above their international market price, while at the same time selling their products, be they agricultural products such as wheat or hogs, forestry products, oil, gas, potash, coal, etc., in an open international market place. Given that most western Canadians live within a short distance of the American border and either visit the United States personally or communicate with neighbours who have recently returned from the U.S., they are constantly reminded of the practical costs of Canadian tariff policy.

Even though Canadian tariffs have been reduced considerably during the past two decades and manufacturing activity in western Canada has increased, western Canadians continue to pay more to maintain Canada's tariffs than they benefit. Canadian tariffs cost western Canada nearly 372 million dollars in 1983 alone, while at the same time benefiting central Canadians by over 474 million dollars.[4] Given tariff reductions over the past several decades and the modest increases in manufacturing throughout western Canada during this same time period, it is understandable why Canadian tariff policy has been particularly aggravating to westerners.

Transportation Policy

National transportation policy constitutes a third set of national policies which western Canadians have found to be blatantly discriminatory. Since time when the federal government utilized western lands to pay for the building of the Canadian Pacific Railway in the late 1800s and permitted the railways to charge discriminatory freight rates, national transportation policy has been particularly aggravating for Alberta, Saskatchewan, and Manitoba. British Columbia, on the other hand, has never been concerned about transportation rates because the province is not landlocked and is favoured by competition between water transportation and rail to obtain optimal cost-benefits.[5]

Whether one picks up a Canadian agriculture magazine of the early 1900s, a contemporary economic analysis of the 1984 Western Grain Transportation Act, or listens to a speech by a western manufacturer, western grievances regarding national transportation policies are an integral part of the discussion. The basic complaint centres around freight rate structures and programs which impose high rates on goods shipped into the three western land-locked provinces and encourages the shipment of non-processed goods out of the region.

The National Interest

Whether it be economists analysing voluntary export quotas on Japanese autos or federal revenue expenditure patterns, or the 1986 Auditor General's report focusing on grants handled by the Department of Regional and Industrial expansion, examples of regionally discriminatory practices by the national government abound.[6] After having examined these and other federal government practices in a 1987 report prepared for the Canada West Foundation entitled "The Western Economy and Canadian Unity," McCormick and Elton conclude that the concept of "national interest" utilized by the national government often excludes the concerns and aspirations of western Canadians. They note: "The term 'the national interest' often takes on ominous overtones for western Canadians. When they hear it invoked, it is much like getting a phone call and being asked if you are sitting down: they know that bad news is on the way."[7]

Western Alienation

As a result of a broad range of policies such as those cited above, a longstanding and widespread disaffection with the national government has become embedded in the very heart of western Canada's political culture. This shared attitude, often referred to as western alienation, exists among a broad cross-section of western residents and has persisted regardless of the party in power or the number of western MPs on the government side of the House. Survey research over the 1979-85 period undertaken for the Canada West Foundation indicates that 4 of every 5 western Canadians believe the Canadian political system favours Ontario and Quebec. These sentiments have lead approximately one in twenty western Canadians to advocate separation or union with the United States. But approximately four out of five westerners continue to identify strongly with the Canadian political system while simultaneously expressing discontent over real and apparent discriminatory tendencies.

While there have been many attempts to explain western alienation, it is probably best symbolized by the 1914 Prairie Grain Grower's Guide cartoon of the mulch cow being fed in the West and milked in Ontario and Quebec. This cartoon is an example of a sentiment that is just as prevalent in the 1980s as it was when it first appeared over sixty years ago.[8]

REGIONAL COOPERATION

Although residents of the prairie provinces developed a strong regional identity in the early decades of this century, it has only been in the last two decades that a significant amount of formal cooperation between western provincial governments has taken place. The establishment of the Prairie Economic Council in 1965 by the provinces of Manitoba, Saskatchewan, and Alberta, followed by the creation of the Western Premiers Conference in 1973, which included British Columbia, are the most significant examples of formal interprovincial relations.

The Prairie Economic Council was created to provide a forum for the discussion of broad social and economic issues common to the region and where needed to permit cooperation on joint ventures. During the 1965-73 period, the Council met on twelve separate occasions and more than 200 items appeared on their agenda. These included water resource issues, tourism, freight rates, resource production, environmental regulation, power generation, educational programs, and highway construction. These discussions led to the initiation of a number of significant regional programs, such as the rationalization of university training programs for veterinary medicine, optometry, and occupational therapy, and the creation of a Prairie Provinces Water Board to administer an agreement allocating fresh water supplies throughout the prairie region.[9]

The creation of the Western Premiers Conference and the inclusion of British Columbia in the regional forum was occasioned by the January 1973 federal government Throne Speech, which proposed a Western Economic Opportunities Conference (WEOC). This initiative was taken by the newly elected minority Liberal Government, whose western representation had been reduced from 28 MPs in 1968 to 7 in 1972. Ottawa proposed WEOC to discuss western economic grievances and hopefully establish an agenda for future economic development and diversification.[10]

The federal WEOC initiative was greeted with considerable enthusiasm by the four western premiers, who in preparation for the conference immediately set their public servants to work preparing joint position papers on transportation, agriculture, economic development and capital financing, and regional financial institutions. While the conference was clearly a historical event (it is the only regional federal-provincial conference that has been held to date), the meeting fell far short of attaining the expectations of either the federal or provincial governments. Rather than setting the stage for what the federal Throne Speech referred to as "concrete programs for stimulating and broadening the economic and industrial base of Western Canada," the meeting ended with few concrete accomplishments beyond commitments by the federal government to review rail rates, provide provinces with data on railway operating costs, and amend the Bank Act to permit limited provincial government ownership of equity stock in chartered banks. The creation of the Western Premiers Conference, although a byproduct, was in retrospect the most noteworthy accomplishment of WEOC.[11]

Since 1973 the western premiers have met annually to discuss the coordination of regional policies and positions on federal-provincial relations. These efforts at regional cooperation have generated activities such as a joint trade mission to Latin America (1975), the creation of a jointly administered and financed Prairie Agricultural Machinery Institute (1974), a manpower training rationalization study (1979-82), and several interprovincial committees to deal with transportation and industrial development issues. Yet the most important function performed by the Western Premiers Conference has been that of providing a mechanism and forum for coordinating the western provinces' interactions with the federal government. For example, in 1976 the western premiers "expressed their concern over the increasing tendency of the government of Canada to legislate in subject areas which historically and constitutionally had been considered to be within the provincial sphere."[12] This concern resulted in the production of three reports during the 1977-79 period which delineated dozens of policies, programs, and actions where the western provinces felt the federal government was intruding in areas of provincial jurisdiction.[13]

FEDERAL-PROVINCIAL CONFLICTS

While there were a number of disagreements between individual western provinces and the federal government during the 1945-70 period (e.g., Alberta's stringent opposition to Medicare in 1968, British Columbia's confrontation with Ottawa over the Columbia River Treaty, etc.), there were three important factors in the late 1960s and early 1970s which led to increased confrontation between the western provinces and the federal government.

First, the late 1960s and early 1970s was a period of economic malaise in western Canada. All four western provinces had sought rapid economic development through an open-door investment policy, unrestricted resource development, and limited environmental controls. Yet each of the provinces was in a mild

recession with job creation relatively stagnant, incomes falling somewhat, and generally a weak demand for the west's resource production.[14]

The second factor which generated change in federal-provincial relations was that the 1969-72 period was one of rapid political change. In 1969, the NDP in Manitoba not only chose a new leader during the election campaign, but succeeded in defeating the governing Conservative party. In 1971 the Liberal government in Saskatchewan was defeated by the NDP lead by Allan Blakeney, and the 36-year reign of the Social Credit party in Alberta came to an end when Albertans elected a Progressive Conservative party headed by Peter Lougheed. In 1972 the winds of political change made a clean sweep of the west when the twenty year reign of W. A. C. Bennett in British Columbia came to an end with the election of a New Democratic Party government headed by Dave Barrett.

In addition to these fundamental changes in provincial politics, the Liberal Party's fortunes in western Canada were dealt a severe blow in the 1972 federal election when their representation was reduced from 26 to 7 Members of Parliament. With four new premiers with new mandates to improve the economic performance of their provinces and a shift in partisan representation from the west in Ottawa, the stage was set for considerable change in federal-provincial relations.

The third factor influencing federal-provincial relations during the early 1970s was the turmoil over constitutional change generated by demands emanating from Quebec for greater provincial autonomy. The western provinces clearly had not actively sought increased provincial autonomy during the 1960s, but rather had focused on increasing federal government contributions to shared-cost programs. However, the growing sophistication of the western provincial bureaucracies, accompanied by a need for greater control over economic development, and the subsequent conflict over resource management and revenues of the 1973-76 period all played a role in convincing western leaders to seek both the protection and expansion of provincial constitutional powers.

The opening shots of the decade-long battle between the western provinces and Ottawa were taken at the July 1973 Western Economic Opportunities Conference. While the four position papers presented to the federal government by the western premiers detailed western grievances, some dating before the turn of the century (e.g., discrimination in transportation freight rates), the federal government's lack of response made it clear that there would be little change. National policies and programs which had frustrated westerners for so long would not undergo any fundamental changes. Thus, when the additional frustrations brought on by conflicts over resource revenues, which emerged within weeks of WEOC in September, 1973, were added to the list of western grievances, a recipe for outright hostilities had been created.

The Oil and Gas Wars

The war over oil and gas revenues struck at the very heart of western provinces-Ottawa relations. While the battle was primarily one between Alberta's Conservative Premier Peter Lougheed and Liberal Prime Minister Pierre Trudeau, it was joined from time to time by NDP Premier Allan Blakeney and by British Columbia's Social Credit Premier Bill Bennett. Manitoba for the most part was not a significant player in the debate since it has little oil and gas production and thus tended to view the issue more from the perspective of a consumer than that of a producer.

Formally the bone of contention between the western provinces (primarily Alberta) and Ottawa was the question of provincial jurisdictional rights over natural resources versus the federal government's regulation of interprovincial and international trade.

This formal debate over jurisdictional responsibilities, while important, should not be construed to be the real heart of the conflict. The real issue was over which government would have the political power to regulate the oil and gas industry and thereby obtain the largest share of the billions of dollars of resource revenues which were to be generated from the sale of these resources.

During the twelve year period commencing with the September 1973 federal government announcement of a freeze on the domestic price of oil (followed ten days later with the announcement of an export tax on crude oil destined for the U.S.) and ending with the 1985 signing of the Western Accord, the battle for oil and gas revenues included a bewildering array of issues and activities. On a nearly continuous basis during the 1973-76 period and again from 1978-82, one or more of the following was taking place: (1) conferences between first ministers and/or energy ministers and their officials; (2) debates over whether and under what circumstances negotiations should be bilateral (i.e. between Alberta and Ottawa only) or multilateral (i.e. involving all ten provinces); (3) passage of a wide variety of provincial and/or federal legislation seeking to control the production, sale, and pricing of oil and gas; (4) temporary pricing agreements between the provinces and the federal government (e.g., 60-180 day pricing agreements) accompanied by premature assumptions that the battle was over; (5) constitutional court challenges; (6) disruptions in oil supplies; (7) the nearly spontaneous development of huge separatist rallies in Calgary and Edmonton.[15]

From an Alberta perspective, the battle with Ottawa over control and regulation of oil and gas was a life and death struggle. The following excerpts from a speech by Peter Lougheed to the Canadian Club of Calgary at the outset of confrontations is an excellent example of the frustration and disenchantment over the federal government's decision to set domestic prices and impose an export tax on oil:

This [the imposition of an oil export tax] appears to be the most discriminatory action taken by a federal government against a particular province in the entire history of Confederation. The natural resources of the provinces are owned by the provinces under the terms of Confederation. The action taken by Ottawa strikes at the very roots of Confederation. And why just an export tax on oil? Why not on lumber from British Columbia, potash from Saskatchewan, nickel from Manitoba, pulp and paper, asbestos, and gold from Ontario and Quebec? Why Alberta oil? . . . We are going to be forced to take certain actions we do not want to take and would not otherwise take . . . . We have to try to protect the Alberta public interest—not from the public interest of Canada as a whole—but from central and eastern Canadian domination of the West.[16]

As a result of a mixture of bilateral (Alberta-Ottawa) and multilateral negotiations (all ten provinces and Ottawa), and notwithstanding the inordinately high profile given such things as inflammatory bumper stickers declaring "Let the eastern bastards freeze in the dark," a series of temporary pricing agreements were reached during the 1973-76 period through compromises on the part of both the producing provinces and the federal government. These compromises resulted in the producing provinces retaining control over much of the revenues generated from increased oil and gas prices and provided both Alberta and Saskatchewan with revenue surpluses worth hundreds of millions of dollars. These monies were used to establish savings trust funds which were used to facilitate economic development and diversification, and provide a financial cushion to make up for the loss of revenues that would take place when the resource base was depleted.

The federal government, on the other hand, not only clearly maintained its control over interprovincial and international trade, but also obtained adequate revenues to provide central and eastern Canadian consumers with oil and gas at well below the international market price. While the arrangements regarding regulation of the oil and gas industry and the sharing of revenues were not totally satisfactory to either the western provinces, the federal government, or the consuming provinces, they did provide for temporary relief from a highly contentious and divisive issue in federal-provincial relations.

With the second dramatic increase in international oil prices in 1979 the uneasy truce between the western provinces and Ottawa was shattered. The battle over oil revenues played an important role in such significant political events as the defeat of Joe Clark's nine month old minority government, the creation of a National Energy Policy, and the establishment of a vibrant separatist movement centred in Alberta. It also generated other important events regarding federal-provincial relations that heretofore had not taken place. For example, the Alberta premier held meetings with federal members of Parliament from his province in an effort to influence Joe Clark's government in 1979. The first joint Alberta-British Columbia cabinet meeting was held in the summer of 1980 to show western solidarity on the resource issue. In addition, Alberta's premier held a number of bilateral meetings not only with other western premiers, but also with premiers in Atlantic Canada.[17]

At the annual Premiers Conference held in Winnipeg in August of 1980, Lougheed succeeded in obtaining the support of nine of the ten provinces regarding Alberta's claim that the federal government should not interfere with provincial regulation of the production and sale of natural resources. The lone dissenting province was Ontario, which in 1979 had released a report entitled "Oil Pricing and Security: A Policy Framework for Canada." This report argued that consuming provinces should participate in the setting of oil prices, and that royalties and taxes generated from oil and gas should flow to the federal treasury for distribution across the country.[18] Not surprisingly, the report did not advocate provinces sharing their revenues generated from other natural resources, such as electricity.

It should be noted that the producing provinces on numerous occasions over the 1974-80 period had stated that they were willing to provide oil to other Canadians at below an artificially high international price in return for a reasonable rate of return for the production of a depleting resource. Thus the Ontario argument that consumers should set the price for the products they consume and also obtain the funds generated from their production was tantamount to the Ontario government flipping a coin and saying to western Canadians, "heads we win, tails you lose."

Notwithstanding widespread support among other provinces for Alberta's position the federal government brought down its National Energy Policy in October 1980. Alberta's response was immediate and calculated. First, Lougheed went on province-wide television and announced that unless Ottawa and Alberta could reach a settlement on oil pricing, Alberta would "turn down the taps" beginning five months hence (April 1, 1981) and further reduce oil production by the same amount on June 1 and September 1. To foreclose the possibility of the federal government using its emergency powers Lougheed was careful to assure Canadians that, while Alberta would not produce and sell this depleting resource at the fire sale prices specified in the National Energy Policy, Alberta would restore production immediately should a shortage of oil develop. This left the federal government in the position of being unable to stop the reduction of production and having to purchase the shortfall of oil on the international market.

Lougheed ended his thirty minute television address on an emotional note by appealing to Albertans' sense of independence:

Who will ultimately decide? It won't be Peter or Pierre—it will be you, as Albertans—you who will determine whether or not you want to see more and more of your lives directed and controlled in Ottawa or whether you want to see a fair portion of the decision-making determined by Albertans in Alberta. If you choose the latter, I believe, over time, we will have a stronger Canada and a better Canada.[19]

The second action was to launch a carefully structured case challenging the constitutionality of the federal government's export tax on natural gas. The Alberta case was based upon gas production from a specific well located on crown land and owned by the Alberta government. The Alberta argument was that the federal government's export tax was illegal because one government cannot tax another. Although it took some time for the courts to render their decision, Alberta won the case before the Supreme Court on a six to three decision.[20]

The third action taken by Alberta was that of an extensive public relations campaign to inform Canadians of the discriminatory nature of the NEP. The campaign consisted primarily of an extensive speaking tour and media awareness briefings by the premier, his energy minister and officials, and a number of prominent oil industry executives and public-spirited Albertans. Ontario was targeted as the primary area and speeches were given to Canadian clubs, Chamber of Commerce gatherings, universities, etc. In addition, newspaper editors were visited and reporters given extraordinary access to Lougheed.

Shortly after Alberta's first round of oil production cutbacks in April 1981, a series of unpublicized bilateral meetings began between key officials of Alberta and the federal government in an effort to arrive at an acceptable compromise on oil pricing. Because no deal had been struck by June 1, oil production was reduced by another 60 000 barrels per day, requiring the federal government to increase subsidies to central Canadian refineries which now had to buy more oil on the international market. By September 1, the day the third reduction in oil production was to take place, Alberta and Ottawa announced that an accommodation had been reached and a five year oil pricing agreement had been negotiated. While the war was not over, an uneasy peace had been declared. Premier Lougheed and Prime

Minister Trudeau held a public signing cere-mony and drank a toast to one another.[21]

It wasn't until four years later, following the defeat of the Liberals and the election of Brian Mulroney's Conservative government, which obtained most of western Canada's seats, that the NEP would be dismantled and replaced by an agreement between Alberta, Saskatchewan, British Columbia, and the federal government. The agreement, called the Western Accord, re-placed federal pricing regulations with interna-tional market discipline.[22] Ironically, within months of the Western Accord international oil prices tumbled to approximately one-third their 1986 price, and western producers and western provincial governments found themselves facing massive cutbacks in energy exploration and lay-offs within the industry of a magnitude never before experienced. Thus by the summer of 1986 the federal government found itself facing de-mands from both Saskatchewan and Alberta for federal loan guarantees and investments in oil sands projects and refineries.

At the same time that the decade-long war over oil and gas production and pricing was taking place, primarily between Ottawa and Al-berta, Saskatchewan was doing battle with Ot-tawa through the Courts over provincial taxation powers regarding natural resources. At issue was the constitutionality of Saskatchewan's mineral income tax and royalty surcharges passed by the Saskatchewan legislature in 1973, and the prov-ince's ability to pro-ration potash production. The Supreme court ruling on the taxation issue, handed down in November 1977, ruled in favour of the plaintiff, Canadian Industrial Gas and Oil Ltd. (CIGOL), on the grounds that provincial legislatures did not have the authority to fix the price of goods to be exported from the province because this involved interprovincial or interna-tional trade and commerce, which were the ex-clusive responsibility of the federal government.[23] This decision effectively put at risk $580 million in taxes which had already been collected by Saskatchewan from 1973

through 1977 and already spent by the Saskatche-wan government on, among other things, the purchase of potash mines. Premier Blakeney an-nounced that in spite of the Court decision his government would not return the funds to the oil companies and appealed for help from the fed-eral government to find a means of obtaining a settlement with the industry. Following closely on the heels of the oil taxation case, the Supreme Court ruled in 1978 that the province's legislation dealing with the pro-rationing of potash produc-tion among the various potash mines in Saskatch-ewan (many of them now owned by the provincial government) was also unconstitutional because almost all of Saskatchewan's potash was exported and the province's pro-rationing scheme inter-fered with international trade. Because the fed-eral government had intervened in this case on behalf of the plaintiff and challenged the provin-cial legislation, the Saskatchewan premier di-rectly attacked the federal government for attempting to wrest control of natural resources from the provinces through influencing these Supreme Court decisions. The premier then went on to vow that, rather than change Sas-katchewan's approach to the management of their resources, he would seek constitutional changes to reinforce provincial control over natural re-sources and permit the kinds of actions which the Supreme Court had found unconstitutional.[24]

THE STRUGGLE OVER CONSTITUTIONAL CHANGE

Constitutional issues were not placed on the western Canadian political agenda by westerners or their governments. They were introduced to the west by Quebec and the federal government in the late 1960s. The agenda for the initial round of constitutional discussions, starting with the Ontario government-sponsored Confederation of Tomorrow conference in 1967 and followed by a series of federal government-sponsored consti-tutional conferences in 1968-71, dealt primarily with Quebec issues. The western provinces simply used the conferences as an opportunity to air traditional grievances regarding lack of attention from Ottawa, and voice their concern over Quebec and federal government proposals concerning language, a charter of rights, and the division of powers between the two governments.[25]

One of the more significant aspects of western involvement in these early conferences was the symbolic gesture made to British Columbia in 1971, when the constitutional conference was held in that province to commemorate its 100th year in Confederation. The amending formula, which was tentatively agreed to at that meeting and thus labeled the Victoria formula, did no more than give formal recognitition to the west as a region by specifying that changes to the constitution would require the concurrence of at least two of the western provinces containing at least 50 percent of the region's population. The acceptance of that formula by western governments is indicative of the desire they had to resolve the constitutional issues and get on with the more pressing issues of economic development and diversification. There was thus no real concern in the west when Quebec subsequently rejected the formula.[26]

By the time constitutional matters were again revived in late 1976, following the Parti Québécois victory in Quebec, western Canadians and their governments, particularly in Saskatchewan, Alberta, and British Columbia were anxious to place a number of important items on the constitutional reform agenda. For Saskatchewan and Alberta control over natural resources was of greatest importance. For British Columbia it was the need for fundamental change to national institutions.

In the fall of 1978 British Columbia released a series of nine position papers dealing with the need for constitutional change. The list included acceptance of British Columbia as a distinctive region of Canada, reform of the Senate, reform of the Supreme Court, improved instruments for federal-provincial relations, a Bill of Rights for Canada, language rights, the distribution of legislative powers, and an amending formula for the constitution. From a B.C. perspective, Senate reform was the most important of the nine items. This recommendation was based upon B.C. Premier Bill Bennett's belief that "the federal government, in formulating national policy, does not understand and, therefore, does not take account of important regional needs and aspirations, including those of British Columbia."[27] Bennett felt that the solution to federal inattention to regional matters was to be found, not in decentralizing power, but in providing for a greater provincial voice in national institutions.

There were four essential elements of the B.C. proposal for Senate reform. First, the primary purpose of the Senate would be to institutionalize federal-provincial participation in the national law-making process and to review legislation enacted by the House of Commons. Second, members of the Senate would be appointed and removed by provincial governments, with the leading Senator from each province being a provincial cabinet minister. Third, the powers of the Senate would be divided into two categories. The first category would contain those items of crucial importance to provinces over which the Senate would exercise an absolute veto, such as appointments to the Supreme Court, amendments to the constitution, federal spending in areas of provincial jurisdiction, etc. The second category would consist of federal government jurisdictional responsibilities over which the Senate would only have a three month suspensive veto. Fourth, defeat of a government bill by the Senate would not defeat the government.[28]

With some variations on specifics, British Columbia's proposal for the establishment of what became known as the "House of the Provinces model" was advocated by a number of organizations during the 1978-80 period, such as the Canada West Foundation, the Ontario Advisory Committee on Constitutional Reform, the national Conservative party, and the federal government's Task Force on Canadian unity.[29]

Initially none of the other three western provinces showed any interest in promoting the B.C. proposal for Senate reform. When Alberta brought out its document on Constitutional reform in October 1978, there was no mention of Senate reform, but instead a definite emphasis upon changes in the division of powers, the institutionalization of federal-provincial conferences, the establishment of an amending formula which treated all provinces equally, and changes to the selection and appointment procedures for the Supreme Court.[30]

Although neither Saskatchewan or Manitoba produced specific constitutional proposals, it is clear from the pronouncements of their premiers that neither were enthusiastic about B.C.'s key proposal regarding Senate reform. Manitoba focused upon language issues and opposed the entrenchment of a Charter of Rights, while Saskatchewan chose to undertake the role of honest broker in the debate and emphasized the need to enhance provincial management and taxation of natural resources.[31]

During the course of the intense federal-provincial negotiations on constitutional matters during the 1978-82 period, all of the above items on the western provinces agenda were debated extensively. When the final agreement was reached in late 1981, two key western issues were included in Canada's new constitution. First, Alberta's version of the amending formula was entrenched in the constitution. This formula recognized the equality of the provinces, denying any one province an absolute veto by requiring the assent of two-thirds of the provinces containing 50 percent of the country's population for key constitutional reforms.[32]

The second major western issue included in the Constitution Act, 1982 was Saskatchewan's desire to have provincial powers over natural resources increased. The constitutional problems that Saskatchewan experienced in the mid-1970s over taxation and regulation of resource production were effectively resolved in Section 92a of the Constitution. This provides for provincial indirect taxation of resources and the ability to regulate resource production even though it may impact interprovincial or international trade. The only limitation now placed upon provincial control of natural resources is that provincial taxation and regulation practices must apply equally across the country.[33]

MEECH LAKE

Following the enactment of the Canada Act in 1982 constitutional debate was shelved in western Canada as it was throughout the country. Once again economic issues dominated federal-provincial relations as western provinces sought ways and means of stimulating economic development and diversification. Of particular concern was the need for increased international trade in general and in particular the establishment of a free trade agreement with the United States. Because both of these issues are primarily within the jurisdictional responsibilities of the federal government, the western premiers, both individually and through the Western Premiers Conferences and the annual Premiers Conference, exhorted the federal government to take action which would further these objectives.[34]

While these economic matters dominated centre stage in federal-provincial relations during the 1982-86 period, a number of highly publicized events pertaining to federal-provincial relations took place which influenced the western provinces' attitude towards further constitutional reforms. In each of these events the centripetal and centrifugal forces working upon western Canadians and their governments are evident and played a part in shaping provincial government behaviour regarding the federal government.

The first event was the creation in 1983 of a special legislative committee of the Alberta legislature to examine ways and means to reform Canada's Senate. Although the Alberta government had not paid much attention to the B.C. proposals on institutional reform in 1978-80, the position changed in response to considerable public pressure exerted by those advocating senate reform based upon a Triple E formula (elected, equal representation from each province, and effective powers). In 1985 the committee reported back to the Alberta legislature and recommended the creation of a Triple E Senate as a necessary element of effective regional representation within the national government.[35]

The demand for Senate reform was based upon two considerations. First, Senate reform advocates utilized the same argument that British Columbia had used in 1978. They pointed to the federal government's inability and/or unwillingness to deal effectively with the needs and aspirations of the west because the structure of the existing parliamentary system and the dominant majoritarian principle and practices contained therein dictate that the concerns and aspirations of central Canada (i.e., Ontario and Quebec) must take precedence over the western or Atlantic hinterlands. The second basic argument used by advocates of Senate reform was that many of the concerns of western Canadians can only be dealt with by the national government, given federal jurisdiction over such matters as transportation, international trade, etc., and therefore some way had to be found to obtain meaningful regional representation within the national government. A Triple E Senate was seen as the best means of dealing with these two problems.[36]

Little interest was paid to this initiative outside Alberta as even the British Columbia government, which had championed Senate reform only four years earlier, refrained from placing the issue on their agenda. Similarly, in Saskatchewan and Manitoba no extensive debate over Senate reform took place within government circles. Saskatchewan was preoccupied with a serious recession in the farm community and the need for federal assistance, and Manitoba was primarily concerned with reductions in federal

spending, particularly with regards to equalization payments.[37]

The second event affecting the attitudes of the western provinces to constitutional reform was a decision by the federal government to award a military fighter aircraft maintenance contract to Quebec rather than Manitoba. The decision to award the F-18 military fighter aircraft maintenance contract to Canadair of Montreal rather than Bristol Aerospace of Winnipeg, even though the latter submitted a better bid, was seen as blatant discrimination and a devastating blow to the Manitoba economy. This action gave concrete and immediate evidence to the argument made by those advocating Senate reform that the federal government discriminates against the west in favour of Quebec. It therefore forced Manitobans, who by in large are supportive of federal spending due to their status as a beneficiary of equalization payments and other federal fiscal programs, to seek some means to ensure that similar discriminatory acts would not take place in the future.[38] Equally important, it created considerable animosity between the government of Manitoba and the federal government.

The third event was an attack on the federal government's procurement practices by parliament's Auditor General, western print media, and the government of British Columbia. The following statement by B.C. Premier Bill Van der Zalm at the 1986 annual First Ministers Conference held in Vancouver is a good example of the content and rationale for these criticisms.

In addition to its tariff and deficit policies the federal government has consistently reaped more income from British Columbia than it returns in the form of expenditures, investment, and employment. Examples of British Columbia not getting its 'fair share' are not hard to find. Your government, Prime Minister, spends billions of dollars annually—approximately $12 billion in fact over the past five years—through its procurement process. In 1985-86, of those billions of dollars, British Columbia companies and manufacturers received only 5.3 percent of the major contracts though we represent 11.4 percent of the people in Canada.[39]

Because similar data regarding federal spending is available regarding each of the four western provinces, Premier Van der Zalm's frustration with federal procurement policies is shared by all western provinces and serves to reinforce a strong sense of inequity which does little to endear the federal government to western premiers, particularly when the west is in a recession and experiencing much higher levels of unemployment than central Canada. This issue provided yet another concrete and contemporary example of what Senate reform advocates were complaining about.

The fourth event which helped shape the mindset of western premiers was the refusal of the federal government to provide financial aid to further develop Alberta and Saskatchewan's oil industry. Alberta's Premier Don Getty expressed his frustration at the lack of federal government appreciation for the situation in the oil industry by noting that in 1986 over 25 000 people had lost their jobs in the oil industry, that investment had been cut by over four billion dollars, and that Canada's future security of oil supply was threatened. What should have been the federal response to this situation?

When it became evident that a vital Canadian industry and part of Canada was hurting badly, we would have liked to have seen the federal government quickly assess all of its policy tools which could have helped. Isn't that, after all, what being a part of Canada is all about? The federal government could have considered how to help the tremendous loss of cash flow in our industry by restoring earned depletion or by reviewing the need for an increase in the investment tax credit incentive for energy investments. These two measures alone would have had a dramatic impact on the industry's ability to reinvest to develop future supplies of crude oil and natural gas for all Canadians. In fact, what was in

the last federal budget was a reduction in the investment tax credit in Alberta. A reduction! Not help—less help. Our system must respond better than that.[40]

The fifth event was the announcement of a billion dollar federal deficiency payment to farmers in 1986 to help them cope with a dramatic fall in international grain prices. Saskatchewan Premier Grant Devine was one of the primary advocates of this federal grant-in-aid and, politically speaking, the greatest beneficiary of the program: it played no small part in the reelection of his government in 1986. For Saskatchewan farmers, for Grant Devine, and to a lesser extent for Alberta and Manitoba grain farmers, who also benefited from the program, it was concrete evidence of the benefits of Confederation and a good reason to support the federal government.

An analysis of the five events discussed above indicates the extent to which there are stresses and strains on federal-provincial relations in the west, accompanied by periodic benefits. Three of the five events leading up to the Meech Lake meeting (i.e., the F-18 contract, federal procurement practices, and oil industry aid) generated considerable animosity between western provinces and the federal government. The growth of support for the creation of a Triple E Senate was spurred on by the fact that these three events provided ample evidence of federal government discrimination and inattention regarding the Canadian west.

Concurrent with the high profile examples of federal government discrimination and inattention, the farm deficiency payment provided evidence of federal largesse towards the west. Thus, at the same time westerners were becoming more convinced that the Canadian federal system didn't work for them, they were provided with concrete evidence that it does work, at least sometimes. It is the continued existence of these sometimes discriminatory, sometimes beneficial federal programs and policies that generates the often seemingly schizophrenic behaviour of western Canadians who are alienated from their national government and yet seek to obtain greater participation in national decision-making.

There are literally dozens of joint federal-provincial programs between each of the western provinces and Ottawa which have been initiated by one province or by the federal government and function without raising public or political consternation.[41] Unlike some members of the public, western provincial leaders are well aware of the scope of these ongoing federal-provincial programs, yet they frequently choose to openly challenge the federal system. This behaviour indicates that there are considerable improvements still needed before Canada's federal system is capable of meeting the needs of its citizens regardless of their place of residence.

Given the foregoing, it is not hard to understand why Alberta Premier Don Getty went to

Meech Lake in April 1987 with the ultimatum that while he was as interested as anyone in finding a way to have the Quebec provincial government sign the constitution, he would not agree to any constitutional changes that did not include some movement towards meaningful Senate reform. Similarly, it is not hard to understand why Manitoba Premier Howard Pawley indirectly threatened to scrap the Meech Lake Accord by insisting upon the continuation of strong federal government constitutional powers regarding spending powers in areas of provincial jurisdiction. Both positions are indicative of western aspirations to play a meaningful role in national decision-making and underlines the strong commitment of westerners to Canada—not Canada as it has existed, but a Canada with a reformed federal system that guarantees balance, equity, and fairness for all Canadians.

Notes

1. David K. Elton, "Alberta and the Federal Government in Historical Perspective, 1905-1977," in Carlo Caldarola, ed., *Society and Politics in Alberta* (Toronto: Methuen, 1979), 109-10.

2. *Ibid.*

3. *Ibid.*

4. "International Trade: Problems and Prospects," *Western Perspectives* (Calgary: Canada West Foundation, November 1985), 10.

5. T. D. Regehr, "Western Canada and the Burden of National Transportation Policies," in David Jay Bercuson, ed., *Canada and the Burden of Unity* (Toronto: Macmillan, 1977), 115-42.

6. Peter McCormick and David Elton, "The Western Economy and Canadian Unity," *Western Perspectives* (Calgary: Canada West Foundation, 1987), 1.

7. *Ibid.*, 12.

8. For a detailed examination of western alienation, see David Elton and Roger Gibbins, "Western Alienation and Political Culture," in Richard Schultz et al., eds., third edition, *The Canadian Political Process* (Toronto: Holt, Rinehart and Winston, 1982), 82-97.

9. "Report on Regional Co-operation," Western Premiers Conference, 1981, 2.

10. Howard R. Penniman, ed., *Canada At The Polls: The General Election of 1974* (Washington: American Enterprise Institute for Public Policy Research, 1975), 294-6.

11. "Follow-up on The Western Economic Opportunities Conference" (Calgary: Canada West Foundation, 1974), 23.

12. "Regional Report on Co-operation," 7.

13. *Ibid.*

14. J. F. Conway, *The West: The History of a Region in Confederation* (Toronto: James Lorimer, 1983), 185-9.

15. For a comprehensive overview of these events, see *Canadian Annual Review* (Toronto: University of Toronto Press, 1973-82).

16. David G. Wood, *The Lougheed Legacy* (Toronto: Key Porter Books, 1985), 147.

17. *Ibid.*, 172-4.

18. *Ibid.*, 159.

19. *Ibid.*, 175.

20. Sheilagh M. Dunn, *The Year in Review 1981: Intergovernmental Relations in Canada* (Kingston: Institute of Intergovernmental Affairs, Queen's University, 1982), 124.

21. *Ibid.*, 123-30.

22. *Canadian News Facts*, Vol. 19 (Toronto: Marpep Publishing, 1985), p. 3228.

23. *Ibid.*, Vol. 11, 1977, 18544-56.

24. *Ibid.*, Vol. 12, 1978, 2021.

25. Elton, "Alberta and the Federal Government," 121-7.

26. *Ibid.*

27. *British Columbia's Constitutional Proposals* (Victoria: Government of British Columbia, 1978), Paper #3, 7-8.

28. *Ibid.*, 33-4.

29. Peter McCormick, Ernest Manning, and Gordon Gibson, *Regional Representation* (Calgary: Canada West Foundation, 1981), 66-83.

30. *Harmony in Diversity: a New Federalism for Canada* (Edmonton: Government of Alberta, 1978), 1-18.

31. Douglas Brown, *The Federal Year in Review: 1977-78* (Kingston: Institute of Intergovernmental Relations, Queen's University, 1979), 66-7.

32. Department of Federal and Intergovernmental Affairs, *Sixth Annual Report* (Edmonton: Government of Alberta, 1979), 20.

33. *A Consolidation of the Constitution Acts 1867 to 1982* (Ottawa: Department of Justice, 1982), Section 92a, 33.

34. For a detailed discussion, see Western Premiers Conference Communiqués, 1982-85 (Office of the Premier, Government of Saskatchewan).

35. *Strengthening Canada: Reform of Canada's Senate*, Report of the Alberta Select Committee on Upper House Reform (Edmonton: Government of Alberta, 1985), 5-6.

36. Canadian Committee for a Triple E Senate, "A Triple E Senate is Essential for Canada" (Calgary, 1986), 1-4.

37. See opening statements by Premiers Grant Devine of Saskatchewan and Howard Pawley of Manitoba, First Ministers Conference, Vancouver, November 20-21, 1986 (mimeographed).

38. *Alberta Report*, November 17, 1986, 10-9.

39. Premier William N. Van der Zalm, Opening Statement, First Ministers Conference, Vancouver, November 20-21, 1986 (mimeographed), 4-5.

40. Premier Don Getty, Opening Statement, First Ministers Conference, Vancouver, November 20-21, 1986 (mimeographed), 6.

41. Department of Federal and Intergovernmental Affairs, *Eleventh Annual Report* (Edmonton: Government of Alberta, 1984), 50-1.

Selected Readings

Blake, Donald E., and Elkins, David J. "B.C. in Confederation." In Peter M. Leslie, ed., *Canada: The State of the Federation 1986*. Kingston: Institute of Intergovernmental Relations, Queen's University, 1986, 21-44.

Doern, G. Bruce, and Toner, Glen. *The Politics of Energy: The Development and Implementation of the NEP*. Toronto: Methuen, 1985.

Gibbons, Roger. "Alberta: Looking Back, Looking Forward." In Peter M. Leslie, ed. *Canada: The State of the Federation* 1985. Kingston: Institute of Intergovernmental Relations, Queen's University, 1985, 121-34.

Hawkes, David C., and Pollard, Bruce C. "The Evolution of Canada's New Energy Policy." In Peter M. Leslie, ed. *Canada: The State of the Federation 1986*. Kingston: Institute of Intergovernmental Relations, Queen's University, 1986, 151-66.

McCormick, Peter, and Elton, David. "The Western Economy and Canadian Unity." *Western Perspectives*. Calgary: Canada West Foundation, 1987.

Stevenson, Garth, and Pratt, Larry, eds. *Western Separatism: Myths, Realities and Dangers*. Edmonton: Hurtig, 1981.

SECTION SEVEN

PERSPECTIVES ON POLITICAL AND CONSTITUTIONAL REFORM

In the aftermath of the 1981 Constitutional Accord, both politicians and the Canadian public have demonstrated little enthusiasm for the renewal of constitutional negotiations. However, the fact remains that the Constitution Act of 1982 was never officially sanctioned by either the Government or the National Assembly of Quebec. Moreover the Constitution Act of 1982 contained no significant changes in the distribution of powers. Proposals recommending significant changes in the distribution of powers and in the reform of central institutions such as the Senate, the House of Commons, and the Supreme Court that were advanced by the Continuing Committee of Officials on the Constitution, the Pépin-Robarts Task Force on Canadian Unity, and private research organizations such as the Canada West Foundation were left at the negotiating table.

Despite the lack of enthusiasm for a renewal of constitutional negotiations, it would appear that the issue of constitutional reform has become a permanent feature of Canada's political landscape. Social, economic, and institutional tensions within the Canadian federal state continue to produce a never-ending list of constitutional issues which require some form of intergovernmental resolution.

Several basic questions underlie the debate concerning the reform of the Canadian federal system: Is the existence of the Canadian state based on a cultural compact between two linguistic communities? If so, to what extent and in what form should this compact be expressed? Should the Province of Quebec assume a "special status" within Confederation based on its historic position as the "homeland" of French Canadians? Alternatively, what role should the federal government play in the protection of linguistic minorities? These matters relate to *dualism*—the relationship between Canada's English- and French-speaking communities.

What powers does the federal government need in order to pursue "nation-building" objectives and to ensure minimum national standards of social service? In the debate over policy priorities and goals, should national or regional interests prevail? Should regional interests be expressed through a division of decision-making powers between federal and provincial governments (interstate federalism) or through

365

the reform of the institutions of intrastate federalism? These questions relate to *regionalism* and reflect the debate about the appropriate degree of centralization or decentralization within the Canadian federation.

The first essay in this section, by Richard Simeon, provides an overview of the future evolution of the Canadian federal state. In his explanation of the matrix of national and international forces which pull the Canadian nation simultaneously in the direction of both greater centralization and decentralization, Simeon summarizes many of the themes pursued by other writers in this volume. It is Simeon's contention that "extraordinary innovation, adaptability, and accommodation" will continue to characterize the Canadian approach to the problems of federalism.

Thomas Courchene's article is an excerpt from his larger study for the Royal Commission on the Economic Union and Development Prospects for Canada (the MacDonald Commission). Courchene adds a new dimension to the discussion of constitutional reform by examining how governmental responsibilities can be reallocated to enhance the efficient management of the Canadian economy. Courchene provides a reminder that significant political change can still be accomplished through the application of a wide range of policy instruments falling short of the formal amendment of the Constitution Act.

F. C. Engelmann addresses the fundamental issue of the compatability between federalism and parliamentary government. He concludes that tensions within the Canadian federal state could be reduced if the mechanisms of intrastate federalism were strengthened to reflect more fully two complementary but yet competing principles—"majority rule" and "concurrent majorities." His article evaluates past proposals to reform both the role and the composition of the Canadian Senate to reflect the existence of territorial majorities, thereby complementing the principle of "majority rule" as expressed in the House of Commons.

The Constitutional Accord of 1987 attempted to accommodate many of Quebec's traditional concerns by proposing that every province receive a veto power over any future reforms to central political institutions such as the Senate, the House of Commons and the Supreme Court. Writing from the perspective of a working journalist, Rory Leishman examines the provisions of the proposed constitutional amendment, documents the political strategies employed by federal and provincial politicians, and assesses the possible implications of the Accord.

22. CONSIDERATIONS ON CENTRALIZATION AND DECENTRALIZATION

Richard Simeon

The themes of centralization and decentralization have been fundamental to debate about Canadian federalism since its inception. Each generation has pursued these themes within the context of current preoccupations, and current views about the role of the state. Today, we are ringing our own changes on the questions of centralization and decentralization, but the answers are elusive and complex.

Even the relatively straightforward empirical question—how decentralized is Canada; is it the most decentralized western country?—is extraordinarily difficult to answer. Different criteria and different measurement techniques produce very different answers. And often those answers are self-serving ones, designed to bolster some political point: either to make the argument that we are clearly so fragmented and decentralized that the tide must be turned or that we are in the grip of a militant centralization which must be reversed. As Richard Bird writes, "it is neither helpful nor correct to claim that we know how decentralized Canada is—much less to conclude that it is too decentralized, decentralizing too fast, more decentralized than other countries, or whatever."[1]

But difficult as the empirical question is to answer, it is not even the most important question. Two others are much more fundamental.

First, *why* centralization or decentralization? What are the forces—social, cultural, economic, institutional—that account for why one country seems more or less decentralized than another; or why a country seems to be centralizing at some times and decentralizing at others. Specifically, what accounts for the widely noted Canadian "exceptionalism"—the view that in some sense at least we have resisted the centralizing trend that has affected most other federal countries? Or why, after a period of dramatic centralization in the wartime and postwar period, did we witness powerful centrifugal pressures in Canadian federalism in the 1960s and 1970s?

Those may be historians' questions, but the answers to them are also crucial for prediction. We can ask how these same forces are likely to play through in the future: Are social and economic conditions in the last years of this century likely to push us towards greater concentrations of central power or to strengthen the thrust for dispersed authority, and more local autonomy? Or will these forces produce both simultaneously? Is there one set of apparent imperatives bred by technological changes or by Canada's perilous position in an uncertain world? Does this in turn breed its own set of countervailing forces, such as a search for local control over one's own affairs in response to the trends towards homogenization, rationalizaton, centralization? It is worth remembering that the sometimes contradictory themes of bureaucracy versus participatory democracy, or efficiency versus equity, or the increasing scale of organi-

Richard Simeon, "Considerations on Centralization and Decentralization," *Canadian Public Administration* 29:3 (1986): 445-461. Reprinted by permission of The Institute of Public Administration Canada.

zation versus "small is beautiful," all have the same roots.

So I want to cast the straws and speculate about some of the trends for the future. But to the extent these trends are contradictory or ambiguous, we also have an element of choice. Economic and social forces are not in fact immutable imperatives; rather they take form in the actions of governments and citizens.

So the second question is a more normative one: how can we think about the desirability of turning in a more centralizing or in a more decentralizing direction? Centralization and decentralization are seldom valued for their own sake. They are judged in terms of how well they serve other values. Are they consistent with our conceptions of democracy, of the character of the political community which we seek, with effectiveness or efficiency?[2] What, in short, are the consequences of moving in one direction or another?

If it is hard to describe levels of centralization, and harder to predict them, it is even more difficult to relate centralization to these other and more fundamental values. Decentralization has been held to enhance democracy and to frustrate it; to improve efficiency and to frustrate it; to account for big government and to account for less government; and so on. Indeed, the Australian political scientist Rufus Davis concludes that we cannot infer, from knowing that a system is federal, whether it is likely to be strong or weak in war; potent or impotent in satisfying demands; efficient or inefficient in the provision of services; faithful or faithless in the pursuit of liberty.

Questions like Does federalism promote or inhibit economic growth? Promote or inhibit freedom? Foster or limit participation? Produce more or less conflict? or Result in higher or lower decision-making costs? cannot be asked with any profit, he argues.[3] In Canada, Richard Bird has recently made the same observation. Even if we could measure it, the degree of decentralization as a criterion for assessing the quality of government is useless.[4]

The same obviously could be said of a debate about centralization and decentralization. Indeed, I think it may well be true that ultimately one's judgments about the virtues or defects of highly decentralized systems are to a large extent aesthetic ones, which precede data and argument. To the ancient theme—from Plato to Rousseau to George Woodcock—that democracy is only possible in small states, is the contrary view that only large, inclusive units can liberate people from the tyrannies of parochialism.[5]

It is also true that to deal sensibly with choices about decentralization, theorizing in the abstract is unlikely to get us very far. The inevitability or the desirability of centralization or decentralization has meaning only in relation to specific systems, in specific contexts, with particular social and economic traditions, political cultures, and political institutions. We may not get far asking whether we are for a tilt towards greater centralization *in general*, but that does not prevent us from asking the same question about Canada in the late twentieth century.

Indeed, to pose the global question—to centralize or to decentralize—is often unhelpful. This is because as soon as we approach the real world we find that in some areas we may want to do one and in some the other. We may even want to do both. As many writers have pointed out, modern society is a maze-like collection of organizations, public and private, bound together by multiple threads of dependence and interdependence, interacting through a multiplicity of relationships of mutual influence and mutual constraint, cooperation and competition, dominance and subordination—in short, a politics of "endless, intricate bargaining."[6]

While debates about centralization and decentralization in Canada have focused mainly on the division of powers between Ottawa and the provinces, we need to cast the net much wider. For example, we should be looking at decentralization, devolution, deconcentration, and dispersal within government; at centralization and decentralization within municipalities and between them and the provinces.

Even at the federal level we have complex mixtures. "National" policy often emerges from the efforts of individual provinces and municipalities, just as federal government policies are often regionally differentiated and keyed to local needs and influences. Equalization is profoundly centralizing. It is a program of the national government based on the idea that all citizens wherever they live should have access to comparable levels of service at comparable levels of taxation. But equally it is profoundly decentralizing. Without conditions, it gives the poorer provinces the resources with which to pursue provincial goals, giving them the capacity to effectively use the jurisdictional authority they possess. Similarly, we have been able to combine the virtue of a highly coordinated tax system with a great deal of flexibility and autonomy, and, despite the many recent disagreements, a reasonably advanced welfare state with much provincial freedom. Throughout the Canadian policy process federal action is required to allow provinces to meet their goals, and vice versa. And, of course, if there is some truth to the view that in federal-provincial terms Canada is relatively decentralized, at the same time in provincial-municipal terms it is among the most centralized. Powers are much dispersed between federal and provincial governments, but, unlike the United States, relatively centralized and concentrated within them.

In this paper I want to weave together two sets of questions: Which direction are larger social, economic, and political forces likely to push us? And, to the extent we have a choice, which vision is most attractive, to tilt towards centralization, or to tilt towards greater dispersal of authority and influence? But first a little history.

About fifty years ago Harold Laski asserted that the epoch of federalism was over: he saw the federal form of state as unsuitable to an era of modernization. That view set the tone for much of the thinking about centralization and decen-

tralization in the depression, wartime, and postwar periods in Canada as elsewhere. Modernization and centralization went hand in hand. The forces of modernization—economic, social, and political—and their accompanying shifts in political attitudes and in the new expansive role of the state rendered centralization inevitable. Centralization was felt to be a necessity if the state was to be able to take on the new responsibilities which modernization thrust upon it.

There were many elements to the argument. Sociologically, modernization was felt to lead to the erosion of traditional cultural loyalties and greater attachments to the nation state; it would result in a political polarization based not on factors such as religion and language, but on functional, economic relationships, related to class and sectoral interest. Hence we could look for a politics of left versus right rather than of regionalism. Modern communications and transportation were increasing mobility and eroding local particularities.

The economy was coming to be dominated by large national and transnational corporations, not tied to a local space. They required a uniform national market in which to operate. These large business organizations were being countered by large national and international unions and other functionally oriented associations of all kinds. Such factors increased interdependencies, externalities and spill-overs, and led to new political coalitions, the chief thrust of which was the "impulse to uniformity."

These economic, social, and political developments also embodied new roles for the state which it was felt only the central governments had the capacity to carry out. The scale and reach of the state must match the scale and reach of the social and economic organizations which the state had to regulate and serve. In particular, the new responsibility for management of the economy along Keynesian lines seemed to require that the central government control the lion's share of revenues and expenditures in order to carry out demand management. And the welfare state, with its emphasis on equality and redistribution, equally seemed to be something only a powerful national government could achieve. And these forces were cumulative: "Centralization, in short, breeds further centralization."[7]

Decentralizing impulses therefore were weak. Decentralized institutions were seen to be barriers to effective adaptation to a modernized world—at best to be worked around, at worst to be displaced or transformed. In Canada, in the postwar period, we moved a considerable distance along this path. Indeed, in a famous article published in 1958, Alec Corry confidently predicted that initiative had decisively shifted to the centre. In the future federalism would remain, but primarily as a shell, with provinces able only to weave minor variations around national themes.[8]

Canadian federalism adapted to the new roles of the state, in part through a limited set of constitutional changes and in part through use of the federal spending power, either to initiate purely federal programs such as family allowances or to achieve national purposes through shared-cost programs. Through tax rentals Ottawa came to dominate the fiscal system; it equally dominated the broad field of social security.

But the presence of Quebec, the preoccupation of the federal government with national unity in the face of a still highly regionalized society, and the difficulties of achieving constitutional change all meant that the federal framework remained intact. Centralization proceeded less far in Canada than in a number of other countries.

The era of centralization was thus, apparently, both incomplete and short-lived. Most discussions of Canadian federalism suggested a dramatic reversal of the centralizing trends. In 1967, Donald Smiley wrote of the "attenuation of federal power," and a few years later argued that "the story of Canadian federalism since the late fifties is the story of the steady attrition of the power of the central government."[9]

In some ways this is correct. Throughout the period provincial and local spending increased considerably faster than at the federal level; hence the federal share of revenues and expenditures declined. Provincial governments became larger, more confident, more assertive, more anxious to see themselves as agents of economic growth, less willing to defer to federal leadership. The funding of established programs gave the federal government much less control over the ever-increasing financial transfers it made to the provinces.

But attenuation is perhaps too strong a term, at least if it is to be interpreted as federal powerlessness. In the 1960s and 1970s we saw the second great wave of social policy innovation: medicare, the Canada and Quebec Pension Plans, and others. We saw a massive increase of federal industrial and regional development activities. We saw moves towards bilingualism, vigorous defence of federal constitutional powers before courts in cases like CIGOL, and aggressive wage and price controls, not to mention the later National Energy Program. While provincial influence over federal policy-making undoubtedly increased, there were no formal institutional changes in that direction and no constitutional additions to provincial authority. As many have observed, the question was not so much one of a power shift from Ottawa back to the provinces, but rather of the emergence of the provinces as powerful rivals—fiscally, bureaucratically, and in terms of popular support—to the federal government.

Nor was Canada quite as exceptional as we sometimes think. In a number of other federal countries provincial-local spending was also growing faster than federal spending; so many of the services demanded by a growing, more affluent, younger population were those usually provided at the local level, such as schools, hospitals, roads, and the like. Moreover, strong regionalist movements emerged to mount a powerful challenge to the centralized modern state in countries as diverse as Belgium, Spain, Britain, Italy, and France.[10]

This prompts the question of why the predictions of the modernization theorists seem to have been confounded. In part the answer may simply lie in the failure of the modernizers to recognize the ability of the forces they saw as obsolete to persist and to use institutional levers, such as the BNA Act, to resist the trends they found uncomfortable. In part it lies in some of the failures of modernization. By the 1960s we had realized that a politics focused on aggregate management did not automatically filter down to improve the lot of peripheral areas; in other words, we rediscovered regional disparities. And this led some to reject the liberal economic model that in a free economy there would be a natural tendency for incomes to equalize across the country. Greater weight was given to theories which emphasized that economic activity tends to concentrate in the centre, and that a modern economy is characterized by relations of dependency and exploitation between centre and periphery.

Modernization, indeed, sometimes had very different effects than those predicted. If it facilitated communication, for instance, it also heightened awareness of difference and inequality. If it embodied an expansive responsibility for the state, it also led to greater expectations and a greater tendency to "blame" the state for inequality and call on it for further redress. If modernization led to centralization, to professionalism and rationalism in public affairs, it also provoked a counter-reaction as people searched for distinctiveness, preservation of traditional values, and greater control over their own lives.[11]

And when modernization coincided with and reinforced historic linguistic or territorial cleavages, the effects, as we saw in Quebec, could be explosive. French-English conflict in the 1960s and 1970s and the emergence of Quebec governments' demands for greater powers—which was the source of the most powerful decentralizing trends—was caused precisely by

the economic and social modernization of the province.[12] Similarly, Roger Gibbins identifies an interesting paradox: it was precisely as the prairie provinces were becoming more diverse, more modern, more like Ontario in important respects, that conflict and demands for decentralization intensified.[13]

Finally, the modernization theorists may well have identified the right factors, but in Canada, with its historic regional cleavages and its position in the global and North American context, such factors may have had a different effect. Thus, if the spread of common cultural values is part of modernization and integration, the culture into which Canadians were being led was not a pan-Canadian one, but a North American one. If communications were knitting people together into larger and larger units, again the cultural organizations at work were largely American ones. If economic integration leads to centralization, then the Canadian experience is one of only limited integration along east-west lines, but rather integration along north-south ones. We might even argue that much modernization in Canada is not centralizing but the reverse, and indeed that the most powerful challenges to central dominance and to the formation of powerful national coalitions of interests around the central government come not from the provinces, but from outside the country.

Thus, the social and economic forces at work in Canada, both domestic and international, seemed to be moving the country to a situation in which regional and linguistic conflicts were heightened and federal power was challenged. Provinces were asserting the need for decentralization, not only to gain greater control in some areas, but also to gain a greater voice in decision-making at the centre.

If societal forces proved to be disintegrative, or at least ambiguous, contrary to the expectations of Corry and others, these were powerfully reinforced by the institutions of Canadian federalism and parliamentary government. Indeed,

Smiley argues that the growth of government, manifested through expansion at both federal and provincial levels, led to a politics dominated by the "intergovernmental lobby" of executive federalism. It is in this intergovernmental dynamic, more than in underlying group and party forces which are relatively underdeveloped in Canada, that we find the primary impetus for centralization and decentralization in Canada.[14]

Debates about centralization and decentralization during the 1970s came to be framed largely in terms of community-based criteria. Decentralization was seen to be essential to Quebec nation-building and, less clearly, to the development of the other provincial communities. Centralization was defined in terms of maintaining the integrity of the Canadian union in the face of these fissiparous tendencies.

Hence, did one celebrate regionalism and dualism or condemn them? Were they to be embraced and responded to by devolution of powers or to be rejected in favour of an assertion of the primacy of the national community, of the national majority, and of the federal government as the embodiment of that community? Today, we are seeing the debates framed much more sharply in terms of the consequences for effectiveness and efficiency in policy and in terms of alternative conceptions of democratic values.

In light of the dominant views about centralization prevalent from the depression to the 1950s, it was striking that intellectual opinion came to be so sympathetic to a somewhat decentralist vision. The 1979 Pépin-Robarts Report, for example, seemed to express the conventional wisdom of the time, at least among political scientists. Very soon afterwards another conventional wisdom took its place: the view that the appropriate response to regionalism and dualism was not decentralization, but rather greater sensitivity to regional interests at the centre. But that, too, was in a sense decentralizing, since it denied the legitimacy of national majorities exercising power in their own interests, seeking to

temper it by giving greater weight to smaller parts of the country.

THE FUTURE

If this analysis of the forces and debates at work in the past is roughly right, what of the future? Can we identify some of the forces at work, and assess their potential for fostering centralization or decentralization and for the ways in which they will be debated? How will we weave together the constants of Canadian life—federalism, regionalism, language—with the contemporary forces of economic challenges, international interdependence, changing cleavages and values, and dilemmas of big government?

There are no clear answers. It is possible to build a persuasive case for the idea that future pressures are likely to be more integrative and centralizing; but equally, a case can be made that they are likely to be more disintegrative and decentralizing. Indeed, it is not a matter of either-or; they will probably be both.

Let us look at some possible "societal factors." Surely one of the most important of postwar trends—one that is almost certain to continue—is what we might call the politicization of society, something which is both cause and result of the expansion of the activities of governments. By politicization I mean both a proliferation in the number and variety of organized interests, as well as their tendency to become increasingly mobilized, asserting their claims on the state. I refer not only to the traditional interests of business and labour (which are themselves becoming more diverse and fragmented) but also to the explosion of newer interests built around issues such as women's rights, the environment, and the like. The dominant characteristic of the evolving society is one of a bewildering plurality and complexity, a fragmentation and diversification of interests, some of which are territorially based, others not.[15] If this is right, which way are these interest groups going to push us? To the extent that the issues they organize around are phrased in symbolic, abstract, universal terms—that is, in the language of rights, which our new Charter of Rights and Freedoms so strongly encourages, rather than in terms of services and programs—they may have a centralizing influence, since at least some of their demands are likely to be hostile to local particularities.

But to the extent that the many movements voice demands that fall outside the existing categories of jurisdiction and make their demands indiscriminately on all governments, their effect is neither centralizing nor decentralizing. The result may rather be ever more overlapping and complexity of government activities as both orders respond to the pressures upon them. More fundamentally, a common feature of the new movements is a search for greater individual and group autonomy. This brings with it a clear demand to open up the processes of intergovernmental relations to greater public scrutiny and participation, as we saw with the mobilization of women in the constitutional debate or the debate over the Canadian Health Act. Another result is that many of these groups are likely to call for radical decentralization, for more grass roots decision-making in town, neighbourhood, and workplace. This may be as much a challenge to the provinces as it is to Ottawa.

One response to "overloaded governments"—to the apparent fragmentation of society and the resulting cacophony of voices—is to argue the need for greater centralization to try to bring some order and coherence and to counteract centrifugal forces. But there is another response. It suggests that in such a fragmented society, decentralized systems, with multiple points of access and decision-making, are likely to be more resilient, more flexible, more able to contain social conflict than are rigid centralized instititions, where all demands and conflicts are focused on a single authority. In such a situation

the danger is that government will either be paralysed by the competing demands made on it, or it will feel the need to become more authoritarian and repressive. Decentralization is thus not only potentially more open and democratic, but also much better able to manage the divisions of a complex society. Overload can be managed by spreading the response to demands over more centres of power; conflicts can be contained before they engulf the whole society.

What about some of the economic challenges facing Canada? Many would argue that these are as serious and fundamental as they were in the depression or postwar reconstruction. Adaptation to new circumstances, innovation, flexibility, competitiveness, and the need for adjustment have become the new by-words. What Tom Courchene has called "slowth" is likely to be with us for a long time, spawning continuing restraint in government expenditure into the foreseeable future. We face a continuing politics of scarcity with potentially bitter debates over the distribution of the burdens and costs of adjustment. The dynamics of future economic development of Canada are not likely to reduce regional economic inequalities. Conditions of scarcity and restraint are likely to enhance interprovincial competition for investment and strain the national commitment to redistribution.

Just as earlier economic crises led often to the view that federalism and decentralization were luxuries that we could not afford and that the new requirements of government made stronger central control over the economy essential, so some argue today that the need for economic renewal demands a centralization of economic powers. There is some support for this in public opinion polls. When people are asked who is responsible for basic economic policy, they see it as a national responsibility and tend to hold the federal government to account.

One argument is that decentralization may inhibit the necessary adjustments, such as moving people from lower to higher growth regions and from sunrise to sunset industries. The more political units, the more the places there are for the losers to appeal to for subsidy and protection. To win votes, governments will compete to bail-out industries rather than to foster necessary changes. A decentralized political system in this view is thus prone to greater rigidity. What is unsatisfactory about this line of thought is that it is not really an argument about decentralization but about political democracy generally. Its supporters imply that economic decisions should be depoliticized and insulated from public pressure, either by enforcing the discipline of the marketplace or by turning power over to the central planners.

A more common argument in Canada is that our economic challenges require far more effective economic planning—some form of comprehensive industrial policy, a New National Policy. Furthermore, it is argued, the tools and levers for such industrial policy-making are no longer those of taxing, spending, and tariffs, all of which are fully available to the central government, but the more direct tools of education, labour relations, financial markets, and the like, many of which are in provincial hands. Thus, if Keynesian economics called for fiscal centralization, the new politics of industrial strategy calls for centralization, or at least coordination, of much more. How, it may be asked, can we have a coordinated, consistent industrial strategy, one that effectively links the strengths of different regions and is sensitive to the question of regional fairness, if the tools are scattered among a multiplicity of governments?

Market-oriented economists reject this prescription. For them, economic growth requires less rather than more intervention and reliance on market rather than planning mechanisms. Their scepticism about intervention spills over into a deep scepticism about centralization, except perhaps as it may be required to police the common market and prevent provinces erecting internal barriers to trade. Thus Albert Breton has recently argued that federalism fosters dynamism. Decentralization is thus not a barrier to

economic growth, a hurdle to be overcome, but a positive virtue. Similarly, Tom Courchene has recently argued that economic adaptation in the future will require a tilt towards the market and away from intervention, to private and away from public activity, to decentralization and away from centralization. The virtues of smaller units are the traditional virtues attributed to decentralized government: governments closer to the ground are better informed about local preferences and conditions and therefore better able to make appropriate decisions. Therefore in an age of uncertainty about what works best, the opportunities for innovation and experiment that local governments provide become more compelling.

Multiple power centres, exploring many policy options, are less likely to make the spectacular errors associated with putting all one's eggs in the same basket. Conversely, in this market model it is felt that provincial governments, lacking the power to print money and more subject to the discipline of competition, will be more likely to pursue restraint and limit their manipulation of the economy. Many arguments for decentralization are thus closely linked to suspicion of intervention in general. And a direct analogy between political and economic markets is made: if competition fosters efficiency and growth in the marketplace, then competition among governments has similar advantages for innovative, responsive policy. The economists thus disagree among themselves. For some, like Courchene, decentralization is likely to lead to more effective adjustment; for others, like Mancur Olson, it can simply entrench the forces which resist it.

A closely related set of forces concern Canada's position in the world economy. The international environment appears ever more pressing and threatening as we face increasing competition, pressure from newly industrializing countries, the internationalization of capital markets which gives individual countries less and less ability to control their own destinies, rising protectionism from the United States and elsewhere, and so on. The growing awareness of these forces could be powerfully centralizing. International crises traditionally result in a rallying around the centre and a diminution in regional differences; people look to the national government to define the national interest in response to the outside world. We sense the need to "get our acts together," to "speak with one voice" in international councils, and to assert our national sovereignty and distinctiveness through a greater government role in what Alan Cairns calls its "symbolic function."

But this is not always the case. In an economy as regionally divided as ours, international forces can, as the energy crisis so dramatically demonstrated, affect different parts of the country in different ways, greatly exacerbating regional divisions, dividing rather than uniting Canadians. Developing a national position in international trade negotiations involves difficult regional trade-offs.

And if international forces seem to call on a greater federal role, those same forces at the same time constrain it: national governments have less and less freedom to chart their own course in response to their own domestic requirements. The growth of international constraints has greatly diminished the benefits of belonging to a large central state, especially one as open as Canada. Indeed, it could be argued that it is not the provinces but these external forces that have most tightly limited the federal government's capacity to act in the recent past. This in turn may be one reason citizens have turned to the provinces for a greater role in economic development—and, indeed, a more active role in international trade relationships. Global interdependence, the potential obsolescence of the nation-state, and the growth of subnational identities and power centres may thus all go together.

Just as the call for an industrial policy often involves the call for greater central control in policy areas now predominantly provincial, so the need for Canada to bargain internationally can lead in the same direction. International trade issues now no longer focus primarily on the tariff—a matter clearly in federal jurisdiction—but on the so-called non-tariff barriers—subsidies, quotas, procurement, product standards, and the like. Again, these lie largely in provincial jurisdiction. If Ottawa is to participate effectively in such negotiations, it might therefore be argued, it needs greater ability to constrain provincial policies of these kinds.

Similarly, former Prime Minister Trudeau and others have argued that effective Canadian competition abroad requires development of world-scale, efficient plants and the collective efforts of all Canadian regions—goals that can be frustrated by interprovincial barriers to trade, by eleven separate provincial industrial strategies, and by provinces negotiating abroad on their own. This is the contemporary version of the "functional argument" for centralization, a somewhat different one from that advanced in the depression and postwar period.

Constitutionally, the federal government cannot enforce treaties whose provisions affect provincial jurisdiction. The lesson would appear to be recognition of the need for closer federal-provincial cooperation in international trade negotiations and perhaps a constitutional amendment which spells out more clearly the treaty-making power. This could provide for a provincial role in ratifying treaties which affect their powers in return for the assurance that any treaty so signed would then be enforceable against provincial action. Nowhere will this cooperation be more important than in any negotiations with the United States over freer trade. The provincial role in negotiating such an arrangement, and then in any joint body to police the treaty, will be crucial.

Any such treaty may well have the long-term effect not of strengthening either Ottawa or the provinces, but rather of constraining and limiting both, since the quid pro quo for the security of access we seek in the United States will undoubtedly be strong limitations on Canadian industrial and regional development policies, both federally and provincially. It is by no means clear that a free-trade agreement would strengthen federal power compared to the provinces; indeed, to the extent it constrained Ottawa more than the provinces, it could enhance the tendency to look to the provinces for economic action.

Other forces will also affect the pressures towards either centralization or decentralization. Developments in technology and communications, for example, are Janus-headed. They embody the potential for great centralization, increasing the capacity for surveillance, information-gathering, and control; and at the same time they increase the potential for localized, dispersed development. Indeed, it has been suggested that, if the central thrust of the mass-production based industrial revolution was towards centralization and larger and larger scale of operations, both in the organization of the economy and in the organization of political life, then the central thrust of the postindustrial revolution, centred on diversity, flexibility, and the small scale, will be decentralizing. This argument might suggest that at both the corporate and the governmental level, massive organizations are now obsolete, paralysed by their own gigantic size and the multitude of demands made on them, unable to respond quickly and sensitively. The economies of scale have been exhausted, we now become more aware of the diseconomies of cumbersome organizations and of the danger of inflexibility, remoteness, lack of information about local contexts and opportunities, and the like. The link between efficiency, effectiveness, and centralization has been broken.

In this sense it is interesting to note that a few years ago the dominant view on both right and left was one of centralizing: on the left, the sense that class, organized nationally and internationally, was the dominant force and that centralization was essential to achieve redistribution and economic planning; on the right, the need to create the conditions for large-scale accumulation, to create larger markets, and to practise Keynesian economic management.

The right lost faith in big government, planning, hierarchy, Keynesian economics, and cen-

tralization, and has rediscovered the virtues of small fragmented markets, both political and economic. So has the left; many theorists of "social democracy" have lost faith in bureaucratic centralization, seeking responsiveness and popular control through decentralization. Big government, Cairns reminds us, "has joined the lengthening queue of gods that failed." If that is true, then the impulse to say "if it is important, centralize it," will also have disappeared.

In a sense the great debates of the future in Canada, as elsewhere, will turn on whether the modernization theorists have it right that the ineluctable forces push towards larger and larger scale, higher and higher degrees of interdependence, the emergence of larger and larger corporate actors rationalized on a national and global scale, greater and greater homogenization of culture and attitudes, and the erosion of particularisms. If so, the argument that to regulate and manage such developments we need a parallel scale of governmental organization, at least nationally and increasingly internationally as well, will be strong. Or on the other hand, if the underlying dynamics are leading instead towards increased differentiation, diversity, fragmentation, the reassertion of local community, and the like, then the more appropriate political response is decentralization.

More likely, both trends are happening—each feeding the other, opposite sides of the same coin. The increased localism of politics is a reaction against these homogenizing tendencies; and the push for more effective central decision-making mechanisms is a reaction against the fragmentation of a complex society. If so, the great challenge for political theorists will be to find a creative synthesis between the two tendencies. The forces for and against centralization—whether at the societal or the governmental level—are thus in constant tension, not so much as opposing forces as in a dialectic.

The thrust to master interdependence by strengthening the centre is challenged by dynamism from the peripheries; and, relatedly, the search for bureaucratic rationality is challenged by the participatory impulse. As Sydney Tarrow remarks: as policy-making migrates to the centre, "citizens turn more and more not to 'functional' representation, but to the territorial institutions around them, reinforcing the territorial dimension in representation, just as it is being displaced in policy-making and administration."[16]

In this model of a society at once fragmented and interdependent, both united and divided by a complex set of divisions, the traditional centralist-decentralist dichotomy does not fit. R. A. Dahl is right when he argues that "only a complex polity, consisting of a number of interrelated units, has the capacity to respond to the collective preferences of the citizens of nation-states."

These speculations may seem far removed from the specific dilemmas faced by Canadians as they think about the division of powers or mechanisms of intergovernmental relations to deal with economic development, control of pollution, saving the forests, or rescuing the fishing industry. But the Canadian case does have some important lessons.

First, if Canadian history shows us anything, it is the *persistence* of regional and linguistic differences. This means that no proposal for sweeping centralization, or indeed decentralization, has any chance of acceptance. But that does not prevent much discussion of more specific shifts of responsibilities, not only through constitutional changes, but also through the myriad devices of flexibility that Canadian federalism has produced.

Equally, if one thing is clear it is that no country as diverse as Canada can be governed solely from the centre. Our social structure, buttressed by our constitution, means that we will always be relatively decentralized and that our policy-making will arise out of the interplay between federal and provincial governments and the interests of the populations they represent. Whatever progress we make towards ensuring the sensitivity and responsiveness of the federal government to regional interests—and that is indeed essential—it can never be a substitute for vital, active provincial and local governments. No single set of common policies will work for a country like Canada.

Secondly, if the challenge for many countries is to respond politically to increased fragmentation and diversity, Canada may provide valuable lessons. Without sacrificing the vitality and responsiveness of federalism, Canadian governments have in the past adapted to shifting political concerns and shifting conceptions of the role of the state. Despite frequent confrontation and apparent bottlenecks, it is hard to make the case that federalism has been a rigid barrier to innovation and responsiveness to citizen interests. The idea that federalism has been a strait-jacket, either on the aspirations and goals of the federal government or on those of provinces such as Quebec or Alberta, is hard to sustain. Let us be more positive: federalism has been a source of extraordinary innovation, adaptability, and accommodation. The dynamic tension between centralism and decentralization is written into the BNA Act itself and has continued to dominate Canadian politics, as it will in the future.

This has meant that we have a great deal of experience at managing a complex society, weaving together the disparate elements in the interorganizational bargaining that is at the heart of policy-making. And that has given us a strength and resilience in the face of competing interests, a sense that centralization and decentralization may not be antithetical. We may be better equipped than most countries to solve the dilemmas posed by the contending forces of centralization and decentralization and by the realization that the key requirements are neither one nor the other, but rather the management of interdependence with all the skills of bargaining, negotiation, and compromise that necessarily entails. The decision-making costs of such diversity are no doubt high; the costs of not doing so are almost certainly higher.

Notes

1. Richard M. Bird, "Federal Finance in Comparative Perspective," in David Conklin, *Ottawa and the Provinces: The Distribution of Money and Power* (Toronto: Ontario Economic Council, 1985), 137-77.

2. Richard Simeon, "Criteria for Choice in Federal Systems," *Queen's Law Journal* 8:1-2 (1982-83): 131-57.

3. S. Rufus Davis, *The Federal Principle: A Journey Through Time in Quest of a Meaning* (Berkeley: University of California Press, 1978), 209-12.

4. Preston King, *Federalism and Federation* (Baltimore: Johns Hopkins University Press, 1982), 136.

5. Reginald Whitaker, *Federalism and Democratic Theory* (Kingston: Institute of Intergovernmental Relations, 1983); Robert A. Dahl and Edward Tufte, *Size and Democracy* (Stanford: Stanford University Press, 1973), 7.

6. Robert Leonardi, et al., "Devolution as a Political Process: The Case of Italy," *Publius* 11 (Winter 1981): 97; M. J. C. Vile, "Federal Theory and the New Federalism," in Dean Jaensch, ed., *The Politics of New Federalism* (Adelaide: Australian Political Science Association, 1972), 1-14; James W. Fesler, "Approaches to the Understanding of Decentralization," *Journal of Politics* 27 (1965): 557.

7. Samuel Beer, "The Modernization of American Federalism," *Publius* 3 (1973): 49-95.

8. J. A. Corry, "Constitutional Trends and Federalism," in A. R. M. Lower, et al., *Evolving Canadian Federalism* (Durham: Duke University Press, 1958), 92-125.

9. Donald V. Smiley, *The Canadian Political Nation-ality* (Toronto: Methuen Publications, 1967), 47; and *Canada in Question: Federalism in Seventies*, 2d ed. (Toronto: McGraw-Hill Ryerson, 1976), 120.

10. Milton J. Esman, *Ethnic Conflict in the Western World* (Ithaca: Cornell University Press, 1977); Edward A. Tiryakian and Ronald Rogowski, eds., *New Nationalisms in the Developed West* (Boston: Allen and Unwin, 1984).

11. Arend Lijphart, in Esman, *Ethnic Conflict*; Stein Rokkan and Derek Urwin, *Economy, Territory, Identity* (London: Sage, 1983).

12. Donald E. Blake and Richard Simeon, "Regional Preferences: Citizens' Views of Public Policy," in David J. Elkins and Richard Simeon, eds., *Small Worlds: Provinces and Parties in Canadian Political Life* (Toronto: Methuen Publications, 1980), 101-2; see also Donald Smiley, "Public Sector Politics, Modernization and Federalism: The Canadian and American Experiences," *Publius* 14 (1984): 39-59.

13. Roger Gibbins, *Prairie Politics and Society: Regionalism in Decline* (Toronto: Butterworth, 1980).

14. Donald Smiley, "Public Sector Politics," 39-59.

15. In this and the following sections, I am much influenced by Thomas Hueglin, *Federalism and Fragmentation: A Comparative View of Political Accommodation in Canada* (Kingston: Institute of Intergovernmental Relations, 1984).

16. Sydney Tarrow, "Introduction," in S. Tarrow, Peter Katzenstein, and Louis G. Graziano, eds., *Territorial Politics in Industrial Nations* (New York and London: Praeger, 1978), 3.

Selected Readings

Banting, K., and Simeon, R., eds. *And No One Cheered: Federalism, Democracy and the Constitution Act*. Toronto: Methuen, 1983.

Banting, K., and Simeon, R., eds. *Redesigning the State: The Politics of Constitutional Change in Industrial Nations*. Toronto: University of Toronto Press, 1985.

Cairns, A. C. "Recent Federalist Constitutional Proposals: A Review Essay." *Canadian Public Policy* 5:3 (Summer 1979): 348-65.

Careless, A. "The Struggle for Jurisdiction: Regionalism versus Rationalism." *Publius* 14:1 (Winter 1984): 61-79.

Stein, M. B. "Canadian Constitutional Reform, 1972-1982: A Comparative Case Analysis over Time." *Publius* 14:1 (Winter 1984): 121-41.

23. ECONOMIC MANAGEMENT AND THE DISTRIBUTION OF POWERS

Thomas J. Courchene

What is striking about the manner in which the Canadian federation approaches the allocation of powers is the incredibly rich variety of arrangements that currently exist. This is most evident in the income security area where the arrangements encompass the three "classical" approaches to structuring a federalism: unilateralism or the separation-of-powers approach (as reflected in old age security (OAS) and guaranteed income supplement (GIS) for Ottawa and programs like Ontario's guaranteed annual income system (GAINS) for the provinces); cooperative federalism (as reflected in the workings of the Canada Assistance Plan); and intrastate federalism, multiple vetoes, or the system of checks and balances (as reflected in the operations of the Canada Pension Plan). While this variety is not typical of all policy areas, it is nonetheless illustrative of the difficulty of approaching the division of powers from a *single* conceptual framework. It would be equally difficult, and perhaps even foolhardy, to attempt to redesign the division of powers from any one conceptual framework.

Further to this point, analysis suggests that the institutions and structures of our federation appear to be continually evolving in order to meet the needs of the time. Even a selected survey of some of the ways in which process and structure have evolved reveals this diversity and dynamism:

— Some powers have been transferred by constitutional amendment from the provinces to Ottawa (e.g., unemployment insurance, old age pensions).

— Some powers have been transferred from Ottawa to the provinces (e.g., the federal enabling legislation which has allowed the provinces to establish marketing boards that interfere with interprovincial trade).

— Some new institutions have been created which, while not enshrined in the Constitution, nonetheless derive their existence from parallel sets of legislation at both levels of government (e.g., the Canada Pension Plan).

— New institutions and structures have developed that do not have either a legislative or constitutional framework but which clearly have become an integral component of the practice, if not the art, of Canadian federalism (e.g., executive federalism and the first ministers' conference).

— Other institutions and/or programs have emerged which have become so much a part of the practice of federalism that they have been enshrined in the Constitution (e.g., equalization).

Thomas J. Courchene, "Economic Management and the Distribution of Powers," in his *Economic Management and the Division of Powers*, vol. 67 of *Research Studies of the Royal Commission on the Economic Union and Development Prospects for Canada* (Toronto: University of Toronto Press, 1986), 229–241. Reprinted by permission of University of Toronto Press. ©Minister of Supply and Services Canada. The essay has been abridged and edited to suit the needs of this volume.

— More important than any of these specific items is the fact that over the past 40 years the framework of the BNA Act has permitted the system to centralize dramatically in wartime; to create national programs in the socio-economic areas in the 1960s; to move toward considerable decentralization in the mid-1970s; and perhaps to begin another round of centralization in the 1980s. The principal instrumentality in most of this change was the federal-provincial transfer system and the exercise of the federal spending power. However, the provinces too have taken initiatives that have led to some of these changes (e.g., the establishment of a separate personal income tax in Quebec in 1954).

In addition to these initiatives, which tend to be associated with changes in the structure (either de facto or de jure) of federalism, the review of the various policy areas reveals a wide range of practices or processes that lend further support to the variety of arrangements permitted or encouraged by the existing constitutional framework:

— In the area of securities legislation the federal government probably has the constitutional right to become a major regulatory player. Thus far, however, it has deferred to the provincial regulatory authorities.
— Federal-provincial agreements have frequently been developed in areas where there is a constitutional void or where constitutional authority is unclear. One example of this relates to the securing of the Canadian economic union where, at least in comparison with some other federations, our constitution does not appear to provide much help. Yet the generally accepted formula for allocating the profits of multi-province businesses across the various jurisdictions implies that in terms of this aspect of tax harmonization we are better off than, say, the Swiss and the U.S. federations where, ironically, they do have stronger constitutional provisions for ensuring a domestic economic union.

— This leads to the more general point that, for certain policy issues, there may be avenues other than constitutional amendment or enshrinement that on occasion may be the preferred route to take.

To be sure, the above series of observations may cast a particularly rosy hue on the evolution of the division of powers. It is not meant to minimize the many problems on the constitutional front but rather to emphasize that there are many avenues that can be utilized to rectify problems which arise. Although it might appear that the evolution is in some sense "optimal," this is not my intention. For example, the federal enabling legislation for provincial marketing boards is, in my opinion, a retrograde measure.

Apart from these concerns, the above summary is deficient in yet another way—its focus is principally (and deliberately) on structure and practice and not on economic management. . . . Again, it seems appropriate to proceed in point form.

— The optimal assignment of powers will in all likelihood depend on the overall economic goals pursued by the federation. A change in the nature of the economic policy objectives will probably call for a corresponding change in the division of powers (either de jure or de facto).
— In any federation, there will always be some things that each level of government is prohibited from doing. However, this is not an important issue if the pursuit of these particular objectives does not make economic sense. For example, the provinces do not have a direct role in the conduct of monetary policy (i.e., monetary policy is not regionalized). This ought to be of no concern, since economic theory and practice indicate that monetary policy ought to be centralized.
— Relatedly, there are powers that can be exercised only in certain circumstances. Wage and price controls are a good example: Ottawa

has the authority to enact such controls in an emergency but not in the ordinary course of events. From my economic perspective, this situation does not warrant a redress since "in the normal course of events" it is hard to argue for a system of controls.

— There are often alternative ways to accomplish any policy goal. While some of these may run afoul of the constitution, others are likely to be *intra vires*. Economists refer to this as the principle of effective market classification or the optimal policy instrument calculus. With respect to the wage and price control example, the federal government has the power to impose wage controls on its own employees and on those sectors falling under federal jurisdiction (e.g., transportation). Similarly, the provinces can follow suit if they wish. Since the private sector can be counted on to respond to economic conditions, this is probably all that is warranted in terms of the powers to implement controls. However, there are other instances where it seems clear that the wrong policy instrument was utilized. The regional aspects of unemployment insurance as well as the special UI provisions for fishermen would probably fall into this category. If the role of UI is seen principally as a distributional role, then an instrument more suited to distribution is to be preferred. If it is an anti-migration policy, again the federal government should have tackled the problem (rigid wage rates across provinces) rather than the symptom (unemployment). In general, economic analysis would suggest that distributional instruments should be used to tackle distributional problems. Unemployment insurance can be viewed as tampering with re-source allocation in order to handle a distributional problem.

— If one level of federal government is assigned the responsibility for achieving a particular objective, then the constitutional arrangements should ensure that it has the ability to address this objective in the optimal manner.

— Underlying all these comments is the more important requirement that the federation be able to adjust its structures and processes to accommodate the required economic adjustment. The comfortable economic niche in which Canada found itself during the decade of the 1960s has clearly vanished. The nations that will succeed in the 1990s are those that can allocate or reallocate resources with speed and efficiency to the sunrise industries. This is especially true for the small, open economies like Canada. Hence, the constitutional framework must be capable of adapting to altered economic circumstances. Thus, the particular structure of powers at any point in time is probably not as important as the ability of this structure to accommodate new economic goals. In this sense, process is every bit as critical as structure.

— There is another reason why process may dominate structure. In our increasingly interdependent world, the role of government has likewise become more pervasive. A given assignment of powers no longer guarantees one level of government full freedom to act with respect to, say, sphere X since actions by the other level of government elsewhere in the complex system will surely rebound back on policy area X.

— In tandem, these concerns have led me in the direction of endorsing Carl Friedrich's notion of federalism . . . : "federalism should not be seen only as a static pattern or design, characterized by a particular and precisely fixed division of powers between government levels. Federalism is also and perhaps primarily the process . . . of adopting joint policies and making joint decisions on joint problems."[1]

This emphasis on federalism as a process takes on added weight in light of the variety of structures in federal countries, to which I now turn.

CROSS-FEDERATION COMPARISONS

*   *   *

One comparison that would initially appear to be particularly revealing is that between Canada and Australia, the only other industrialized federation with a British-type parliamentary system. . . . Australia can be viewed as falling, along with Canada, in the "interstate federalism" category: some of the processes developed by the Australians (e.g., executive federalism) also exist in Canada. However, as Richard Bird notes:

> Had Australia not been established initially as a federal country, it seems most unlikely that it would be one today. Of all the countries examined its fiscal policies are by far the most centralized . . . the impulse toward uniformity in this homogeneous country . . . runs deep.[2]

The German federation is also highly centralized, even to the point where the constitution does not permit differential tax rates on the major shared taxes. Although the various states or *Laender* do have some input into federal policies, the German federation is decentralized principally in the sense that there is decentralized implementation of national legislation. We could argue that this is more consistent with a unitary state with a structure of local governments than with the notion of federalism that is characteristic of, say, Canada and Switzerland. Even so, there may be a good deal that we can learn from the German experience, particularly in those policy areas where Canada goes some way toward the joint implementation model. To quote Bird again:

> Despite our up-and-down experience with using the federal spending power to slip (or bludgeon) a federal presence into the designated functions of the provinces, it may not be beyond the human mind to work out at least some limited "joint" tasks in Canada—"joint" in the sense of involv-

ing federal financing but provincial execution of essentially provincial expenditures, all subject to agreement by both sides on a basis of equality. Such an approach might prove valuable in such fields as higher education, health care, and technical retraining—in all of which both federal and provincial interests are obvious.[3]

In other words, we do not have to adopt the German institutional framework (intrastate federalism et al.) in order to see virtue in having some of our processes of federalism imitate those in the German federation.

In terms of the degree of decentralization, the Swiss and U.S. federations may provide more in the way of a role model. The diversity in these two federations leads Bird to two intriguing insights with respect to the operation of the Canadian system. With respect to the United States, he observes that "the U.S. system suggests how much more diversity in many respects—for instance, in local tax systems—can be tolerated than is generally considered to be the case in Canada." Even more insightful are his reflections on the Swiss model:

> Although Switzerland hardly offers readily transferable solutions to Canada's problems, a close look at its experience may provide the most illuminating of all possible comparisons for Canadians, in part because it suggests that some of the problems and solutions currently discussed in Canada may, when viewed from a different perspective, reverse their positions. As in a well-known optical illusion, when looked at in a slightly different way, background may become foreground and the foreground background—or problems (such as, say, tax diversity) may become solutions while solutions (such as tax harmonization) may become problems![4]

The Notion of "Balance" in a Federation

More generally, it seems that each federation has gone through a process of internal "coexistence." In some cases this coexistence was forced upon the system by the constitution itself. For example, the Australian Commonwealth found that it was prevented by the constitution from nationalizing airlines and banks and from creating national marketing boards. It eventually found a way around these restrictions by utilizing to the fullest its power to make grants to the states and by creating new institutions like the Australian Loan Council. In other federations, the co-existence is essentially directed "against" the constitution. For example, in the Swiss case the internal market provision in its constitution is such that the federal government has authority to harmonize the fiscal system and to put an end to the so-called tax jungle. But the cultural, historical, and political (local democracy) traditions of the Swiss not only have prevented this from occurring but . . . the issue of the potential inefficiency arising from the tax jungle is not even widely discussed, except outside of Switzerland.

In other words, there is a "balance" that appears to have developed in each federation—a balance between centralization and decentralization, between the role of citizens and the role of governments, between uniformity and diversity, and so on. As any review of cross-federation approaches will demonstrate, this balance is struck at different places for different policies for different countries, and the balance is clearly time dependent. Moreover, the nature of the balance operating in one federation in comparison with another can be much more than the positioning of the "fulcrum" in the two countries. Consider the internal common market issue. The Canadian government was quite correct to point out (in the constitutional discussions in 1980) that the Canadian provinces have more freedom to enact policies that may fragment the internal common market than is the case for the states of most other federations. However, what it did not point out (or at least did not emphasize) was that this was also true of the Canadian government: the federal governments of other federations tend

to be more constrained by their constitutions in terms of implementing policies that give preference to one region or one state over other regions or states. Hence, there will be more regionally distortive policies in Canada implemented by *both* levels of government than we would find, say, in Australia. But the process is not explosive (although some may argue that it has gone too far), since each level of government in Canada has the power to escalate and, therefore, to generate dead-weight loss. This, too, is balance, albeit a balance that may be typically Canadian in the sense that it is probably born more of the particular economic geography of the provinces than of ideology.

There is a second element to any notion of balance that is probably important—that while the formal constitution is typically an important determinant of these trade-offs, there are other factors that will almost of necessity come into play. This was clearly evident in the example of Switzerland and its approach (or lack of approach) to tax harmonization. In turn, this suggests that the notion of balance is supported not only by the structure but also by the processes of the federation.

Several implications follow from this notion of balance. First of all, it tends to provide a different perspective from which to view certain features of federalism. Consider, for example, the "opting-out provision" in our fiscal arrangements, a feature that is probably unique to the Canadian federation. No doubt, it represents to many an undesirable feature in our federal structure. It is well recognized that opting-out allows Quebec more flexibility on its fiscal side than would otherwise be the case. However, what is not so well recognized is that opting-out also permits the remaining nine provinces to have a more harmonized (and perhaps more centralized!) fiscal structure than would otherwise be possible. Thus, in striking the balance between harmony and diversity, and perhaps between centralization and decentralization as well, the opting-out provision allows at the same time more diversity (for Quebec) and more harmony (for the remaining nine provinces) than would be the case if all provinces were made to toe some common intermediate line.

A second implication of this focus on balance is that changes in the formal constitution may not be the only, or the most appropriate, manner by which to usher in any desired changes. In some areas, like securities regulation, the federal government can (constitutionally) play a major role, but it has decided thus far to leave securities regulation to the provinces. Hence, in this area changes in the de facto division of powers will likely arise because of perceived economic or political needs. Much the same is like to characterize other areas as well . . .

The problem with a dramatic shift in the formal distribution of powers is that it will almost assuredly set in motion a veritable chain reaction of adjustments on the part of both levels of government until some new "balance" is restored. Moreover, it is far from clear that the final outcome will be predictable. This does not mean that dramatic changes are necessarily to be avoided. What it does mean, however, is that any such constitutional change will eventually have to be filtered through the political, economic, cultural, and geographical compromises inherent in the federation in order that a new set of structures and processes replace the old.

In this context, it is instructive to devote some time to the one element of the new Constitution that clearly has altered the traditional balance in the Canadian federation—the Canadian Charter of Rights and Freedoms. Surely this Charter will bring about dramatic changes in the practice of federalism in Canada. For one thing, it will "republicanize" the federation in the sense that it represents a move away from parliamentary democracy: there are now some things with respect to which no parliament can legislate. Moreover, as the Canadian public becomes more accustomed to the role of a bill of rights, my guess is that they will move to expand its

application. For example, a move to include private property in the bill of rights (i.e., to move it more in the direction of an economic bill of rights) may well represent one way to secure an internal common market. However, the implications of securing a Canadian economic union via a bill of economic rights are vastly different from securing it, for example, via enlarging a federal head of power. The result would be a "decentralization" or powers, but it would represent a transfer of power to citizens (and to the courts) and away from both levels of government. Should this occur, it will have substantial implications for the governments' role in the economy, particularly on the allocation front (e.g., regional policy). It will take decades, rather than years, for the federation to generate a new "balance" in the wake of such a development. Nonetheless, I, for one, would welcome such an extension of the charter.

TOWARD AN ECONOMIC CONSTITUTION

Finally, I want to focus on what economics and economic management might tell us about constitutional redesign. Unfortunately, apart from some obvious areas like monetary policy, I think the answer is "not much" (or at least not as much as I had anticipated prior to embarking on this study). Experience elsewhere indicates that both centralized and decentralized federations can be effective on the economic front. Moreover, if Canadians wish to decentralize further, this change need not imply constitutional redesign. Among the alternative options open are

— legislative changes within the existing constitutional framework (e.g., the CPP experience);

— an increase in the proportion of provincial revenues that arise from own-source taxation as distinct from federal transfers;

— an increase in the proportion of federal transfers to the provinces that are unconditional; and

— an increase in the range of policy areas on which the provinces must be consulted (e.g., allowing provincial input into appointments for national bodies).

Nonetheless, there are several areas where economics suggests that new arrangements may be appropriate. Basically, however, most of these can be treated under the rubric of a new economic constitution rather than a new Constitution Act.

Toward this goal of providing an economic constitution for Canada, let me suggest the following items. First, there ought to be a recognition and indeed a commitment that it is desirable to enhance the Canadian economic union. I have suggested that the preferable route to follow here may be a federal-province "code of economic conduct" rather than a formal change in the constitutional allocation of powers. Whatever the mechanisms, however, there is need for a reorientation of policy in several areas. One approach that would appear to have merit is to attempt to enhance those aspects of the internal common market that will facilitate our ability to penetrate foreign markets. For example, portability of pensions and portability of social services across provinces will enhance labour mobility resource allocation . . . If the provinces are unwilling or unable to guarantee these mobility rights, then Ottawa should enforce them via its expenditure power (as a condition for federal-provincial transfers). A similar recommendation applies to the markets for capital. . . . If the provinces become embroiled in a beggar-thy-neighbour approach to regulating the capital markets, Ottawa can and should step in to ensure that the national market for capital is not balkanized. Therefore, enhancing the ability of goods, services, labour, and capital to move free and freely within the federation is the first component of an economic constitution. An important corollary is that any such enhanced domestic integration should not be accompanied by decreasing international integration. One of the principal conclusions of the internal economic union chapter was that the costs of impediments on the international front exceeded those on the domestic front.

Second, an economic constitution should strive to remove duplication and waste—to "disentangle" where feasible. The views of the former treasurer of Ontario on this subject effectively capture the essence of this point:

> This [the reduction of waste and duplication] is neither a new issue nor a new concern in Canada. In my view, much of the wasteful duplication among governments was the product of political conflict between Ottawa and the provinces in recent years.
>
> Most of the provinces have well-developed programs to support small business and cost-effective initiatives to assist the young unemployed. But too often, Ottawa developed its own set of programs—duplicating provincial efforts. And in the areas where the federal government developed a program . . . to meet a local or regional concern, the province involved would probably launch its own similar initiative. Surely, as a fundamental tenet of our new economic constitution, we can agree that if one level of government is best equipped or situated to deal with a problem, the other level should provide complementary resources and support to make that program work even better—rather than operating a separate program of its own.
>
> That may require both levels of government to "give up turf" on occasion. Canadians now expect us to subordinate narrow partisan interests to the interests of effectiveness and efficiency.[5]

The requirement to "give up turf" is clearly central to effective disentanglement. It may well be that this can be accomplished by mutually agreeable trades within the existing framework, but the parties may also require safeguards of a nature that would call for legislative action or even a formal reallocation of powers. Nonetheless, the politics and economics of fiscal restraint and economic exigency will continue to exert pressure for rationalization and/or disentanglement in some areas.

The third component of an economic constitution would be to ensure that the existing structures and processes of federalism are such as to enable overall policy to reflect the economic needs of the 1990s. From my perspective, the next decade will place a premium on flexibility and adjustment, and the range of socio-economic policies should serve to encourage rather than inhibit this adjustment. Once again, constitutional change may not be the desirable route to follow, particularly in light of the tremendous interdependence that characterizes the policy actions in this area. Moreover, the existing set of arrangements already run the gamut from unilateralism to intrastate federalism. Thus, getting the division of powers "right" is not as important as getting the policy "right": indeed the role of the former should be to facilitate the latter.

A fourth component relates to the optimal instrument assignment. Once there is agreement on the objectives to be pursued by the two levels of government, it is critical to ensure that each level has at its disposal the policy instruments appropriate to achieve the objective.

We could add many more components to this notion of an economic constitution. Moreover, the reader's list would no doubt differ from mine. But, what becomes clear is that any such package will become more in the nature of a design for appropriate policy than a design for appropriate structure. Structure becomes a problem only if it prevents, or makes very costly, the achievement of appropriate policy. In my view, it is difficult to find many cases where our poor economic performance can be blamed on the straitjacket imposed by the constitutional framework (energy policy is probably the exception). . . . Phrased differently, inadequacies in economic management in our federation are, in the main, a matter of the failure of policy, not structure. This is not intended to rule out formal changes in structure but to suggest that the first priority on the economic management front is to decide on the appropriate policy stance. Once this is clear, the question of structural redesign will become both more obvious and less controversial.

Thus, my overall conclusion is that structure is secondary to policy: the structure and processes should adjust to the economic needs of the federation rather than the situation where the economic policies of the federation come to be determined by structural and constitutional considerations. Constitutional redesign, formulated in the abstract, is not the route to take. As Yogi Berra once proclaimed: "if you don't know where you're going, you may end up somewhere else."

Notes

1. Cited in Richard Bastien, *Federalism and Decentralization: Where Do We Stand?* (Ottawa: Supply and Services Canada, 1981), 48.

2. Richard Bird, "Federal Finance in Comparative Perspective," in T. J. Courchene, D. W. Conklin, and G. C. A. Cook, eds., *Ottawa and the Province: The Distribution of Money and Power.* (Toronto: Ontario Economic Council, 1985), 167.

3. *Ibid.*, 168.

4. *Ibid.*, 170-1.

5. Larry Grossman, Ministry of Industry and Tourism, Government of Ontario, "Remarks at the Primrose Club Luncheon," Toronto, Ontario, September 25, 1984, 5-6.

Selected Readings

Canada. *Report of the Royal Commission on the Economic Union and Development Prospects for Canada.* Vol. 3. Ottawa: Supply and Services Canada, 1985.

Canada. *Securing the Canadian Economic Union in the Constitution, A Discussion Paper.* Ottawa: Supply and Services Canada, 1980.

Courchene, T. J. "The Political Economy of Canadian Constitution Making: The Canadian Economic Union Issue." *Public Choice* 4: 1 (1984): 201–49.

Safarin, A. E. *Canadian Federalism and Economic Integration.* Ottawa: Information Canada, 1974.

Trebilcock, M. J., Prichard, J. R. S., Courchene, T. J., and Whalley, J. *Federalism and the Canadian Economic Union.* Toronto: University of Toronto Press for the Economic Council of Canada, 1983.

Whyte, J. D. "Constitutional Aspects of Economic Development Policy." In Richard Simeon, research coordinator, *Division of Powers and Public Policy.* Background Study for the Royal Commission on the Economic Union and Development Prospects for Canada. Vol 61. Toronto: University of Toronto Press, 1985, 29-69.

24. A PROLOGUE TO STRUCTURAL REFORM OF THE GOVERNMENT OF CANADA

Frederick C. Englemann

The Canadian constitutional debate has been going on during the entire professional life of most currently active Canadian political scientists. It came to a crisis, but hardly a thorough resolution, during the years 1980–82. We emerged from this crisis with a patriated constitution, an amending formula, and a Charter of Rights and Freedoms. The only significant institutional change was the limiting of the Senate's role in constitutional amendments. Yet from 1968 on, more than a dozen reports and literally thousands of printed pages have been devoted to thorough structural change.[1] The failure to act on any of these was recognized by the government of Canada in 1982 with the launching of the Royal Commission on the Economic Union and Development Prospects for Canada. In addition to its chief economic objectives, the Macdonald Commission was charged with examining the institutional structure of the government of Canada. Canadian political scientists can be proud of the fact that a past president of their association, Alan Cairns, was charged with presiding over research for this task.

The Commission followed the Special Joint Committee of the Senate and of the House of Commons on Senate Reform,[2] the Alberta Select Special Committee on Upper House Reform,[3] and the Canada West Foundation[4] in proposing, as the centrepiece of structural reform, an elective Senate. The elective Senate proposed by the Macdonald Commission[5] would be made up of 144 senators elected by proportional representation from 23 six-menber constituencies—one for Prince Edward Island, four each from Ontario and Quebec and two each from the remaining provinces, and six senators from the Territories. This Senate would be restricted to a suspensive veto of six months. This provision is to safeguard the prime position of the House of Commons and, more important, a prime minister and cabinet based on the support of the House of Commons.

Throughout the years of debate, some of us[6] have gone so far as to doubt the feasibility of a permanent, successful symbiosis between the parliamentary system of government and a federal system crowned by an elective Senate. The main problem is that of a double instead of the present single popular mandate. After all is said, any duplication of the popular mandate flies in the face of the principle of majority rule. This majority principle, first voiced clearly by John Locke,[7] is one of two alternate principles of democratic government. The alternative is some form of consensual government in which policies have to be negotiated before they can be enacted. Our oldest federal sisters, the United States and Switzerland, have governmental structures based on this consensual, or at least negotiating principle.

The only true hybrid, at least in the first world, of federalism with an elected Senate and parliamentary government is the Commonwealth of Australia. The Australian founding fathers realized that a parliamentary system with two elected houses could lead to deadlock. Their way of re-

Frederick C.Englemann, "A Prologue to Structural Reform of the Government of Canada," *Canadian Journal of Political Science* 19:4 (1986): 667–678. Reprinted by permission of the Canadian Political Science Association and the author. The essay has been revised by the author to suit the needs of this volume.

solving such a deadlock was, of course, the process of double dissolution, of the dissolution of the Senate as well as the House of Representatives, with a joint sitting of the new houses to resolve the legislative deadlock, but with the fate of the government depending entirely on the composition of the new House of Representatives. In 1975, the intention of a relatively unpopular government to stay in office without getting a fresh mandate, but to obtain a new Senate, led to the first dismissal of a government[8] in the history of first-world British parliamentary government since the dismissal of the Fox-North ministry by George III in 1783—a power, as Lowell wrote in 1908, that responsible government has "practically made obsolete."[9] If the representatives of the Crown had not, shall we say, won the ensuing election, heaven only knows what would have happened to Australia's governmental structure. The spectre of having Mme. Sauvé dismiss Mr. Mulroney should be sufficient to make Canadians pause before instituting a parliamentary system with two elective chambers.

But, some will retort I am drawing a false picture. The proposed elective Senate is to have a *suspensive* veto, not the absolute one of the Australian Senate; thus there is no need for a deadlock. My answer is based on close to five decades of watching cabinet governments. I was not surprised when the intricate deadlock resolving mechanism of the Australian constitution blew a fuse in 1975. We should never underestimate two factors: the intention of prime minister and cabinet to stay in office and the determination—let us call it partisan determination—of any elective official to stay in office and use his or her power. The mitigation of the suspensive veto may well be drowned out by the partisanship of senators, who could use the suspensive veto as a matter of course in order to force a government enjoying the confidence of the House of Commons into a premature election. I would say, then, that those backing the Macdonald Commission solution are taking the proposed suspensive veto too lightly, especially in view of Peter Aucoin's well-placed emphasis on party government.[10] Donald Smiley and Ronald

Watts[11] recognize the momentum of any elective body but, once having pointed out the difficulties involved—"attempting to reconcile intrastate federalism with the Westminster model is akin to trying to square the constitutional circle"[12]—they essentially ignore their own reservations in the end by proposing an elective Senate.

At this point, let me concede that I am not trying to improve on the work of the eminent colleagues who worked for the Macdonald Commission. I am not presenting a solution, but a prologue: a prologue which states the problem in a way none of them has. My prologue calls for a principle: for asking the first question first before we attempt to restructure the government of Canada. The first question, I submit, is this: *do we or do we not want to maintain majority rule in the government of Canada?* I call this the first question because the chief characteristic of the British parliamentary system is that, like no other system in existence, it institutionalizes majority rule. In order to approximate perfection, majority rule must be based on a *single* system of elective representation, on the popular election of the House of Commons only.

The purpose of most of our structural reformers is clear: they want to make the decision-making process at the federal level more responsive to the various regions of Canada. The periphery, from where I hail, does not want decisions affecting all Canadians made by a majority which may well represent—as it did after the election of 1980—primarily the central provinces of Ontario and Quebec. The improvement of regional representation is the hallmark of the many reform proposals. In bringing some of the proposed structural changes in line with my basic question, we must find whether improved regional representation in the government of Canada—or intrastate federalism, as the experts have come to call it—is or is not compatible with majority rule. If it is, we can reform without asking the basic question. If it is not, we must decide whether we want to preserve our parliamentary system of institutionalized majority rule.

I submit that *some* changes—some improvements of intrastate federalism—are possible without jeopardizing majority rule. The mildest among these is the addition of some extra seats, elected by proportional representation (PR) to the House of Commons. I am not going into the entire area of reform of Commons representation, in which William Irvine is the leading scholar,[13] because I restrict myself to more effective regional representation. Without going into arithmetic detail, the number of PR seats should be large enough so that any party likely to form the government could be expected to elect at least one member from a province now having 10 or more seats. This was not the case in several elections prior to 1984. I say "ten seats" because Prince Edward Island has a tendency to represent both major parties in the House of Commons, and accommodating it might necessitate an unduly high number of PR seats.

Those objecting to the partial election of the House of Commons by PR on the grounds that the PR members would not be "the honourable member from somewhere" and would thus be second-class members should take a look at the role and prestige of those members of the German lower house, the Bundestag, elected from Land lists by proportional representation. These members are assigned to a constituency or constituencies captured by another party and work hard on representing their partisans in such an area—hardly a second-class job.[14] Similar developments could take place in Canada.

Other reforms compatible with majority rule would strengthen regional interests by loosening the requirements of parliamentary government where they are most rigid: by loosening the firm nexus of policy and cabinet tenure, making it necessary for a government to win each policy vote in order to stay in office. The Mother of Parliaments has in fact loosened this nexus,[15] making it possible to defeat the cabinet on a policy matter yet sustaining it on a subsequent motion of want of confidence. Many of us remember Prime Minister Pearson's defeat in the House just before the 1968 convention which made Pierre Trudeau leader and, effectively, prime minister. The Liberals got away with Pearson's staying in office. We thus even have a Canadian precedent for allowing governments to lose policy votes, provided they maintain confidence in a subsequent vote. Here again, since it is regional interests that the reformers I am talking about want to protect, governments could emphasize that they want the Commons to tolerate their defeat on matters of a regional nature, again of course subject to their maintaining the confidence of the House.

From here on, we enter the area of formal constitutional change. As these lines are written, it is uncertain whether reform of the Senate requires the amending formula (Parliament—or, after a six months' wait, the House of Commons alone—and two-thirds of the provinces containing 50 percent of Canada's population) or the formula of the Meech Lake agreement, which requires provincial unanimity for institutional change. What both formulae require—like the approach to Westminster prior to 1982—is the support of the government of Canada. Extant proposals generally do not worry about the problem of securing such a support.

The hypertrophy of federal cabinet involvement in constitutional change was bared starkly in 1980, when Trudeau capriciously announced that patriation of the British North America Act was going to involve not just patriation and an amending formula, but also the substantive change of the Charter of Rights and Freedoms. Such an intention was unheard of in the entire history of liberal democracy. In none of them had constitutions been changed by the action of the caucus of the governing party alone. In this connection, we must remember that Ed Broadbent's promise of support almost broke up the New Democratic party caucus. As we all remember, eight of the provinces rebelled and, with the support of a palpable but not legally binding interpretation by the Supreme Court of Canada, gained the federal cabinet's agreement to negotiate the settlement which became reality on April 17, 1982.

Both the amending formula worked out by this process and the proposed Meech Lake formula probably make it insufficient to call a federal-provincial conference to change our structure of government. The either eight or eleven governments required to agree may not bring about a discussion of first principles, or changes based on *any* principle. For the kind of discussion proposed here to take place, a third authority would have to be added to Canada and the provinces: the people. Those who are tied to the events preceding 1867 may call me unCanadian. But things have changed since then. Canada has become a nation, as Trudeau finally recognized when he proposed a referendum on his constitutional changes. As a nation, Canada itself, not only our governments, has something to say about our Constitution.

If any structural changes beyond those I have mentioned already are to be considered, whether compatible with the Westminster model or not, I propose that a constitutional mini-convention be convened. I say mini-convention because its task would be confined to initiating and proposing structural change. Without prescribing the composition of this mini-convention, I would suggest that it be composed of members elected in the provinces, about one-half from such interests (and experts) as business, labour, agriculture, law, and political science, and one-half representative of the public at large. It could make one single or alternative proposals. It would then meet with a federal-provincial conference and attempt to persuade, depending on the adoption of Meech Lake, all eleven or the required eight governments necessary for amending the constitution, or negotiate a proposal with this federal-provincial conference. The entire effort would take time, possibly a year, but it would have to be employed once only.

At least one of the more thorough structural changes which might involve the process I have just proposed would not negate the essentials of majority rule: a Bundesrat for Canada, a second chamber in which provinces are represented not by members but by delegates of the provincial governments. Since I was among those proposing

a Bundesrat in 1978,[16] I am mindful of everything that has been said against a Bundesrat solution. What I am proposing now is a Bundesrat with modest powers. It would have no suspensive veto at all. In fact, it would deal with ordinary legislation. In matters of joint or overlapping jurisdiction, to be worked out by the proposed mini-convention, the Canadian Bundesrat would have a veto, which could be overriden only by a joint sitting with the House of Commons. The Bundesrat-type body would have no more votes (possibly fewer) than one-half of the membership of the House of Commons. Structural details for this Canadian Bundesrat would also be worked out in negotiations by the admittedly and intentionally cumbersome process I outlined for the determination of its powers.

The kind of Bundesrat I propose would not refute majority rule in Ottawa. It would simply, by mutual agreement, exempt some areas from majority rule—areas which the process I propose would clearly mark as areas of great regional concern. The Bundesrat solution would also give Canada one capability it now lacks: a place in which representatives of federal and provincial bureaucracies could meet regularly. Does Canada need such meetings, since our provincial servants do not, like their German counterparts, administer federal laws? My answer is that our provincial public servants do not lack a sense of Canada, and they can contribute to national unity. Not all of the constitutional solution of 1982 is a great thing. But it was largely provincial public servants—even more than groups making submissions in 1981— who modified Trudeau's attempt to impose personally a constitution on Canada.

We need not go as far as a Bundesrat-type solution, but I submit that it is as far as we *can* go in reforming without destroying responsible government or, as Aucoin calls it, party government. I know that it will not placate my Triple E Senate friends in Alberta, who want an elective, equal, and effective Senate. What I am saying now is not directed at our Macdonald Commission colleagues, because they want a Single E Senate:

elected, but not equal and, because of its suspensive veto, not effective in the book of the Triple E people. My only objection to the Single E Senate, as mentioned earlier, is that elected people who do not agree with majority decisions will find ways to thwart them. Many of the Triple E people want a Senate like the one they watch south of the border. To them I say that a US-type Senate is totally incompatible with the majority rule core of responsible government. They have to drop the other shoe and come out—a few of them actually do—for a Canadian Congress, with two co-equal houses. They feel that if America is too large and diverse for majority rule, so is Canada.

Now if professors Smiley and Watts are willing to think the unthinkable and contemplate questioning the parliamentary system, why not I, who was not privileged to be born under the aegis of the daughter of the Mother of Parliaments? The obvious place to look for an alternative is south of the border. The United States was an unpopular model in the 1860s, but already two generations ago, William Bennett Munro identified the United States as the second most important source of Canadian government and politics.[17] The beauty of the American system is that it gives representation not only to provinces or regions, but also to a number of interests. Because of the complex decision-making machinery—committees in both houses, the two houses, and possibly a conference committee—every interest is potentially represented. In Canada, this would mean English, French, Third Canadians and all ethnicities, native peoples, women, the elderly, the young, regions, provinces, sub-provincial regions—from northern Ontario to southern Alberta to Vancouver Island to Cape Breton Island—and, of course, all kinds of economic and social interests. If this brings on the spectre of policy immobilism, such a spectre would have impressed me more before Joe Clark and Erik Nielsen invented bell-ringing against majority governments.

But in presenting—not proposing—a congressional system, I have to face the clincher: would not a congressional system require an elected president? Let me face this question without, for the moment, worrying about maintaining the monarchy. A U.S.-type presidential election in our nation with two founding races, with the language of one spoken by the majority of the population, might well endanger national unity. The phenomenon to be avoided then, is having a French versus English election, or no francophone presidents at all. It can be avoided. We Canadians could, for instance, elect the lower house every two years, and one-half of the Senate every four years. Every six years we could elect a president and a vice-president for one nonrenewable term, with the understanding that in the first campaign, there would be only anglophone candidates, only francophone candidates in the next campaign, and alternation thereafter. A virtue would soon emerge from necessity. Under such circumstances, presidential elections would not be incompatible with Canada's bilingual and bicultural nature. A great by-product would be the early bilingualization of all political parties in the country.

Please remember once more that I am not trying to be prescriptive, but that I am presenting alternatives. Having been a citizen of republics for most of my life, I may be accused of neglecting the monarchist sentiment of Canadians. An Angus Reid poll in early 1986 showed a firm monarchist majority in anglophone Canada, and of course the constitution requires unanimous consent of the provinces to abolish the monarchy. Cleary, we cannot have a president and maintain a monarchy. But do we have to jettison the idea of a Congress simply because we want to preserve the monarchy? Here again, I can propose a way out. Switzerland has never had a monarch, but the Swiss system of government is not incompatible with monarchy. It has two independent legislative houses and an independent executive[18] and is well worth examining for Canadians who want to preserve the monarchy but want to subordinate responsible government to effective regional representation.

Many Canadians would reject the Swiss alternative for Canada on at least three grounds. First, Switzerland is a small country in which government, compared to Canada, is a bit of a family affair. Second, the Swiss have consociational government. While they have political parties and partisan elections, they can hardly be said to have party government. Third, Swiss cantons, compared to the Helvetian Confederation, are even more powerful than Canadian provinces, and direct democracy in Switzerland makes many decisions which cannot be made within the machinery of government. Now I admit that proposing the Swiss system for Canada is a bit of a *tour de force*. Once again, I must ask my readers to remember that I am not being prescriptive, but that I present alternatives. The Swiss alternative would give Canada the American flexibility in policy-making with the protection of regions and other interests, and it is thoroughly compatible with keeping the monarch as the head of state.

The core of Swiss government is the Bundesrat. Because of the unfortunate homonym with the German second chamber, let me refer to it as the Federal Council. This Federal Council (in Switzerland, of seven members) is elected one at a time at the beginning of each Parliament by the National Council, representing the population, and the Standerat (Council of the Estates), representing the cantons. Since 1959, the parties have agreed on a formula giving two seats each to the Social, Free, and Christian Democrats and one to the Swiss People's Party. The Council makes majority decisions on which its proposals to parliament are based. There is no party discipline, though Social Democrats tend to behave in unison, and no executive solidarity. Outvoted members may try to block proposals in Parliament or by means of a proposal submitted to a popular vote in the direct democratic process.

Having just mentioned the party discipline of the Social Democrats, I hope I have shown that this peculiar institutional structure tolerates diverse group behaviour. It could equally tolerate

uniform group behaviour, that is, party discipline practised by all involved parties. If Canada had a Congress and it had the power to elect a multi-member executive, party majorities in these executives would be rare. Had such a body been elected by a two-elected-houses Parliament in 1984, there would have been a Progressive Conservative majority. With Liberals and possibly New Democrats gaining in the provinces, a Progressive Conservative majority of 1984 dimensions might be required in 1988 to maintain this majority in the executive. Certainly, this adaptation of the Swiss system to Canada would give adequate regional representation: in the second chamber and probably also in the executive. Policy-making would probably proceed in a manner not unlike the American one. There remains, of course, the objection regarding vetoes and possible inaction. I would, however, urge those making comparisons with what Canada has now to look not only at the pure Westminster model, but also at the way it was applied to the Mulroney-Wilson budget of 1985, despite a Commons majority of 211-71.

How would the monarchy come into play? The multi-member executive, which would for reasons of federalism and Canada's size have to be considerably larger than that of Switzerland, would simply be appointed by the governor general, just as she now appoints the leader of the party commanding a majority of the House of Commons. The British monarchy has shown stupendous adaptability since 1215. The adoption of a Swiss system by Canada would certainly not destroy it.

Am I simply offering the choice between a German and a Swiss Bundesrat? This is not so. All I have done is present alternatives to please all those who are persuaded that regional representation in Ottawa is inadequate: first, for those who want to hold on to majority rule and then for those who want to give it up.

There is one more fly in the ointment. Would not the combination of separation of powers in Ottawa and parliamentary government in the provinces fragment Canada hopelessly? Quite possibly such fragmentation would occur. Those fearing it yet preferring strong regional representation should prefer the adapted German over the Swiss Bundesrat.

I agree with the First Ministers who met at Meech Lake that the structure of Canadian government needs changing. Because the regions of Canada have no place in the structure of the government of Canada, our premiers are looked to more and more as persons who can provide regional opposition. Their opposition to Ottawa reached a high point in the late Trudeau years and was mitigated only by the support Trudeau received from premiers William Davis and Richard Hatfield—national heroes to some, traitors to others. The "Gang of Eight" was a more effective opposition to Trudeau's single-handed effort to give us a constitution than Her Majesty's Loyal Opposition under Joe Clark, not because Clark and his Progressive Conservatives were not trying hard, but because the majority principle stamped them as losers before they even began to oppose. Premiers' opposition to Ottawa is unhealthy because it pits whole provinces, not buffered by their interaction in some kind of Bundesrat, against the government of Canada. We may want effective regional opposition, but not in the form of diplomatic threats to national unity. Canada is better off when regional opposition is *within* the structure of our federal government and not carried simply by many, most, or all of our ten provinces.

Potential opposition of Ontario, Quebec, Alberta, or British Columbia to Ottawa is not the only aspect of the status quo, though the only one with a centrifugal threat to the country. The other part of the status quo, erroneously thought to aid peripheral interests by the majority of the Fathers of Confederation, is, of course, the Senate. I became a bit of an expert on the Senate of Canada when I wrote my senior essay on it 45 years ago.[19] At that time, I was just learning the basic facts about the government of Canada. Closer observation during the past 25 years and the acquaintance of a few of our more able senators and the occa-

sional writings of others have done little or nothing to modify the devastating impression the Senate of Canada made on me, then a stateless student in the United States, in 1942. It remains a mystery to me how the Fathers could seriously think that a body appointed in fact by the prime minister, as central a figure as any federation has, could protect the interests of the provinces. Well over a thousand purely partisan appointments—many hundreds of them patronage appointments pure and simple—have shaped this body that showed its few signs of life during 119 years *not* because regions were to be protected, but because the party with a Senate majority was out of office.

Provinces, whether red, blue, or a different hue, can expect a tinker's damn in protection from the Senate of 1867. We should recognize the committee and task-force work of some senators, but we should also recognize that the Red Chamber has not dared thwart majority rule for a quarter of a century, even now when some of the honourable senators might dream of doing so for the only reason it has been dreamed about for many decades: the reason of party. And as far as revising legislation goes, it does not require a separate chamber. Of this our 10 provinces offer proof.

The status quo, then, is hardly satisfactory. This brings us back to where I started: structural reform. And once again I return to where I began: the first question for reformers should be whether or not we want to maintain a government "similar in principle to that of the United Kingdom." As Canadians ponder whether to reform the structure of the federal government, the question we must face is once more: "Is regional diversity compatible with majority rule and thus with the parliamentary system?" If not, anything goes, patterned after the American or the Swiss system or something completely new, which might emerge from the interaction of a mini-convention and the first ministers. If the answer is that there *is* basic compatibility between Canadian diversity and the parliamentary system, then the maximum safe modification of our federal governmental structure is some kind of a

German Bundesrat solution, which would give the aggregate of the provinces a veto over what negotiations determine are their affairs in Ottawa. Once again, let me emphasize that I have made every effort not to be prescriptive, only to pose first questions first.

There are more strains between federalism and responsible government than the Fathers of Confederation anticipated. A majority of them thought they had conquered regional problems and they did not anticipate a regime of 11 first ministers. The legislative union a majority thought it had created was suitable for majoritarian parliamentary government. As we know only too well, things have changed. Today, the compatibility or incompatibility of federalism and parliamentary government is the first task we must face as we proceed to reform the structure of our federal government.

Notes

1. This is not the place to present a complete bibliography of these reports. The central document of the Trudeau government is *A Time for Action* (Ottawa: Information Canada, 1978). Possibly the most balanced proposal is *A Future Together*, the report of the (Pépin-Robarts) Task Force on Canadian Unity (Ottawa: Information Canada, 1979). Prominent secondary sources are Edward McWhinney, *Canada and the Constitution, 1979–1982* (Toronto: University of Toronto Press, 1982), David Milne, *The New Canadian Constitution* (Toronto: Lorimer, 1982) and Keith Banting and Richard Simeon, eds., *And No One Cheered* (Toronto: Methuen, 1983).

2. *Report of the Special Joint Committee of the Senate and the House of Commons on Senate Reform* (Ottawa: Queen's Printer, 1984).

3. *Strengthening Canada: Reform of Canada's Senate. Report of the Alberta Select Special Committee on Senate Reform* (Edmonton: The Clerk's Office, Legislature, 1985).

4. Peter McCormick, Ernest C. Manning, and Gordon Gibson, *Regional Representation: The Canadian Partnership* (Calgary: Canada West Foundation, 1981).

5. *Report of the Royal Commission on the Economic Union and Development Prospects for Canada*, vol. 3 (Ottawa: Supply and Services Canada, 1985), 89.

6. While Douglas V. Verney was one of the scholars who for some time pointed to the difficulty of combining the federal and parliamentary systems, I had not, when delivering this address, read his *Three Civilizations, Two Cultures, One State* (Durham: Duke University Press, 1986). I have since done so, and found the book replete with statements of the problematic posed here, especially in chaps. 1, 4, 5, 9, 10, and 11.

7. The clearest statement of Locke's majority principle is Willmoore Kendall, *John Locke and the Doctrine of Majority-Rule* (Urbana: University of Illinois Press, 1941).

8. For a thorough Canadian analysis of the Australian crisis, see D. V. Smiley, *An Elected Senate for Canada?* (Kingston: Institute of Intergovernmental Relations, Queen's University, 1985).

9. A. Lawrence Lowell, *The Government of England,* rev. ed. (New York: Macmillan, 1920), 1, 32.

10. Peter Aucoin, "Regionalism, Party and National Government," in Peter Aucoin, ed., *Party Government and Regional Representation in Canada* (Toronto: University of Toronto Press, 1985), 137.

11. D. V. Smiley and R. L. Watts, *Intrastate Federalism in Canada* (Toronto: University of Toronto Press, 1985), chap. 3.

12. *Ibid.*, 32.

13. W. P. Irvine, *Does Canada Need a New Electoral System?* (Kingston: Institute of Intergovernmental Relations, Queen's University, 1979).

14. While interviewing members of the Bundestag on the Great Coalition of 1966–1969 in 1969, I was greatly impressed by the volume and intensity of work done by PR-elected members in this area.

15. For a discussion of recent British developments along this line, see Philip Norton, ed., *Parliament in the 1980s* (Oxford: Blackwell, 1985).

16. D. Elton, F. C. Engelmann, and P. McCormick, *Alternatives* (Calgary: Canada West Foundation, 1978).

17. W. B. Munro, *American Influences on Canadian Government* (Toronto: Macmillan, 1929).

18. For a sophisticated treatment of Swiss government, see Jürg Steiner, *Amicable Agreement versus Majority Rule: Conflict Resolution in Switzerland* (Chapel Hill: University of North Carolina Press, 1974).

19. F. C. Engelmann, "The Canadian Senate: The Story of a Quixotic Chamber" (unpublished A.B. thesis, University of California at Los Angeles, 1942).

Selected Readings

Alberta. Select Committee on Upper House Reform. *Strengthening Canada*. Edmonton, 1985.

Aucoin, Peter, research coordinator. *Party Government and Regional Representation in Canada*. Research study prepared for the Royal Commission on the Economic Union and Development Prospects for Canada. Vol. 36. Toronto: University of Toronto Press, 1985.

Cairns, A. C. *From Interstate to Intra-State Federalism*. Kingston: Institute of Intergovernmental Affairs, Queen's University, 1979.

Gibbins, Roger. *Senate Reform: Moving Towards the Slippery Slope*. Kingston: Institute of Intergovernmental Relations, Queen's University, 1983.

Smiley, D. V., and Watts, R. L. *Intra-State Federalism in Canada*. Research studies prepared for the Royal Commission on the Economic Union and Development Prospects for Canada. Vol. 39. Toronto: University of Toronto Press, 1985.

25. QUEBEC AND THE CONSTITUTION: COMPLETING THE PATRIATION PROCESS

Rory Leishman

It's déjà vu all over again.   — Yogi Berra

*

Mr. Speaker, I rise to report to the House on the meeting of First Ministers yesterday at Meech Lake. I am honoured to inform the House that at about 10 p.m. last night the Premiers and I reached unanimous agreement in principle on a constitutional package which will allow Quebec to rejoin the Canadian Constitutional family . . . .

This agreement enhances the Confederation bargain and strengthens, I believe, the federal nature of Canada. Although it remains to be formalized, it represents in the judgment of First Ministers from all political stripes and from all areas of the country an historic accomplishment.

The Meech Lake agreement springs from the Canadian tradition of honourable compromise and is a tribute to the statesmanship and leadership of all First Ministers demonstrated yesterday at Meech Lake. Our task, simply put, was to settle a constitutional impasse which was incompletely resolved in 1981. Our task was to attempt to reconcile Quebec's distinct needs with the interests of all other provinces and the good of the country as a whole. . . .

Mr. Speaker, the Meech Lake agreement is good for Canada and good for Canadians.

— Prime Minister Brian Mulroney, *House of Commons Debates*, vol. 129, no. 112 (May 1, 1987), 5628-9.

*

It would be difficult to imagine a more total bungle.

During earlier attempts to Canadianize the Constitution, Prime Ministers Mackenzie King, Saint-Laurent, Diefenbaker, Pearson, and

Trudeau had acted as if it couldn't be done without the unanimous consent of the provinces . . . . But since 1982, Canada had its Constitution, including a Charter which was binding on the provinces as well as the federal government . . . . From then on, "Canada's constitutional evolution" could have taken place without preconditions and without blackmail, on the basis of give and take among equals . . . . With the assurance of a creative equilibrium between the provinces and the central government, the federation was set to last a thousand years!

Alas, only one eventuality hadn't been foreseen: that one day the government of Canada might fall into the hands of a weakling. It has now happened. And the Right Honourable Brian Mulroney, PC, MP, with the complicity of 10 provincial premiers, has already entered into history as the author of a constitutional document which, if it is accepted by the people and their legislators, will render the Canadian state totally impotent. That would destine it, given the dynamics of power, to eventually be governed by eunuchs.

— Pierre Trudeau, *The Toronto Star*, May 27, 1987.

*

Meech Lake: triumph or disaster? Any reasonable answer to that question requires reconsideration of some fundamental constitutional issues which date from the beginning of Confederation. Throughout the history of Canadian federalism, many of the same issues and arguments have kept recurring. In the 1970s, Canada came perilously close to splitting apart over constitutional disagreements: A similar crisis could well develop

---

An original essay written especially for this volume.

in the 1990s, especially if lessons from the past are blithely ignored in preparing for the future.

Independence for Quebec is currently a dormant, but far from dead issue. Parti Québécois leader Pierre-Marc Johnson now speaks vaguely of "national affirmation" rather than outright independence as the party's immediate goal, but sovereignty remains the PQ's ultimate and most cherished objective for Quebec. At a meeting of the party's tenth biennial convention on June 13, 1987, the 900 delegates in attendance voted almost unanimously in favour of reaffirming Quebec independence as the primary goal of the party.[1] As approved by the convention, article 1 of the PQ program now states: "The fundamental objective of the Parti Québécois is to achieve Quebec sovereignty by democratic means. Only the advent of political sovereignty can allow the Quebec people to fulfill itself completely. Sovereignty will be accompanied by freely accepted associations with other countries."

Nowhere in this revised program is there any mention of sovereignty-association, the awkward phrase coined by former party leader René Lévesque. Article 2 makes plain that by sovereignty for Quebec, the party means "exclusive control of our laws, taxes, and institutions and the ability to have relations on a basis of equality with foreign countries," including Canada.

In a speech to a group of French parliamentarians in Paris in November 1986, Quebec Intergovernmental Affairs Minister Gil Remillard insisted that the independence movement is still very much alive in Quebec. It could return in an even more dangerous form, he warned, if the current Quebec government with its strong commitment to federalism cannot return the province to its rightful place as a major partner in the Canadian federation. In his opinion, Quebec's stature within Canada was diminished during the struggle over patriation of the Canadian constitution. "As you know," he reminded the French legislators, "the government of Quebec did not adhere to the Constitution Act, 1982, a law which was imposed upon it and to which it has refused, and will always refuse, to subscribe. No Quebec government, no matter what its political tendency," he emphasized, "could adhere to the Constitution Act, 1982 in its present text."[2]

On other occasions, Quebec Premier Robert Bourassa had said much the same thing. Every party leader in Quebec and Ottawa would agree with Remillard that the Constitution Act, 1982 must be substantially amended in order to win Quebec's adherence.

Prime Minister Brian Mulroney has been especially anxious for a settlement of this issue. During an election campaign speech at Sept-Isles, Quebec on August 6, 1984, he promised to take concrete steps "to convince the Quebec National Assembly to give its consent to the new Canadian Constitution with honour and enthusiasm."[3] Many times, he reiterated that pledge, going so far at a press conference on December 19, 1986, as to rank constitutional reform with trade and tax reform as "the stuff of which major decisions are made."

"This is history," the prime minister added, "you win some and you lose some. I think it's very important we try and win this one very badly for the following reason. We're only part of a country while an important province representing an official language group of Canada is not part of the constitutional process."[4]

Once again, Canadians asked a familiar question: What does Quebec want? In February 1985, the policy commission of the Quebec Liberal Party outlined a comprehensive answer in "Maitriser l'avenir" ("Mastering Our Future"), a policy program prepared for the upcoming provincial election.[5] Among other things, this document spelled out five changes required to make the Constitution Act, 1982 acceptable to the Quebec government.

More than two years later, the Meech Lake agreement in principle turned out to be based precisely on these five points advanced in the Quebec Liberal Party's election platform, together with some additional federal concessions to demands made by other provinces. For this reason, it's convenient to examine the April 30, 1987 Meech Lake agreement point by point, beginning with a statement of the initial Quebec position, as summarized by Remillard,[6] and followed by the Meech Lake response.[7]

POINT 1: DISTINCT SOCIETY

Quebec Position

First of all, the Canadian constitution must explicitly recognize the Canadian duality and the distinct character of Quebec society.

Meech Lake Agreement

(1) The Constitution of Canada shall be interpreted in a manner consistent with

a) the recognition that the existence of French-speaking Canada, centred in but not limited to Quebec, and English-speaking Canada, concentrated outside Quebec but also present in Quebec, constitutes a fundamental characteristic of Canada; and

b) the recognition that Quebec constitutes within Canada a distinct society.

(2) Parliament and the provincial legislatures, in the exercise of their respective powers, are committed to preserving the fundamental characteristic of Canada referred to in paragraph (1)(a).

(3) The role of the legislature and Government of Quebec to preserve and promote the distinct identity of Quebec referred to in paragraph (1)(b) is affirmed.

Few elements of the Meech Lake agreement seem to have aggravated former prime minister Pierre Trudeau more than this first section on Quebec as a distinct society. In a scathing denunciation of the entire agreement published by *The Toronto Star* on May 27, 1987, he said flatly: "Those Canadians who fought for a single Canada, bilingual and bicultural, can say goodbye to their dream."

In the aftermath of that warning, coming up with precise wording to denote Quebec as a distinct society proved to be one of the difficult issues which prolonged the marathon all-day and all-night meeting in the Langevin Bloc on Parliament Hill on June 2 and 3, 1987, when the First Ministers finally agreed on a text for the proposed Constitution Amendment, 1987.[8] Instead of "French-speaking Canada" and "English-speaking Canada", this, the Langevin amendment, refers to "French- and English-speaking Canadians"—a refinement evidently meant to dispel any two-nations connotation and to reaffirm Canada as a single, although officially bilingual, country. That helped clear up some confusion, but nowhere in either the Meech Lake agreement or the Langevin amendment is there any precise definition of what is meant by Quebec as a "distinct society." The phrase could refer to language, to culture, or to any aspect of Quebec history and society which differs from the rest of the country.

The implications of this section for official language rights are particularly obscure. Section 23 of the existing Canadian Charter of Rights and Freedoms provides that any child in Quebec with at least one parent who received primary school instruction in the English language anywhere in Canada has a right to attend an English-language school. By invoking the "distinct society" clause of the Langevin amendment, could the Quebec government once again limit access to English-language schools essentially only to the children of native-born anglophone Quebecers as provided in the province's Bill 101?

Premier Howard Pawley of Manitoba, for one, seems to have feared such a possibility. According to a leaked negotiating document published by *Le Devoir* on June 2, his government proposed that the "distinct society" article should include a provision specifying that it "does not diminish guarantees provided by the Canadian Charter of Rights and Freedoms."[9] Instead, the Langevin amendment contains a new subsection 2.(4), which provides that:

> Nothing in this section derogates from the powers, rights or privileges of Parliament or the Government of Canada, or of the legislatures or governments of the provinces, including any powers, rights or privileges relating to language.

In other words, the Langevin amendment offers to protect not the language rights of Canadians, but the language powers of the federal and provincial governments. Trudeau, for one, is bound to be dismayed. In his *Toronto Star* article, he maintained that if, as the amendment proposes, the role of the legislature and government of Quebec is to preserve and promote the distinct identity of Quebec, "it is easy to predict what future awaits anglophones living in Quebec and what treatment will continue to be accorded to francophones living in provinces where they are fewer in number than Canadians of Ukrainian or German origin."[10]

Responding in *The Globe and Mail* on May 30, Senator Lowell Murray, Minister for Federal and Provincial Relations in the Mulroney government, noted that Trudeau himself once proposed that "the distinctive character of Quebec society" should be acknowledged in a preamble to the Constitition. That is true enough, but the language proposed by Trudeau was far more precise than the Constitution Amendment, 1987.

Specifically, in Bill C-60, an abortive amendment law initiated by Trudeau in 1978, he suggested that "a permanent national commitment to the endurance and self-fulfillment of the Canadian French-speaking society centred in but not limited to Quebec" should be recognized in the constitution as one of the aims of the Canadian federation.[11] Another, no less important aim stated in that bill was "to ensure throughout Canada equal respect for English and French as

the country's principal spoken languages."[12] In this way, Trudeau's bill would have upheld the bilingual character of Canada, while affirming that both the Parliament of Canada and the legislature of Quebec—not just Quebec alone, as in the Meech Lake agreement—have a responsibility to nurture Canada's French-speaking society centred in Quebec.

As it is now, only the courts can tell us to what extent, if any, the anglophone minority in Quebec could end up with lesser rights than francophones elsewhere in the country under terms of the ambiguous language of the "distinct society" article of the Langevin amendment. The confusion, though, could still be diminished and the fundamental national principle of equal minority language rights throughout the country could yet be safeguarded if the Constitution Amendment, 1987, were itself amended prior to adoption after the manner proposed by Pawley.

POINT 2: THE AMENDING FORMULA

Quebec Position

> In order for (Quebec's) specificity to be respected, we must have assurance that no amendment to the constitution will be able to change the rules of the federalist game without the consent of Quebec.

Meech Lake Agreement

> Maintain the current general amending formula set out in section 38, which requires the consent of Parliament and at least two-thirds of the provinces representing at least fifty percent of the population;
> guarantee reasonable compensation in all cases where a province opts out of an amendment transferring provincial jurisdiction to Parliament;

because opting out of constitutional amendments to matters set out in section 42 of the Constitution Act, 1982 is not possible, require the consent of Parliament and all the provinces for such amendments.

In "Mastering Our Future," the Quebec Liberal Party indicated that it would prefer that the general amendment formula of section 38 should be abolished in favour of an alternative formula granting Quebec a universal veto over all constitutional matters. Something close to such a veto would have been accorded to Quebec under terms of the abortive Fulton-Favreau Formula in 1964 and the amendment formula of the Victoria Charter in 1971.[13] However, on April 16, 1981, former Quebec premier René Lévesque abandoned Quebec's historic claim to an amendment veto by joining with seven other colleagues in a "gang of eight" then opposed to an unilateral patriation initiative by Trudeau. Under terms of an agreement among these dissenters, Levesque endorsed the so-called Vancouver amending formula, which would have required general amendments to have the approval of no more than Parliament and the legislatures of just seven provinces containing only half the population of Canada. At the time, Lévesque explained that he was willing reluctantly to go alone with this formula, because it also specified that any province could opt-out of any amendment transferring powers from provincial to federal jurisdiction with full financial compensation from the federal government.

Barely five months later, the Supreme Court of Canada ruled that Quebec might have an amendment veto as a matter of constitutional convention, but not in point of law.[14] And in Nov. 1981, Levesque was abandoned by his seven dissenting colleagues, who endorsed the existing amendment formula contained in the Constitution Act, 1982. Much like the Vancouver agreement, Section 38 of that act provides for a general amending formula requiring approval by the House of Commons and the legislatures of at

least two-thirds of the provinces with at least fifty percent of the population of all the provinces. Also, it allows any province to opt-out of an amendment transferring provincial legislative powers or proprietary rights to Parliament. Section 40 requires the government of Canada to provide reasonable compensation to an opting-out province, but—in marked contrast to the general requirement of the Vancouver amending formula—only in the case of amendments relating to education or other cultural matters. In addition, Section 41 gives each province an amendment veto, but only over a very restricted list of subjects—namely, the office of the Queen, the Governor General, and the Lieutenant Governor of a province; the right of a province to a number of members in the House of Commons not less than the number of Senators by which the province was entitled to be represented in 1982; subject to individual agreements between Ottawa and a province, the use of the English or the French language; the composition of the Supreme Court of Canada; and an amendment to this part. Furthermore, section 42(1) specifies that the general formula of section 38 shall apply to the following matters:

(a) the principle of proportionate representation of the provinces in the House of Commons prescribed by the Constitution of Canada;

(b) the powers of the Senate and the method of selecting Senators;

(c) the number of members by which a province is entitled to be represented in the Senate and the residence qualifications of Senators;

(d) subject to paragraph 41(d), the Supreme Court of Canada;

(e) the extension of existing provinces into the territories; and

(f) notwithstanding any other law or practice, the establishment of new provinces.

Considering that Lévesque had abandoned Quebec's historic claim to a veto in 1981 and that the Supreme Court of Canada had ruled out such a right in law, the Quebec Liberal position as explained in "Mastering Our Future" included a fall-back position on the amendment question. If other first ministers prove unwilling to concede a blanket veto to Quebec, this document suggested that an acceptable alternative for Quebec, "in the spirit of the present opting-out formula, would be to extend the principle of financial compensation to all matters involving the sharing of jurisdictions, and to include a formal right of veto on matters listed in Section 42(1) of the Constitution Act, 1982."[15]

As it happened, Premiers Brian Peckford of Newfoundland, John Buchanan of Nova Scotia, and Howard Pawley of Manitoba all publicly repudiated any idea of a universal constitutional veto for Quebec and Ontario as proposed by Bourassa at the annual premiers conference in Edmonton on August 12, 1986.[16] As planned, Bourassa then retreated to the fall-back position of the Quebec Liberal Party, which was accepted in total by Mulroney and the other provincial premiers during the Meech Lake meeting. The Langevin amendment stipulates that Canada must provide reasonable compensation to any province which opts-out of any amendment transferring provincial legislative powers to Parliament under terms of section 38(1) and extends to each province a veto over all subjects mentioned in both section 41 and 42(1) of the Constitution Act, 1982.

More than a few constitutional experts consider that the Constitution is already too difficult to amend and adjust to changing social and political conditions. Referring to the existing amendment formula, Peter Hogg, a professor of constitutional law at the Osgoode Law School, has written: "I expect that it will be difficult to secure any amendment to the Constitution, because of the high level of agreement required by the general amending procedure."[17] Former Senator Eugene Forsey concurs and also contends that the Meech Lake agreement would make the existing amendment formula "still more rigid,

make many of its most important provisions totally unchangeable except by unanimous consent of the provincial legislatures, which may not truly represent, on these matters, the people of their respective provinces. "Is that," he asks, "what we really want?"[18]

A federal study entitled, "The Canadian Constitution and Constitutional Amendment," which was prepared while Trudeau was prime minister and released in August 1978, suggested that Canada might well wish to follow the Swiss and Australian practice of having amendments ratified directly by the people in a regionally weighted referendum.[19] In January 1979, the Pépin-Robarts "Task Force on Canadian Unity" advanced a similar proposal.[20] It's an idea which should yet get serious consideration, although Canada would now seem to be locked into an amendment formula that subjects the text of the Constitution almost completely to the executive power of just 11 first ministers, who usually have enough political clout to dominate their respective legislatures.

POINT 3: IMMIGRATION

Quebec Position

With regard to immigration, our birth rate after having been one of the highest in the world is now the second lowest after that of West Germany; we must, in consequence, hold the powers necessary for us to guarantee a demographic evolution capable of preserving our role as a major partner in the Canadian federation.

Meech Lake Agreement

Provide under the Constitution that the Government of Canada shall negotiate an immigration agreement appropriate to the needs and circumstances of a province that so requests and that, once concluded, the agreement may be entrenched at the request of the province;

such agreements must recognize the federal

government's power to set national standards and objectives relating to immigration, such as the ability to determine general categories of immigrants, to establish overall levels of immigration and prescribe categories of inadmissible persons;

under the foregoing provisions, conclude in the first instance an agreement with Quebec that would:

incorporate the principle of the Cullen-Couture agreement on the selection abroad and in Canada of independent immigrants, visitors for medical treatment, students and temporary workers, and on the selection of refugees abroad and economic criteria for family reunification and assisted relatives;

guarantee that Quebec will receive a number of immigrants, including refugees, within the annual total established by the federal government for all of Canada proportionate to its share of the population of Canada, with the right to exceed that figure by five per cent for demographic reasons; and

provide an undertaking by Canada to withdraw services (except citizenship services) for the reception and integration (including linguistic and cultural) of all foreign nationals wishing to settle in Quebec where services are to be provided by Quebec, with such withdrawal to be accompanied by reasonable compensation;

nothing in the foregoing should be construed as preventing the negotiation of similar agreements with other provinces.

Section 95 of the Constitution Act, 1867, provides for joint federal-provincial jurisdiction over immigration, with primacy accorded to Parliament in the event of conflict between federal and provincial legislation. However, on Feb. 20, 1978, Bud Cullen, then federal immigration minister, and his Quebec counterpart, Jacques Couture, voluntarily agreed to establish an intergovernmental committee to regulate immigration levels into Quebec in accordance with provincial needs.[21] In "Mastering Our Future," the Quebec Liberal Party suggested that what the province now needs is "the constitutional right to have an equal say with Ottawa as regards the

selection and the number of immigrants settling in Quebec each year."[22]

In response to this request, both the Meech Lake agreement and the Langevin amendment would constitutionally entrench the principles of the Cullen-Couture agreement for Quebec and any other province which might want it. In addition, Mulroney has agreed to have Canada pay the government of Quebec or any other province to assume federal responsibility for the reception and integration (linguistic and cultural) of foreign nationals who choose to settle within the borders of the province. Taking both of these concessions together, it is evident that Mulroney has surrendered significantly more federal authority over immigration to the provinces than the Quebec Liberals originally sought in "Mastering Our Future."

POINT 4: FEDERAL SPENDING POWER

Quebec Position

In order that Quebec might fully control its development, it's necessary that the federal spending power should be delimited. No financial intervention by the federal government in a field of provincial jurisdiction should take place without the consent of the province concerned.

Meech Lake Agreement

Stipulate that Canada must provide reasonable compensation to any province that does not participate in a future national shared-cost program in an area of exclusive provincial jurisdiction if that province undertakes its own initiative or programs compatible with national objectives.

The spending power of Parliament is not spelled out in the constitution and has been only imprecisely defined by the courts. Yet most, but by no means all, constitutional authorities would agree that just as Parliament can raise money by any mode or system of taxation, it also has authority to make grants out of the federal treasury to governments, groups, or individuals for any purpose and subject to any conditions, even in areas within the direct legislative jurisdiction of the provinces.[23] On this basis, the federal spending power has taken on crucial constitutional significance over the past thirty years, having been used by Parliament to establish national shared-cost or conditional-grant programs within areas of provincial administrative jurisdiction such as health, welfare, post-secondary education, and roads. Provincial governments, regardless of their own priorities, have had to go along with these plans by Parliament for fear of losing out on sometimes hundreds of millions of dollars in federal grants.

Of course, such federal intrusions on provincial turf have not always been welcomed. At one time or another, it seems that a premier in every province in the country has raised objections to some use by Parliament of the federal spending power.

For example, at a constitutional conference in February 1969, an angry Premier John Robarts of Ontario told Trudeau: "Medicare is a glowing example of a Machiavellian scheme that is in my humble opinion one of the greatest political frauds that has been perpetrated on the people of this country. The position is this: you are taxing our people in Ontario to the tune of $225 million a year to pay for a plan for which we get nothing because it has a low priority in our plans for Ontario."[24] At the time Robarts much preferred a more limited insurance plan devised by his government, but bowing to financial pressure, Ontario joined the federal program just eight months later, followed shortly thereafter by three other provincial holdouts Quebec, Prince Edward Island, and New Brunswick.

Earlier, in the 1950s, Trudeau himself had gone to bat for his arch political enemy, Quebec Premier Maurice Duplessis, in opposition to federal conditional grants for provincial universi-

ties. In an article published in *Cité Libre* in February 1957, the future prime minister with a centralist reputation contended that as a matter of federalist principle, "no government has the right to interfere with the administration of other governments in those areas not within its own jurisdiction."[25] A provincial government should not get mixed up in matters of federal jurisdiction, such as foreign aid, he argued, but "a provincial government with sufficient tax resources is answerable only to its electorate, never to the federal government, for the regulation and financing of education, and this would be true no matter how ruinous its policies. From these principles it inevitably follows," concluded Trudeau, "that the total resources available to the Canadian Treasury must be divided among the federal and provincial governments in such a way as to allow each government to look after its share of the common good as it sees fit."[26]

Bourassa could not have said it any more forcibly. In "Mastering Our Future," Quebec Liberals proposed a constitutional amendment forbidding the federal government from introducing any new national shared-cost programs, such as day-care, without approval in advance by at least seven provinces having at least fifty percent of the population of the country as specified in section 38 of the Constitution Act, 1982.[27] Had such a limit on the federal spending power been in effect in the 1960s, the introduction of a national medicare program in anything like its present form would have been impossible, yet in 1969, Trudeau himself advanced a proposal for requiring a national consensus for introducing new shared-cost programs, based on a close approximation to the general amending formula included two years later in the Victoria Charter.[28]

In addition to such a consensus requirement, the Quebec Liberals in "Mastering Our Future" also insisted upon a constitutional amendment specifying that the conditions which Parliament can set down for provincial participation in a shared-cost program "should cover only the broad norms to be respected by the provinces as regards the programs to be set up. In no way, should they prescribe regulations relative to the administration of such programs."[29]

Here, then, was a specific proposal for constitutional change which should have been acceptable to Mulroney and all of the provincial premiers, to say nothing of Trudeau. Instead, with regard to shared-cost programs, the Meech Lake Agreement provides that any province can opt out with reasonable compensation from all future shared-cost programs, subject only to the vaguely worded requirement that it "undertakes its own initiative or programs compatible with national objectives."

What does such ambiguous language mean? If such an amendment had been in effect in 1966, could Robarts have blocked the federal medical care act? Or could former Prime Minister Lester Pearson have pressed ahead with the national medicare legislation, because it would still have been up to Parliament alone to determine "national objectives" for shared-cost programs?

In *The Toronto Star* polemic on May 27, Trudeau took the view that an amendment based on the Meech Lake agreement would so drastically limit the spending power that each province would be left to decide for itself if a provincial initiative or program is compatible with national objectives. Parliament would no longer be able to set down even broadly defined national standards for health, education, or welfare programs.

Not so, insists Mulroney. During question period in the House of Commons on May 4, he said firmly: "With regard to the spending power, I can give my honourable friend the assurance that the right, obligation, and authority of the Parliament of Canada to conduct national affairs with respect to spending are uninhibited and unfettered. At all times we can act in the national interest."[30]

However, on this point, Bourassa seems to agree with Trudeau. At a meeting of the General Council of the Quebec Liberal Party on May 24, the Quebec premier disclosed that it was he who

insisted on the word "initiative" in the Meech Lake statement on the spending power. An initiative, Bourassa explained, is different from a program, and "objectives" are not the same as criteria or norms. "It is precisely in order to have flexibility, a margin for manoeuvre, and to take our priorities into account, that we have given preference to the word 'initiative'," said Bourassa. By way of an example, he suggested that if the federal government were to introduce a new conditional grant program for child care, Quebec could opt out with reasonable compensation by promoting much the same "objectives" through the "initiative" of carrying on a family policy specifically aimed at promoting a higher birth rate within Quebec.[31]

So there we have it. In Bourassa's judgment, under terms of the Langevin amendment, any effort to elevate the birth rate in one province would be tantamount to the expansion of day-care centres in another: both provinces, if they chose to opt out of a national day-care program initiated under the spending power of Parliament, would be entitled to reasonable financial compensation from the federal treasury.

So much for Mulroney's assurances about the federal spending power remaining "uninhibited and unfettered." He might be right, but it would seem to be a daunting challenge for any advocate to bring the Supreme Court of Canada around to such a viewpoint, given the imprecise wording of the Langevin amendment.

However, if Bourassa and Trudeau are right, adoption of the Meech Lake principles would make it impossible to introduce any new shared-cost programs like medicare without the unanimous approval of not just seven, but all 10 provincial governments as well as Ottawa. Moreover, this confederal consensus would have to be reached without the federal government wielding any kind of financial stick to help get recalcitrant provinces into line.

At least initially, the ambiguity of the Meech Lake agreement on the spending power did not sit well with New Democratic Party leader Ed Broadbent. During debate in the House of Commons on May 11, he suggested a straightforward way of ending the confusion: Mulroney should make sure that his view will prevail, Broadbent suggested, by seeing to it that the constitutional text based on Mcech Lake makes it crystal clear that an opting-out province cannot qualify for reasonable compensation, unless it carries on a program or initiative compatible with national objectives "as established by the Parliament of Canada."[32]

In the interests of precision, it's regrettable that Broadbent's clarifying subamendment was rejected. The Langevin amendment essentially reiterates the Meech Lake statement and if anything confuses matters more with a supplementary qualification providing that "nothing in this section extends the legislative powers of the Parliament of Canada or of the legislatures of the provinces."

What does this enigmatic assertion mean? It is probably intended simply as an additional signal to the courts that the federal spending power should be given only a restricted interpretation.

Precise answers to all such questions and the many others raised by the imprecise language of the spending power provisions can only be provided by the Supreme Court of Canada. Mulroney, Bourassa, and the other premiers evidently could not agree on precise proposals for the spending power, so they smothered over their differences in obscure equivocations which leave many of the toughest questions on these most sensitive political matters to the judicial system.

Already, though, Mulroney's assurances notwithstanding, it seems evident that the Langevin amendment would seriously curtail the power of Parliament to establish new shared-cost programs. It's a question of precisely how much. In a *Globe and Mail* article on June 15, Senator Lowell Murray affirmed that the Langevin amendment "will increase the bargaining power" of the provinces. "The major change in this area is that flexibility and cooperation will be the new ground rules for implementing na-

tional joint programs," he explained. "New national shared-cost programs will continue to be established—the change will, above all, place a premium on collaboration."[33]

Trudeau has put the matter somewhat differently. Opting out of all new shared-cost programs with full compensation, he maintains, "will enable the provinces to finish off the balkanization of languages and cultures with the balkanization of social services. After all, what provincial politician will not insist on distributing in his own way (what remains, really, of 'national objectives?') and to the advantage of his constituents, the money he'll be getting painlessly from the federal treasury?"[34]

POINT 5: THE SUPREME COURT

Quebec Position

> Concerning the Supreme Court of Canada, which is the final arbitrator of our federation, we insist upon constitutional recognition of the guarantee that three of the nine judges of this court should come from the bar or the judiciary of Quebec and be appointed with the participation of the Quebec government.

Meech Lake Agreement

> Entrench the Supreme Court and the requirement that at least three of the nine justices appointed be from the civil bar;
>
> provide that, where there is a vacancy on the Supreme Court, the federal government shall appoint a person from a list of candidates proposed by the provinces and who is acceptable to the federal government.

Under terms of the existing Constitution Act, 1867, Parliament has exclusive jurisdiction over all aspects of the Supreme Court of Canada, including the appointment of judges. The provinces have no legal right to intervene.

Nonetheless, the Supreme and Exchequers Court Act requires that three of the nine judges on the Supreme Court of Canada should come from among members of the Quebec civil bar, so there has been little opposition to the Quebec proposal that this practice should be constitutionally entrenched. Much more controversial are the Meech Lake and parallel Langevin requirements that future appointments to the top court can only be made by the federal government from among candidates nominated by the provinces, and that once the Langevin amendment is adopted, any additional amendments changing this appointment procedure to the Supreme Court must have unanimous federal and provincial consent.

In Trudeau's opinion, such an appointment arrangement will transfer "supreme judicial power to the provinces, since Canada's highest court will eventually be composed entirely of persons put forward by the provinces."[35] Again, Senator Murray disagrees. As he sees it, the Meech Lake provision for provincial participation in the nomination of Supreme Court judges "is really a form of double veto, with Quebec and the other provinces having the right to submit a list of candidates, and the federal government having the right to ask for a new list until such time as it agrees to a candidate and then proceeds to appointment. This procedure," he insists, "is based on the Victoria Charter and especially on Bill C-60, proposed by Trudeau."[36]

However, that last assertion is somewhat misleading. Unlike Trudeau's previous proposal, neither the Meech Lake agreement nor the proposed Langevin amendment has anything to say about how to break a deadlock in the event that the federal and provincial governments cannot agree on a Supreme Court nominee.

This is a serious deficiency. The Langevin amendment specifies that the three judges from Quebec can only be nominated by the Quebec government. Consider what such a provision would have meant during the tenure of former Quebec premier René Lévesque, when three judges from Quebec, Julien Chouinard, Antonio Lamer, and Gerald Le Dain, were appointed to the Supreme Court of Canada. It's a safe bet that not one of them would have been nominated by Levesque, who probably would have preferred judges with much more decentralist, if not outright separatist opinions.

Trudeau, at least, would never have gone for such nominees. The result, under terms of the Langevin amendment, would have been an intractable deadlock.

In contrast, the abortive Victoria Charter and Bill C-60, as endorsed by Trudeau, both included a complex deadlock-breaking mechanism which would have quickly forced the provinces to make a final decision from among at least three nominees of the federal attorney general.[37] However, even this limited form of provincial participation evoked some controversy. In *Quebec and the Constitution: 1960-1978*, Edward McWhinney, a law professor who once served as a constitutional adviser to both Bourassa and former Quebec premier Jean-Jacques Bertrand, expressed the opinion that consulting provincial attorneys general on Supreme Court appointments, "would add complexity and delays, and inevitably screen out the more sparkling judicial personalities, such as Duff, Rand, Laskin, and Pigeon, of our time."[38]

In comparison, the Langevin formula would give the provinces even greater influence over Supreme Court appointments. If the government of Ontario, for example, were to refuse to nominate anyone with somewhat centralist views—even a distinguished candidate like the late chief justice Bora Laskin—the federal cabinet could still opt for the next best candidate put up by one of the other English-speaking provinces. However, under terms of the Langevin amendment, only the Quebec government can nominate candidates from the Quebec civil bar, yet the act says nothing about how deadlocks between Ottawa and Quebec over such appointments might be resolved. Here, another potentially explosive political dilemma has simply been dumped into the lap of the Supreme Court of Canada.

CONCLUSIONS

> Prime Minister Mulroney as a great conciliator? Really, Mulroney had nothing to conciliate; it was an open bar and each province helped itself.
>
> — Lysianne Gagnon in *La Presse*, Saturday, May 2, 1987

In addition to Quebec's five points, the Meech Lake agreement and Langevin amendment also include a requirement that, pending a complete overhaul of the Senate, vacancies in the upper chamber for any province must be filled by persons nominated by the government of that province and acceptable to the federal cabinet; but again, there is no provision for breaking deadlocks. In addition, both documents stipulate that any additional amendments to "the powers of the Senate and the method of selecting Senators" shall require unanimous federal and provincial consent.

It might be wondered why Premier Don Getty of Alberta would have gone along with this last provision, inasmuch as Ontario or any one of the other provinces—to say nothing of the House of Commons—is almost certain never to go along with a Triple E (elected, equal, and effective) Senate.

However, Getty and the other provincial premiers stand to gain in another way: Senators nominated by the provinces are bound to be more responsive to provincial outlooks, particularly when they clash with the central vision of the federal government and the House of Commons. Moreover, if the Langevin amendment is adopted, the Senate promises to be much more influential than in the past. Under the Constitution Act, 1982, the upper chamber has a suspensive veto over most constitutional amendments,[39] but it can hold up all other legislation approved

by the House of Commons indefinitely. In practice, though, Senators have been inhibited from exercising that veto on many issues, or for very long, out of concern that the House of Commons could retaliate by insisting on a constitutional amendment under Section 42 reducing the powers of the Senate to no more than a limited suspensive veto over all legislation approved by the lower chamber. The Langevin amendment would effectively eliminate that threat by giving each province a veto over any additional amendment affecting senatorial powers.

Trudeau has expressed concern that this arrangement will give the provinces "an absolute right of veto over Parliament, since the Senate will eventually be composed entirely of persons who owe their appointments to the provinces."[40] That judgment might be somewhat exaggerated, but it could be that the Senate provisions of the Langevin amendment will have a greater impact on the Constitution than any of the five points conceded specifically to Quebec.

In view of all these federal concessions and the promise to consider still more constitutional reforms demanded by the provinces, it's understandable that Mulroney should have won the plaudits of his fellow first ministers: He simply surrendered to whatever demand all of them could manage to agree upon, and in the process, seriously undermined some of the essential powers of Parliament.

Concern has also been expressed about the impact of the Langevin amendment on the judiciary. Adoption of the Canadian Charter of Rights and Freedoms has already weighed down the Supreme Court of Canada with considerable political responsibilities. The reputation of the judiciary for political independence and impartiality is bound to be compromised to the extent that the courts also become embroiled in attempts to define the federal spending power or the implications of Quebec as a distinct society under the deliberately vague and ambiguous terms of the Langevin amendment.

In response to such criticisms, Mulroney would maintain that the Langevin accord, for all its weaknesses, is better than nothing. Failure to have won Bourassa's support for a revised Canadian constitution would have seriously undermined national unity. Parliament might be marginally weaker, but the country will be much stronger as a result of the Meech Lake exercise in cooperative federalism.

One thing is certain: this controversy is bound to go on. Even if the Langevin amendment is quickly ratified and duly proclaimed, the fundamental issues underlying this constitutional controversy will still be long and hotly debated. Anyone who thinks this matter is essentially over and done with would do well to recall the immortal words of Yogi Berra: "It ain't over 'til it's over."

Notes

1. See the report by Robert Mackenzie in *The Toronto Star*, June 14, 1987.

2. See "Notes pour une allocution du ministre des relations internationales du Québec," Monsieur Gil Remillard, devant les Parlementaires Francais, Paris, Nov. 26, 1986. (Unless otherwise indicated, all translations from the French used in this article have been made by the author.)

3. Speech by Mr. Mulroney, Sêpt-Iles, August 6, 1984, as reported in "Federal Statements on the Quebec Constitutional Issue," Office of the Prime Minister, Ottawa, May, 1987.

4. Mulroney, press conference statement as reported in *The London Free Press*, Dec. 20, 1986.

5. See *Maitriser l'avenir, Programme politique*, Commission politique, Parti liberal du Québec, Document de travail, Fevrier, 1985. (This document has been translated by the party with the title: *Mastering Our Future, Policy Program*, Policy Commission, Quebec Liberal Party (Working Paper, February, 1985), 49-59.

6. See Remillard, "Notes."

7. For the text of the Meech Lake agreement, see "Background Information on the Meech Lake Agreement," Office of the Prime Minister, Ottawa, May 1987.

8. For the sake of brevity, this document will be referred to simply as "the Langevin amendment." For the complete text and an official federal commentary, see "A Guide to the Constitutional Accord," Office of the Prime Minister, Ottawa, June 3, 1987.

9. See *Le Devoir*, June 2, 1987. The lack of any such guarantee in the Langevin amendment is all the more ominous inasmuch as section 95B(3) of the immigration article does specifically state that the Canadian Charter of Rights and Freedoms applies with respect to immigration agreements between Canada and a province.

10. *The Toronto Star*, May 27, 1987.

11. Lowell Murray, *The Globe and Mail*, May 30, 1987.

12. See Bill 60 (1978), Preamble and Part 1. A convenient source for the text of documents relating to constitutional reform is the summary government document entitled: *Proposals on the Constitution: 1971-78*, Collation by the Canadian Intergovernmental Conference Secretariat, Ottawa, December, 1978. (Referred to hereinafter as *Secretariat Proposals*.)

13. For a complete text of both formulae, see *Secretariat Proposals*, 364-71. For an interesting brief discussion and analysis of these formulae, see The Special Joint Committee of the Senate and of the House of Commons on the Constitution of Canada, *Final Report*, Ottawa, 1972, 9, 10.

14. See *In the Matter of an Act for Expediting the Decision of Constitutional and Other Provincial Questions, Being R.S.M. 1970, c. C-180*, Supreme

Court of Canada, decision of September 28, 1981.

15. See "Mastering Our Future," 54.

16. See a report on this meeting in *The London Free Press*, August 13, 1986.

17. Peter Hogg, *Constitutional Law of Canada* (Toronto: Carswell, 1985), 75.

18. Eugene Forsey, "Vague Aspects of the Meech Deal Pose a Big Threat," *The Globe and Mail*, June 1, 1987.

19. See *Secretariat Proposals*, 383.

20. Jean-Luc Pépin and John Robarts, co-chairmen, *The Task Force on Canadian Unity: A Future Together* (Ottawa: Supply and Services Canada, 1979), 102-4.

21. This administrative agreement is a singular example of flexible and cooperative federalism within a framework of constitutional rigidity. See Edward McWhinney, *Quebec and the Constitution: 1960-1978* (Toronto: University of Toronto Press, 1979), 109.

22. *Mastering Our Future*, 47-9.

23. For a discussion of constitutional issues relating to the spending power of Parliament, see Hogg, *Constitutional Law*, 123-6. For a dissenting viewpoint by two University of Montreal law professors questioning the existence of the spending power as usually understood, see André Lajoie and Jacques Fremont, "Des Amendements Inacceptables : Le Pouvoir Federal de Dépenser," *Le Devoir*, May 14, 1987, 11.

24. Robarts as quoted in Malcolm Taylor, *Health In-*

surance and Canadian Public Policy (Montreal: McGill-Queen's University Press, 1978), 375.

25. This English translation is from Pierre Elliott Trudeau, *Federalism and the French Canadians* (Toronto: Macmillan, 1968), 80.

26. *Ibid.*

27. See *Mastering Our Future*, 50-1.

28. See Pierre Trudeau, *Federal-Provincial Grants and the Spending Power of Parliament* (Ottawa: Government of Canada, 1969), 40, 42. For a parallel discussion of this same issue, see the Special Joint Committee of the Senate and of the House of Commons on the Constitution of Canada, *Final Report*, Ottawa, 1972, 50-3.

29. See *Mastering Our Future*, 51.

30. *House of Commons Debates*, Monday, May 4, 1987, 5688.

31. See a report on this speech and a subsequent press conference in *Le Devoir*, May 25, 1987.

32. *House of Commons Debates*, Monday, May 11, 1987, 5940.

33. *The Globe and Mail*, June 15, 1987.

34. *The Toronto Star*, May 27, 1987.

35. Trudeau, *Federal-Provincial Grants*.

36. Murray, *The Globe and Mail*, May 30, 1987.

37. See *Secretariat Proposals*, 369-71, 381.

38. McWhinney, *Quebec*, 123.

39. See Section 47(1) of the Constitution Act, 1982.

40. *The Toronto Star*, May 27, 1987.

Selected Readings

Boismenu, Gerard, "Backing Down or Compromising on the Future: Quebec's Constitutional Proposals." In Peter M. Leslie, ed. *Canada: The State of the Federation 1985*. Kingston: Institute of Intergovernmental Relations, Queen's University, 1985, 47-82.

Canada. Task Force on Canadian Unity. *A Future Together: Observations and Recommendations*. Ottawa: Supply and Services Canada, 1979.

Leslie, Peter M. "Quebec and the Constitutional Issue." In Peter M. Leslie, ed., *Canada: The State of the Federation 1986*. Kingston: Institute of Intergovernmental Relations, Queen's University, 1986, 65-105.

Olling, R. D., and Westmacott, M. W., eds., *The Confederation Debate: The Constitution in Crisis*. Dubuque, Iowa: Kendell/Hunt, 1980.

APPENDIX

1987 CONSTITUTIONAL ACCORD

INTRODUCTION

In April 1987, a First Ministers Conference was convened at the Meech Lake residence of the Prime Minister of Canada. The meeting produced an agreement to amend the Canadian constitution in accordance with certain proposals presented by the Province of Quebec. This agreement in principle has come to be known as the *Meech Lake Accord*.

The First Ministers came together for a second time in June 1987 at the Langevin Block offices of the Prime Minister in Ottawa. This marathon meeting sought to clarify the meaning of certain controversial sections of the Meech Lake Accord and sanction a final legal text for a formal amendment to the Constitution Act. Limited, though important, changes were made to the wording of the text.

Some commentators immediately dubbed the revised agreement the *Langevin Accord* or the *Langevin Amendment*. However, because the basic tenets of the April agreement remained untouched, the descriptive title *Meech Lake Accord* has also continued in general use.

The following appendix contains the complete text of the June 1987 Constitutional Accord, the parliamentary motion to be tabled in the Parliament of Canada and each provincial legislature, and the annotated schedule listing the specific changes to be made to the Constitution Act.

At the time of publication, the National Assembly of Quebec has ratified the Constitutional Accord and the federal government and the remaining provinces are beginning the constitutional amending process as stipulated in the Constitution Act, 1982. As presently constituted, the proposed amendment will require the approval of all eleven legislative bodies.

1987 CONSTITUTIONAL ACCORD

WHEREAS first ministers, assembled in Ottawa, have arrived at a unanimous accord on constitutional amendments that would bring about the full and active participation of Quebec in Canada's constitutional evolution, would recognize the principle of equality of all the provinces, would provide new arrangements to foster greater harmony and cooperation between the Government of Canada and the governments of the provinces and would require that annual first ministers' conferences on the state of the Canadian economy and such other matters as may be appropriate be convened and that annual constitutional conferences composed of first ministers be convened commencing not later than December 31, 1988.

AND WHEREAS first ministers have also reached unanimous agreement on certain additional commitments in relation to some of those amendments;

NOW THEREFORE the Prime Minister of Canada and the first ministers of the provinces commit themselves and the governments they represent to the following:

1. The Prime Minister of Canada will lay or cause to be laid before the Senate and House of Commons, and the first ministers of the provinces will lay or cause to be laid before their legislative assemblies, as soon as possible, a resolution, in the form appended hereto, to authorize a proclamation to be issued by the Governor General under the Great Seal of Canada to amend the Constitution of Canada.

2. The Government of Canada will, as soon as possible, conclude an agreement with the Government of Quebec that would
   (a) incorporate the principles of the Cullen-Couture agreement on the selection abroad and in Canada of independent immigrants, visitors for medical treatment, students and temporary workers, and on the selection of refugees abroad and economic criteria for family reunification and assisted relatives,
   (b) guarantee that Quebec will receive a number of immigrants, including refugees, within the annual total established by the federal government for all of Canada proportionate to its share of the population of Canada, with the right to exceed that figure by five percent for demographic reasons, and
   (c) provide an undertaking by Canada to withdraw services (except citizenship services) for the reception and integration (including linguistic and cultural) of all foreign nationals wishing to settle in Quebec where services are to be provided by Quebec, with such withdrawal to be accompanied by reasonable compensation.

and the Government of Canada and the Government of Quebec will take the necessary steps to give the agreement the force of law under the proposed amendment relating to such agreements.

3. Nothing in this Accord should be construed as preventing the negotiation of similar agreements with other provinces relating to immigration and the temporary admission of aliens.

4. Until the proposed amendment relating to appointments to the Senate comes into force, any person summoned to fill a vacancy in the Senate shall be chosen from among persons whose names have been submitted by the government of the province to which the vacancy relates and must be acceptable to the Queen's Privy Council for Canada.

MOTION FOR A RESOLUTION TO AUTHORIZE AN AMENDMENT TO THE CONSTITUTION OF CANADA

WHEREAS the *Constitution Act, 1982* came into force on April 17, 1982, following an agreement between Canada and all the provinces except Quebec;

AND WHEREAS the Government of Quebec has established a set of five proposals for constitutional change and has stated that amendments to give effect to those proposals would enable Quebec to resume a full role in the constitutional councils of Canada;

AND WHEREAS the amendment proposed in the schedule hereto sets out the basis on which Quebec's five constitutional proposals may be met;

AND WHEREAS the amendment proposed in the schedule hereto also recognizes the principle of the equality of all the provinces, provides new arrangements to foster greater harmony and cooperation between the Government of Canada and the governments of the provinces and requires that conferences be convened to consider important constitutional, economic and other issues;

AND WHEREAS certain portions of the amendment proposed in the schedule hereto relate to matters referred to in section 41 of the *Constitution Act, 1982*;

AND WHEREAS section 41 of the *Constitution Act, 1982* provides that an amendment to the Constitution of Canada may be made by proclamation issued by the Governor General under the Great Seal of Canada where so authorized by resolutions of the Senate and the House of Commons and of the legislative assembly of each province;

NOW THEREFORE the (Senate) (House of Commons) (legislative assembly) resolves that an amendment to the Constitution of Canada be authorized to be made by proclamation issued by Her Excellency the Governor General under the Great Seal of Canada in accordance with the schedule hereto.

SCHEDULE

CONSTITUTION AMENDMENT, 1987

Constitution Act, 1982

1. The *Constitution Act, 1867* is amended by adding thereto, immediately after section 1 thereof, the following section:

Interpretation

"2.(1) The Constitution of Canada shall be interpreted in a manner consistent with

(a) the recognition that the existence of French-speaking Canadians, centred in Quebec but also present elsewhere in Canada, and English-speaking Canadians, concentrated outside Quebec but also present in Quebec, constitutes a fundamental characteristic of Canada; and

(b) the recognition that Quebec constitutes within Canada a distinct society.

Role of Parliament and legislatures

(2) The role of the Parliament of Canada and the provincial legislatures to preserve the fundamental characteristic of Canada referred to in paragraph (1)(a) is affirmed.

Role of legislature and Government of Quebec

(3) The role of the legislature and Government of Quebec to preserve and promote the distinct identity of Quebec referred to in paragraph (1)(b) is affirmed.

Rights of legislatures and governments preserved

(4) Nothing in this section derogates from the powers, rights or privileges of Parliament or the Government of Canada, or of the legislatures or governments of the provinces, including any powers, rights or privileges relating to language."

2. The said Act is further amended by adding thereto, immediately after section 24 thereof, the following section:

Names to be submitted

"25.(1) Where a vacancy occurs in the Senate, the government of the province to which the vacancy relates may, in relation to that vacancy, submit to the Queen's Privy Council for Canada the names of persons who may be summoned to the Senate.

Choice of Senators from names submitted

(2) Until an amendment to the Constitution of Canada is made in relation to the Senate pursuant to section 41 of the *Constitution Act, 1982*, the person summoned to fill a vacancy in the Senate shall be chosen from among persons whose names have been submitted under subsection (1) by the government of the province to which the vacancy relates and must be acceptable to the Queen's Privy Council for Canada."

3. The said Act is further amended by adding thereto, immediately after section 95 thereof, the following heading and sections:

"Agreements on Immigration and Aliens

Commitment to
negotiate

95A. The Government of Canada shall, at the request of the government of any province, negotiate with the government of that province for the purpose of concluding an agreement relating to immigration or the temporary admission of aliens into that province that is appropriate to the needs and circumstances of that province.

Agreements

95B. (1) Any agreement concluded between Canada and a province in relation to immigration or the temporary admission of aliens into that province has the force of law from the time it is declared to do so in accordance with subsection 95C(1) and shall from that time have effect notwithstanding class 25 of section 91 or section 95.

Limitation

(2) An agreement that has the force of law under subsection (1) shall have effect only so long and so far as it is not repugnant to any provision of an Act of the Parliament of Canada that sets national standards and objectives relating to immigration or aliens, including any provision that establishes general classes of immigrants or relates to levels of immigration for Canada or that prescribes classes of individuals who are inadmissible into Canada.

Application of
Charter

(3) The *Canadian Charter of Rights and Freedoms* applies in respect of any agreement that has the force of law under subsection (1) and in respect of anything done by the Parliament or Government of Canada, or the legislature or government of a province, pursuant to any such agreement.

Proclamation
relating to
agreements

95C.(1) A declaration that an agreement referred to in subsection 95B(1) has the force of law may be made by proclamation issued by the Governor General under the Great Seal of Canada only where so authorized by resolutions of the Senate and House of Commons and of the legislative assembly of the province that is a party to the agreement.

Amendment of
agreements

(2) An amendment to an agreement referred to in subsection 95B(1) may be made by proclamation issued by the Governor General under the Great Seal of Canada only where so authorized.

(a) by resolutions of the Senate and House of Commons and of the legislative assembly of the province that is a party to the agreement; or

(b) in such other manner as is set out in the agreement.

Application of sections 46 to 48 of *Constitution Act, 1982*

95D. Sections 46 to 48 of the *Constitution Act, 1982* apply, with such modifications as the circumstances require, in respect of any declaration made pursuant to subsection 95C(1), any amendment to an agreement made pursuant to subsection 95C(2) or any amendment made pursuant to section 95E.

Amendments to sections 95A to 95D or this section

95E. An amendment to sections 95A to 95D or this section may be made in accordance with the procedure set out in subsection 38(1) of the *Constitution Act, 1982*, but only if the amendment is authorized by resolutions of the legislative assemblies of all the provinces that are, at the time of the amendment, parties to an agreement that has the force of law under subsection 95B(1)."

4. The said Act is further amended by adding thereto, immediately preceding section 96 thereof, the following heading:

"General"

5. The said Act is further amended by adding thereto, immediately preceding section 101 thereof, the following heading:

"Courts Established by the Parliament of Canada"

6. The said Act is further amended by adding thereto, immediately after section 101 thereof, the following heading and sections:

"Supreme Court of Canada"

Supreme Court continued

101A.(1) The court existing under the name of the Supreme Court of Canada is hereby continued as the general court of appeal for Canada, and as an additional court for the better administration of the laws of Canada, and shall continue to be a superior court of record.

Constitution of Court

(2) The Supreme Court of Canada shall consist of a chief justice to be called the Chief Justice of Canada and eight other judges, who shall be appointed by the Governor General in Council by letters patent under the Great Seal.

Who may be appointed judges

101B.(1) Any person may be appointed a judge of the Supreme Court of Canada who, after having been admitted to the bar of any province or territory, has, for a total of at least ten years, been a judge of any court in Canada or a member of the bar of any province or territory.

Three judges from Quebec

(2) At least three judges of the Supreme Court of Canada shall be appointed from among persons who, after having been admitted to the bar of Quebec, have, for a total of at least ten years, been judges of any court of Quebec or of any court established by the Parliament of Canada, or members of the bar of Quebec.

Names may
be submitted

101C.(1) Where a vacancy occurs in the Supreme Court of Canada, the government of each province may, in relation to that vacancy, submit to the Minister of Justice of Canada the names of any of the persons who have been admitted to the bar of that province and are qualified under section 101B for appointment to that court.

Appointment from
names submitted

(2) Where an appointment is made to the Supreme Court of Canada, the Governor General in Council shall, except where the Chief Justice is appointed from among members of the Court, appoint a person whose name has been submitted under subsection (1) and who is acceptable to the Queen's Privy Council for Canada.

Appointment
from Quebec

(3) Where an appointment is made in accordance with subsection (2) of any of the three judges necessary to meet the requirement set out in subsection 101B(2), the Governor General in Council shall appoint a person whose name has been submitted by the Government of Quebec.

Appointment from
other provinces

(4) Where an appointment is made in accordance with subsection (2) otherwise than as required under subsection (3), the Governor General in Council shall appoint a person whose name has been submitted by the government of a province other than Quebec.

Tenure, salaries, etc.
of judges

101D. Sections 99 and 100 apply in respect of the judges of the Supreme Court of Canada.

Relationship to
section 101

101E.(1) Sections 101A to 101D shall not be construed as abrogating or derogating from the powers of the Parliament of Canada to make laws under section 101 except to the extent that such laws are inconsistent with those sections.

References to the
Supreme Court
of Canada

(2) For greater certainty, section 101A shall not be construed as abrogating or derogating from the powers of the Parliament of Canada to make laws relating to the reference of questions of law or fact, or any other matters, to the Supreme Court of Canada."

7. The said Act is further amended by adding thereto, immediately after section 106 thereof, the following section:

Shared-cost program

"106A.(1) The Government of Canada shall provide reasonable compensation to the government of a province that chooses not to participate in a national shared-cost program that is established by the Government of Canada after the coming into force of this section in an area of exclusive provincial jurisdiction, if the province carries on a program or initiative that is compatible with the national objectives.

Legislative power
not extended

(2) Nothing in this section extends the legislative powers of the Parliament of Canada or of the legislatures of the provinces."

8. The said Act is further amended by adding thereto the following heading and sections:

"XII—Conferences on the Economy and Other Matters

Conferences on
the economy and
other matters

148. A conference composed of the Prime Minister of Canada and the first ministers of the provinces shall be convened by the Prime Minister of Canada at least once a year to discuss the state of the Canadian economy and such other matters as may be appropriate.

XIII—References

Reference includes
amendments

149. A reference to this Act shall be deemed to include a reference to any amendments thereto."

Constitution Act, 1982

9. Sections 40 to 42 of the *Constitution Act, 1982* are repealed and the following substituted therefor:

Compensation

"40. Where an amendment is made under subsection 38(1) that transfers legislative powers from provincial legislatures to Parliament, Canada shall provide reasonable compensation to any province to which the amendment does not apply.

Amendment by
unanimous consent

41. An amendment to the Constitution of Canada in relation to the following matters may be made by proclamation issued by the Governor General under the Great Seal of Canada only where authorized by resolutions of the Senate and House of Commons and of the legislative assembly of each province:

(a) the office of the Queen, the Governor General and the Lieutenant Governor of a province;

(b) the powers of the Senate and the method of selecting Senators;

(c) the number of members by which a province is entitled to be represented in the Senate and the residence qualifications of Senators;

(d) the right of a province to a number of members in the House of Commons not less than the number of Senators by which the province *was* entitled to be represented on *April 17, 1982*;

(e) the principle of proportionate representation of the provinces in the House of Commons prescribed by the Constitution of Canada;

(f) subject to section 43, the use of the English or the French language;

(g) the Supreme Court of Canada;

(h) the extension of existing provinces into the territories;

(i) notwithstanding any other law or practice, the establishment of new provinces;

(j) an amendment to this Part."

10. Section 44 of the said Act is repealed and the following substituted therefor:

Amendments by Parliament

"44. Subject to section 41, Parliament may exclusively make laws amending the Constitution of Canada in relation to the executive government of Canada or the Senate and House of Commons."

11. Subsection 46(1) of the said Act is repealed and the following substituted therefor:

Initiation of amendment procedures

"46.(1) The procedures for amendment under sections 38, 41 and 43 may be initiated either by the Senate or the House of Commons or by the legislative assembly of a province."

12. Subsection 47(1) of the said Act is repealed and the following substituted therefor:

Amendments without Senate resolution

"47.(1) An amendment to the Constitution of Canada made by proclamation under section 38, 41 or 43 may be made without a resolution of the Senate authorizing the issue of the proclamation if, within one hundred and eighty days after the adoption by the House of Commons of a resolution authorizing its issue, the Senate has not adopted such a resolution and if, at any time after the expiration of that period, the House of Commons again adopts the resolution."

13. Part VI of the said Act is repealed and the following substituted therefor:

"Part VI
Constitutional Conferences

Constitutional conference

50.(1) A constitutional conference composed of the Prime Minister of Canada and the first ministers of the provinces shall be convened by the Prime Minister of Canada at least once each year, commencing in 1988.

Agenda

(2) The conferences convened under subsection (1) shall have included on their agenda the following matters:

(a) Senate reform, including the role and functions of the Senate, its powers, the method of selecting Senators and representation in the Senate;

(b) roles and responsibilities in relation to fisheries; and

(c) such other matters as are agreed upon."

14. Subsection 52(2) of the said Act is amended by striking out the word "and" at the end of paragraph (b) thereof, by adding the word "and " at the end of paragraph (c) thereof and by adding thereto the following paragraph:

"(d) any other amendment to the Constitution of Canada."

15. Section 61 of the said Act is repealed and the following substituted therefor:

References

"61. *A reference to the Constitution Act, 1982, or* a reference to the *Constitution Acts 1867 to 1982*, shall be deemed to include a reference to *any amendment thereto.*"

General

Multi-cultural
heritage and
aboriginal peoples

16. Nothing in section 2 of the *Constitution Act, 1867* affects section 25 or 27 of the *Canadian Charter of Rights and Freedoms*, section 35 of the *Constitution Act, 1982* or class 24 of section 91 of the *Constitution Act, 1867.*

CITATION

Citation

17. This amendment may be cited as the *Constitution Amendment, 1987.*

Index